# ACCOUNTING AND FINANCE
## for Non-Specialists

Visit the *Accounting and Finance for Non-Specialists*, seventh edition, MyAccountingLab at **www.myaccountinglab.com** to find valuable **student** learning material including:

- Diagnostic Tests designed to determine your strengths and weaknesses.
- A personalised Study Plan containing practice questions and support materials.
- Interactive Study Guide containing further activities and exercise material.

**Seventh Edition**

# ACCOUNTING AND FINANCE
## for Non-Specialists

**Peter Atrill**
and
**Eddie McLaney**

**Financial Times
Prentice Hall
is an imprint of**

Harlow, England • London • New York • Boston • San Francisco • Toronto • Sydney • Singapore • Hong Kong
Tokyo • Seoul • Taipei • New Delhi • Cape Town • Madrid • Mexico City • Amsterdam • Munich • Paris • Milan

**Pearson Education Limited**

Edinburgh Gate
Harlow
Essex CM20 2JE
England

and Associated Companies throughout the world

*Visit us on the World Wide Web at:*
www.pearsoned.co.uk

First published 1995 by Prentice Hall Europe
Second edition published 1997
Third edition published 2001 by Pearson Education Limited
Fourth edition published 2004
Fifth edition published 2006
Sixth edition published 2008
**Seventh edition published 2011**

© Prentice Hall Europe 1995
© Pearson Education Limited 2001, 2011

ISBN: 978-0-273-74588-4

**British Library Cataloguing-in-Publication Data**
A catalogue record for this book is available from the British Library

**Library of Congress Cataloging-in-Publication Data**
Atrill, Peter.
   Accounting and finance for non-specialists / Peter Atrill and Eddie McLaney.
-- 7th ed.
      p. cm.
   ISBN 978-0-273-74588-4 (pbk.)
   1. Accounting.   2. Financial Statements.   I. McLaney, E. J.   II. Title.
   HF5636.A87 2011
   657--dc22

                                                          2010037454

10  9  8  7  6  5  4  3  2  1
14  13  12  11

Typeset in 9/12.5pt Stone Serif by 35
Printed by Ashford Colour Press Ltd., Gosport

# Brief Contents

Preface                                                          xv
Guided tour of the book                                          xviii
Guided tour of MyAccountingLab                                   xxi
Acknowledgements                                                 xxiii

 1  Introduction to accounting and finance                        l

## Part 1 Financial accounting                                    27

 2  Measuring and reporting financial position                    29
 3  Measuring and reporting financial performance                 70
 4  Accounting for limited companies                              112
 5  Measuring and reporting cash flows                            158
 6  Analysing and interpreting financial statements               186

## Part 2 Management accounting                                   237

 7  Cost-volume-profit analysis                                   239
 8  Full costing                                                  276
 9  Budgeting                                                     312

## Part 3 Financial management                                    353

10  Making capital investment decisions                           355
11  Financing a business                                          402
12  Managing working capital                                      453

Appendix A: Glossary of key terms                                 498
Appendix B: Solutions to self-assessment questions               511
Appendix C: Solutions to review questions                        522
Appendix D: Solutions to selected exercises                      535
Appendix E: Present value table                                   563
Index                                                             565

# Contents

Preface                                                          xv
  How to use this book                                 xvi
  Integrated assessment material                       xvi
  End-of-chapter assessment material                   xvi
Guided tour of the book                                          xviii
Guided tour of MyAccountingLab                                   xxi
Acknowledgements                                                 xxiii

**1  Introduction to accounting and finance**                    1
  Introduction                                         1
  Learning outcomes                                    1
  What are accounting and finance?                     2
  Who are the users of accounting information?         3
  Providing a service                                  5
  But . . . is it material?                            7
  Weighing up the costs and benefits                   7
  Accounting as an information system                  9
  Management accounting and financial accounting       10
  Scope of this book                                   12
  Has accounting become too interesting?               12
  The changing face of accounting                      14
  How are businesses managed?                          15
  What is the financial objective of a business?       15
  Balancing risk and return                            19
  Not-for-profit organisations                         20
  Why do I need to know anything about accounting and finance?   21
  Summary                                              22
  Key terms                                            24
  Further reading                                      24
  Review questions                                     25

## Part 1 FINANCIAL ACCOUNTING

### 2 Measuring and reporting financial position 29

Introduction 29
Learning outcomes 29
Making financial decisions 30
The major financial statements – an overview 30
The statement of financial position 35
The effect of trading transactions 42
Classifying assets 44
Classifying claims 47
Statement layouts 48
Self-assessment question 2.1 50
Capturing a moment in time 50
The role of accounting conventions 51
Money measurement 55
Valuing assets 58
Meeting user needs 63
Summary 64
Key terms 66
Further reading 66
Review questions 67
Exercises 67

### 3 Measuring and reporting financial performance 70

Introduction 70
Learning outcomes 70
What does it mean? 71
The income statement 71
Different roles 73
Income statement layout 74
Further issues 75
Recognising revenue 78
Recognising expenses 83
Depreciation 87
Costing inventories 97
Trade receivables problems 101
Self-assessment question 3.1 103
Uses and usefulness of the income statement 104
Summary 105
Key terms 107

Further reading 107
Review questions 107
Exercises 108

## 4 Accounting for limited companies 112

Introduction 112
Learning outcomes 112
The main features of limited companies 113
Managing a company 119
The UK Corporate Governance Code 121
Financing limited companies 123
Raising share capital 131
Borrowings 131
Withdrawing equity 132
The main financial statements 136
Dividends 138
Additional financial statements 138
The directors' duty to account 141
The need for accounting rules 142
Sources of accounting rules 143
The auditors' role 145
The directors' report 145
Creative accounting 146
Self-assessment question 4.1 148
Summary 149
Key terms 152
Reference 152
Further reading 152
Review questions 153
Exercises 153

## 5 Measuring and reporting cash flows 158

Introduction 158
Learning outcomes 158
The statement of cash flows 159
Why is cash so important? 160
The main features of the statement of cash flows 161
A definition of cash and cash equivalents 161
The relationship between the main financial statements 163
The form of the statement of cash flows 163
The normal direction of cash flows 166
Preparing the statement of cash flows 167

| | |
|---|---|
| What does the statement of cash flows tell us? | 175 |
| Self-assessment question 5.1 | 177 |
| Summary | 178 |
| Key terms | 179 |
| Further reading | 180 |
| Review questions | 180 |
| Exercises | 180 |

## 6 Analysing and interpreting financial statements

| | 186 |
|---|---|
| Introduction | 186 |
| Learning outcomes | 186 |
| Financial ratios | 187 |
| Financial ratio classifications | 188 |
| The need for comparison | 189 |
| Calculating the ratios | 190 |
| A brief overview | 192 |
| Profitability | 193 |
| Efficiency | 200 |
| Relationship between profitability and efficiency | 205 |
| Liquidity | 207 |
| Financial gearing | 209 |
| Self-assessment question 6.1 | 215 |
| Investment ratios | 217 |
| Trend analysis | 224 |
| Using ratios to predict future outcomes | 226 |
| Limitations of ratio analysis | 226 |
| Summary | 228 |
| Key terms | 230 |
| Further reading | 230 |
| Review questions | 230 |
| Exercises | 231 |

## Part 2 MANAGEMENT ACCOUNTING

## 7 Cost-volume-profit analysis

| | 239 |
|---|---|
| Introduction | 239 |
| Learning outcomes | 239 |
| Cost behaviour | 240 |
| Fixed cost | 240 |
| Variable cost | 242 |

Semi-fixed (semi-variable) cost 243
Finding the break-even point 245
Contribution 250
Margin of safety 251
Achieving a target profit 254
Operating gearing 255
Profit-volume charts 257
Failing to break even 257
Weaknesses of break-even analysis 258
Using contribution to make decisions: marginal analysis 261
Self-assessment question 7.1 269
Summary 270
Key terms 271
Further reading 271
Review questions 272
Exercises 272

## 8 Full costing 276

Introduction 276
Learning outcomes 276
Why do managers want to know the full cost? 277
What is full costing? 278
Single-product businesses 279
Multi-product businesses 280
Direct and indirect cost 280
Job costing 282
Overheads as service renderers 285
How job costing works 286
Batch costing 296
Full (absorption) cost as the break-even price 297
Self-assessment question 8.1 297
Activity-based costing 298
Using full (absorption) cost information 306
Summary 306
Key terms 308
Further reading 308
Review questions 309
Exercises 309

## 9 Budgeting 312

Introduction 312
Learning outcomes 312

| | |
|---|---|
| Budgets and budgeting | 313 |
| How budgets link with strategic plans and objectives | 313 |
| Time horizon of plans and budgets | 316 |
| Limiting factors | 316 |
| Budgets and forecasts | 317 |
| Periodic and continual budgets | 317 |
| How budgets link to one another | 318 |
| How budgets help managers | 321 |
| Using budgets in practice | 323 |
| Incremental and zero-base budgeting | 325 |
| Preparing the cash budget | 327 |
| Preparing other budgets | 331 |
| Non-financial measures in budgeting | 334 |
| Self-assessment question 9.1 | 334 |
| Budgeting for control | 335 |
| Measuring variances from budget | 336 |
| Making budgetary control effective | 343 |
| Behavioural issues | 344 |
| Summary | 345 |
| Key terms | 346 |
| Reference | 346 |
| Further reading | 346 |
| Review questions | 347 |
| Exercises | 347 |

## Part 3 FINANCIAL MANAGEMENT

## 10 Making capital investment decisions 355

| | |
|---|---|
| Introduction | 355 |
| Learning outcomes | 355 |
| The nature of investment decisions | 356 |
| Investment appraisal methods | 357 |
| Accounting rate of return (ARR) | 359 |
| Payback period (PP) | 364 |
| Net present value (NPV) | 368 |
| Why NPV is better | 377 |
| Internal rate of return (IRR) | 379 |
| Some practical points | 384 |
| Investment appraisal in practice | 388 |
| Self-assessment question 10.1 | 391 |
| Summary | 393 |

Key terms   395
Further reading   395
Review questions   396
Exercises   396

## 11   Financing a business   402

Introduction   402
Learning outcomes   402
Sources of finance   403
Sources of internal finance   403
Long-term sources of internal finance   403
Short-term sources of internal finance   405
Sources of external finance   407
Long-term sources of external finance   408
Gearing and long-term financing decisions   423
Share issues   426
The role of the Stock Exchange   431
The Alternative Investment Market   435
Short-term sources of external finance   436
Long-term versus short-term borrowing   440
Providing long-term finance for the small business   441
Self-assessment question 11.1   444
Summary   446
Key terms   447
References   448
Further reading   448
Review questions   448
Exercises   448

## 12   Managing working capital   453

Introduction   453
Learning outcomes   453
What is working capital?   454
The scale of working capital   456
Managing inventories   458
Managing receivables   470
Self-assessment question 12.1   475
Managing cash   479
Managing trade payables   487
Summary   490
Key terms   492
Further reading   493

Review questions                                                    493
Exercises                                                          494

**Appendix A: Glossary of key terms**                              498
**Appendix B: Solutions to self-assessment questions**             511
**Appendix C: Solutions to review questions**                      522
**Appendix D: Solutions to selected exercises**                    535
**Appendix E: Present value table**                                563
Index                                                              565

# Preface

This text provides an introduction to accounting and finance. It is aimed primarily at students who are not majoring in accounting or finance but who are, nevertheless, studying introductory-level accounting and finance as part of their course in business, economics, hospitality management, tourism, engineering, or some other area. Students who are majoring in either accounting or finance should, however, find the book a useful introduction to the main principles, which can serve as a foundation for further study. The text does not focus on the technical aspects, but rather examines the basic principles and underlying concepts and the ways in which accounting statements and financial information can be used to improve the quality of decision making. To reinforce this practical emphasis, there are, throughout the text, numerous illustrative extracts with commentary from company reports, survey data and other sources.

In this seventh edition, we have taken the opportunity to make improvements that have been suggested by both students and lecturers who used the previous edition. We have brought up to date and expanded the number of examples from real life. We have continued to reflect the latest developments in the international rules relating to the main financial statements. We have also made reference to changes in financing methods that have emerged recently and to the financial crisis that they have partly led to.

The text is written in an 'open-learning' style. This means that there are numerous integrated activities, worked examples and questions throughout the text to help you to understand the subject fully. You are encouraged to interact with the material and to check your progress continually. Irrespective of whether you are using the book as part of a taught course or for personal study, we have found that this approach is more 'user-friendly' and makes it easier for you to learn.

We recognise that most of you will not have studied accounting or finance before, and we have therefore tried to write in a concise and accessible style, minimising the use of technical jargon. We have also tried to introduce topics gradually, explaining everything as we go. Where technical terminology is unavoidable we try to provide clear explanations. In addition, you will find all of the key terms highlighted in the text, and then listed at the end of each chapter with a page reference. All of these key terms are also listed alphabetically, with a concise definition, in the Glossary towards the end of the book (Appendix A). This should provide a convenient point of reference from which to revise.

A further important consideration in helping you to understand and absorb the topics covered is the design of the text itself. The page layout and colour scheme have been carefully considered to allow for the easy navigation and digestion of material. The layout features a large-page format, an open design, and clear signposting of the various features and assessment material. More detail about the nature and use of these features is given in the 'How to use this book' section below; and the main points are also summarised, using example pages from the text, in the guided tour on pages xviii–xx.

We hope that you find the book both readable and helpful.

## How to use this book

We have organised the chapters to reflect what we consider to be a logical sequence and, for this reason, we suggest that you work through the text in the order in which it is presented. We have tried to ensure that earlier chapters do not refer to concepts or terms that are not explained until a later chapter. If you work through the chapters in the 'wrong' order, you will probably encounter concepts and terms that were explained previously.

Irrespective of whether you are using the book as part of a lecture/tutorial-based course or as the basis for a more independent mode of study, we advocate following broadly the same approach.

### Integrated assessment material

Interspersed throughout each chapter are numerous **Activities**. You are strongly advised to attempt all of these questions. They are designed to simulate the sort of quick-fire questions that your lecturer might throw at you during a lecture or tutorial. Activities serve two purposes:

- to give you the opportunity to check that you understand what has been covered so far;
- to encourage you to think about the topic just covered, either to see a link between that topic and others with which you are already familiar, or to link the topic just covered to the next.

The answer to each Activity is provided immediately after the question. This answer should be covered up until you have deduced your solution, which can then be compared with the one given.

Towards the middle/end of each chapter, except for Chapter 1, there is a **self-assessment question**. This is more comprehensive and demanding than most of the Activities, and is designed to give you an opportunity to check and apply your understanding of the core coverage of the chapter. The answer to each of these questions is provided in Appendix B at the end of the book. As with the Activities, it is important that you attempt each question thoroughly before referring to the solution. If you have difficulty with a self-assessment question, you should go over the relevant chapter again.

### End-of-chapter assessment material

At the end of each chapter there are four **review questions**. These are short questions requiring a narrative answer or discussion within a tutorial group. They are intended to help you assess how well you can recall and critically evaluate the core terms and concepts covered in each chapter. Answers to these questions are provided in Appendix C at the end of the book.

At the end of each chapter, except for Chapter 1, there are five **exercises**. These are mostly computational and are designed to reinforce your knowledge and understanding. Exercises are graded as either 'basic' or 'more advanced' according to their level of difficulty. The basic-level questions are fairly straightforward; the more advanced ones can be quite demanding but are capable of being successfully completed if you have worked conscientiously through the chapter and have attempted the basic exercises. Answers to three of the exercises in each chapter are provided in Appendix D at the end of the book. A coloured exercise number identifies these three questions. Here, too, a thorough attempt should be made to answer each exercise before referring to the solution. Answers to the other two exercises are provided in a separate Instructors' Manual.

# Guided tour of the book

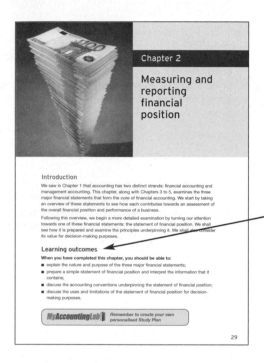

**Learning outcomes**
Bullet points at the start of each chapter show what you can expect to learn from that chapter, and highlight the core coverage.

**Key terms**
The key concepts and techniques in each chapter are highlighted in colour where they are first introduced, with an adjacent icon in the margin to help you refer back to the most important points.

**Examples**
At frequent intervals throughout most chapters, there are numerical examples that give you step-by-step workings to follow through to the solution.

## 'Real World' illustrations

Integrated throughout the text, these illustrative examples highlight the practical application of accounting concepts and techniques by real businesses, including extracts from company reports and financial statements, survey data and other interesting insights from business.

## Activities

These short questions, integrated throughout each chapter, allow you to check your understanding as you progress through the text. They comprise either a narrative question requiring you to review or critically consider topics, or a numerical problem requiring you to deduce a solution. A suggested answer is given immediately after each activity.

## Bullet point chapter summary

Each chapter ends with a 'bullet point' summary. This highlights the material covered in the chapter and can be used as a quick reminder of the main issues.

## Self-assessment questions

Towards the end of most chapters you will encounter one of these questions, allowing you to attempt a comprehensive question before tackling the end-of-chapter assessment material. To check your understanding and progress, solutions are provided at the end of the book.

## Key terms summary

At the end of each chapter, there is a listing (with page references) of all the key terms, allowing you to easily refer back to the most important points.

## Further reading

This section comprises a listing of relevant chapters in other textbooks that you might refer to in order to pursue a topic in more depth or gain an alternative perspective.

## Review questions

These short questions encourage you to review and/or critically discuss your understanding of the main topics covered in each chapter, either individually or in a group. Solutions to these questions can be found at the end of the book.

## Exercises

These comprehensive questions appear at the end of most chapters. The more advanced questions are separately identified. Solutions to some of the questions (those with coloured numbers) are provided at the end of the book, enabling you to assess your progress. Solutions to the remaining questions are available online for lecturers only. Additional exercises can be found within MyAccountingLab at **www.myaccountinglab.com**.

# Guided tour of MyAccountingLab

## What is MyAccountingLab? *MyAccountingLab*

**MyAccountingLab** for *Accounting and Finance for Non-Specialists*, Seventh Edition, enables you to assess your learning and provides you with a personalised Study Plan that identifies the areas where you need to focus to improve your grades. Specific tools are provided to direct your study in the most efficient way.

Access to **MyAccountingLab** is provided with every new purchase of the main text.

**MyAccountingLab contains the following resources for students**:

- A personalised Study Plan with extensive self-testing so that you can see the areas where you need to focus.

- A range of multiple choice problems and extended exercises for each section of the textbook. Many exercises contain figures which are re-populated every time you attempt them, to allow for unlimited practice at key concepts.

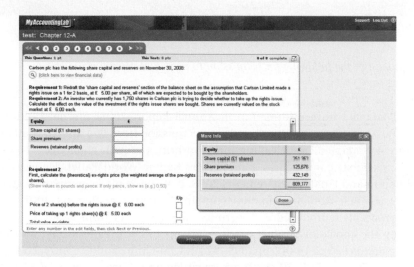

- Links to the online textbook from every question in the Study Plan, to assist your learning.
- Additional resources organised by chapter, including an online version of the full textbook which you can annotate, highlight, and bookmark as you please. You will also find Glossary Flashcards amongst the chapter resources.

**MyAccountingLab for lecturers:**

- The MyAccountingLab gradebook automatically records each student's perform-ance on all tests, homework and Study Plan material. Reports on student progress can be generated, organised by student or chapter.
- Lecturers can use MyAccountingLab to build their own tests, quizzes and home-work assignments from the question base provided.
- Many questions are generated algorithmically, containing different values each time they are used.
- If you are a lecturer and would like more information about MyAccountingLab, please contact your local Pearson representative at **www.pearsoned.co.uk/ replocator** or visit **www.myaccountinglab.com**.

**Additional lecturer resources** can be downloaded from the lecturer website at **www.pearsoned.co.uk/atrill**

# Acknowledgements

*We are grateful to the following for permission to reproduce copyright material:*

## Figures
Figure 3.1 adapted from information in Annual Report 2008, Arsenal Holdings plc, Notes to the Accounts, p. 36, reproduced with permission from The Arsenal Football Club plc; Figure 4.1 adapted from 'Falling inflation brings growth challenge', 14 October 2009, www.kamcity.com, figures compiled by Kantar World Panel; Figure 5.3 from Annual Report and Financial Statements 2008, p. 4, Tesco plc, copyright © Tesco PLC; Figure 7.9 adapted from information contained in Annual Reports 2002 to 2008, British Airways plc reproduced with permission; Figure 8.11 from 'A Survey of factors influencing the choice of product costing systems in UK organisations', *Management Accounting Research*, Vol 18 (4), pp. 399–424 (M. Al-Omiri and C. Drury 2007), copyright © 2007 Elsevier Ltd. All rights reserved; Figure 9.5 from *Financial Management and Working Capital Practices in UK SMEs*, Figure 16, Manchester Business School (F. Chittenden, P. Poutziouris and N. Michaelas 1998) p. 22, by kind permission of the authors; Figure 10.5 adapted from 'How do CFOs make capital budgeting and capital structure decisions?', *Journal of Applied Corporate Finance*, Vol 15 (1), pp. 8–23 (R. Graham and C. Harvey 2002), copyright © 2002, John Wiley and Sons; Figure 11.4 from Finance and Leasing Association Annual Review 2009, p. 9, www.fla.org.uk, copyright © Finance and Leasing Association; Figure 11.9 adapted from Client sales: domestic invoice discounting and factoring, 2001 to 2008, www.abfa.org.uk, copyright © Asset Based Finance Association; Figure 11.11 from *British Enterprise: Thriving or Surviving?*, Centre for Business Research, University of Cambridge (A. Cosh and A. Hughes 2007) reproduced with permission of the authors.

## Text
Extract 1.3 from 'Business big shot: Kate Swann of WH Smith', *The Times*, 27/01/2009, p. 39 (Ian King), http://business.timesonline.co.uk/tol/business/movers_and_shakers/article5594430.ece; Extract 2.1 from Sandeep Sud Business Link 'Balance sheets: the basics', 14/04/2010, © Crown copyright 2010; Extract 2.4 from Marks and Spencer plc Annual Report 2009, Marks and Spencer plc, note 14 Notes to the financial statements, copyright © Marks and Spencer plc; Extract 3.1 adapted from information in Annual Report 2008. Arsenal Holdings plc, Notes to the Accounts, p. 36, reproduced with permission from The Arsenal Football Club plc; Extract 3.2 from Annual Report and Accounts 2009, p. 71, TUI Travel plc, www.tuitravelplc.com, copyright © TUI Travel plc; Extract 3.6 from 'JJB massages results to boost profits', *Accountancy Age*, p. 3 reproduced with permission; Extract 4.4 from The UK Corporate Governance Code, FSA,

www.fsa.org.uk, copyright © Financial Services Authority 2010. Use of any FSA material does not indicate any endorsement or promotion of this publication by the FSA, and any views or opinions stated in this publication are not necessarily those of the FSA; Extract 6.10 from Annual Report 2009, Marks and Spencer plc, copyright © Marks and Spencer plc; Extract 10.9 from 'The theory-practice gap in capital budgeting: evidence from the United Kingdom', *Journal of Business Finance and Accounting*, Vol 27 (5), pp. 603–626 (GC Arnold and PD Hatzopoulos 2000), copyright © 2000, John Wiley and Sons; Extract 11.14 from 'Internet FD is in the money after flotation', *Accountancy Age*, p. 3 (Jetuah, D.), reproduced by permission; Extract 11.16 from Financial Statistics, *Share Ownership Survey 2008*, p. 1 (Office for National Statistics 2010), Crown Copyright material is reproduced with the permission of the Controller, Office of Public Sector Information (OPSI); Extract 12.2 adapted from REL/CFO Europe 2009, '*Europe Working Capital Survey*', p. 2 (www.relconsult.com 2009); Extract 12.10 adapted from 13 August 2008, www.atradius.us/news/press-releases, copyright © Atradius Trade Credit Insurance, Inc.; Extracts 12.12 and 12.14 adapted from 'Dash for cash' *CFO Europe magazine*, 08/07/2008 (Karaian, J.), reprinted with permission from CFO, www.cfo.com, copyright © CFO Publishing LLC. All rights reserved. Foster Printing Service: 866-879-9144, www.marketingreprints.com. License #13788.

**The Financial Times**

Extract 1.1 adapted from 'Cohort to restructure', *The Financial Times*, 09/12/2009 (Lemer, J.), copyright © The Financial Times Ltd; Extract 1.5 from 'Fair Shares?', *The Financial Times*, 11/06/2005 (Skapinker, M.), copyright © The Financial Times Ltd; Extract 1.7 adapted from 'Appetite for risks drives industry', *The Financial Times*, 27/06/2007 (Fidler, S.), copyright © The Financial Times Ltd; Extract 2.5 adapted from 'Akzo Nobel defends ICI takeover', *The Financial Times*, 24/02/2009 (Steen, M.), copyright © The Financial Times Ltd; Extract 3.8 from 'SMEs write off more bad debt', *The Financial Times*, 12/03/2010 (Moules, J.), copyright © The Financial Times Ltd; Extract 4.1 from 'Monotub Industries in a spin as founder gets Titan for £1', *The Financial Times*, 23/01/2003 (Urquhart, L.), copyright © The Financial Times Ltd; Extract 5.1 from 'Companies learn to care for cash', *The Financial Times*, 02/10/2009 (Sakoui, A.), copyright © The Financial Times Ltd; Extract 6.4 adapted from 'Costs vibrate as VW accelerates', *The Financial Times*, 29/03/2010 (Schafer, D.), copyright © The Financial Times Ltd; Extract 6.5 adapted from 'Small businesses hit at late Whitehall payments', *The Financial Times*, 02/02/2010 (Guthrie, J.), copyright © The Financial Times Ltd; Extract 6.6 adapted from 'Gearing levels set to plummet', *The Financial Times*, 10/02/2009 (Grant, J.), copyright © The Financial Times Ltd; Extract 7.4 adapted from 'Nick Reilly Head of Opel and Vauxhall', *The Financial Times*, 28/12/2009 (Milne, R.), copyright © The Financial Times Ltd; Extract 7.5 adapted from 'Chelsea owner axes £340m of debt', *The Financial Times*, 31/12/2009 (Kavanagh, M.), copyright © The Financial Times Ltd; Extract 7.6 adapted from Yahoo faces battle to keep up with its sleeker rivals, 25 January 2010. Low-cost car to challenge Tata Nano. 11 November 2009. Comet's festive sales dampened by competition 10 January 2010, *The Financial Times* (Menn, J. Leahy, J. Bintiff, E.), copyright © The Financial Times Ltd; Extract 10.4

adapted from 'Case study: power efficiency' *The Financial Times*, 25/11/2009 (Jaggi, R.), copyright © The Financial Times Ltd; Extract 10.6 adapted from 'Bond seeks funds in London to min African diamonds', *The Financial Times*, 22/04/2007 (Bream, R.), copyright © The Financial Times Ltd; Extract 10.11 from 'Satellites need space to earn', *The Financial Times*, 14/07/2003 (Burt, T.), copyright © The Financial Times Ltd; Extract 11.2 adapted from 'Man Utd's first bond suffers from lack of support', *The Financial Times*, 03/02/2010 (Sakoui, A. and Blitz, R.), copyright © The Financial Times Ltd; Extract 11.5 adapted from 'Significant doubt' over EMI's viability', *The Financial Times*, 05/02/2010 (Edgecliffe-Johnson, A. and Davoudi, S.), copyright © The Financial Times Ltd; Extract 11.8 from 'Seeds of Woolworths' demise sown long ago', *The Financial Times*, 29/11/2008 (Rigby, E.), copyright © The Financial Times Ltd; Extract 11.10 adapted from 'King fails to soothe lenders', *The Financial Times*, 23/01/2008 (Strauss, D.), copyright © The Financial Times Ltd; Extract 11.12 adapted from 'Blacks set to raise £20m in share sale', *The Financial Times*, 05/02/2010 (O'Doherty, J.), copyright © The Financial Times Ltd; Extract 12.4 adapted from 'Wal-Mart aims for further inventory cuts', *The Financial Times*, 19/04/2006 (Birchall, J.), copyright © The Financial Times Ltd.

In some instances we have been unable to trace the owners of copyright material, and we would appreciate any information that would enable us to do so.

# Chapter 1

# Introduction to accounting and finance

## Introduction

Welcome to the world of accounting and finance! In this opening chapter we provide a broad outline of these subjects. We begin by considering the roles of accounting and finance and then go on to identify the main users of financial information. We shall see how both accounting and finance can be valuable tools in helping these users improve the quality of their decisions. In subsequent chapters, we develop this decision-making theme by examining in some detail the kinds of financial reports and methods used to aid decision making.

For many of you, accounting and finance are not the main focus of your studies and you may well be asking 'Why do I need to study these subjects?' So, after we have considered the key features of accounting and finance, we shall go on to discuss why some understanding of them is likely to be relevant to you.

## Learning outcomes

**When you have completed this chapter, you should be able to:**

- explain the nature and roles of accounting and finance;
- identify the main users of financial information and discuss their needs;
- distinguish between financial accounting and management accounting;
- explain why an understanding of accounting and finance is likely to be relevant to your needs.

 **Remember to create your own personalised Study Plan**

1

## What are accounting and finance?

Let us start our study of accounting and finance by trying to understand the purpose of each. Accounting is concerned with collecting, analysing and communicating financial information. The ultimate aim is to help those using this information to make more informed decisions. If the financial information that is communicated is not capable of improving the quality of decisions made, there would be no point in producing it.

Accounting information should be useful to anyone wishing to make decisions and plans about businesses, including those who control and manage them. Thus, the managers of businesses may need accounting information to decide whether to:

- develop new products or services (as with a computer manufacturer developing a new range of computers);
- increase or decrease the price or quantity of existing products or services (as with a telecommunications business changing its mobile phone call and text charges);
- borrow money to help finance the business (as with a supermarket wishing to increase the number of stores it owns);
- increase or decrease the operating capacity of the business (as with a beef farming business reviewing the size of its herd); and
- change the methods of purchasing, production or distribution (as with a clothes retailer switching from UK to overseas suppliers).

The information provided should help in identifying and assessing the financial consequences of these sorts of decisions.

Though managers are likely to be important users of accounting information relating to their particular business, they are by no means the only users. There are others outside the business who may also need accounting information. These users will be considered in some detail a little later but examples include those deciding whether to:

- invest or disinvest in the ownership of the business (for example, investors who buy or sell shares);
- lend money to the business (for example, a bank providing a loan);
- offer credit facilities (for example, a supplier of goods or services offering delayed payment).

Sometimes the impression is given that the purpose of accounting is simply to prepare financial reports on a regular basis. While it is true that accountants undertake this kind of work, it does not represent an end in itself. As already mentioned, the ultimate aim of the accountant's work is to give people better financial information on which to base their decisions. This decision-making perspective of accounting fits in with the theme of this book and shapes the way in which we deal with each topic.

Finance (or financial management), like accounting, exists to help decision makers. It is concerned with the ways in which funds for a business are raised and invested. This lies at the very heart of what a business is about. In essence, a business exists to raise funds from investors (owners and lenders) and then to use those funds to make investments (in equipment, premises, inventories and so on) in an attempt to make the business, and its owners, wealthier. It is important that funds are raised in a way that is appropriate to the particular needs of the business. An understanding of finance should help in identifying:

- the main forms of finance available;
- the costs and benefits of each form of finance;
- the risks associated with each form of finance; and
- the role of financial markets in supplying finance.

Once the funds are raised, they must be invested in a way that will provide the business with a worthwhile return. An understanding of finance should help in evaluating

- the returns from that investment; and
- the risks associated with that investment.

Businesses tend to raise and invest funds in large amounts for long periods of time. The quality of the investment decisions made can, therefore, have a profound impact on the fortunes of the business.

There is little point in trying to make a sharp distinction between accounting and finance. We have already seen that both are concerned with the financial aspects of decision making. There is considerable overlap between the two subjects: for example, accounting reports are a major source of information for financing and investment decision making. In this book, we shall not emphasise the distinctions between accounting and finance.

## Who are the users of accounting information?

For accounting information to be useful, the accountant must be clear *for whom* the information is being prepared and *for what purpose* the information will be used. There are likely to be various groups of people (known as 'user groups') with an interest in a particular organisation, in the sense of needing to make decisions about it. For the typical private sector business, the more important of these groups are shown in Figure 1.1. Take a look at this figure and then try Activity 1.1.

### Activity 1.1

Ptarmigan Insurance plc (PI) is a large motor insurance business. Taking the user groups identified in Figure 1.1, suggest, for each group, the sorts of decisions likely to be made about PI and the factors to be taken into account when making these decisions.

Your answer may be along the following lines:

| User group | Decision |
|---|---|
| Customers | Whether to take further motor policies with PI. This might involve an assessment of PI's ability to continue in business and to meet their needs, particularly in respect of any insurance claims made. |

→

| User group | Decision |
|---|---|
| Competitors | How best to compete against PI or, perhaps, whether to leave the market on the grounds that it is not possible to compete profitably with PI. This might involve competitors using PI's performance in various respects as a 'benchmark' when evaluating their own performance. They might also try to assess PI's financial strength and to identify significant changes that may signal PI's future actions (for example, raising funds as a prelude to market expansion). |
| Employees | Whether to continue working for PI and, if so, whether to demand higher rewards for doing so. The future plans, profits and financial strength of the business are likely to be of particular interest when making these decisions. |
| Government | Whether PI should pay tax and, if so, how much, whether it complies with agreed pricing policies, whether financial support is needed and so on. In making these decisions an assessment of PI's profits, sales revenues and financial strength would be made. |
| Community representatives | Whether to allow PI to expand its premises and/or whether to provide economic support for the business. When making such decisions, PI's ability to continue to provide employment for the community and its willingness to use community resources and to fund environmental improvements are likely to be important considerations. |
| Investment analysts | Whether to advise clients to invest in PI. This would involve an assessment of the likely risks and future returns associated with PI. |
| Suppliers | Whether to continue to supply PI and, if so, whether to supply on credit. This would involve an assessment of PI's ability to pay for any goods and services supplied. |
| Lenders | Whether to lend money to PI and/or whether to require repayment of any existing loans. PI's ability to pay the interest and to repay the principal sum would be important factors in such decisions. |
| Managers | Whether the performance of the business needs to be improved. Performance to date would be compared with earlier plans or some other 'benchmark' to decide whether action needs to be taken. Managers may also wish to decide whether there should be a change in PI's future direction. This would involve looking at PI's ability to perform and at the opportunities available to it. |
| Owners | Whether to invest more in PI or to sell all, or part, of the investment currently held. This would involve an assessment of the likely risks and returns associated with PI. Owners may also be involved with decisions on rewarding senior managers. The financial performance of the business would normally be considered when making such a decision. |

Although this answer covers many of the key points, you may have identified other decisions and/or other factors to be taken into account by each group.

**Figure 1.1** Main users of financial information relating to a business

Several user groups have an interest in accounting information relating to a business. The majority of these are outside the business but, nevertheless, have a stake in it. This is not meant to be an exhaustive list of potential users; however, the groups identified are normally the most important.

## Providing a service

One way of viewing accounting is as a form of service. Accountants provide economic information to their 'clients', who are the various users identified in Figure 1.1. The quality of the service provided is determined by the extent to which the needs of the various user groups have been met. To meet these users' needs, it can be argued that accounting information should possess certain key qualities, or characteristics: relevance, reliability, comparability and understandability.

■ Relevance. It must be possible for accounting information to influence decisions. Unless this characteristic is present, there is really no point in producing the information. The information may be relevant to the prediction of future events (for example, in predicting how much profit is likely to be earned next year) or relevant in helping to confirm past events (for example, in establishing how much profit was earned last year). The role of accounting in confirming past events is important because users often wish to check the accuracy of earlier predictions that they have made. The accuracy of earlier predictions may help users to judge the accuracy of current predictions. To influence a decision, the information must, of course, be available when the decision is being made. Thus, relevant information must be timely.

■ Reliability. Accounting should be free from significant error or bias. It should be capable of being relied upon by managers to represent what it is supposed to represent. Though both relevance and reliability are very important, the problem that we often face in accounting is that information that is highly relevant may not be very reliable. Similarly, that which is reliable may not be very relevant.

### Activity 1.2

To illustrate this last point, let us assume that a manager has to sell a custom-built machine owned by the business and has recently received a bid for it. This machine is very unusual and there is no ready market for it.

What information would be relevant to the manager when deciding whether to accept the bid? How reliable would that information be?

The manager would probably like to know the current market value of the machine before deciding whether or not to accept the bid. The current market value would be highly relevant to the final decision, but it might not be very reliable because the machine is unique and there is likely to be little information concerning market values.

When seeking to strike the right balance between relevance and reliability, the needs of users should be the overriding consideration.

■ Comparability. This quality will enable users to identify changes in the business over time (for example, the trend in sales revenue over the past five years). It will also help them to evaluate the performance of the business in relation to similar businesses. Comparability is achieved by treating items that are basically the same in the same manner for accounting purposes. Comparability may also be enhanced by making clear the policies adopted in measuring and presenting the information.

■ Understandability. Accounting reports should be expressed as clearly as possible and should be understood by those at whom the information is aimed.

### Activity 1.3

Do you think that accounting reports should be understandable to those who have not studied accounting?

It would be very useful if accounting reports could be understood by everyone. This, however, is unrealistic, as complex financial events and transactions cannot normally be expressed in simple terms. It is probably best that we regard accounting reports in the same way that we regard a report written in a foreign language. To understand either of these, we need to have had some preparation. Generally speaking, accounting reports assume that the user not only has a reasonable knowledge of business and accounting but is also prepared to invest some time in studying the reports.

Despite the answer to Activity 1.3, the onus is clearly on accountants to provide information in a way that makes it as understandable as possible to non-accountants.

## But . . . is it material?

The qualities, or characteristics, that have just been described will help us to decide whether accounting information is potentially useful. If a particular piece of information has these qualities then it may be useful. However, this does not automatically mean that it should be reported to users. We also have to consider whether the information is material, or significant. This means that we should ask whether its omission or misrepresentation in the accounting reports would really alter the decisions that users make. Thus, in addition to possessing the characteristics mentioned above, accounting information must also cross the threshold of materiality. If the information is not regarded as material, it should not be included within the reports as it will merely clutter them up and, perhaps, interfere with the users' ability to interpret the financial results. The type of information and amounts involved will normally determine whether it is material.

## Weighing up the costs and benefits

Having read the previous sections you may feel that, when considering a piece of accounting information, provided the four main qualities identified are present and it is material it should be gathered and made available to users. Unfortunately, there is one more hurdle to jump. Something may still exclude a piece of accounting information from the reports even when it is considered to be useful. Consider Activity 1.4.

### Activity 1.4

Suppose an item of information is capable of being provided. It is relevant to a particular decision, it is also reliable, comparable, can be understood by the decision maker concerned and is material.

Can you think of the reason why, in practice, you might choose not to produce, or discover, the information?

The reason is that you judge the cost of doing so to be greater than the potential benefit of having the information. This cost–benefit issue will limit the amount of accounting information provided.

In theory, a particular item of accounting information should only be produced if the costs of providing it are less than the benefits, or value, to be derived from its use. In practice, however, these costs and benefits are often difficult to assess.

To illustrate the practical problems of establishing the value of information, let us assume that someone has collided with our car in a car park and dented one of the doors and scraped the paintwork. We want to have the dent taken out and the door resprayed at a local garage. We know that the nearest garage would charge £250 but we believe that other local garages may offer to do the job for a lower price. The only way of finding out the prices at other garages is to visit them, so that they can see the extent of the damage. Visiting the garages will involve using some petrol and will take up some of our time. Is it worth the cost of finding out the price for the job at the various local garages? The answer, as we have seen, is that if the cost of discovering the price is less than the potential benefit, it is worth having that information.

To identify the various prices for the job, there are several points to be considered, including:

■ How many garages shall we visit?
■ What is the cost of petrol to visit each garage?
■ How long will it take to make all the garage visits?
■ At what price do we value our time?

The economic benefit of having the information on the price of the job is probably even harder to assess. The following points need to be considered:

■ What is the cheapest price that we might be quoted for the job?
■ How likely is it that we shall be quoted a price cheaper than £250?

**Figure 1.2** The characteristics that influence the usefulness of accounting information

There are four main qualitative characteristics that influence the usefulness of accounting information. In addition, however, accounting information should be material and the benefits of providing the information should outweigh the costs.

As we can imagine, the answers to these questions may be far from clear – remember that we have only contacted the local garage so far. When assessing the value of accounting information we are confronted with similar problems.

Producing accounting information can be very costly; however, the costs are often difficult to quantify. The direct, out-of-pocket costs, such as salaries of accounting staff, are not really a problem to identify, but these are only part of the total costs involved. There are also less direct costs such as the cost of the user's time spent on analysing and interpreting the information contained in reports.

The economic benefit of having accounting information is even harder to assess. It is possible to apply some 'science' to the problem of weighing the costs and benefits, but a lot of subjective judgement is likely to be involved. No one would seriously advocate that the typical business should produce no accounting information. At the same time, no one would advocate that every item of information that could be seen as possessing one or more of the key characteristics should be produced, irrespective of the cost of producing it.

The characteristics that influence the usefulness of accounting information, and which have been discussed in this section, and the preceding section are set out in Figure 1.2.

## Accounting as an information system

We have already seen that accounting can be seen as the provision of a service to 'clients'. Another way of viewing accounting is as a part of the business's total information system. Users, both inside and outside the business, have to make decisions concerning the allocation of scarce economic resources. To ensure that these resources are efficiently allocated, users need economic information on which to base decisions. It is the role of the accounting system to provide this information.

The accounting information system should have certain features that are common to all valid information systems within a business. These are:

- identifying and capturing relevant information (in this case financial information);
- recording, in a systematic way, the information collected;
- analysing and interpreting the information collected; and
- reporting the information in a manner that suits the needs of users.

The relationship between these features is set out in Figure 1.3.

**Figure 1.3 The accounting information system**

There are four sequential stages of an accounting information system. The first two stages are concerned with preparation, whereas the last two stages are concerned with using the information collected.

Given the decision-making emphasis of this book, we shall be concerned primarily with the final two elements of the process: the analysis and reporting of accounting information. We shall consider the way in which information is used by, and is useful to, users rather than the way in which it is identified and recorded.

Efficient accounting systems are an essential ingredient of an efficient business. When the accounting systems fail, the results can be disastrous. Real World 1.1 provides an example of one such failure and its impact on the business.

---

### Real World 1.1

## System failure

Cohort, the defence services group, will shift its focus towards internal restructuring and away from the external expansion strategy it has followed in recent years in the wake of serious accounting problems, according to Andy Thomis, chief executive.

'[Acquisitions and international expansion] will follow in due course . . . at the moment we've got to sort the problems out and restore shareholder value,' Mr Thomis said.

Last week Cohort surprised the market with a profits warning and said it would miss full year results expectations. An IT changeover and accounting errors caused it to significantly overstate income on certain contracts at its SCS unit.

Since then the shares have slumped more than 40 per cent to around 95p.

Mr Thomis said he had suspended the financial controller of SCS, which provides consultancy services to the Ministry of Defence, pending the results of an ongoing investigation, and would take further steps to cut costs.

The comments came as Cohort reported its results for the six months to the end of October. Over the period, pre-tax profits fell by more than half to £1.2 million.

*Source*: 'Cohort to restructure', *The Financial Times*, 09/12/2009 (Lemer, J.), copyright © The Financial Times Ltd.

---

## Management accounting and financial accounting

Accounting is usually seen as having two distinct strands. These are:

- management accounting, which seeks to meet the accounting needs of managers; and
- financial accounting, which seeks to meet those of all of the other users identified earlier in the chapter (see Figure 1.1).

The difference in their targeted user groups has led to each strand of accounting developing along different lines. The main areas of difference are as follows.

- *Nature of the reports produced.* Financial accounting reports tend to be general-purpose, that is, they contain financial information that will be useful for a broad range of users and decisions rather than being specifically designed for the needs of a particular group or set of decisions. Management accounting reports, on the other hand, are often specific-purpose reports. They are designed with a particular decision in mind and/or for a particular manager.

- *Level of detail.* Financial accounting reports provide users with a broad overview of the performance and position of the business for a period. As a result, information is aggregated and detail is often lost. Management accounting reports, however, often provide managers with considerable detail to help them with a particular operational decision.
- *Regulations.* Financial accounting reports, for many businesses, are subject to accounting regulations that try to ensure that they are produced with standard content and in a standard format. The law and accounting rule makers impose these regulations. As management accounting reports are for internal use only, there are no regulations from external sources concerning the form and content of the reports. They can be designed to meet the needs of particular managers.
- *Reporting interval.* For most businesses, financial accounting reports are produced on an annual basis, though some large businesses produce half-yearly reports and a few produce quarterly ones. Management accounting reports may be produced as frequently as required by managers. In many businesses, managers are provided with certain reports on a daily, weekly or monthly basis, which allows them to check progress frequently. In addition, special-purpose reports will be prepared when required (for example, to evaluate a proposal to purchase a piece of equipment).
- *Time orientation.* Financial accounting reports reflect the performance and position of the business for the past period. In essence, they are backward-looking. Management accounting reports, on the other hand, often provide information concerning future performance as well as past performance. It is an oversimplification, however, to suggest that financial accounting reports never incorporate expectations concerning the future. Occasionally, businesses will release projected information to other users in an attempt to raise capital or to fight off unwanted takeover bids. Even preparation of the routine financial accounting reports typically requires making some judgements about the future, as we shall see in Chapter 3.
- *Range and quality of information.* Financial accounting reports concentrate on information that can be quantified in monetary terms. Management accounting also produces such reports, but is also more likely to produce reports that contain information of a non-financial nature, such as physical volume of inventories, number of sales orders received, number of new products launched, physical output per employee and so on. Financial accounting places greater emphasis on the use of objective, verifiable evidence when preparing reports. Management accounting reports may use information that is less objective and verifiable, but nevertheless provide managers with the information they need.

We can see from this that management accounting is less constrained than financial accounting. It may draw from a variety of sources and use information that has varying degrees of reliability. The only real test to be applied when assessing the value of the information produced for managers is whether or not it improves the quality of the decisions made.

The distinctions between management accounting and financial accounting suggest that there are differences between the information needs of managers and those of other users. While differences undoubtedly exist, there is also a good deal of overlap between these needs.

## Activity 1.5

Can you think of any areas of overlap between the information needs of managers and those of other users?

We thought of two points:

■ Managers will, at times, be interested in receiving a historical overview of business operations of the sort provided to other users.
■ Other users would be interested in receiving information relating to the future, such as the planned level of profits, and non-financial information, such as the state of the sales order book and the extent of product innovations.

The distinction between the two areas of accounting reflects, to some extent, the differences in access to financial information. Managers have much more control over the form and content of information they receive. Other users have to rely on what managers are prepared to provide or what must be provided to satisfy the financial reporting regulations. Though the scope of financial accounting reports has increased over time, fears concerning loss of competitive advantage and user ignorance concerning the reliability of forecast data have led businesses to resist providing other users with the same detailed and wide-ranging information as is available to managers.

## Scope of this book

This book covers both financial accounting and management accounting topics. Broadly speaking, the next five chapters (Part 1, Chapters 2 to 6) are concerned with financial accounting topics and the following three (Part 2, Chapters 7 to 9) with management accounting topics. The final part of the book (Part 3, Chapters 10 to 12) is concerned with the financial management of the business, that is, the chapters examine issues relating to the financing and investing activities of the business. As we have seen, accounting information is usually vitally important for these kinds of decisions.

## Has accounting become too interesting?

In recent years, accounting has become front-page news and has been a major talking point among those connected with the world of business. Unfortunately, the attention that accounting has attracted has been for all the wrong reasons. We have seen that investors rely on financial reports to help to keep an eye both on their investment and on the performance of the managers. What, though, if the managers provide misleading financial reports to investors? Recent revelations suggest that the managers of some large businesses have been doing just this.

Two of the most notorious cases have been those of:

■ Enron, an energy-trading business based in Texas, which was accused of entering into complicated financial arrangements in an attempt to obscure losses and to inflate profits; and

■ WorldCom, a major long-distance telephone operator in the US, which was accused of reclassifying $3.9 billion of expenses so as to falsely inflate the profit figures that the business reported to its owners (shareholders) and to others.

In the wake of these scandals, there was much closer scrutiny by investment analysts and investors of the financial reports that businesses produce. This led to further businesses, in both the US and Europe, being accused of using dubious accounting practices to bolster reported profits.

Accounting scandals can have a profound effect on all those connected with the business. The Enron scandal, for example, ultimately led to the collapse of the company, which, in turn, resulted in lost jobs and large financial losses for lenders, suppliers and investors. Confidence in the world of business can be badly shaken by such events and this can pose problems for society as a whole. Not surprisingly, therefore, the relevant authorities tend to deal severely with those who perpetrate such scandals. For example, in the US, Bernie Ebbers, the former chief executive of WorldCom, received twenty-five years in prison for his part in the fraud.

Various reasons have been put forward to explain this spate of scandals. Some scandals may have been caused by the pressures on managers to meet unrealistic expectations of investors for continually rising profits, others by the greed of unscrupulous executives whose pay is linked to financial performance. However, they may all reflect a particular economic environment.

Real World 1.2 offers the view that, when all appears to be going well with a business, people can be quite gullible and over-trusting.

## Real World 1.2

### The thoughts of Warren Buffett

Warren Buffett is one of the world's shrewdest and most successful investors. He believes that the accounting scandals mentioned above were perpetrated during the 'new economy boom' of the late 1990s when confidence was high and exaggerated predictions were being made concerning the future. He states that during that period

> You had an erosion of accounting standards. You had an erosion, to some extent, of executive behaviour. But during a period when everybody 'believes', people who are inclined to take advantage of other people can get away with a lot.

He believes that the worst is now over and that the 'dirty laundry' created during this heady period was later washed away when the washing machine entered the 'rinse cycle'.

*Source:* 'Buffett expects markets to get worse', *The Times*, 26 September 2002, p. 25, John Ashworth.

Whatever the causes, the result of these accounting scandals has been to undermine the credibility of financial statements and to introduce much stricter regulations concerning the quality of financial information. We shall return to this issue in later chapters when we consider the financial statements.

## The changing face of accounting

Over the past three decades, the environment within which businesses operate has become increasingly turbulent and competitive. Various reasons have been identified to explain these changes, including:

- the increasing sophistication of customers;
- the development of a global economy where national frontiers become less important;
- rapid changes in technology;
- the deregulation of domestic markets (for example, electricity, water and gas);
- increasing pressure from owners (shareholders) for competitive economic returns; and
- the increasing volatility of financial markets.

This new, more complex, environment has brought new challenges for managers and other users of accounting information. Their needs have changed and both financial accounting and management accounting have had to respond. To meet the changing needs of users there has been a radical review of the kind of information to be reported.

The changing business environment has given added impetus to the search for a clear framework and principles upon which to base financial accounting reports. Various attempts have been made to clarify the purpose of financial accounting reports and to provide a more solid foundation for the development of accounting rules. The frameworks and principles that have been developed try to address fundamental questions such as:

- Who are the users of financial accounting information?
- What kinds of financial accounting reports should be prepared and what should they contain?
- How should items such as profit and asset values be measured?

In response to criticisms that the financial reports of some businesses are not clear enough to users, accounting rule makers have tried to improve reporting rules to ensure that the accounting policies of businesses are more comparable and more transparent and that they portray economic reality more faithfully. While this has had a generally beneficial effect, the recent accounting scandals have highlighted the limitations of accounting rules in protecting investors and others.

The internationalisation of businesses has created a need for accounting rules to have an international reach. It can no longer be assumed that users of accounting information relating to a particular business are based in the country in which the business operates or are familiar with the accounting rules of that country. Thus, there has been increasing harmonisation of accounting rules across national frontiers.

Management accounting has also changed by becoming more outward-looking in its focus. In the past, information provided to managers has been largely restricted to that collected within the business. However, the attitude and behaviour of customers and rival businesses have now become the object of much information-gathering. Increasingly, successful businesses are those that are able to secure and maintain competitive advantage over their rivals.

To obtain this advantage, businesses have become more 'customer driven' (that is, concerned with satisfying customer needs). This has led to the production of management accounting information that provides details of customers and the market, such as customer evaluation of services provided and market share. In addition, information about the costs and profits of rival businesses, which can be used as 'benchmarks' by which to gauge competitiveness, is gathered and reported.

To compete successfully, businesses must also find ways of managing costs. The cost base of modern businesses is under continual review and this, in turn, has led to the development of more sophisticated methods of measuring and controlling costs.

## How are businesses managed?

We have already seen that the environment in which businesses operate has become increasingly turbulent and competitive. The effect of these environmental changes has been to make the role of managers more complex and demanding. It has meant that managers have had to find new ways to manage their business. This has increasingly  led to the introduction of strategic management.

Strategic management is designed to provide a business with a clear sense of purpose and to ensure that appropriate action is taken to achieve that purpose. The action taken should link the internal resources of the business to the external environment of competitors, suppliers, customers and so on. This should be done in such a way that any business strengths, such as having a skilled workforce, are exploited and any weaknesses, such as being short of investment finance, are not exposed. To achieve this requires the development of strategies and plans that take account of the business's strengths and weaknesses, as well as the opportunities offered and threats posed by the external environment. Access to a new, expanding market is an example of an opportunity; the decision of a major competitor to reduce prices is an example of a threat. This topic will be considered in more depth in Chapter 9 when we consider business planning and budgeting.

## What is the financial objective of a business?

A business is normally created to enhance the wealth of its owners. Throughout this book we shall assume that this is its main objective. This may come as a surprise, as there are other objectives that a business may pursue that are related to the needs of others associated with the business. For example, a business may seek to provide good working conditions for its employees, or it may seek to conserve the environment for the local community. While a business may pursue these objectives, it is normally set up with a view to increasing the wealth of its owners. In practice, the behaviour of businesses over time appears to be consistent with this objective.

Real World 1.3 explains how one well-known business has changed its focus in order to improve profits for its owners.

### Real World 1.3

## Profiting from change

It speaks volumes for the work done by Kate Swann in turning around W H Smith that when she became chief executive five years ago, the company was being spoken of in similar terms to Woolworths. Comments such as 'You wouldn't invent it if you were starting out today' and 'What is it actually for these days?' were typical among analysts, as they were with Woolies. Indeed, many thought that W H Smith was beyond help and argued that the supermarkets were eating away at sales.

Ms Swann has defied the sceptics, achieving an impressive turnaround. The company's magazine and newspaper distribution division was hived off as a separate entity and new outlets were opened at airports and railway stations – so much so that sales by W H Smith's travel unit now threaten to overtake those of its traditional high street stores. Lines with lower profit margins, such as CDs and DVDs, have been cleared from the shelves to make way for items with higher profit margins, such as stationery.

The last plank of the strategy was in evidence again in yesterday's update, in which Ms Swann reported that sales in the nine weeks to 17 January were down by 7 per cent in the high street stores and by 2 per cent in the travel stores, partly because W H Smith is continuing to reduce its exposure to the entertainment category.

That was the bad news. The good news was that, although sales overall were down, the reduced focus on entertainment was good for profits. W H Smith made an extra 2p of profit in every £1 of sales, compared with the same period a year earlier, a stunning achievement given the deflation hitting the high street.

*Source*: 'Business big shot: Kate Swann of WH Smith', *The Times*, 27 January 2009, p. 39 (Ian King), http://business.timesonline.co.uk/tol/business/movers_and_shakers/article5594430.ece.

Within a market economy there are strong competitive forces at work that ensure that failure to enhance owners' wealth will not be tolerated for long. Competition for the funds provided by the owners and competition for managers' jobs will normally mean that the owners' interests will prevail. If the managers do not provide the expected increase in ownership wealth, the owners have the power to replace the existing management team with a new team that is more responsive to owners' needs.

Does this mean that the needs of other groups associated with the business (employees, customers, suppliers, the community and so on) are not really important? The answer to this question is certainly no, if the business wishes to survive and prosper over the longer term. Satisfying the needs of other groups will normally be consistent with increasing the wealth of the owners over the longer term.

The importance of customers to a business cannot be overstated. Dissatisfied customers will take their business to another supplier and this will, in turn, lead to a loss of wealth for the owners of the business losing the customers. Real World 1.4 provides an illustration of the way in which one business acknowledges the link between customer satisfaction and creating wealth for its owners.

## Checking out Sainsbury's objectives

J. Sainsbury plc is a leading food retailer that recognises the importance of customers to increasing the wealth of the owners (shareholders) as follows:

Our objective is to serve customers well and thereby provide shareholders with good, sustainable financial returns.

*Source*: Investor FAQs, www.j-sainsbury.co.uk, November 2009, p. 2.

A dissatisfied workforce may result in low productivity, strikes and so forth, which will in turn have an adverse effect on owners' wealth. Similarly, a business that upsets the local community by unacceptable behaviour, such as polluting the environment, may attract bad publicity, resulting in a loss of customers. It may also attract heavy fines.

Real World 1.5 provides an example of how two businesses responded to potentially damaging allegations.

## The price of clothes

US clothing and sportswear manufacturers Gap and Nike have many of their clothes produced in Asia where labour tends to be cheap. However, some of the contractors that produce clothes on behalf of the two companies have been accused of unacceptable practices.

Campaigners visited the factories and came up with damaging allegations. The factories were employing minors, they said, and managers were harassing female employees.

Nike and Gap reacted by allowing independent inspectors into the factories. They promised to ensure their contractors obeyed minimum standards of employment. Earlier this year, Nike took the extraordinary step of publishing the names and addresses of all its contractors' factories on the internet. The company said it could not be sure all the abuse had stopped. It said that if campaigners visited its contractors' factories and found examples of continued malpractice, it would take action.

Nike and Gap said the approach made business sense. They needed society's approval if they were to prosper. Nike said it was concerned about the reaction of potential US recruits to the campaigners' allegations. They would not want to work for a company that was constantly in the news because of the allegedly cruel treatment of those who made its products.

*Source*: 'Fair shares?', *The Financial Times*, 11/06/2005 (Skapinker, M.), copyright © The Financial Times Ltd.

It is important to recognise that generating wealth for the owners is not the same as seeking to maximise the current year's profit. Wealth creation is a longer-term concept, which relates not only to this year's profit but to that of future years as well. In the short term, corners can be cut and risks taken that improve current profit at the expense of future profit. Real World 1.6 provides some examples of how emphasis on short-term profit can be damaging.

## Short-term gains, long-term problems

For many years, under the guise of defending capitalism, we have been allowing ourselves to degrade it. We have been poisoning the well from which we have drawn wealth.

We have misunderstood the importance of values to capitalism. We have surrendered to the idea that success is pursued by making as much money as the law allowed without regard to how it was made.

Thirty years ago, retailers would be quite content to source the shoes they wanted to sell as cheaply as possible. The working conditions of those who produced them was not their concern.

Then headlines and protests developed. Society started to hold them responsible for previously invisible working conditions.

Companies like Nike went through a transformation. They realised they were polluting their brand. Global sourcing became visible. It was no longer viable to define success simply in terms of buying at the lowest price and selling at the highest.

Financial services and investment are today where footwear was thirty years ago. Public anger at the crisis will make visible what was previously hidden.

Take the building up of huge portfolios of loans to poor people on US trailer parks. These loans were authorised without proper scrutiny of the circumstances of the borrowers. Somebody else then deemed them fit to be securitised and so on through credit default swaps and the rest without anyone seeing the transaction in terms of its ultimate human origin.

Each of the decision makers thought it okay to act like the thoughtless footwear buyer of the 1970s. The price was attractive. There was money to make on the deal. Was it responsible? Irrelevant. It was legal, and others were making money that way.

And the consequences for the banking system if everybody did it? Not our problem.

Now we are paying the price in trillions of dollars for that imprudent attitude.

One senior investment banker whose business has survived the crisis in good shape recently confirmed this analysis to me. Again and again new product ideas had been put in front of him, without any prior thought about their ethical content.

The consumer has had a profound shock. Surely we could have expected the clever and wise people who invested our money to be better at risk management than they have shown themselves to be in the present crisis?

How could they have been so gullible in not challenging the bankers whose lending proved so flaky? How could they have believed that the levels of bonuses that were, at least in part, coming out of their savings could have been justified in 'incentivising' a better performance? How could they have believed that a 'better' performance would be one that is achieved for one bank without regard to its effect on the whole banking system? Where was the stewardship from those exercising investment on their behalf?

The answer has been that very few of them do exercise that stewardship. Most have stood back and said it doesn't really pay them to do so.

> The failure of stewardship comes from the same mindset that created the irresponsible lending in the first place. We are back to the mindset that has allowed us to poison the well: never mind the health of the system as a whole, I'm making money out of it at the moment.
>
> Responsibility means awareness for the system consequences of our actions. It is not a luxury. It is the cornerstone of prudence.
>
> *Source*: Goyder, M., 'How we've poisoned the well of wealth', *The Financial Times*, 15 February 2009.

## Balancing risk and return

All decision making involves the future, and business decision making is no exception. The only thing certain about the future, however, is that we cannot be sure what will happen. Things may not turn out as planned and this risk should be carefully considered when making financial decisions.

As in other aspects of life, risk and return tend to be related. Evidence shows that returns relate to risk in something like the way shown in Figure 1.4.

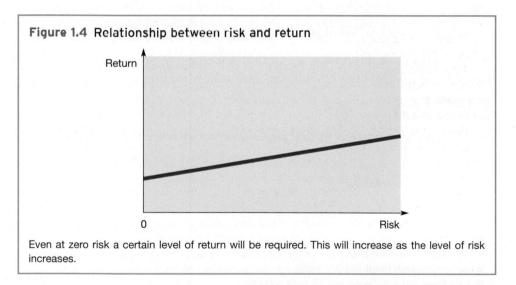

**Figure 1.4 Relationship between risk and return**

Even at zero risk a certain level of return will be required. This will increase as the level of risk increases.

This relationship between risk and return has important implications for setting financial objectives for a business. The owners will require a minimum return to induce them to invest at all, but will require an additional return to compensate for taking risks; the higher the risk, the higher the required return. Managers must be aware of this and must strike the appropriate balance between risk and return when setting objectives and pursuing particular courses of action.

Real World 1.7 describes how some businesses have been making higher-risk investments in pursuit of higher returns.

### Real World 1.7

## Appetite for risk drives businesses

Over the last few years, companies from the US and western Europe, joined increasingly by competitors from China and India, have looked to new markets abroad both to source and sell their products.

Driven by intensifying competition at home, companies have been drawn into direct investment in markets that not long ago were considered beyond the pale. But in the drive to increase returns, they have also been forced to accept higher risks.

Over time, the balance between risk and reward changes. For example, companies flooded into Russia early in the decade. But recently returns have fallen, largely due to booming raw materials prices. Meanwhile the apparent risk of investing in Russia has grown significantly.

As the risk/reward calculation has changed in Russia, companies have looked to other countries such as Libya and Vietnam where the rewards may be substantial, and the threats, though high, may be more manageable.

*Source*: adapted from 'Appetite for risk drives industry', *The Financial Times*, 27/06/2007 (Fidler, S.), copyright © The Financial TImes Ltd.

## Not-for-profit organisations

Though the focus of this book is accounting as it relates to private sector businesses, there are many organisations that do not exist mainly for the pursuit of profit.

### Activity 1.6

Can you think of at least four types of organisation that are not primarily concerned with making profits?

We thought of the following:

- charities
- clubs and associations
- universities
- local government authorities
- national government departments
- churches
- trade unions.

All of these organisations need to produce accounting information for decision-making purposes. Once again, various user groups need this information to help them to make decisions. These user groups are often the same as, or similar to, those identified for private sector businesses. They may have a stake in the future viability of the organisation and may use accounting information to check that the wealth of the organisation is being properly controlled and used in a way that is consistent with its objectives.

Real World 1.8 provides an example of the importance of accounting to relief agencies.

## Accounting for disasters

In the aftermath of the Asian tsunami more than £400 million was raised from charitable donations. It was important that his huge amount of money for aid and reconstruction was used as efficiently and effectively as possible. That did not just mean medical staff and engineers. It also meant accountants.

The charity that exerts financial control over aid donations is Mango: Management Accounting for Non-Governmental Organisations (NGOs). It provides accountants in the field and it provides the back-up, such as financial training and all the other services that should result in really robust financial management in a disaster area.

The world of aid has changed completely as a result of the tsunami. According to Mango's director, Alex Jacobs, 'Accounting is just as important as blankets. Agencies have been aware of this for years. But when you move on to a bigger scale there is more pressure to show the donations are being used appropriately.'

More recently, the earthquake in Haiti led to a call from Mango for French-speaking accountants to help support the relief programme and to help in the longer-term rebuilding of Haiti.

*Sources*: adapted from Bruce, R., 'Tsunami: finding the right figures for disaster relief', FT.com, 7 March 2005; Bruce, R., 'The work of Mango: coping with generous donations', FT.com, 27 February 2006; and Grant, P., 'Accountants needed in Haiti', *Accountancy Age*, 5 February 2010.

## Why do I need to know anything about accounting and finance?

If you are planning a career in accounting or finance, you will be clear as to why you are now studying these subjects.

If your career plans do not lie in that direction, you may be asking yourself at this point 'Why do I need to study accounting and finance? I don't intend to become an accountant!' Well, from the explanation of what accounting and finance is about, which has broadly been the subject of this chapter, it should be clear that the accounting/finance function within a business is a central part of its management information system. On the basis of information provided by the system, managers make decisions concerning the allocation of resources. These decisions may concern whether to:

- continue with certain business operations;
- invest in particular projects; or
- sell particular products.

Such decisions can have a profound effect on all those connected with the business. It is important, therefore, that *all* those who intend to work in a business should have a fairly clear idea of certain important aspects of accounting and finance. These aspects include

- how accounting reports should be read and interpreted;
- how financial plans are made;
- how investment decisions are made; and
- how businesses are financed.

Many, perhaps most, students have a career goal of being a manager within a business – perhaps a personnel manager, production manager, marketing manager or IT manager. If you are one of these students, an understanding of accounting and finance is very important. When you become a manager, even a junior one, it is almost certain that you will have to use financial reports to help you to carry out your management tasks. It is equally certain that it is largely on the basis of financial information and reports that your performance as a manager will be judged.

As a manager, it is likely that you will be expected to help in forward planning for the business. This will often involve the preparation of projected financial statements and setting of financial targets. If you do not understand what the financial statements really mean and the extent to which the financial information is reliable, you will find yourself at a distinct disadvantage to others who know their way round the system. As a manager, you will also be expected to help decide how the limited resources available to the business should be allocated between competing options. This will require an ability to evaluate the costs and benefits of the different options available. Once again, an understanding of accounting and finance is important to carrying out this management task.

This is not to say that you cannot be an effective and successful personnel, production, marketing or IT manager unless you are also a qualified accountant. It does mean, however, that you need to become a bit 'streetwise' in accounting and finance in order to succeed. This book should give you that street wisdom.

## Summary

The main points of this chapter may be summarised as follows.

### What are accounting and finance?

- Accounting provides financial information to help various user groups make better judgements and decisions.
- Finance is concerned with the financing and investing activities of the business and is also concerned with improving the quality of user decisions.

### Accounting and user needs

- For accounting to be useful, there must be a clear understanding of *for whom* and *for what purpose* the information will be used.
- Owners, managers and lenders are important user groups, but there are several others.

### Providing a service

- Accounting can be viewed as a form of service as it involves providing financial information required by the various users.

- To provide a useful service, accounting must possess certain qualities, or characteristics. These are relevance, reliability, comparability and understandability. In addition, accounting information must be material.

- Providing a service to users can be costly and financial information should be produced only if the cost of providing the information is less than the benefits gained.

### Accounting information

- Accounting is part of the total information system within a business. It shares the features that are common to all information systems within a business, which are the identification, recording, analysis and reporting of information.

### Management accounting and financial accounting

- Accounting has two main strands – management accounting and financial accounting.

- Management accounting seeks to meet the needs of the business's managers, and financial accounting seeks to meet the needs of the other user groups.

- These two strands differ in terms of the types of reports produced, the level of reporting detail, the time horizon, the degree of regulation and the range and quality of information provided.

### Is accounting too interesting?

- In recent years, there has been a wave of accounting scandals in the US and Europe.

- This appears to reflect a particular economic environment, although other factors may also play a part.

### The changing face of accounting

- Changes in the economic environment have led to changes in the nature and scope of accounting.

- Financial accounting has improved its framework of rules and there has been greater international harmonisation of accounting rules.

- Management accounting has become more outward-looking, and new methods for managing costs have emerged.

### How are businesses managed?

- Strategic management has been increasingly adopted to cope with the more complex and more competitive business environment.

- It is designed to provide a clear sense of purpose and to ensure that any action taken is consistent with this purpose.

### What is the financial objective of a business?

- The key financial objective is to enhance the wealth of the owners. To achieve this objective, the needs of other groups connected with the business, such as employees, cannot be ignored.

- When setting financial objectives, the right balance must be struck between risk and return.

### Why study accounting?

- Everyone connected with business should be a little 'streetwise' about accounting and finance because they exert such an enormous influence over business operations.

**MyAccountingLab** | Now check your progress in your personal Study Plan

 **Key terms**

| | |
|---|---|
| accounting p. 2 | materiality p. 7 |
| finance p. 2 | accounting information system p. 9 |
| relevance p. 5 | management accounting p. 10 |
| reliability p. 6 | financial accounting p. 10 |
| comparability p. 6 | strategic management p. 15 |
| understandability p. 6 | |

## Further reading

If you would like to explore the topics covered in this chapter in more depth, we recommend the following books:

Atrill, P. and McLaney, E., *Management Accounting for Decision Makers* (6th edn), Financial Times Prentice Hall, 2009, chapter 1.

Elliot, B. and Elliot, J., *Financial Accounting and Reporting* (13th edn), Financial Times Prentice Hall, 2010, chapter 7.

Horngren, C., Bhimani, A., Datar, S. and Foster, G., *Management and Cost Accounting* (4th edn), Prentice Hall, 2007, chapter 1.

McLaney, E., *Business Finance: Theory and Practice* (9th edn), Prentice Hall, 2011, chapters 1 and 2.

# ? Review questions

Solutions to these questions can be found at the back of the book, in Appendix C.

**1.1** What is the purpose of providing accounting information?

**1.2** Identify the main users of accounting information for a university. For what purposes would different user groups need information? Is there a major difference in the ways in which accounting information for a university would be used compared with that of a private sector business?

**1.3** Management accounting has been described as 'the eyes and ears of management'. What do you think this expression means?

**1.4** Financial accounting statements tend to reflect past events. In view of this, how can they be of any assistance to a user in making a decision when decisions, by their very nature, can only be made about future actions?

# Part 1

# FINANCIAL ACCOUNTING

**2** Measuring and reporting financial position

**3** Measuring and reporting financial performance

**4** Accounting for limited companies

**5** Measuring and reporting cash flows

**6** Analysing and interpreting financial statements

## Chapter 2

# Measuring and reporting financial position

## Introduction

We saw in Chapter 1 that accounting has two distinct strands: financial accounting and management accounting. This chapter, along with Chapters 3 to 5, examines the three major financial statements that form the core of financial accounting. We start by taking an overview of these statements to see how each contributes towards an assessment of the overall financial position and performance of a business.

Following this overview, we begin a more detailed examination by turning our attention towards one of these financial statements: the statement of financial position. We shall see how it is prepared and examine the principles underpinning it. We shall also consider its value for decision-making purposes.

## Learning outcomes

**When you have completed this chapter, you should be able to:**

- explain the nature and purpose of the three major financial statements;
- prepare a simple statement of financial position and interpret the information that it contains;
- discuss the accounting conventions underpinning the statement of financial position;
- discuss the uses and limitations of the statement of financial position for decision-making purposes.

 *Remember to create your own personalised Study Plan*

## Making financial decisions

We have just seen that a key purpose of this chapter is to show how the statement of financial position may help users. So, let us begin by providing an example of its value for decision making. Real World 2.1 describes how the statement of financial position of a small business was used by a bank when considering whether to grant a loan.

---

### Real World 2.1

### A sound education

Sandeep Sud is a qualified solicitor who also runs a school uniform business based in Hounslow, in partnership with his parents. The business, which has four full-time employees, uses its statement of financial position to gauge how the business is progressing. It has also been a key factor in securing a bank loan for the improvement and expansion of the business premises.

According to Sandeep,

Having a strong statement of financial position helped when it came to borrowing. When we first applied for a refurbishment loan we couldn't provide up-to-date accounts to the bank manager. This could have been a problem, but we quickly got our accounts in order and the loan was approved straight away. Because our statement of financial position was strong, the bank thought we were a good risk. Although we decided not to draw down on the loan – because we used cash flow instead – it did open our eyes to the importance of a strong statement of financial position.

*Source*: adapted from 'Balance sheets: the basics', www.businesslink.gov.uk, accessed 14 April 2010.

---

Before we consider this financial statement in detail, however, we should first gain an overview of all three major financial accounting statements. This will help us to understand the role of each as well as their interrelationships.

## The major financial statements – an overview

The major financial accounting statements aim to provide a picture of the financial position and performance of a business. To achieve this, a business's accounting system will normally produce three financial statements on a regular, recurring basis. These three statements are concerned with answering the following questions relating to a particular period:

- What cash movements took place?
- How much wealth was generated?
- What is the accumulated wealth of the business at the end of the period and what form does it take?

To address each of the above questions, there is a separate financial statement. The financial statements are:

- the statement of cash flows,
- the income statement (also known as the profit and loss account), and
- the statement of financial position (also known as the balance sheet).

Together they provide an overall picture of the financial health of the business.

Perhaps the best way to introduce these financial statements is to look at an example of a very simple business. From this we shall be able to see the sort of information that each of the statements can usefully provide. It is, however, worth pointing out that, while a simple business is our starting point, the principles for preparing the financial statements apply equally to the largest and most complex businesses. Thus, we shall frequently encounter these principles again in later chapters.

## Example 2.1

Paul was unemployed and unable to find a job. He therefore decided to embark on a business venture. With Christmas approaching, he decided to buy gift wrapping paper from a local supplier and to sell it on the corner of his local high street. He felt that the price of wrapping paper in the high street shops was too high. This provided him with a useful business opportunity.

He began the venture with £40 of his own money, in cash. On Monday, Paul's first day of trading, he bought wrapping paper for £40 and sold three-quarters of it for £45 cash.

### What cash movements took place in Paul's business during Monday?

For Monday, a *statement of cash flows* showing the cash movements (that is, cash in and cash out) for the day can be prepared as follows:

**Statement of cash flows for Monday**

|  | £ |
|---|---|
| Opening balance (cash introduced) | 40 |
| Cash from sales of wrapping paper | 45 |
| Cash paid to buy wrapping paper | (40) |
| Closing balance of cash | 45 |

The statement shows that Paul placed £40 cash into the business. The business received £45 cash from customers, but paid £40 cash to buy the wrapping paper. This left £45 of cash by Monday evening. Note that we are taking the standard approach found in the financial statements of showing figures to be deducted (in this case the £40 paid out) in brackets. We shall take this approach consistently throughout the chapters dealing with financial statements.

**How much wealth (that is, profit) was generated by the business during Monday?**

An *income statement* (*profit and loss account*) can be prepared to show the wealth (profit) generated on Monday. The wealth generated arises from trading and will be the difference between the value of the sales made and the cost of the goods (that is, wrapping paper) sold.

**Income statement (profit and loss account) for Monday**

| | £ |
|---|---|
| Sales revenue | 45 |
| Cost of goods sold (¾ of £40) | (30) |
| Profit | 15 |

Note that it is only the cost of the wrapping paper *sold* that is matched against (and deducted from) the sales revenue in order to find the profit, not the whole of the cost of wrapping paper acquired. Any unsold inventories (in this case ¼ of £40 = £10) will be charged against the future sales revenue that they generate.

**What is the accumulated wealth on Monday evening and what form does it take?**

To establish the accumulated wealth at the end of Monday's trading, we can draw up a *statement of financial position* (*balance sheet*) for Paul's business. This statement will also list the forms of wealth held at the end of that day.

**Statement of financial position (balance sheet)**
**as at Monday evening**

| | £ |
|---|---|
| Cash (closing balance) | 45 |
| Inventories of goods for resale (¼ of £40) | 10 |
| Total assets | 55 |
| Equity | 55 |

Note the terms 'assets' and 'equity' that appear in the above statement. 'Assets' are business resources (things of value to the business) and include cash and inventories. 'Equity' is the word used in accounting to describe the investment, or stake, of the owner(s) – in this case Paul – in the business. Both of these terms will be discussed in some detail a little later in this chapter.

We can see from the financial statements in Example 2.1 that each statement provides part of a picture of the financial performance and position of the business. We begin by showing the cash movements. Cash is a vital resource that is necessary for any business to function effectively. It is required to meet debts that become due and to acquire other resources (such as inventories). Cash has been described as the 'lifeblood' of a business.

Reporting cash movements alone, however, is not enough to portray the financial health of the business. To find out how much profit was generated, we need an income statement. It is important to recognise that cash and profits rarely move in unison. During Monday, for example, the cash balance increased by £5, but the profit generated, as shown in the income statement, was £15. The cash balance did not increase in line with profit because part of the wealth generated (£10) was held in the form of inventories.

The statement of financial position that was drawn up as at the end of Monday's trading provides an insight into the total wealth of the business. This wealth can be held in various forms. For this business, wealth is held in the form of cash and inventories (also known as stock). Hence, when drawing up the statement of financial position, both forms will be listed. For a large business, many other forms of wealth may be held, such as property, equipment, motor vehicles and so on.

Let us now continue with our example.

<table>
<tr><td>Example 2.2</td></tr>
</table>

On Tuesday, Paul bought more wrapping paper for £20 cash. He managed to sell all of the new inventories and all of the earlier inventories, for a total of £48.

The statement of cash flows for Tuesday will be as follows:

**Statement of cash flows for Tuesday**

|  | £ |
|---|---|
| Opening balance (from Monday evening) | 45 |
| Cash from sales of wrapping paper | 48 |
| Cash paid to buy wrapping paper | (20) |
| Closing balance | 73 |

The income statement for Tuesday will be as follows:

**Income statement for Tuesday**

|  | £ |
|---|---|
| Sales revenue | 48 |
| Cost of goods sold (£20 + £10) | (30) |
| Profit | 18 |

The statement of financial position as at Tuesday evening will be:

**Statement of financial position as at Tuesday evening**

|  | £ |
|---|---|
| Cash (closing balance) | 73 |
| Inventories | – |
| Total assets | 73 |
| Equity | 73 |

We can see that the total business wealth increased to £73 by Tuesday evening. This represents an increase of £18 (that is, £73 – £55) over Monday's figure – which, of course, is the amount of profit made during Tuesday as shown on the income statement.

### Activity 2.1

On Wednesday, Paul bought more wrapping paper for £46 cash. However, it was raining hard for much of the day and sales were slow. After Paul had sold half of his total inventories for £32, he decided to stop trading until Thursday morning.

Have a go at drawing up the three financial statements for Paul's business for Wednesday.

**Statement of cash flows for Wednesday**

| | £ |
|---|---|
| Opening balance (from the Tuesday evening) | 73 |
| Cash from sales of wrapping paper | 32 |
| Cash paid to buy wrapping paper | (46) |
| Closing balance | 59 |

**Income statement for Wednesday**

| | £ |
|---|---|
| Sales revenue | 32 |
| Cost of goods sold (½ of £46) | (23) |
| Profit | 9 |

**Statement of financial position as at Wednesday evening**

| | £ |
|---|---|
| Cash (closing balance) | 59 |
| Inventories (½ of £46) | 23 |
| Total assets | 82 |
| Equity | 82 |

Note that the total business wealth has increased by £9 (that is, the amount of Wednesday's profit) even though the cash balance has declined. This is because the business is holding more of its wealth in the form of inventories rather than cash, compared with the position on Tuesday evening.

By Wednesday evening, the equity stood at £82. This arose from Paul's initial investment of £40, plus his profits for Monday (£15), Tuesday (£18) and Wednesday (£9). This represents Paul's total investment in his business at that time. The equity of most businesses will similarly be made up of injections of funds by the owner plus any accumulated profits.

We can see that the income statement and statement of cash flows are both concerned with measuring flows (of wealth and cash respectively) during a particular period. The statement of financial position, however, is concerned with the financial position at a particular moment in time. Figure 2.1 illustrates this point.

**Figure 2.1** The relationship between the statement of financial position, the income statement and the statement of cash flows

The income statement and statement of cash flows are concerned with measuring flows of wealth and cash (respectively) over time. The statement of financial position, however, is concerned with measuring the amount of wealth at a particular moment in time.

The three financial statements discussed are often referred to as the final accounts of the business.

For external users (that is, virtually all users except the managers of the business concerned), these statements are normally backward-looking because they are based on information concerning past events and transactions. This can be useful in providing feedback on past performance and in identifying trends that provide clues to future performance. However, the statements can also be prepared using projected data to help assess likely future profits, cash flows and so on. The financial statements are normally prepared on a projected basis for internal decision-making purposes only. Managers are usually reluctant to publish these projected statements for external users, as they may reveal valuable information to competitors.

Now that we have an overview of the financial statements, we shall consider each one in detail. The remainder of this chapter is devoted to the statement of financial position. Chapter 3 looks at the income statement and Chapter 5 looks at the statement of cash flows. (Chapter 4 looks at the statements of financial position and income statements of limited companies.)

## The statement of financial position

We saw a little earlier that this statement shows the forms in which the wealth of a business is held and how much wealth is held in each form. We can, however, be more specific about the nature of this statement by saying that it sets out the assets of a business, on the one hand, and the claims against the business, on the other. Before looking at the statement of financial position in more detail, we need to be clear about what these terms mean.

## Assets

An asset is essentially a resource held by a business. For a particular item to be treated as an asset for accounting purposes, it should have the following characteristics:

- *A probable future benefit must exist.* This simply means that the item must be expected to have some future monetary value. This value can arise through its use within the business or through its hire or sale. Thus, an obsolete piece of equipment that could be sold for scrap would still be considered an asset, whereas an obsolete piece of equipment that could not be sold for scrap would not be regarded as one.
- *The business must have the right to control the resource.* Unless the business controls the resource, it cannot be regarded as an asset for accounting purposes. Thus, for a business offering holidays on barges, the canal system may be a very valuable resource, but as the business will not be able to control the access of others to the canal system, it cannot be regarded as an asset of the business. (However, the barges owned by the business would be regarded as assets.)
- *The benefit must arise from some past transaction or event.* This means that the transaction (or other event) giving rise to a business's right to the benefit must have already occurred and will not arise at some future date. Thus an agreement by a business to buy a piece of equipment at some future date would not mean the item is currently an asset of the business.
- *The asset must be capable of measurement in monetary terms.* Unless the item can be measured in monetary terms, with a reasonable degree of reliability, it will not be regarded as an asset for inclusion on the statement of financial position. Thus, the title of a magazine (for example *Hello!* or *Vogue*) that was created by its publisher may be extremely valuable to that publishing business, but this value is usually difficult to quantify. It will not, therefore, be treated as an asset.

Note that all four of these conditions must apply. If one of them is missing, the item will not be treated as an asset for accounting purposes and will not, therefore, appear on the statement of financial position.

We can see that these conditions will strictly limit the kind of items that may be referred to as 'assets' in the statement of financial position. Certainly not all resources exploited by a business will be assets of the business for accounting purposes. Some, like the canal system or the magazine title *Hello!*, may well be assets in a broader sense, but not for accounting purposes. Once an asset has been acquired by a business, it will continue to be considered an asset until the benefits are exhausted or the business disposes of it in some way.

## Activity 2.2

Indicate which of the following items could appear as an asset on the statement of financial position of a business. Explain your reasoning in each case.

1 £1,000 owed to the business by a customer who is unable to pay.
2 A patent, bought from an inventor, that gives the business the right to produce a new product. Production of the new product is expected to increase profits over the period during which the patent is held.
3 A new marketing director, whom the business had recently hired, who is confidently expected to increase profits by over 30 per cent during the next three years.
4 A recently purchased machine that will save the business £10,000 each year. It is already being used by the business but it has been acquired on credit and is not yet paid for.

Your answer should be along the following lines.

1 Under normal circumstances, a business would expect a customer to pay the amount owed. Such an amount is therefore typically shown as an asset under the heading 'trade receivables' (or 'debtors'). However, in this particular case the customer is unable to pay. As a result, the item is incapable of providing future benefits and the £1,000 owing would not be regarded as an asset. Debts that are not paid are referred to as 'bad debts'.
2 The patent would meet all of the conditions set out above and would therefore be regarded as an asset.
3 The new marketing director would not be considered as an asset. One argument for this is that the business does not have exclusive rights of control over the director. (Nevertheless, it may have an exclusive right to the services that the director provides.) Perhaps a stronger argument is that the value of the director cannot be measured in monetary terms with any degree of reliability.
4 The machine would be considered an asset even though it is not yet paid for. Once the business has agreed to buy the machine and has accepted it, the machine represents an asset even though payment is still outstanding. (The amount outstanding would be shown as a claim, as we shall see below.)

The sorts of items that often appear as assets in the statement of financial position of a business include:

- property
- plant and equipment
- fixtures and fittings
- patents and trademarks
- trade receivables (debtors)
- investments outside the business.

### Activity 2.3

**Can you think of two additional items that might appear as assets in the statement of financial position of a typical business?**

You may be able to think of a number of other items. Two that we have met so far, because they were held by Paul's wrapping-paper business (in Example 2.1), are inventories and cash.

Note that an asset does not have to be a physical item – it may be a non-physical item that gives a right to certain benefits. Assets that have a physical substance and can be touched (such as inventories) are referred to as tangible assets. Assets that have no physical substance but which, nevertheless, provide expected future benefits (such as patents) are referred to as intangible assets.

## Claims

A claim is an obligation of the business to provide cash, or some other form of benefit, to an outside party. It will normally arise as a result of the outside party providing assets for use by the business. There are essentially two types of claim against a business:

- **Equity**. This represents the claim of the owner(s) against the business. This claim is sometimes referred to as the *owner's capital*. Some find it hard to understand how the owner can have a claim against the business, particularly when we consider the example of a sole-proprietor-type business where the owner *is*, in effect, the business. For accounting purposes, however, a clear distinction is made between the business and the owner(s). The business is viewed as being quite separate from the owner. It is seen as a separate entity with its own separate existence and when financial statements are prepared, they relate to the business rather than to the owner(s). Viewed from this perspective, any funds contributed by the owner will be seen as coming from outside the business and will appear as a claim against the business in its statement of financial position.

  The equity section of the statement of financial position is broadly the same irrespective of the type of business concerned. We shall see in Chapter 4 that, with limited companies, the total equity figure must be analysed according to how each part of it first arose. For example, companies must make a distinction between that part of it that arose from retained earnings (or profits) and that part that arose from the owners putting in cash to start up the business, usually by buying shares in the company.

- **Liabilities**. Liabilities represent the claims of all individuals and organisations other than the owner(s). They arise from past transactions or events such as supplying goods or lending money to the business. A liability will be settled through an outflow of assets (usually cash).

Once a claim from the owners or outsiders has been incurred by a business, it will remain as an obligation until it is settled.

Now that the meanings of the terms *assets*, *equity* and *liabilities* have been established, we can consider the relationship between them. This relationship is quite straightforward. If a business wishes to acquire assets, it must raise the necessary funds from somewhere. It may raise these funds from the owner(s), or from other outside parties, or from both. Example 2.3 illustrates this relationship.

## Example 2.3

Jerry and Company is a new business that was created by depositing £20,000 in a bank account on 1 March. This amount was raised partly from the owner (£6,000) and partly from borrowing (£14,000). Raising funds in this way will give rise to a claim on the business by both the owner (equity) and the lender (liability). If a statement of financial position of Jerry and Company is prepared following the above transactions, it will appear as follows:

**Jerry and Company**
**Statement of financial position as at 1 March**

|  | £ |
|---|---|
| **ASSETS** | |
| Cash at bank | 20,000 |
| | |
| Total assets | 20,000 |
| **EQUITY AND LIABILITIES** | |
| Equity | 6,000 |
| Liabilities – borrowing | 14,000 |
| Total equity and liabilities | 20,000 |

We can see from the statement of financial position that the total claims (equity and liabilities) are the same as the total assets. Thus:

**Assets = Equity + Liabilities**

This equation – which we shall refer to as the *accounting equation* – will always hold true. Whatever changes may occur to the assets of the business or the claims against it, there will be compensating changes elsewhere that will ensure that the statement of financial position always 'balances'. By way of illustration, consider the following transactions for Jerry and Company:

| | |
|---|---|
| 2 March | Bought a motor van for £5,000, paying by cheque. |
| 3 March | Bought inventories (that is, goods to be sold) on one month's credit for £3,000. (This means that the inventories were bought on 3 March, but payment will not be made to the supplier until 3 April.) |
| 4 March | Repaid £2,000 of the amount borrowed to the lender, by cheque. |
| 6 March | Owner introduced another £4,000 into the business bank account. |

→

39

A statement of financial position may be drawn up after each day in which transactions have taken place. In this way, we can see the effect of each transaction on the assets and claims of the business. The statement of financial position as at 2 March will be:

**Jerry and Company**
**Statement of financial position as at 2 March**

|  | £ |
|---|---|
| **ASSETS** | |
| Cash at bank (20,000 – 5,000) | 15,000 |
| Motor van | 5,000 |
| **Total assets** | 20,000 |
| **EQUITY AND LIABILITIES** | |
| Equity | 6,000 |
| Liabilities – borrowing | 14,000 |
| **Total equity and liabilities** | 20,000 |

As we can see, the effect of buying the motor van is to decrease the balance at the bank by £5,000 and to introduce a new asset – a motor van – to the statement of financial position. The total assets remain unchanged. It is only the 'mix' of assets that has changed. The claims against the business remain the same because there has been no change in the way in which the business has been funded.

The statement of financial position as at 3 March, following the purchase of inventories, will be:

**Jerry and Company**
**Statement of financial position as at 3 March**

|  | £ |
|---|---|
| **ASSETS** | |
| Cash at bank | 15,000 |
| Motor van | 5,000 |
| Inventories | 3,000 |
| **Total assets** | 23,000 |
| **EQUITY AND LIABILITIES** | |
| Equity | 6,000 |
| Liabilities – borrowing | 14,000 |
| Liabilities – trade payable | 3,000 |
| **Total equity and liabilities** | 23,000 |

The effect of buying inventories has been to introduce another new asset (inventories) to the statement of financial position. Furthermore, the fact that the goods have not yet been paid for means that the claims against the business will be increased by the £3,000 owed to the supplier, who is referred to as a trade payable (or trade creditor) on the statement of financial position.

## Activity 2.4

Try drawing up a statement of financial position for Jerry and Company as at 4 March.

The statement of financial postion as at 4 March, following the repayment of part of the borrowing, will be:

**Jerry and Company**
**Statement of financial position as at 4 March**

|  | £ |
|---|---|
| **ASSETS** | |
| Cash at bank (15,000 – 2,000) | 13,000 |
| Motor van | 5,000 |
| Inventories | 3,000 |
| Total assets | 21,000 |
| **EQUITY AND LIABILITIES** | |
| Equity | 6,000 |
| Liabilities – borrowing (14,000 – 2,000) | 12,000 |
| Liabilities – trade payable | 3,000 |
| Total equity and liabilities | 21,000 |

The repayment of £2,000 of the borrowing will result in a decrease in the balance at the bank of £2,000 and a decrease in the lender's claim against the business by the same amount.

## Activity 2.5

Try drawing up a statement of financial position as at 6 March for Jerry and Company.

The statement of financial position as at 6 March, following the introduction of more funds, will be:

**Jerry and Company**
**Statement of financial position as at 6 March**

|  | £ |
|---|---|
| **ASSETS** | |
| Cash at bank (13,000 + 4,000) | 17,000 |
| Motor van | 5,000 |
| Inventories | 3,000 |
| Total assets | 25,000 |
| **EQUITY AND LIABILITIES** | |
| Equity (6,000 + 4,000) | 10,000 |
| Liabilities – borrowing | 12,000 |
| Liabilities – trade payable | 3,000 |
| Total equity and liabilities | 25,000 |

The introduction of more funds by the owner will result in an increase in the equity of £4,000 and an increase in the cash at bank by the same amount.

Example 2.3 illustrates the point that the accounting equation (assets equals equity plus liabilities) will always hold true, because it reflects the fact that, if a business wishes to acquire more assets, it must raise funds equal to the cost of those assets. The funds raised must be provided by the owners (equity), or by others (liabilities) or by a combination of the two. Hence the total cost of assets acquired should always equal the total equity plus liabilities.

It is worth pointing out that businesses do not normally draw up a statement of financial position after each day, as shown in the example above. We have done this to illustrate the effect on the statement of financial position of each transaction. In practice, a statement of financial position for a business is usually prepared at the end of a defined reporting period.

Determining the length of the reporting period will involve weighing up the costs of producing the information against the perceived benefits of the information for decision-making purposes. In practice, the reporting period will vary between businesses; it could be monthly, quarterly, half-yearly or annually. For external reporting purposes, an annual reporting period is the norm (although certain businesses, typically larger ones, report more frequently than this). However, for internal reporting purposes to managers, monthly financial statements may be prepared.

## The effect of trading transactions

In Example 2.3, we dealt with the effect on the statement of financial position of a number of different types of transactions that a business might undertake. These transactions covered the purchase of assets for cash and on credit, the repayment of borrowing and the injection of equity. However, one form of transaction (trading transactions) has not yet been considered. To deal with the effect of trading transactions on the statement of financial position, let us return to Jerry and Company.

### Example 2.4

The statement of financial position that we drew up for Jerry and Company as at 6 March was as follows:

**Jerry and Company**
**Statement of financial position as at 6 March**

|  | £ |
|---|---|
| **ASSETS** | |
| Cash at bank | 17,000 |
| Motor van | 5,000 |
| Inventories | 3,000 |
| **Total assets** | 25,000 |
| **EQUITY AND LIABILITIES** | |
| Equity | 10,000 |
| Liabilities – borrowing | 12,000 |
| Liabilities – trade payable | 3,000 |
| **Total equity and liabilities** | 25,000 |

On 7 March, the business managed to sell all of the inventories for £5,000 and received a cheque immediately from the customer for this amount. The statement of financial position on 7 March, after this transaction has taken place, will be:

**Jerry and Company**
**Statement of financial position as at 7 March**

| | £ |
|---|---|
| **ASSETS** | |
| Cash at bank (17,000 + 5,000) | 22,000 |
| Motor van | 5,000 |
| Inventories (3,000 – 3,000) | – |
| Total assets | 27,000 |
| **EQUITY AND LIABILITIES** | |
| Equity (10,000 + (5,000 – 3,000)) | 12,000 |
| Liabilities – borrowing | 12,000 |
| Liabilities – trade payable | 3,000 |
| Total equity and liabilities | 27,000 |

We can see that the inventories (£3,000) have now disappeared from the statement of financial position, but the cash at bank has increased by the selling price of the inventories (£5,000). The net effect has therefore been to increase assets by £2,000 (that is, £5,000 less £3,000). This increase represents the net increase in wealth (the profit) that has arisen from trading. Also note that the equity of the business has increased by £2,000, in line with the increase in assets. This increase in equity reflects the fact that increases in wealth, as a result of trading or other operations, will be to the benefit of the owners and will increase their stake in the business.

## Activity 2.6

What would have been the effect on the statement of financial position if the inventories had been sold on 7 March for £1,000 rather than £5,000?

The statement of financial position on 7 March would then have been:

**Jerry and Company**
**Statement of financial position as at 7 March**

| | £ |
|---|---|
| **ASSETS** | |
| Cash at bank (17,000 + 1,000) | 18,000 |
| Motor van | 5,000 |
| Inventories (3,000 – 3,000) | – |
| Total assets | 23,000 |
| **EQUITY AND LIABILITIES** | |
| Equity (10,000 + (1,000 – 3,000)) | 8,000 |
| Liabilities – borrowing | 12,000 |
| Liabilities – trade payable | 3,000 |
| Total equity and liabilities | 23,000 |

→

> As we can see, the inventories (£3,000) will disappear from the statement of financial position but the cash at bank will rise by only £1,000. This will mean a net reduction in assets of £2,000. This reduction represents a loss arising from trading and will be reflected in a reduction in the equity of the owners.

We can see that any decrease in wealth (that is, a loss) arising from trading or other transactions will lead to a reduction in the owner's stake in the business. If the business wished to maintain the level of assets as at 6 March, it would be necessary to obtain further funds from the owners or from borrowing, or both.

What we have just seen means that the accounting equation can be extended as follows:

**Assets (at the end = Equity (amount at the start of the period**
**of the period)        + profit (or − loss) for the period)**
**                        + Liabilities (at the end of the period)**

(This is assuming that the owner makes no injections or withdrawals of equity during the period.)

Any funds introduced or withdrawn by the owner for living expenses or other reasons also affect equity. If the owners withdrew £1,500 for their own use, the equity of the owners would be reduced by £1,500. If these drawings were in cash, the balance of cash would decrease by £1,500 in the statement of financial position.

Note that, like all statement of financial position items, the amount of equity is cumulative. This means that any profit made that is not taken out as drawings by the owner(s) remains in the business. These retained (or 'ploughed-back') earnings have the effect of expanding the business.

## Classifying assets

On the statement of financial position, assets and claims are usually grouped into categories. This is designed to help users, as a haphazard listing of these items could be confusing. Assets may be categorised as being either current or non-current.

### Current assets

Current assets are basically assets that are held for the short term. To be more precise, they are assets that meet any of the following conditions:

- they are held for sale or consumption during the business's normal operating cycle;
- they are expected to be sold within the next year;
- they are held principally for trading;
- they are cash, or near equivalents to cash such as easily marketable, short-term investments.

The operating cycle of a business is the time between buying and/or creating a product or service and receiving the cash on its sale. For most businesses, this will be less than a year.

The most common current assets are inventories (stock), trade receivables (customers who owe amounts for goods or services supplied on credit) and cash.

It is worth making the point here that most sales made by most businesses are made on credit. This is to say that the goods pass to, or the service is rendered to, the customer at one point but the customer pays later. Retail sales are the only significant exception to this general point.

For businesses that sell goods, rather than render a service, the current assets of inventories, trade receivables and cash are interrelated. They circulate within a business as shown in Figure 2.2. We can see that cash can be used to buy inventories, which are then sold on credit. When the credit customers (trade receivables) pay, the business receives an injection of cash and so on.

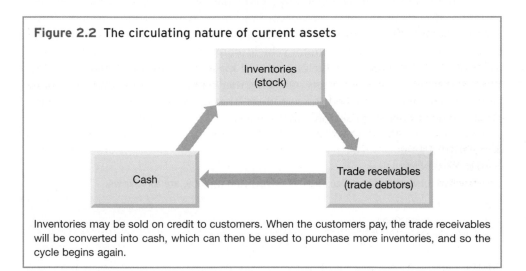

**Figure 2.2 The circulating nature of current assets**

Inventories
(stock)

Cash

Trade receivables
(trade debtors)

Inventories may be sold on credit to customers. When the customers pay, the trade receivables will be converted into cash, which can then be used to purchase more inventories, and so the cycle begins again.

For purely service businesses, the situation is similar, except that inventories are not involved.

## Non-current assets

Non-current assets (also called fixed assets) are simply assets that do not meet the definition of current assets. They tend to be held for long-term operations.

This distinction between assets that are continuously circulating within the business (current) and assets used for long-term operations (non-current) may be helpful when trying to assess the appropriateness of the mix of assets held. Most businesses will need a certain amount of both types of asset to operate effectively.

## Activity 2.7

Can you think of two examples of assets that may be classified as non-current assets for an insurance business?

Examples of assets that may be defined as being non-current are:

■ property
■ furniture
■ motor vehicles
■ computers
■ computer software
■ reference books.

This is not an exhaustive list. You may have thought of others.

It is important to appreciate that how a particular asset is classified (that is, between current and non-current) may vary according to the nature of the business. This is because the *purpose* for which a particular type of asset is held may differ from business to business. For example, a motor vehicle manufacturer will normally hold inventories of the finished motor vehicles produced for resale; it would, therefore, classify them as part of the current assets. On the other hand, a business that uses motor vehicles for delivering its goods to customers (that is, as part of its long-term operations) would classify them as non-current assets.

## Activity 2.8

The assets of Kunalun and Co., a large advertising agency, are as follows:

■ cash at bank
■ fixtures and fittings
■ office equipment
■ motor vehicles
■ property
■ computer equipment
■ work in progress (that is, partly completed work for clients).

Which of these do you think should be defined as non-current assets and which should be defined as current assets?

Your answer should be as follows:

| Non-current assets | Current assets |
|---|---|
| Fixtures and fittings | Cash at bank |
| Office equipment | Work in progress |
| Motor vehicles | |
| Property | |
| Computer equipment | |

## Classifying claims

As we have already seen, claims are normally classified into equity (owner's claim) and liabilities (claims of outsiders). Liabilities are further classified as either current or non-current.

### Current liabilities

➡ Current liabilities are basically amounts due for settlement in the short term. To be more precise, they are liabilities that meet any of the following conditions:

- they are expected to be settled within the business's normal operating cycle;
- they are held principally for trading purposes;
- they are due to be settled within a year after the date of the relevant statement of financial position;
- there is no right to defer settlement beyond a year after the date of the relevant statement of financial position.

### Non-current liabilities

➡ Non-current liabilities represent amounts due that do not meet the definition of current liabilities and so represent longer-term liabilities.

It is quite common for non-current liabilities to become current liabilities. For example, borrowings to be repaid eighteen months after the date of a particular statement of financial position will appear as a non-current liability, but will appear as a current liability in the statement of financial position in the following year.

This classification of liabilities between current and non-current helps to highlight those financial obligations that must shortly be met. Users can compare the amount of current liabilities with the amount of current assets (that is, the assets that either are cash or will turn into cash within the normal operating cycle) to see whether a business can cover its maturing obligations.

The classification of liabilities between current and non-current should also help to indicate how long-term finance is raised. If a business relies on long-term borrowings to finance the business, the financial risks associated with the business will increase. This is because these borrowings will bring a commitment to make periodic interest payments and capital repayments. The business may be forced to stop trading if this commitment is not fulfilled. Thus, when raising long-term finance, a business must try to strike the right balance between non-current liabilities and owner's equity. We shall consider this issue in more detail in Chapter 6.

### Activity 2.9

Can you think of one example of a current liability and one of a non-current liability? →

An example of a current liability would be amounts owing to suppliers for goods supplied on credit (trade payables) or a bank overdraft (a form of short-term bank borrowing that is repayable on demand). An example of a non-current liability would be long-term borrowings.

# Statement layouts

Now that we have looked at the classification of assets and liabilities, we shall consider the layout of the statement of financial position. Although there is an almost infinite number of ways in which the same information on assets and claims could be presented, we shall consider two basic layouts. The first of these follows the style that we adopted with Jerry and Company earlier (see pages 39 to 43). A more comprehensive example of this style is shown in Example 2.5.

## Example 2.5

**Brie Manufacturing**
**Statement of financial position as at 31 December 2009**

|  | £000 |
|---|---|
| **ASSETS** | |
| **Non-current assets** | |
| Property | 45 |
| Plant and equipment | 30 |
| Motor vans | 19 |
|  | 94 |
| **Current assets** | |
| Inventories | 23 |
| Trade receivables | 18 |
| Cash at bank | 12 |
|  | 53 |
| **Total assets** | 147 |
| **EQUITY AND LIABILITIES** | |
| Equity | 60 |
| **Non-current liabilities** | |
| Long-term borrowings | 50 |
| **Current liabilities** | |
| Trade payables | 37 |
| **Total equity and liabilities** | 147 |

The non-current assets have a total of £94,000, which together with the current assets total of £53,000 gives a total of £147,000 for assets. Similarly, the equity totals £60,000, which together with the £50,000 for non-current liabilities and £37,000 for current liabilities gives a total for equity and liabilities of £147,000.

Within each category of asset (non-current and current) shown in Example 2.5, the items are listed in reverse order of liquidity (nearness to cash). Thus, the assets that are furthest from cash come first and the assets that are closest to cash come last. In the case of non-current assets, property is listed first as this asset is usually the most difficult to turn into cash, and motor vans are listed last as there is usually a ready market for them. In the case of current assets, we have already seen that inventories are converted to trade receivables and then trade receivables are converted to cash. Hence, under the heading of current assets, inventories are listed first, followed by trade receivables and finally cash itself. This ordering of assets is a normal practice, which is followed irrespective of the layout used.

Note that, in addition to a grand total for assets held, subtotals for non-current assets and current assets are shown. Subtotals are also used for non-current liabilities and current liabilities when more than one item appears within these categories.

This layout is the most popular in practice in the UK.

A slight variation from the standard layout illustrated in Example 2.5 is as shown in Example 2.6.

### Example 2.6

**Brie Manufacturing**
**Statement of financial position as at 31 December 2009**

|  | £000 |
|---|---:|
| **ASSETS** | |
| **Non-current assets** | |
| Property | 45 |
| Plant and equipment | 30 |
| Motor vans | 19 |
|  | 94 |
| **Current assets** | |
| Inventories | 23 |
| Trade receivables | 18 |
| Cash at bank | 12 |
|  | 53 |
| **Total assets** | 147 |
| **LIABILITIES** | |
| **Non-current liabilities** | |
| Long-term borrowings | (50) |
| **Current liabilities** | |
| Trade payables | (37) |
| **Total liabilities** | (87) |
| Net assets | 60 |
| **EQUITY** | 60 |

We can see that the total liabilities are deducted from the total assets. This derives a figure for net assets – which is equal to equity. Using this format, the basic accounting equation is rearranged so that

49

$$\text{Assets} - \text{Liabilities} = \text{Equity}$$

This rearranged equation highlights the fact that equity represents the residual interest of the owner(s) after deducting all liabilities of the business.

**? Self-assessment question 2.1**

The following information relates to Simonson Engineering as at 30 September 2010:

|  | £ |
|---|---|
| Plant and machinery | 25,000 |
| Trade payables | 18,000 |
| Short-term borrowings | 26,000 |
| Inventories | 45,000 |
| Property | 72,000 |
| Long-term borrowings | 51,000 |
| Trade receivables | 48,000 |
| Equity at 1 October 2009 | 117,500 |
| Cash in hand | 1,500 |
| Motor vehicles | 15,000 |
| Fixtures and fittings | 9,000 |
| Profit for the year to 30 September 2010 | 18,000 |
| Drawings for the year to 30 September 2010 | 15,000 |

**Required:**
Prepare a statement of financial position for the business using the standard layout illustrated in Example 2.5.

The solution to this question can be found at the back of the book, in Appendix B.

## Capturing a moment in time

As we have already seen, the statement of financial position reflects the assets, equity and liabilities of a business at *a specified point in time*. It has been compared to a photograph. A photograph 'freezes' a particular moment in time and will represent the situation only at that moment. Hence, events may be quite different immediately before and immediately after the photograph was taken. When examining a statement of financial position, therefore, it is important to establish the date for which it has been drawn up. This information should be prominently displayed in the heading to the statement, as shown above in Examples 2.5 and 2.6. When we are trying to assess current financial position, the more recent the statement of financial position date, the better.

A business will normally prepare a statement of financial position as at the close of business on the last day of its annual reporting period. In the UK, businesses are free to choose their accounting year. When making a decision on which year-end date to choose, commercial convenience can often be a deciding factor. For example, a business operating in the retail trade may choose to have a year-end date early in the calendar year (for example, 31 January) because trade tends to be slack during that period and more staff time is available to help with the tasks involved in the preparation of the annual financial statements (such as checking the amount of inventories held). Since trade is slack, it is also a time when the amount of inventories held by the retail business is likely to be unusually low as compared with other times of the year. Thus the statement of financial position, though showing a fair view of what it purports to show, may not show a picture of what is more typically the position of the business over the rest of the year.

## The role of accounting conventions

As we saw in Chapter 1, accounting has a number of rules or conventions that have evolved over time. They have evolved as attempts to deal with practical problems experienced by preparers and users of financial statements, rather than to reflect some theoretical ideal. In preparing the statements of financial position earlier, we have followed various accounting conventions, though they have not been explicitly mentioned. We shall now identify and discuss the major conventions that we have applied.

### Business entity convention

For accounting purposes, the business and its owner(s) are treated as being quite separate and distinct. This is why owners are treated as being claimants against their own business in respect of their investment. The business entity convention must be distinguished from the legal position that may exist between businesses and their owners. For sole proprietorships and partnerships, the law does not make any distinction between the business and its owner(s). For limited companies, on the other hand, there is a clear legal distinction between the business and its owners. (As we shall see in Chapter 4, the limited company is regarded as having a separate legal existence.) For accounting purposes, these legal distinctions are irrelevant and the business entity convention applies to all businesses.

### Historic cost convention

The historic cost convention holds that the value of assets shown on the statement of financial position should be based on their acquisition cost (that is, historic cost). This method of measuring asset value takes preference over other methods based on some form of current value. Many people, however, find the historic cost convention difficult to support, as outdated historic costs are unlikely to help in the assessment of the current financial position. It is often argued that recording assets at their current value would provide a more realistic view of financial position and would be relevant for a wide range of decisions. However, a system of measurement based on current values can present a number of problems.

The term 'current value' can be defined in different ways. It can be defined broadly as either the current replacement cost or the current realisable value (selling price)

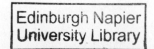

of an asset. These two types of valuation may result in quite different figures being produced to represent the current value of an item. Furthermore, the broad terms 'replacement cost' and 'realisable value' can be defined in different ways. We must therefore be clear about what kind of current value accounting we wish to use.

Current values, however defined, are often difficult to establish with any real degree of objectivity. Activity 2.10 illustrates the practical problems associated with current value accounting.

### Activity 2.10

Plumber and Company has some motor vans that are used by staff when visiting customers' premises to carry out work. It is now the last day of the business's reporting period. If it were decided to show the vans on the statement of financial position at a current value (rather than a value based on their historic cost), how might the business arrive at a suitable value and how reliable would this figure be?

Two ways of deriving a current value are to find out:

– how much would have to be paid to buy vans of a similar type and condition (current replacement cost);
– how much a motor van dealer would pay for the vans, were the business to sell them (current realisable value).

Both options will normally rely on opinion and so a range of possible values could be produced for each. For example, both the cost to replace the vans and the proceeds of selling them is likely to vary from one dealer to another. Moreover, the range of values for each option could be significantly different from one option to the other. (The selling prices of the vans are likely to be lower than the amount required to replace them.) Thus, any value finally decided upon could arouse some debate.

The figures produced under a system of current value accounting may be heavily dependent on the opinion of managers. Unless these figures are capable of some form of independent verification, there is a danger that the financial statements will lose their credibility among users. The motor vans discussed in Activity 2.10 are less of a problem than many types of asset. There is a ready market for motor vans, which means that a value can be obtained by contacting a dealer. For a custom-built piece of equipment, however, identifying a replacement cost, or worse still a selling price, could be very difficult.

By reporting assets at their historic cost, it is argued that more reliable information is produced. Reporting in this way reduces the need for judgements, as the amount paid for a particular asset is usually a matter of demonstrable fact. Information based on past costs, however, may not always be relevant to the needs of users.

Later in the chapter, we shall consider the valuation of assets in the statement of financial position in more detail. We shall see that the historic cost convention is not always rigidly adhered to. Departures from this convention are becoming more frequent.

## Prudence convention

➡ The prudence convention holds that caution should be exercised when making accounting judgements. The application of this convention normally involves recording all losses at once and in full; this refers to both actual losses and expected losses. Profits, on the other hand, are recognised only when they actually arise. Greater emphasis is, therefore, placed on expected losses than on expected profits. To illustrate the application of this convention, let us assume that certain inventories held by a business prove unpopular with customers and so a decision is made to sell them below their original cost. The prudence convention requires that the expected loss from future sales be recognised immediately rather than when the goods are eventually sold. If, however, these inventories could have been sold above their original cost, profit would only be recognised at the time of sale.

The prudence convention evolved to counteract the excessive optimism of some managers and is designed to prevent an overstatement of financial position and performance. Applying this convention, however, requires judgement. This means that the way in which it is applied by preparers of financial statements may differ over time and between businesses. Where excessive prudence is applied, it will lead to an understatement of profits and financial position.

### Activity 2.11

What might be the effect of applying excessive prudence on the quality of user decisions?

Being excessively prudent will tend to obscure the underlying financial reality and may lead to poor decisions being made. The owners, for example, may sell their stake in the business at a lower price than they would have received if a more balanced view of the financial health of the business had been presented.

In recent years, the prudence convention has weakened its grip on accounting and has become a less dominant force. Nevertheless, it remains an important convention.

## Going concern convention

➡ The going concern convention holds that the financial statements should be prepared on the assumption that a business will continue operations for the foreseeable future, unless there is evidence to the contrary. In other words, it is assumed that there is no intention, or need, to sell off the non-current assets of the business. Where a business is in financial difficulties, however, non-current assets may have to be sold in order to repay those who have enforceable claims against the business.

The realisable (sale) value of many non-current assets is often much lower than the values reported in the statement of financial position. Thus, if a forced sale of assets were to occur, significant losses would arise. These anticipated losses would need to be fully reported were a business's going concern status to be called into question. Where, however, there is no expectation that non-current assets need be sold, they can continue to be shown at their reported values.

## Dual aspect convention

The dual aspect convention asserts that each transaction has two aspects, both of which will affect the statement of financial position. Thus, the purchase of a motor car for cash results in an increase in one asset (motor car) and a decrease in another (cash). The repayment of borrowings results in the decrease in a liability (borrowings) and the decrease in an asset (cash).

### Activity 2.12

What are the two aspects of each of the following transactions?

1  Purchasing £1,000 of inventories on credit.
2  Owner withdrawing £2,000 in cash.
3  Paying a supplier for £1,000 of inventories bought on credit a few weeks earlier.

Your answer should be as follows:

1  Inventories increase by £1,000, trade payables increase by £1,000.
2  Equity reduces by £2,000, cash reduces by £2,000.
3  Trade payables reduce by £1,000, cash reduces by £1,000.

Recording the dual aspect of each transaction ensures that the statement of financial position will continue to balance.

Figure 2.3 summarises the main accounting conventions that exert an influence on the construction of the statement of financial position.

**Figure 2.3  Accounting conventions influencing the statement of financial position**

These are the key accounting conventions relating to the statement of financial position.

## Money measurement

We saw earlier that a resource will only be regarded as an asset and included on the statement of financial position if it can be measured in monetary terms, with a reasonable degree of reliability. Some resources of a business, however, do not meet this criterion and so are excluded from the statement of financial position. As a result, the scope of the statement of financial position is limited.

### Activity 2.13

Can you think of resources of a business that cannot usually be measured reliably in monetary terms?

In answering this activity you may have thought of the following:

- the quality of the human resources of the business
- the reputation of the business's products
- the location of the business
- the relationship a business enjoys with its customers.

There have been occasional attempts to measure and report resources of a business that are normally excluded from the statement of financial position so as to provide a more complete picture. These attempts, however, invariably fail the reliability test. We saw in Chapter 1 that a lack of reliability affects the quality of financial statements. Unreliable measurement can lead to inconsistency in reporting and can create uncertainty among users of the financial statements, which in turn undermines those statements' credibility.

We shall now discuss some key resources of a business that normally defy reliable measurement.

## Goodwill and brands

Some intangible non-current assets are similar to tangible non-current assets: they have a clear and separate identity and the cost of acquiring the asset can be reliably measured. Examples normally include patents, trademarks, copyrights and licences. Other intangible non-current assets, however, are quite different. They lack a clear and separate identity and reflect a hotchpotch of attributes, which are part of the essence of the business. Goodwill and product brands are often examples of assets that lack a clear and separate identity.

The term 'goodwill' is often used to cover various attributes such as the quality of the products, the skill of employees and the relationship with customers. The term 'product brands' is also used to cover various attributes, such as the brand image, the quality of the product, the trademark and so on. Where goodwill and product brands have been generated internally by the business, it is often difficult to determine their cost or to measure their current market value or even to be clear that they really exist. They are, therefore, excluded from the statement of financial position.

When they are acquired through an 'arm's-length transaction', however, the problems of uncertainty about their existence and measurement are resolved. (An arm's-length transaction is one that is undertaken between two unconnected parties.) If goodwill is acquired when taking over another business, or if a business acquires a particular product brand from another business, these items will be separately identified and a price agreed for them. Under these circumstances, they can be regarded as assets (for accounting purposes) by the business that acquired them and included on the statement of financial position.

To agree a price for acquiring goodwill or product brands means that some form of valuation must take place and this raises the question as to how it is done. Usually, the valuation will be based on estimates of future earnings from holding the asset – a process that is fraught with difficulties. Nevertheless, a number of specialist businesses now exist that are prepared to take on this challenge. Real World 2.2 shows how one specialist business ranked and valued the top ten brands in the world for 2009.

---

### Real World 2.2

## Brand leaders

Millward Brown Optimor, part of WPP marketing services group, recently produced a report that ranked and valued the top ten world brands for 2009 as follows:

| Ranking | Brand | Value ($m) |
|---|---|---|
| 1 | Google | 100,039 |
| 2 | Microsoft | 76,249 |
| 3 | Coca-Cola | 67,625 |
| 4 | IBM | 66,622 |
| 5 | McDonalds | 66,575 |
| 6 | Apple | 63,113 |
| 7 | China Mobile | 61,283 |
| 8 | GE (General Electric) | 59,793 |
| 9 | Vodafone | 53,727 |
| 10 | Marlboro | 49,460 |

We can see that the valuations placed on the brands are quite staggering.

*Source*: Millward Brown Optimor, BrandZ Top 100 Most Valuable Global Brands 2009, www.millwardbrown.com.

---

## Human resources

Attempts have been made to place a monetary measurement on the human resources of a business, but without any real success. There are, however, certain limited circumstances in which human resources are measured and reported in the statement of financial position. These circumstances normally arise with professional football clubs. While football clubs cannot own players, they can own the rights to the players' services. Where these rights are acquired by compensating other clubs for releasing the players from their contracts, an arm's-length transaction arises and the amounts paid provide a reliable basis for measurement. This means that the rights to services can be regarded as an asset of the club for accounting purposes (assuming, of course, the player will also bring benefits to the club).

Real World 2.3 describes how one leading club reports its investment in players on the statement of financial position.

### Real World 2.3

## Spurs players appear on the pitch and on the statement of financial position

Tottenham Hotspur Football Club (Spurs) has acquired several key players as a result of paying transfer fees to other clubs. In common with most UK football clubs, Spurs reports the cost of acquiring the rights to the players' services on its statement of financial position. The club's statement as at 30 June 2009 shows the cost of registering its squad of players at about £197 million. The club treats a proportion of each players' transfer fee as an expense each year. The exact proportion depends on the length of the particular player's contract.

The £197 million does not include 'home-grown' players such as Ledley King, because Spurs did not pay a transfer fee for them and so no clear-cut value can be placed on their services. On the surface, this is correct. However, due to capitalising cost of agents fee, a small element of Ledley King was included in the £197 million, and is allowed under FA rules. During the year to 30 June 2009, the club was very active in the transfer market and fifteen players were signed, including Jermain Defoe from Portsmouth. Defoe had previously been with Spurs and was only away at Portsmouth for 17–18 months. Fifteen players left the club (including Dimitar Berbatov to go to Manchester United), earning it transfer fees totalling £73 million.

The item of players' registrations is shown as an intangible asset in the statement of financial position as it is the rights to services, not the players, that are the assets. It is shown net of depreciation (or amortisation as it is usually termed for non-current assets). The carrying amount at 30 June 2009 was £128 million and represented 44 per cent of Spurs assets, as shown in the statement of financial position.

*Source*: Tottenham Hotspur plc Annual Report 2009.

## Monetary stability

When using money as the unit of measurement, we normally fail to recognise the fact that it will change in value over time. In the UK and throughout much of the world, however, inflation has been a persistent problem. This has meant that the value of money has declined in relation to other assets. In past years, high rates of inflation have resulted in statements of financial position which were prepared on a historic cost basis reflecting figures for assets that were much lower than if current values were employed. Rates of inflation have been relatively low in recent years and so the disparity between historic cost values and current values has been less pronounced. Nevertheless, it can still be significant and has added fuel to the debate concerning how to measure asset values on the statement of financial position. It is to this issue that we now turn.

## Valuing assets

As we saw earlier, when preparing the statement of financial position, the historic cost convention is normally applied for the reporting of assets. However, this point requires further explanation as, in practice, it is not simply a matter of recording each asset on the statement of financial position at its original cost. We shall see that things are a little more complex than this. Before discussing the valuation rules in some detail, however, we should point out that these rules are based on International Financial Reporting Standards, which are rules that are generally accepted throughout much of the world. The nature and role of financial reporting standards will be discussed in detail in Chapter 4.

### Tangible non-current assets (property, plant and equipment)

 Tangible non-current assets normally consist of property, plant and equipment. We shall refer to them in this way from now on. This is a rather broad term that includes items such as land and buildings, motor vehicles and fixtures and fittings. All of these items are, in essence, the 'tools' used by the business to generate wealth, that is, they are used to produce or supply goods and services or for administration purposes. They tend to be held for the longer term, which means for more than one reporting period.

Initially these items are recorded at their historic cost, which will include any amounts spent on getting them ready for use. However, they will normally be used up over time as a result of wear and tear, obsolescence and so on. The amount used up, which is referred to as *depreciation*, must be measured for each reporting period for which the assets are held. Although we shall leave a detailed examination of depreciation until Chapter 3, we need to know that when an asset has been depreciated, this must be reflected in the statement of financial position.

The total depreciation that has accumulated over the period since the asset was acquired must be deducted from its cost. This net figure (that is, the cost of the asset less the total depreciation to date) is referred to as the *carrying amount*. It is sometimes also known as *net book value* or *written-down value*. The procedure just described is not really a contravention of the historic cost convention. It is simply recognition of the fact that a proportion of the historic cost of the non-current asset has been consumed in the process of generating benefits for the business.

Although using historic cost (less any depreciation) is the standard or 'benchmark' treatment for recording these assets, an alternative is allowed. Property, plant and equipment can be recorded using fair values provided that these values can be measured reliably. The fair values, in this case, are the current market values (that is, the exchange values in an arm's-length transaction). The use of fair values, rather than depreciated cost figures, can provide users with more up-to-date information, which may well be more relevant to their needs. It may also place the business in a better light, as assets such as property (real estate) may have increased significantly in value over time. Of course, increasing the statement of financial position value of an asset does not make that asset more valuable. However, perceptions of the business may be altered by such a move.

One consequence of revaluing non-current assets is that the depreciation charge will be increased. This is because the depreciation charge is based on the increased value of the asset.

Real World 2.4 shows that one well-known business revalued its land and buildings and, by doing so, greatly improved the look of its statement of financial position.

### Real World 2.4

## Marks marks up land and buildings

The statement of financial position of Marks and Spencer plc, a major high street retailer, as at 28 March 2009 reveals land and buildings at a carrying amount, or net book value, of £2,458 million. These land and buildings were revalued by a firm of independent surveyors five years earlier and this has been reflected in subsequent statements of financial position. The effect of the revaluation was to give an uplift of £530.9 million against the previous carrying amount.

*Source*: Marks and Spencer plc Annual Report 2009, Notes to the financial statements, Note 14, www.marksandspencer.com.

### Activity 2.14

Refer to the statement of financial position of Brie Manufacturing shown earlier in Example 2.5 (page 48). What would be the effect of revaluing the property to a figure of £110,000 on the statement of financial position?

The effect on the statement of financial position would be to increase the figure for the property to £110,000 and the gain on revaluation (that is, £110,000 − £45,000 = £65,000) would be added to equity, as it is the owner(s) who will benefit from the gain. The revised statement of financial position would therefore be as follows:

**Brie Manufacturing**
**Statement of financial position as at 31 December 2009**

|  | £000 |
|---|---:|
| **ASSETS** | |
| **Non-current assets (property, plant and equipment)** | |
| Property | 110 |
| Plant and equipment | 30 |
| Motor vans | 19 |
|  | 159 |
| **Current assets** | |
| Inventories | 23 |
| Trade receivables | 18 |
| Cash at bank | 12 |
|  | 53 |
| **Total assets** | 212 |
| **EQUITY AND LIABILITIES** | |
| **Equity** (60 + 65) | 125 |
| **Non-current liabilities** | |
| Long-term borrowings | 50 |
| **Current liabilities** | |
| Trade payables | 37 |
| **Total equity and liabilities** | 212 |

Once assets are revalued, the frequency of revaluation then becomes an important issue as assets recorded at out-of-date values can mislead users. Using out-of-date revaluations on the statement of financial position is the worst of both worlds. It lacks the objectivity and verifiability of historic cost; it also lacks the realism of current values. Where fair values are used, revaluations should therefore be frequent enough to ensure that the carrying amount of the revalued asset does not differ materially from its fair value at the statement of financial position date.

When an item of property, plant or equipment is revalued on the basis of fair values, all assets within that particular group must be revalued. Thus, it is not acceptable to revalue some items of property but not others. Although this provides some degree of consistency within a particular group of assets, it does not, of course, prevent the statement of financial position from containing a mixture of valuations.

## Intangible non-current assets

For these assets, the 'benchmark treatment' is, once again, that they are measured initially at historic cost. What follows, however, will depend on whether the asset has a finite or an infinite useful life. (Purchased goodwill is an example of an asset that could have an infinitely useful life, though this is not always the case.) Where the asset has a finite life, any amortisation following acquisition will be deducted from its cost.

Where, however, the asset has an infinite life, it will not be amortised. Instead, it will be tested annually to see whether there has been any fall in value. This point is discussed in more detail in the following section.

Once again, the alternative of revaluing intangible assets using fair values is available. However, this can only be used where an active market exists, which allows fair values to be properly determined. In practice, this is a rare occurrence.

## The impairment of non-current assets

There is always a risk that both types of non-current asset (tangible and intangible) may suffer a significant fall in value. This may be due to factors such as changes in market conditions, technological obsolescence and so on. In some cases, this fall in value may lead to the carrying amount of the asset being higher than the amount that could be recovered from the asset through its continued use or through its sale. When this occurs, the asset value is said to be impaired and the general rule is to reduce the value on the statement of financial position to the recoverable amount. Unless this is done, the asset value will be overstated. This type of impairment in value should not be confused with routine depreciation, arising from, say, wear and tear due to normal usage.

### Activity 2.15

With which one of the accounting conventions that we discussed earlier is this accounting treatment of impaired assets consistent?

The answer is the prudence convention, which states that actual or anticipated losses should be recognised in full.

In many situations, a business may use either historic cost, less any depreciation, or a value-based measure when reporting its non-current assets. However, where the value-based measure is the impaired value and is smaller than the historic-cost-based value, the business has no choice; the use of depreciated historic cost is not an option.

Real World 2.5 provides an example of where the application of the 'impairment rule', as it is called, resulted in huge write-downs (that is, reductions in the statement of financial position value of the assets) for one large business.

### Real World 2.5

## Painting a rosy picture

Akzo Nobel, the Dutch paints and chemicals company, on Tuesday defended its £8bn (€11.6bn) acquisition of ICI in 2007 after it took a €1.2bn (€1.5bn) impairment charge on the former UK industrial giant because of sharply lower paint sales.

The company saw the volume of paint sold fall by 10 per cent in the fourth quarter, with even steeper declines in Asia, one of the areas where ICI had been strong. This prompted the move to slash growth estimates and fair value for ICI.

'It's not a world of high growth any more, it's a world with completely different challenges,' said Hans Wijers, chief executive. 'We expect 2009 to be an uncertain year with a lot of volatility [and] with challenging volume circumstances.'

The €1.2bn impairment charge cuts into the €4.4bn of goodwill the company recorded when it acquired ICI and its Dulux brand name, but Akzo defended its previous assumptions as conservative.

'Could we have anticipated that the world economy would go down so much?' Mr Wijers said. 'I'm not sorry about [the ICI] transaction. It was the right thing to do at the right time and the company has become much stronger because of it.'

*Source*: adapted from 'Akzo Nobel defends ICI takeover', *The Financial Times*, 24/02/2009 (Steen, M.), copyright © The Financial Times Ltd.

We saw earlier that intangible, non-current assets with infinite lives must be tested annually to see whether there has been any impairment. Other non-current assets, however, must also be tested where events suggest that impairment has taken place.

## Inventories

It is not only non-current assets that run the risk of a significant fall in value. The inventories of a business could also suffer this fate, which could be caused by factors such as reduced selling prices, obsolescence, deterioration, damage and so on. Where a fall in value means that the amount likely to be recovered from the sale of the inventories will be lower than their cost, this loss must be reflected in the statement of financial position. Thus, if the net realisable value (that is, selling price less any selling costs) falls below the historic cost of inventories held, the former should be used as the basis of valuation. This reflects, once again, the influence of the prudence convention on the statement of financial position.

Real World 2.6 reveals how one well-known business wrote down the inventories of one of its products following a sharp reduction in selling prices.

### Real World 2.6

## You're fired!

'You're fired!' is what some investors might like to tell Amstrad, run by Apprentice star Sir Alan Sugar. Shares in the company fell nearly 10 per cent as it revealed that sales of its much-vaunted videophone have failed to take off.

Amstrad launched the E3, a phone allowing users to hold video calls with each other, in a blaze of publicity last year. But, after cutting the price from £99 to £49, Amstrad sold just 61,000 E3s in the year to June and has taken a £5.7m stock (inventories) write-down.

*Source*: 'Amstrad (AMT)', *Investors Chronicle*, 7 October 2005.

The published financial statements of large businesses will normally show the basis on which inventories are valued. Real World 2.7 shows how one business reports this information.

## Reporting inventories

The 2009 annual report of Ted Baker plc, a leading designer clothes brand, includes the following explanation concerning inventories:

Inventories and work in progress are stated at the lower of cost and net realisable value. Cost includes materials, direct labour and inward transportation costs. Net realisable value is based on estimated selling price, less further costs expected to be incurred to completion and disposal. Provision is made for obsolete, slow moving or defective items where appropriate.

*Source*: Ted Baker plc Report and Accounts 2009, p. 44.

## Meeting user needs

The statement of financial position is the oldest of the three main financial statements and many businesses prepare one on a regular basis, even where there is no regulation requiring it to be produced. This suggests that it is regarded as providing useful information. There are various ways in which the statement of financial position may help users, including the following:

- *It provides insights about how the business is financed and how its funds are deployed.* The statement of financial position shows how much finance is contributed by the owners and how much is contributed by outside lenders. It also shows the different kinds of assets acquired and how much is invested in each kind.
- *It can provide a basis for assessing the value of the business.* Since the statement of financial position lists, and places a value on, the various assets and claims, it can provide a starting point for assessing the value of the business. It is, however, severely limited in the extent to which it can do this. We have seen earlier that accounting rules may result in assets being shown at their historic cost and that the restrictive definition of assets may exclude certain business resources from the statement of financial position. Ultimately, the value of a business will be based on its ability to generate wealth in the future. Because of this, assets need to be valued on the basis of their wealth-generating potential. Also, other business resources that do not meet the restrictive definition of assets, such as brand values, need to be similarly valued and included.
- *Relationships between assets and claims can be assessed.* It can be useful to look at relationships between various statement of financial position items, for example the relationship between how much wealth is tied up in current assets and how much

is owed in the short term (current liabilities). From this relationship, we can see whether the business has sufficient short-term assets to cover its maturing obligations. We shall look at this and other relationships between statement of financial position items in some detail in Chapter 6.

■ *Performance can be assessed.* The effectiveness of a business in generating wealth can usefully be assessed against the amount of investment that was involved. Knowing the relationship between profit earned during a period and the value of the net assets invested can be helpful to many users, particularly owners and managers. This and similar relationships will also be explored in detail in Chapter 6.

## Summary

The main points of this chapter may be summarised as follows.

### The major financial statements

■ There are three major financial statements: the statement of cash flows, the income statement (profit and loss account) and the statement of financial position (balance sheet).

■ The statement of cash flows shows the cash movements over a particular period.

■ The income statement shows the wealth (profit) generated over a particular period.

■ The statement of financial position shows the accumulated wealth at a particular point in time.

### The statement of financial position

■ This sets out the assets of the business, on the one hand, and the claims against those assets, on the other.

■ Assets are resources of the business that have certain characteristics, such as the ability to provide future benefits.

■ Claims are obligations on the part of the business to provide cash, or some other benefit, to outside parties.

■ Claims are of two types: equity and liabilities.

■ Equity represents the claim(s) of the owner(s) and liabilities represent the claims of others, apart from the owner.

■ The statement of financial position reflects the accounting equation:

$$\text{Assets} = \text{Equity} + \text{Liabilities}$$

### Classification of assets and liabilities

■ Assets are normally categorised as being current or non-current.

■ Current assets are cash or near cash or are held for sale or consumption in the normal course of business, or for trading, or for the short term.

- Non-current assets are assets that are not current assets. They are normally held for the long-term operations of the business.

- Liabilities are normally categorised as being current or non-current liabilities.

- Current liabilities represent amounts due in the normal course of the business's operating cycle, or are held for trading, or are to be settled within a year of, or cannot be deferred for at least a year after, the end of the reporting period.

- Non-current liabilities represent amounts due that are not current liabilities.

## Statement of financial position layouts

- The standard layout begins with assets at the top of the statement of financial position and places equity and liabilities underneath.

- A variation of the standard layout begins with the assets at the top of the statement of financial position. From the total assets figure are deducted the non-current and current liabilities to arrive at a net assets figure. Equity is placed underneath.

## Accounting conventions

- Accounting conventions are the rules of accounting that have evolved to deal with practical problems experienced by those preparing financial statements.

- The main conventions relating to the statement of financial position include business entity, historic cost, prudence, going concern and dual aspect.

## Money measurement

- Using money as the unit of measurement limits the scope of the statement of financial position.

- Certain resources such as goodwill, product brands and human resources are difficult to measure. An 'arm's-length transaction' is normally required before such assets can be reliably measured and reported on the statement of financial position.

- Money is not a stable unit of measurement – it changes in value over time.

## Asset valuation

- The 'benchmark treatment' is to show property, plant and equipment at historic cost less any amounts written off for depreciation. However, fair values may be used rather than depreciated cost.

- The 'benchmark treatment' for intangible non-current assets is to show the items at historic cost. Only assets with a finite life will be amortised (depreciated) and fair values will rarely be used.

- Where the recoverable amount from non-current assets is below their carrying amount, this lower amount is reflected in the statement of financial position.

- Inventories are shown at the lower of cost or net realisable value.

> **The usefulness of the statement of financial position**
> - It shows how finance has been raised and how it has been deployed.
> - It provides a basis for valuing the business, though the conventional statement of financial position can only be a starting point.
> - Relationships between various statement of financial position items can usefully be explored.
> - Relationships between wealth generated and wealth invested can be helpful indicators of business effectiveness.

**MyAccountingLab** | *Now check your progress in your personal Study Plan*

## → Key terms

statement of cash flows p. 31
income statement p. 31
statement of financial position p. 31
inventories p. 33
final accounts p. 35
assets p. 36
claims p. 36
tangible assets p. 38
intangible assets p. 38
equity p. 38
liabilities p. 38
trade payables p. 40
current assets p. 44

trade receivables p. 45
non-current (fixed) assets p. 45
current liabilities p. 47
non-current liabilities p. 47
accounting conventions p. 51
business entity convention p. 51
historic cost convention p. 51
prudence convention p. 53
going concern convention p. 53
dual aspect convention p. 54
property, plant and equipment p. 58
fair values p. 59

## Further reading

If you would like to explore the topics covered in this chapter in more depth, we recommend the following books:

Elliott, B. and Elliott, J., *Financial Accounting and Reporting* (13th edn), Financial Times Prentice Hall, 2010, chapters 16 and 18.

IASC Foundation Education, *A Guide through IFRS 2009*, July 2009, IAS 16, IAS 36 and IAS 38.

KPMG, *Insights into IFRS* (6th edn, 2009/10), Sweet and Maxwell, 2009, sections 1.2, 3.2, 3.3, 3.8 and 3.10.

# Review questions

Solutions to these questions can be found at the back of the book, in Appendix C.

**2.1** An accountant prepared a statement of financial position for a business. In this statement, the equity of the owner was shown next to the liabilities. This confused the owner, who argued: 'My equity is my major asset and so should be shown as an asset on the statement of financial position.' How would you explain this misunderstanding to the owner?

**2.2** 'The statement of financial position shows how much a business is worth.' Do you agree with this statement? Explain the reasons for your response.

**2.3** What is meant by the accounting equation? How does the form of this equation differ between the two statement of financial position layouts mentioned in the chapter?

**2.4** In recent years there have been attempts to place a value on the 'human assets' of a business in order to derive a figure that can be included on the statement of financial position. Do you think humans should be treated as assets? Would 'human assets' meet the conventional definition of an asset for inclusion on the statement of financial position?

# Exercises

Exercise 2.5 is more advanced than Exercises 2.1 to 2.4. Those with coloured numbers have solutions at the back of the book, in Appendix D.

If you wish to try more exercises, visit the website at www.myaccountinglab.com.

**2.1** On Thursday, the fourth day of his business venture, Paul, the street trader in wrapping paper (see earlier in the chapter, pages 31–34), bought more inventories for £53 cash. During the day he sold inventories that had cost £33 for a total of £47.

**Required:**
Draw up the three financial statements for Paul's business venture for Thursday.

**2.2** While on holiday in Bridlington, Helen had her credit cards and purse stolen from the beach while she was swimming. She was left with only £40, which she had kept in her hotel room, but she had three days of her holiday remaining. She was determined to continue her holiday and decided to make some money to enable her to do so. She decided to sell orange juice to holidaymakers using the local beach. On day 1 she bought 80 cartons of orange juice at £0.50 each for cash and sold 70 of these at £0.80 each. On the following day she bought 60 cartons at £0.50 each for cash and sold 65 at £0.80 each. On the third and final day she bought another 60 cartons at £0.50 each for cash. However, it rained and, as a result, business was poor. She managed to sell 20 at £0.80 each but sold off the rest of her inventories at £0.40 each.

**Required:**
Prepare an income statement and statement of cash flows for each day's trading and prepare a statement of financial position at the end of each day's trading.

**2.3** On 1 March, Joe Conday started a new business. During March he carried out the following transactions:

| | |
|---|---|
| 1 March | Deposited £20,000 in a bank account. |
| 2 March | Bought fixtures and fittings for £6,000 cash and inventories £8,000 on credit. |
| 3 March | Borrowed £5,000 from a relative and deposited it in the bank. |
| 4 March | Bought a motor car for £7,000 cash and withdrew £200 in cash for his own use. |
| 5 March | A further motor car costing £9,000 was bought. The motor car bought on 4 March was given in part exchange at a value of £6,500. The balance of purchase price for the new car was paid in cash. |
| 6 March | Conday won £2,000 in a lottery and paid the amount into the business bank account. He also repaid £1,000 of the borrowings. |

**Required:**

Draw up a statement of financial position for the business at the end of each day.

**2.4** The following is a list of the assets and claims of Crafty Engineering Ltd at 30 June last year:

| | £000 |
|---|---|
| Trade payables | 86 |
| Motor vehicles | 38 |
| Long-term borrowing from Industrial Finance Co. | 260 |
| Equipment and tools | 207 |
| Short-term borrowings | 116 |
| Inventories | 153 |
| Property | 320 |
| Trade receivables | 185 |

**Required:**

(a) Prepare the statement of financial position of the business as at 30 June last year from the above information using the standard layout. (*Hint*: There is a missing item that needs to be deduced and inserted.)

(b) Discuss the significant features revealed by this financial statement.

**2.5** The statement of financial position of a business at the start of the week is as follows:

| | £ |
|---|---|
| **ASSETS** | |
| Property | 145,000 |
| Furniture and fittings | 63,000 |
| Inventories | 28,000 |
| Trade receivables | 33,000 |
| **Total assets** | 269,000 |
| **EQUITY AND LIABILITIES** | |
| Equity | 203,000 |
| Short-term borrowing (bank overdraft) | 43,000 |
| Trade payables | 23,000 |
| **Total equity and liabilities** | 269,000 |

During the week the following transactions take place:

(a) Inventories sold for £11,000 cash; these inventories had cost £8,000.
(b) Sold inventories for £23,000 on credit; these inventories had cost £17,000.
(c) Received cash from trade receivables totalling £18,000.
(d) The owners of the business introduced £100,000 of their own money, which was placed in the business bank account.
(e) The owners brought a motor van, valued at £10,000, into the business.
(f) Bought inventories on credit for £14,000.
(g) Paid trade payables £13,000.

**Required:**

Show the statement of financial position after all of these transactions have been reflected.

## Chapter 3

# Measuring and reporting financial performance

## Introduction

In this chapter, we continue our examination of the major financial statements by looking at the income statement. This statement was briefly considered in Chapter 2 and we shall now look at it in some detail. We shall see how it is prepared and how it links with the statement of financial position. We shall also consider some of the key measurement problems to be faced when preparing the income statement.

## Learning outcomes

**When you have completed this chapter, you should be able to:**

- discuss the nature and purpose of the income statement;
- prepare an income statement from relevant financial information and interpret the information that it contains;
- discuss the main recognition and measurement issues that must be considered when preparing the income statement;
- explain the main accounting conventions underpinning the income statement.

**MyAccountingLab** Remember to create your own personalised Study Plan

## What does it mean?

Tate and Lyle plc, whose business is sweeteners, starches and sugar refining, reported sales revenue of £3,553 million and a profit of £70 million for the year ended on 31 March 2009. To understand fully the significance of these figures, we must be clear about the nature of revenue and profit. This means that we must be able to answer questions such as:

- Does the sales revenue of £3,553 million represent the cash generated from sales for the period?
- What is the relationship between the sales revenue and the profit for the period?
- Can the profit for the period of £70 million be measured with complete accuracy and certainty?
- Does the profit figure of £70 million mean that the business had £70 million more in the bank at the end of the year than it had at the beginning?
- How can the sales revenue and profit figures help in assessing performance?

The answers to these and other questions are covered in the chapter.

## The income statement

In Chapter 2 we considered the statement of financial position (balance sheet). We saw that it sets out the wealth of a business, at a particular moment in time, and who contributed that wealth. However, it is not usually enough for users of financial statements to have information relating only to this aspect of financial health. Businesses exist to generate wealth, or profit, and it is the profit generated *during a period* that is the concern of many users. The main purpose of the income statement – or profit and loss account, as it is sometimes called – is to measure and report how much profit (wealth) the business has generated over a period. It also helps users to gain some impression of how that profit was made. As with the statement of financial position, which we examined in Chapter 2, the principles of preparation are the same irrespective of whether the income statement is for a sole proprietorship business or for a limited company.

The measurement of profit requires that the total revenue of the business, generated during a particular period, is identified. Revenue is simply a measure of the inflow of economic benefits arising from the ordinary activities of a business. These benefits will result in either an increase in assets (such as cash or amounts owed to the business by its customers) or a decrease in liabilities. Different forms of business enterprise will generate different forms of revenue. Some examples of the different forms that revenue can take are as follows:

- sales of goods (for example, by a manufacturer)
- fees for services (for example, of a solicitor)
- subscriptions (for example, of a club)
- interest received (for example, on an investment fund).

Real World 3.1 shows the various forms of revenue generated by a leading football club.

**Real World 3.1**

## Gunning for revenue

Arsenal Football Club generated total revenue of £313 million for the year ended 31 May 2009. Like other leading clubs, it relies on various forms of revenue to sustain its success. Figure 3.1 shows the contribution of each form of revenue for the year. The high level of revenue from property development is unusual for a football club, even for Arsenal. It arises from the fact that the club is developing its former home Highbury Stadium for residential accommodation following its move to the Emirates Stadium.

**Figure 3.1** Arsenal's revenue for the year ended 31 May 2009

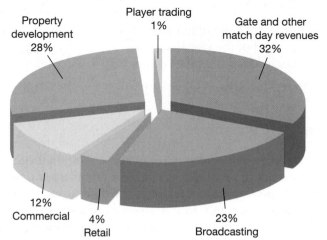

Gate receipts and broadcasting tend to be Arsenal's main forms of revenue, although commercial activities (including sponsorship and events) are also significant. During this particular year, there was a lot of income from property development. Between them, gate receipts, broadcasting and commercial activities accounted for 93 per cent of total revenue other than property development.

*Source*: based on information in Arsenal Holdings plc Annual Report 2009, Note 3 to the financial statements.

The total expenses relating to each period must also be identified. Expense is really the opposite of revenue. It represents the outflow of economic benefits arising from the ordinary activities of a business. This loss of benefits will result in either a decrease in assets (such as cash) or an increase in liabilities (such as amounts owed to suppliers). Expenses are incurred in the process of generating, or attempting to generate, revenue. The nature of the business will again determine the type of expenses that will be incurred. Examples of some of the more common types of expenses are:

■ the cost of buying, or making, the goods that are sold during the period concerned
– known as *cost of sales* or *cost of goods sold*
■ salaries and wages

- rent and rates
- motor vehicle running expenses
- insurance
- printing and stationery
- heat and light
- telephone and postage.

The *income statement* simply shows the total revenue generated during a particular period and deducts from this the total expenses incurred in generating that revenue. The difference between the total revenue and total expenses will represent either profit (if revenue exceeds expenses) or loss (if expenses exceed revenue). Thus, we have:

> **Profit (or loss) for the period = Total revenue for the period less Total expenses incurred in generating that revenue**

The period over which profit or loss is normally measured is usually known as the reporting period, but is sometimes called the 'accounting period' or 'financial period'.

## Different roles

The income statement and the statement of financial position should not be viewed in any way as substitutes for one another. Rather they should be seen as performing different roles. The statement of financial position, as we have seen, sets out the position at a single moment in time: it is a 'snapshot' of the make-up of the wealth held by the business. The income statement, on the other hand, is concerned with the *flow* of wealth over a period of time. The two statements are, however, closely related.

The income statement links the statements of financial position at the beginning and the end of a reporting period. Thus, at the start of a new reporting period, the statement of financial position shows the opening wealth position of the business. After an appropriate period, an income statement is prepared to show the wealth generated over that period. A statement of financial position is then also prepared to reveal the new wealth position at the end of the period. This statement of financial position will reflect the changes in wealth that have occurred since the previous statement of financial position was drawn up.

We saw in Chapter 2 (page 44) that the effect on the statement of financial position of making a profit (or loss) means that the accounting equation can be extended as follows:

> **Assets (at the end of the period) = Equity (amount at the start of the period**
> **+ profit (or − loss) for the period)**
> **+ Liabilities (at the end of the period)**

(This is assuming that the owner makes no injections or withdrawals of equity during the period.)

The amount of profit or loss for the period affects the statement of financial position as an adjustment to equity.

The above equation can be extended to:

Assets (at the end of the period) = Equity (amount at the start of the period)
+ (sales revenue − expenses for the period)
+ Liabilities (at the end of the period)

In theory, it would be possible to calculate the profit (or loss) for the period by making all adjustments for revenue and expenses through the equity section of the statement of financial position. However, this would be rather cumbersome. A better solution is to have an 'appendix' to the equity section, in the form of an income statement. By deducting expenses from revenue for the period, the income statement derives the profit (or loss) by which the equity figure in the statement of financial position needs to be adjusted. This profit (or loss) figure represents the net effect of trading for the period. Through this 'appendix', users are presented with a detailed and more informative view of performance.

## Income statement layout

The layout of the income statement will vary according to the type of business to which it relates. To illustrate an income statement, let us consider the case of a retail business (that is, a business that buys goods in their completed state and resells them). This type of business usually has straightforward operations and, as a result, the income statement is relatively easy to understand.

Example 3.1 sets out a typical layout for the income statement of a retail business.

### Example 3.1

**Better-Price Stores**
**Income statement for the year ended 31 October 2009**

|  | £ |
|---|---:|
| Sales revenue | 232,000 |
| Cost of sales | (154,000) |
| **Gross profit** | 78,000 |
| Salaries and wages | (24,500) |
| Rent and rates | (14,200) |
| Heat and light | (7,500) |
| Telephone and postage | (1,200) |
| Insurance | (1,000) |
| Motor vehicle running expenses | (3,400) |
| Depreciation – fixtures and fittings | (1,000) |
| Depreciation – motor van | (600) |
| **Operating profit** | 24,600 |
| Interest received from investments | 2,000 |
| Interest on borrowings | (1,100) |
| **Profit for the year** | 25,500 |

We saw in Chapter 2 that brackets are used to denote when an item is to be deducted. This convention is used by accountants in preference to + or − signs and will be used throughout the text.

The above income statement provides three measures of profit. Let us now consider each.

## Gross profit

The first part of the income statement is concerned with calculating the gross profit for the period. We can see that revenue, which arises from selling the goods, is the first item to appear. The cost of sales (also called cost of goods sold) for the period is deducted from sales revenue. This gives the gross profit, which represents the profit from buying and selling goods, without taking into account any other revenues or expenses associated with the business.

## Operating profit

Other expenses (overheads) that have been incurred in operating the business (salaries and wages, rent and rates and so on) are then deducted from the gross profit.

The resulting figure is known as the operating profit for the reporting period. This represents the wealth generated during the period from the normal activities of the business. It does not take account of any income that the business may have from activities that are not included in its normal operations. Better-Price Stores in Example 3.1 is a retailer, so the interest on some spare cash that the business has invested is not part of its operating profit. Costs of financing the business are also ignored in the calculation of the operating profit.

## Profit for the year

Having established the operating profit, we add any non-operating income (such as interest receivable) and deduct any interest payable on borrowings made by the business, to arrive at the profit for the year (or net profit). This is the income that is attributable to the owner(s) of the business and which will be added to the equity figure in the statement of financial position. As can be seen, profit for the year is a residual: that is, the amount remaining after deducting all expenses incurred in generating the sales revenue for the period and taking account of non-operating income.

## Further issues

Having set out the main principles involved in preparing an income statement, we need to consider some further points.

## Cost of sales

The cost of sales (or cost of goods sold) figure for a period can be identified in different ways. In some businesses, the cost of sales amount for each individual sale is identified at the time of the transaction. Each item of sales revenue is closely matched with the relevant cost of that sale and so identifying the cost of sales figure for inclusion in the income statement is not a problem. Many large retailers (for example, supermarkets) have point-of-sale (checkout) devices that not only record each sale but also simultaneously pick up the cost of the goods that are the subject of the particular sale. Other businesses that sell a relatively small number of high-value items (for example, an engineering business that produces custom-made equipment) also tend to match sales revenue with the cost of the goods sold, at the time of the sale. However, some businesses (for example, small retailers) do not usually find it practical to match each sale to a particular cost of sales figure as the reporting period progresses. Instead, therefore, they identify the cost of sales figure at the end of the reporting period.

### Deriving the cost of sales after the end of the reporting period

To understand how this is done, we need to remember that the cost of sales figure represents the cost of goods that were *sold* by the business during the period rather than the cost of goods that were *bought* by that business during the period. Part of the goods bought during a particular period may remain in the business, as inventories, at the reporting period end. These will normally be sold in the next period. To derive the cost of sales for a period, we need to know the amount of opening and closing inventories for the period and the cost of goods bought during the period. Example 3.2 illustrates how the cost of sales is derived.

### Example 3.2

Better-Price Stores, which we considered in Example 3.1 above, began the annual reporting period with unsold inventories of £40,000 and during that year bought inventories at a cost of £189,000. At the end of the year, unsold inventories of £75,000 were still held by the business.

The opening inventories at the beginning of the year *plus* the goods bought during the year will represent the total goods available for resale. Thus:

|  | £ |
|---|---|
| Opening inventories | 40,000 |
| Purchases (goods bought) | 189,000 |
| Goods available for resale | 229,000 |

The closing inventories will represent that portion of the total goods available for resale that remains unsold at the end of the year. Thus, the cost of goods actually sold during the annual reporting period must be the total goods available for resale *less* the inventories remaining at the end of the year. That is:

|  | £ |
|---|---|
| Goods available for resale | 229,000 |
| Closing inventories | (75,000) |
| Cost of sales (or cost of goods sold) | 154,000 |

These calculations are sometimes shown on the face of the income statement as in Example 3.3.

## Example 3.3

|  | £ | £ |
|---|---:|---:|
| Sales revenue | | 232,000 |
| Cost of sales: | | |
| Opening inventories | 40,000 | |
| Purchases (goods bought) | 189,000 | |
| Closing inventories | (75,000) | (154,000) |
| **Gross profit** | | 78,000 |

This is just an expanded version of the first section of the income statement for Better-Price Stores, as set out in Example 3.1. We have simply included the additional information concerning inventories balances and purchases for the year provided in Example 3.2.

## Classifying expenses

The classifications for the revenue and expense items, as with the classifications of various assets and claims in the statement of financial position, are often a matter of judgement by those who design the accounting system. Thus, the income statement set out in Example 3.1 could have included the insurance expense with the telephone and postage expense under a single heading – say, 'general expenses'. Such decisions are normally based on how useful a particular classification will be to users. This will usually mean that expense items of material size will be shown separately. For businesses that trade as limited companies, however, there are rules that dictate the classification of various items appearing in the financial statements for external reporting purposes. These rules will be discussed in Chapter 4.

## Activity 3.1

The following information relates to the activities of H & S Retailers for the year ended 30 April 2010:

|  | £ |
|---|---:|
| Motor vehicle running expenses | 1,200 |
| Closing inventories | 3,000 |
| Rent and rates payable | 5,000 |
| Motor vans – cost less depreciation | 6,300 |
| Annual depreciation – motor vans | 1,500 |
| Heat and light | 900 |
| Telephone and postage | 450 |
| Sales revenue | 97,400 |
| Goods purchased | 68,350 |
| Insurance | 750 |
| Loan interest payable | 620 |
| Balance at bank | 4,780 |
| Salaries and wages | 10,400 |
| Opening inventories | 4,000 |

→

> Prepare an income statement for the year ended 30 April 2010. (*Hint*: Not all items listed should appear in the income statement.)

Your answer to this activity should be as follows:

**H & S Retailers**
**Income statement for the year ended 30 April 2010**

|  | £ | £ |
|---|---:|---:|
| Sales revenue |  | 97,400 |
| Cost of sales: |  |  |
|    Opening inventories | 4,000 |  |
|    Purchases | 68,350 |  |
|    Closing inventories | (3,000) | (69,350) |
| **Gross profit** |  | 28,050 |
| Salaries and wages |  | (10,400) |
| Rent and rates |  | (5,000) |
| Heat and light |  | (900) |
| Telephone and postage |  | (450) |
| Insurance |  | (750) |
| Motor vehicle running expenses |  | (1,200) |
| Depreciation – motor vans |  | (1,500) |
| **Operating profit** |  | 7,850 |
| Loan interest |  | (620) |
| **Profit for the year** |  | 7,230 |

Note that neither the motor vans nor the bank balance are included in this statement, because they are both assets and so neither revenues nor expenses.

## The reporting period

We have seen already that for reporting to those outside the business, a financial reporting cycle of one year is the norm, though some large businesses produce a half-yearly, or interim, financial statement to provide more frequent feedback on progress. For those who manage a business, however, it is probably essential to have much more frequent feedback on performance. Thus it is quite common for income statements to be prepared on a quarterly, a monthly, a weekly or even a daily basis in order to show how things are progressing.

## Recognising revenue

A key issue in the measurement of profit concerns the point at which revenue is recognised. Revenue arising from the sale of goods or provision of a service could be recognised at various points. Where, for example, a motor car dealer receives an order for a new car from one of its customers, the associated revenue could be recognised by the dealer:

- at the time that the order is placed by the customer;
- at the time that the car is collected by the customer; or
- at the time that the customer pays the dealer.

These three points could well be quite far apart, particularly where the order relates to a specialist car that is sold to the customer on credit.

The point chosen is not simply a matter of academic interest: it can have a profound impact on the total revenues recognised for a particular reporting period. This, in turn, could have a profound effect on profit. If the sale transaction straddled the end of a reporting period, the choice made between the three possible times for recognising the revenue could determine whether it is included as revenue of the earlier reporting period or the later one.

When dealing with the sale of goods or the provision of services, the main criteria for recognising revenue are that:

- the amount of revenue can be measured reliably; and
- it is probable that the economic benefits will be received.

An additional criterion, however, must be applied where the revenue comes from the sale of goods, which is that:

- ownership and control of the items should pass to the buyer.

Activity 3.2 provides an opportunity to apply these criteria to a practical problem.

## Activity 3.2

A manufacturing business sells goods on credit (that is, the customer pays for the goods some time after they are received). Below are four points in the production/selling cycle at which revenue might be recognised by the business:

1 when the goods are produced;
2 when an order is received from the customer;
3 when the goods are delivered to, and accepted by, the customer;
4 when the cash is received from the customer.

A significant amount of time may elapse between these different points. At what point do you think the business should recognise revenue?

All of the three criteria mentioned above will usually be fulfilled at Point 3: when the goods are passed to, and accepted by, the customer. This is because:

- the selling price and the settlement terms will have been agreed and therefore the amount of revenue can be reliably measured;
- delivery and acceptance of the goods leads to ownership and control passing to the buyer;
- transferring ownership gives the seller legally enforceable rights that makes it probable that the buyer will pay.

We can see that the effect of applying these criteria is that a sale on credit is usually recognised *before* the cash is received. Thus, the total sales revenue figure shown in the income statement may include sales transactions for which the cash has yet to be received. The total sales revenue figure in the income statement for a period will often, therefore, be different from the total cash received from sales during that period.

For cash sales (that is sales where cash is paid at the same time as the goods are transferred), there will be no difference in timing between reporting sales revenue and the cash being received.

Real World 3.2 sets out the revenue recognition criteria for the travel business, TUI Travel plc (which owns First Choice, Thompson, Exodus and many other well-known names). We can see that, although clients may pay for flights or holidays some time before they go, any money received in advance of the departure date, or use of the service, is not treated as revenue until later.

---

### Real World 3.2

### Selling point

*(i) Revenue recognition*
Revenue is recognised in the income statement when the significant risks and rewards of ownership have been transferred to the buyer.

Travel agency commissions and other revenues received from the sale of third-party products are recognised when they are earned, typically on receipt of final payment. Revenue in respect of in-house product is recognised on the date of departure. Revenue from individual travel modules directly booked by the customer with airline, hotels and incoming agencies is recognised when the customer departs or uses the respective service.

No revenue is recognised if there are significant uncertainties regarding recovery of the consideration due, associated costs or possible return of goods.

*(ii) Client monies received in advance (deferred income)*
Client monies received at the balance sheet (statement of financial position) date relating to holidays commencing and flights departing after the year end is deferred and included within trade and other payables.

*Source*: TUI Travel plc Annual Report and Accounts 2009, Notes to the consolidated statements, p. 4, www.tuitravelplc.com.

---

## Long-term contracts

Some contracts, both for goods and for services, can last for more than one reporting period. If the business providing the goods or service were to wait until the contract is completely fulfilled before recognising revenue, the income statement could give a misleading impression of the wealth generated in the various reporting periods covered by the contract. This is a particular problem for businesses that undertake major long-term contracts, where a single contract could represent a large proportion of their total activities.

## Construction contracts

Construction contracts often extend over a long period of time. Suppose that a customer enters into a contract with a builder to have a new factory built that will take three years to complete. In such a situation, it is possible to recognise revenue *before* the factory is completed provided that the building work can be broken down into a number of stages and each stage can be measured reliably. Let us assume that building the factory could be broken down into the following stages:

Stage 1 – clearing and levelling the land and putting in the foundations
Stage 2 – building the walls
Stage 3 – putting on the roof
Stage 4 – putting in the windows and completing all the interior work.

Each stage can be awarded a separate price with the total for all the stages being equal to the total contract price for the factory. This means that, as each stage is completed, the builder can recognise the price for that stage as revenue and bill the customer accordingly. This is provided that the outcome of the contract as a whole can be estimated reliably.

If the builder were to wait until the factory was completed before recognising revenue, the income statement covering the final year of the contract would recognise all of the revenue on the contract, and the income statements for each preceding year would recognise no revenue. This would give a misleading impression, as it would not reflect the work done during each period.

Real World 3.3 sets out the revenue recognition criteria for one large business engaged in long-term contracts.

### Real World 3.3

## Contract revenue

AMEC plc is an international business offering consultancy, engineering and project management services. The point at which revenue on long-term contracts is recognised by the business is as follows:

> As soon as the outcome of a long-term contract can be estimated reliably, contract revenue and expenses are recognised in the income statement in proportion to the stage of completion of the contract. The stage of completion is assessed by reference to surveys of work performed. When the outcome of a contract cannot be estimated reliably, revenue is recognised only to the extent of contract costs incurred that it is probable will be recoverable, and contract costs are expensed as incurred. An expected loss on a contract is recognised immediately in the income statement.

*Source*: AMEC plc Annual Report and Accounts 2009, Notes to Consolidated Accounts, p. 68.

## Services

Revenue from contracts for services may also be recognised in stages. Suppose a consultancy business has a contract to install a new computer system for the government, which will take several years to complete. Revenue can be recognised *before* the contract is completed as long as the contract can be broken down into stages and the particular stages of completion can be measured reliably. This is really the same approach as that used in the construction contract mentioned above.

Sometimes a continuous service is provided to a customer; for example, a telecommunications business may provide open access to the Internet to those who subscribe to the service. In this case, revenue is usually recognised as the service is rendered. Benefits from providing the service are usually assumed to flow evenly over time and so revenue is recognised evenly over the subscription period.

Where it is not possible to break down a service into particular stages of completion, or to assume that benefits from providing the service accrue evenly over time, revenue will not usually be recognised until the service is fully completed. A solicitor handling a house purchase for a client would normally be one such example.

Real World 3.4 provides an example of how one major business recognises revenue from providing services.

### Real World 3.4

## Sky-high broadcasting revenue

British Sky Broadcasting Group plc is a major satellite broadcaster that generates various forms of revenue. Here are the ways in which some of its revenues are recognised:

- Pay-per-view revenues – when the event (movie or football match) is viewed
- Subscription services, including Sky TV and Sky Broadband – as the services are provided
- Advertising revenues – when the advertising is broadcast
- Installation, hardware and service revenue – when the goods and services are delivered.

*Source*: based on information in British Sky Broadcasting Group plc Annual Report and Accounts 2009, p. 78.

When a service is provided, there will normally be a timing difference between the recognition of revenue and the receipt of cash. Revenue for providing services is often recognised before the cash is received, as with the sale of goods on credit. However, there are occasions when it is the other way around, usually because the service provider demands payment before rendering the service.

### Activity 3.3

Can you think of any examples where cash may be demanded in advance of a service being provided? (*Hint*: Try to think of services that you may use.)

Examples of cash being received in advance of the service being provided may include:

- rent received from letting premises
- telephone line rental charges
- TV licence (BBC) or subscription (for example, Sky) fees
- subscriptions received for the use of health clubs or golf clubs.

You may have thought of others.

## Recognising expenses

Having decided on the point at which revenue is recognised, we can now turn to the issue of the recognition of expenses. The matching convention of accounting is designed to provide guidance concerning the recognition of expenses. This convention states that expenses should be matched to the revenue that they helped to generate. In other words, the expenses associated with a particular item of revenue must be taken into account in the same reporting period as that in which the item of revenue is included. Applying this convention may mean that a particular expense reported in the income statement for a period may not be the same figure as the cash paid for that item during the period. The expense reported might be either more or less than the cash paid during the period. Let us consider two examples that illustrate this point.

### When the expense for the period is more than the cash paid during the period

#### Example 3.4

Domestic Ltd sells household electrical appliances. It pays its sales staff a commission of 2 per cent of sales revenue generated. Total sales revenue for last year amounted to £300,000. This will mean that the commission to be paid in respect of the sales for the year will be £6,000. However, by the end of the year, the amount of sales commission that had actually been paid to staff was £5,000. If the business reported only the amount paid, it would mean that the income statement would not reflect the full expense for the year. This would contravene the matching convention because not all of the expenses associated with the revenue of the year would have been matched in the income statement. This will be remedied as follows:

■ Sales commission expense in the income statement will include the amount paid plus the amount outstanding (that is, £6,000 = £5,000 + £1,000).
■ The amount outstanding (£1,000) represents an outstanding liability at the end of the year and will be included under the heading accrued expenses, or 'accruals', in the statement of financial position. As this item will have to be paid within twelve months of the year end, it will be treated as a current liability.
■ The cash will already have been reduced to reflect the commission paid (£5,000) during the period.

These points are illustrated in Figure 3.2.

In principle, all expenses should be matched to the period in which the sales revenue to which they relate is reported. However, it is sometimes difficult to match certain expenses to sales revenue in the same precise way that we have matched

**Figure 3.2  Accounting for sales commission**

Income statement

Statement of cash flows

Sales commission expense
£6,000

Cash £5,000

Accrual £1,000

Statement of financial position at year end

This illustrates the main points of Example 3.4. We can see that the sales commission expense of £6,000 (which appears in the income statement) is made up of a cash element of £5,000 and an accrued element of £1,000. The cash element appears in the statement of cash flows and the accrued element will appear as a year-end liability in the statement of financial position.

sales commission to sales revenue. It is unlikely, for example, that electricity charges incurred can be linked directly to particular sales in this way. As a result, the electricity charges incurred by, say, a retailer would be matched to the *period* to which they relate. Example 3.5 illustrates this.

## Example 3.5

Domestic Ltd, a retailer, has reached the end of its annual reporting period and has only paid for electricity for the first three-quarters of the year (amounting to £1,900). This is simply because the electricity company has yet to send out bills for the quarter that ends on the same date as Domestic Ltd's year end. The amount of Domestic Ltd's bill for the last quarter is £500. In this situation, the amount of the electricity expense outstanding is dealt with as follows:

■ Electricity expense in the income statement will include the amount paid, plus the amount of the bill for the last quarter (that is, £1,900 + £500 = £2,400) in order to cover the whole year.

■ The amount of the outstanding bill (£500) represents a liability at the end of the year and will be included under the heading 'accruals' or 'accrued expenses' in the statement of financial position. This item would normally have to be paid within twelve months of the year end and will, therefore, be treated as a current liability.

■ The cash will already have been reduced to reflect the electricity paid (£1,900) during the period.

This treatment will mean that the correct figure for the electricity expense for the year will be included in the income statement. It will also have the effect of showing that, at the end of the annual reporting period, Domestic Ltd owed the amount of the last quarter's electricity bill. Dealing with the outstanding amount in this way reflects the dual aspect of the item and will ensure that the accounting equation is maintained.

Domestic Ltd may wish to draw up its income statement before it is able to discover how much it owes for the last quarter's electricity. In this case it is quite normal to make a reasonable estimate of the amount of the bill and to use this estimated amount as described above.

## Activity 3.4

How will the payment of the electricity bill for the last quarter be dealt with in the accounting records of Domestic Ltd?

When the electricity bill is eventually paid, it will be dealt with as follows:

■ Reduce cash by the amount of the bill.
■ Reduce the amount of the accrued expense as shown on the statement of financial position by the same amount.

If an estimated figure is used and there is a slight error in the estimate, a small adjustment (either negative or positive depending on the direction of the error) can be made to the following year's expense. Dealing with the estimation error in this way is not strictly correct, but the amount is likely to be insignificant.

## Activity 3.5

Can you think of other expenses for a retailer, apart from electricity charges, that cannot be linked directly to sales revenue and for which matching will therefore be done on a time basis?

You may have thought of the following examples:

■ rent and rates
■ insurance
■ interest payments
■ licence fees payable
■ wages and salaries (apart from any sales commission or similar payments).

This is not an exhaustive list. You may have thought of others.

## When the amount paid during the period is more than the full expense for the period

It is not unusual for a business to be in a situation where it has paid more during the year than the full expense for that year. Example 3.6 illustrates how we deal with this.

### Example 3.6

Images Ltd, an advertising agency, normally pays rent for its premises quarterly in advance (on 1 January, 1 April, 1 July and 1 October). On the last day of the last annual reporting period (31 December), it paid the next quarter's rent (£4,000) to the following 31 March, which was a day earlier than required. This would mean that a total of five quarters' rent was paid during the year. If Images Ltd reports all of the cash paid as an expense in the income statement, this would be more than the full expense for the year. This would contravene the matching convention because a higher figure than the expenses associated with the revenue of the year would appear in the income statement.

The problem is overcome by dealing with the rental payment as follows:

- Show the rent for four quarters as the appropriate expense in the income statement (that is, 4 × £4,000 = £16,000).
- The cash (that is, 5 × £4,000 = £20,000) would already have been paid during the year.
- Show the quarter's rent paid in advance (£4,000) as a prepaid expense under assets in the statement of financial position. (The rent paid in advance will appear as a current asset in the statement of financial position, under the heading prepaid expenses or 'prepayments'.)

In the next reporting period, this prepayment will cease to be an asset and will become an expense in the income statement of that period. This is because the rent prepaid relates to the next period and will be 'used up' during it.

These points are illustrated in Figure 3.3.

In practice, the treatment of accruals and prepayments will be subject to the materiality convention of accounting. This convention states that, where the amounts involved are immaterial, we should consider only what is reasonable. This may mean that an item will be treated as an expense in the reporting period in which it is paid, rather than being strictly matched to the revenue to which it relates. For example, a business may find that, at the end of a reporting period, a bill of £5 has been paid for stationery that has yet to be delivered. For a business of any size, the time and effort involved in recording this as a prepayment would not be justified by the little effect that this would have on the measurement of profit or financial position. The amount would, therefore, be treated as an expense when preparing the income statement for the current reporting period and ignored in the following period.

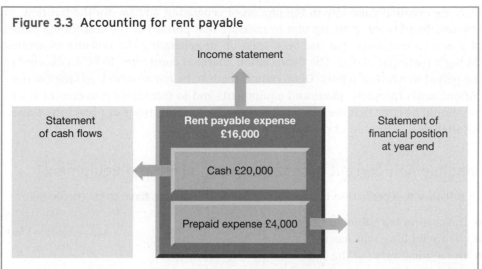

**Figure 3.3** Accounting for rent payable

Income statement

Statement of cash flows

Rent payable expense £16,000

Cash £20,000

Prepaid expense £4,000

Statement of financial position at year end

This illustrates the main points of Example 3.6. We can see that the rent expense of £16,000 (which appears in the income statement) is made up of four quarters' rent at £4,000 per quarter. This is the amount that relates to the period and is 'used up' during the period. The cash paid of £20,000 (which appears in the statement of cash flows) is made up of the cash paid during the period, which is five quarters at £4,000 per quarter. Finally, the prepayment of £4,000 (which appears on the statement of financial position) represents the payment made on 31 December and relates to the next annual reporting period.

## Profit, cash and accruals accounting

As we have just seen, revenue does not usually represent cash received, and expenses are not the same as cash paid. As a result, the profit figure (that is, total revenue minus total expenses) will not normally represent the net cash generated during a period. It is therefore important to distinguish between profit and liquidity. Profit is a measure of achievement, or productive effort, rather than a measure of cash generated. Although making a profit will increase wealth, as we have already seen in Chapter 2, cash is only one form in which that wealth may be held.

The above points are reflected in the accruals convention of accounting, which asserts that profit is the excess of revenue over expenses for a period, not the excess of cash receipts over cash payments. Leading on from this, the approach to accounting that is based on the accruals convention is frequently referred to as accruals accounting. Thus, the statement of financial position and the income statement are both prepared on the basis of accruals accounting. The statement of cash flows, on the other hand, is not, as it simply deals with cash receipts and payments.

## Depreciation

The expense of depreciation, which appeared in the income statement in Activity 3.1, requires further explanation. Most non-current assets do not have a perpetual existence.

They are eventually used up in the process of generating revenue for the business. In essence, depreciation is an attempt to measure that portion of the cost (or fair value) of a non-current asset that has been used up in generating the revenue recognised during a particular period. The depreciation charge is considered to be an expense of the period to which it relates. Depreciation tends to be relevant both to tangible non-current assets (property, plant and equipment) and to intangible non-current assets. We should be clear that the principle is the same for both types of non-current asset. We shall deal with each of the two in turn.

## Tangible non-current assets (property, plant and equipment)

To calculate a depreciation charge for a period, four factors have to be considered:

- the cost (or fair value) of the asset
- the useful life of the asset
- the residual value of the asset
- the depreciation method.

### The cost (or fair value) of the asset

The cost of an asset will include all costs incurred by the business to bring the asset to its required location and to make it ready for use. Thus, in addition to the costs of acquiring the asset, any delivery costs, installation costs (for example, setting up a new machine) and legal costs incurred in the transfer of legal title (for example, in purchasing property) will be included as part of the total cost of the asset. Similarly, any costs incurred in improving or altering an asset in order to make it suitable for its intended use within the business will also be included as part of the total cost.

### Activity 3.6

Andrew Wu (Engineering) Ltd bought a new motor car for its marketing director. The invoice received from the motor car supplier showed the following:

|  | £ |
|---|---|
| New BMW 325i | 26,350 |
| Delivery charge | 80 |
| Alloy wheels | 660 |
| Sun roof | 200 |
| Petrol | 30 |
| Number plates | 130 |
| Road fund licence | 120 |
|  | 27,570 |
| Part exchange – Reliant Robin | (1,000) |
| Amount outstanding | 26,570 |

What is the total cost of the new car that will be treated as part of the business's property, plant and equipment?

The cost of the new car will be as follows:

|  | £ |
|---|---|
| New BMW 325i | 26,350 |
| Delivery charge | 80 |
| Alloy wheels | 660 |
| Sun roof | 200 |
| Number plates | 130 |
|  | 27,420 |

This cost includes delivery charges, which are necessary to bring the asset into use. It also includes number plates, as they are a necessary and integral part of the asset. Improvements (alloy wheels and sun roof) are also regarded as part of the total cost of the motor car. The petrol and road fund licence, however, represent costs of operating the asset rather than a part of the total cost of acquiring it and making it ready for use. These amounts will, therefore, be charged as an expense in the period incurred (although part of the cost of the licence may be regarded as a prepaid expense in the period incurred).

The part-exchange figure shown is part payment of the total amount outstanding and so is not relevant to a consideration of the total cost.

The fair value of an asset was defined in Chapter 2 as the exchange value that could be obtained in an arm's-length transaction. As we saw, assets may be revalued to fair value only if this can be measured reliably. When a revaluation is carried out, all items within the same class must be revalued and revaluations must be kept up to date.

## The useful life of the asset

A tangible non-current asset has both a *physical life* and an *economic life*. The physical life will be exhausted through the effects of wear and tear and/or the passage of time. It is possible, however, for the physical life to be extended considerably through careful maintenance, improvements and so on. The economic life is decided by the effects of technological progress and by changes in demand. After a while, the benefits of using the asset may be less than the costs involved. This may be because the asset is unable to compete with newer assets, or because it is no longer relevant to the needs of the business. The economic life of a non-current tangible asset may be much shorter than its physical life. For example, a computer may have a physical life of eight years, but an economic life of just three years.

It is the economic life that will determine the expected useful life for the purpose of calculating depreciation. Forecasting the economic life, however, may be extremely difficult in practice: both the rate at which technology progresses and shifts in consumer tastes can be swift and unpredictable.

## Residual value (disposal value)

When a business disposes of a tangible non-current asset that may still be of value to others, some payment may be received. This payment will represent the residual value, or *disposal value*, of the asset. To calculate the total amount to be depreciated, the residual value must be deducted from the cost (or fair value) of the asset. The likely amount to be received on disposal can, once again, be difficult to predict. The best guide is often past experience of similar assets sold.

### Depreciation methods

Once the amount to be depreciated (that is, the cost, or fair value, of the asset less any residual value) has been estimated, the business must select a method of allocating this depreciable amount between the annual reporting periods covering the asset's useful life. Although there are various ways in which the total depreciation may be allocated and, from this, a depreciation charge for each year derived, there are really only two methods that are commonly used in practice.

→ The first of these is known as the straight-line method. This method simply allocates the amount to be depreciated evenly over the useful life of the asset. In other words, an equal amount of depreciation is charged for each year that the asset is held.

### Example 3.7

To illustrate this method, consider the following information:

| | |
|---|---|
| Cost of machine | £78,124 |
| Estimated residual value at the end of its useful life | £2,000 |
| Estimated useful life | 4 years |

To calculate the depreciation charge for each year, the total amount to be depreciated must be calculated. This will be the total cost less the estimated residual value: that is, £78,124 – £2,000 = £76,124. Having done this, the annual depreciation charge can be derived by dividing the amount to be depreciated by the estimated useful life of the asset of four years. The calculation is therefore:

$$\frac{£76,124}{4} = £19,031$$

Thus, the annual depreciation charge that appears in the income statement in relation to this asset will be £19,031 for each of the four years of the asset's life.

The amount of depreciation relating to the asset will be accumulated for as long as the asset continues to be owned by the business. This accumulated depreciation figure will increase each year as a result of the annual depreciation amount charged to the income statement. This accumulated amount will be deducted from the cost of the asset on the statement of financial position. At the end of the second year, for example, the accumulated depreciation will be £19,031 × 2 = £38,062. The asset details will appear on the statement of financial position as follows:

| | £ |
|---|---|
| Machine at cost | 78,124 |
| Accumulated depreciation | (38,062) |
| | 40,062 |

As we saw in Chapter 2, the balance of £40,062 shown above is referred to as the carrying amount (sometimes also known as the written-down value or net book value) of the asset. It represents that portion of the cost (or fair value) of the asset that has still to be charged as an expense (written off) in future years. It must be emphasised that this figure does not, except by coincidence, represent the current market value, which may be quite different. The only point at which the carrying amount is intended to equal the market value of the asset is immediately before it is to be disposed of. Thus in Example 3.7, at the end of the four-year life of the machine, the carrying amount would be £2,000 – its estimated disposal value.

The straight-line method derives its name from the fact that the carrying amount of the asset at the end of each year, when plotted against time, will result in a straight line, as shown in Figure 3.4.

**Figure 3.4** Graph of carrying amount against time using the straight-line method

The carrying amount of the asset declines by a constant amount each year. This is because the straight-line method provides a constant depreciation charge each year. The result, when plotted on a graph, is a straight line.

The second approach to calculating annual depreciation which is found in practice is referred to as the reducing-balance method. This method applies a fixed percentage rate of depreciation to the carrying amount of the asset each year. The effect of this will be high annual depreciation charges in the early years and lower charges in the later years. To illustrate this method, let us take the same information that was used in Example 3.7. By using a fixed percentage of 60 per cent of the carrying amount to determine the annual depreciation charge, the effect will be to reduce the carrying amount to £2,000 after four years.

The calculations will be as follows:

|  | £ |
|---|---|
| Cost of machine | 78,124 |
| Year 1 Depreciation charge (60%* of cost) | (46,874) |
| Carrying amount | 31,250 |
| Year 2 Depreciation charge (60% of carrying amount) | (18,750) |
| Carrying amount | 12,500 |
| Year 3 Depreciation charge (60% of carrying amount) | (7,500) |
| Carrying amount | 5,000 |
| Year 4 Depreciation charge (60% of carrying amount) | (3,000) |
| Residual value | 2,000 |

\* Box 3.1 explains how to derive the fixed percentage.

---

**Box 3.1**
**Deriving the fixed percentage**

Deriving the fixed percentage to be applied requires the use of the following formula:

$$P = (1 - \sqrt[n]{R/C}) \times 100\%$$

where: $P$ = the depreciation percentage
$n$ = the useful life of the asset (in years)
$R$ = the residual value of the asset
$C$ = the cost, or fair value, of the asset.

The fixed percentage rate will, however, be given in all examples used in this text.

---

We can see that the pattern of depreciation is quite different between the two methods. If we plot the carrying amount of the asset, which has been derived using the reducing-balance method, against time, the result will be as shown in Figure 3.5.

**Figure 3.5** Graph of carrying amount against time using the reducing-balance method

Under the reducing-balance method, the carrying amount of an asset falls by a larger amount in the earlier years than in the later years. This is because the depreciation charge is based on a fixed percentage of the carrying amount.

### Activity 3.7

Assume that the machine used in the example above was owned by a business that made a profit before depreciation of £40,000 for each of the four years in which the asset was held.

Calculate the profit for the business for each year under each depreciation method, and comment on your findings.

Your answer should be as follows:

**Straight-line method**

|  | (a)<br>Profit before<br>depreciation<br>£ | (b)<br>Depreciation<br>£ | (a – b)<br>Profit<br>£ |
|---|---|---|---|
| Year 1 | 40,000 | 19,031 | 20,969 |
| Year 2 | 40,000 | 19,031 | 20,969 |
| Year 3 | 40,000 | 19,031 | 20,969 |
| Year 4 | 40,000 | 19,031 | 20,969 |

**Reducing-balance method**

|  | (a)<br>Profit before<br>depreciation<br>£ | (b)<br>Depreciation<br>£ | (a – b)<br>Profit/(loss)<br>£ |
|---|---|---|---|
| Year 1 | 40,000 | 46,874 | (6,874) |
| Year 2 | 40,000 | 18,750 | 21,250 |
| Year 3 | 40,000 | 7,500 | 32,500 |
| Year 4 | 40,000 | 3,000 | 37,000 |

The straight-line method of depreciation results in a constant profit figure over the four-year period. This is because both the profit before depreciation and the depreciation charge are constant over the period. The reducing-balance method, however, results in a changing profit figure over time, despite the fact that in this example the pre-depreciation profit is the same each year. In the first year a loss is reported and, thereafter, a rising profit.

Although the *pattern* of profit over the four-year period will be quite different, depending on the depreciation method used, the *total* profit for the period (£83,876) will remain the same. This is because both methods of depreciating will allocate the same amount of total depreciation (£76,124) over the four-year period. It is only the amount allocated *between years* that will differ.

In practice, the use of different depreciation methods may not have such a dramatic effect on profits as suggested in Activity 3.7. This is because businesses typically have more than one depreciating non-current asset. Where a business replaces some of its assets each year, the total depreciation charge calculated under the reducing-balance method will reflect a range of charges (from high through to low), as assets will be at different points in the replacement cycle. This could mean that each year's total depreciation charge may not be significantly different from the total depreciation charge that would be derived under the straight-line method.

### Selecting a depreciation method

How does a business choose which depreciation method to use for a particular asset? The answer is the one that best matches the depreciation expense to the pattern of economic benefits that the asset provides. Where these benefits are provided evenly over time (buildings, for example), the straight-line method is usually appropriate. Where assets lose their efficiency (as with certain types of machinery), the benefits provided will decline over time and so the reducing-balance method may be more appropriate. Where the pattern of economic benefits provided by the asset is uncertain, the straight-line method is normally chosen.

There is an International Financial Reporting Standard (International Accounting Standard) which deals with the depreciation of property, plant and equipment. As we shall see in Chapter 4, the purpose of financial reporting standards is to narrow areas of accounting difference and to try to ensure that information provided to users is transparent and comparable. The relevant standard endorses the view that the depreciation method chosen should reflect the pattern of economic benefits provided but does not specify particular methods to be used. It states that the useful life, depreciation method and residual values of non-current assets should be reviewed at least annually and adjustments made where appropriate.

Real World 3.5 sets out the depreciation policies of Thorntons plc.

---

**Real World 3.5**

## Sweet talk on depreciation policies

Thorntons plc, the manufacturer and retailer of confectionery, uses the straight-line method to depreciate all its property, plant and equipment, other than land and assets in the course of construction. The financial statements for the year ended 30 June 2009 show the period over which different classes of assets are depreciated as follows:

| | |
|---|---|
| Long leasehold and freehold premises | 50 years |
| Short leasehold land and buildings | Period of the lease |
| Other plant, vehicles and equipment | 3 to 15 years |
| Retail fixtures and fittings | Up to 10 years |

We can see that there are wide variations in the expected useful lives of the various assets held.

*Source*: Thorntons plc Annual Report and Accounts 2009, p. 49.

It seems that Thorntons plc is typical of UK businesses in that most use the straight-line approach. The reducing-balance method is not very much used.

The approach taken to calculating depreciation is summarised in Figure 3.6.

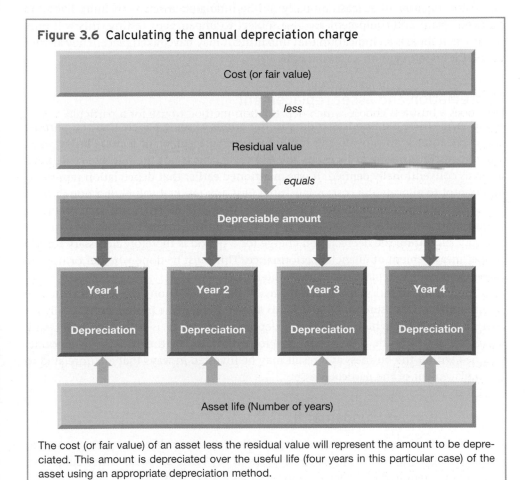

**Figure 3.6** Calculating the annual depreciation charge

The cost (or fair value) of an asset less the residual value will represent the amount to be depreciated. This amount is depreciated over the useful life (four years in this particular case) of the asset using an appropriate depreciation method.

## Depreciating intangible assets

Where an intangible asset has a finite life, the approach taken for the depreciation (or amortisation as it is usually called with intangibles) is broadly the same as that for property, plant and equipment (tangible non-current assets). The asset is amortised (depreciated) over its useful life and the amortisation method used should reflect the pattern of benefits provided. Some differences arise, however, because of the valuation problems surrounding these assets. Intangible assets are reported initially at cost but can, in principle, be revalued to fair value. However, this rarely occurs as there is usually no active market from which to establish fair values. For similar reasons, the residual value of an intangible asset is normally assumed to be zero.

We saw in Chapter 2 that some intangible assets, which may include acquired goodwill, have an infinite useful life. These assets are not amortised but instead are tested for impairment at least annually. While intangible assets with finite lives and property, plant and equipment are also subject to impairment testing, this will only occur when there is an indication that impairment may have taken place. They are not tested for impairment on a routine basis.

## Depreciation and asset replacement

There seems to be a misunderstanding in the minds of some people that the purpose of depreciation is to provide the funds for the replacement of a non-current asset when it reaches the end of its useful life. However, this is not the purpose of depreciation as conventionally defined. It was mentioned earlier that depreciation represents an attempt to allocate the cost or fair value (less any residual value) of a non-current asset over its expected useful life. The resulting depreciation charge in each reporting period represents an expense, which is then used in the calculation of profit for the period. Calculating the depreciation charge for a period is therefore necessary for the proper measurement of financial performance. This must be done whether or not the business intends to replace the asset in the future.

If there is an intention to replace the asset, the depreciation charge in the income statement will not ensure that liquid funds are set aside by the business specifically for this purpose. Although the effect of a depreciation charge is to reduce profit and, therefore, to reduce the amount available for withdrawal by the owners, the amounts retained within the business as a result may be invested in ways that are unrelated to the replacement of the particular asset.

## Depreciation and judgement

From what we have just seen about depreciation, it seems that accounting is not as precise and objective as it sometimes appears to be. There are areas where subjective judgement is required and depreciation provides a good illustration of this.

### Activity 3.8

What kinds of judgements must be made to calculate a depreciation charge for a period?

You may have thought of the following:

- the expected residual or disposal value of the asset
- the expected useful life of the asset
- the choice of depreciation method.

Making different judgements on these matters would result in a different pattern of depreciation charges over the life of the asset and, therefore, in a different pattern of reported profits. However, underestimations or overestimations that are made in relation to the above will be adjusted for in the final year of an asset's life. As a result, the total depreciation charge (and total profit) over the asset's life will not be affected by estimation errors.

Real World 3.6 describes the effect of extending the useful life of property, plant and equipment on the short-term profits of one large business.

## Real World 3.6

### Sports massage

JJB Sports plc, a leading retailer, reported interim financial results for the six months ended 30 June 2005 that caused some disquiet among investors and analysts. The business changed the estimates for the useful life of its property, plant and equipment when calculating depreciation. It explained that this was due to new requirements to adopt International Financial Reporting Standards (IFRSs) when preparing financial statements. The article below, however, suggests that not everyone believed this.

#### JJB massages results to boost profits
High street retailer JJB Sports massaged last week's disappointing interim results by changing its depreciation calculations, in order to boost flagging profits by £4.3 million.

Analysts admitted that they were caught on the hop, as the company reported a 35.8% drop in operating profits from £27.4 million to £17.6 million for six months ended June 2005 on revenues down 6% to £340.4 million. Operating profits would have plummeted even further to £14.3 million had the company not changed its accounting for depreciation. 'The company explained the change as coming out of its IFRS conversion review, but it was clearly there for other reasons,' said Teather & Greenwood retail analyst Sanjay Vidyarthi.

JJB said that an impairment review ahead of its IFRS transition had forced a rethink on the carrying value of property, plant and equipment.

It concluded that these items had useful economic lives that more closely matched the length of the short-term lease of the property, rather than the 10-year economic life which had formed the basis of the depreciation charge in previous reporting periods.

Richard Ratner, head of equity research at Seymour Pierce, said: 'They said the way they had depreciated assets previously was not correct but I haven't seen any other companies make this kind of change.'

JJB's share price fell from 168.2p before the results to 164.7p at the end of last week.

*Source*: 'JJB massages results to boost profits', *Accountancy Age*, 20 October 2005, p. 3.

## Costing inventories

The way in which we measure the cost of inventories (or stock) is important because the cost of inventories sold during a reporting period will affect the calculation of profit. Furthermore, the cost of remaining inventories held at the end of the reporting period can affect the portrayal of wealth in the statement of financial position. It is tempting to think that determining the cost of inventories used or still held is pretty straightforward. However, during a period of changing prices, it can be a problem.

To determine the cost of the inventories sold and the cost of the inventories remaining at the end of the reporting period, an assumption must be made about the way in which inventories are physically handled. This assumption need not have anything to do with how the inventories are *actually* handled. It is concerned only with providing useful accounting information.

Three common assumptions used are:

- first in, first out (FIFO), in which it is assumed that the earliest acquired inventories held are the first to be used;
- last in, first out (LIFO), in which it is assumed that the latest acquired inventories held are the first to be used; and
- weighted average cost (AVCO), in which it is assumed that inventories acquired lose their separate identity and go into a 'pool'. Any issues of inventories from this pool will reflect the weighted average cost of inventories held.

Example 3.8 provides a simple illustration of the way in which each method is applied.

## Example 3.8

A business commenced on 1 May to supply oil to factories. During the first month, the following transactions took place:

|  | Tonnes | Cost per tonne |
|---|---|---|
| May   2 Purchased | 10,000 | £10 |
| May 10 Purchased | 20,000 | £13 |
| May 18 Sold | 9,000 | |

### First in, first out (FIFO)

Using the first in, first out approach, 9,000 tonnes of the 10,000 tonnes bought on 2 May are treated as if these are the ones to be sold. The remaining inventories bought on 2 May (1,000 tonnes) and the inventories bought on 10 May (20,000 tonnes) will become the closing inventories. Thus we have:

| Cost of sales | (9,000 @ £10 per tonne) | £90,000 |
|---|---|---|
| Closing inventories | | |
| | | £ |
| | (1,000 @ £10 per tonne) | 10,000 |
| | (20,000 @ £13 per tonne) | 260,000 |
| | | 270,000 |

### Last in, first out (LIFO)

Using the last in, first out approach, 9,000 tonnes of the inventories bought on 10 May will be treated as if these are the first to be sold. The earlier inventories bought on

2 May (10,000 tonnes) and the remainder of the inventories bought on 10 May (11,000 tonnes) will become the closing inventories. Thus we have:

| | | |
|---|---|---|
| Cost of sales | (9,000 @ £13 per tonne) | £117,000 |
| Closing inventories | | |
| | | £ |
| | (11,000 @ £13 per tonne) | 143,000 |
| | (10,000 @ £10 per tonne) | 100,000 |
| | | 243,000 |

## Weighted average cost (AVCO)

Since newly acquired inventories are treated, for accounting purposes, as if they lose their separate identity, any issues should reflect the weighted average cost of inventories held. Using this approach, a weighted average cost, based on the quantities of each batch purchased, is calculated. The weighted average cost is then used to derive both the cost of goods sold and the cost of remaining inventories held. This simply means that the cost of the inventories bought on 2 May and 10 May are added together and then divided by the total number of tonnes to obtain the weighted average cost per tonne. That is:

Average cost = $((10,000 \times £10) + (20,000 \times £13))/(10,000 + 20,000) = £12$ per tonne

Both the cost of sales and the value of the closing inventories are then based on this average cost per tonne. Thus we have:

| | | |
|---|---|---|
| Cost of sales | (9,000 @ £12 per tonne) | £108,000 |
| Closing inventories | (21,000 @ £12 per tonne) | £252,000 |

### Activity 3.9

Suppose that the 9,000 tonnes of inventories in Example 3.8 were sold for £15 a tonne.

(a) Calculate the gross profit for the period under each of the three costing methods.
(b) What do you note about the different profit and closing inventories valuations when using each method, when prices are rising?

Your answer should be along the following lines:

(a) Gross profit calculation:

| | FIFO £000 | LIFO £000 | AVCO £000 |
|---|---|---|---|
| Sales revenue (9,000 @ £15) | 135 | 135 | 135 |
| Cost of sales | (90) | (117) | (108) |
| Gross profit | 45 | 18 | 27 |
| Closing inventories figure | 270 | 243 | 252 |

→

(b) These figures show that FIFO will give the highest gross profit during a period of rising prices. This is because sales revenue is matched with the earlier (and cheaper) purchases. LIFO will give the lowest gross profit because sales revenue is matched against the more recent (and dearer) purchases. The AVCO method will normally give a figure that is between these two extremes.

The closing inventories figure in the statement of financial position will be highest with the FIFO method. This is because the cost of oil still held will be based on the more recent (and dearer) purchases. LIFO will give the lowest closing inventories figure as the oil held will be based on the earlier (and cheaper) purchases. Once again, the AVCO method will normally give a figure that is between these two extremes. During a period of falling prices, the position of FIFO and LIFO is reversed.

The different costing methods will only have an effect on the reported profit from one reporting period to the next. The figure derived for closing inventories will be carried forward and matched with sales revenue in a later period. Thus, if the cheaper purchases of inventories are matched to sales revenue in the current period, it will mean that the dearer purchases will be matched to sales revenue in a later period. Over the life of the business, therefore, the total profit will be the same either way.

## Inventories – some further issues

We saw in Chapter 2 that the convention of prudence requires that inventories be valued at the lower of cost and net realisable value. (The net realisable value of inventories is the estimated selling price less any further costs necessary to complete the goods and any costs involved in selling and distributing them.) In theory, this means that the valuation method applied to inventories could switch each year, depending on which of cost and net realisable value is the lower. In practice, however, the cost of the inventories held is usually below the current net realisable value – particularly during a period of rising prices. It is, therefore, the cost figure that will normally appear in the statement of financial position.

### Activity 3.10

Can you think of any circumstances where the net realisable value will be lower than the cost of inventories held, even during a period of generally rising prices?

The net realisable value may be lower where:

- goods have deteriorated or become obsolete;
- there has been a fall in the market price of the goods;
- the goods are being used as a 'loss leader';
- bad buying decisions have been made.

There is an International Financial Reporting Standard that deals with inventories. It states that, when preparing financial statements for external reporting, the cost of inventories should normally be determined using either FIFO or AVCO. The LIFO approach is not an acceptable method to use for external reporting. The standard also requires the 'lower of cost and net realisable value' rule to be used and so endorses the application of the prudence convention.

Real World 3.7 sets out the inventories costing methods of one well-known supermarket business.

### Real World 3.7

## Buy one, get one free

J Sainsbury plc, the supermarket chain, employs two methods of costing inventories and the particular method applied depends on where the inventories are located. The business reports:

> Inventories are valued at the lower of cost and net realisable value. Inventories at warehouses are valued on a first-in, first-out basis. Those at retail outlets are valued at calculated average cost prices.

*Source*: J Sainsbury plc Annual Report 2009, p. 49.

 Costing inventories and depreciation provide two examples where the consistency convention must be applied. This convention holds that once a particular method of accounting is selected, it should be applied consistently over time. Thus, it would not be acceptable to switch from, say, FIFO to AVCO between periods (unless exceptional circumstances make it appropriate). The purpose of this convention is to help users make valid comparisons of performance and position from one period to the next.

### Activity 3.11

Reporting inventories in the financial statements provides a further example of the need to apply subjective judgement. For the inventories of a retail business, what are the main areas where judgement is required?

The main areas are:

- the choice of cost method (FIFO, LIFO, AVCO);
- deducing the net realisable value figure for inventories held.

## Trade receivables problems

We have seen that, when businesses sell goods or services on credit, revenue will usually be recognised before the customer pays the amounts owing. Recording the dual aspect of a credit sale will involve increasing sales revenue and increasing trade receivables by the amount of the revenue from the credit sale.

With this type of sale there is always the risk that the customer will not pay the amount due, however reliable they might have appeared to be at the time of the sale.

When it becomes reasonably certain that the customer will never pay, the debt owed is considered to be a bad debt and this must be taken into account when preparing the financial statements.

## Activity 3.12

When preparing the financial statements, what would be the effect on the income statement, and on the statement of financial position, of not taking into account the fact that a debt is bad?

The effect would be to overstate the assets (trade receivables) on the statement of financial position and to overstate profit in the income statement, as the revenue which has been recognised will not result in any future benefit.

To provide a more realistic picture of financial performance and position, the bad debt must be 'written off'. This will involve reducing the trade receivables and increasing expenses (by creating an expense known as 'bad debts written off') by the amount of the bad debt.

The matching convention requires that the bad debt is written off in the same period as the sale that gave rise to the debt is recognised.

Note that, when a debt is bad, the accounting response is not simply to cancel the original sale. If this were done, the income statement would not be so informative. Reporting the bad debts as an expense can be extremely useful in assessing management performance.

## Activity 3.13

The treatment of bad debts represents a further example where judgement is needed to derive an appropriate expense figure.

What will be the effect of different judgements concerning the appropriate amount of bad debts expense on the profit for a particular period and on the total profit reported over the life of the business?

Judgement is often required in deriving a figure for bad debts incurred during a period. There may be situations where views will differ concerning whether or not a debt is irrecoverable. The decision concerning whether or not to write off a bad debt will have an effect on the expenses for the period and, therefore, on the reported profit. However, over the life of the business the total reported profit would not be affected, as incorrect judgements in one period will be adjusted for in a later period.

Suppose that a debt of £100 was written off in a period and that, in a later period, the amount owing was actually received. The increase in expenses of £100 in the period in which the bad debt was written off would be compensated for by an increase in revenue of £100 when the amount outstanding was finally received (bad debt recovered). If, on the other hand, the amount owing of £100 was never written off in the first place, the profit for the two periods would not be affected by the bad debt adjustment and would, therefore, be different – but the total profit for the two periods would be the same.

Real World 3.8 describes the recent rise in bad debts among small and medium-sized businesses.

## Real World 3.8

## Bad debts getting worse

The average amount of bad debt being written off by small and medium-sized businesses has doubled in twelve months to £2,529, according to research by Barclays.

The bank's annual late payments survey, covering 1,000 small and medium-sized businesses, found that, on any given day, about £9 billion was owed to such companies, although this is £1 billion less than in the previous year. Although 18 per cent of those asked said that late payers were a threat to the company's survival, this was down from 32 per cent in the same survey in 2008.

One in six of the company heads interviewed said they had cancelled more debt in 2009 than in the previous twelve months.

*Source*: 'SMEs write off more bad debt', *The Financial Times*, 12/03/2010 (Moules, J.), copyright © The Financial Times Ltd.

Let us now try to bring together some of the points that we have raised in this chapter through a self-assessment question.

## ? Self-assessment question 3.1

TT and Co. is a new business that started trading on 1 January 2009. The following is a summary of transactions that occurred during the first year of trading:

1 The owners introduced £50,000 of equity, which was paid into a bank account opened in the name of the business.

2 Premises were rented from 1 January 2009 at an annual rental of £20,000. During the year, rent of £25,000 was paid to the owner of the premises.

3 Rates (a tax on business premises) were paid during the year as follows:

|   |   |
|---|---|
| For the period 1 January 2009 to 31 March 2009 | £500 |
| For the period 1 April 2009 to 31 March 2010 | £1,200 |

4 A delivery van was bought on 1 January 2009 for £12,000. This is expected to be used in the business for four years and then to be sold for £2,000.

5 Wages totalling £33,500 were paid during the year. At the end of the year, the business owed £630 of wages for the last week of the year.

6 Electricity bills for the first three quarters of the year were paid totalling £1,650. After 31 December 2009, but before the financial statements had been finalised for the year, the bill for the last quarter arrived showing a charge of £620.

7 Inventories totalling £143,000 were bought on credit.

8 Inventories totalling £12,000 were bought for cash.

9 Sales revenue on credit totalled £152,000 (cost of sales £74,000).

→

10 Cash sales revenue totalled £35,000 (cost of sales £16,000).
11 Receipts from trade receivables totalled £132,000.
12 Payments to trade payables totalled £121,000.
13 Van running expenses paid totalled £9,400.

At the end of the year it was clear that a credit customer (trade receivable) who owed £400 would not be able to pay any part of the debt. All of the other trade receivables were expected to settle in full.

The business uses the straight-line method for depreciating non-current assets.

**Required:**
Prepare an income statement for the year to 31 December 2009 and a statement of financial position as at that date.

**The solution to this question can be found at the back of the book, in Appendix B.**

## Uses and usefulness of the income statement

The income statement, like the statement of financial position, has been around for a long time. Most large businesses prepare an income statement on a frequent basis (monthly or even more frequently). There is, however, no rule requiring this statement to be produced more frequently than once, or in some cases twice, a year. The income statement is, therefore, regarded as capable of providing useful information. In particular, this statement may help in revealing:

- *How effective the business has been in generating wealth.* Since wealth generation is the primary reason for most businesses to exist, assessing how much wealth has been created is an important issue. Although different judgements concerning depreciation, inventories and bad debts may affect the calculation of profit for a period, this problem should not be overstated. For most businesses in most years, the effect of making different judgements would probably not significantly affect the final profit figure.
- *How the profit was derived.* For some users, the only item of concern may be the final profit figure, or *bottom line* as it is sometimes called. While this is a primary measure of performance, and its importance is difficult to overstate, the income statement contains other information that should also be of interest. To evaluate business performance effectively, it is important to discover how the profit figure was derived. Thus the level of sales revenue, the nature and amount of expenses incurred and the profit, in relation to sales revenue, are also important to an understanding of business performance. The analysis and interpretation of financial statements are considered in detail in Chapter 6.

## Summary

The main points of this chapter may be summarised as follows.

### The income statement (profit and loss account)

- The income statement measures and reports how much profit (or loss) has been generated over a period.

- Profit (or loss) for the period is the difference between the total revenue and total expenses for the period.

- The income statement links the statements of financial position at the beginning and end of a reporting period.

- Normally, the income statement will first calculate gross profit and then deduct any overheads for the period. The final figure derived is the profit (or loss) for the period.

- Gross profit represents the difference between the sales revenue for the period and the cost of sales.

### Expenses and revenue

- Cost of sales may be identified either by matching the cost of each sale to the particular sale or, in the case of retail and wholesaling businesses, by adjusting the goods bought during the period to take account of opening and closing inventories.

- Classifying expenses is often a matter of judgement, although there are rules for businesses that operate as limited companies.

- Revenue is recognised when the amount of revenue can be measured reliably and it is probable that the economic benefits will be received.

- Where there is a sale of goods, there is an additional criterion that ownership and control must pass to the buyer before revenue can be recognised.

- Revenue can be recognised after partial completion provided that a particular stage of completion can be measured reliably.

- The matching convention states that expenses should be matched to the revenue that they help generate.

- A particular expense reported in the income statement may not be the same as the cash paid. This will result in accruals or prepayments appearing in the statement of financial position.

- The materiality convention states that where the amounts are immaterial, we should consider only what is expedient.

- 'Accruals accounting' is preparing the income statement and statement of financial position following the accruals convention, which says that profit = revenue less expenses (not cash receipts less cash payments).

### Depreciation of non-current assets

- Depreciation requires a consideration of the cost (or fair value), useful life and residual value of an asset. It also requires a consideration of the method of depreciation.

- The straight-line method of depreciation allocates the amount to be depreciated evenly over the useful life of the asset.

- The reducing-balance method applies a fixed percentage rate of depreciation to the carrying amount of an asset each year.

- The depreciation method chosen should reflect the pattern of benefits associated with the asset.

- Depreciation is an attempt to allocate the cost (or fair value), less the residual value, of an asset over its useful life. It does not provide funds for replacement of the asset.

### Costing inventories

- The way in which we derive the cost of inventories is important in the calculation of profit and the presentation of financial position.

- The first in, first out (FIFO) method approaches matters as if the earliest inventories held are the first to be used.

- The last in, first out (LIFO) method approaches matters as if the latest inventories are the first to be used.

- The weighted average cost (AVCO) method applies an average cost to all inventories used.

- When prices are rising, FIFO gives the lowest cost of sales figure and highest closing inventories figure and LIFO gives the highest cost of sales figure and the lowest closing inventories figure. AVCO gives figures for cost of sales and closing inventories that lie between FIFO and LIFO.

- When prices are falling, the positions of FIFO and LIFO are reversed.

- Inventories are shown at the lower of cost and net realisable value.

- When a particular method of accounting, such as an inventories costing method, is selected, it should be applied consistently over time.

### Bad debts

- Where it is reasonably certain that a credit customer will not pay, the debt is regarded as 'bad' and written off.

### Uses of the income statement

- It provides a profit figure.

- It provides information on how the profit was derived.

*MyAccountingLab* Now check your progress in your personal Study Plan

→ **Key terms**

| | |
|---|---|
| profit p. 71 | depreciation p. 87 |
| revenue p. 71 | residual value p. 89 |
| expense p. 72 | straight-line method p. 90 |
| reporting period p. 73 | carrying amount p. 91 |
| gross profit p. 75 | written-down value p. 91 |
| operating profit p. 75 | net book value p. 91 |
| profit for the year p. 75 | reducing-balance method p. 91 |
| cost of sales p. 75 | amortisation p. 95 |
| matching convention p. 83 | first in, first out (FIFO) p. 98 |
| accrued expenses p. 83 | last in, first out (LIFO) p. 98 |
| prepaid expenses p. 86 | weighted average cost (AVCO) p. 98 |
| materiality convention p. 86 | consistency convention p. 101 |
| accruals convention p. 87 | bad debt p. 102 |
| accruals accounting p. 87 | |

## Further reading

If you would like to explore the topics covered in this chapter in more depth, we recommend the following books:

Elliott, B. and Elliott, J., *Financial Accounting and Reporting* (13th edn), Financial Times Prentice Hall, 2010, chapters 2, 16, 19 and 20.

IASC Foundation Education, *A Guide through IFRS 2009*, July 2009, IAS 2, IAS 16, IAS 18, IAS 36 and IAS 38.

KPMG, *Insights into IFRS* (6th edn, 2009/10), Sweet and Maxwell, 2009, sections 3.2, 3.3, 3.8, 3.10 and 4.2.

## ? Review questions

Solutions to these questions can be found at the back of the book, in Appendix C.

**3.1** 'Although the income statement is a record of past achievement, the calculations required for certain expenses involve estimates of the future.' What does this statement mean? Can you think of examples where estimates of the future are used?

**3.2** 'Depreciation is a process of allocation and not valuation.' What do you think is meant by this statement?

**3.3** What is the convention of consistency? Does this convention help users in making a more valid comparison between businesses?

**3.4** 'An asset is similar to an expense.' Do you agree?

# ✳ Exercises

Exercises 3.4 and 3.5 are more advanced than Exercises 3.1 to 3.3. Those with coloured numbers have solutions at the back of the book, in Appendix D.

If you wish to try more exercises, visit the website at www.myaccountinglab.com.

**3.1** You have heard the following statements made. Comment critically on them.

(a) 'Equity only increases or decreases as a result of the owners putting more cash into the business or taking some out.'
(b) 'An accrued expense is one that relates to next year.'
(c) 'Unless we depreciate this asset we shall be unable to provide for its replacement.'
(d) 'There is no point in depreciating the factory building. It is appreciating in value each year.'

**3.2** Singh Enterprises, which started business on 1 January 2007, has an annual reporting period to 31 December and uses the straight-line method of depreciation. On 1 January 2007 the business bought a machine for £10,000. The machine had an expected useful life of four years and an estimated residual value of £2,000. On 1 January 2008 the business bought another machine for £15,000. This machine had an expected useful life of five years and an estimated residual value of £2,500. On 31 December 2009 the business sold the first machine bought for £3,000.

**Required:**
Show the relevant income statement extract and statement of financial position extract for the years 2007, 2008 and 2009.

**3.3** The owner of a business is confused and comes to you for help. The financial statements for the business, prepared by an accountant, for the last reporting period revealed a profit of £50,000. However, during the reporting period the bank balance declined by £30,000. What reasons might explain this apparent discrepancy?

**3.4** The following is the statement of financial position of TT and Co. at the end of its first year of trading (from Self-assessment question 3.1):

**Statement of financial position as at 31 December 2009**

|  | £ |
|---|---:|
| **ASSETS** | |
| **Non-current assets** | |
| *Property, plant and equipment* | |
| Delivery van at cost | 12,000 |
| Depreciation | (2,500) |
| | 9,500 |
| **Current assets** | |
| Inventories | 65,000 |
| Trade receivables | 19,600 |
| Prepaid expenses* | 5,300 |
| Cash | 750 |
| | 90,650 |
| **Total assets** | 100,150 |
| **EQUITY AND LIABILITIES** | |
| **Equity** | |
| Original | 50,000 |
| Retained earnings | 26,900 |
| | 76,900 |
| **Current liabilities** | |
| Trade payables | 22,000 |
| Accrued expenses† | 1,250 |
| | 23,250 |
| **Total equity and liabilities** | 100,150 |

* The prepaid expenses consisted of rates (£300) and rent (£5,000).
† The accrued expenses consisted of wages (£630) and electricity (£620).

During 2010, the following transactions took place:

1 The owners withdrew equity in the form of cash of £20,000.
2 Premises continued to be rented at an annual rental of £20,000. During the year, rent of £15,000 was paid to the owner of the premises.
3 Rates on the premises were paid during the year as follows: for the period 1 April 2010 to 31 March 2011 £1,300.
4 A second delivery van was bought on 1 January 2010 for £13,000. This is expected to be used in the business for four years and then to be sold for £3,000.
5 Wages totalling £36,700 were paid during the year. At the end of the year, the business owed £860 of wages for the last week of the year.
6 Electricity bills for the first three quarters of the year and £620 for the last quarter of the previous year were paid totalling £1,820. After 31 December 2010, but before the financial statements had been finalised for the year, the bill for the last quarter arrived showing a charge of £690.
7 Inventories totalling £67,000 were bought on credit.

→

8 Inventories totalling £8,000 were bought for cash.
9 Sales revenue on credit totalled £179,000 (cost £89,000).
10 Cash sales revenue totalled £54,000 (cost £25,000).
11 Receipts from trade receivables totalled £178,000.
12 Payments to trade payables totalled £71,000.
13 Van running expenses paid totalled £16,200.

The business uses the straight-line method for depreciating non-current assets.

**Required:**
Prepare an income statement for the year to 31 December 2010 and a statement of financial position as at that date.

**3.5** The following is the statement of financial position of WW Associates as at 31 December 2008:

**Statement of financial position as at 31 December 2008**

|  | £ |
|---|---:|
| **ASSETS** | |
| **Non-current assets** | |
| Machinery | 25,300 |
| **Current assets** | |
| Inventories | 12,200 |
| Trade receivables | 21,300 |
| Prepaid expenses (rates) | 400 |
| Cash | 8,300 |
|  | 42,200 |
| **Total assets** | 67,500 |
| **EQUITY AND LIABILITIES** | |
| **Equity** | |
| Original | 25,000 |
| Retained earnings | 23,900 |
|  | 48,900 |
| **Current liabilities** | |
| Trade payables | 16,900 |
| Accrued expenses (wages) | 1,700 |
|  | 18,600 |
| **Total equity and liabilities** | 67,500 |

During 2009, the following transactions took place:

1 The owners withdrew equity in the form of cash of £23,000.
2 Premises were rented at an annual rental of £20,000. During the year, rent of £25,000 was paid to the owner of the premises.
3 Rates on the premises were paid during the year for the period 1 April 2009 to 31 March 2010 and amounted to £2,000.
4 Some machinery (a non-current asset), which was bought on 1 January 2008 for £13,000, has proved to be unsatisfactory. It was part-exchanged for some new machinery on 1 January 2009 and WW Associates paid a cash amount of £6,000.

The new machinery would have cost £15,000 had the business bought it without the trade-in.

5 Wages totalling £23,800 were paid during the year. At the end of the year, the business owed £860 of wages.

6 Electricity bills for the four quarters of the year were paid totalling £2,700.

7 Inventories totalling £143,000 were bought on credit.

8 Inventories totalling £12,000 were bought for cash.

9 Sales revenue on credit totalled £211,000 (cost £127,000).

10 Cash sales revenue totalled £42,000 (cost £25,000).

11 Receipts from trade receivables totalled £198,000.

12 Payments to trade payables totalled £156,000.

13 Van running expenses paid totalled £17,500.

The business uses the reducing-balance method of depreciation for non-current assets at the rate of 30 per cent each year.

**Required:**

Prepare an income statement for the year ended 31 December 2009 and a statement of financial position as at that date.

## Chapter 4

# Accounting for limited companies

## Introduction

Most businesses in the UK, except the very smallest, operate in the form of limited companies. About two and a quarter million limited companies now exist and they account for the majority of UK business activity and employment. The economic significance of this type of business is not confined to the UK; it can be seen in most of the world's developed countries.

In this chapter we consider the nature of limited companies and how they differ from sole proprietorship businesses and partnerships. We examine the ways in which the owners provide finance, as well as the rules governing the way in which limited companies must account to their owners and to other interested parties. We shall also see how the financial statements, which were discussed in the previous two chapters, are prepared for this type of business.

## Learning outcomes

**When you have completed this chapter, you should be able to:**

- discuss the nature of the limited company;
- describe the main features of the equity (owners' claim) in a limited company;
- discuss the framework of rules designed to safeguard the interests of shareholders;
- explain how the income statement and statement of financial position of a limited company differ in detail from those of sole proprietorships and partnerships.

 *Remember to create your own personalised Study Plan*

## The main features of limited companies

### Legal nature

Let us begin our examination of limited companies by discussing their legal nature. A limited company has been described as an artificial person that has been created by law. This means that a company has many of the rights and obligations that 'real' people have. It can, for example, sue or be sued by others and can enter into contracts in its own name. This contrasts sharply with other types of businesses, such as sole proprietorships and partnerships (that is, unincorporated businesses), where it is the owner(s) rather than the business that must sue, enter into contracts and so on, because the business has no separate legal identity.

With the rare exceptions of those that are created by Act of Parliament or by Royal Charter, all UK companies are created (or *incorporated*) by registration. To create a company the person or persons wishing to create it (usually known as *promoters*) fill in a few simple forms and pay a modest registration fee. After having ensured that the necessary formalities have been met, the Registrar of Companies, a UK government official, enters the name of the new company on the Registry of Companies. Thus, in the UK, companies can be formed very easily and cheaply (for about £100).

A limited company may be owned by just one person, but most have more than one owner and some have many owners. The owners are usually known as *members* or *shareholders*. The ownership of a company is normally divided into a number, frequently a large number, of shares, each of equal size. Each owner, or shareholder, owns one or more shares in the company. Large companies typically have a very large number of shareholders. For example, at 31 March 2009, BT Group plc, the telecommunications business, had nearly 1.2 million different shareholders.

Since a limited company has its own legal identity, it is regarded as being quite separate from those that own and manage it. It is worth emphasising that this legal separateness of owners and the company has no connection whatsoever with the business entity convention of accounting, which we discussed in Chapter 2. This accounting convention applies equally well to all business types, including sole proprietorships and partnerships where there is certainly no legal distinction between the owner(s) and the business.

The legal separateness of the limited company and its shareholders leads to two important features of the limited company: perpetual life and limited liability. These are now explained.

### Perpetual life

A company is normally granted a perpetual existence and so will continue even where an owner of some, or even all, of the shares in the company dies. The shares of the deceased person will simply pass to the beneficiary of his or her estate. The granting of perpetual existence means that the life of a company is quite separate from the lives of those individuals who own or manage it. It is not, therefore, affected by changes in ownership that arise when individuals buy and sell shares in the company.

Though a company may be granted a perpetual existence when it is first formed, it is possible for either the shareholders or the courts to bring this existence to an end. When this is done, the assets of the company are usually sold to generate cash to meet the outstanding liabilities. Any surplus arising after all liabilities have been met will then be used to pay the shareholders. Shareholders may agree to end the life of a company where it has achieved the purpose for which it was formed or where they feel that the company has no real future. The courts may bring the life of a company to an end where creditors have applied to the courts for this to be done because they have not been paid amounts owing.

Where shareholders agree to end the life of a company, it is referred to as a 'voluntary liquidation'. Real World 4.1 describes the demise of one company by this method.

### Real World 4.1

## Monotub Industries in a spin as founder gets Titan for £1

Monotub Industries, maker of the Titan washing machine, yesterday passed into corporate history with very little ceremony and with only a whimper of protest from minority shareholders.

At an extraordinary meeting held in a basement room of the group's West End headquarters, shareholders voted to put the company into voluntary liquidation and sell its assets and intellectual property to founder Martin Myerscough for £1. [The shares in the company were at one time worth 650p each.]

The only significant opposition came from Giuliano Gnagnatti who, along with other shareholders, has seen his investment shrink faster than a wool twin-set on a boil wash.

The not-so-proud owner of 100,000 Monotub shares, Mr Gnagnatti, the managing director of an online retailer, described the sale of Monotub as a 'free gift' to Mr Myerscough. This assessment was denied by Ian Green, the chairman of Monotub, who said the closest the beleaguered company had come to a sale was an offer for £60,000 that gave no guarantees against liabilities, which are thought to amount to £750,000.

The quiet passing of the washing machine, eventually dubbed the Titanic, was in strong contrast to its performance in many kitchens.

Originally touted as the 'great white goods hope' of the washing machine industry with its larger capacity and removable drum, the Titan ran into problems when it kept stopping during the spin cycle, causing it to emit a loud bang and leap into the air.

Summing up the demise of the Titan, Mr Green said: 'Clearly the machine had some revolutionary aspects, but you can't get away from the fact that the machine was faulty and should not have been launched with those defects.'

The usually-vocal Mr Myerscough, who has promised to pump £250,000 into the company and give Monotub shareholders £4 for every machine sold, refused to comment on his plans for the Titan or reveal who his backers were. But . . . he did say that he intended to 'take the Titan forward'.

*Source*: 'Monotub Industries in a spin as founder gets Titan for £1', *The Financial Times*, 23/01/2003 (Urquhart, L.), copyright © The Financial Times Ltd.

## Limited liability

Since the company is a legal person in its own right, it must take responsibility for its own debts and losses. This means that, once the shareholders have paid what they have agreed to pay for the shares, their obligation to the company, and to the company's creditors, is satisfied. Thus shareholders can limit their losses to the amount that they have paid, or agreed to pay, for their shares. This is of great practical importance to potential shareholders since they know that what they can lose, as part owners of the business, is limited.

Contrast this with the position of sole proprietors or partners. They cannot 'ring-fence' assets that they do not want to put into the business. If a sole proprietorship or partnership business finds itself in a position where liabilities exceed the business assets, the law gives unsatisfied creditors the right to demand payment out of what the sole proprietor or partner may have regarded as 'non-business' assets. Thus the sole proprietor or partner could lose everything – house, car, the lot. This is because the law sees Jill, the sole proprietor, as being the same as Jill the private individual. The shareholder, by contrast, can lose only the amount committed to that company. Legally, the business operating as a limited company, in which Jack owns shares, is not the same as Jack himself. This is true even if Jack were to own all of the shares in the company.

Real World 4.2 gives an example of a well-known case where the shareholders of a particular company were able to avoid any liability to those that had lost money as a result of dealing with the company.

### Real World 4.2

## Carlton and Granada 1 – Nationwide Football League 0

Two television broadcasting companies, Carlton and Granada, each owned 50 per cent of a separate company, ITV Digital (formerly ON Digital). ITV Digital signed a contract to pay the Nationwide Football League (in effect the three divisions of English football below the Premiership) more than £89 million on both 1 August 2002 and 1 August 2003 for the rights to broadcast football matches over three seasons. ITV Digital was unable to sell enough subscriptions for the broadcasts and collapsed because it was unable to meet its liabilities. The Nationwide Football League tried to force Carlton and Granada (ITV Digital's only shareholders) to meet ITV Digital's contractual obligations. It was unable to do so because the shareholders could not be held legally liable for the amounts owing.

Carlton and Granada merged into one business in 2003, but at the time of ITV Digital were two independent companies.

### Activity 4.1

The fact that shareholders can limit their losses to that which they have paid, or have agreed to pay, for their shares is of great practical importance to potential shareholders.

Can you think of any practical benefit to a private sector economy, in general, of this ability of shareholders to limit losses?

Business is a risky venture – in some cases very risky. People in a position to invest money will usually be happier to do so when they know the limit of their liability. If investors are given limited liability, new businesses are more likely to be formed and existing ones are likely to find it easier to raise more finance. This is good for the private sector economy and may ultimately lead to the generation of greater wealth for society as a whole.

Although limited liability has this advantage to the providers of equity finance (the shareholders), it is not necessarily to the advantage of others who have a stake in the business, like the Nationwide Football League clubs (see Real World 4.2). Limited liability is attractive to shareholders because they can, in effect, walk away from the unpaid debts of the company if their contribution has not been sufficient to meet those debts. This is likely to make any individual, or another business, that is considering entering into a contract, wary of dealing with the limited company. This can be a real problem for smaller, less established companies. Suppliers may insist on cash payment before delivery of goods or the rendering of a service. Alternatively, they may require a personal guarantee from a major shareholder that the debt will be paid before allowing trade credit. In the latter case, the supplier circumvents the company's limited liability status by demanding the personal liability of an individual. Larger, more established companies, on the other hand, tend to have built up the confidence of suppliers.

## Legal safeguards

Various safeguards exist to protect individuals and businesses contemplating dealing with a limited company. These include the requirement to indicate limited liability status in the name of the company. By doing this, an alert is issued to prospective suppliers and lenders.

A further safeguard is the restrictions placed on the ability of shareholders to withdraw their equity from the company. These restrictions are designed to prevent shareholders from protecting their own investment and, as a result, leaving lenders and suppliers in an exposed position. We shall consider this point in more detail later in the chapter.

Finally, limited companies are required to produce annual financial statements (which include the income statement, statement of financial position and statement of cash flows) and to make these publicly available. This means that anyone interested can gain an impression of the financial performance and position of the company. The form and content of these statements are considered in some detail later in this chapter and in Chapter 5, which considers the statement of cash flows.

## Public and private companies

When a company is registered with the Registrar of Companies, it must be registered either as a public or as a private company. The main practical difference between these is that a public limited company can offer its shares for sale to the general public, but a private limited company is restricted from doing so. A public limited company must signal its status to all interested parties by having the words 'public limited company', or its abbreviation 'plc', in its name. For a private limited company, the word 'limited' or 'Ltd' must appear as part of its name.

Private limited companies tend to be smaller businesses where the ownership is divided among relatively few shareholders who are usually fairly close to one another

– for example, a family company. Numerically, there are vastly more private limited companies in the UK than there are public ones. Of the 2.25 million UK limited companies now in existence, only 9,600 (representing 0.4 per cent of the total) are public limited companies.

Since individual public companies tend to be larger, they are often economically more important. In some industry sectors, such as banking, insurance, oil refining and grocery retailing, they are completely dominant. Although some large private limited companies exist, many private limited companies are little more than the vehicle through which one-person businesses operate.

Real World 4.3 shows the extent of market dominance of public limited companies in one particular business sector.

---

**Real World 4.3**

## A big slice of the market

The grocery sector is dominated by four large players: Tesco, Sainsbury, Morrison and Asda. The first three are public limited companies and the fourth, Asda, is owned by a large US public company, Wal-Mart. Figure 4.1 shows the share of the grocery market enjoyed by each, during the 12-week period which ended on 24 January 2010.

**Figure 4.1** Market share of the four largest grocers: 12 weeks to 24 January 2010

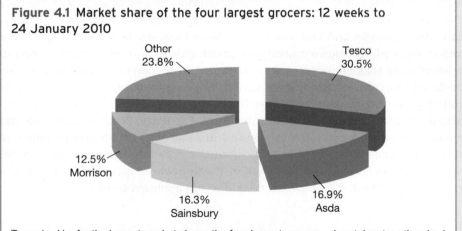

Other
23.8%

Tesco
30.5%

12.5%
Morrison

16.3%
Sainsbury

16.9%
Asda

Tesco had by far the largest market share; the four largest grocers, when taken together, had more than 75 per cent of the total market during the period.

*Source*: compiled from information in Mills, E., 'Tesco's grocery market share rises to 30.5% in 12 weeks – Kantar', Dow Jones Newswires, 2 February 2010.

---

## Taxation

Another consequence of the legal separation of the limited company from its owners is that companies must be accountable to the tax authorities for tax on their profits and gains. This leads to the reporting of tax in the financial statements of limited companies. The charge for tax is shown in the income statement. The tax charge for a particular year is based on that year's profit. Since only 50 per cent of a company's tax liability is due for payment during the year concerned, the other 50 per cent will appear on the end-of-year statement of financial position as a short-term liability. This will be illustrated a little later in the chapter. The tax position of companies contrasts with that of sole proprietorships and partnerships, where tax is levied not on the business but on the owner(s). Thus tax does not impact on the financial statements of unincorporated businesses, but is an individual matter between the owner(s) and the tax authorities.

→    Companies are charged corporation tax on their profits and gains. The percentage rates of tax tend to vary from year to year, but have recently been 28 per cent for larger companies and 21 per cent for smaller companies. These rates of tax are levied on the company's taxable profit, which is not necessarily the same as the profit shown on the income statement. This is because tax law does not, in every respect, follow the normal accounting rules. Generally, however, the taxable profit and the company's accounting profit are pretty close to one another.

## Transferring share ownership: the role of the Stock Exchange

We have already seen that shares in a company may be transferred from one owner to another. The desire of some shareholders to sell their shares, coupled with the desire of others to buy those shares, has led to the existence of a formal market in which shares can be bought and sold. The London Stock Exchange and similar organisations around the world provide a marketplace in which shares in public companies may be bought and sold. Share prices are determined by the laws of supply and demand, which are, in turn, determined by investors' perceptions of the future economic prospects of the companies concerned. Only the shares of certain companies (*listed* companies) may be traded on the London Stock Exchange. Less than 1,100 UK companies are listed. This represents only about 1 in 2,000 of all UK companies (public and private) and roughly one in nine public limited companies. However, many of these listed companies are massive. Nearly all of the 'household-name' UK businesses (for example, Tesco, Next, BT, Vodafone, BP and so on) are listed companies.

### Activity 4.2

If, as has been pointed out earlier, the change in ownership of shares does not directly affect the particular company, why do many public companies actively seek to have their shares traded in a recognised market?

The main reason is that investors are generally very reluctant to pledge their money unless they can see some way in which they can turn their investment back into cash. In theory, the shares of a particular company may be very valuable because the company has bright prospects. However, unless this value is capable of being turned into cash, the benefit to the shareholders is dubious. After all, we cannot spend shares; we normally need cash.

This means that potential shareholders are much more likely to be prepared to buy new shares from the company (thereby providing the company with new investment finance) where they can see a way of liquidating their investment (turning it into cash) as and when they wish. Stock Exchanges provide the means of liquidation.

Although the buying and selling of 'second-hand' shares does not provide the company with cash, the fact that the buying and selling facility exists will make it easier for the company to raise new share capital when it needs to do so.

## Managing a company

A limited company may have legal personality, but it is not a human being capable of making decisions and plans about the business and exercising control over it. People must undertake these management tasks. The most senior level of management of a company is the board of directors.

The shareholders elect directors (by law there must be at least one director for a private limited company and two for a public limited company) to manage the company on a day-to-day basis on behalf of those shareholders. In a small company, the board may be the only level of management and consist of all of the shareholders. In larger companies, the board may consist of ten or so directors out of many thousands of shareholders. Indeed, directors are not even required to be shareholders. Below the board of directors of the typical large company could be several layers of management comprising thousands of people.

In recent years, the issue of corporate governance has generated much debate. The term is used to describe the ways in which companies are directed and controlled. The issue of corporate governance is important because, with larger companies, those who own the company (that is, the shareholders) are usually divorced from the day-to-day control of the business. The shareholders employ the directors to manage the company for them. Given this position, it may seem reasonable to assume that the best interests of shareholders will guide the directors' decisions. However, in practice this does not always seem to be the case. The directors may be more concerned with pursuing their own interests, such as increasing their pay and 'perks' (such as expensive motor cars, overseas visits and so on) and improving their job security and status. As a result, a conflict can occur between the interests of shareholders and the interests of directors.

Where directors pursue their own interests rather than those of shareholders, there is clearly a problem for the shareholders. However, it may also be a problem for society as a whole. Where investors feel that their funds are likely to be mismanaged, they will be reluctant to invest. A shortage of funds will mean that companies can make fewer investments. Furthermore, the costs of finance will increase as companies compete for what funds are available. Thus, a lack of concern for shareholders can have a profound effect on the performance of individual companies and, with this, the health of the economy. To avoid these problems, most competitive market economies have a framework of rules to help monitor and control the behaviour of directors.

These rules are usually based around three guiding principles:

■ *Disclosure*. This lies at the heart of good corporate governance. An OECD report (see reference 1 at the end of chapter for details) summed up the benefits of disclosure as follows:

> Adequate and timely information about corporate performance enables investors to make informed buy-and-sell decisions and thereby helps the market reflect the value of a corporation [company] under present management. If the market determines that present management is not performing, a decrease in stock [share] price will sanction management's failure and open the way to management change.

■ *Accountability*. This involves defining the roles and duties of the directors and establishing an adequate monitoring process. In the UK, company law requires that the directors of a company act in the best interests of the shareholders. This means, among other things, that they must not try to use their position and knowledge to make gains at the expense of the shareholders. The law also requires larger companies to have their annual financial statements independently audited. The purpose of an independent audit is to lend credibility to the financial statements prepared by the directors. We shall consider this point in more detail later in the chapter.

■ *Fairness*. Directors should not be able to benefit from access to 'inside' information that is not available to shareholders. As a result, both the law and the London Stock Exchange place restrictions on the ability of directors to buy and sell the shares of the company. One example of these restrictions is that the directors cannot buy or sell shares immediately before the announcement of the annual trading results of the company or before the announcement of a significant event, such as a planned merger or the loss of the chief executive.

These principles are set out in Figure 4.2.

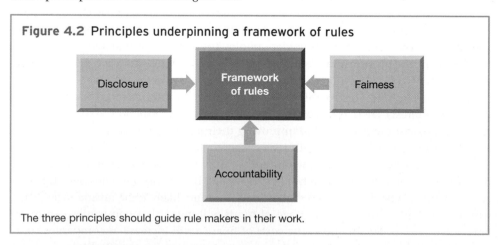

**Figure 4.2 Principles underpinning a framework of rules**

The three principles should guide rule makers in their work.

## Strengthening the framework of rules

The number of rules designed to safeguard shareholders has increased considerably over the years. This has been in response to weaknesses in corporate governance procedures, which have been exposed through well-publicised business failures and frauds, excessive pay increases to directors and evidence that some financial reports were being 'massaged' so as to mislead shareholders. (This last point will be discussed later in the chapter.)

Many believe, however, that the shareholders must shoulder some of the blame for any weaknesses. Not all shareholders in large companies are private individuals owning just a few shares each. In fact, ownership, by market value, of the shares listed on the London Stock Exchange is dominated by investing institutions such as insurance businesses, banks, pension funds and so on. These are often massive operations, owning large quantities of the shares of the companies in which they invest. These institutional investors employ specialist staff to manage their portfolios of shares in various companies. It has been argued that the large institutional shareholders, despite their size and relative expertise, have not been very active in corporate governance matters. Thus, there has been little monitoring of directors. However, things seem to be changing. There is increasing evidence that institutional investors are becoming more proactive in relation to the companies in which they hold shares.

## The UK Corporate Governance Code

During the 1990s there was a real effort by the accountancy profession and the London Stock Exchange to address the problems of poor corporate governance mentioned earlier. A Code of Best Practice on Corporate Governance emerged in 1992. This was concerned with accountability and financial reporting. In 1995, a separate code of practice emerged which dealt with directors' pay and conditions. These two codes were revised, 'fine tuned' and amalgamated to produce the Combined Code, which was issued in 1998. Every few years, the impact and effectiveness of the Code has been reviewed and this has resulted in revisions being made. In 2010, the Combined Code changed its name to the 'UK Corporate Governance Code'.

The UK Corporate Governance Code has the backing of the London Stock Exchange. This means that companies listed on the London Stock Exchange must 'comply or explain'. That is, they must comply with the requirements of the UK Code or must give their shareholders good reason why they do not. Failure to do one or other of these can lead to the company's shares being suspended from listing.

### Activity 4.3

Why might being suspended from listing be an important sanction against a non-compliant company?

A major advantage of a Stock Exchange listing is that it enables investors to sell their shares whenever they wish. A company that is suspended from listing would find it hard and, therefore, expensive to raise funds from investors because there would be no ready market for the shares.

The UK Code sets out a number of principles relating to such matters as the role of the directors, their relations with shareholders and their accountability. Real World 4.4 outlines some of the more important of these.

---

**Real World 4.4**

## The UK Corporate Governance Code

The key elements of the UK Code are as follows:

- Every listed company should have a board of directors that is collectively responsible for its success.
- There should be a clear division of responsibilities between the chairman and the chief executive officer of the company to try to ensure that a single person does not have unbridled power.
- There should be an appropriate balance of skills, experience, independence and knowledge to enable the board to carry out its duties effectively.
- The board should receive timely information that is of sufficient quality to enable it to carry out its duties. All board members should refresh their skill regularly and new board members should receive induction.
- Appointments to the board should be the subject of rigorous, formal and transparent procedures and should be drawn from a broad talent pool.
- All directors should submit themselves for re-election at regular intervals, subject to satisfactory performance.
- Remuneration levels should be sufficient to attract, retain and motivate directors of the appropriate quality and should take account of individual and company performance.
- There should be formal and transparent procedures for developing policy on directors' remuneration.
- The board should try to ensure that a satisfactory dialogue with shareholders occurs.
- Boards should use the annual general meeting to communicate with investors and encourage their participation.
- Institutional shareholders should use their votes and enter into a dialogue with the company based on a mutual understanding of objectives.
- The board should publish a balanced and understandable assessment of the company's position and future prospects.
- The board should define the company's risk appetite and tolerance and should maintain a sound risk management system.
- Formal and transparent arrangements for applying financial reporting and internal control principles and for maintaining an appropriate relationship with auditors should be in place.
- The board should undertake a formal and rigorous examination of its own performance each year, which will include its committees and individual directors.

*Source*: www.fsa.org.uk.

---

Strengthening the framework of rules in this way has been generally agreed to have improved the quality of information available to shareholders. It has also resulted in better checks on the powers of directors and provided greater transparency in corporate affairs. However, rules can only be a partial answer. A balance must be struck between the need to protect shareholders and the need to encourage the entrepreneurial spirit of directors – which could be stifled under a welter of rules. This implies that rules should not be too tight, and so unscrupulous directors may still find ways around them.

## Financing limited companies

### Equity (the owners' claim)

The equity of a sole proprietorship is normally encompassed in one figure on the statement of financial position. With companies, this is usually a little more complicated, although in essence the same broad principles apply. With a company, equity is divided between shares (for example, the original investment), on the one hand, and reserves (that is, profits and gains subsequently made), on the other. There is also the possibility that there will be more than one type of shares and of reserves. Thus, within the basic divisions of share capital and reserves, there might well be further subdivisions. This might seem quite complicated, but we shall shortly consider the reasons for these subdivisions and all should become clearer.

### The basic division

When a company is first formed, those who take steps to form it (the promoters) will decide how much needs to be raised by the potential shareholders to set the company up with the necessary assets to operate. Example 4.1 acts as a basis for illustration.

### Example 4.1

Some friends decide to form a company to operate an office cleaning business. They estimate that the company will need £50,000 to obtain the necessary assets. Between them, they raise the cash, which they use to buy shares in the company, on 31 March 2009, with a nominal value (or par value) of £1 each.

At this point the statement of financial position of the company would be:

**Statement of financial position as at 31 March 2009**

| | £ |
|---|---|
| Net assets (all in cash) | 50,000 |
| **Equity** | |
| Share capital | |
| 50,000 shares of £1 each | 50,000 |

The company now buys the necessary non-current assets (vacuum cleaners and so on) and inventories (cleaning materials) and starts to trade. During the first year, the company makes a profit of £10,000. This, by definition, means that the equity expands by £10,000. During the year, the shareholders (owners) make no drawings of their equity, so at the end of the year the summarised statement of financial position looks like this:

**Statement of financial position as at 31 March 2010**

|  | £ |
| --- | --- |
| Net assets (various assets less liabilities*) | <u>60,000</u> |
| **Equity** | |
| Share capital | |
| 50,000 shares of £1 each | 50,000 |
| Reserves (revenue reserve) | <u>10,000</u> |
| **Total equity** | <u>60,000</u> |

\* We saw in Chapter 2 that Assets = Equity + Liabilities. We also saw that this can be rearranged so that Assets − Liabilities = Equity.

→ The profit is shown in a reserve, known as a revenue reserve, because it arises from generating revenue (making sales). Note that we do not simply merge the profit with the share capital: we must keep the two amounts separate (to satisfy company law). The reason for this is that there is a legal restriction on the maximum drawings of their
→ equity (or payment of a dividend) that the shareholders can make. This is defined by the amount of revenue reserves, and so it is helpful to show these separately. We shall look at why there is this restriction, and how it works, a little later in the chapter.

## Share capital

### Ordinary shares

Shares represent the basic units of ownership of a business. All companies issue
→ ordinary shares. Ordinary shares are often known as *equities*. The nominal value of such shares is at the discretion of the people who start up the company. For example, if the initial share capital is to be £50,000, this could be two shares of £25,000 each, 5 million shares of one penny each or any other combination that gives a total of £50,000. All shares must have equal value.

### Activity 4.4

The initial financial requirement for a new company is £50,000. There are to be two equal shareholders. Would you advise them to issue two shares of £25,000 each? Why?

Such large-denomination shares tend to be unwieldy. Suppose that one of the shareholders wanted to sell her shareholding. She would have to find one buyer. If there were shares of smaller denomination, it would be possible to sell part of the shareholding to various potential buyers. Furthermore, it would be possible to sell just part of the holding and retain a part.

In practice, £1 is the normal maximum nominal value for shares. Shares of 25 pence each and 50 pence each are probably the most common.

### Altering the nominal value of shares

As we have already seen, the promoters of a new company may make their own choice of the nominal or par value of the shares. This value need not be permanent. At a later date the shareholders can decide to change it.

Suppose that a company has 1 million ordinary shares of £1 each and a decision is made to change the nominal value of the shares from £1 to £0.50, in other words to halve the value. This would lead the company to issue each shareholder with a new share certificate (the shareholders' evidence of ownership of their shares) for exactly twice as many shares, each with half the nominal value. The result would be that each shareholder retains a holding of the same total nominal value. This process is known, not surprisingly, as splitting the shares. The opposite, reducing the number of shares and increasing their nominal value per share to compensate, is known as consolidating. Since each shareholder would be left, after a split or consolidation, with exactly the same proportion of ownership of the company's assets as before, the process should not increase the value of the total shares held.

Splitting is fairly common. The objective is probably to avoid individual shares becoming too valuable and thus unwieldy, as discussed in the answer to Activity 4.4. If a company trades successfully, the value of each share is likely to rise and, in time, could increase to a level that makes the shares less marketable. Splitting would solve this problem. Consolidating is relatively rare.

Real World 4.5 provides an example of a share split by one business.

---

**Real World 4.5**

## Doing the splits

A G Barr, the Scottish based maker of soft drinks, including Tizer and Irn Bru, had a share split in September 2009, as announced by the business in its half-yearly report:

> As previously announced, the 2 for 1 share split, which is aimed at improving liquidity and marketability of the company's shares became effective on 21 September.

*Source*: A G Barr plc Interim Report, August 2009, p. 3.

---

### Preference shares

Some companies not only issue ordinary shares, but also have other classes of shares, preference shares being the most common. Preference shares guarantee that *if a dividend is paid*, the preference shareholders will be entitled to the first part of it up to a maximum value. This maximum is normally defined as a fixed percentage of the nominal value of the preference shares. If, for example, a company issues 10,000 preference shares of £1 each with a dividend rate of 6 per cent, this means that the preference shareholders are entitled to receive the first £600 (that is, 6 per cent of £10,000) of any dividend that is paid by the company for a year. The excess over £600 goes to the ordinary shareholders. Normally, any undistributed profits and gains also accrue to the ordinary shareholders.

The ordinary shareholders are the primary risk takers as they are entitled to share in the profits of the company only after other claims have been satisfied. There are no upper limits, however, on the amount by which they may benefit. The potential rewards available to ordinary shareholders reflect the risks that they are prepared to take. Since ordinary shareholders take most of the risks, power normally resides in their hands. Usually, only the ordinary shareholders are able to vote on issues that affect the company, such as who the directors should be.

It is open to the company to issue shares of various classes – perhaps with some having unusual and exotic conditions – but in practice it is rare to find other than straightforward ordinary and preference shares. Although a company may have different classes of shares whose holders have different rights, within each class all shares must be treated equally. The rights of the various classes of shareholders, as well as other matters relating to a particular company, are contained in that company's set of rules, known as the 'articles and memorandum of association'. A copy of these rules must be lodged with the Registrar of Companies, who makes it available for inspection by the general public.

## Reserves

As we have already seen, reserves are profits and gains that a company has made and which still form part of the shareholders' equity. One reason that past profits and gains may not continue to be part of equity is that they have been paid out to shareholders (as dividends and so on). Another reason is that reserves will be reduced by the amount of any losses that the company might suffer. In the same way that profits increase equity, losses reduce it.

### Activity 4.5

**Are reserves amounts of cash? Can you think of a reason why this is an odd question?**

To deal with the second point first, it is an odd question because reserves are a claim, or part of one, on the assets of the company, whereas cash is an asset. So reserves cannot be cash.

Reserves are classified as either revenue reserves or capital reserves. In Example 4.1 we came across one type of reserve, the revenue reserve. We should recall that this reserve represents the company's retained trading profits and gains on the disposal of non-current assets. It is worth mentioning that retained earnings, as they are most often called, represent overwhelmingly the largest source of new finance for UK companies. For most companies they amount to more than share issues and borrowings combined.

Capital reserves arise for two main reasons:

- issuing shares at above their nominal value (for example, issuing £1 shares at £1.50);
- revaluing (upwards) non-current assets.

Where a company issues shares at above their nominal value, UK law requires that the excess of the issue price over the nominal value be shown separately.

## Activity 4.6

Can you think why shares might be issued at above their nominal value? (*Hint*: This would not usually happen when a company is first formed and the initial shares are being issued.)

Once a company has traded and has been successful, the shares would normally be worth more than the nominal value at which they were issued. If additional shares are to be issued to new shareholders to raise finance for further expansion, unless they are issued at a value higher than the nominal value, the new shareholders will be gaining at the expense of the original ones.

Example 4.2 shows how this works.

## Example 4.2

Based on future prospects, the net assets of a company are worth £1.5 million. There are currently 1 million ordinary shares in the company, each with a face (nominal) value of £1. The company wishes to raise an additional £0.6 million of cash for expansion and has decided to raise it by issuing new shares. If the shares are issued for £1 each (that is 600,000 shares), the total number of shares will be

$$1.0m + 0.6m = 1.6m$$

and their total value will be the value of the existing net assets plus the new injection of cash:

$$£1.5m + £0.6m = £2.1m$$

This means that the value of each share after the new issue will be

$$£2.1m/1.6m = £1.3125$$

The current value of each share is

$$£1.5m/1.0m = £1.50$$

so the original shareholders will lose

$$£1.50 - £1.3125 = £0.1875 \text{ a share}$$

and the new shareholders will gain

$$£1.3125 - £1.0 = £0.3125 \text{ a share}$$

The new shareholders will, no doubt, be delighted with this outcome; the original ones will not.

Things could be made fair between the two sets of shareholders described in Example 4.2 by issuing the new shares at £1.50 each. In this case it would be necessary to issue 400,000 shares to raise the necessary £0.6 million. £1 a share of the £1.50 is the nominal value and will be included with share capital in the statement of financial position (£400,000 in total). The remaining £0.50 is a share premium, which will be shown as a capital reserve known as the share premium account (£200,000 in total).

It is not clear why UK company law insists on the distinction between nominal share values and the premium. In some other countries (for example, the United States) with similar laws governing the corporate sector, there is not the necessity of distinguishing between share capital and share premium. Instead, the total value at which shares are issued is shown as one comprehensive figure on the company's statement of financial position. Real World 4.6 shows the equity of one well-known business.

---

**Real World 4.6**

### Funding Thorntons

Thorntons plc, the chocolate maker and retailer, had the following share capital and reserves as at 27 June 2009:

|                                    | £m     |
|------------------------------------|--------|
| Share capital (10p ordinary shares) | 6,835  |
| Share premium                      | 13,752 |
| Retained earnings                  | 8,151  |
| **Total equity**                   | **28,738** |

Note how the nominal share capital figure is only about half as much as the share premium account figure. This implies that Thorntons has issued shares at higher prices than the 10p a share nominal value. This reflects its trading success since the company was first formed. In 2008, retained earnings (profits) had made up over 40 per cent of the total for share capital and reserves. By 2009, this had reduced to around 28 per cent. This reduction was mainly caused by a loss suffered by the company pension fund during the year.

*Source*: Thorntons plc Annual Report 2009, p. 45.

---

## Bonus shares

It is always open to a company to take reserves of any kind (irrespective of whether they are capital or revenue) and turn them into share capital. This will involve transferring the desired amount from the reserve concerned to share capital and then distributing the appropriate number of new shares to the existing shareholders. New shares arising from such a conversion are known as bonus shares. Issues of bonus shares used to be quite frequently encountered in practice, but more recently they are much less common. Example 4.3 illustrates this aspect of share issues.

## Example 4.3

The summary statement of financial position of a company at a particular point in time is as follows:

**Statement of financial position**

| | £ |
|---|---|
| Net assets (various assets less liabilities) | 128,000 |
| Equity | |
| Share capital | |
| 50,000 shares of £1 each | 50,000 |
| Reserves | 78,000 |
| Total equity | 128,000 |

The company decides that it will issue existing shareholders with one new share for every share currently owned by each shareholder. The statement of financial position immediately following this will appear as follows:

**Statement of financial position**

| | £ |
|---|---|
| Net assets (various assets less liabilities) | 128,000 |
| Equity | |
| Share capital | |
| 100,000 shares of £1 each (50,000 + 50,000) | 100,000 |
| Reserves (78,000 − 50,000) | 28,000 |
| Total equity | 128,000 |

We can see that the reserves have decreased by £50,000 and share capital has increased by the same amount. Share certificates for the 50,000 ordinary shares of £1 each, which have been created from reserves, will be issued to the existing shareholders to complete the transaction.

## Activity 4.7

A shareholder of the company in Example 4.3 owned 100 shares before the bonus issue. How will things change for this shareholder as regards the number of shares owned and the value of the shareholding?

The answer should be that the number of shares would double, from 100 to 200. Now the shareholder owns one five-hundredth of the company (that is, 200/100,000). Before the bonus issue, the shareholder also owned one five-hundredth of the company (that is, 100/50,000). The company's assets and liabilities have not changed as a result of the bonus issue and so, logically, one five-hundredth of the value of the company should be identical to what it was before. Thus, each share is worth half as much.

A *bonus issue* simply takes one part of the equity (a reserve) and puts it into another part (share capital). The transaction has no effect on the company's assets or liabilities, so there is no effect on shareholders' wealth.

Note that a bonus issue is not the same as a share split. A split does not affect the reserves.

## Activity 4.8

Can you think of any reasons why a company might want to make a bonus issue if it has no direct economic consequence?

We think that there are three possible reasons:

- *Share price*. To lower the value of each share without reducing the shareholders' collective or individual wealth. This has a similar effect to share splitting.
- *Shareholder confidence*. To provide the shareholders with a 'feel-good factor'. It is believed that shareholders like bonus issues because they seem to make them better off, although in practice they should not affect their wealth.
- *Lender confidence*. Where reserves arising from operating profits and/or realised gains on the sale of non-current assets are used to make the bonus issue, it has the effect of taking part of that portion of the shareholders' equity that could be drawn by the share-holders, as drawings (or dividends), and locking it up. The amount transferred becomes part of the permanent equity base of the company. (We shall see a little later in this chapter that there are severe restrictions on the extent to which shareholders may make drawings from their equity.) An individual or business contemplating lending money to the company may insist that the dividend payment possibilities are restricted as a condition of making the loan. This point will be explained shortly.

Real World 4.7 cites a recent example of a bonus share issue. Given the discussion above, the rationale provided for the bonus issue is particularly interesting (and perplexing!).

## Real World 4.7

### It's a bonus?

Medusa Mining is a gold producer that is listed on various international stock markets. In 2010, it announced a one-for-ten bonus issue of shares to all shareholders of the company.

In a statement, the company said it had achieved several significant milestones in the last calendar year and the bonus issue is in recognition of the invaluable support the company has received from its shareholders. The bonus issue was also designed to encourage greater liquidity in Medusa shares.

Geoff Davis, managing director of Medusa, said: 'The board is extremely pleased to be in a position to reward shareholders as a result of the company having rapidly expanded its production over the last twelve months and having met all targets on time.'

*Source*: adapted from 'Medusa Mining', www.proactiveinvestors.co.uk, 8 March 2010.

## Share capital jargon

Before leaving our detailed discussion of share capital, it might be helpful to clarify some of the jargon relating to shares that is used in company financial statements.

Share capital that has been issued to shareholders is known as the issued share capital (or allotted share capital). Sometimes, but not very often, a company may not require shareholders to pay the whole amount that is due to be paid for the shares at the time of issue. This may happen where the company does not need the money all at once. Some money would normally be paid at the time of issue and the company would 'call' for further instalments until the shares were fully paid shares. That part of the total issue price that has been 'called' is known as the called-up share capital. That part that has been called and paid is known as the paid-up share capital.

## Raising share capital

Once the company has made its initial share issue to start business (usually soon after the company is first formed) it may decide to make further issues of new shares. These may be:

- *rights issues* – issues made to existing shareholders, in proportion to their existing shareholding;
- *public issues* – issues made to the general investing public; or
- *private placings* – issues made to selected individuals who are usually approached and asked if they would be interested in taking up new shares.

During its lifetime a company may use all three of these approaches to raising funds through issuing new shares (although only public companies can make appeals to the general public).

We shall explore the ways that companies can raise new share capital in more detail in Chapter 11.

## Borrowings

Most companies borrow money to supplement that raised from share issues and ploughed-back profits. Company borrowing is often on a long-term basis, perhaps on a ten-year contract. Lenders may be banks and other professional providers of loan finance. Many companies borrow in such a way that small investors, including private individuals, are able to lend small amounts. This is particularly the case with the larger, Stock Exchange listed, companies and involves them making a *loan notes* issue, which, though large in total, can be taken up in small slices by individual investors, both private individuals and investing institutions, such as pension funds and insurance companies. In some cases, these slices of loans can be bought and sold through the Stock Exchange. This means that investors do not have to wait the full term of their loan to obtain repayment, but can sell their slice of it to another would-be lender at intermediate points in the term of the loan. Loan notes are often known as *loan stock* or *debentures*.

Some of the features of loan notes financing, particularly the possibility that the loan notes may be traded on the Stock Exchange, can lead to a misunderstanding that loan notes are shares by another name. We should be clear that this is not the case. It is the shareholders who own the company and, therefore, who share in its losses and profits. Holders of loan notes lend money to the company under a legally binding contract that normally specifies the rate of interest, the interest payment dates and the date of repayment of the loan itself.

Usually, long-term loans are secured on assets of the company. This would give the lender the right to seize the assets concerned, sell them and satisfy the repayment obligation, should the company fail to pay either its interest payments or the repayment of the loan itself, on the dates specified in the contract between the company and the lender. A mortgage granted to a private individual buying a house or a flat is a very common example of a secured loan.

Long-term financing of companies can be depicted as in Figure 4.3.

**Figure 4.3 Sources of long-term finance for a typical limited company**

Companies derive their long-term finance from three sources: new share issues, retained earnings and long-term borrowings. For a typical company, the sum of the first two (jointly known as 'equity finance') exceeds the third. Retained earnings usually exceed each of the other two in terms of the amount of finance raised in most years.

It is important to the prosperity and stability of a company that it strikes a suitable balance between finance provided by the shareholders (equity) and from borrowing. This topic will be explored in Chapter 6. Equity and loan notes are, of course, not the only forms of finance available to a company. In Chapter 11, we consider other sources of finance available to businesses, including companies.

## Withdrawing equity

Companies, as we have seen, are legally obliged to distinguish, on the statement of financial position, between that part of the shareholders' equity that may be withdrawn and that part which may not. The withdrawable part consists of profits arising from trading (retained profits or earnings) and from the disposal of non-current assets. It is represented in the statement of financial position by *revenue reserves*.

It is important to appreciate that the total of revenue reserves appearing in the statement of financial position is rarely the total of all trading profits and profits on disposals of non-current assets generated by the company. This total will normally have been reduced by at least one of the following three factors:

- corporation tax paid on those profits
- any dividends paid
- any losses from trading and the disposal of non-current assets.

The non-withdrawable part consists of share capital plus profits arising from shareholders buying shares in the company and from upward revaluations of assets still held. It is represented in the statement of financial position by *share capital* and *capital reserves*.

Figure 4.4 shows the important division between the part of the shareholders' equity that can be withdrawn as a dividend and the part that cannot.

**Figure 4.4** Availability for dividends of various parts of the shareholders' equity

Share capital
(at nominal or
par value)

*Not available
for dividend*

Capital
reserves

**Revenue
reserves**

*Available
for dividend*

Total equity finance of limited companies consists of share capital, capital reserves and revenue reserves. Only the revenue reserves (which arise from realised profits and gains) can be used to fund a dividend. In other words, the maximum legal dividend is the amount of the revenue reserves.

The law does not specify how large the non-withdrawable part of a particular company's shareholders' equity should be. However, when seeking to impress prospective lenders and credit suppliers, the larger this part, the better. Those considering doing business with the company must be able to see from the company's statement of financial position how large it is.

### Activity 4.9

Why are limited companies required to distinguish different parts of their shareholders' equity, whereas sole proprietorship and partnership businesses are not?

The reason stems from the limited liability that company shareholders enjoy but which owners of unincorporated businesses do not. If a sole proprietor or partner withdraws all of the equity, or even an amount in excess of this, the position of the lenders and credit suppliers of the business is not weakened since they can legally enforce their claims against the sole proprietor or partner as an individual. With a limited company, the business and the owners are legally separated and such a right to enforce claims against individuals does not exist. To protect the company's lenders and credit suppliers, however, the law insists that the shareholders cannot normally withdraw a specific part of their equity.

Let us now look at an example that illustrates how this protection of creditors works.

### Example 4.4

The summary statement of financial position of a company at a particular date is as follows:

**Statement of financial position**

|  | £ |
| --- | --- |
| Total assets | 43,000 |
| **Equity** | |
| Share capital | |
| 20,000 shares of £1 each | 20,000 |
| Reserves (revenue) | 23,000 |
| Total equity | 43,000 |

A bank has been asked to make a £25,000 long-term loan to the company. If the loan were to be made, the statement of financial position immediately following would appear as follows:

**Statement of financial position (after the loan)**

|  | £ |
| --- | --- |
| Total assets (£43,000 + £25,000) | 68,000 |
| **Equity** | |
| Share capital | |
| 20,000 shares of £1 each | 20,000 |
| Reserves (revenue) | 23,000 |
|  | 43,000 |
| **Non-current liability** | |
| Borrowings – loan | 25,000 |
| Total equity and liabilities | 68,000 |

As things stand, there are assets with a total carrying amount of £68,000 to meet the bank's claim of £25,000. It would be possible and perfectly legal, however, for the company to pay a dividend (withdraw part of the shareholders' equity) equal to the total revenue reserves (£23,000). The statement of financial position would then appear as follows:

**Statement of financial position**

|  | £ |
|---|---|
| Total assets (£68,000 – £23,000) | 45,000 |
| Equity |  |
| Share capital |  |
| 20,000 shares of £1 each | 20,000 |
| Reserves (revenue) (£23,000 – £23,000) | – |
|  | 20,000 |
| Non-current liabilities |  |
| Borrowings – bank loan | 25,000 |
| Total equity and liabilities | 45,000 |

This leaves the bank in a very much weaker position, in that there are now total assets with a carrying amount of £45,000 to meet a claim of £25,000. Note that the difference between the amount of the borrowings (bank loan) and the total assets equals the equity (share capital and reserves) total. Thus, the equity represents a margin of safety for lenders and suppliers. The larger the amount of the equity withdrawable by the shareholders, the smaller is the potential margin of safety for lenders and suppliers.

As we have already seen, the law says nothing about how large the margin of safety must be. It is up to each company to decide what is appropriate.

As a practical footnote to Example 4.4, it is worth pointing out that long-term lenders would normally seek to secure a loan against an asset of the company, such as land.

## Activity 4.10

Would you expect a company to pay all of its revenue reserves as a dividend? What factors might be involved with a dividend decision?

It would be rare for a company to pay all of its revenue reserves as a dividend: the fact that it is legally possible does not necessarily make it a good idea. Most companies see ploughed-back profits as a major – usually *the* major – source of new finance. The factors that tend most to influence the dividend decision are likely to include:

- the availability of cash to pay a dividend; it would not be illegal to borrow to pay a dividend, but it would be unusual and, possibly, imprudent;
- the needs of the business for finance for new investment;
- the expectations of shareholders concerning the amount of dividends to be paid.

You may have thought of others.

If we look back at Real World 4.6 (page 128), we can see that at 27 June 2009, Thorntons plc could legally have paid a dividend totalling £8,151 million. Of course, the company did not do this, presumably because the funds concerned were tied up in property, plant and equipment and other assets, not lying around in the form of unused cash.

## The main financial statements

As we might expect, the financial statements of a limited company are, in essence, the same as those of a sole proprietor or partnership. There are, however, some differences of detail. We shall now consider these. Example 4.5 sets out the income statement and statement of financial position of a limited company.

### Example 4.5

**Da Silva plc**
**Income statement for the year ended 31 December 2010**

|  | £m |
|---|---|
| Revenue | 840 |
| Cost of sales | (520) |
| **Gross profit** | 320 |
| Wages and salaries | (98) |
| Heat and light | (18) |
| Rent and rates | (24) |
| Motor vehicle expenses | (20) |
| Insurance | (4) |
| Printing and stationery | (12) |
| Depreciation | (45) |
| Audit fee | (4) |
| **Operating profit** | 95 |
| Interest payable | (10) |
| **Profit before taxation** | 85 |
| Taxation | (24) |
| **Profit for the year** | 61 |

**Statement of financial position as at 31 December 2010**

|  | £m |
|---|---|
| **ASSETS** | |
| **Non-current assets** | |
| Property, plant and equipment | 203 |
| Intangible assets | 100 |
|  | 303 |
| **Current assets** | |
| Inventories | 65 |
| Trade receivables | 112 |
| Cash | 36 |
|  | 213 |
| **Total assets** | 516 |

|  | £m |
|---|---|
| **EQUITY AND LIABILITIES** | |
| **Equity** | |
| Ordinary shares of £0.50 each | 200 |
| Share premium account | 30 |
| Other reserves | 50 |
| Retained earnings | 25 |
|  | 305 |
| **Non-current liabilities** | |
| Borrowings | 100 |
| **Current liabilities** | |
| Trade payables | 99 |
| Taxation | 12 |
|  | 111 |
| **Total equity and liabilities** | 510 |

Let us now go through these statements and pick up those aspects that are unique to limited companies.

## The income statement

There are several features in the income statement that need consideration.

### Profit

We can see that, following the calculation of operating profit, two further measures of profit are shown.

- The first of these is the profit before taxation. Interest charges are deducted from the operating profit to derive this figure. In the case of a sole proprietor or partnership business, the income statement would end here.

- The second measure of profit is the profit for the year. As the company is a separate legal entity, it is liable to pay tax (known as corporation tax) on the profits generated. (This contrasts with the sole proprietor business where it is the owner rather than the business that is liable for the tax on profits, as we saw earlier in the chapter.) This measure of profit represents the amount that is available for the shareholders.

### Audit fee

Companies beyond a certain size are required to have their financial statements audited by an independent firm of accountants, for which a fee is charged. As we shall see later in this chapter, the purpose of the audit is to lend credibility to the financial statements. Although it is also open to sole proprietors and partnerships to have their financial statements audited, relatively few do, so this is an expense that is most often seen in the income statements of companies.

## The statement of financial position

The main points for consideration in the statement of financial position are as follows.

### Taxation

The amount that appears as part of the current liabilities represents 50 per cent of the tax on the profit for the year 2010. It is, therefore, 50 per cent (£12 million) of the charge that appears in the income statement (£24 million); the other 50 per cent (£12 million) will already have been paid. The unpaid 50 per cent will be paid shortly after the statement of financial position date. These payment dates are set down by law.

### Other reserves

This will include any reserves that are not separately identified on the face of the statement of financial position. It may include a *general reserve*, which normally consists of trading profits that have been transferred to this separate reserve for reinvestment ('ploughing back') into the operations of the company. It is not at all necessary to set up a separate reserve for this purpose. The trading profits could remain unallocated and still swell the retained earnings of the company. It is not entirely clear why directors decide to make transfers to general reserves, since the profits concerned remain part of the revenue reserves. As such, they still remain available for dividend. The most plausible explanation seems to be that directors feel that placing profits in a separate reserve indicates an intention to invest the funds, represented by the reserve, permanently in the company and, therefore, not to use them to pay a dividend. Of course, the retained earnings appearing on the statement of financial position are also a reserve, but that fact is not indicated in its title.

## Dividends

We have already seen that dividends represent drawings by the shareholders of the company. Dividends are paid out of the revenue reserves and should be deducted from these reserves (usually retained earnings) when preparing the statement of financial position. Shareholders are often paid an annual dividend, perhaps in two parts. An 'interim' dividend may be paid part way through the year and a 'final' dividend shortly after the year end.

Dividends declared by the directors during the year but still unpaid at the year end *may* appear as a liability in the statement of financial position. To be recognised as a liability, however, they must be properly authorised before the year-end date. This normally means that the shareholders must approve the dividend.

## Additional financial statements

In the sections below, we turn our attention to two new financial statements that must be provided by those companies that are subject to International Financial

Reporting Standards. We shall consider the nature and role of these standards a little later in the chapter.

## Statement of comprehensive income

The statement of comprehensive income extends the conventional income statement to include certain other gains and losses that affect shareholders' equity. It may be presented either in the form of a single statement or as two separate statements, comprising an income statement (like the one shown in Example 4.5) and a statement of comprehensive income.

This new statement attempts to overcome the perceived weaknesses of the conventional income statement. In broad terms, the conventional income statement shows all *realised* gains and losses for the period. It also shows some unrealised losses. However, gains, and some losses, that remain *unrealised* (because the asset is still held) tend not to pass through the income statement, but will go, instead, directly to a reserve. We saw, in an earlier chapter, an example of such an unrealised gain.

### Activity 4.11

**Can you think of this example?**

The example that we met earlier is where a business revalues its land and buildings. The gain arising is not shown in the conventional income statement, but is transferred to a revaluation reserve, which forms part of the equity. (See example in Activity 2.14 on page 59.) Land and buildings are not the only assets to which this rule relates, but revaluations of these types of asset are, in practice, the most common examples of unrealised gains.

An example of an unrealised gain, or loss, that has not been mentioned so far, arises from exchange differences when the results of foreign operations are translated into UK currency. Any gain, or loss, bypasses the income statement and is taken directly to a currency translation reserve.

A weakness of conventional accounting is that there is no robust principle that we can apply to determine precisely what should, and what should not, be included in the income statement. Thus, on the one hand, losses arising from the impairment of non-current assets normally appear in the income statement. On the other hand, losses arising from translating the carrying value of assets expressed in an overseas currency (because they are owned by an overseas branch) do not. This difference in treatment, which is ingrained in conventional accounting, is difficult to justify.

The statement of comprehensive income ensures that all gains and losses, both realised and unrealised, are reported within a single statement. To do this, it extends the conventional income statement by including unrealised gains, as well as any unrealised losses not yet reported, immediately below the measure of profit for the year. An illustration of this statement is shown in Example 4.6.

### Example 4.6

**Malik plc**
**Statement of comprehensive income for the year ended 31 July 2010**

|  | £m |
|---|---:|
| Revenue | 97.2 |
| Cost of sales | (59.1) |
| **Gross profit** | 38.1 |
| Other income | 3.5 |
| Distribution expenses | (16.5) |
| Administration expenses | (11.2) |
| Other expenses | (2.4) |
| **Operating profit** | 11.5 |
| Finance charges | (1.8) |
| **Profit before tax** | 9.7 |
| Tax | (2.4) |
| **Profit for the year** | 7.3 |
| *Other comprehensive income* | |
| Revaluation of property, plant and equipment | 6.6 |
| Foreign currency translation differences for foreign operations | 4.0 |
| Tax on other comprehensive income | (2.6) |
| Other comprehensive income for the year, net of tax | 8.0 |
| **Total comprehensive income for the year** | 15.3 |

This example adopts a single-statement approach to presenting comprehensive income. The alternative two-statement approach simply divides the information shown above into two separate parts. The income statement, which is the first statement, begins with the revenue for the year and ends with the profit for the year. The statement of comprehensive income, which is the second statement, begins with the profit for the year and ends with the total comprehensive income for the year.

## Statement of changes in equity

→ The statement of changes in equity aims to help users to understand the changes in share capital and reserves that took place during the period. It reconciles the figures for these items at the beginning of the period with those at the end of the period. This is achieved by showing the effect on the share capital and reserves of total comprehensive income as well as the effect of share issues and purchases during the period. The effect of dividends during the period may also be shown in this statement, although dividends can be shown in the notes instead.

To see how a statement of changes in equity may be prepared, let us consider Example 4.7.

## Example 4.7

At 1 January 2010 Miro plc had the following equity:

**Miro plc**

|  | £m |
|---|---|
| Share capital (£1 ordinary shares) | 100 |
| Revaluation reserve | 20 |
| Translation reserve | 40 |
| Retained earnings | 150 |
| **Total equity** | **310** |

During 2010, the company made a profit for the year from normal business operations of £42 million and reported an upward revaluation of property, plant and equipment of £120 million (net of any tax that would be payable were the unrealised gains to be realised). The company also reported a £10 million loss on exchange differences on translating the results of foreign operations. To strengthen its financial position, the company issued 50 million ordinary shares during the year at a premium of £0.40. Dividends for the year were £27 million.

This information for 2010 can be set out in a statement of changes in equity as follows:

**Statement of changes in equity for the year ended 31 December 2010**

|  | Share capital | Share premium | Revaluation reserve | Translation reserve | Retained earnings | Total |
|---|---|---|---|---|---|---|
|  | £m | £m | £m | £m | £m | £m |
| Balance as at 1 January 2010 | 100 | – | 20 | 40 | 150 | 310 |
| Changes in equity for 2010 |  |  |  |  |  |  |
| Issue of ordinary shares (Note 1) | 50 | 20 | – | – | – | 70 |
| Dividends (Note 2) | – | – | – | – | (27) | (27) |
| Total comprehensive income for the year (Note 3) | – | – | 120 | (10) | 42 | 152 |
| Balance at 31 December 2010 | 150 | 20 | 140 | 30 | 165 | 505 |

Notes:
1 The premium on the share price is transferred to a specific reserve.
2 We have chosen to show dividends in the statement of changes in equity rather than in the notes. They represent an appropriation of equity and are deducted from retained earnings.
3 The effect of each component of comprehensive income on the various components of shareholders' equity must be separately disclosed. The revaluation gain and the loss on translating foreign operations are each allocated to a specific reserve. The profit for the year is added to retained earnings.

## The directors' duty to account

With most large companies, it is not possible for all shareholders to take part in the management of the company, nor do most of them wish to be involved. Instead, they appoint directors to act on their behalf. This separation of ownership from day-to-day control creates the need for directors to be accountable for their stewardship (management) of the company's assets. Thus, the law requires that directors:

■ maintain appropriate accounting records
■ prepare annual financial statements and a directors' report and make these available to all shareholders and to the public at large.

The financial statements are made available to the public by submitting a copy to the Registrar of Companies (Department of Trade and Industry), who allows any interested person to inspect them. In addition, listed companies are required to publish their financial statements on their website.

### Activity 4.12

Why does the law require directors to account in this way and who benefits from these requirements?

We thought of the following benefits and beneficiaries:

■ *To inform and protect shareholders*. If shareholders do not receive information about the performance and position of their investment, they will have problems in appraising their investment. Under these circumstances, they would probably be reluctant to invest and this, in turn, would affect the functioning of the private sector.
■ *To inform and protect suppliers of labour, goods, services and finance, particularly those supplying credit (loans) or goods and services on credit*. Individuals and organisations would be reluctant to engage in commercial relationships, such as supplying goods or lending money, where a company does not provide information about its financial health. The fact that a company has limited liability increases the risks involved in dealing with the company. An unwillingness to engage in commercial relationships with limited companies will, once again, affect the functioning of the private sector.
■ *To inform and protect society more generally*. Some companies exercise enormous power and influence in society generally, particularly on a geographically local basis. For example, a particular company may be the dominant employer and purchaser of commercial goods and services in a particular town or city. Legislators have tended to take the view that society has the right to information about the company and its activities.

## The need for accounting rules

If we accept the need for directors to prepare and publish financial statements, we should also accept the need for a framework of rules concerning how these statements are prepared and presented. Without rules, there is a much greater risk that unscrupulous directors will adopt accounting policies and practices that portray an unrealistic view of financial health. There is also a much greater risk that the financial statements will not be comparable over time or with those of other businesses. Accounting rules can narrow areas of differences and reduce the variety of accounting methods. This should help ensure that businesses treat similar transactions in a similar way.

Accounting rules should help to provide greater confidence in the integrity of financial statements. This, in turn, may help a business to raise funds and to build stronger relationships with customers and suppliers. Users must be realistic, however, about what can be achieved through regulation. Problems of manipulation and of concealment can still occur even within a highly regulated environment and examples of both will be considered later in the chapter. The scale of these problems, however, should be reduced where there is a practical set of rules.

Problems of comparability can also still occur as accounting is not a precise science. Judgements and estimates must be made when preparing financial statements and these may hinder comparisons. Furthermore, no two companies are identical and the accounting policies adopted may vary between companies for entirely valid reasons.

## Sources of accounting rules

In recent years there have been increasing trends towards the internationalisation of business and the integration of financial markets. These trends have helped to strengthen the case for the international harmonisation of accounting rules. By adopting a common set of rules, users of financial statements should be better placed to compare the financial health of companies based in different countries. It should also relieve international companies of some of the burden of preparing financial statements as different financial statements would no longer have to be prepared to comply with the rules of different countries in which a particular company operates.

The International Accounting Standards Board (IASB) is an independent body that is at the forefront of the move towards harmonisation. The Board, which is based in the UK, is dedicated to developing a single set of high-quality, global accounting rules. These rules aim to provide transparent and comparable information in financial statements. They are known as International Financial Reporting Standards (IFRSs) or International Accounting Standards (IASs) and deal with key issues such as:

- what information should be disclosed;
- how information should be presented;
- how assets should be valued; and
- how profit should be measured.

### Activity 4.13

We have already come across some IASs and IFRSs in earlier chapters. Try to recall at least two topics where International Financial Reporting Standards were mentioned.

We came across financial reporting standards when considering:

- the valuation and impairment of assets (Chapter 2);
- depreciation and impairment of non-current assets (Chapter 3);
- the valuation of inventories (Chapter 3).

In recent years, several important developments have greatly increased the authority of the IASB. The first major development came when the European Commission required nearly all companies listed on the stock exchanges of EU member states to adopt IFRSs for reporting periods commencing on or after 1 January 2005. As a result, nearly 7,000 companies in 25 different countries switched to IFRSs. Further developments have occurred since and there are now more than 100 countries that either require or permit the use of IFRSs. Although non-listed UK companies are not currently required to adopt IFRSs, they have the option to do so. Some informed observers believe, however, that IFRSs will soon become a requirement for all UK companies.

The EU requirement to adopt IFRSs, mentioned earlier, overrides any laws in force in member states that could either hinder or restrict compliance with them. The ultimate aim is to achieve a single framework of accounting rules for companies from all member states. The EU recognises that this will be achieved only if individual governments do not add to the requirements imposed by the various IFRSs. Thus, it seems that accounting rules developed within individual EU member countries will eventually disappear. For the time being, however, the EU accepts that the governments of member states may need to impose additional disclosures for some corporate governance matters and regulatory requirements.

In the UK, company law requires disclosure relating to various corporate governance issues. There is, for example, a requirement to disclose details of directors' remuneration in the published financial statements, which goes beyond anything required by IFRSs. Furthermore, the Financial Services Authority (FSA), in its role as the UK (Stock Exchange) listing authority, imposes rules on Stock Exchange listed companies. These include the requirement to publish a condensed set of interim (half-year) financial statements in addition to the annual financial statements.

Figure 4.5 sets out the main sources of accounting rules for Stock Exchange listed companies discussed above. While company law and the FSA still play an important role, in the longer term IFRSs seem set to become the sole source of company accounting rules.

**Figure 4.5** Sources of external accounting rules for a UK public limited company listed on the London Stock Exchange

International Financial Reporting Standards provide the basic framework of accounting rules for nearly all Stock Exchange listed companies. These rules are augmented by company law and by the Financial Services Authority (FSA) in its role as the UK listing authority.

## The auditors' role

Shareholders are required to elect a qualified and independent person or, more usually, a firm to act as auditors. The auditors' main duty is to report whether, in their opinion, the financial statements do what they are supposed to do, namely to show a true and fair view of the financial performance, position and cash flows of the company. To be able to form such an opinion, auditors must carefully scrutinise the annual financial statements and the underlying evidence upon which they are based. In particular, they will examine the accounting principles followed, the accounting estimates made and the robustness of the company's internal control systems. The auditors' opinion must be included with the financial statements sent to the shareholders and to the Registrar of Companies.

The relationship between the shareholders, the directors and the auditors is illustrated in Figure 4.6. This shows that the shareholders elect the directors to act on their behalf, in the day-to-day running of the company. The directors are then required to 'account' to the shareholders on the performance, position and cash flows of the company, on an annual basis. The shareholders also elect auditors, whose role it is to give the shareholders an independent view of the truth and fairness of the financial statements prepared by the directors.

**Figure 4.6** **The relationship between the shareholders, the directors and the auditors**

The directors are appointed by the shareholders to manage the company on the shareholders' behalf. The directors are required to report each year to the shareholders, principally by means of financial statements, on the company's performance, position and cash flows. To give greater confidence in the statements, the shareholders also appoint auditors to investigate the reports and to express an opinion on their reliability.

## The directors' report

In addition to preparing the financial statements, UK law requires the directors to prepare an annual report to shareholders and other interested parties. The directors' report will contain both financial and non-financial information, which goes beyond that contained in the financial statements. The information to be disclosed is diverse and will include the names of those who were directors during the year, the principal activities of the company and any recommended dividend. The most important element of the report, however, is probably the business review. This is aimed at helping shareholders to assess how well the directors have performed. It should provide an analysis of financial performance and position and should also set out the principal risks and uncertainties facing the business.

In addition to disclosing the above information, the directors' report must contain a declaration that the directors are not aware of any other information that the auditors might need in preparing their audit report. Furthermore, the report must declare that the directors have taken steps to ensure that the auditors are aware of all relevant information. The auditors do not carry out an audit of the directors' report. However, they will check to see that the information in the report is consistent with that contained in the audited financial statements.

For companies listed on the Stock Exchange, the law also requires the publication of an annual directors' remuneration report. This should help shareholders to assess whether the rewards received by directors are appropriate.

 ## Creative accounting

Despite the proliferation of accounting rules and the independent checks that are imposed, concerns over the quality of published financial statements surface from time to time. There are occasions when directors apply particular accounting policies, or structure particular transactions, in such a way as to portray a picture of financial health that is in line with what they want users to see, rather than what is a true and fair view of financial position and performance. Misrepresenting the performance and position of a business in this way is referred to as creative accounting and it poses a major problem for accounting rule makers and for society generally.

### Activity 4.14

**Why might the directors of a company engage in creative accounting?**

There are many reasons including:

- to get around restrictions (for example, to report sufficient profit to pay a dividend);
- to avoid government action (for example, the taxation of excessive profits);
- to hide poor management decisions;
- to achieve sales revenue or profit targets, thereby ensuring that performance bonuses are paid to the directors;
- to attract new share capital or long-term borrowing by showing an apparently healthy financial position; and
- to satisfy the demands of major investors concerning levels of return.

## Creative accounting methods

The ways in which unscrupulous directors can manipulate the financial statements are many and varied. However, they usually involve adopting novel or unorthodox practices for reporting key elements of the financial statements such as revenue, expenses, assets and liabilities. They may also involve the use of complicated or obscure transactions in an attempt to hide the underlying economic reality. The manipulation carried out may be designed either to bend the rules or to break them.

Many creative accounting methods are designed to overstate the revenue for a period. These methods often involve the early recognition of sales revenue or the reporting of sales transactions that have no real substance. Real World 4.8 provides examples of both types of revenue manipulation.

---

**Real World 4.8**

### Overstating revenue

*Channel stuffing*: A business, usually with considerable market power, may pressurise its distributors to accept more goods than is needed to meet normal sales demand. In this way, the business can record additional sales for a period even though there has effectively been only a transfer of inventories from the business to its distributors. This method of artificially increasing sales is also known as 'trade loading'.

*Pre-dispatching*: Normally, revenue for credit sales is recognised when goods have been passed to, and accepted by, the customer. To boost sales and profits for a period, however, some businesses have been known to recognise revenue as soon as the order for goods has been received.

*Hollow swaps*: Telecom businesses may agree to sell unused fibre optic capacity to each other – usually at the same price. Although this will not increase profits, it will increase revenues and give an impression that the business is growing.

*Round tripping*: Energy businesses may agree to buy and sell energy between each other. Again this is normally for the same price and so no additional profits will be made. It will, however, boost revenues to give a false impression of business growth. This method is also known as 'in and out trading'.

*Source*: based on information in 'Dirty laundry: how companies fudge the numbers', *The Times, Business Section*, 22/09/2002.

---

Some years ago there was a wave of creative accounting scandals, particularly in the US but also in Europe; however, it seems that this wave has now subsided. The quality of financial statements is improving and, it is to be hoped, trust among investors and others is being restored. As a result of the actions taken by various regulatory bodies and by accounting rule makers, creative accounting has become a more risky and difficult process for those who attempt it. However, it will never disappear completely and a further wave of creative accounting scandals may occur in the future. The recent wave coincided with a period of strong economic growth and, during good economic times, investors and auditors become less vigilant. Thus, the opportunity to manipulate the figures becomes easier. We must not, therefore, become too complacent. Things may change again when we next experience a period of strong growth.

## ? Self-assessment question 4.1

This question requires you to correct some figures on a set of company financial statements. It should prove useful practice for the material that you covered in Chapters 2 and 3, as well as helping you to become familiar with the financial statements of a company.

Presented below is a draft set of simplified financial statements for Pear Limited for the year ended 30 September 2010.

### Income statement for the year ended 30 September 2010

|  | £000 |
| --- | --- |
| Revenue | 1,456 |
| Cost of sales | (768) |
| **Gross profit** | 688 |
| Salaries | (220) |
| Depreciation | (249) |
| Other operating costs | (131) |
| **Operating profit** | 88 |
| Interest payable | (15) |
| **Profit before taxation** | 73 |
| Taxation at 30% | (22) |
| **Profit for the year** | 51 |

### Statement of financial position as at 30 September 2010

| ASSETS | £000 |
| --- | --- |
| **Non-current assets** | |
| *Property, plant and equipment* | |
| Cost | 1,570 |
| Depreciation | (690) |
| | 880 |
| **Current assets** | |
| Inventories | 207 |
| Trade receivables | 182 |
| Cash at bank | 21 |
| | 410 |
| **Total assets** | 1,290 |
| **EQUITY AND LIABILITIES** | |
| **Equity** | |
| Share capital | 300 |
| Share premium account | 300 |
| Retained earnings at beginning of year | 104 |
| Profit for year | 51 |
| | 755 |
| **Non-current liabilities** | |
| Borrowings (10% loan notes repayable 2014) | 300 |
| **Current liabilities** | |
| Trade payables | 88 |
| Other payables | 20 |
| Taxation | 22 |
| Borrowings (bank overdraft) | 105 |
| | 235 |
| **Total equity and liabilities** | 1,290 |

The following information is available:

1 Depreciation has not been charged on office equipment with a carrying amount of £100,000. This class of assets is depreciated at 12 per cent a year using the reducing-balance method.
2 A new machine was purchased, on credit, for £30,000 and delivered on 29 September 2010 but has not been included in the financial statements. (Ignore depreciation.)
3 A sales invoice to the value of £18,000 for September 2010 has been omitted from the financial statements. (The cost of sales figure is stated correctly.)
4 A dividend of £25,000 had been approved by the shareholders before 30 September 2010, but was unpaid at that date. This is not reflected in the financial statements.
5 The interest payable on the loan notes for the second half-year was not paid until 1 October 2010 and has not been included in the financial statements.
6 An allowance for trade receivables is to be made at the level of 2 per cent of trade receivables.
7 An invoice for electricity to the value of £2,000 for the quarter ended 30 September 2010 arrived on 4 October and has not been included in the financial statements.
8 The charge for taxation will have to be amended to take account of the above information. Make the simplifying assumption that tax is payable shortly after the end of the year, at the rate of 30 per cent of the profit before tax.

**Required:**
Prepare a revised set of financial statements for the year ended 30 September 2010 incorporating the additional information in 1 to 8 above. (Work to the nearest £1,000.)

**The solution to this question can be found at the back of the book, in Appendix B.**

## Summary

The main points of this chapter may be summarised as follows.

### Main features of a limited company

- It is an artificial person that has been created by law.
- It has a separate life to its owners and is granted a perpetual existence.
- It must take responsibility for its own debts and losses but its owners are granted limited liability.
- A public company can offer its shares for sale to the public; a private company cannot.
- It is governed by a board of directors, which is elected by the shareholders.
- Corporate governance is a major issue.

### Financing the limited company

- The share capital of a company can be of two main types: ordinary shares and preference shares.

- Holders of ordinary shares (equities) are the main risk takers and are given voting rights; they form the backbone of the company.

- Holders of preference shares are given a right to a fixed dividend before ordinary shareholders receive a dividend.

- Reserves are profits and gains made by the company and form part of the ordinary shareholders' equity.

- Borrowings provide another major source of finance.

### Share issues

- Bonus shares are issued to existing shareholders when part of the reserves of the company is converted into share capital. No funds are raised.

- Rights issues give existing shareholders the right to buy new shares in proportion to their existing holding.

- Public issues are made direct to the general investing public.

- Private placings are share issues to particular investors.

- The shares of public companies may be bought and sold on a recognised Stock Exchange.

### Reserves

- Reserves are of two types: revenue reserves and capital reserves.

- Revenue reserves arise from trading profits and from realised profits on the sale of non-current assets.

- Capital reserves arise from the issue of shares above their nominal value or from the upward revaluation of non-current assets.

- Revenue reserves can be withdrawn as dividends by the shareholders whereas capital reserves normally cannot.

### Financial statements of limited companies

- The financial statements of limited companies are based on the same principles as those of sole proprietorship and partnership businesses. However, there are some differences in detail.

- The income statement has three measures of profit displayed after the gross profit figure: operating profit, profit before taxation and profit for the year.

- The income statement also shows audit fees and tax on profits for the year.

- Any unpaid tax and unpaid, but authorised, dividends will appear in the statement of financial position as current liabilities.

- The statement of comprehensive income extends the income statement to include all gains and losses, both realised and unrealised.

- The statement of changes in equity reconciles the equity figure at the beginning of a reporting period with that at the end.
- The share capital plus the reserves make up 'equity'.
- Limited companies subject to International Financial Reporting Standards must produce a statement of comprehensive income and statement of changes in equity.

### Directors' duty

- The directors have a duty to
  - maintain appropriate accounting records;
  - prepare and publish financial statements and a directors' report.

### The need for accounting rules

- Accounting rules are necessary to
  - avoid unacceptable accounting practices;
  - improve the comparability of financial statements.

### Accounting rules

- The International Accounting Standards Board (IASB) has become an important source of rules.
- Company law and the London Stock Exchange are also sources of rules for UK companies.

### Other statutory reports

- The auditors' report provides an opinion by independent auditors concerning whether the financial statements provide a true and fair view of the financial health of a business.
- The directors' report contains information of a financial and a non-financial nature, which goes beyond that contained in the financial statements.

### Creative accounting

- Despite the accounting rules in place there have been examples of creative accounting by directors.
- This involves using accounting practices to show what the directors would like users to see rather than what is a fair representation of reality.

 *Now check your progress in your personal Study Plan*

## → Key terms

limited company p. 113
shares p. 113
limited liability p. 116
public limited company p. 116
private limited company p. 116
corporation tax p. 118
directors p. 119
corporate governance p. 119
UK Corporate Governance Code p. 121
reserves p. 123
nominal value p. 123
par value p. 123
revenue reserve p. 124
dividend p. 124
ordinary shares p. 124
splitting p. 125
consolidating p. 125
preference shares p. 125
capital reserves p. 126
share premium account p. 128

bonus shares p. 128
issued share capital p. 131
allotted share capital p. 131
fully paid shares p. 131
called-up share capital p. 131
paid-up share capital p. 131
profit before taxation p. 137
profit for the year p. 137
statement of comprehensive income
    p. 139
statement of changes in equity p. 140
International Financial Reporting
    Standards p. 143
International Accounting Standards
    p. 143
auditors p. 145
directors' report p. 145
business review p. 146
creative accounting p. 146

## Reference

1 Business Sector Advisory Group on Corporate Governance, *Corporate Governance: Improving Competitiveness and Access to Capital in Global Markets*, OECD, 1998.

## Further reading

If you would like to explore the topics covered in this chapter in more depth, we recommend the following books:

Elliott, B. and Elliott, J., *Financial Accounting and Reporting* (13th edn), Financial Times Prentice Hall, 2010, chapter 10.
IASC Foundation Education, *A Guide through IFRS 2009*, July 2009, IAS 1.
Thomas, A. and Ward, A., *Introduction to Financial Accounting* (6th edn), McGraw-Hill, 2009, chapter 29.

Review questions

Solutions to these questions can be found at the back of the book, in Appendix C.

**4.1** How does the liability of a limited company differ from the liability of a real person, in respect of amounts owed to others?

**4.2** Some people are about to form a company, as a vehicle through which to run a new business. What are the advantages to them of forming a private limited company rather than a public one?

**4.3** What is a reserve? Distinguish between a revenue reserve and a capital reserve.

**4.4** What is a preference share? Compare the main features of a preference share with those of

(a) an ordinary share; and
(b) loan notes.

## ✳ Exercises

Exercises 4.4 and 4.5 are more advanced than Exercises 4.1 to 4.3. Those with coloured numbers have solutions at the back of the book, in Appendix D.

> If you wish to try more exercises, visit the website at www.myaccountinglab.com.

**4.1** Comment on the following quote:

> Limited companies can set a limit on the amount of debts that they will meet. They tend to have reserves of cash, as well as share capital and they can use these reserves to pay dividends to the shareholders. Many companies have preference as well as ordinary shares. The preference shares give a guaranteed dividend. The shares of many companies can be bought and sold on the Stock Exchange. Shareholders selling their shares can represent a useful source of new finance to the company.

**4.2** The following information was extracted from the financial statements of I. Ching (Booksellers) plc for the year to 31 December 2009:

|  | £m |
|---|---|
| Finance charges | 40 |
| Cost of sales | 460 |
| Distribution expenses | 110 |
| Revenue | 943 |
| Administration expenses | 212 |
| Other expenses | 25 |
| Gain on revaluation of property, plant and equipment | 20 |
| Loss on foreign currency translations on foreign operations | 15 |
| Tax on profit for the year | 24 |
| Tax on other components of comprehensive income | 1 |

**Required:**

Prepare a statement of comprehensive income for the year ended 31 December 2009.

**4.3** Briefly explain each of the following expressions that you have seen in the financial statements of a limited company:

(a) dividend
(b) audit fee
(c) share premium account.

**4.4** Presented below is a draft set of financial statements for Chips Limited.

**Chips Limited**
**Income statement for the year ended 30 June 2010**

|  | £000 |
|---|---|
| Revenue | 1,850 |
| Cost of sales | (1,040) |
| **Gross profit** | 810 |
| Depreciation | (220) |
| Other operating costs | (375) |
| **Operating profit** | 215 |
| Interest payable | (35) |
| **Profit before taxation** | 180 |
| Taxation | (60) |
| **Profit for the year** | 120 |

## Statement of financial position as at 30 June 2010

| | Cost £000 | Depreciation £000 | £000 |
|---|---|---|---|
| **ASSETS** | | | |
| **Non-current assets** | | | |
| *Property, plant and equipment* | | | |
| Buildings | 800 | (112) | 688 |
| Plant and equipment | 650 | (367) | 283 |
| Motor vehicles | 102 | (53) | 49 |
| | 1,552 | (532) | 1,020 |
| **Current assets** | | | |
| Inventories | | | 950 |
| Trade receivables | | | 420 |
| Cash at bank | | | 16 |
| | | | 1,386 |
| **Total assets** | | | 2,406 |
| **EQUITY AND LIABILITIES** | | | |
| **Equity** | | | |
| Ordinary shares of £1, fully paid | | | 800 |
| Reserves at beginning of the year | | | 248 |
| Profit for the year | | | 120 |
| | | | 1,168 |
| **Non-current liabilities** | | | |
| Borrowings (secured 10% loan notes) | | | 700 |
| **Current liabilities** | | | |
| Trade payables | | | 361 |
| Other payables | | | 117 |
| Taxation | | | 60 |
| | | | 538 |
| **Total equity and liabilities** | | | 2,406 |

The following additional information is available:

1 Purchase invoices for goods received on 29 June 2010 amounting to £23,000 have not been included. This means that the cost of sales figure in the income statement has been understated.

2 A motor vehicle costing £8,000 with depreciation amounting to £5,000 was sold on 30 June 2010 for £2,000, paid by cheque. This transaction has not been included in the company's records.

3 No depreciation on motor vehicles has been charged. The annual rate is 20 per cent of cost at the year end.

4 A sale on credit for £16,000 made on 1 July 2010 has been included in the financial statements in error. The cost of sales figure is correct in respect of this item.

5 A half-yearly payment of interest on the secured loan due on 30 June 2010 has not been paid.

6 The tax charge should be 30 per cent of the reported profit before taxation. Assume that it is payable, in full, shortly after the year end.

**Required:**

Prepare a revised set of financial statements incorporating the additional information in 1 to 6 above. (Work to the nearest £1,000.)

**4.5** Rose Limited operates a small chain of retail shops that sell high-quality teas and coffees. Approximately half of sales are on credit. Abbreviated and unaudited financial statements are given below.

**Rose Limited**
**Income statement for the year ended 31 March 2010**

|  | £000 |
|---|---|
| Revenue | 12,080 |
| Cost of sales | (6,282) |
| **Gross profit** | 5,798 |
| Labour costs | (2,658) |
| Depreciation | (625) |
| Other operating costs | (1,003) |
| **Operating profit** | 1,512 |
| Interest payable | (66) |
| **Profit before taxation** | 1,446 |
| Taxation | (434) |
| **Profit for the year** | 1,012 |

**Statement of financial position as at 31 March 2010**

|  | £000 |
|---|---|
| **ASSETS** | |
| Non-current assets | 2,728 |
| **Current assets** | |
| Inventories | 1,583 |
| Trade receivables | 996 |
| Cash | 26 |
|  | 2,605 |
| **Total assets** | 5,333 |
| **EQUITY AND LIABILITIES** | |
| **Equity** | |
| Share capital (50p shares, fully paid) | 750 |
| Share premium | 250 |
| Retained earnings | 1,468 |
|  | 2,468 |
| **Non-current liabilities** | |
| Borrowings – secured loan notes (2014) | 300 |
| **Current liabilities** | |
| Trade payables | 1,118 |
| Other payables | 417 |
| Tax | 434 |
| Borrowings – overdraft | 596 |
|  | 2,565 |
| **Total equity and liabilities** | 5,333 |

Since the unaudited financial statements for Rose Limited were prepared, the following information has become available:

1 An additional £74,000 of depreciation should have been charged on fixtures and fittings.
2 Invoices for credit sales on 31 March 2010 amounting to £34,000 have not been included; cost of sales is not affected.
3 Trade receivables totalling £21,000 are recognised as having gone bad, but they have not yet been written off.
4 Inventories which had been purchased for £2,000 have been damaged and are unsaleable. This is not reflected in the financial statements.
5 Fixtures and fittings to the value of £16,000 were delivered just before 31 March 2010, but these assets were not included in the financial statements and the purchase invoice had not been processed.
6 Wages for Saturday-only staff, amounting to £1,000, have not been paid for the final Saturday of the year. This is not reflected in the financial statements.
7 Tax is payable at 30 per cent of profit after taxation. Assume that it is payable shortly after the year end.

**Required:**
Prepare revised financial statements for Rose Limited for the year ended 31 March 2010, incorporating the information in 1 to 7 above. (Work to the nearest £1,000.)

## Chapter 5

# Measuring and reporting cash flows

## Introduction

This chapter is devoted to the third major financial statement identified in Chapter 2: the statement of cash flows. This statement reports the movements of cash over a period and the effect of these movements on the cash position of the business. It is an important financial statement because cash is vital to the survival of a business. Without cash, a business cannot operate.

In this chapter, we shall see how the statement of cash flows is prepared and how the information that it contains may be interpreted. We shall also see why the deficiencies of the income statement in identifying and explaining cash flows make a separate statement necessary.

The statement of cash flows is being considered after the chapter on limited companies because the format of the statement requires an understanding of this type of business. Nearly all limited companies are required to provide a statement of cash flows for shareholders and other users as part of their annual financial reports.

## Learning outcomes

**When you have completed this chapter, you should be able to:**

- discuss the crucial importance of cash to a business;
- explain the nature of the statement of cash flows and discuss how it can be helpful in identifying cash flow problems;
- prepare a statement of cash flows;
- interpret a statement of cash flows.

 **Remember to create your own personalised Study Plan**

# The statement of cash flows

The statement of cash flows is a fairly recent addition to the annual published financial statements. Until relatively recently, companies were only required to publish an income statement and a statement of financial position (balance sheet). The prevailing view seems to have been that all the financial information needed by users would be contained within these two statements. This view may have been based partly on the assumption that if a business were profitable, it would also have plenty of cash. Although in the long run this is likely to be true, it is not necessarily true in the short to medium term.

We saw in Chapter 3 that the income statement sets out the revenue and expenses, rather than the cash receipts and cash payments, for the period. This means that profit (or loss), which represents the difference between the revenue and expenses for the period, may have little or no relation to the cash generated for the period. To illustrate this point, let us take the example of a business making a sale (generating a revenue). This may well lead to an increase in wealth that will be reflected in the income statement. However, if the sale is made on credit, no cash changes hands – at least not at the time of sale. Instead, the increase in wealth is reflected in another asset: an increase in trade receivables. Furthermore, if an item of inventories is the subject of the sale, wealth is lost to the business through the reduction in inventories. This means an expense is incurred in making the sale, which will be shown in the income statement. Once again, however, no cash has changed hands at the time of sale. For such reasons, the profit and the cash generated for a period will rarely go hand in hand.

Activity 5.1 should help to underline how profit and cash for a period may be affected differently by particular transactions or events.

## Activity 5.1

The following is a list of business/accounting events. In each case, state the effect (increase, decrease or none) on both profit and cash.

|  | | *Effect* | |
|---|---|---|---|
|  | | on profit | on cash |
| 1 | Repayment of borrowings | _____ | _____ |
| 2 | Making a profitable sale on credit | _____ | _____ |
| 3 | Buying a current asset on credit | _____ | _____ |
| 4 | Receiving cash from a credit customer (trade receivable) | _____ | _____ |
| 5 | Depreciating a non-current asset | _____ | _____ |
| 6 | Buying some inventories for cash | _____ | _____ |
| 7 | Making a share issue for cash | _____ | _____ |

→

You should have come up with the following:

|  |  | Effect | |
|---|---|---|---|
|  |  | on profit | on cash |
| 1 | Repayment of borrowings | none | decrease |
| 2 | Making a profitable sale on credit | increase | none |
| 3 | Buying a current asset on credit | none | none |
| 4 | Receiving cash from a credit customer (trade receivable) | none | increase |
| 5 | Depreciating a non-current asset | decrease | none |
| 6 | Buying some inventories for cash | none | decrease |
| 7 | Making a share issue for cash | none | increase |

The reasons for these answers are as follows:

1 Repaying borrowings requires that cash be paid to the lender. This means that two figures in the statement of financial position will be affected, but none in the income statement.
2 Making a profitable sale on credit will increase the sales revenue and profit figures. No cash will change hands at this point, however.
3 Buying a current asset on credit affects neither the cash balance nor the profit figure.
4 Receiving cash from a credit customer increases the cash balance and reduces the credit customer's balance. Both of these figures are on the statement of financial position. The income statement is unaffected.
5 Depreciating a non-current asset means that an expense is recognised. This causes the carrying amount of the asset, as it is recorded on the statement of financial position, to fall by an amount equal to the amount of the expense. No cash is paid or received.
6 Buying some inventories for cash means that the value of inventories held will increase and the cash balance will decrease by a similar amount. Profit is not affected.
7 Making a share issue for cash increases the shareholders' equity and increases the cash balance; profit is unaffected.

It is clear from the above that if we are to gain insights about cash movements over time, the income statement is not the place to look. Instead we need a separate financial statement. This fact has become widely recognised in recent years and in 1991 a UK financial reporting standard, FRS 1, emerged that required all but the smallest companies to produce and publish a statement of cash flows. This standard has been superseded for listed companies from 2005 by the International Financial Reporting (Accounting) Standard IAS 7. The two standards have broadly similar requirements. This chapter follows the provisions of IAS 7.

## Why is cash so important?

It is worth asking why cash is so important. After all, cash is just an asset that the business needs to help it to function. In that sense, it is no different from inventories or non-current assets.

The reason for the importance of cash is that people and organisations will not normally accept anything other than cash in settlement of their claims. If a business wants to employ people, it must pay them in cash. If it wants to buy a new non-current asset to exploit a business opportunity, the seller of the asset will normally insist on being paid in cash, probably after a short period of credit. When businesses fail, it is their inability to find the cash to pay the amounts owed that really pushes them under. These factors lead to cash being the pre-eminent business asset. Cash is what analysts tend to watch most carefully when assessing the ability of businesses to survive and/or to take advantage of commercial opportunities.

During an economic downturn, the ability to generate cash takes on even greater importance. Banks become more cautious in their lending and those businesses with weak cash flows often find it difficult to obtain finance. Real World 5.1 describes how the recent financial crisis has led to greater emphasis on cash flows.

**Real World 5.1**

### Cash is king

As the number of corporate failures has risen, there is one line that bankers continue to echo: it is not a fall in profits that leads to failure, but a lack of cash. In too many situations, companies and their investors have been focused on profits, but in an environment where liquidity is tight and confidence thin, cash is king.

'Cash management is incredibly important and even very large and stable businesses are taking it very seriously. Those that don't are doing so at their peril, as their customers and suppliers will be taking [cash] more seriously than they are,' says David Sage, working capital management partner at Ernst & Young. 'Poor cash management is one of the key reasons why nine out of ten companies fail when they do.'

While credit market conditions have improved in recent months, the retrenchment in bank lending is still a big challenge for many businesses. 'Banks are adopting more cautious lending policies and placing greater pressure on companies to mitigate cash needs through their own self-help measures,' says Ian Devlin, an associate partner in Deloitte's reorganisation services team.

Source: 'Companies learn to care for cash', *The Financial Times*, 02/10/2009 (Sakoui, A.), copyright © The Financial Times Ltd.

## The main features of the statement of cash flows

The statement of cash flows is a summary of the cash receipts and payments over the period concerned. All payments of a particular type, for example cash payments to acquire additional non-current assets or other investments, are added together to give just one figure that appears in the statement. The net total of the statement is the net increase or decrease in the cash (and cash equivalents) of the business over the period. The statement is basically an analysis of the business's cash (and cash equivalents) movements for the period.

## A definition of cash and cash equivalents

IAS 7 defines cash as notes and coins in hand and deposits in banks and similar institutions that are accessible to the business on demand. Cash equivalents are short-term, highly liquid investments that are readily convertible to known amounts of cash and which are subject to an insignificant risk of changes of value. Cash equivalents are held for the purpose of meeting short-term cash commitments rather than for investment or other purposes.

Activity 5.2 should clarify the types of items that fall within the definition of 'cash equivalents'.

## Activity 5.2

At the end of its reporting period, Zeneb plc's statement of financial position included the following items:

1 *A bank deposit account where one month's notice of withdrawal is required*. This deposit was made because the business has a temporary cash surplus that it will need to use in the short term for operating purposes.
2 *Ordinary shares in Jones plc (a Stock Exchange listed business)*. These were acquired because Zeneb plc had a temporary cash surplus and its directors believed that the share represents a good short-term investment. The funds invested will need to be used in the short term for operating purposes.
3 *A bank deposit account that is withdrawable instantly*. This represents an investment of surplus funds that are not seen as being needed in the short term.
4 *An overdraft on the business's bank current account*.

Which (if any) of these four items would be included in the figure for cash and cash equivalents?

Your response should have been as follows:

1 A cash equivalent because the deposit is part of the business's normal cash management activities and there is little doubt about how much cash will be obtained when the deposit is withdrawn.
2 Not a cash equivalent. Although the investment was made as part of normal cash management, there is a significant risk that the amount expected (hoped for!) when the shares are sold may not actually be forthcoming.
3 Not a cash equivalent because this represents an investment that will not be used to meet short-term commitments.
4 This is cash itself, though a negative amount of it. The only exception to this classification would be where the business is financed in the longer term by an overdraft, when it would be part of the financing of the business, rather than negative cash.

As can be seen from the answers to Activity 5.2, whether a particular item falls within the definition of cash and cash equivalent depends on two factors:

■ the nature of the item; and
■ why it has arisen.

In practice, it is not usually difficult to decide whether an item is a cash equivalent.

## The relationship between the main financial statements

The statement of cash flows is now accepted, along with the income statement and the statement of financial position, as a major financial statement. The relationship between the three statements is shown in Figure 5.1. The statement of financial position reflects the combination of assets (including cash) and claims (including the shareholders' equity) of the business *at a particular point in time*. The statement of cash flows and the income statement explain the *changes over a period* to two of the items in the statement of financial position. The statement of cash flows explains the changes to cash. The income statement explains changes to equity, arising from trading operations.

**Figure 5.1** The relationship between the statement of financial position, the income statement and the statement of cash flows

The statement of financial position shows the position, at a particular point in time, of the business's assets and claims. The income statement explains how, over a period between two statements of financial position, the equity figure in the first statement of financial position has altered as a result of trading operations. The statement of cash flows also looks at changes over the reporting period, but this statement explains the alteration in the cash (and cash equivalent) balances from the first to the second of the two consecutive statements of financial position.

## The form of the statement of cash flows

The standard layout of the statement of cash flows is summarised in Figure 5.2. Explanations of the terms used in the statement of cash flows are given below.

**Figure 5.2** Standard layout of the statement of cash flows

This is the standard layout for the statement of cash flows as required by IAS 7 *Statement of cash flows*.

## Cash flows from operating activities

This is the net inflow or outflow from trading operations, after tax payments (or receipts) and cash paid to meet financing costs. It is equal to the sum of cash receipts from trade receivables and cash receipts from cash sales, where relevant, less the sums paid to buy inventories, to pay rent, to pay wages and so on. From this are also deducted payments for interest on the business's borrowings, corporation tax and dividends paid.

Note that it is the amounts of cash received and paid during the period that feature in the statement of cash flows, not the revenue and expenses for that period. It is, of course, the income statement that deals with the revenue and expenses. Similarly the tax and dividend payments that appear in the statement of cash flows are those made during the reporting period of the statement. Companies normally pay tax on their profits in four equal instalments. Two of these are during the annual reporting period concerned and the other two are during the following year. As a result, by the end of each annual reporting period, half of the tax will have been paid and the remainder will be a current liability at the end of the year, to be paid off during the following year. During any annual reporting period, therefore, the tax payment would normally equal 50 per cent of the previous year's tax charge and 50 per cent of that of the current year.

The net figure for this section is intended to indicate the net cash flows for the period that arose from normal day-to-day trading activities, after taking account of the tax that has to be paid on them and the cost of servicing the finance (equity and borrowings) needed to support them.

## Cash flows from investing activities

This section of the statement is concerned with cash payments made to acquire additional non-current assets and with cash receipts from the disposal of non-current assets. These non-current assets will tend to be the usual items such as buildings and machinery. They might also be loans made by the business or shares in another company bought by the business.

This section also includes cash receipts *arising from* financial investments (loans and equities) made outside the business. These receipts are interest on loans made by the business and dividends from shares in other companies that are owned by the business.

## Cash flows from financing activities

This part of the statement is concerned with the long-term financing of the business. So here we are considering borrowings (other than very short–term) and finance from share issues. This category is concerned with repayment/redemption of finance as well as with the raising of it. It is permissible under IAS 7 to include dividend payments made by the business here, as an alternative to including them in 'Cash flows from operating activities'.

This section shows the net cash flows from raising and/or paying back long-term finance.

## Net increase or decrease in cash and cash equivalents

The total of the statement must, of course, be the net increase or decrease in cash and cash equivalents over the period concerned.

The effect on a business's cash and cash equivalents of its various activities is shown in Figure 5.3. As explained there, the arrows show the *normal* direction of cash flow for the typical healthy, profitable business in a typical year.

**Figure 5.3 Diagrammatical representation of the statement of cash flows**

Various activities of the business each have their own effect on its cash and cash equivalent balances, either positive (increasing them) or negative (reducing them). The net increase or decrease in the cash and cash equivalent balances over a period will be the sum of these individual effects, taking account of the direction (cash in or cash out) of each activity.

Note that the direction of the arrow shows the *normal* direction of the cash flow in respect of each activity. In certain circumstances, each of these arrows could be reversed in direction.

## The normal direction of cash flows

Normally 'operating activities' provide positive cash flows, that is, they help to increase the business's cash resources. In fact, for most UK businesses, in most time periods, cash generated from day-to-day trading, even after deducting tax, interest and dividends, is overwhelmingly the most important source of new finance.

### Activity 5.3

Last year's statement of cash flows for Angus plc showed a negative cash flow from operating activities. What could be the reason for this and should the business's management be alarmed by it? (*Hint*: We think that there are two broad possible reasons for a negative cash flow.)

The two reasons are:

■ The business is unprofitable. This leads to more cash being paid out to employees, to suppliers of goods and services, for interest and so on than is received from trade receivables in respect of sales. This would be particularly alarming, because a major expense for most businesses is depreciation of non-current assets. Since depreciation does not lead to a cash flow, it is not considered in 'net cash inflows from operating activities'. This means that a negative operating cash flow might well indicate a very much larger trading loss – in other words, a significant loss of the business's wealth; something to concern management.

■ The other reason might be less alarming. A business that is expanding its activities (level of sales revenue) would tend to spend quite a lot of cash relative to the amount of cash coming in from sales. This is because it will probably be expanding its assets (non-current and current) to accommodate the increased demand. For example, a business may well need to have inventories in place before additional sales can be made. Similarly staff have to be employed and paid. Even when the additional sales are made, those sales would normally be made on credit, with the cash inflow lagging behind the sale. All of this means that, in the first instance, in cash flow terms, the business would not necessarily benefit from the additional sales revenue. This is particularly likely to be true of a new business, which would be expanding inventories and other assets from zero. It would also need to employ and pay staff. Expansion typically causes cash flow strains for the reasons just explained. This can be a particular problem because the business's increased profitability might encourage a feeling of optimism, which could lead to lack of attention being paid to the cash flow problem.

Investing activities typically cause net negative cash flows. This is because many types of non-current asset wear out and many that do not wear out become obsolete. Also, businesses tend to seek to expand their asset base. When a business sells some non-current assets, the sale will give rise to positive cash flows, but in net terms the cash flows are normally negative with cash spent on new assets outweighing that received from disposal of old ones.

Financing can go in either direction, depending on the financing strategy at the time. Since businesses seek to expand, there is a general tendency for this area to lead to cash coming into the business rather than leaving it.

Real World 5.2 shows the summarised statement of cash flows of Tesco plc, the UK-based supermarket.

---

**Real World 5.2**

## Cashing in

Like many larger companies, Tesco produces summary versions of its financial statements for users who do not want all of the detail. The summary statement of cash flows for the business for the year ended 28 February 2009 shows the cash flows of the business under each of the headings described above.

### Summarised statement of cash flows for the year ended 28 February 2009

|  | £m |
|---|---|
| Cash generated from operations | 4,978 |
| Interest paid | (562) |
| Corporation tax paid | (456) |
| **Net cash from operating activities** | 3,960 |
| **Net cash used in investing activities** | (5,974) |
| **Cash flows from financing activities** | |
| Dividends paid | (883) |
| Other net cash flows from financing activities | 4,498 |
| **Net cash from financing activities** | 3,615 |
| **Net increase in cash and cash equivalents** | 1,601 |

Source: Tesco Annual Review 2009, www.tescocorporate.com, p. 24.

---

As we shall see shortly, more detailed information under each of the main headings is provided in the statement of cash flows presented to shareholders and other users.

# Preparing the statement of cash flows

## Deducing net cash flows from operating activities

The first section of the statement of cash flows is the 'cash flows from operating activities'. There are two approaches that can be taken to deriving this figure: the direct method and the indirect method.

### The direct method

→ The direct method involves an analysis of the cash records of the business for the period, picking out all payments and receipts relating to operating activities. These are summarised to give the total figures for inclusion in the statement of cash flows. Done on a computer, this is a simple matter, but not many businesses adopt the direct method.

### The indirect method

→ The indirect method is the more popular method. It relies on the fact that, broadly, sales revenue gives rise to cash inflows and expenses give rise to outflows. This means that the profit for the year figure will be closely linked to the net cash flows from operating activities. Since businesses have to produce an income statement in any case, information from it can be used as a starting point to deduce the cash flows from operating activities.

Of course, within a particular reporting period, profit for the year will not normally equal the net cash inflows from operating activities. We saw in Chapter 3 that, when sales are made on credit, the cash receipt occurs some time after the sale. This means that sales revenue made towards the end of an annual reporting period will be included in that year's income statement. However, most of the cash from those sales will flow into the business, and should be included in the statement of cash flows, in the following year. Fortunately it is easy to deduce the cash received from sales if we have the relevant income statement and statements of financial position, as we shall see in Activity 5.4.

### Activity 5.4

How can we deduce the cash inflows from sales using the income statement and statement of financial position for the business?

The statement of financial position will tell us how much was owed in respect of credit sales at the beginning and end of the year (trade receivables). The income statement tells us the sales revenue figure. If we adjust the sales revenue figure by the increase or decrease in trade receivables over the year, we deduce the cash from sales for the year.

### Example 5.1

The sales revenue figure for a business for the year was £34 million. The trade receivables totalled £4 million at the beginning of the year, but had increased to £5 million by the end of the year.

Basically, the trade receivables figure is dictated by sales revenue and cash receipts. It increases when a sale is made and decreases when cash is received from a credit customer. If, over the year, the sales revenue and the cash receipts had been equal, the beginning-of-year and end-of-year trade receivables figures would have been equal. Since the trade receivables figure increased, it must mean that less cash was received than sales revenues were made. This means that the cash receipts from sales must be £33 million (that is, 34 – (5 – 4)).

Put slightly differently, we can say that as a result of sales, assets of £34 million flowed into the business during the year. If £1 million of this went to increasing the asset of trade receivables, this leaves only £33 million that went to increase cash.

The same general point is true in respect of nearly all of the other items that are taken into account in deducing the operating profit figure. The exception is depreciation. This is not necessarily associated with any movement in cash during the reporting period.

All of this means that we can take the profit before taxation (that is, the profit after interest but before taxation) for the year, add back the depreciation and interest expense, charged in arriving at that profit, and adjust this total by movements in inventories, trade (and other) receivables and payables. If we then go on to deduct payments made during the reporting period for taxation, interest on borrowings and dividends, we have the net cash from operating activities.

## Example 5.2

The relevant information from the financial statements of Dido plc for last year is as follows:

|  | £m |
|---|---|
| Profit before taxation (after interest) | 122 |
| Depreciation charged in arriving at profit before taxation | 34 |
| Interest expense | 6 |
| At the beginning of the year: | |
| Inventories | 15 |
| Trade receivables | 24 |
| Trade payables | 18 |
| At the end of the year: | |
| Inventories | 17 |
| Trade receivables | 21 |
| Trade payables | 19 |

The following further information is available about payments during last year:

|  | £m |
|---|---|
| Taxation paid | 32 |
| Interest paid | 5 |
| Dividends paid | 9 |

→

169

The cash flow from operating activities is derived as follows:

|  | £m |
|---|---|
| Profit before taxation (after interest) | 122 |
| Depreciation | 34 |
| Interest expense | 6 |
| Increase in inventories (17 − 15) | (2) |
| Decrease in trade receivables (21 − 24) | 3 |
| Increase in trade payables (19 − 18) | 1 |
| **Cash generated from operating activities** | 164 |
| Interest paid | (5) |
| Taxation paid | (32) |
| Dividends paid | (9) |
| **Net cash from operating activities** | 118 |

As we can see, the net increase in working capital* (that is, current assets less current liabilities), as a result of trading, was £162 million (that is, 122 + 34 + 6). Of this, £2 million went into increased inventories. More cash was received from trade receivables than sales revenue was made. Similarly, less cash was paid to trade payables than purchases were made of goods and services on credit. Both of these had a favourable effect on cash. Over the year, therefore, cash increased by £164 million. When account was taken of the payments for interest, tax and dividends, the net cash from operating activities was £118 million (inflow).

Note that we needed to adjust the profit before taxation (after interest) by the depreciation and interest expenses to derive the profit before depreciation, interest and taxation.

* Working capital is a term widely used in accounting and finance, not just in the context of the statement of cash flows. We shall encounter it several times in later chapters.

We should be clear why it is necessary to add back an amount for interest at the start of the derivation of cash flow from operating activities only to deduct an amount for interest further down. The reason is that the first is the interest expense for the year, whereas the second is the amount of cash paid out for interest during the year. These may well be different amounts, as was the case in Example 5.2.

The indirect method of deducing the net cash flow from operating activities is summarised in Figure 5.4.

**Figure 5.4** The indirect method of deducing the net cash flows from operating activities

Determining the net cash flow from operating activities first involves adding back the depreciation and the interest expenses to the profit before taxation. Next, adjustment is made for increases or decreases in inventories, trade receivables and trade payables. Lastly, cash paid for interest, taxation and dividends is deducted.

\* Note that dividends could alternatively be included under the heading 'Cash flows from financing activities'.

## Activity 5.5

The relevant information from the financial statements of Pluto plc for last year is as follows:

|  | £m |
|---|---|
| Profit before taxation (after interest) | 165 |
| Depreciation charged in arriving at operating profit | 41 |
| Interest expense | 21 |
| At the beginning of the year: | |
|   Inventories | 22 |
|   Trade receivables | 18 |
|   Trade payables | 15 |
| At the end of the year: | |
|   Inventories | 23 |
|   Trade receivables | 21 |
|   Trade payables | 17 |

The following further information is available about payments during last year:

|  | £m |
|---|---|
| Taxation paid | 49 |
| Interest paid | 25 |
| Dividends paid | 28 |

What figure should appear in the statement of cash flows for 'Cash flows from operating activities'?

Net cash inflows from operating activities:

|  | £m |
|---|---|
| Profit before taxation (after interest) | 165 |
| Depreciation | 41 |
| Interest expense | 21 |
| Increase in inventories (23 − 22) | (1) |
| Increase in trade receivables (21 − 18) | (3) |
| Increase in trade payables (17 − 15) | 2 |
| **Cash generated from operating activities** | 225 |
| Interest paid | (25) |
| Taxation paid | (49) |
| Dividends paid | (28) |
| **Net cash from operating activities** | 123 |

## Deducing the other areas of the statement of cash flows

We can now go on to take a look at the preparation of a complete statement of cash flows through Example 5.3.

## Example 5.3

Torbryan plc's income statement for the year ended 31 December 2010 and the statements of financial position as at 31 December 2009 and 2010 are as follows:

### Income statement for the year ended 31 December 2010

|  | £m |
|---|---|
| Revenue | 576 |
| Cost of sales | (307) |
| **Gross profit** | 269 |
| Distribution expenses | (65) |
| Administrative expenses | (26) |
|  | 178 |
| Other operating income | 21 |
| **Operating profit** | 199 |
| Interest receivable | 17 |
|  | 216 |
| Interest payable | (23) |
| **Profit before taxation** | 193 |
| Taxation | (46) |
| **Profit for the year** | 147 |

### Statements of financial position as at 31 December 2009 and 2010

|  | 2009 £m | 2010 £m |
|---|---|---|
| **ASSETS** | | |
| **Non-current assets** | | |
| *Property, plant and equipment* | | |
| Land and buildings | 241 | 241 |
| Plant and machinery | 309 | 325 |
|  | 550 | 566 |
| **Current assets** | | |
| Inventories | 44 | 41 |
| Trade receivables | 121 | 139 |
|  | 165 | 180 |
| **Total assets** | 715 | 746 |
| **EQUITY AND LIABILITIES** | | |
| **Equity** | | |
| Called-up ordinary share capital | 150 | 200 |
| Share premium account | – | 40 |
| Retained earnings | 26 | 123 |
|  | 176 | 363 |
| **Non-current liabilities** | | |
| Borrowings – loan notes | 400 | 250 |
| **Current liabilities** | | |
| Borrowings (all bank overdraft) | 68 | 56 |
| Trade payables | 55 | 54 |
| Taxation | 16 | 23 |
|  | 139 | 133 |
| **Total equity and liabilities** | 715 | 746 |

→

During 2010, the business spent £95 million on additional plant and machinery. There were no other non-current-asset acquisitions or disposals. A dividend of £50 million was paid on ordinary shares during the year. The interest receivable revenue and the interest payable expense for the year were equal to the cash inflow and outflow respectively.

The statement of cash flows would be as follows:

**Torbryan plc**
**Statement of cash flows for the year ended 31 December 2010**

| | £m |
|---|---:|
| *Cash flows from operating activities* | |
| Profit before taxation (after interest) (see Note 1 below) | 193 |
| Adjustments for: | |
| Depreciation (Note 2) | 79 |
| Interest receivable (Note 3) | (17) |
| Interest payable (Note 4) | 23 |
| Increase in trade receivables (139 – 121) | (18) |
| Decrease in trade payables (55 – 54) | (1) |
| Decrease in inventories (44 – 41) | 3 |
| **Cash generated from operations** | 262 |
| Interest paid | (23) |
| Taxation paid (Note 5) | (39) |
| Dividend paid | (50) |
| **Net cash from operating activities** | 150 |
| *Cash flows from investing activities* | |
| Payments to acquire tangible non-current assets | (95) |
| Interest received (Note 3) | 17 |
| **Net cash used in investing activities** | (78) |
| *Cash flows from financing activities* | |
| Repayments of loan notes (Note 6) | (150) |
| Issue of ordinary shares (Note 7) | 90 |
| **Net cash used in financing activities** | (60) |
| **Net increase in cash and cash equivalents** | 12 |
| Cash and cash equivalents at 1 January 2010 (Note 8) | (68) |
| **Cash and cash equivalents at 31 December 2010** | (56) |

To see how this relates to the cash of the business at the beginning and end of the year it can be useful to provide a reconciliation as follows:

**Analysis of cash and cash equivalents during the year ended**
**31 December 2010**

| | £m |
|---|---:|
| Overdraft balance at 1 January 2010 | (68) |
| Net cash inflow | 12 |
| Overdraft balance at 31 December 2010 | (56) |

Notes:

1 This is simply taken from the income statement for the year.

2 Since there were no disposals, the depreciation charges must be the difference between the start and end of the year's plant and machinery (non-current assets) values, adjusted by the cost of any additions.

|  | £m |
|---|---|
| Carrying amount at 1 January 2010 | 309 |
| Additions | 95 |
|  | 404 |
| Depreciation (balancing figure) | (79) |
| Carrying amount at 31 December 2010 | 325 |

3 Interest receivable must be taken away to work towards the profit before crediting it, because it is not part of operations but of investing activities. The cash inflow from this source appears under the 'Cash flows from investing activities' heading.

4 Interest payable expense must be taken out, by adding it back to the profit figure. We subsequently deduct the cash paid for interest payable during the year. In this case the two figures are identical.

5 Taxation is paid by companies 50 per cent during their annual reporting period and 50 per cent in the following period. As a result the 2010 payment would have been half the tax on the 2009 profit (that is, the figure that would have appeared in the current liabilities at the end of 2009), plus half of the 2010 taxation charge (that is, $16 + (\frac{1}{2} \times 46) = 39$). Probably the easiest way to deduce the amount paid during the year to 31 December 2010 is by following this approach:

|  | £m |
|---|---|
| Taxation owed at start of the year (from the statement of financial position as at 31 December 2009) | 16 |
| Taxation charge for the year (from the income statement) | 46 |
|  | 62 |
| Taxation owed at the end of the year (from the statement of financial position as at 31 December 2010) | (23) |
| Taxation paid during the year | 39 |

This follows the logic that if we start with what the business owed at the beginning of the year, add the increase in what was owed as a result of the current year's taxation charge and then deduct what was owed at the end, the resulting figure must be what was paid during the year.

6 It has been assumed that the loan notes were redeemed for the value shown on the statement of financial position. This is not, however, always the case.

7 The share issue raised £90 million, of which £50 million went into the share capital total on the statement of financial position and £40 million into share premium.

8 There were no 'cash equivalents', just cash (though negative).

## What does the statement of cash flows tell us?

The statement of cash flows tells us how the business has generated cash during the reporting period and where that cash has gone. Since cash is properly regarded as the lifeblood of just about any business, this is potentially very useful information.

Tracking the sources and uses of cash over several years could show financing trends that a reader of the statements could use to help to make judgements about the likely future behaviour of the business.

Looking specifically at the statement of cash flows for Torbryan plc in Example 5.3, we can see the following:

■ Net cash flow from operations was strong, much larger than the profit for the year figure, after taking account of the dividend paid. This would be expected because depreciation is deducted in arriving at profit. Working capital has absorbed some cash, which would be unsurprising if there had been an expansion of activity (sales revenue) over the year. From the information supplied, however, we do not know whether there was an expansion or not. (We have only one year's income statement.)

■ There was a net outflow of cash for investing activities, but this would not be unusual. Many items of property, plant and equipment have limited lives and need to be replaced with new ones. The expenditure during the year was not out of line with the depreciation expense for the year, which is to be expected for a business with a regular replacement programme for non-current assets.

■ There was a fairly major outflow of cash to redeem some borrowings, partly offset by the proceeds of a share issue. This presumably represents a change of financing strategy. Together with the ploughed-back profit from trading, there has been a significant shift in the equity/borrowings balance.

Real World 5.3 looks at the statement of cash flows of an emerging business, LiDCO Group plc, that is experiencing negative cash flows as it seeks to establish a profitable market for its products.

### Real World 5.3

## Not losing heart

LiDCO Group plc has its shares listed on the Alternative Investment Market (AIM). AIM is a junior market of the London Stock Exchange that specialises in the shares of smaller, up-and-coming businesses.

LiDCO makes highly sophisticated equipment for monitoring the hearts of cardiac patients, typically in hospitals and clinics. The business was started by doctors and scientists. It has spent £6.8 million over ten years developing its products, obtaining registration for their use from both the UK and US authorities and creating manufacturing facilities.

LiDCO's statement of cash flows for the year to 31 January 2009 was as follows:

|  | £000 |
|---|---|
| Net cash outflow from operating activities | (1,204) |
| *Cash flows from investing activities* | |
| Purchase of property, plant and equipment | (208) |
| Purchase of intangible fixed assets | (447) |
| Interest received | 57 |
| Net cash used in investing activities | (598) |
| *Cash flows from financing activities* | |
| Convertible loan repayment | (553) |
| Invoice discounting financing facility | 364 |
| Net cash outflow from financing activities | (189) |
| Net decrease in cash and cash equivalents | (1,991) |

[Note that this was adapted from the statement that appeared in the business's annual report. Some more detail was supplied in the way of notes to the accounts.]

To put these figures into context, the sales revenue for the year was £4.53 million. This means that the net cash outflow from operating activities was equal to 27 per cent of the revenue figure. (This was an improvement, since it was 30 per cent in 2008, nearly 40 per cent in 2007 and over 50 per cent in 2006.) Such cash flow profiles are fairly typical of 'high-tech' businesses that have enormous start-up costs to bring their products to the market in sufficient quantities to yield a profit. Of course, not all such businesses achieve this, but LiDCO seems confident of success.

*Sources*: LiDCO Group plc Annual Report 2009 and AIM company profile, www.londonstockexchange.com.

## ? Self-assessment question 5.1

Touchstone plc's income statements for the years ended 31 December 2009 and 2010 and the statements of financial position as at 31 December 2009 and 2010 are as follows:

### Income statements for the years ended 2009 and 2010

|  | 2009 £m | 2010 £m |
|---|---|---|
| Revenue | 173 | 207 |
| Cost of sales | (96) | (101) |
| Gross profit | 77 | 106 |
| Distribution expenses | (18) | (20) |
| Administrative expenses | (24) | (26) |
| Other operating income | 3 | 4 |
| Operating profit | 38 | 64 |
| Interest payable | (2) | (4) |
| Profit before taxation | 36 | 60 |
| Taxation | (8) | (16) |
| Profit for the year | 28 | 44 |

### Statements of financial position as at 31 December 2009 and 2010

|  | 2009 £m | 2010 £m |
|---|---|---|
| **ASSETS** | | |
| **Non-current assets** | | |
| *Property, plant and equipment* | | |
| Land and buildings | 94 | 110 |
| Plant and machinery | 53 | 62 |
|  | 147 | 172 |
| **Current assets** | | |
| Inventories | 25 | 24 |
| Treasury bills (short-term investments) | – | 15 |
| Trade receivables | 16 | 26 |
| Cash at bank and in hand | 4 | 4 |
|  | 45 | 69 |
| Total assets | 192 | 241 |

→

|  | 2009 £m | 2010 £m |
|---|---|---|
| **EQUITY AND LIABILITIES** | | |
| **Equity** | | |
| Called-up ordinary share capital | 100 | 100 |
| Retained earnings | 30 | 56 |
|  | 130 | 156 |
| **Non-current liabilities** | | |
| Borrowings – loan notes (10%) | 20 | 40 |
| **Current liabilities** | | |
| Trade payables | 38 | 37 |
| Taxation | 4 | 8 |
|  | 42 | 45 |
| **Total equity and liabilities** | 192 | 241 |

Included in 'cost of sales', 'distribution expenses' and 'administrative expenses', depreciation was as follows:

|  | 2009 £m | 2010 £m |
|---|---|---|
| Land and buildings | 5 | 6 |
| Plant and machinery | 6 | 10 |

There were no non-current asset disposals in either year.

The interest payable expense equalled the cash payment made during the year, in both cases.

The business paid dividends on ordinary shares of £14 million during 2009 and £18 million during 2010.

The Treasury bills represent a short-term investment of funds that will be used shortly in operations. There is insignificant risk that this investment will lose value.

**Required:**
Prepare a statement of cash flows for the business for 2010.

**The solution to this question can be found at the back of the book, in Appendix B.**

## Summary

The main points of this chapter may be summarised as follows.

### The need for a statement of cash flows

■ Cash is important because no business can operate without it.

■ The statement of cash flows is specifically designed to reveal movements in cash over a period.

■ Cash movements cannot be readily detected from the income statement, which focuses on revenue and expenses rather than on cash receipts and cash payments.

- Profit (or loss) and cash generated for the period are rarely equal.
- The statement of cash flows is a primary financial statement, along with the income statement and the statement of financial position.

## Preparing the statement of cash flows

- The layout of the statement contains three categories of cash movement:
  - cash flows from operating activities;
  - cash flows from investing activities;
  - cash flows from financing activities.
- The total of the cash movements under these three categories will provide the net increase or decrease in cash and cash equivalents for the period.
- A reconciliation can be undertaken to check that the opening balance of cash and cash equivalents plus the net increase (or decrease) for the period equals the closing balance.

## Calculating the cash generated from operations

- The net cash flows from operating activities can be derived by either the direct method or the indirect method.
- The direct method is based on an analysis of the cash records for the period, whereas the indirect method uses information contained within the income statement and statements of financial position of the business.
- The indirect method takes the net operating profit for the period, adds back any depreciation charge and then adjusts for changes in inventories, receivables and payables during the period.

## Interpreting the statement of cash flows

- The statement of cash flows shows the main sources and uses of cash.
- Tracking the cash movements over several periods may reveal financing and investing patterns and may help predict future management action.

 **Now check your progress in your personal Study Plan**

 **Key terms**

direct method p. 168
indirect method p. 168
working capital p. 170

## Further reading

If you would like to explore the topics covered in this chapter in more depth, we recommend the following books:

Elliott, B. and Elliott, J., *Financial Accounting and Reporting* (13th edn), Financial Times Prentice Hall, 2010, chapter 27.
IASC Foundation Education, *A Guide through IFRS 2009*, July 2009, IAS 7.
KPMG, *Insights into IFRS* (6th edn 2009/10), Sweet and Maxwell, 2009, section 2.3.

## ? Review questions

**Solutions to these questions can be found at the back of the book, in Appendix C.**

**5.1** The typical business outside the service sector has about 50 per cent more of its resources tied up in inventories than in cash, yet there is no call for a 'statement of inventories flows' to be prepared. Why is cash regarded as more important than inventories?

**5.2** What is the difference between the direct and indirect methods of deducing cash generated from operations?

**5.3** Taking each of the categories of the statement of cash flows in turn, in which direction would you normally expect the cash flow to be? Explain your answer.

(a) Cash flows from operating activities.
(b) Cash flows from investing activities.
(c) Cash flows from financing activities.

**5.4** What causes the profit for the year not to equal the net cash inflow?

## ✳ Exercises

**Exercises 5.3 to 5.5 are more advanced than 5.1 and 5.2. Those with coloured numbers have solutions at the back of the book, in Appendix D.**

> If you wish to try more exercises, visit the website at www.myaccountinglab.com.

**5.1** How will each of the following events ultimately affect the amount of cash?

(a) An increase in the level of inventories.
(b) A rights issue of ordinary shares.
(c) A bonus issue of ordinary shares.
(d) Writing off part of the value of some inventories.

(e) The disposal of a large number of the business's shares by a major shareholder.

(f) Depreciating a non-current asset.

**5.2** The following information has been taken from the financial statements of Juno plc for last year and the year before last:

|  | Year before last £m | Last year £m |
|---|---|---|
| Operating profit | 156 | 187 |
| Depreciation charged in arriving at operating profit | 47 | 55 |
| Inventories held at the end of: | 27 | 31 |
| Trade receivables at the end of: | 24 | 23 |
| Trade payables at the end of: | 15 | 17 |

**Required:**

What is the figure for cash generated from operations for Juno plc for last year?

**5.3** Torrent plc's income statement for the year ended 31 December 2010 and the statements of financial position as at 31 December 2009 and 2010 are as follows:

### Income statement for the year ended 31 December 2010

|  | £m |
|---|---|
| Revenue | 623 |
| Cost of sales | (353) |
| **Gross profit** | 270 |
| Distribution expenses | (71) |
| Administrative expenses | (30) |
| Rental income | 27 |
| **Operating profit** | 196 |
| Interest payable | (26) |
| **Profit before taxation** | 170 |
| Taxation | (36) |
| **Profit for the year** | 134 |

### Statements of financial position as at 31 December 2009 and 2010

|  | 2009 £m | 2010 £m |
|---|---|---|
| **ASSETS** | | |
| **Non-current assets** | | |
| *Property, plant and equipment* | | |
| Land and buildings | 310 | 310 |
| Plant and machinery | 325 | 314 |
|  | 635 | 624 |
| **Current assets** | | |
| Inventories | 41 | 35 |
| Trade receivables | 139 | 145 |
|  | 180 | 180 |
| **Total assets** | 815 | 804 |

→

|  | 2009 £m | 2010 £m |
|---|---|---|
| **EQUITY AND LIABILITIES** | | |
| **Equity** | | |
| Called-up ordinary share capital | 200 | 300 |
| Share premium account | 40 | – |
| Revaluation reserve | 69 | 9 |
| Retained earnings | 123 | 197 |
|  | 432 | 506 |
| **Non-current liabilities** | | |
| Borrowings – loan notes | 250 | 150 |
| **Current liabilities** | | |
| Borrowings (all bank overdraft) | 56 | 89 |
| Trade payables | 54 | 41 |
| Taxation | 23 | 18 |
|  | 133 | 148 |
| **Total equity and liabilities** | 815 | 804 |

During 2010, the business spent £67 million on additional plant and machinery. There were no other non-current asset acquisitions or disposals.

There was no share issue for cash during the year. The interest payable expense was equal in amount to the cash outflow. A dividend of £60 million was paid.

**Required:**
Prepare the statement of cash flows for Torrent plc for the year ended 31 December 2010.

**5.4**   Chen plc's income statements for the years ended 31 December 2009 and 2010 and the statements of financial position as at 31 December 2009 and 2010 are as follows:

**Income statements for the years ending 31 December 2009 and 2010**

|  | 2009 £m | 2010 £m |
|---|---|---|
| Revenue | 207 | 153 |
| Cost of sales | (101) | (76) |
| **Gross profit** | 106 | 77 |
| Distribution expenses | (22) | (20) |
| Administrative expenses | (20) | (28) |
| **Operating profit** | 64 | 29 |
| Interest payable | (4) | (4) |
| **Profit before taxation** | 60 | 25 |
| Taxation | (16) | (6) |
| **Profit for the year** | 44 | 19 |

**Statements of financial position as at 31 December 2009 and 2010**

|  | 2009 £m | 2010 £m |
|---|---|---|
| **ASSETS** | | |
| **Non-current assets** | | |
| *Property, plant and equipment* | | |
| Land and buildings | 110 | 130 |
| Plant and machinery | 62 | 56 |
| | 172 | 186 |
| **Current assets** | | |
| Inventories | 24 | 25 |
| Trade receivables | 26 | 25 |
| Cash at bank and in hand | 19 | – |
| | 69 | 50 |
| **Total assets** | 241 | 236 |
| **EQUITY AND LIABILITIES** | | |
| **Equity** | | |
| Called-up ordinary share capital | 100 | 100 |
| Retained earnings | 56 | 57 |
| | 156 | 157 |
| **Non-current liabilities** | | |
| Borrowings – loan notes (10%) | 40 | 40 |
| **Current liabilities** | | |
| Borrowings (all bank overdraft) | – | 2 |
| Trade payables | 37 | 34 |
| Taxation | 8 | 3 |
| | 45 | 39 |
| **Total equity and liabilities** | 241 | 236 |

Included in 'cost of sales', 'distribution expenses' and 'administrative expenses', depreciation was as follows:

|  | 2009 £m | 2010 £m |
|---|---|---|
| Land and buildings | 6 | 10 |
| Plant and machinery | 10 | 12 |

There were no non-current asset disposals in either year. The amount of cash paid for interest equalled the expense in both years. Dividends were paid totalling £18 million in each year.

**Required:**
Prepare a statement of cash flows for the business for 2010.

$\rightarrow$

**5.5** The following financial statements for Brownstone plc are a slightly simplified set of published accounts. Brownstone plc is an engineering business that developed a new range of products in 2007. These products now account for 60 per cent of its turnover.

### Income statement for the years ended 31 March

|  | Notes | 2009 £m | 2010 £m |
|---|---|---|---|
| Revenue |  | 7,003 | 11,205 |
| Cost of sales |  | (3,748) | (5,809) |
| **Gross profit** |  | 3,255 | 5,396 |
| Operating expenses |  | (2,205) | (3,087) |
| **Operating profit** |  | 1,050 | 2,309 |
| Interest payable | 1 | (216) | (456) |
| **Profit before taxation** |  | 834 | 1,853 |
| Taxation |  | (210) | (390) |
| **Profit for the year** |  | 624 | 1,463 |

### Statements of financial position as at 31 March

|  | Notes | 2009 £m | 2010 £m |
|---|---|---|---|
| **ASSETS** |  |  |  |
| **Non-current assets** |  |  |  |
| *Property, plant and equipment* | 2 | 4,300 | 7,535 |
| Intangible assets | 3 | – | 700 |
|  |  | 4,300 | 8,235 |
| **Current assets** |  |  |  |
| Inventories |  | 1,209 | 2,410 |
| Trade receivables |  | 641 | 1,173 |
| Cash at bank |  | 123 | – |
|  |  | 1,973 | 3,583 |
| **Total assets** |  | 6,273 | 11,818 |
| **EQUITY AND LIABILITIES** |  |  |  |
| **Equity** |  |  |  |
| Share capital |  | 1,800 | 1,800 |
| Share premium |  | 600 | 600 |
| Capital reserves |  | 352 | 352 |
| Retained profits |  | 685 | 1,748 |
|  |  | 3,437 | 4,500 |
| **Non-current liabilities** |  |  |  |
| Borrowings – bank loan (repayable 2013) |  | 1,800 | 3,800 |
| **Current liabilities** |  |  |  |
| Trade payables |  | 931 | 1,507 |
| Taxation |  | 105 | 195 |
| Borrowings (all bank overdraft) |  | – | 1,816 |
|  |  | 1,036 | 3,518 |
| **Total equity and liabilities** |  | 6,273 | 11,818 |

Notes:

1 The expense and the cash outflow for interest payable are equal.

2 The movements in property, plant and equipment during the year are set out below.

|  | Land and buildings £m | Plant and machinery £m | Fixtures and fittings £m | Total £m |
|---|---|---|---|---|
| **Cost** |  |  |  |  |
| At 1 April 2009 | 4,500 | 3,850 | 2,120 | 10,470 |
| Additions | – | 2,970 | 1,608 | 4,578 |
| Disposals | – | (365) | (216) | (581) |
| At 31 March 2010 | 4,500 | 6,455 | 3,512 | 14,467 |
| **Depreciation** |  |  |  |  |
| At 1 April 2009 | 1,275 | 3,080 | 1,815 | 6,170 |
| Charge for year | 225 | 745 | 281 | 1,251 |
| Disposals | – | (305) | (184) | (489) |
| At 31 March 2010 | 1,500 | 3,520 | 1,912 | 6,932 |
| **Carrying amount** |  |  |  |  |
| At 31 March 2010 | 3,000 | 2,935 | 1,600 | 7,535 |

3 Intangible assets represent the amounts paid for the goodwill of another engineering business acquired during the year.

4 Proceeds from the sale of non-current assets in the year ended 31 March 2010 amounted to £54 million.

5 Dividends were paid on ordinary shares of £300 million in 2009 and £400 million in 2010.

**Required:**

Prepare a statement of cash flows for Brownstone plc for the year ended 31 March 2010. (*Hint*: A loss (deficit) on disposal of non-current assets is simply an additional amount of depreciation and should be dealt with as such in preparing the statement of cash flows.)

## Chapter 6

# Analysing and interpreting financial statements

## Introduction

In this chapter we shall consider the analysis and interpretation of the financial statements that we discussed in Chapters 2 and 3. We shall see how financial (or accounting) ratios can help in assessing the financial health of a business. We shall also consider the problems that are encountered when applying this technique.

Financial ratios can be used to examine various aspects of financial position and performance and are widely used for planning and control purposes. They can be very helpful to managers in a wide variety of decision areas, such as profit planning, pricing, working capital management and financial structure.

## Learning outcomes

**When you have completed this chapter, you should be able to:**

■ identify the major categories of ratios that can be used for analysis purposes;

■ calculate key ratios for assessing the financial performance and position of a business;

■ explain the significance of the ratios calculated;

■ discuss the limitations of ratios as a tool of financial analysis.

*MyAccountingLab* **Remember to create your own personalised Study Plan**

# Financial ratios

Financial ratios provide a quick and relatively simple means of assessing the financial health of a business. A ratio simply relates one figure appearing in the financial statements to some other figure appearing there (for example, operating profit in relation to the amount invested in the business (capital employed)) or, perhaps, to some resource of the business (for example, operating profit per employee, sales revenue per square metre of selling space and so on).

Ratios can be very helpful when comparing the financial health of different businesses. Differences may exist between businesses in the scale of operations. This means that a direct comparison of, say, the operating profit generated by each business may be misleading. By expressing operating profit in relation to some other measure (for example, capital employed), the problem of scale is eliminated. A business with an operating profit of, say, £10,000 and capital employed of £100,000 can be compared with a much larger business with an operating profit of, say, £80,000 and capital employed of £1,000,000 by the use of a simple ratio. The operating profit to capital employed ratio for the smaller business is 10 per cent (that is, (10,000/100,000) × 100%) and the same ratio for the larger business is 8 per cent (that is, (80,000/1,000,000) × 100%). These ratios can be directly compared whereas comparison of the absolute operating profit figures would be much less meaningful. The need to eliminate differences in scale through the use of ratios can also apply when comparing the performance of the same business over time.

By calculating a small number of ratios it is often possible to build up a revealing picture of the position and performance of a business. It is not surprising, therefore, that ratios are widely used by those who have an interest in businesses and business performance. Although ratios are not difficult to calculate, they can be difficult to interpret. It is important to appreciate that they are really only the starting point for further analysis.

Ratios help to highlight the financial strengths and weaknesses of a business, but they cannot, by themselves, explain why those strengths or weaknesses exist or why certain changes have occurred. Only a detailed investigation will reveal these underlying reasons. Ratios tend to enable us to know which questions to ask, rather than provide the answers.

Ratios can be expressed in various forms, for example as a percentage or as a proportion. The way that a particular ratio is presented will depend on the needs of those who will use the information. Although it is possible to calculate a large number of ratios, only a few, based on key relationships, tend to be helpful to a particular user. Many ratios that could be calculated from the financial statements (for example, rent payable in relation to current assets) may not be considered because there is no clear or meaningful relationship between the two items.

There is no generally accepted list of ratios that can be applied to the financial statements, nor is there a standard method of calculating many ratios. Variations in both the choice of ratios and their calculation will be found in practice. However, it is important to be consistent in the way in which ratios are calculated for comparison purposes. The ratios that we shall discuss here are those that are widely used. They are popular because many consider them to be among the more important for decision-making purposes.

## Financial ratio classifications

Ratios can be grouped into categories, with each category relating to a particular aspect of financial performance or position. The following five broad categories provide a useful basis for explaining the nature of the financial ratios to be dealt with:

- *Profitability*. Businesses generally exist with the primary purpose of creating wealth for their owners. Profitability ratios provide insights relating to the degree of success in achieving this purpose. They express the profit made (or figures bearing on profit, such as sales revenue or overheads) in relation to other key figures in the financial statements or to some business resource.
- *Efficiency*. Ratios may be used to measure the efficiency with which particular resources have been used within the business. These ratios are also referred to as *activity* ratios.
- *Liquidity*. It is vital to the survival of a business that there are sufficient liquid resources available to meet maturing obligations (that is, amounts owing that must be paid in the near future). Some liquidity ratios examine the relationship between liquid resources held and amounts due for payment in the near future.
- *Financial gearing*. This is the relationship between the contribution to financing the business, made by the owners of the business, and the amount contributed by others, in the form of loans. The level of gearing has an important effect on the degree of risk associated with a business, as we shall see. Gearing is, therefore, something that managers must consider when making financing decisions. Gearing ratios tend to highlight the extent to which the business uses borrowings.
- *Investment*. Certain ratios are concerned with assessing the returns and performance of shares in a particular business from the perspective of shareholders who are not involved with the management of the business.

The analyst must be clear *who* the target users are and *why* they need the information. Different users of financial information are likely to have different information needs, which will in turn determine the ratios that they find useful. For example, shareholders are likely to be particularly interested in their returns in relation to the level of risk associated with their investment. Profitability, investment and gearing ratios will, therefore, be of particular interest. Long-term lenders are concerned with the long-term viability of the business and, to help them to assess this, the profitability and gearing ratios of the business are also likely to be of particular interest. Short-term lenders, such as suppliers of goods and services on credit, may be interested in the ability of the business to repay the amounts owing in the short term. As a result, the liquidity ratios should be of interest.

We shall consider ratios falling into each of the five categories (profitability, efficiency, liquidity, gearing and investment) a little later in the chapter.

## The need for comparison

Merely calculating a ratio will not tell us very much about the position or performance of a business. For example, if a ratio revealed that a retail business was generating £100 in sales revenue per square metre of floor space, it would not be possible to deduce from this information alone whether this particular level of performance was good, bad or indifferent. It is only when we compare this ratio with some 'benchmark' that the information can be interpreted and evaluated.

### Activity 6.1

Can you think of any bases that could be used to compare a ratio you have calculated from the financial statements of your business for a particular period?
   We feel that there are three sensible possibilities.

You may have thought of the following bases:

■  past periods for the same business
■  similar businesses for the same or past periods
■  planned performance for the business.

We shall now take a closer look at these three in turn.

## Past periods

By comparing the ratio we have calculated with the same ratio, but for a previous period, it is possible to detect whether there has been an improvement or deterioration in performance. Indeed, it is often useful to track particular ratios over time (say, five or ten years) to see whether it is possible to detect trends. The comparison of ratios from different periods brings certain problems, however. In particular, there is always the possibility that trading conditions were quite different in the periods being compared. There is the further problem that, when comparing the performance of a single business over time, operating inefficiencies may not be clearly exposed. For example, the fact that sales revenue per employee has risen by 10 per cent over the previous period may at first sight appear to be satisfactory. This may not be the case, however, if similar businesses have shown an improvement of 50 per cent for the same period or had much better sales revenue per employee ratios to start with. Finally, there is the problem that inflation may have distorted the figures on which the ratios are based.

Inflation can lead to an overstatement of profit and an understatement of asset values, as will be discussed later in the chapter.

## Similar businesses

In a competitive environment, a business must consider its performance in relation to that of other businesses operating in the same industry. Survival may depend on its ability to achieve comparable levels of performance. A useful basis for comparing a particular ratio, therefore, is the ratio achieved by similar businesses during the same period. This basis is not, however, without its problems. Competitors may have different year ends and so trading conditions may not be identical. They may also have different accounting policies, which can have a significant effect on reported profits and asset values (for example, different methods of calculating depreciation or valuing inventories). Finally, it may be difficult to obtain the financial statements of competitor businesses. Sole proprietorships and partnerships, for example, are not obliged to make their financial statements available to the public. In the case of limited companies, there is a legal obligation to do so. However, a diversified business may not provide a breakdown of activities that is sufficiently detailed to enable analysts to compare the activities with those of other businesses.

## Planned performance

Ratios may be compared with the targets that management developed before the start of the period under review. The comparison of planned performance with actual performance may be a useful way of revealing the level of achievement attained. However, the planned levels of performance must be based on realistic assumptions if they are to be useful for comparison purposes.

Planned performance is likely to be the most valuable benchmark against which managers may assess their own business. Businesses tend to develop planned ratios for each aspect of their activities. When formulating its plans, a business may usefully take account of its own past performance and the performance of other businesses. There is no reason, however, why a particular business should seek to achieve either its own previous performance or that of other businesses. Neither of these may be seen as an appropriate target.

Analysts outside the business do not normally have access to the business's plans. For these people, past performance and the performances of other, similar, businesses may provide the only practical benchmarks.

## Calculating the ratios

Probably the best way to explain financial ratios is through an example. Example 6.1 provides a set of financial statements from which we can calculate important ratios.

## Example 6.1

The following financial statements relate to Alexis plc, which operates a wholesale carpet business.

### Statements of financial position (balance sheets) as at 31 March

| | 2009<br>£m | 2010<br>£m |
|---|---|---|
| **ASSETS** | | |
| **Non-current assets** | | |
| *Property, plant and equipment (at cost less depreciation)* | | |
| Land and buildings | 381 | 427 |
| Fixtures and fittings | 129 | 160 |
| | 510 | 587 |
| **Current assets** | | |
| Inventories at cost | 300 | 406 |
| Trade receivables | 240 | 273 |
| Cash at bank | 4 | – |
| | 544 | 679 |
| **Total assets** | 1,054 | 1,266 |
| **EQUITY AND LIABILITIES** | | |
| **Equity** | | |
| £0.50 ordinary shares (Note 1) | 300 | 300 |
| Retained earnings | 263 | 234 |
| | 563 | 534 |
| **Non-current liabilities** | | |
| Borrowings – 9% loan notes (secured) | 200 | 300 |
| **Current liabilities** | | |
| Trade payables | 261 | 354 |
| Taxation | 30 | 2 |
| Short-term borrowings (all bank overdraft) | – | 76 |
| | 291 | 432 |
| **Total equity and liabilities** | 1,054 | 1,266 |

### Income statements for the year ended 31 March

| | 2009<br>£m | 2010<br>£m |
|---|---|---|
| Revenue (Note 2) | 2,240 | 2,681 |
| Cost of sales (Note 3) | (1,745) | (2,272) |
| **Gross profit** | 495 | 409 |
| Operating expenses | (252) | (362) |
| **Operating profit** | 243 | 47 |
| Interest payable | (18) | (32) |
| **Profit before taxation** | 225 | 15 |
| Taxation | (60) | (4) |
| **Profit for the year** | 165 | 11 |

→

**Notes:**

1 The market value of the shares of the business at the end of the year was £2.50 for 2009 and £1.50 for 2010.
2 All sales and purchases are made on credit.
3 The cost of sales figure can be analysed as follows:

|  | 2009 £m | 2010 £m |
|---|---|---|
| Opening inventories | 241 | 300 |
| Purchases (Note 2) | 1,804 | 2,378 |
|  | 2,045 | 2,678 |
| Closing inventories | (300) | (406) |
| Cost of sales | 1,745 | 2,272 |

4 At 31 March 2008, the trade receivables stood at £223 million and the trade payables at £183 million.
5 A dividend of £40 million had been paid to the shareholders in respect of each of the years.
6 The business employed 13,995 staff at 31 March 2009 and 18,623 at 31 March 2010.
7 The business expanded its capacity during 2010 by setting up a new warehouse and distribution centre in the north of England.
8 At 1 April 2008, the total of equity stood at £438 million and the total of equity and non-current liabilities stood at £638 million.

## A brief overview

Before we start our detailed look at the ratios for Alexis plc (see Example 6.1), it is helpful to take a quick look at what information is obvious from the financial statements. This will usually pick up some issues that the ratios may not be able to identify. It may also highlight some points that could help us in our interpretation of the ratios. Starting at the top of the statement of financial position, the following points can be noted:

■ *Expansion of non-current assets.* These have increased by about 15 per cent (from £510 million to £587 million). Note 7 mentions a new warehouse and distribution centre, which may account for much of the additional investment in non-current assets. We are not told when this new facility was established, but it is quite possible that it was well into the year. This could mean that not much benefit was reflected in terms of additional sales revenue or cost saving during 2010. Sales revenue, in fact, expanded by about 20 per cent (from £2,240 million to £2,681 million), and this is greater than the expansion in non-current assets.

■ *Major expansion in the elements of working capital.* Inventories increased by about 35 per cent, trade receivables by about 14 per cent and trade payables by about 36 per cent between 2009 and 2010. These are major increases, particularly in inventories and payables (which are linked because the inventories are all bought on credit – see Note 2).

■ *Reduction in the cash balance.* The cash balance fell from £4 million (in funds) to a £76 million overdraft, between 2009 and 2010. The bank may be putting the business under pressure to reverse this, which could raise difficulties.

- *Apparent debt capacity*. Comparing the non-current assets with the long-term borrowings implies that the business may well be able to offer security on further borrowing. This is because potential lenders usually look at the value of assets that can be offered as security when assessing loan requests. Lenders seem particularly attracted to land and buildings as security. For example, at 31 March 2010, non-current assets had a carrying amount (the value at which they appeared in the statement of financial position) of £587 million, but long-term borrowing was only £300 million (though there was also an overdraft of £76 million). Carrying amounts are not normally, of course, market values. On the other hand, land and buildings tend to have a market value higher than their value as shown on the statement of financial position, due to inflation in property values.
- *Lower operating profit*. Though sales revenue expanded by 20 per cent between 2009 and 2010, both cost of sales and operating expenses rose by a greater percentage, leaving both gross profit and, particularly, operating profit massively reduced. The level of staffing, which increased by about 33 per cent (from 13,995 to 18,623 employees – see Note 6), may have greatly affected the operating expenses. (Without knowing when the additional employees were recruited during 2010, we cannot be sure of the effect on operating expenses.) Increasing staffing by 33 per cent must put an enormous strain on management, at least in the short term. It is not surprising, therefore that 2010 was not successful for the business – not, at least, in profit terms.

Having had a quick look at what is fairly obvious, without calculating any financial ratios, we shall now go on to calculate and interpret some.

## Profitability

The following ratios may be used to evaluate the profitability of the business:

- return on ordinary shareholders' funds
- return on capital employed
- operating profit margin
- gross profit margin.

We shall now look at each of these in turn.

### Return on ordinary shareholders' funds (ROSF)

The return on ordinary shareholders' funds ratio compares the amount of profit for the period available to the owners with the owners' average stake in the business during that same period. The ratio (which is normally expressed in percentage terms) is as follows:

$$\text{ROSF} = \frac{\text{Profit for the year (net profit) less any preference dividend}}{\text{Ordinary share capital + Reserves}} \times 100$$

The profit for the year (less preference dividend (if any)) is used in calculating the ratio, as this figure represents the amount of profit that is attributable to the owners.

In the case of Alexis plc, the ratio for the year ended 31 March 2009 is

$$ROSF = \frac{165}{(438 + 563)/2} \times 100 = 33.0\%$$

Note that, when calculating the ROSF, the average of the figures for ordinary share-holders' funds as at the beginning and at the end of the year has been used. It is prefer-able to use an average figure as this is likely to be more representative. This is because the shareholders' funds did not have the same total throughout the year, yet we want to compare it with the profit earned during the whole period. We know, from Note 8, that the total of the shareholders' funds at 1 April 2008 was £438 million. By a year later, however, it had risen to £563 million, according to the statement of financial position as at 31 March 2009.

The easiest approach to calculating the average amount of shareholders' funds is to take a simple average based on the opening and closing figures for the year. This is often the only information available, as is the case with Example 6.1. Averaging in this way is generally valid for all ratios that combine a figure for a period (such as profit for the year) with one taken at a point in time (such as shareholders' funds).

Where not even the beginning-of-year figure is available, it is usually acceptable to use just the year-end figure. This is not ideal but, provided that this approach is con-sistently adopted, it should provide ratios that are useful.

## Activity 6.2

Calculate the ROSF for Alexis plc for the year to 31 March 2010.

The ratio for 2010 is

$$ROSF = \frac{11}{(563 + 534)/2} \times 100 = 2.0\%$$

Broadly, businesses seek to generate as high a value as possible for this ratio, pro-vided that it is not achieved at the expense of potential future returns by, for example, taking on more risky activities. In view of this, the 2010 ratio is very poor by any stand-ards; a bank deposit account will normally yield a better return than this. We need to try to find out why things went so badly wrong in 2010. As we look at other ratios, we should find some clues.

## Return on capital employed (ROCE)

→ The return on capital employed ratio is a fundamental measure of business perform-ance. This ratio expresses the relationship between the operating profit generated during a period and the average long-term capital invested in the business.

The ratio is expressed in percentage terms and is as follows:

$$ROCE = \frac{\text{Operating profit}}{\text{Share capital + Reserves + Non-current liabilities}} \times 100$$

Note, in this case, that the profit figure used is the operating profit (that is, the profit *before* interest and taxation), because the ratio attempts to measure the returns to all suppliers of long-term finance before any deductions for interest payable on borrowings, or payments of dividends to shareholders, are made.

For the year to 31 March 2009, the ratio for Alexis plc is

$$\text{ROCE} = \frac{243}{(638 + 763)/2} \times 100 = 34.7\%$$

(The capital employed figure at 1 April 2008 is given in Note 8).

ROCE is considered by many to be a primary measure of profitability. It compares inputs (capital invested) with outputs (operating profit). This comparison is vital in assessing the effectiveness with which funds have been deployed. Once again, an average figure for capital employed should be used where the information is available.

### Activity 6.3

Calculate the ROCE for Alexis plc for the year to 31 March 2010.

The ratio for 2010 is

$$\text{ROCE} = \frac{47}{(763 + 834)/2} \times 100 = 5.9\%$$

This ratio tells much the same story as ROSF, namely a poor performance, with the return on the assets being less than the rate that the business has to pay for most of its borrowed funds (that is, 9 per cent for the loan notes).

Real World 6.1 shows how financial ratios are used by businesses as a basis for setting profitability targets.

### Real World 6.1

## Targeting profitability

The ROCE ratio is widely used by businesses when establishing targets for profitability. These targets are sometimes made public and here are some examples:

Tesco plc, the supermarket business, in 2004 set a target to achieve a growth in ROCE of 2 per cent from its 2004 figure of 10.4 per cent. It achieved this with 12.5 per cent in 2006 and increased it further in 2007. Tesco then set a further 2 per cent target growth for ROCE for 2008 and beyond. The business achieved a 13 per cent rate of ROCE in 2009. Tesco uses performance against a target ROCE as a basis of rewarding its senior managers, indicating the importance that the business attaches to this measure of performance.

BSkyB plc, the satellite broadcaster, has a target ROCE of 15 per cent by 2011 for its broadband operation.

Air France-KLM, the world's largest airline (on the basis of sales revenue), has set itself the target of achieving a ROCE of 7 per cent.

BMW, the car maker, has a long-term target ROCE in excess of 26 per cent.

*Sources*: information taken from Tesco plc Annual Report 2009; 'BSkyB/triple play'; *The Financial Times*, 12 July 2006; Air France-KLM, press release, 14 February 2008; 'BMW adds to carmakers' gloom', FT.com, 1 August 2008.

Real World 6.2 provides some indication of the levels of ROCE achieved by UK businesses.

---

**Real World 6.2**

## Achieving profitability

UK businesses reported an average ROCE of 11.6 per cent for the second quarter of 2009. This was down on the record rate of 15.1 per cent for the first quarter of 2007, which was the highest level of ROCE since the Office of National Statistics first kept records.

Service sector businesses were much the more successful with an average ROCE of 15.6 per cent, compared with 6.7 per cent among manufacturers. These compare with 15.7 per cent for service businesses and 10.2 per cent for manufacturers, averaged over 2006, 2007 and 2008. This suggests that, despite the recession, UK service businesses are maintaining their profitability quite well. Manufacturers, on the other hand, have suffered a large fall in profitability compared with that of recent years.

The difference in ROCE between the two sectors is accounted for by the higher capital intensity of manufacturing, according to the Office of National Statistics.

*Source*: information taken from Office of National Statistics, 'Corporate profitability', www.statistics.gov.uk/cci, 17 October 2009.

---

## Operating profit margin

→ The operating profit margin ratio relates the operating profit for the period to the sales revenue. The ratio is expressed as follows:

$$\text{Operating profit margin} = \frac{\text{Operating profit}}{\text{Sales revenue}} \times 100$$

The operating profit (that is, profit before interest and taxation) is used in this ratio as it represents the profit from trading operations before the interest payable expense is taken into account. This is often regarded as the most appropriate measure of operational performance, when used as a basis of comparison, because differences arising from the way in which the business is financed will not influence the measure.

For the year ended 31 March 2009, Alexis plc's operating profit margin ratio is

$$\text{Operating profit margin} = \frac{243}{2,240} \times 100 = 10.8\%$$

This ratio compares one output of the business (operating profit) with another output (sales revenue). The ratio can vary considerably between types of business. For example, supermarkets tend to operate on low prices and, therefore, low operating profit margins. This is done in an attempt to stimulate sales and thereby increase the total amount of operating profit generated. Jewellers, on the other hand, tend to have high operating profit margins but have much lower levels of sales volume. Factors such as the degree of competition, the type of customer, the economic climate and industry characteristics (such as the level of risk) will influence the operating profit margin of a business. This point is picked up again later in the chapter.

## Activity 6.4

Calculate the operating profit margin for Alexis plc for the year to 31 March 2010.

The ratio for 2010 is

$$\text{Operating profit margin} = \frac{47}{2,681} \times 100 = 1.8\%$$

Once again, a very weak performance compared with that of 2009. In 2009 for every £1 of sales revenue an average of 10.8p (that is, 10.8 per cent) was left as operating profit, after paying the cost of the carpets sold and other expenses of operating the business. For 2010, however, this had fallen to only 1.8p for every £1. It seems that the reason for the poor ROSF and ROCE ratios was partially, perhaps wholly, a high level of expenses relative to sales revenue. The next ratio should provide us with a clue as to how the sharp decline in this ratio occurred.

Real World 6.3 describes how one well-known business targets the operating profit margin.

## Real World 6.3

### Operating profit margin taking off at BA

British Airways plc, the airline business, exceeded its 10 per cent operating profit margin target during the year to 31 March 2008. This target had been in existence since 2002.

The year to 31 March 2009 was rather less successful with the company sustaining an operating loss equal to 2.4 per cent of its sales revenue. The business put this down to 'incredibly difficult trading conditions' brought about by the recession.

*Source*: British Airways plc Annual Report 2009.

## Gross profit margin

The gross profit margin ratio relates the gross profit of the business to the sales revenue generated for the same period. Gross profit represents the difference between sales revenue and the cost of sales. The ratio is therefore a measure of profitability in buying (or producing) and selling goods or services before any other expenses are taken into account. As cost of sales represents a major expense for many businesses, a change in this ratio can have a significant effect on the 'bottom line' (that is, the profit for the year). The gross profit margin ratio is calculated as follows:

$$\textbf{Gross profit margin} = \frac{\textbf{Gross profit}}{\textbf{Sales revenue}} \times 100$$

For the year to 31 March 2009, the ratio for Alexis plc is

$$\text{Gross profit margin} = \frac{495}{2,240} \times 100 = 22.1\%$$

**Activity 6.5**

Calculate the gross profit margin for Alexis plc for the year to 31 March 2010.

The ratio for 2010 is

$$\text{Gross profit margin} = \frac{409}{2,681} \times 100 = 15.3\%$$

The decline in this ratio means that gross profit was lower *relative* to sales revenue in 2010 than it had been in 2009. Bearing in mind that

 **Gross profit = Sales revenue – Cost of sales (or cost of goods sold)**

this means that cost of sales was higher *relative* to sales revenue in 2010 than in 2009. This could mean that sales prices were lower and/or that the purchase cost of carpets sold had increased. It is possible that both sales prices and purchase prices had reduced, but the former at a greater rate than the latter. Similarly they may both have increased, but with sales prices having increased at a lesser rate than the cost of the carpets.

Clearly, part of the decline in the operating profit margin ratio is linked to the dramatic decline in the gross profit margin ratio. Whereas, after paying for the carpets sold, for each £1 of sales revenue 22.1p was left to cover other operating expenses and leave an operating profit in 2009, this was only 15.3p in 2010.

The profitability ratios for the business over the two years can be set out as follows:

|  | 2009 | 2010 |
|---|---|---|
|  | % | % |
| ROSF | 33.0 | 2.0 |
| ROCE | 34.7 | 5.9 |
| Operating profit margin | 10.8 | 1.8 |
| Gross profit margin | 22.1 | 15.3 |

**Activity 6.6**

What do you deduce from a comparison of the declines in the operating profit and gross profit margin ratios?

It occurs to us that the decline in the operating profit margin was 9 percentage points (that is, from 10.8 per cent to 1.8 per cent), whereas that of the gross profit margin was only 6.8 percentage points (that is, from 22.1 per cent to 15.3 per cent). This can only mean that operating expenses were greater compared with sales revenue in 2010 than they had been in 2009. The declines in both ROSF and ROCE were caused partly, therefore, by the business incurring higher inventories purchasing costs relative to sales revenue and partly through higher operating expenses compared with sales revenue. We should need to compare these ratios with the planned levels for them before we could usefully assess the business's success.

The analyst must now carry out some investigation to discover what caused the increases in both cost of sales and operating expenses, relative to sales revenue, from 2009 to 2010. This will involve checking on what has happened with sales and inventories prices over the two years. Similarly, it will involve looking at each of the individual areas that make up operating expenses to discover which ones were responsible for the increase, relative to sales revenue. Here, further ratios, for example, staff expenses (wages and salaries) to sales revenue, could be calculated in an attempt to isolate the cause of the change from 2009 to 2010. In fact, as we discussed when we took an overview of the financial statements, the increase in staffing may well account for most of the increase in operating expenses.

Real World 6.4 discusses how high operating costs may adversely affect the future profitability of a leading car maker.

## Real World 6.4

### VW accelerates but costs vibrate

Volkswagen's fervent quest to overtake Japanese rival Toyota by 2018 threatens to exacerbate its already high cost structure and to hamper profitability in the coming years, analysts and industry executives have warned. The industry executives and analysts argue that VW's growth initiative – which involves a huge investment of €26.6 billion ($35.7 billion) in the next three years, the €16 billion takeovers of Porsche and its Salzburg dealership and a €1.7 billion stake in Japanese small car specialist Suzuki – will put the car maker back on a low-profit-margin track.

So far, VW, Europe's largest car maker, has been one of the most successful during the crisis. The Wolfsburg-based manufacturer posted a €911 million profit after tax and a 1.2 per cent profit margin in 2009 at a time when many others were making losses. VW is now aiming for an industry-leading pre-tax profit margin of more than 8 per cent in 2018, by which time it wants to become the world's leading car producer 'economically as well as ecologically', Martin Winterkorn, VW's chief executive, has said. The car maker wants to lift its sales from 6.3 million cars in the past year to more than 10 million by 2018.

While few dispute that VW could overtake Toyota – which sold almost 9 million cars in 2009 – in terms of sales, the profitability target remains in doubt. 'There should be more doubt in the market about the sustainability of VW's profits,' says Philippe Houchois, analyst at UBS.

In spite of its success, VW's cost structure is still in dire straits, particularly in Germany. With its 370,000 global workforce, the partly state-owned car maker trails almost all global rivals when it comes to statistics such as revenues or vehicles per employee. 'People forget that despite their large scale, VW has some of the worst cost-structures in the industry. They have abysmal labour productivity and high plant costs,' says Max Warburton, analyst at research firm Sanford Bernstein.

Mr Warburton says high margins have been the exception at VW. '2007–2008 represented a brief period of temporary profit maximisation delivered by a [now departed] temporary management team who made temporary, emergency cost cuts,' he says. VW disputes that it has taken its eye off cost-cutting. Hans Dieter Pötsch, the car maker's chief financial officer, says that 'by optimising our purchasing and increasing productivity . . . we have reached cost cuts of €1 billion throughout 2009'. In addition, he points to the car maker's ongoing productivity improvement target of 10 per cent each year.

VW's profit figures for last year paint a dark picture of the car maker's cost structures. At least three of its nine brands – Seat, Bentley and Lamborghini, and probably also Bugatti whose results are not disclosed – were lossmaking, and are not expected to return to profit this year. VW's light truck operations only posted a profit after a one-off gain from the sale of its Brazil operations. Operating profit at the group's core brand, VW, was crimped by 79 per cent to €561 million, in spite of the marque benefiting hugely from European scrapping incentive programmes.

*Source*: adapted from 'Costs vibrate as VW accelerates', *The Financial Times*, 29/03/2010 (Schäfer, D.), copyright © The Financial Times Ltd.

## Efficiency

Efficiency ratios are used to try to assess how successfully the various resources of the business are managed. The following ratios consider some of the more important aspects of resource management:

- average inventories turnover period
- average settlement period for trade receivables
- average settlement period for trade payables
- sales revenue to capital employed
- sales revenue per employee.

We shall now look at each of these in turn.

### Average inventories turnover period

Inventories often represent a significant investment for a business. For some types of business (for example, manufacturers and certain retailers), inventories may account for a substantial proportion of the total assets held (see Real World 12.1, page 456).  The average inventories turnover period ratio measures the average period for which inventories are being held. The ratio is calculated as follows:

$$\text{Average inventories turnover period} = \frac{\text{Average inventories held}}{\text{Cost of sales}} \times 365$$

The average inventories for the period can be calculated as a simple average of the opening and closing inventories levels for the year. However, in the case of a highly seasonal business, where inventories levels may vary considerably over the year, a monthly average may be more appropriate, should this information be available.

In the case of Alexis plc, the inventories turnover period for the year ended 31 March 2009 is

$$\text{Average inventories turnover period} = \frac{(241 + 300)/2}{1,745} \times 365 = 56.6 \text{ days}$$

(The opening inventories figure was taken from Note 3 to the financial statements.)

This means that, on average, the inventories held are being 'turned over' every 56.6 days. So, a carpet bought by the business on a particular day would, on average, have been sold about eight weeks later. A business will normally prefer a short inventories turnover period to a long one, because holding inventories has costs, for example the opportunity cost of the funds tied up. When judging the amount of inventories to carry, the business must consider such things as the likely demand for them, the possibility of supply shortages, the likelihood of price rises, the amount of storage space available for them, and their perishability/susceptibility to obsolescence.

This ratio is sometimes expressed in terms of weeks or months rather than days. Multiplying by 52 or 12, rather than 365, will achieve this.

### Activity 6.7

Calculate the average inventories turnover period for Alexis plc for the year ended 31 March 2010.

The ratio for 2010 is

$$\text{Average inventories turnover period} = \frac{(300 + 406)/2}{2,272} \times 365 = 56.7 \text{ days}$$

The inventories turnover period is virtually the same in both years.

## Average settlement period for trade receivables

Selling on credit is the norm for most businesses, except for retailers. Trade receivables are a necessary evil. A business will naturally be concerned with the amount of funds tied up in trade receivables and try to keep this to a minimum. The speed of payment can have a significant effect on the business's cash flow. The average settlement period for trade receivables ratio calculates how long, on average, credit customers take to pay the amounts that they owe to the business. The ratio is as follows:

$$\textbf{Average settlement period for trade receivables} = \frac{\textbf{Average trade receivables}}{\textbf{Credit sales revenue}} \times \textbf{365}$$

A business will normally prefer a shorter average settlement period to a longer one as, once again, funds are being tied up that may be used for more profitable purposes. Although this ratio can be useful, it is important to remember that it produces an *average* figure for the number of days for which debts are outstanding. This average may be badly distorted by, for example, a few large customers who are very slow or very fast payers.

Since all sales made by Alexis plc are on credit, the average settlement period for trade receivables for the year ended 31 March 2009 is

$$\text{Average settlement period for trade receivables} = \frac{(223 + 240)/2}{2,240} \times 365 = 37.7 \text{ days}$$

(The opening trade receivables figure was taken from Note 4 to the financial statements.)

### Activity 6.8

Calculate the average settlement period for Alexis plc's trade receivables for the year ended 31 March 2010.

The ratio for 2010 is

$$\text{Average settlement period for trade receivables} = \frac{(240 + 273)/2}{2,681} \times 365 = 34.9 \text{ days}$$

On the face of it, this reduction in the settlement period is welcome. It means that less cash was tied up in trade receivables for each £1 of sales revenue in 2010 than in 2009. Only if the reduction were achieved at the expense of customer goodwill or a high direct financial cost might the desirability of the reduction be questioned. For example, the reduction may have been due to chasing customers too vigorously or as a result of incurring higher expenses, such as discounts allowed to customers who pay quickly.

## Average settlement period for trade payables

→ The average settlement period for trade payables ratio measures how long, on average, the business takes to pay those who have supplied goods and services on credit. The ratio is calculated as follows:

$$\text{Average settlement period for trade payables} = \frac{\text{Average trade payables}}{\text{Credit purchases}} \times 365$$

This ratio provides an average figure, which, like the average settlement period for trade receivables ratio, can be distorted by the payment period for one or two large suppliers.

As trade payables provide a free source of finance for the business, it is perhaps not surprising that some businesses attempt to increase their average settlement period for trade payables. However, such a policy can be taken too far and result in a loss of goodwill of suppliers.

For the year ended 31 March 2009, Alexis plc's average settlement period for trade payables is

$$\text{Average settlement period for trade payables} = \frac{(183 + 261)/2}{1,804} \times 365 = 44.9 \text{ days}$$

(The opening trade payables figure was taken from Note 4 to the financial statements and the purchases figure from Note 3.)

## Activity 6.9

Calculate the average settlement period for trade payables for Alexis plc for the year ended 31 March 2010.

The ratio for 2010 is

$$\text{Average settlement period for trade payables} = \frac{(261 + 354)/2}{2{,}378} \times 365 = 47.2 \text{ days}$$

There was an increase, between 2009 and 2010, in the average length of time that elapsed between buying inventories and services and paying for them. On the face of it, this is beneficial because the business is using free finance provided by suppliers. This is not necessarily advantageous, however, if it is leading to a loss of supplier goodwill that could have adverse consequences for Alexis plc.

Real World 6.5 is an extract from an article that describes how small businesses have been affected by larger customers delaying payments during the recent recession.

## Real World 6.5

### Taking credit where it's not due

Late payment is a significant cause of ill will between small businesses and larger customers. By extending payment periods, usually through simple foot-dragging, debtors are able to draw on a plentiful supply of free credit. But this complicates financial planning for creditors and in extreme cases can trigger their insolvency. Successive governments have struggled to defeat the problem because small entrepreneurs are reluctant to exercise such sanctions as charging interest on late payments.

Payment periods crept up during the recession as large companies hoarded cash. The average payment period in the private sector is 52 days, according to the Federation of Small Businesses, which said that most invoices specify payment within 30 days. Companies House data show that some businesses can take six months or more to meet their debts.

*Source*: adapted from 'Small businesses hit at late Whitehall payments', *The Financial Times*, 02/02/2010 (Guthrie, J.), copyright © The Financial Times Ltd.

## Sales revenue to capital employed

The sales revenue to capital employed ratio (or net asset turnover ratio) examines how effectively the assets of the business are being used to generate sales revenue. It is calculated as follows:

$$\frac{\text{Sales revenue to}}{\text{capital employed ratio}} = \frac{\text{Sales revenue}}{\text{Share capital + Reserves + Non-current liabilities}}$$

Generally speaking, a higher sales revenue to capital employed ratio is preferred to a lower one. A higher ratio will normally suggest that assets are being used more productively in the generation of revenue. However, a very high ratio may suggest that the business is 'overtrading on its assets', that is, it has insufficient assets to sustain the level of sales revenue achieved. When comparing this ratio for different businesses, factors such as the age and condition of assets held, the valuation bases for assets and whether assets are leased or owned outright can complicate interpretation.

A variation of this formula is to use the total assets less current liabilities (which is equivalent to long-term capital employed) in the denominator (lower part of the fraction). The identical result is obtained.

For the year ended 31 March 2009 this ratio for Alexis plc is

$$\text{Sales revenue to capital employed} = \frac{2,240}{(638 + 763)/2} = 3.20 \text{ times}$$

---

### Activity 6.10

Calculate the sales revenue to capital employed ratio for Alexis plc for the year ended 31 March 2010.

The ratio for 2010 is

$$\text{Sales revenue to capital employed} = \frac{2,681}{(763 + 834)/2} = 3.36 \text{ times}$$

---

This seems to be an improvement, since in 2010 more sales revenue was being generated for each £1 of capital employed (£3.36) than was the case in 2009 (£3.20). Provided that overtrading is not an issue and that the additional sales are generating an acceptable profit, this is to be welcomed.

## Sales revenue per employee

The sales revenue per employee ratio relates sales revenue generated during a reporting period to a particular business resource, labour. It provides a measure of the productivity of the workforce. The ratio is

$$\text{Sales revenue per employee} = \frac{\textbf{Sales revenue}}{\textbf{Number of employees}}$$

Generally, businesses would prefer to have a high value for this ratio, implying that they are using their staff efficiently.

For the year ended 31 March 2009, the ratio for Alexis plc is

$$\text{Sales revenue per employee} = \frac{£2,240m}{13,995} = £160,057$$

## Activity 6.11

Calculate the sales revenue per employee for Alexis plc for the year ended 31 March 2010.

The ratio for 2010 is

$$\text{Sales revenue per employee} = \frac{£2,681m}{18,623} = £143,962$$

This represents a fairly significant decline and probably one that merits further investigation. As we discussed previously, the number of employees had increased quite notably (by about 33 per cent) during 2010 and the analyst will probably try to discover why this had not generated sufficient additional sales revenue to maintain the ratio at its 2009 level. It could be that the additional employees were not appointed until late in the year ended 31 March 2010.

The efficiency, or activity, ratios may be summarised as follows:

|  | 2009 | 2010 |
|---|---|---|
| Average inventories turnover period | 56.6 days | 56.7 days |
| Average settlement period for trade receivables | 37.7 days | 34.9 days |
| Average settlement period for trade payables | 44.9 days | 47.2 days |
| Sales revenue to capital employed (net asset turnover) | 3.20 times | 3.36 times |
| Sales revenue per employee | £160,057 | £143,962 |

## Activity 6.12

What do you deduce from a comparison of the efficiency ratios over the two years?

We feel that maintaining the inventories turnover period at the 2009 level might be reasonable, though whether this represents a satisfactory period can probably only be assessed by looking at the business's planned inventories period. The inventories turnover period for other businesses operating in carpet retailing, particularly those regarded as the market leaders, may have been helpful in formulating the plans. On the face of things, a shorter receivables collection period and a longer payables payment period are both desirable. On the other hand, these may have been achieved at the cost of a loss of the goodwill of customers and suppliers, respectively. The increased net asset turnover ratio seems beneficial, provided that the business can manage this increase. The decline in the sales revenue per employee ratio is undesirable but, as we have already seen, is probably related to the dramatic increase in the level of staffing. As with the inventories turnover period, these other ratios need to be compared with the planned standard of efficiency.

# Relationship between profitability and efficiency

In our earlier discussions concerning profitability ratios, we saw that return on capital employed (ROCE) is regarded as a key ratio by many businesses. The ratio is

$$ROCE = \frac{\text{Operating profit}}{\text{Long-term capital employed}} \times 100$$

where long-term capital comprises share capital plus reserves plus non-current liabilities. This ratio can be broken down into two elements, as shown in Figure 6.1. The first ratio is the operating profit margin ratio and the second is the sales revenue to capital employed (net asset turnover) ratio, both of which we discussed earlier.

**Figure 6.1 The main elements of the ROCE ratio**

The ROCE ratio can be divided into two elements: operating profit to sales revenue and sales revenue to capital employed. By analysing ROCE in this way, we can see the influence of both profitability and efficiency on this important ratio.

By breaking down the ROCE ratio in this manner, we highlight the fact that the overall return on funds employed within the business will be determined both by the profitability of sales and by efficiency in the use of capital.

### Example 6.2

Consider the following information, for last year, concerning two different businesses operating in the same industry:

|  | Antler plc | Baker plc |
|---|---|---|
|  | £m | £m |
| Operating profit | 20 | 15 |
| Average long-term capital employed | 100 | 75 |
| Sales revenue | 200 | 300 |

The ROCE for each business is identical (20 per cent). However, the manner in which that return was achieved by each business was quite different. In the case of Antler plc, the operating profit margin is 10 per cent and the sales revenue to capital employed ratio is 2 times (so ROCE = 10% × 2 = 20%). In the case of Baker plc, the operating profit margin is 5 per cent and the sales revenue to capital employed ratio is 4 times (and so ROCE = 5% × 4 = 20%).

Example 6.2 demonstrates that a relatively high sales revenue to capital employed ratio can compensate for a relatively low operating profit margin. Similarly, a relatively low sales revenue to capital employed ratio can be overcome by a relatively high operating profit margin. In many areas of retail and distribution (for example, supermarkets and delivery services), the operating profit margins are quite low but the ROCE can be high, provided that the assets are used productively (that is, low margin, high sales revenue to capital employed).

## Activity 6.13

Show how the ROCE ratio for Alexis plc can be analysed into the two elements for each of the years 2009 and 2010. What conclusions can you draw from your figures?

|  | ROCE | = | Operating profit margin | × | Sales revenue to capital employed |
|---|---|---|---|---|---|
| 2009 | 34.7% | | 10.8% | | 3.20 |
| 2010 | 5.9% | | 1.8% | | 3.36 |

As we can see, the relationship between the three ratios holds for Alexis plc for both years. The small apparent differences arise because the three ratios are stated here only to one or two decimal places.

Although the business was more effective at generating sales revenue (sales revenue to capital employed ratio increased) in 2010 than in 2009, in 2010 it fell well below the level necessary to compensate for the sharp decline in the effectiveness of each sale (operating profit margin). As a result, the 2010 ROCE was well below the 2009 value.

## Liquidity

Liquidity ratios are concerned with the ability of the business to meet its short-term financial obligations. The following ratios are widely used:

■ current ratio
■ acid test ratio.

These two ratios will now be considered.

### Current ratio

The current ratio compares the 'liquid' assets (that is, cash and those assets held that will soon be turned into cash) of the business with the current liabilities. The ratio is calculated as follows:

$$\text{Current ratio} = \frac{\text{Current assets}}{\text{Current liabilities}}$$

Some people seem to believe that there is an 'ideal' current ratio (usually 2 times or 2:1) for all businesses. However, this fails to take into account the fact that different types of business require different current ratios. For example, a manufacturing business will often have a relatively high current ratio because it has to hold inventories of finished goods, raw materials and work in progress. It will also normally sell goods on credit, thereby giving rise to trade receivables. A supermarket chain, on the other hand, will have a relatively low ratio, as it will hold only fast-moving inventories of finished goods and all of its sales will be made for cash (no credit sales). (See Real World 12.1 on page 456.)

The higher the ratio, the more liquid the business is considered to be. As liquidity is vital to the survival of a business, a higher current ratio might be thought to be preferable to a lower one. If a business has a very high ratio, however, it may be that excessive funds are tied up in cash or other liquid assets and are not, therefore, being used as productively as they might otherwise be.

As at 31 March 2009, the current ratio of Alexis plc is

$$\text{Current ratio} = \frac{544}{291} = 1.9 \text{ times (or 1.9:1)}$$

## Activity 6.14

Calculate the current ratio for Alexis plc as at 31 March 2010.

The ratio as at 31 March 2010 is

$$\text{Current ratio} = \frac{679}{432} = 1.6 \text{ times (or 1.6:1)}$$

Although this is a decline from 2009 to 2010, it is not necessarily a matter of concern. The next ratio may provide a clue as to whether there seems to be a problem.

## Acid test ratio

The acid test ratio is very similar to the current ratio, but it represents a more stringent test of liquidity. For many businesses, inventories cannot be converted into cash quickly. (Note that, in the case of Alexis plc, the inventories turnover period was about 57 days in both years (see pages 200–201).) As a result, it may be better to exclude this particular asset from any measure of liquidity. The acid test ratio is a variation of the current ratio, but excluding inventories.

The minimum level for this ratio is often stated as 1.0 times (or 1:1; that is, current assets (excluding inventories) equal current liabilities). In many highly successful businesses that are regarded as having adequate liquidity, however, it is not unusual for the acid test ratio to be below 1.0 without causing particular liquidity problems. (See Real World 12.1 on page 456.)

The acid test ratio is calculated as follows:

$$\text{Acid test ratio} = \frac{\text{Current assets (excluding inventories)}}{\text{Current liabilities}}$$

The acid test ratio for Alexis plc as at 31 March 2009 is

$$\text{Acid test ratio} = \frac{544 - 300}{291} = 0.8 \text{ times (or 0.8:1)}$$

We can see that the 'liquid' current assets do not quite cover the current liabilities, so the business may be experiencing some liquidity problems.

## Activity 6.15

Calculate the acid test ratio for Alexis plc as at 31 March 2010.

The ratio as at 31 March 2010 is

$$\text{Acid test ratio} = \frac{679 - 406}{432} = 0.6 \text{ times (or 0.6:1)}$$

The 2010 ratio is significantly below that for 2009. The 2010 level may well be a cause for concern. The rapid decline in this ratio should lead to steps being taken, at least, to stop it falling further.

The liquidity ratios for the two-year period may be summarised as follows:

|  | 2009 | 2010 |
|---|---|---|
| Current ratio | 1.9 | 1.6 |
| Acid test ratio | 0.8 | 0.6 |

## Activity 6.16

What do you deduce from the liquidity ratios set out above?

Although it is not possible to make a totally valid judgement without knowing the planned ratios, there appears to have been a worrying decline in liquidity. This is indicated by both of these ratios. The apparent liquidity problem may, however, be planned, short-term and linked to the expansion in non-current assets and staffing. It may be that when the benefits of the expansion come on stream, liquidity will improve. On the other hand, short-term claimants may become anxious when they see signs of weak liquidity. This anxiety could lead to steps being taken to press for payment. This could cause problems for Alexis plc.

# Financial gearing

Financial gearing occurs when a business is financed, at least in part, by borrowing instead of by finance provided by the owners (the shareholders) as equity. A business's level of gearing (that is, the extent to which it is financed from sources that require a fixed return) is an important factor in assessing risk. Where a business borrows, it takes on a commitment to pay interest charges and make capital repayments. Where the borrowing is heavy, this can be a significant financial burden; it can increase the risk of the business becoming insolvent. Nevertheless, most businesses are geared to some extent. (Costain Group plc, the building and construction business, is a rare example of a UK business with no borrowings.)

Given the risks involved, we may wonder why a business would want to take on gearing (that is, to borrow). One reason may be that the owners have insufficient funds, so the only way to finance the business adequately is to borrow from others. Another reason is that gearing can be used to increase the returns to owners. This is possible provided that the returns generated from borrowed funds exceed the cost of paying interest. Example 6.3 illustrates this point.

## Example 6.3

The long-term capital structures of two new businesses, Lee Ltd and Nova Ltd, are as follows:

|  | Lee Ltd £000 | Nova Ltd £000 |
|---|---|---|
| £1 ordinary shares | 100 | 200 |
| 10% loan notes | 200 | 100 |
|  | 300 | 300 |

In their first year of operations, they each make an operating profit (that is, profit before interest and taxation) of £50,000. The tax rate is 30 per cent of the profit before taxation but after interest.

Lee Ltd would probably be considered relatively highly geared, as two-thirds of its long-term financing comes from borrowing. Nova Ltd is much lower-geared. The profit available to the shareholders of each business in the first year of operations will be:

|  | Lee Ltd £000 | Nova Ltd £000 |
|---|---|---|
| Operating profit | 50 | 50 |
| Interest payable | (20) | (10) |
| Profit before taxation | 30 | 40 |
| Taxation (30%) | (9) | (12) |
| Profit for the year (available to ordinary shareholders) | 21 | 28 |

The return on ordinary shareholders' funds (ROSF) for each business will be:

$$\text{Lee Ltd} \qquad \frac{21,000}{100,000} \times 100 = 21\% \qquad \text{Nova Ltd} \qquad \frac{28,000}{200,000} \times 100 = 14\%$$

We can see that Lee Ltd, the more highly geared business, has generated a better ROSF than Nova Ltd. This is despite the fact that the ROCE (return on capital employed) is identical for both businesses (that is, (£50,000/£300,000) × 100 = 16.7%).

Note that at the £50,000 level of operating profit, the shareholders of both Lee Ltd and Nova Ltd benefit from gearing. Were the two businesses totally reliant on equity financing, the profit for the year (the profit after taxation) would be £35,000 (that is, £50,000 less 30 per cent taxation), giving an ROSF of 11.7 per cent (that is, £35,000/£300,000). Both businesses generate higher ROSFs than this as a result of financial gearing.

An effect of gearing is that returns to shareholders become more sensitive to changes in operating profits. For a highly geared business, a change in operating profits will lead to a proportionately greater change in the ROSF ratio.

## Activity 6.17

Assume that the operating profit was 20 per cent higher for each business than stated above (that is, an operating profit of £60,000). What would be the effect of this on ROSF?

The revised profit available to the shareholders of each business in the first year of operations will be:

|  | Lee Ltd | Nova Ltd |
|---|---|---|
|  | £000 | £000 |
| Operating profit | 60 | 60 |
| Interest payable | (20) | (10) |
| Profit before taxation | 40 | 50 |
| Taxation (30%) | (12) | (15) |
| Profit for the year (available to ordinary shareholders) | 28 | 35 |

The ROSF for each business will now be:

$$\text{Lee Ltd} \qquad\qquad \text{Nova Ltd}$$

$$\frac{28,000}{100,000} \times 100 = 28\% \qquad \frac{35,000}{200,000} \times 100 = 17.5\%$$

We can see that for Lee Ltd, the higher-geared business, the returns to shareholders have increased by a third (from 21 per cent to 28 per cent), whereas for the lower-geared business, Nova Ltd, the benefits of gearing are less pronounced, increasing by only a quarter (from 14 per cent to 17.5 per cent). The effect of gearing can, of course, work in both directions. So, for a highly geared business, a small decline in operating profit will bring about a much greater decline in the returns to shareholders.

The reason that gearing tends to be beneficial to shareholders is that interest rates for borrowings are low by comparison with the returns that the typical business can earn. On top of this, interest expenses are tax-deductible, in the way shown in Example 6.3 and Activity 6.17, which makes the effective cost of borrowing quite cheap. It is debatable whether the apparent low interest rates really are beneficial to the shareholders. Some argue that since borrowing increases the risk to shareholders, there is a hidden cost of borrowing. What are not illusory, however, are the benefits to the shareholders of the tax-deductibility of interest on borrowings.

The effect of gearing is like that of two intermeshing cogwheels of unequal size (see Figure 6.2). The movement in the larger cog (operating profit) causes a more than proportionate movement in the smaller cog (returns to ordinary shareholders).

**Figure 6.2** The effect of financial gearing

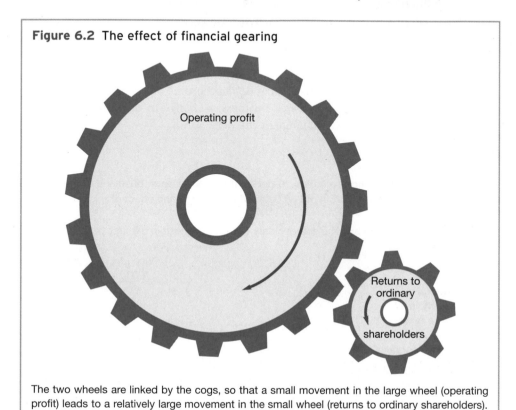

The two wheels are linked by the cogs, so that a small movement in the large wheel (operating profit) leads to a relatively large movement in the small wheel (returns to ordinary shareholders).

Two ratios are widely used to assess gearing:

- gearing ratio
- interest cover ratio.

## Gearing ratio

The gearing ratio measures the contribution of long-term lenders to the long-term capital structure of a business:

$$\text{Gearing ratio} = \frac{\text{Long-term (non-current) liabilities}}{\text{Share capital} + \text{Reserves} + \text{Long-term (non-current) liabilities}} \times 100$$

The gearing ratio for Alexis plc, as at 31 March 2009, is

$$\text{Gearing ratio} = \frac{200}{(563 + 200)} \times 100 = 26.2\%$$

This is a level of gearing that would not normally be considered to be very high.

## Activity 6.18

Calculate the gearing ratio of Alexis plc as at 31 March 2010.

The ratio as at 31 March 2010 is

$$\text{Gearing ratio} = \frac{300}{(534 + 300)} \times 100 = 36.0\%$$

This is a substantial increase in the level of gearing over the year.

## Interest cover ratio

→ The interest cover ratio measures the amount of operating profit available to cover interest payable. The ratio may be calculated as follows:

$$\text{Interest cover ratio} = \frac{\text{Operating profit}}{\text{Interest payable}}$$

The ratio for Alexis plc for the year ended 31 March 2009 is

$$\text{Interest cover ratio} = \frac{243}{18} = 13.5 \text{ times}$$

This ratio shows that the level of operating profit is considerably higher than the level of interest payable. This means that a large fall in operating profit could occur before operating profit levels failed to cover interest payable. The lower the level of operating profit coverage, the greater the risk to lenders that interest payments will not be met. There will also be a greater risk to the shareholders that the lenders will take action against the business to recover the interest due.

## Activity 6.19

Calculate the interest cover ratio of Alexis plc for the year ended 31 March 2010.

The ratio for the year ended 31 March 2010 is

$$\text{Interest cover ratio} = \frac{47}{32} = 1.5 \text{ times}$$

Alexis plc's gearing ratios are:

|  | 2009 | 2010 |
|---|---|---|
| Gearing ratio | 26.2% | 36.0% |
| Interest cover ratio | 13.5 times | 1.5 times |

## Activity 6.20

**What do you deduce from a comparison of Alexis plc's gearing ratios over the two years?**

The gearing ratio altered significantly. This is mainly due to the substantial increase in the contribution of long-term lenders to the financing of the business.

The interest cover ratio has declined dramatically from a position where operating profit covered interest 13.5 times in 2009, to one where operating profit covered interest only 1.5 times in 2010. This was partly caused by the increase in borrowings in 2010, but mainly caused by the dramatic decline in profitability in that year. The latter situation looks hazardous; only a small decline in future profitability would leave the business with insufficient operating profit to cover the interest payments. The gearing ratio at 31 March 2010 would not necessarily be considered to be very high for a business that was trading successfully. It is the low profitability that is the problem.

Without knowing what the business planned these ratios to be, it is not possible to reach a valid conclusion on Alexis plc's gearing.

Real World 6.6 consists of extracts from an article that discusses the likely lowering of gearing levels in the face of the recession. It explains that many businesses seem likely to issue additional ordinary shares (equity), either through making a rights issue or some public issue, and use the resulting funds to reduce borrowing as a means of reducing gearing.

## Real World 6.6

### Changing gear

When Stuart Siddall was corporate treasurer of AMEC four years ago, analysts were critical when the engineering group swung from having substantial net debt on its balance sheet [statement of financial position] to sitting on a huge cash pile after completing disposals.

'The analysts were saying "this is inefficient balance sheet management",' says Mr Siddall.

Companies back then were expected to be highly geared, with net debt to shareholders' funds at historically high levels.

How times have changed. With a wave of rights issues and other equity issuance now expected from the UK's non-financial companies – and with funds from these being used to pay down debt – the pendulum is rapidly swinging back in favour of more conservative balance sheet management. Gearing levels are set to fall dramatically, analysts say. 'There is going to be an appreciable and material drop in gearing, by about a quarter or a third over the next three years,' predicts Mr Siddall, now chief executive of the Association of Corporate Treasurers.

Historically, gearing levels – as measured by net debt as a proportion of shareholders' funds – have run at an average of about 30 per cent over the past 20 years.

Peak levels (around 45 per cent) were reached in the past few years as companies took advantage of cheap credit. Current predictions see it coming down to about 20 per cent – and staying there for a good while to come.

Graham Secker, managing director of equity research at Morgan Stanley, says 'This is going to be a relatively long-term phenomenon.'

One of the most immediate concerns to heavily indebted companies is whether, in a recessionary environment, they will be able to generate the profit and cash flows to service their debts.

Gearing levels vary from sector to sector as well. Oil companies prefer low levels given their exposure to the volatility of oil prices. BP's net debt to shareholders' funds ratio of 21 per cent is at the low end of a 20 to 30 per cent range it considers prudent.

Miners' gearing is on a clear downward trend already. Xstrata, the mining group, stressed last month that its £4.1 billion rights issue would cut gearing from 40 per cent to less than 30 per cent. A week later, BHP said its $13 billion of first-half cash flows had cut gearing to less than 10 per cent. Rio Tinto, which had gearing of 130 per cent at the last count in August 2008, is desperately trying to cut it by raising fresh equity.

Utilities tend to be highly geared because they can afford to borrow more against their typically reliable cash flows. But even here the trend is downwards.

Severn Trent, the UK water group, says its appropriate long-term gearing level is 60 per cent. But 'given ongoing uncertainties . . . it is prudent in the near term to retain as much liquidity and flexibility as possible'. It does not expect to pursue that target until credit markets improve.

Reducing gearing is not easy, especially for the most indebted companies that need to the most: shareholders will be more reluctant to finance replacement equity in companies with highly leveraged balance sheets.

The supply of fresh equity will also be constrained, not only by a glut of demand from companies but by the squeeze on investor money from a wave of government bond issuance.

Richard Jeffrey, chief investment officer at Cazenove Capital Management, says there is a risk of the government making it more difficult to raise money to improve balance sheets. 'That is of extreme concern because that could become a limitation, longer term, in the capital that companies have to fund investment.'

*Source*: adapted from 'Gearing levels set to plummet', *The Financial Times*, 10/02/2009 (Grant, J.), copyright © The Financial Times Ltd.

## ? Self-assessment question 6.1

Both Ali plc and Bhaskar plc operate electrical stores throughout the UK. The financial statements of each business for the year ended 30 June 2010 are as follows:

**Statements of financial position as at 30 June 2010**

|  | Ali plc £m | Bhaskar plc £m |
|---|---|---|
| ASSETS |  |  |
| Non-current assets |  |  |
| Property, plant and equipment (cost less depreciation) |  |  |
| Land and buildings | 360.0 | 510.0 |
| Fixtures and fittings | 87.0 | 91.2 |
|  | 447.0 | 601.2 |
| Current assets |  |  |
| Inventories | 592.0 | 403.0 |
| Trade receivables | 176.4 | 321.9 |
| Cash at bank | 84.6 | 91.6 |
|  | 853.0 | 816.5 |
| Total assets | 1,300.0 | 1,417.7 |

|  | Ali plc £m | Bhaskar plc £m |
|---|---|---|
| **EQUITY AND LIABILITIES** | | |
| **Equity** | | |
| £1 ordinary shares | 320.0 | 250.0 |
| Retained earnings | 367.6 | 624.6 |
|  | 687.6 | 874.6 |
| **Non-current liabilities** | | |
| Borrowings – loan notes | 190.0 | 250.0 |
| **Current liabilities** | | |
| Trade payables | 406.4 | 275.7 |
| Taxation | 16.0 | 17.4 |
|  | 422.4 | 293.1 |
| **Total equity and liabilities** | 1,300.0 | 1,417.7 |

### Income statements for the year ended 30 June 2010

|  | Ali plc £m | Bhaskar plc £m |
|---|---|---|
| Revenue | 1,478.1 | 1,790.4 |
| Cost of sales | (1,018.3) | (1,214.9) |
| **Gross profit** | 459.8 | 575.5 |
| Operating expenses | (308.5) | (408.6) |
| **Operating profit** | 151.3 | 166.9 |
| Interest payable | (19.4) | (27.5) |
| **Profit before taxation** | 131.9 | 139.4 |
| Taxation | (32.0) | (34.8) |
| **Profit for the year** | 99.9 | 104.6 |

All purchases and sales were on credit. Ali plc had announced its intention to pay a dividend of £135 million and Bhaskar plc £95 million in respect of the year. The market values of a share in Ali plc and Bhaskar plc at the end of the year were £6.50 and £8.20 respectively.

**Required:**
For each business, calculate two ratios that are concerned with each of the following aspects:

- profitability
- efficiency
- liquidity
- gearing.

What can you conclude from the eight ratios that you have calculated?

**The solution to this question can be found at the back of the book, in Appendix B.**

# Investment ratios

There are various ratios available that are designed to help shareholders assess the returns on their investment. The following are widely used:

- dividend payout ratio
- dividend yield ratio
- earnings per share
- price/earnings ratio.

## Dividend payout ratio

The dividend payout ratio measures the proportion of earnings that a business pays out to shareholders in the form of dividends. The ratio is calculated as follows:

$$\text{Dividend payout ratio} = \frac{\text{Dividends announced for the year}}{\text{Earnings for the year available for dividends}} \times 100$$

In the case of ordinary shares, the earnings available for dividend will normally be the profit for the year (that is, the profit after taxation) less any preference dividends relating to the year. This ratio is normally expressed as a percentage.

The dividend payout ratio for Alexis plc for the year ended 31 March 2009 is

$$\text{Dividend payout ratio} = \frac{40}{165} \times 100 = 24.2\%$$

The information provided by this ratio is often expressed slightly differently as the dividend cover ratio. Here the calculation is

$$\text{Dividend cover ratio} = \frac{\text{Earnings for the year available for dividends}}{\text{Dividends announced for the year}}$$

In the case of Alexis plc for 2009 it would be 165/40 = 4.1 times. That is to say, the earnings available for dividend cover the actual dividend paid by just over four times.

### Activity 6.21

Calculate the dividend payout ratio of Alexis plc for the year ended 31 March 2010.

The ratio for 2010 is

$$\text{Dividend payout ratio} = \frac{40}{11} \times 100 = 363.6\%$$

This would normally be considered to be a very alarming increase in the ratio over the two years. Paying a dividend of £40 million in 2010 would probably be widely regarded as very imprudent.

## Dividend yield ratio

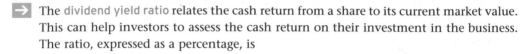 The dividend yield ratio relates the cash return from a share to its current market value. This can help investors to assess the cash return on their investment in the business. The ratio, expressed as a percentage, is

$$\text{Dividend yield} = \frac{\text{Dividend per share}/(1 - t)}{\text{Market value per share}} \times 100$$

where $t$ is the 'dividend tax credit' rate of income tax. This requires some explanation. In the UK, investors who receive a dividend from a business also receive a tax credit. As this tax credit can be offset against any tax liability arising from the dividends received, the dividends are effectively issued net of income tax, at the dividend tax credit rate.

Investors may wish to compare the returns from shares with the returns from other forms of investment. As these other forms of investment are usually quoted on a 'gross' (that is, pre-tax) basis it is useful to 'gross up' the dividend to make comparison easier. We can achieve this by dividing the dividend per share by $(1 - t)$, where $t$ is the 'dividend tax credit' rate of income tax.

Using the 2009/10 dividend tax credit rate of 10 per cent, the dividend yield for Alexis plc for the year ended 31 March 2009 is

$$\text{Dividend yield} = \frac{0.067^*/(1 - 0.10)}{2.50} \times 100 = 3.0\%$$

\* Dividend proposed/number of shares = 40/(300 × 2) = £0.067 dividend per share (the 300 is multiplied by 2 because they are £0.50 shares). The share's market value is given in Note 1 to Example 6.1 (page 192).

### Activity 6.22

Calculate the dividend yield for Alexis plc for the year ended 31 March 2010.

The ratio for 2010 is

$$\text{Dividend yield} = \frac{0.067^*/(1 - 0.10)}{1.50} \times 100 = 4.9\%$$

\* 40/(300 × 2) = £0.067.

## Earnings per share

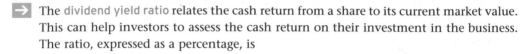 The earnings per share (EPS) ratio relates the earnings generated by the business, and available to shareholders, during a period, to the number of shares in issue. For equity (ordinary) shareholders, the amount available is the profit for the year (profit after taxation) less any preference dividend, where applicable. The ratio for equity shareholders is calculated as follows:

$$\text{Earnings per share} = \frac{\text{Earnings available to ordinary shareholders}}{\text{Number of ordinary shares in issue}}$$

In the case of Alexis plc, the earnings per share for the year ended 31 March 2009 is as follows:

$$\text{EPS} = \frac{£165m}{600m} = 27.5p$$

Many investment analysts regard the EPS ratio as a fundamental measure of share performance. The trend in earnings per share over time is used to help assess the investment potential of a business's shares.

It is not usually very helpful to compare the EPS of one business with that of another. Differences in financing arrangements (for example, in the nominal value of shares issued) can render any such comparison meaningless. However, it can be very useful to monitor the changes that occur in this ratio for a particular business over time.

## Activity 6.23

Calculate the earnings per share of Alexis plc for the year ended 31 March 2010.

The ratio for 2010 is

$$\text{EPS} = \frac{£11m}{600m} = 1.8p$$

## Price/earnings (P/E) ratio

The price/earnings ratio relates the market value of a share to the earnings per share. This ratio can be calculated as follows:

$$\text{P/E ratio} = \frac{\text{Market value per share}}{\text{Earnings per share}}$$

The P/E ratio for Alexis plc as at 31 March 2009 is

$$\text{P/E ratio} = \frac{£2.50}{27.5p^*} = 9.1 \text{ times}$$

* The EPS figure (27.5p) was calculated above.

This ratio indicates that the market value of the share is 9.1 times higher than its current level of earnings. The ratio is a measure of market confidence in the future of a business. The higher the P/E ratio, the greater the confidence in the future earning power of the business and, consequently, the more investors are prepared to pay in relation to the earnings stream of the business.

P/E ratios provide a useful guide to market confidence concerning the future and they can, therefore, be helpful when comparing different businesses. However, differences in accounting policies between businesses can lead to different profit and earnings per share figures. This can distort comparisons.

## Activity 6.24

Calculate the P/E ratio of Alexis plc as at 31 March 2010.

The ratio for 2010 is

$$\text{P/E ratio} = \frac{\pounds1.50}{1.8p} = 83.3 \text{ times}$$

The investment ratios for Alexis plc over the two-year period are as follows:

|  | 2009 | 2010 |
|---|---|---|
| Dividend payout ratio | 24.2% | 363.6% |
| Dividend yield ratio | 3.0% | 4.9% |
| Earnings per share | 27.5p | 1.8p |
| P/E ratio | 9.1 times | 83.3 times |

## Activity 6.25

What do you deduce from the investment ratios set out above?
   Can you offer an explanation why the share price has not fallen as much as it might have done, bearing in mind the very poor (relative to 2009) trading performance in 2010?

We thought that, although the EPS has fallen dramatically and the dividend payment for 2010 seems very imprudent, the share price seems to have held up remarkably well (fallen from £2.50 to £1.50). This means that dividend yield and P/E value for 2010 look better than those for 2009. This is an anomaly of these two ratios, which stems from using a forward-looking value (the share price) in conjunction with historic data (dividends and earnings). Share prices are based on investors' assessments of the business's future. It seems with Alexis plc that, at the end of 2010, the 'market' was not happy with the business, relative to 2009. This is evidenced by the fact that the share price had fallen by £1 a share. On the other hand, the share price has not fallen as much as profit for the year. It appears that investors believe that the business will perform better in the future than it did in 2010. This may well be because they believe that the large expansion in assets and employee numbers that occurred in 2010 will yield benefits in the future; benefits that the business was not able to generate during 2010.

Real World 6.7 gives some information about the shares of several large, well-known UK businesses. This type of information is provided on a daily basis by several newspapers, notably *The Financial Times*.

## Real World 6.7

# Market statistics for some well-known businesses

The following data were extracted from the *Financial Times* of 2 April 2010, relating to the previous day's trading of the shares of some well-known businesses on the London Stock Exchange.

| Share | Price | Chng | 2009/10 | | Y'ld | P/E | Volume |
|---|---|---|---|---|---|---|---|
| | | | High | Low | | | 000s |
| BP | 631.30 | +7.9 | 640.10 | 400 | 6.4 | 11.5 | 75,461 |
| J D Wetherspoon | 513 | +7.50 | 543.57 | 266.36 | 2.3 | 14.4 | 533 |
| ITV | 62.95 | +2.20 | 63.85 | 16.50 | – | 18.9 | 58,787 |
| Marks and Spencer | 371.90 | +1.80 | 412.70 | 209.50 | 4.0 | 11.6 | 7,874 |
| Rolls-Royce | 611 | +15.50 | 611.50 | 242.01 | 2.2 | 5.1 | 9,007 |
| Vodafone | 151.70 | –0.30 | 153.80 | 111.20 | 5.2 | 8.1 | 298,865 |

The column headings are as follows:

Price      Mid-market price in pence (that is, the price midway between buying and selling price) of the shares at the end of trading on 1 April 2010

Chng      Gain or loss in the mid-market price during 1 April 2010

High/Low      Highest and lowest prices reached by the share during the year ended on 1 April 2010

Y'ld      Gross dividend yield, based on the most recent year's dividend and the current share price

P/E      Price/earnings ratio, based on the most recent year's (after-tax) profit for the year and the current share price

Volume      The number of shares (in thousands) that were bought/sold on 1 April 2010.

So, for example for BP, the oil business:

- the shares had a mid-market price of £6.313 each at the close of Stock Exchange trading on 1 April 2010;
- the shares had increased in price by 7.9 pence during trading on 1 April 2010;
- the shares had highest and lowest prices during the previous year of £6.401 and £4.00, respectively;
- the shares had a dividend yield, based on the 1 April 2010 price (and the dividend for the most recent year) of 6.4 per cent;
- the shares had a P/E ratio, based on the 1 April 2010 price (and the after-taxation earnings per share for the most recent year) of 11.5;
- during trading in the shares on 1 April 2010, 75,461 of the business's shares had changed hands from one investor to another.

Note that one of the businesses shown above (ITV) does not have a dividend yield figure. This is because it has not paid a dividend recently.

*Source: The Financial Times, 2 April 2010.*

Real World 6.8 shows how investment ratios can vary between different industry sectors.

## Yielding dividends

Investment ratios can vary significantly between businesses and between industries. To give some indication of the range of variations that occur, the average dividend yield ratios and average P/E ratios for listed businesses in twelve different industries are shown in Figures 6.3 and 6.4, respectively.

These dividend yield ratios are calculated from the current market value of the shares and the most recent year's dividend paid.

Some industries tend to pay out lower dividends than others, leading to lower dividend yield ratios. The average for all Stock Exchange listed businesses was 3.12 (as is shown in Figure 6.3), but there is a wide variation with chemicals at 2.18 and electricity at 5.22.

Some types of businesses tend to invest heavily in developing new products, hence their tendency to pay low dividends compared with their share prices. Some of the inter-industry differences in the dividend yield ratio can be explained by the nature of the calculation of

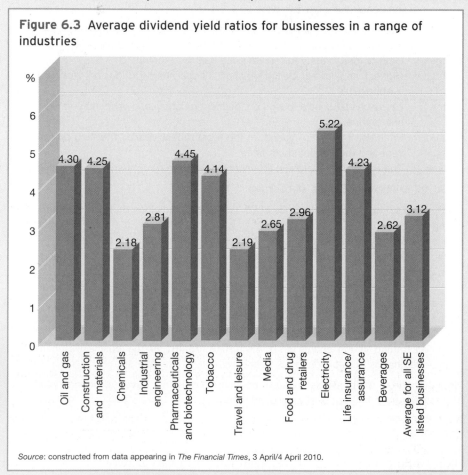

**Figure 6.3** Average dividend yield ratios for businesses in a range of industries

*Source*: constructed from data appearing in *The Financial Times*, 3 April/4 April 2010.

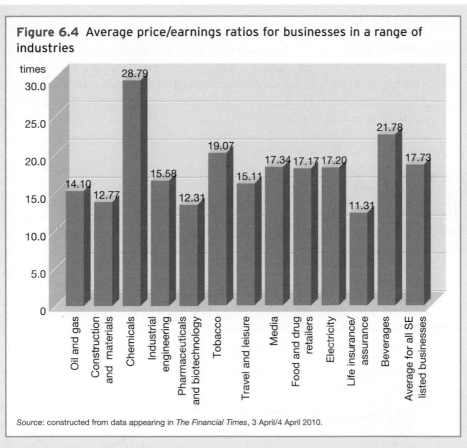

**Figure 6.4** Average price/earnings ratios for businesses in a range of industries

*Source*: constructed from data appearing in *The Financial Times*, 3 April/4 April 2010.

the ratio. The prices of shares at any given moment are based on expectations of their economic futures; dividends are actual past events. A business that had a good trading year recently may have paid a dividend that, in the light of investors' assessment of the business's economic future, may be high (a high dividend yield).

The P/E ratios are calculated from the current market value of the shares and the most recent year's earnings per share (EPS).

Businesses that have a high share price relative to their recent historic earnings have high P/E ratios. This may be because their future is regarded as economically bright, which may be the result of investing heavily in the future at the expense of recent profits (earnings). On the other hand, high P/Es also arise where businesses have recent low earnings but investors believe that their future is brighter. The average P/E for all Stock Exchange listed businesses was 17.73, but for life assurance it was as low as 11.31 and for chemicals as high as 28.79.

At 3 April 2010, P/E ratios were at a fairly high level. Share prices were quite high, as a result of a strong recovery in share prices from their low point in February 2009. At the same time, the recession had led to fairly low reported profits. (Remember that P/Es are based on current share prices and recent reported profits.)

*Source*: *The Financial Times*, 3 April/4 April 2010.

## Trend analysis

It is often helpful to see whether ratios are indicating trends. Key ratios can be plotted on a graph to provide a simple visual display of changes occurring over time. The trends occurring within a business may, for example, be plotted against trends for rival businesses or for the industry as a whole for comparison purposes. An example of trend analysis is shown in Real World 6.9.

### Real World 6.9

### Trend setting

In Figure 6.5 the current ratio of three of the UK's leading supermarkets is plotted over time. We can see that the current ratio of Tesco plc has risen over the period but it was, nevertheless, consistently lower than that of its main rivals, until 2005, when it overtook Morrison; in 2009, it overtook Sainsbury. Sainsbury seems to be following the opposite trend, with its current ratio on a fairly consistent downward path. With well-managed businesses like Sainsbury and Tesco, it seems highly probable that these trends are the result of deliberate policy.

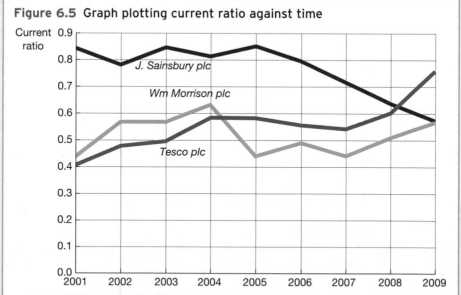

**Figure 6.5** Graph plotting current ratio against time

The current ratio for three leading UK supermarkets is plotted for the financial years ended during 2001 to 2009. This enables comparison to be made regarding the ratio, both for each of the three businesses over time and between the businesses.

*Source:* ratios calculated from information in the annual reports of the three businesses for the years 2001 to 2009.

Many larger businesses publish certain key financial ratios as part of their annual reports to help users identify significant trends. These ratios typically cover several years' activities. Real World 6.10 shows part of the table of 'key performance measures' of Marks and Spencer plc (M and S), the well-known UK high street store.

---

**Real World 6.10**

## Key performance measures of Marks and Spencer plc

| | | 2009<br>52 weeks | 2008<br>52 weeks | 2007<br>52 weeks | 2006<br>53 weeks | 2005<br>52 weeks |
|---|---|---|---|---|---|---|
| Gross margin | $\dfrac{\text{Gross profit}}{\text{Revenue}}$ | 37.2% | 38.6% | 38.9% | 38.3% | 34.7% |
| Net margin | $\dfrac{\text{Operating profit}}{\text{Revenue}}$ | 9.6% | 13.4% | 12.2% | 10.9% | 8.0% |
| Net margin excluding property disposals and exceptional items | | 8.5% | 12.1% | 12.2% | 11.0% | 8.7% |
| Profitability | $\dfrac{\text{Profit before tax}}{\text{Revenue}}$ | 7.8% | 12.5% | 10.9% | 9.6% | 6.7% |
| Profitability excluding property disposals and exceptional items | | 6.7% | 11.2% | 11.2% | 9.6% | 7.4% |
| Basic earnings per share | $\dfrac{\text{Basic earnings}}{\text{Weighted average ordinary shares in issue}}$ | 32.3p | 49.2p | 39.1p | 31.3p | 17.6p |
| Earnings per share adjusted for property disposals and exceptional items | | 28.0p | 43.6p | 40.4p | 31.4p | 19.2p |
| Dividend per share declared in respect of the year | | 17.8p | 22.5p | 18.3p | 14.0p | 12.1p |
| Dividend cover | $\dfrac{\text{Profit attributable to shareholders}}{\text{Dividends payable}}$ | 1.8× | 2.3× | 2.1× | 2.2× | 2.9× |
| Return on equity | $\dfrac{\text{Profit attributable to shareholders}}{\text{Average equity shareholders' funds}}$ | 25.2% | 45.6% | 46.3% | 50.0% | 35.1% |

*Source*: Marks and Spencer plc Annual Report 2009. Reproduced by kind permission of Marks and Spencer plc.

---

M and S's return on equity (return on ordinary shareholders' funds) in 2009 was significantly less good than it had been during the previous three years. The net margin fell significantly in 2009 from a recent peak in 2008, though the gross margin was fairly stable after 2005. M and S felt that its problems in 2009 were substantially related to difficult trading conditions in a major recession.

## Using ratios to predict future outcomes

Financial ratios, based on current or past performance, are often used to help predict the future, though both the choice of ratios and the interpretation of results are normally dependent on the judgement of the analyst. Attempts have been made, however, to develop a more rigorous and systematic approach to the use of ratios for prediction purposes. In particular, researchers have shown an interest in the use of ratios to predict financial distress in a business. By financial distress we mean a business getting into financial difficulties or even being made 'bankrupt' and forced out of existence. Several methods and models using ratios have been developed that are claimed to predict future financial distress. Researchers have also developed ratio-based models with which to assess the supposed vulnerability of a business to takeover by another business. These areas, of course, are of interest to all those connected with the business. In the future, it is likely that further ratio-based models will be developed that predict other aspects of future performance.

## Limitations of ratio analysis

Although ratios offer a quick and useful method of analysing the position and perform-ance of a business, they are not without their problems and limitations. We shall now review some of the shortcomings of financial ratio analysis.

### Quality of financial statements

It must always be remembered that ratios are based on financial statements. The results of ratio analysis are, therefore, dependent on the quality of these underlying statements. Ratios will inherit the limitations of the financial statements on which they are based. In Chapter 2 we saw that one important limitation of financial state-ments is their failure to include all resources controlled by the business. Internally generated goodwill and brands, for example, are excluded from the statement of finan-cial position because they fail to meet the strict definition of an asset. This means that, even though these resources may be of considerable value, key ratios such as ROSF, ROCE and the gearing ratio will fail to acknowledge their presence.

There is also the problem of deliberate attempts to make the financial statements misleading. We discussed this problem of *creative accounting* in Chapter 4.

### Inflation

A persistent, though recently less severe, problem, in most countries is that the finan-cial results of businesses can be distorted as a result of inflation. One effect of inflation is that the reported value of assets held for any length of time may bear little relation to current values. Generally speaking, the reported value of assets will be understated in current terms during a period of inflation as they are usually reported at their original cost (less any amounts written off for depreciation). This means that comparisons, either between businesses or between periods, will be hindered. A difference in, say, ROCE may simply be owing to the fact that assets shown in one of the statements of financial position being compared were acquired more recently (ignoring the effect of depreciation on the asset values). Another effect of inflation is to distort the measurement of profit. In the calculation of profit, sales revenue is often matched with costs incurred at an earlier time. This is because there is often a time lag between acquiring a particular resource and using it to help generate sales revenue. For example, inventories may well be acquired several months before they are sold. During a period of inflation, this will mean that the expense does not reflect prices that are current at the time of the sale. The cost of sales figure is usually based on the historic cost of the inventories concerned. As a result, expenses will be understated in the income statement and this, in turn, means that profit will be overstated. One effect of this will be to distort the profitability ratios discussed earlier.

## Overreliance on ratios

It is important not to rely exclusively on ratios, thereby losing sight of information contained in the underlying financial statements. As we saw earlier in the chapter, some items reported in these statements can be vital in assessing position and performance. For example, the total sales revenue, capital employed and profit figures may be useful in assessing changes in absolute size that occur over time, or in assessing differences in scale between businesses. Ratios do not provide such information. When comparing one figure with another, ratios measure relative performance and position and, therefore, provide only part of the picture. When comparing two businesses, therefore, it will often be useful to assess the absolute size of profits, as well as the relative profitability of each business. For example, Business A may generate £1 million operating profit and have a ROCE of 15 per cent and Business B may generate £100,000 operating profit and have a ROCE of 20 per cent. Although Business B has a higher level of profitability, as measured by ROCE, it generates lower total operating profits. This may well be useful information for the analyst.

## The basis for comparison

We saw earlier that if ratios are to be useful, they require a basis for comparison. Moreover, it is important that the analyst compares like with like. Where the comparison is with another business, there can be difficulties. No two businesses are identical: the greater the differences between the businesses being compared, the greater the limitations of ratio analysis. Furthermore, any differences in accounting policies, financing methods (gearing levels) and reporting year ends will add to the problems of making comparisons between businesses.

## Ratios relating to the statement of financial position

Because the statement of financial position is only a 'snapshot' of the business at a particular moment in time, any ratios based on statement of financial position figures, such as the liquidity ratios, may not be representative of the financial position of the business for the year as a whole. For example, it is common for a seasonal business to have a financial year end that coincides with a low point in business activity. As a result, inventories and trade receivables may be low at the year end. This means that the liquidity ratios may also be low. A more representative picture of liquidity can only really be gained by taking additional measurements at other points in the year.

Real World 6.11 points out another way in which ratios are limited.

---

**Real World 6.11**

## Remember, it's people that really count . . .

Lord Weinstock (1924–2002) was an influential industrialist whose management style and philosophy helped to shape management practice in many UK businesses. During his long and successful reign at GEC plc, a major engineering business, Lord Weinstock relied heavily on financial ratios to assess performance and to exercise control. In particular, he relied on ratios relating to sales revenue, expenses, trade receivables, profit margins and inventories turnover. However, he was keenly aware of the limitations of ratios and recognised that, ultimately, people produce profits.

In a memo written to GEC managers he pointed out that ratios are an aid to good management rather than a substitute for it. He wrote:

> The operating ratios are of great value as measures of efficiency but they are only the measures and not efficiency itself. Statistics will not design a product better, make it for a lower cost or increase sales. If ill-used, they may so guide action as to diminish resources for the sake of apparent but false signs of improvement.
>
> Management remains a matter of judgement, of knowledge of products and processes and of understanding and skill in dealing with people. The ratios will indicate how well all these things are being done and will show comparison with how they are done elsewhere. But they will tell us nothing about how to do them. That is what you are meant to do.

*Source*: Extract from Aris, S., *Arnold Weinstock and the Making of GEC*, Aurum Press, 1998, published in *The Sunday Times*, 22 February 1998, p. 3.

---

## Summary

The main points of this chapter may be summarised as follows.

### Ratio analysis

- Ratio analysis compares two related figures, usually both from the same set of financial statements.
- It is an aid to understanding what the financial statements really mean.
- It is an inexact science, so results must be interpreted cautiously.
- Past periods, the performance of similar businesses and planned performance are often used to provide benchmark ratios.
- A brief overview of the financial statements can often provide insights that may not be revealed by ratios and/or may help in the interpretation of them.

### Profitability ratios

- Profitability ratios are concerned with effectiveness at generating profit.
- The profitability ratios covered are the return on ordinary shareholders' funds (ROSF), return on capital employed (ROCE), operating profit margin and gross profit margin.

### Efficiency ratios

- Efficiency ratios are concerned with efficiency of using assets/resources.
- The efficiency ratios covered are the average inventories turnover period, average settlement period for trade receivables, average settlement period for trade payables, sales revenue to capital employed and sales revenue per employee.

### Liquidity ratios

- Liquidity ratios are concerned with the ability to meet short-term obligations.
- The liquidity ratios covered are the current ratio and the acid test ratio.

### Gearing ratios

- Gearing ratios are concerned with the relationship between equity and debt financing.
- The gearing ratios covered are the gearing ratio and the interest cover ratio.

### Investment ratios

- Investment ratios are concerned with returns to shareholders.
- The investment ratios covered are the dividend payout ratio, dividend yield ratio, earnings per share and price/earnings ratio.

### Uses of ratios

- Individual ratios can be tracked to detect trends (for example, by plotting them on a graph).
- Ratios can be used to help predict the future, particularly financial distress.

### Limitations of ratio analysis

- Ratios are only as reliable as the financial statements from which they derive.
- Inflation can distort the information.
- Ratios give a restricted vision.
- It can be difficult to find a suitable benchmark (for example, another business) to compare with.
- Some ratios could mislead due to the 'snapshot' nature of the statement of financial position.

 *Now check your progress in your personal Study Plan*

→ **Key terms**

return on ordinary shareholders' funds
   ratio (ROSF) p. 193
return on capital employed ratio
   (ROCE) p. 194
operating profit margin ratio p. 196
gross profit margin ratio p. 197
average inventories turnover period
   ratio p. 200
average settlement period for trade
   receivables ratio p. 201
average settlement period for trade
   payables ratio p. 202
sales revenue to capital employed ratio
   p. 203

sales revenue per employee ratio
   p. 204
current ratio p. 207
acid test ratio p. 208
financial gearing p. 209
gearing ratio p. 212
interest cover ratio p. 213
dividend payout ratio p. 217
dividend cover ratio p. 217
dividend yield ratio p. 218
dividend per share p. 218
earnings per share (EPS) p. 218
price/earnings ratio p. 219

## Further reading

If you would like to explore the topics covered in this chapter in more depth, we recommend the following books:

Elliott, B. and Elliott, J., *Financial Accounting and Reporting* (13th edn), Financial Times Prentice Hall, 2010, chapter 28.

Schoenebeck, K. and Holtzman, M., *Interpreting and Analyzing Financial Statements* (5th edn), Prentice Hall, 2009, chapters 2, 3, 4 and 5.

Wild, J., Subramanyam, K. and Halsey, R., *Financial Statement Analysis* (9th edn), McGraw-Hill, 2006, chapters 8, 9 and 11.

## ? Review questions

**Solutions to these questions can be found at the back of the book, in Appendix C.**

**6.1** Some businesses operate on a low operating profit margin (for example, a supermarket chain). Does this mean that the return on capital employed from the business will also be low?

**6.2** What potential problems arise for the external analyst from the use of statement of financial position figures in the calculation of financial ratios?

**6.3** Two businesses operate in the same industry. One has an inventories turnover period that is longer than the industry average. The other has an inventories turnover period that is shorter than the industry average. Give three possible explanations for each business's inventories turnover period ratio.

**6.4** In the chapter it was mentioned that ratios help to eliminate some of the problems of comparing businesses of different sizes. Does this mean that size is irrelevant when interpreting and analysing the position and performance of different businesses?

# Exercises

Exercises 6.4 and 6.5 are more advanced than 6.1 to 6.3. Those with coloured numbers have solutions at the back of the book, in Appendix D.

If you wish to try more exercises, visit the website at www.myaccountinglab.com.

**6.1** I. Jiang (Western) Ltd has recently produced its financial statements for the current year. The directors are concerned that the return on capital employed (ROCE) had decreased from 14 per cent last year to 12 per cent for the current year.

The following reasons were suggested as to why this reduction in ROCE had occurred:

1 an increase in the gross profit margin;
2 a reduction in sales revenue;
3 an increase in overhead expenses;
4 an increase in amount of inventories held;
5 the repayment of some borrowings at the year end; and
6 an increase in the time taken for credit customers (trade receivables) to pay.

**Required:**
Taking each of these six suggested reasons in turn, state, with reasons, whether each of them could lead to a reduction in ROCE.

**6.2** Amsterdam Ltd and Berlin Ltd are both engaged in retailing, but they seem to take a different approach to it according to the following information:

| Ratio | Amsterdam Ltd | Berlin Ltd |
|---|---|---|
| Return on capital employed (ROCE) | 20% | 17% |
| Return on ordinary shareholders' funds (ROSF) | 30% | 18% |
| Average settlement period for trade receivables | 63 days | 21 days |
| Average settlement period for trade payables | 50 days | 45 days |
| Gross profit margin | 40% | 15% |
| Operating profit margin | 10% | 10% |
| Average inventories turnover period | 52 days | 25 days |

**Required:**
Describe what this information indicates about the differences in approach between the two businesses. If one of them prides itself on personal service and one of them on competitive prices, which do you think is which and why?

**6.3** Conday and Co. Ltd has been in operation for three years and produces antique repro-
duction furniture for the export market. The most recent set of financial statements for the
business is set out as follows:

**Statement of financial position as at 30 November**

| ASSETS | £000 |
|---|---|
| **Non-current assets** | |
| *Property, plant and equipment (cost less depreciation)* | |
| Land and buildings | 228 |
| Plant and machinery | 762 |
| | 990 |
| **Current assets** | |
| Inventories | 600 |
| Trade receivables | 820 |
| | 1,420 |
| **Total assets** | 2,410 |
| **EQUITY AND LIABILITIES** | |
| **Equity** | |
| Ordinary shares of £1 each | 700 |
| Retained earnings | 365 |
| | 1,065 |
| **Non-current liabilities** | |
| Borrowings – 9% loan notes (Note 1) | 200 |
| **Current liabilities** | |
| Trade payables | 665 |
| Taxation | 48 |
| Short-term borrowings (all bank overdraft) | 432 |
| | 1,145 |
| **Total equity and liabilities** | 2,410 |

**Income statement for the year ended 30 November**

| | £000 |
|---|---|
| Revenue | 2,600 |
| Cost of sales | (1,620) |
| **Gross profit** | 980 |
| Selling and distribution expenses (Note 2) | (408) |
| Administration expenses | (194) |
| **Operating profit** | 378 |
| Finance expenses | (58) |
| **Profit before taxation** | 320 |
| Taxation | (95) |
| **Profit for the year** | 225 |

Notes:
1 The loan notes are secured on the freehold land and buildings.
2 Selling and distribution expenses include £170,000 in respect of bad debts.
3 A dividend of £160,000 was paid on the ordinary shares during the year.
4 The directors have invited an investor to take up a new issue of ordinary shares in the business at £6.40 each making a total investment of £200,000. The directors wish to use the
funds to finance a programme of further expansion.

**Required:**

(a) Analyse the financial position and performance of the business and comment on any features that you consider to be significant.

(b) State, with reasons, whether or not the investor should invest in the business on the terms outlined.

**6.4** Threads Limited manufactures nuts and bolts, which are sold to industrial users. The abbreviated financial statements for 2009 and 2010 are as follows:

### Income statements for the year ended 30 June

|  | 2009 | 2010 |
|---|---|---|
|  | £000 | £000 |
| Revenue | 1,180 | 1,200 |
| Cost of sales | (680) | (750) |
| Gross profit | 500 | 450 |
| Operating expenses | (200) | (208) |
| Depreciation | (66) | (75) |
| Operating profit | 234 | 167 |
| Interest | (–) | (8) |
| Profit before taxation | 234 | 159 |
| Taxation | (80) | (48) |
| Profit for the year | 154 | 111 |

### Statements of financial position as at 30 June

|  | 2009 | 2010 |
|---|---|---|
| ASSETS | £000 | £000 |
| Non-current assets |  |  |
| Property, plant and equipment | 702 | 687 |
| Current assets |  |  |
| Inventories | 148 | 236 |
| Trade receivables | 102 | 156 |
| Cash | 3 | 4 |
|  | 253 | 396 |
| Total assets | 955 | 1,083 |
| EQUITY AND LIABILITIES |  |  |
| Equity |  |  |
| Ordinary share capital (£1 shares, fully paid) | 500 | 500 |
| Retained earnings | 256 | 295 |
|  | 756 | 795 |
| Non-current liabilities |  |  |
| Borrowings – bank loan | – | 50 |
| Current liabilities |  |  |
| Trade payables | 60 | 76 |
| Other payables and accruals | 18 | 16 |
| Taxation | 40 | 24 |
| Short-term borrowings (all bank overdraft) | 81 | 122 |
|  | 199 | 238 |
| Total equity and liabilities | 955 | 1,083 |

233

Dividends were paid on ordinary shares of £70,000 and £72,000 in respect of 2009 and 2010, respectively.

**Required:**

(a) Calculate the following financial ratios for *both* 2009 and 2010 (using year-end figures for statement of financial position items):

1  return on capital employed
2  operating profit margin
3  gross profit margin
4  current ratio
5  acid test ratio
6  settlement period for trade receivables
7  settlement period for trade payables
8  inventories turnover period.

(b) Comment on the performance of Threads Limited from the viewpoint of a business considering supplying a substantial amount of goods to Threads Limited on usual trade credit terms.

**6.5** Bradbury Ltd is a family-owned clothes manufacturer based in the south west of England. For a number of years the chairman and managing director was David Bradbury. During his period of office, sales revenue had grown steadily at a rate of 2 to 3 per cent each year. David Bradbury retired on 30 November 2009 and was succeeded by his son Simon. Soon after taking office, Simon decided to expand the business. Within weeks he had successfully negotiated a five-year contract with a large clothes retailer to make a range of sports and leisurewear items. The contract will result in an additional £2 million in sales revenue during each year of the contract. To fulfil the contract, Bradbury Ltd acquired new equipment and premises.

Financial information concerning the business is given below:

**Income statements for the year ended 30 November**

|  | 2009 | 2010 |
|---|---|---|
|  | £000 | £000 |
| Revenue | 9,482 | 11,365 |
| Operating profit | 914 | 1,042 |
| Interest charges | (22) | (81) |
| Profit before taxation | 892 | 961 |
| Taxation | (358) | (386) |
| Profit for the year | 534 | 575 |

**Statements of financial position as at 30 November**

| | 2009 £000 | 2010 £000 |
|---|---|---|
| ASSETS | | |
| Non-current assets | | |
| *Property, plant and equipment* | | |
| Premises at cost | 5,240 | 7,360 |
| Plant and equipment (net) | 2,375 | 4,057 |
| | 7,615 | 11,417 |
| Current assets | | |
| Inventories | 2,386 | 3,420 |
| Trade receivables | 2,540 | 4,280 |
| | 4,926 | 7,700 |
| Total assets | 12,541 | 19,117 |
| EQUITY AND LIABILITIES | | |
| Equity | | |
| Share capital | 2,000 | 2,000 |
| Reserves | 7,813 | 8,268 |
| | 9,813 | 10,268 |
| Non-current liabilities | | |
| Borrowing – loans | 1,220 | 3,675 |
| Current liabilities | | |
| Trade payables | 1,157 | 2,245 |
| Taxation | 179 | 193 |
| Short-term borrowings (all bank overdraft) | 172 | 2,736 |
| | 1,508 | 5,174 |
| Total equity and liabilities | 12,541 | 19,117 |

Dividends of £120,000 were paid on ordinary shares in respect of each of the two years.

**Required:**

(a) Calculate, for each year (using year-end figures for statement of financial position items), the following ratios:
   1 operating profit margin
   2 return on capital employed
   3 current ratio
   4 gearing ratio
   5 trade receivables settlement period
   6 sales revenue to capital employed.

(b) Using the above ratios, and any other ratios or information you consider relevant, comment on the results of the expansion programme.

# Part 2

# MANAGEMENT ACCOUNTING

7  Cost-volume-profit analysis

8  Full costing

9  Budgeting

## Chapter 7

# Cost-volume-profit analysis

## Introduction

This chapter is concerned with the relationship between the volume of activity, cost
and profit. Broadly, costs can be analysed between those that are fixed, relative to the
volume of activity, and those that vary with the volume of activity. We shall consider how
an understanding of this relationship can be used to make decisions and to assess risk,
particularly in the context of short-term decisions.

Though the distinction between financial accounting and management accounting is
rather blurred, and much relating to the financial statements that we have discussed so
far in the book relates to providing information to managers, this chapter is the first that
is clearly in the area of management accounting.

## Learning outcomes

**When you have completed this chapter, you should be able to:**

- distinguish between fixed cost and variable cost and use this distinction to explain
  the relationship between cost, volume and profit;
- prepare a break-even chart and deduce the break-even point for some activity;
- discuss the weaknesses of break-even analysis;
- demonstrate the way in which marginal analysis can be used when making short-term
  decisions.

*MyAccountingLab*    *Remember to create your own
personalised Study Plan*

## Cost behaviour

→ Cost represents the resources that have to be sacrificed to achieve a business objective. The objective may be to make a particular product, to provide a particular service, to operate an IT department and so on. The costs incurred by a business may be classified in various ways and one important way is according to how they behave in relation to changes in the volume of activity. A cost may be classified according to whether it

- remains constant (fixed) when changes occur to the volume of activity; or
- varies according to the volume of activity.

→ These are known as fixed cost and variable cost respectively. Thus, in the case of a restaurant, the manager's salary would normally be a fixed cost while the cost of the unprepared food would be a variable cost.

As we shall see, knowing how much of each type of cost is associated with a particular activity can be of great value to the decision maker.

## Fixed cost

The way in which a fixed cost behaves can be shown by preparing a graph that plots the fixed cost of a business against the level of activity, as in Figure 7.1. The distance OF represents the amount of fixed cost, which stays the same irrespective of the volume of activity.

### Activity 7.1

Can you give some examples of items of cost that are likely to be fixed for a hairdressing business?

We came up with the following:

- rent
- insurance
- cleaning cost
- staff salaries.

These items of cost are likely to be the same irrespective of the number of customers having their hair cut or styled.

Staff salaries (or wages) are often assumed to be a variable cost but in practice they tend to be fixed. Members of staff are not normally paid according to the volume of output and it is unusual to dismiss staff when there is a short-term downturn in activity. Where there is a long-term downturn, or at least it seems that way to management, redundancies may occur with fixed-cost savings. This, however, is true of all types of fixed cost. For example, management may also decide to close some branches to make rental cost savings.

**Figure 7.1** Graph of fixed cost against the volume of activity

As the volume of output increases, the fixed cost stays exactly the same (0F).

There are circumstances in which the labour cost is variable (for example, where staff are paid according to how much output they produce), but this is unusual. Whether labour cost is fixed or variable depends on the circumstances in the particular case concerned.

It is important to be clear that 'fixed', in this context, means only that the cost is unaffected by changes in the volume of activity. Fixed cost is likely to be affected by inflation. If rent (a typical fixed cost) goes up because of inflation, a fixed cost will have increased, but not because of a change in the volume of activity.

Similarly, the level of fixed cost does not stay the same irrespective of the time period involved. Fixed cost elements are almost always *time-based*: that is, they vary with the length of time concerned. The rental charge for two months is normally twice that for one month. Thus, fixed cost normally varies with time, but (of course) not with the volume of output. This means that when we talk of fixed cost being, say, £1,000, we must add the period concerned, say, £1,000 a month.

### Activity 7.2

Does fixed cost stay the same irrespective of the volume of output, even where there is a massive rise in that volume? Think in terms of the rent cost for the hairdressing business.

In fact, the rent is only fixed over a particular range (known as the 'relevant' range). If the number of people wanting to have their hair cut by the business increased, and the business wished to meet this increased demand, it would eventually have to expand its physical size. This might be achieved by opening an additional branch, or perhaps by moving the existing business to larger premises nearby. It may be possible to cope with relatively minor increases in activity by using existing space more efficiently, or by having longer opening hours. If activity continued to expand, however, increased rent charges would seem inevitable.

In practice, the situation described in Activity 7.2 would look something like Figure 7.2.

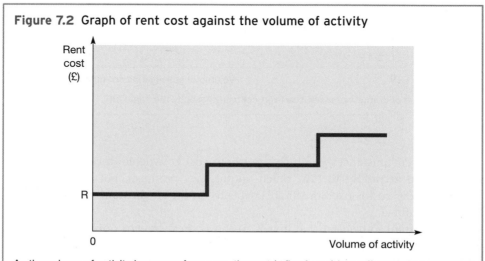

**Figure 7.2  Graph of rent cost against the volume of activity**

As the volume of activity increases from zero, the rent (a fixed cost) is unaffected. At a particular point, the volume of activity cannot increase further without additional space being rented. The cost of renting the additional space will cause a 'step' in the rent cost. The higher rent cost will continue unaffected if volume rises further until eventually another step point is reached.

At lower volumes of activity, the rent cost shown in Figure 7.2 would be OR. As the volume of activity expands, the accommodation becomes inadequate and further expansion requires an increase in premises and, therefore, cost. This higher level of accommodation provision will enable further expansion to take place. Eventually, additional cost will need to be incurred if further expansion is to occur. A fixed cost  that behaves in this way is often referred to as a stepped fixed cost.

## Variable cost

We saw earlier that variable cost varies with the volume of activity. In a manufacturing business, for example, this would include the cost of raw materials used.

Variable cost can be represented graphically as in Figure 7.3. At zero volume of activity, the variable cost is zero. It then increases in a straight line as activity increases.

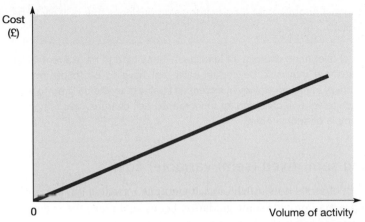

**Figure 7.3** Graph of variable cost against the volume of activity

At zero activity, there is no variable cost. However, as the volume of activity increases, so does the variable cost.

## Activity 7.3

**Can you think of some examples of cost elements that are likely to be variable for a hairdressing business?**

We can think of a couple:

- lotions, sprays and other materials used;
- laundry cost to wash towels used to dry customers' hair.

As with many types of business activity, the variable cost incurred by hairdressers tends to be low in comparison with the fixed cost: that is, fixed cost tends to make up the bulk of total cost.

The straight line for variable cost in Figure 7.3 implies that this type of cost will be the same per unit of activity, irrespective of the volume of activity. We shall consider the practicality of this assumption a little later in this chapter.

## Semi-fixed (semi-variable) cost

In some cases, cost has an element of both fixed and variable cost. This can be described as a semi-fixed (semi-variable) cost. An example might be the electricity cost for the hairdressing business. Some of this will be for heating and lighting, and this part is probably fixed, at least until the volume of activity expands to a point where longer opening hours or larger premises are necessary. The other part of the cost will vary with the volume of activity. Here we are talking about such things as power for hairdryers.

### Activity 7.4

Can you suggest another cost for a hairdressing business that is likely to be semi-fixed (semi-variable)?

We thought of telephone charges for landlines. These tend to have a rental element, which is fixed, and there may also be certain calls that have to be made irrespective of the volume of activity involved. However, increased business would be likely to lead to the need to make more telephone calls and so to increased call charges. You may have thought of another example of such a cost.

## Estimating semi-fixed (semi-variable) cost

Often, it is not obvious how much of each element a particular cost contains. However, past experience may provide some guidance. Let us again take the example of electricity. If we have data on what the electricity cost has been for various volumes of activity, say the relevant data over several three-month periods (electricity is usually billed by the quarter), we can estimate the fixed and variable portions. This may be done graphically, as shown in Figure 7.4. We tend to use past data here purely because they provide us with an estimate of future cost; past cost is not, of course, relevant for its own sake.

**Figure 7.4 Graph of electricity cost against the volume of activity**

Here the electricity bill for a time period (for example, three months) is plotted against the volume of activity for that same period. This is done for a series of periods. A line is then drawn that best 'fits' the various points on the graph. From this line we can then deduce both the cost at zero activity (the fixed element) and the slope of the line (the variable element).

Each of the dots in Figure 7.4 is the electricity charge for a particular quarter plotted against the volume of activity (probably measured in terms of sales revenue) for the same quarter. The diagonal line on the graph is the *line of best fit*. This means that this was the line that best seemed (to us, at least) to represent the data. A better estimate can usually be made using a statistical technique (*least squares regression*), which does not involve drawing graphs and making estimates. In practice though, it probably makes little difference which approach is taken.

From the graph we can say that the fixed element of the electricity cost is the amount represented by the vertical distance from the origin at zero (bottom left-hand corner) to the point where the line of best fit crosses the vertical axis of the graph. The variable cost per unit is the amount that the graph rises for each increase in the volume of activity.

By breaking down semi-fixed cost into its fixed and variable elements in this way, we are left with just two types of cost: fixed cost and variable cost.

Armed with knowledge of how much each element of cost represents for a particular product or service, it is possible to make predictions regarding total and per-unit cost at various projected levels of output. Such predictive information can be very useful to decision makers, and much of the rest of this chapter will be devoted to seeing how, starting with break-even analysis.

## Finding the break-even point

If, for a particular product or service, we know the fixed cost for a period and the variable cost per unit, we can produce a graph like the one shown in Figure 7.5. This graph shows the total cost over the possible range of volume of activity.

**Figure 7.5 Graph of total cost against volume of activity**

The bottom part of the graph represents the fixed cost element. To this is added the wedge-shaped top portion, which represents the variable cost. The two parts together represent total cost. At zero activity, the variable cost is zero, so total cost equals fixed cost. As activity increases so does total cost, but only because variable cost increases. We are assuming that there are no steps in the fixed cost.

The bottom part of Figure 7.5 shows the fixed cost area. Added to this is the variable cost, the wedge-shaped portion at the top of the graph. The uppermost line represents the total cost over a range of volume of activity. For any particular volume, the total cost can be measured by the vertical distance between the graph's horizontal axis and the relevant point on the uppermost line.

Logically, the total cost at zero activity is the amount of the fixed cost. This is because, even where there is nothing going on, the business will still be paying rent, salaries and so on, at least in the short term. As the volume of activity increases from zero, the fixed cost is augmented by the relevant variable cost to give the total cost.

→  If we take this total cost graph in Figure 7.5, and superimpose on it a line representing total revenue over the range of volume of activity, we obtain the break-even chart. This is shown in Figure 7.6.

**Figure 7.6  Break-even chart**

The sloping line starting at zero represents the sales revenue at various volumes of activity. The point at which this finally catches up with the sloping total cost line, which starts at F, is the break-even point (BEP). Below this point a loss is made, above it a profit.

In Figure 7.6, note that, at zero volume of activity (zero sales), there is zero sales revenue. The profit (loss), which is the difference between total sales revenue and total cost, for a particular volume of activity, is the vertical distance between the total sales revenue line and the total cost line at that volume of activity. Where there is no vertical distance between these two lines (total sales revenue equals total cost) the
→  volume of activity is at break-even point (BEP). At this point there is neither profit nor loss; that is, the activity *breaks even*. Where the volume of activity is below BEP, a loss will be incurred because total cost exceeds total sales revenue. Where the business operates at a volume of activity above BEP, there will be a profit, because total sales revenue will exceed total cost. The further below BEP, the higher the loss: the further above BEP, the higher the profit.

Deducing BEPs by graphical means is a laborious business. Since the relationships in the graph are all linear (that is, the lines are all straight), however, it is easy to calculate the BEP.

We know that at BEP (but not at any other point)

**Total sales revenue = Total cost**

The above formula can be expanded so that

**Total sales revenue = Fixed cost + Total variable cost**

If we call the number of units of output at BEP *b*, then

$b$ × Sales revenue per unit = Fixed cost + ($b$ × Variable cost per unit)

so

($b$ × Sales revenue per unit) − ($b$ × Variable cost per unit) = Fixed cost

and

$b$ × (Sales revenue per unit − Variable cost per unit) = Fixed cost

giving

$$b = \frac{\textbf{Fixed cost}}{\textbf{Sales revenue per unit − Variable cost per unit}}$$

If we look back at the break-even chart in Figure 7.6, this formula seems logical. The total cost line starts off at point F, higher than the starting point for the total sales revenues line (zero) by amount F (the amount of the fixed cost). Because the sales revenue per unit is greater than the variable cost per unit, the sales revenue line will gradually catch up with the total cost line. The rate at which it will catch up is dependent on the relative steepness of the two lines. Bearing in mind that the slopes of the two lines are the variable cost per unit and the selling price per unit, the above equation for calculating *b* looks perfectly logical.

Though the BEP can be calculated quickly and simply without resorting to graphs, this does not mean that the break-even chart is without value. The chart shows the relationship between cost, volume and profit over a range of activity and in a form that can easily be understood by non-financial managers. The break-even chart can therefore be a useful device for explaining this relationship.

### Example 7.1

Cottage Industries Ltd makes baskets. The fixed cost of operating the workshop for a month totals £500. Each basket requires materials that cost £2, and each takes one hour to make. The business pays the basket makers £10 an hour. The basket makers are all on contracts such that if they do not work for any reason, they are not paid. The baskets are sold to a wholesaler for £14 each.

What is the BEP for basket making for the business?
The BEP (in number of baskets) is

$$\frac{\text{Fixed cost}}{\text{Sales revenue per unit} - \text{Variable cost per unit}} = \frac{\text{\pounds}500}{\text{\pounds}14 - (\text{\pounds}2 + \text{\pounds}10)}$$

$$= 250 \text{ baskets per month}$$

Note that the BEP must be expressed with respect to a period of time.

Real World 7.1 shows information on the BEPs of two well-known businesses.

**Real World 7.1**

## BE at BA and Ryanair

Commercial airlines seem to pay a lot of attention to their BEPs and their 'load factors', that is, their actual level of activity. Figure 7.7 shows the BEP and load factor for two well-known airlines operating from the UK. British Airways (BA) is a traditional airline. Ryanair is a 'no frills' carrier, which means that passengers receive lower levels of service in return for lower fares. Both operate flights within the UK and from the UK to other European countries. BA also offers worldwide destinations. We can see that both airlines were making operating profits as each had a load factor greater than its BEP. Ryanair had both the higher load factor and the higher break-even point.

**Figure 7.7** Break-even and load factors in the airline industry

*Source*: based on information contained in 2008 annual reports of the two businesses concerned.

## Activity 7.5

Can you think of reasons why the managers of a business might find it useful to know the BEP of some activity that they are planning to undertake?

By knowing the BEP, it is possible to compare the expected, or planned, volume of activity with the BEP and so make a judgement about risk. If the volume of activity is expected only just to exceed the break-even point, this may suggest that it is a risky venture. Only a small fall from the expected volume of activity could lead to a loss.

## Activity 7.6

Cottage Industries Ltd (see Example 7.1) expects to sell 500 baskets a month. The business has the opportunity to rent a basket-making machine. Doing so would increase the total fixed cost of operating the workshop for a month to £3,000. Using the machine would reduce the labour time to half an hour per basket. The basket makers would still be paid £10 an hour.

(a) How much profit would the business make each month from selling baskets
- assuming that the basket-making machine is not rented; and
- assuming that it is rented?
(b) What is the BEP if the machine is rented?
(c) What do you notice about the figures that you calculate?

(a) Estimated monthly profit from basket making:

|  |  | Without the machine | | With the machine | |
| --- | --- | --- | --- | --- | --- |
|  |  | £ | £ | £ | £ |
| Sales revenue | (500 × £14) |  | 7,000 |  | 7,000 |
| Materials | (500 × £2) | (1,000) |  | (1,000) |  |
| Labour | (500 × 1 × £10) | (5,000) |  |  |  |
|  | (500 × ½ × £10) |  |  | (2,500) |  |
| Fixed cost |  | (500) |  | (3,000) |  |
|  |  |  | (6,500) |  | (6,500) |
| Profit |  |  | 500 |  | 500 |

(b) The BEP (in number of baskets) with the machine

$$= \frac{\text{Fixed cost}}{\text{Sales revenue per unit} - \text{Variable cost per unit}}$$

$$= \frac{£3,000}{£14 - (£2 + £5)}$$

$$= 429 \text{ baskets a month}$$

The BEP without the machine is 250 baskets per month (see Example 7.1).
(c) There seems to be nothing to choose between the two manufacturing strategies regarding profit, at the projected sales volume. There is, however, a distinct difference

between the two strategies regarding the BEP. Without the machine, the actual volume of sales could fall by a half of that which is expected (from 500 to 250) before the business would fail to make a profit. With the machine, however, just a 14 per cent fall (from 500 to 429) would be enough to cause the business to fail to make a profit. On the other hand, for each additional basket sold above the estimated 500, an additional profit of only £2 (that is, £14 − (£2 + £10)) would be made without the machine, whereas £7 (that is, £14 − (£2 + £5)) would be made with the machine. (Note that knowledge of the BEP and the planned volume of activity gives some basis for assessing the riskiness of the activity.)

We shall take a closer look at the relationship between fixed cost, variable cost and profit together with any advice that we might give the management of Cottage Industries Ltd after we have briefly considered the notion of contribution.

# Contribution

The bottom part of the break-even formula (sales revenue per unit less variable cost per unit) is known as the contribution per unit. Thus, for the basket-making activity, without the machine the contribution per unit is £2, and with the machine it is £7. This can be quite a useful figure to know in a decision-making context. It is called 'contribution' because it contributes to meeting the fixed cost and, if there is any excess, it then contributes to profit.

We shall see, a little later in this chapter, how knowing the amount of the contribution generated by a particular activity can be valuable in making short-term decisions of various types, as well as being useful in the BEP calculation.

## Contribution margin ratio

The contribution margin ratio is the contribution from an activity expressed as a percentage of the sales revenue, thus:

$$\text{Contribution margin ratio} = \frac{\text{Contribution}}{\text{Sales revenue}} \times 100\%$$

Contribution and sales revenue can both be expressed in per-unit or total terms. For Cottage Industries Ltd (Example 7.1 and Activity 7.6), the contribution margin ratios are, without the machine,

$$\frac{14 - 12}{14} \times 100\% = 14\%$$

and with the machine,

$$\frac{14 - 7}{14} \times 100\% = 50\%$$

The ratio can provide an impression of the extent to which sales revenue is eaten away by variable cost.

## Margin of safety

→ The margin of safety is the extent to which the planned volume of output or sales lies above the BEP. To illustrate how the margin of safety is calculated, we can use the information in Activity 7.6 relating to each option.

|  | Without the machine | With the machine |
|---|---|---|
| Expected volume of sales (number of baskets) | 500 | 500 |
| BEP (number of baskets) | 250 | 429 |
| Margin of safety: | | |
| Expressed as the number of baskets | 250 | 71 |
| Expressed as the percentage of projected volume of sales | 50% | 14% |

The margin of safety can be used as a partial measure of risk.

### Activity 7.7

What advice would you give Cottage Industries Ltd about renting the machine, on the basis of the values for margin of safety?

It is a matter of personal judgement, which in turn is related to individual attitudes to risk, as to which strategy to adopt. Most people, however, would prefer the strategy of not renting the machine, since the margin of safety between the expected volume of activity and the BEP is much greater. Thus, for the same level of return, the risk will be lower without renting the machine.

The relative margins of safety are directly linked to the relationship between the selling price per basket, the variable cost per basket and the fixed cost per month. Without the machine the contribution (selling price less variable cost) per basket is £2; with the machine it is £7. On the other hand, without the machine the fixed cost is £500 a month; with the machine it is £3,000. This means that, with the machine, the contributions have more fixed cost to 'overcome' before the activity becomes profitable. However, the rate at which the contributions can overcome fixed cost is higher with the machine, because variable cost is lower. Thus, with the machine, one more, or one less, basket sold has a greater impact on profit than it does if the machine is not rented. The contrast between the two scenarios is shown graphically in Figures 7.8(a) and 7.8(b).

If we look back to Real World 7.1 (page 248), we can see that Ryanair had a larger margin of safety than that of BA.

Real World 7.2 goes into more detail on the margin of safety and operating profit, over recent years, of one of the two airlines featured in Real World 7.1.

**Figure 7.8** Break-even charts for Cottage Industries' basket-making activities (a) without the machine and (b) with the machine

Without the machine the contribution per basket is low. Thus, each additional basket sold does not make a dramatic difference to the profit or loss. With the machine, however, the opposite is true, and small increases or decreases in the sales volume will have a great effect on the profit or loss.

## Real World 7.2

# BA's margin of safety

As we saw in Real World 7.1, commercial airlines pay a lot of attention to BEPs. They are also interested in their margin of safety (the difference between load factor and BEP).

Figure 7.9 shows BA's margin of safety and its operating profit over a seven-year period. Note that in 2002, BA had a load factor that was below its break-even point and this caused an operating loss. In the other years, the load factors were comfortably greater than the BEP. This led to operating profits.

**Figure 7.9** BA's margin of safety

The margin of safety is expressed as the difference between the load factor and the BEP (for each year), expressed as a percentage of the BEP. Generally, the higher the margin of safety, the higher the operating profit.

*Source*: derived from information in British Airways plc Annual Reports 2002 to 2008.

## Achieving a target profit

In the same way as we can derive the number of units of output necessary to break even, we can calculate the volume of activity required to achieve a particular level of profit. We can expand the equation shown on p. 247 above so that

**Total sales revenue = Fixed cost + Total variable cost + Target profit**

If we let $t$ be the required number of units of output to achieve the target profit, then

$t \times$ Sales revenue per unit = Fixed cost + ($t \times$ Variable cost per unit) + Target profit

so

($t \times$ Sales revenue per unit) − ($t \times$ Variable cost per unit) = Fixed cost + Target profit

and

$t \times$ (Sales revenue per unit − Variable cost per unit) = Fixed cost + Target profit

giving

$$t = \frac{\text{Fixed cost + Target profit}}{\text{Sales revenue per unit − Variable cost per unit}}$$

or

$$t = \frac{\text{Fixed cost + Target profit}}{\text{Contribution per unit}}$$

### Activity 7.8

What volume of activity is required by Cottage Industries Ltd (See Example 7.1 and Activity 7.6) in order to make a profit of £4,000 a month:

(a) assuming that the basket-making machine is not rented; and
(b) assuming that it is rented?

(a) Using the formula above, the required volume of activity without the machine

$$= \frac{\text{Fixed cost + Target profit}}{\text{Contribution per unit}}$$

$$= \frac{£500 + £4,000}{£14 − (£2 + £10)}$$

$$= 2,250 \text{ baskets a month}$$

(b) The required volume of activity with the machine

$$= \frac{£3,000 + £4,000}{£14 − (£2 + £5)} = 1,000 \text{ baskets a month}$$

## Operating gearing

The relationship between contribution and fixed cost is known as operating gearing (or operational gearing). An activity with a relatively high fixed cost compared with its variable cost is said to have high operating gearing. Thus, Cottage Industries Ltd would have higher operating gearing if it used the machine than it would have if not. Renting the machine increases the level of operating gearing quite dramatically because it causes an increase in fixed cost, but at the same time it leads to a reduction in variable cost per basket.

### Operating gearing and its effect on profit

The reason why the word 'gearing' is used in this context is that, as with intermeshing gear wheels of different circumferences, a circular movement in one of the factors (volume of output) causes a more-than-proportionate circular movement in the other (profit) as illustrated by Figure 7.10.

**Figure 7.10 The effect of operating gearing**

Volume of output

Profit

Where operating gearing is relatively high, as in the diagram, a small amount of motion in the volume wheel causes a relatively large amount of motion in the profit wheel. An increase in volume would cause a disproportionately greater increase in profit. The equivalent would also be true of a decrease in activity, however.

Increasing the level of operating gearing makes profit more sensitive to changes in the volume of activity. We can demonstrate operating gearing with Cottage Industries Ltd's basket-making activities as follows:

|  | Without the machine | | | With the machine | | |
|---|---|---|---|---|---|---|
| Volume (number of baskets) | 500 | 1,000 | 1,500 | 500 | 1,000 | 1,500 |
|  | £ | £ | £ | £ | £ | £ |
| Contribution* | 1,000 | 2,000 | 3,000 | 3,500 | 7,000 | 10,500 |
| Fixed cost | (500) | (500) | (500) | (3,000) | (3,000) | (3,000) |
| Profit | 500 | 1,500 | 2,500 | 500 | 4,000 | 7,500 |

* £2 per basket without the machine and £7 per basket with it.

Note that, without the machine (low operating gearing), a doubling of the output from 500 to 1,000 units brings a trebling of the profit. With the machine (high operating gearing), doubling output causes profit to rise by eight times. At the same time, reductions in the volume of output tend to have a more damaging effect on profit where the operating gearing is higher.

## Activity 7.9

What types of business activity are likely to have high operating gearing? (*Hint*: Cottage Industries Ltd might give you some idea.)

Activities that are capital intensive tend to have high operating gearing. This is because renting or owning capital equipment gives rise to additional fixed cost, but it can also give rise to lower variable cost.

Real World 7.3 shows how a very well-known business has benefited from high operating gearing.

## Real World 7.3

### Check out operating gearing

After several years of disappointing trading and loss of market share, in 2004, J Sainsbury plc, the UK supermarket chain, set a plan to improve its profitability and gain market share. During the period from 2005 to 2009, Sainsbury's increased its sales revenue by 25 per cent, but this fed through to a 118 per cent increase in profit. This was partly due to relatively high operating gearing, which caused the profit to increase at a much greater rate than the sales revenue. Quite a lot of retailers' costs are fixed – rent, salaries, heat and light, training and advertising for example.

In its 2009 annual report Sainsbury's Chief Executive, Justin King, said 'Sainsbury's has driven operational gearing from higher sales volumes and the delivery of cost efficiency savings.'

*Source*: J Sainsbury plc Annual Report 2009, p. 17.

## Profit-volume charts

 A slight variant of the break-even chart is the profit-volume (PV) chart. A typical PV chart is shown in Figure 7.11.

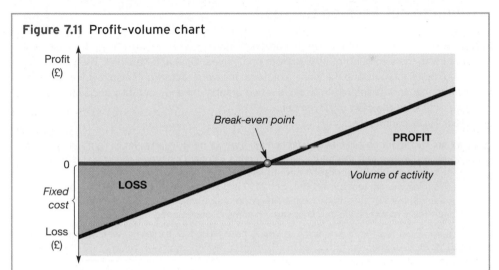

**Figure 7.11 Profit-volume chart**

The sloping line is profit (loss) plotted against activity. As activity increases, so does total contribution (sales revenue less variable cost). At zero activity there is no contribution, so there will be a loss equal in amount to the total fixed cost.

The PV chart is obtained by plotting loss or profit against volume of activity. The slope of the graph is equal to the contribution per unit, since each additional unit sold decreases the loss, or increases the profit, by the sales revenue per unit less the variable cost per unit. At zero volume of activity there are no contributions, so there is a loss equal to the amount of the fixed cost. As the volume of activity increases, the amount of the loss gradually decreases until BEP is reached. Beyond BEP a profit is made, which increases as activity increases.

As we can see, the PV chart does not tell us anything not shown by the break-even chart. It does, however, highlight key information concerning the profit (loss) arising at any volume of activity. The break-even chart shows this as the vertical distance between the total cost and total sales revenue lines. The PV chart, in effect, combines the total sales revenue and total variable cost lines, which means that profit (or loss) is directly readable.

## Failing to break even

Where a business fails to reach its BEP, steps must be taken to remedy the problem: there must be an increase in sales revenue or a reduction in cost, or both of these. Real

World 7.4 discusses how General Motors's subsidiaries, Opel and Vauxhall, are taking severe measures in an attempt to reach their BEPs.

---

**Real World 7.4**

## Trying to get back on the road

Nick Reilly has the toughest job in European industry after being charged by General Motors with the turnround of its European companies, Opel and Vauxhall. The plan so far calls for 8,500 job cuts and the closure of parts of several factories. It also requires aid from governments and savings from workers – two groups unhappy at GM's decision to scrap a sale of Opel at the start of November.

Nick Reilly commented:

> we are taking our cost level down far enough that our break-even point is significantly below where we believe that the future average market will be. Our break-even point is more like 14m to 14.5m now. So, it doesn't have to rise too much before we get into profit.
>
> We think we can reach it in 2011. So, 2010 is going to be another tough year because of the market, but 2011 we think we should get to about break-even, and then in 2012, as the market really recovers, we can start earning some decent money.

*Source*: adapted from 'Nick Reilly head of Opel and Vauxhall', *The Financial Times*, 28/12/2009 (Milne, R.), copyright © The Financial Times Ltd.

---

## Weaknesses of break-even analysis

As we have seen, break-even analysis can provide some useful insights concerning the important relationship between fixed cost, variable cost and the volume of activity. It does, however, have its weaknesses. There are three general problems:

- *Non-linear relationships.* The management accountant's normal approach to break-even analysis assumes that the relationships between sales revenues, variable cost and volume are strictly straight-line ones. In real life, this is unlikely to be the case. We shall look at the reason for this in Activity 7.10. Non-linearity is probably not a major problem, since, as we have just seen,
  - break-even analysis is normally conducted in advance of the activity actually taking place. Our ability to predict future cost, revenue and so on is somewhat limited, so what are probably minor variations from strict linearity are unlikely to be significant, compared with other forecasting errors; and
  - most businesses operate within a narrow range of volume of activity; over short ranges, curved lines tend to be relatively straight.
- *Stepped fixed cost.* Most types of fixed cost are not fixed over all volumes of activity. They tend to be 'stepped' in the way depicted in Figure 7.2. This means that, in practice, great care must be taken in making assumptions about fixed cost. The problem is heightened because most activities will probably involve various types

of fixed cost (for example rent, supervisory salaries, administration cost), all of which are likely to have steps at different points.

■ *Multi-product businesses*. Most businesses do not offer just one product or service. This is a problem for break-even analysis since it raises the question of the effect of additional sales of one product or service on sales of another of the business's products or services. There is also the problem of identifying the fixed cost of one particular activity. Fixed cost tends to relate to more than one activity – for example, two activities may be carried out in the same rented premises. There are ways of dividing the fixed cost between activities, but these tend to be arbitrary, which calls into question the value of the break-even analysis and any conclusions reached.

## Activity 7.10

We saw above that, in practice, relationships between cost, revenue and volume of activity are not necessarily straight-line ones.
Can you think of at least three reasons, with examples, why this may be the case?

We thought of the following:

■ *Economies of scale with labour*. A business may do things more economically where there is a high volume of activity than is possible at lower levels of activity. It may, for example, be possible for employees to specialise and, as a result, to work more efficiently.

■ *Economies of scale with buying goods or services*. A business may find it cheaper to buy goods and services where it is buying in bulk because discounts are often given on large orders.

■ *Diseconomies of scale*. This may mean that the per-unit cost of output is higher at higher levels of activity. For example, it may be necessary to pay higher rates of pay to workers to recruit the additional staff needed at higher volumes of activity.

■ *Lower sales prices at high levels of activity*. Some consumers may only be prepared to buy the particular product or service at a lower price. Thus, it may not be possible to achieve high levels of sales activity without lowering the selling price.

Despite some practical problems, break-even analysis and BEP seem to be widely used. The media frequently refer to the BEP for businesses and activities. For example, there is seemingly constant discussion about Eurotunnel's BEP and whether it will ever be reached. Similarly, the number of people regularly needed to pay to watch a football team so that the club breaks even is often mentioned. This is illustrated in Real World 7.5, which is an extract from an article discussing arrangements being made by Chelsea, the premiership football club, to break even. To help achieve this, the owner, Roman Abramovich, is to cancel his loan to the club, thus cancelling the club's obligation to pay him interest on it.

## Real World 7.5

### Blues to break even

The debt conversion into equity is consistent with a long-term plan agreed with Peter Kenyon, who recently stepped down as chief executive, for 'Phase II' of the Abramovich era aimed at reining in Chelsea's spending on player transfers and wage bills as the club seeks to break even financially.

The tidying up of Chelsea's balance sheet [statement of financial position] also comes soon after publication of a blueprint by Europe's footballing authorities aimed at curbing the ability of club-owners to buy their way to success.

In September, Michel Platini, Uefa's president, set out a three-year plan, entitled Fair Play Agenda, aimed at linking clubs' spending to the revenue they generate, preventing them from accumulating unsustainable levels of debt and controlling the amount spent on transfers and salaries.

Revealing the measures recently, Mr Platini said: 'The basic premise is that clubs should not spend more than they earn,' and claimed he had the support of Mr Abramovich.

*Source*: adapted from 'Chelsea owner axes £340m of debt', *The Financial Times*, 31/12/2009 (Kavanagh, M.), copyright © The Financial Times Ltd.

Real World 7.6 shows specific references to break-even point for three well-known businesses.

## Real World 7.6

### Breaking even is breaking out all over

**America is not online often enough to break even**
The main advertisement part of the business of AOL, the internet service provider, is running at a substantial loss. Tim Armstrong, the former Google employee, who is now CEO at AOL, said, 'We would like to get to break even or better this year.'

**World's cheapest car will have to travel far to break even**
Tata raised the barrier to entry this year with its release of the Nano, whose starting price is about Rs100,000 ($2,150). It is the first car cheap enough to challenge India's burgeoning motorcycle market.

But the Nano's initial production run was fewer than 100,000 units after Tata had to abandon a factory in West Bengal state following protests from farmers.

The Nano is not expected to break even until it reaches production volumes of about 250,000 units a year for three years.

**Comet's sister businesses look set to break even**
Kesa Electricals plc, the London-based group that owns a number of electrical retail businesses around Europe, including Comet in the UK, has lossmaking businesses in Spain, Italy and Turkey. However, sales levels in these businesses have recently picked up leading to expectations that they achieve the group's ambition and break even.

*Sources*: adapted from 'Yahoo faces battle to keep up with its sleeker rivals', 25 January 2010; 'Low-cost car to challenge Tata Nano', 11 November 2009; 'Comet's festive sales dampened by competition', 10 January 2010; *The Financial Times* (Menn, J., Leahy, J., Bintliff, E.), copyright © The Financial Times Ltd.

Real World 7.7 provides a more formal insight as to the extent that managers use break-even analysis in practice.

## Break-even analysis in practice

A survey of management accounting practice in the United States was conducted in 2003. Nearly 2,000 businesses replied to the survey. These tended to be larger businesses, of which about 40 per cent were manufacturers and about 16 per cent financial services; the remainder were across a range of other industries.

The survey revealed that 62 per cent use break-even analysis extensively, with a further 22 per cent considering using the technique in the future.

Though the survey relates to the US and was undertaken several years ago, in the absence of UK evidence, it provides some insight as to what is likely also to be current practice in the UK and elsewhere in the developed world.

*Source*: Ernst and Young, *2003 Survey of Management Accounting*, 2003.

## Using contribution to make decisions: marginal analysis

When we are trying to decide between two or more possible courses of action, *only costs that vary with the decision should be included in the decision analysis.*

### Activity 7.11

A householder wants a house decorated. Two decorators have been asked to price the job. One of them will do the work for £250, the other one wants £300, in both cases on the basis that the householder will supply the materials. It is believed that the two decorators will do an equally good job. The materials will cost £200 irrespective of which decorator does the work. Assuming that the householder wants the house decorated at the lower cost, which decorator should be asked to do the work? Is the cost of the materials relevant to the decision?

Clearly the first of the two decorators should be selected. The cost of the materials is irrelevant because it will be the same in each case. It is only possible to distinguish rationally between courses of action on the basis of differences between them.

In Activity 7.11 a distinction is made between relevant and irrelevant costs. For many decisions that involve relatively small variations from existing practice and/or relatively limited periods of time, fixed cost is not relevant to the decision, because it will be the same irrespective of the decision made. This is because either

- fixed cost elements tend to be impossible to alter in the short term, or
- managers are reluctant to alter them in the short term.

## Activity 7.12

Ali plc owns premises from which it provides a PC repair and maintenance service. There is a downturn in demand for the service and it would be possible for Ali plc to carry on the business from smaller, cheaper premises.

Can you think of any reasons why the business might not immediately move to smaller, cheaper premises?

We thought of broadly three reasons:

1   It is not usually possible to find a buyer for existing premises at very short notice and it may be difficult to find available alternative premises quickly.
2   It may be difficult to move premises quickly where there is, say, delicate equipment to be moved.
3   Management feels that the downturn might not be permanent. It would, therefore, be reluctant to take such a dramatic step and deny itself the opportunity to benefit from a possible revival of trade.

We shall now consider some types of decisions where fixed cost can be regarded as irrelevant. In making these decisions, we should have as our key strategic objective the enhancement of owners' (shareholders') wealth. Since these decisions are short-term in nature, this means that trying to generate as much net cash inflow as possible will normally increase wealth.

In marginal analysis we concern ourselves only with costs and revenues that vary with the decision and so this usually means that fixed cost is ignored. This is because marginal analysis is usually applied only to decisions involving minor alterations in the level of activity. It tends to be true, therefore, that the variable cost per unit will be equal to the marginal cost, which is the additional cost of producing one more unit of output. Whilst this is normally the case, there may be times when producing one more unit will involve a step in the fixed cost. If this occurs, the marginal cost is not just the variable cost; it will include the increment, or step, in the fixed cost as well.

Marginal analysis may be used in four key areas of decision making:

■ pricing/assessing opportunities to enter contracts;
■ determining the most efficient use of scarce resources;
■ make-or-buy decisions; and
■ closing or continuation decisions.

We shall now consider each of these areas in turn.

## Pricing/assessing opportunities to enter contracts

To understand how marginal analysis may be used in assessing an opportunity, let us consider the following activity.

## Activity 7.13

Cottage Industries Ltd (see Example 7.1, page 247) has spare capacity as its basket makers have some spare time. An overseas retail business has offered the business an order for 300 baskets at a price of £13 each.

Without considering any wider issues, should the business accept the order? (Assume that the business does not rent the machine.)

Since the fixed cost will be incurred in any case, it is not relevant to this decision. All we need to do is see whether the price offered will yield a contribution. If it will, the business will be better off by accepting the contract than by refusing it.

|  | £ |
|---|---|
| Additional revenue per unit | 13 |
| Additional cost per unit | (12) |
| Additional contribution per unit | 1 |

For 300 units, the additional contribution will be £300 (that is, 300 × £1). Since no fixed cost increase is involved, irrespective of what else is happening to the business, it will be £300 better off by taking this contract.

As ever with decision making, there are other factors that are either difficult or impossible to quantify. These should be taken into account before reaching a final decision. In the case of Cottage Industries Ltd's decision concerning the overseas customer, these could include the following:

- The possibility that spare capacity will have been 'sold off' cheaply when another customer would have offered a higher price at a later date. It is a matter of commercial judgement as to how likely this will be.
- Selling the same product, but at different prices, could lead to a loss of customer goodwill. The fact that a different price will be set for customers in different countries (that is, in different markets) may be sufficient to avoid this potential problem.
- If the business is going to suffer continually from being unable to sell its full production potential at the 'usual' price, it might be better, in the long run, to reduce capacity and make savings in fixed cost. Using the spare capacity to produce marginal benefits may lead to the business failing to address this issue.
- On a more positive note, the business may see this as a way of breaking into the overseas market. This is something that might be impossible to achieve if the business charges its usual price.

## The most efficient use of scarce resources

Normally, the output of a business is determined by customer demand for the particular goods or services. In some cases, however, output will be restricted by the productive capacity of the business. Limited productive capacity might stem from a shortage of any factor of production – labour, raw materials, space, machine capacity and so on. Such scarce factors are often known as *key* or *limiting* factors.

Where productive capacity acts as a brake on output, management must decide on how best to meet customer demand. That is, it must decide which products, from the range available, should be produced and how many of each should be produced. Marginal analysis can be useful to management in such circumstances. The guiding principle is that the most profitable combination of products will occur where the *contribution per unit of the scarce factor* is maximised. Example 7.2 illustrates this point.

### Example 7.2

A business provides three different services, the details of which are as follows:

| Service (code name) | AX107 | AX109 | AX220 |
|---|---|---|---|
| Selling price per unit (£) | 50 | 40 | 65 |
| Variable cost per unit (£) | (25) | (20) | (35) |
| Contribution per unit (£) | 25 | 20 | 30 |
| Labour time per unit (hours) | 5 | 3 | 6 |

Within reason, the market will take as many units of each service as can be provided, but the ability to provide the service is limited by the availability of labour, all of which needs to be skilled. Fixed cost is not affected by the choice of service provided because all three services use the same facilities.

The most profitable service is AX109 because it generates a contribution of £6.67 (£20/3) an hour. The other two generate only £5.00 each an hour (£25/5 and £30/6). So, to maximise profit, priority should be given to the production that maximises the contribution per unit of limiting factor.

Our first reaction might be that the business should provide only service AX220, as this is the one that yields the highest contribution per unit sold. If so, we would have been making the mistake of thinking that it is the ability to sell that is the limiting factor. If the above analysis is not convincing, we can take a random number of available labour hours and ask ourselves what is the maximum contribution (and, therefore, profit) that could be made by providing each service exclusively. Bear in mind that there is no shortage of anything else, including market demand, just a shortage of labour.

### Activity 7.14

A business makes three different products, the details of which are as follows:

| Product (code name) | B14 | B17 | B22 |
|---|---|---|---|
| Selling price per unit (£) | 25 | 20 | 23 |
| Variable cost per unit (£) | 10 | 8 | 12 |
| Weekly demand (units) | 25 | 20 | 30 |
| Machine time per unit (hours) | 4 | 3 | 4 |

Fixed cost is not affected by the choice of product because all three products use the same machine. Machine time is limited to 148 hours a week.

Which combination of products should be manufactured if the business is to produce the highest profit?

| Product (code name) | B14 | B17 | B22 |
|---|---|---|---|
| Selling price per unit (£) | 25 | 20 | 23 |
| Variable cost per unit (£) | (10) | (8) | (12) |
| Contribution per unit (£) | 15 | 12 | 11 |
| Machine time per unit | 4 hours | 3 hours | 4 hours |
| Contribution per machine hour | £3.75 | £4.00 | £2.75 |
| Order of priority | 2nd | 1st | 3rd |

Therefore produce

| | |
|---|---|
| 20 units of product B17 using | 60 hours |
| 22 units of product B14 using | 88 hours |
| | 148 hours |

This leaves unsatisfied the market demand for a further 3 units of product B14 and 30 units of product B22.

## Activity 7.15

What steps could be taken that might lead to a higher level of contribution for the business in Activity 7.14?

The possibilities for improving matters that occurred to us are as follows:

■ Consider obtaining additional machine time. This could mean obtaining a new machine, subcontracting the machining to another business or, perhaps, squeezing a few more hours a week out of the business's own machine. Perhaps a combination of two or more of these is a possibility.
■ Redesign the products in a way that requires less time per unit on the machine.
■ Increase the price per unit of the three products. This might well have the effect of dampening demand, but the existing demand cannot be met at present, and it may be more profitable in the long run to make a greater contribution on each unit sold than to take one of the other courses of action to overcome the problem.

## Activity 7.16

Going back to Activity 7.14, what is the maximum price that the business concerned would logically be prepared to pay to have the remaining B14s machined by a sub-contractor, assuming that no fixed or variable cost would be saved as a result of the business not doing the machining itself?

Would there be a different maximum if we were considering the B22s?

If the remaining three B14s were subcontracted at no cost, the business would be able to earn a contribution of £15 a unit, which it would not otherwise be able to gain. Any price up to £15 a unit would, therefore, be worth paying to a subcontractor to undertake the machining. Naturally, the business would prefer to pay as little as possible, but anything up to £15 would still make it worthwhile subcontracting the machining.

This would not be true of the B22s because they have a different contribution per unit; £11 would be the relevant figure in their case.

## Make-or-buy decisions

Businesses are frequently confronted by the need to decide whether to produce the product or service that they sell, or to buy it in from some other business. Thus, a producer of electrical appliances might decide to subcontract the manufacture of one of its products to another business, perhaps because there is a shortage of production capacity in the producer's own factory, or because it believes it to be cheaper to subcontract than to make the appliance itself.

It might be just part of a product or service that is subcontracted. For example, the producer may have a component for the appliance made by another manufacturer. In principle, there is hardly any limit to the scope of make-or-buy decisions. Virtually any part, component or service that is required in production of the main product or service, or the main product or service itself, could be the subject of a make-or-buy decision. So, for example, the personnel function of a business, which is normally performed in-house, could be subcontracted. At the same time, electrical power, which is typically provided by an outside electrical utility business, could be generated by the business itself. Obtaining services or products from a subcontractor is often called  outsourcing.

Real World 7.8 discusses the role of Indian businesses in supplying outsourcing services to western businesses, particularly UK and US ones.

### India is the west's back office

Proficiency in the English language, technical skills and low cost helped Indian companies over the past decade plug into the global economy and earn a reputation as the 'world's back office'. Big western companies, particularly in the US, turned to Indian service providers – such as Infosys, Wipro, Genpact and Tata Consultancy Services – to support IT systems and supply back office business processing and staff call centres.

The 'new economy' prospered on little more than some computers, telephone lines and entrepreneurial spirit in the 1990s. But today India has about 50 per cent of the global market for offshore IT and business services.

*Source*: Lamont, J., 'India mines riches as west's back office', FT.com, 29 December 2009.

## Activity 7.17

Shah Ltd needs a component for one of its products. It can subcontract production of the component to a subcontractor who will provide the components for £20 each. Shah Ltd can produce the components internally for total variable cost of £15 per component. Shah Ltd has spare capacity.

Should the component be subcontracted or produced internally?

The answer is that Shah Ltd should produce the component internally, since the variable cost of subcontracting is greater by £5 (that is, £20 – £15) than the variable cost of internal manufacture.

## Activity 7.18

Now assume that Shah Ltd (Activity 7.17) has no spare capacity, so it can only produce the component internally by reducing its output of another of its products. While it is making each component, it will lose contributions of £12 from the other product.

Should the component be subcontracted or produced internally?

The answer is to subcontract. In this case, both the variable cost of production and the 'opportunity' cost of lost contributions must be taken into account.

Thus, the relevant cost of internal production of each component is:

|  | £ |
|---|---|
| Variable cost of production of the component | 15 |
| Opportunity cost of lost production of the other product | 12 |
|  | 27 |

This is obviously more costly than the £20 per component that will have to be paid to the subcontractor.

## Activity 7.19

What factors, other than the immediately financially quantifiable, would you consider when making a make-or-buy decision?

We feel that there are two major factors:

1 The general problems of subcontracting, particularly
   (a) loss of control of quality;
   (b) potential unreliability of supply.
2 Expertise and specialisation. Generally, businesses should focus on their core competences. It is possible for most businesses, with sufficient determination, to do virtually everything themselves. This may, however, require a level of skill and facilities that most businesses neither have nor feel inclined to acquire. For example, though it is true that most businesses could generate their own electricity, their managements tend to take the view that this is better done by a specialist generator business. Specialists can often do things more cheaply, with less risk of things going wrong.

## Closing or continuation decisions

It is quite common for businesses to produce separate financial statements for each department or section, to try to assess their relative performance. Example 7.3 considers how marginal analysis can help decide how to respond where it is found that a particular department underperforms.

### Example 7.3

Goodsports Ltd is a retail shop that operates through three departments, all in the same premises. The three departments occupy roughly equal-sized areas of the premises. The trading results for the year just finished showed the following:

|  | Total £000 | Sports equipment £000 | Sports clothes £000 | General clothes £000 |
|---|---|---|---|---|
| Sales revenue | 534 | 254 | 183 | 97 |
| Cost | (482) | (213) | (163) | (106) |
| Profit/(loss) | 52 | 41 | 20 | (9) |

It would appear that if the general clothes department were to close, the business would be more profitable, by £9,000 a year, assuming last year's performance to be a reasonable indication of future performance.

When the cost is analysed between that part that is variable and that part that is fixed, however, the contribution of each department can be deduced and the following results obtained:

|  | Total £000 | Sports equipment £000 | Sports clothes £000 | General clothes £000 |
|---|---|---|---|---|
| Sales revenue | 534 | 254 | 183 | 97 |
| Variable cost | (344) | (167) | (117) | (60) |
| Contribution | 190 | 87 | 66 | 37 |
| Fixed cost (rent and so on) | (138) | (46) | (46) | (46) |
| Profit/(loss) | 52 | 41 | 20 | (9) |

Now it is obvious that closing the general clothes department, without any other developments, would make the business worse off by £37,000 (the department's contribution). The department should not be closed, because it makes a positive contribution. The fixed cost would continue whether the department was closed or not. As can be seen from the above analysis, distinguishing between variable and fixed cost, and deducing the contribution, can make the picture a great deal clearer.

### Activity 7.20

In considering Goodsports Ltd (in Example 7.3), we saw that the general clothes department should not be closed 'without any other developments'.

What 'other developments' could affect this decision, making continuation either more attractive or less attractive?

The things that we could think of are as follows:

- Expansion of the other departments or replacing the general clothes department with a completely new activity. This would make sense only if the space currently occupied by the general clothes department could generate contributions totalling at least £37,000 a year.
- Subletting the space occupied by the general clothes department. Once again, this would need to generate a net rent greater than £37,000 a year to make it more financially beneficial than keeping the department open.
- Keeping the department open, even if it generated no contribution whatsoever (assuming that there is no other use for the space), may still be beneficial. If customers are attracted into the shop because it has general clothing, they may then buy something from one of the other departments. In the same way, the activity of a sub-tenant might attract customers into the shop. (On the other hand, it might drive them away!)

## ? Self-assessment question 7.1

Khan Ltd can render three different types of service (Alpha, Beta and Gamma) using the same staff. Various estimates for next year have been made as follows:

|  | Alpha | Beta | Gamma |
|---|---|---|---|
| Selling price (£/unit) | 30 | 39 | 20 |
| Variable material cost (£/unit) | 15 | 18 | 10 |
| Other elements of variable cost (£/unit) | 6 | 10 | 5 |
| Share of fixed cost (£/unit) | 8 | 12 | 4 |
| Staff time required (hours/unit) | 2 | 3 | 1 |

Fixed cost for next year is expected to total £40,000.

Required:
(a) If the business were to render only service Alpha next year, how many units of the service would it need to provide in order to break even? (Assume for this part of the question that there is no effective limit to market size and staffing level.)
(b) If the business were to be prepared to render all three services, but has a limited number of staff hours available next year, in which order of preference would the three services come?
(c) If the maximum market for next year for the three services were as follows:

| Alpha | 3,000 units |
|---|---|
| Beta | 2,000 units |
| Gamma | 5,000 units |

what quantities of which service should the business provide next year and how much profit would this be expected to yield?

The answer to this question can be found at the back of the book, in Appendix B.

## Summary

The main points in this chapter may be summarised as follows.

### Cost behaviour

- Fixed cost is independent of the level of activity (for example, rent).
- Variable cost varies with the level of activity (for example, raw materials).
- Semi-fixed (semi-variable) cost is a mixture of fixed and variable cost (for example, electricity).

### Break-even analysis

- The break-even point (BEP) is the level of activity (in units of output or sales revenue) at which total cost (fixed + variable) = total sales revenue.
- Calculation of the BEP is as follows:

$$\text{BEP (in units of output)} = \frac{\text{Fixed cost for the period}}{\text{Contribution per unit}}$$

- Knowledge of the BEP for a particular activity can be used to help assess risk.
- Contribution per unit = sales revenue per unit less variable cost per unit.
- Contribution margin ratio = contribution/sales revenue ($\times$ 100%).
- Margin of safety = excess of planned volume of activity over BEP.
- Calculation of the volume of activity ($t$) required to achieve a target profit is as follows:

$$t = \frac{\text{Fixed cost + Target profit}}{\text{Contribution per unit}}$$

- Operating gearing is the extent to which the total cost of some activity is fixed rather than variable.
- A profit–volume (PV) chart is an alternative approach to a break-even chart, which is easier to understand.
- Economists tend to take a different approach to break-even, taking account of economies (and diseconomies) of scale and of the fact that, generally, to be able to sell large volumes, price per unit tends to fall.

### Weaknesses of BE analysis

- There are non-linear relationships between cost, revenue and volume.
- There may be stepped fixed costs. Most elements of fixed cost are not fixed over all volumes of activity.
- Multi-product businesses have problems in allocating fixed cost to particular activities.

**Marginal analysis (ignores fixed cost where this is not affected by the decision)**

■ In deciding whether to accept or reject special contracts, we consider only the effect on contributions.

■ When resources are scarce, the limiting factor is most effectively used by maximising its contribution per unit.

■ In make-or-buy decisions, we take the action that leads to the highest total contributions.

■ Closing/continuing an activity should be assessed by net effect on total contributions.

 **MyAccountingLab** | *Now check your progress in your personal Study Plan*

### → Key terms

| | |
|---|---|
| cost p. 240 | contribution per unit p. 250 |
| fixed cost p. 240 | contribution margin ratio p. 250 |
| variable cost p. 240 | margin of safety p. 251 |
| stepped fixed cost p. 242 | operating gearing p. 255 |
| semi-fixed (semi-variable) cost p. 243 | profit–volume (PV) chart p. 257 |
| break-even analysis p. 245 | marginal analysis p. 262 |
| break-even chart p. 246 | marginal cost p. 262 |
| break-even point (BEP) p. 246 | outsourcing p. 266 |

## Further reading

If you would like to explore the topics covered in this chapter in more depth, we recommend the following books:

Drury, C., *Management and Cost Accounting* (7th edn), South Western Cengage Learning, 2007, chapter 8.

Hilton, R., *Managerial Accounting* (8th edn), McGraw-Hill Higher Education, 2009, chapter 8.

Horngren, C., Foster, G., Datar, S., Rajan, M. and Ittner, C., *Cost Accounting: A Managerial Emphasis* (13th edn), Prentice Hall International, 2008, chapter 3.

McWatters, C., Zimmerman, J. and Morse, D., *Management Accounting: Analysis and Interpretation*, FT Prentice Hall, 2008, chapter 5.

## ? Review questions

Solutions to these questions can be found at the back of the book, in Appendix C.

**7.1** Define the terms *fixed cost* and *variable cost*. Explain how an understanding of the distinction between fixed cost and variable cost can be useful to managers.

**7.2** What is meant by the *break-even point* for an activity? How is the BEP calculated? Why is it useful to know the BEP?

**7.3** When we say that some business activity has *high operating gearing*, what do we mean? What are the implications for the business of high operating gearing?

**7.4** If there is a scarce resource that is restricting sales, how will the business maximise its profit? Explain the logic of the approach that you have identified for maximising profit.

## ✳ Exercises

Exercises 7.3 to 7.5 are more advanced than 7.1 and 7.2. Those with a coloured number have solutions at the back of the book, in Appendix D.

> If you wish to try more exercises, visit the website at www.myaccountinglab.com.

**7.1** The management of a business is concerned about its inability to obtain enough fully trained labour to enable it to meet its present budget projection.

Information concerning the three services offered by the business is as follows:

| Service | Alpha £000 | Beta £000 | Gamma £000 | Total £000 |
|---|---|---|---|---|
| Variable cost | | | | |
| Materials | 6 | 4 | 5 | 15 |
| Labour | 9 | 6 | 12 | 27 |
| Expenses | 3 | 2 | 2 | 7 |
| Allocated fixed cost | 6 | 15 | 12 | 33 |
| Total cost | 24 | 27 | 31 | 82 |
| Profit | 15 | 2 | 2 | 19 |
| Sales revenue | 39 | 29 | 33 | 101 |

The amount of labour likely to be available amounts to £20,000. All of the variable labour is paid at the same hourly rate. You have been asked to prepare a statement of plans ensuring that at least 50 per cent of the budgeted sales revenues are achieved for each service. The balance of labour is used to produce the greatest profit.

**Required:**

(a) Prepare the statement, with explanations, showing the greatest profit available from the limited amount of skilled labour available, within the constraint stated. *Hint*: Remember that all labour is paid at the same rate.

(b) What steps could the business take in an attempt to improve profitability, in the light of the labour shortage?

**7.2** A hotel group prepares financial statements on a quarterly basis. The senior management is reviewing the performance of one hotel and making plans for next year.

The managers have in front of them the results for this year (based on some actual results and some forecasts to the end of this year):

| Quarter | Sales revenue | Profit/(loss) |
|---------|---------------|---------------|
| | £000 | £000 |
| 1 | 400 | (280) |
| 2 | 1,200 | 360 |
| 3 | 1,600 | 680 |
| 4 | 800 | 40 |
| Total | 4,000 | 800 |

The total estimated number of guest nights for this year is 50,000. The results follow a regular pattern; there are no unexpected cost fluctuations beyond the seasonal trading pattern shown above. For next year, management anticipates an increase in unit variable cost of 10 per cent and a profit target for the hotel of £1 million. These will be incorporated into its plans.

**Required:**

(a) Calculate the total variable and total fixed cost of the hotel for this year. Show the provisional annual results for this year in total, showing variable and fixed cost separately. Show also the revenue and cost per guest night.

(b) (i) If there is no increase in guest nights for next year, what will be the required revenue rate per guest night to meet the profit target?

 (ii) If the required revenue rate per guest night is not raised above this year's level, how many guest nights will be required to meet the profit target?

(c) Outline and briefly discuss the assumptions that are made in typical PV or break-even analysis. Assess whether these assumptions limit its usefulness.

**7.3** A business makes three products, A, B and C. All three products require the use of two types of machine: cutting machines and assembling machines. Estimates for next year include the following:

| | A | B | C |
|---|---|---|---|
| Selling price (£/unit) | 25 | 30 | 18 |
| Sales demand (units) | 2,500 | 3,400 | 5,100 |
| Material cost (£/unit) | 12 | 13 | 10 |
| Variable production cost (£/unit) | 7 | 4 | 3 |
| Time required per unit on cutting machines (hours) | 1.0 | 1.0 | 0.5 |
| Time required per unit on assembling machines (hours) | 0.5 | 1.0 | 0.5 |

Fixed cost for next year is expected to total £42,000. It is the business's policy for each unit of production to absorb these in proportion to its total variable cost.

The business has cutting machine capacity of 5,000 hours a year and assembling machine capacity of 8,000 hours a year.

**Required:**

(a) State, with supporting workings, which products in which quantities the business should plan to make next year on the basis of the above information. *Hint*: First determine which machines will be a limiting factor (scarce resource).

(b) State the maximum price per product that it would be worth the business paying to a subcontractor to carry out that part of the work that could not be done internally.

**7.4** Darmor Ltd has three products, which require the same production facilities. Information about the production cost for one unit of its products is as follows:

|  | X | Y | Z |
|---|---|---|---|
|  | £ | £ | £ |
| Labour: Skilled | 6 | 9 | 3 |
| Unskilled | 2 | 4 | 10 |
| Materials | 12 | 25 | 14 |
| Other elements of variable cost | 3 | 7 | 7 |
| Fixed cost | 5 | 10 | 10 |

All labour and materials are variable costs. Skilled labour is paid £12 an hour and unskilled labour is paid £8 an hour. All references to labour cost above, are based on basic rates of pay. Skilled labour is scarce, which means that the business could sell more than the maximum that it is able to make of any of the three products.

Product X is sold in a regulated market and the regulators have set a price of £30 per unit for it.

**Required:**

(a) State, with supporting workings, the price that must be charged for products Y and Z, such that the business would find it equally profitable to make and sell any of the three products.

(b) State, with supporting workings, the maximum rate of overtime premium that the business would logically be prepared to pay its skilled workers to work beyond the basic time.

**7.5** Gandhi Ltd renders a promotional service to small retailing businesses. There are three levels of service: the 'basic', the 'standard' and the 'comprehensive'. On the basis of past experience, the business plans next year to work at absolute full capacity as follows:

| Service | Number of units of the service | Selling price | Variable cost per unit |
|---|---|---|---|
|  |  | £ | £ |
| Basic | 11,000 | 50 | 25 |
| Standard | 6,000 | 80 | 65 |
| Comprehensive | 16,000 | 120 | 90 |

The business's fixed cost totals £660,000 a year. Each service takes about the same length of time, irrespective of the level.

One of the accounts staff has just produced a report that seems to show that the standard service is unprofitable. The relevant extract from the report is as follows:

*Standard service cost analysis*

|  | £ |
|---|---|
| Selling price per unit | 80 |
| Variable cost per unit | (65) |
| Fixed cost per unit | (20)    (£660,000/(11,000 + 6,000 + 16,000)) |
| Loss | (5) |

The producer of the report suggests that the business should not offer the standard service next year.

**Required:**

(a) Should the standard service be offered next year, assuming that the quantity of the other services could not be expanded to use the spare capacity?

(b) Should the standard service be offered next year, assuming that
  ■ the released capacity could be used to render a new service, the 'Nova':
  ■ customers would be charged £75 per Nova;
  ■ the Nova would have variable cost of £50 per unit; and
  ■ the Nova would take twice as long to deliver as the other three services?

(c) What is the minimum price that could be accepted for the basic service, assuming that the necessary capacity to expand it will come only from not offering the standard service?

## Introduction

Full (absorption) costing is a widely used approach to costing that takes account of all of the cost of producing a particular product or service. In this chapter, we shall see how this approach can be used to deduce the cost of some activity, such as making a unit of product (for example a tin of baked beans), providing a unit of service (for example, a car repair) or creating a facility (for example, building an Olympic athletics stadium). This full cost approach contrasts with the one that we considered in Chapter 7, which concentrated on just the variable cost.

We shall first take a look at the traditional method of full costing and consider the usefulness of full cost for management purposes. We shall then go on to consider activity-based costing, which represents an alternative to the traditional method.

## Learning outcomes

**When you have completed this chapter, you should be able to:**

- discuss the usefulness, for decision-making purposes, of deducing the full cost of a unit of output;
- deduce the full cost of a unit of output both in a single-product environment and in a multi-product environment using the traditional full cost method;
- discuss the problems of charging full cost to jobs in a multi-product environment;
- explain the role and nature of activity-based costing.

 *Remember to create your own personalised Study Plan*

## Why do managers want to know the full cost?

As we saw in Chapter 1, the only point in providing accounting information is to help managers make better decisions. There are broadly four areas where managers use information concerning the full cost of the business's products or services. These are:

- *Pricing and output decisions.* Having full cost information can help managers make decisions on the price to be charged to customers for the business's products or services. Linked to pricing decisions are decisions on the number of units of a product or service that the business should produce.
- *Exercising control.* Managers need information to help them keep the business on course by ensuring that plans are met. Budgets (that is, short-term financial plans) are typically expressed in full cost terms. This means that periodic reports that compare actual performance with budgets need to be expressed in the same full cost terms.
- *Assessing relative efficiency.* Full cost information can help managers compare the cost of doing something in one way, or place, with its cost if done in a different way, or place. For example, a motor car manufacturer may find it useful to compare the cost of building a particular model of car in one of its plants, rather than another. This could help the business decide on where to locate future production.
- *Assessing performance.* The level of profit generated over a period is an important measure of business performance. To measure profit, we need to compare sales revenue with the associated expenses. Where a business makes a product or renders a service, a major expense will be the cost of making the product or rendering the service. Usually, this expense is based on the full cost of whatever is sold. Measuring profit provides managers (and other users) with information that can help them make a whole range of decisions.

Figure 8.1 shows the four uses of full cost information.

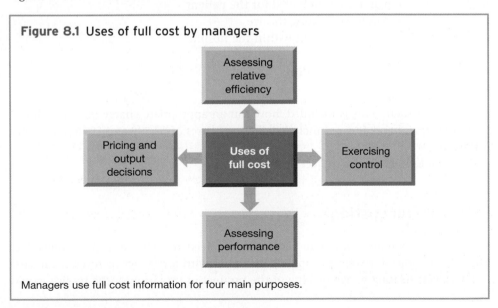

**Figure 8.1 Uses of full cost by managers**

Managers use full cost information for four main purposes.

Now let us consider Real World 8.1.

---

**Real World 8.1**

## Operating cost

An interesting example of the use of full cost for pricing decisions occurs in the National Health Service (NHS). In recent years, the funding of hospitals has radically changed. A new system of Payment by Results requires the Department of Health to produce a list of prices for different types of procedures that involve patient spells in hospital. This list, which is revised annually, reflects the prices that hospitals will be paid by the government for carrying out the different procedures.

The price list included the following figures:

- £7,599 for carrying out a hip replacement operation
- £996 for delivering a baby

These figures are based on the full cost of undertaking each type of procedure. Full cost figures were submitted by all NHS hospitals as part of their annual accounting process and an average for each type of procedure was then calculated. Figures for other procedures on the price list were derived in the same way.

*Source*: Coates, S., 'Tories say reductions in NHS national tariff could save billions', Timesonline, 3 August 2009.

---

When considering the information in Real World 8.1, an important question that arises is 'What does the full cost of each type of procedure include?' Does it simply include the cost of the salaries earned by doctors and nurses during the time spent with the patient or does it also include the cost of other items? If the cost of other items is included, how is it determined? Would it include, for example, a charge for

- the artificial hip and drugs provided for the patient
- equipment used in the operating theatre
- administrative and support staff within the hospital
- heating and lighting
- maintaining the hospital buildings
- laundry and cleaning?

If the cost of such items is included, how can an appropriate charge be determined? If, on the other hand, it is not included, are the figures of £7,599 and £996 potentially misleading?

These questions are the subject of this chapter.

## What is full costing?

➡ Full cost is the total amount of resources sacrificed to achieve a given objective. Thus, if the objective were to supply a customer with a product or service, the cost of all aspects relating to the making of the product or provision of the service would be included as part of the full cost. To derive the full cost figure, we must accumulate the elements of cost incurred and then assign them to the particular product or service.

→ The logic of full costing is that the entire cost of running a facility, say an office, is part of the cost of the output of that office. For example, the rent may be a cost that will not alter merely because we provide one more unit of the service. If the office were not rented, however, there would be nowhere for the staff to work, so rent is an → important element of the cost. A cost unit is one unit of whatever is having its cost determined. This is usually one unit of output of a particular product or service.

In the sections that follow we shall see how full costing is applied to a single-product business and then see how it is done for a multi-product one.

## Single-product businesses

The simplest case for which to deduce the full cost per unit is where the business has only one product or service, that is, each unit of its production is identical. Here it is simply a question of adding up all of the elements of cost of production incurred in a particular period (materials, labour, rent, fuel, power and so on) and dividing this total by the total number of units of output for that period.

### Activity 8.1

Fruitjuice Ltd has just one product, a sparkling orange drink that is marketed as Orange Fizz. During last month the business produced 7,300 litres of the drink. The cost incurred was made up as follows:

|  | £ |
|---|---|
| Ingredients (oranges and so on) | 390 |
| Fuel | 85 |
| Rent of premises | 350 |
| Depreciation of equipment | 75 |
| Labour | 880 |

**What is the full cost per litre of producing Orange Fizz?**

This figure is found by simply adding together all of the elements of cost incurred and then dividing by the number of litres produced:

£(390 + 85 + 350 + 75 + 880)/7,300 = £0.24 per litre

In practice, there can be problems in deciding exactly how much cost was incurred. In the case of Fruitjuice Ltd, for example, how is the cost of depreciation deduced? As we saw in Chapter 3, it is certainly an estimate and so its reliability is open to question. The cost of raw materials may also be a problem. Should we use the 'relevant' cost of the raw materials (in this case, almost certainly the replacement cost), or the actual price paid for them (historic cost)? If the cost per litre is to be used for some decision-making purpose (which it should be, if it is to be deduced), the replacement cost is probably more logical. In practice, however, it seems that historic cost is more often used to deduce full cost. It is not clear why this should be the case.

There can also be problems in deciding precisely how many units of output were produced. If making Orange Fizz is not a very fast process, some of the drink will probably be in the process of being made at any given moment. This, in turn, means that some of the cost incurred last month was for some Orange Fizz that was work in progress at the end of the month, so is not included in last month's output quantity of 7,300 litres. Similarly, part of the 7,300 litres might well have been started and incurred cost in the previous month, yet all of those litres were included in the 7,300 litres that we used in our calculation of the cost per litre. Work in progress is not a serious problem, but some adjustment for the value of opening and closing work in progress for the particular period needs to be made if reliable full cost information is to be obtained.

This approach to full costing, which can be taken where all of the output consists of identical, or near identical items (of goods or services), is often referred to as ➔ process costing.

## Multi-product businesses

Many businesses produce more than one type of product or service. Here, the units of output of the product, or service, will not be identical and so the approach used with litres of Orange Fizz in Activity 8.1 is probably inappropriate. Although it is reasonable to assign an identical cost to units of output that are identical, it is not normally helpful to do this where the units of output are obviously different. It would not be reasonable, for example, to assign the same cost to each car repair carried out by a garage, irrespective of the complexity and size of the repair.

## Direct and indirect cost

To provide full cost information, we need to have a systematic approach to accumulating the elements of cost and then assigning this total cost to particular cost units on some reasonable basis. Where cost units are not identical, the starting point is to separate cost into two categories: direct cost and indirect cost.

➔ Direct cost is the type of cost that can be identified with specific cost units. That is to say, the effect of the cost can be measured in respect of each particular cost unit. The main examples of a direct cost are direct materials and direct labour. Thus, in determining the cost of a car repair by a garage, both the cost of spare parts used in the repair and the cost of the mechanic's time would be part of the direct cost of that repair. Collecting elements of direct cost is a simple matter of having a cost-recording system that is capable of capturing the cost of direct materials used on each job and the cost, based on the hours worked and the rate of pay, of direct workers.

→ Indirect cost (or overheads) includes all other elements of cost, that is, those items that cannot be directly measured in respect of each particular cost unit (job). Thus, the rent of the garage premises would be an indirect cost of a motor car repair.

→ We shall use the terms 'indirect cost' and 'overheads' interchangeably for the remainder of this book. Indirect cost is also sometimes known as common cost because it is common to all of the output of the production unit (for example, office, factory or department) for the period.

Real World 8.2 gives some indication of the relative importance of direct and indirect cost in practice.

---

**Real World 8.2**

## Counting the cost

A recent survey of 176 UK businesses operating in various industries, all with annual sales revenue of more than £50 million, was conducted by Al-Omiri and Drury. They discovered that the total cost of the businesses' output on average is split between direct and indirect cost as follows:

|  | Direct cost (percentage) | Indirect cost (percentage) |
|---|---|---|
| All 176 businesses | 69 | 31 |
| Manufacturing businesses (91) | 75 | 25 |
| Service and retail businesses (85) | 49 | 51 |

For the manufacturers, the 75 per cent direct cost was, on average, made up as follows:

|  | Percentage |
|---|---|
| Direct materials | 52 |
| Direct labour | 14 |
| Other direct costs | 9 |

A more extensive (nearly 2,000 responses), but less recent survey of management accounting practice in the US showed similar results. Like the UK survey (above), this tended to relate to larger businesses. About 40% were manufacturers and about 16% financial services; the remainder were from a range of other industries.

This survey revealed that, of total cost, indirect cost accounted for between 34 per cent for retailers (lowest) and 42 per cent for manufacturers (highest), with other industries' proportion of indirect cost falling within the 34 per cent to 42 per cent range. Financial and commercial businesses showed an average indirect cost percentage of 38 per cent.

*Sources:* Al-Omiri, M. and Drury, C., 'A survey of factors influencing the choice of product costing systems in UK organisations', *Management Accounting Research*, December 2007, pp. 399–424; Ernst and Young, *2003 Survey of Management Accounting*, 2003.

## Activity 8.2

A garage bases its prices on the direct cost of each job (car repair) that it carries out. How could the garage collect the direct cost (labour and materials) information concerning a particular job?

Usually, direct workers are required to record how long was spent on each job. Thus, the mechanic responsible for the job would record the length of time worked on the car by direct workers (that is, the mechanic concerned and any colleagues). The stores staff would normally be required to keep a record of the cost of parts and materials used on each job.

A 'job sheet' will normally be prepared – perhaps on the computer – for each individual job. Staff would need to get into the routine of faithfully recording all elements of direct labour and materials applied to the job.

## Job costing

The term job costing is used to describe the way in which we identify the full cost per cost unit (unit of output or 'job') where the cost units differ. To cost (that is, deduce the full cost of) a particular cost unit, we first identify the direct cost of the cost unit, which, by the definition of direct cost, is fairly straightforward. We then seek to 'charge' each cost unit with a fair share of indirect cost (overheads). Put another way, cost units will absorb overheads. This leads to full costing also being called absorption costing. The absorption process is shown graphically in Figure 8.2.

**Figure 8.2** The relationship between direct cost and indirect cost

The full cost of any particular job is the sum of those cost elements that can be measured specifically in respect of the job (direct cost) and a share of the cost of creating the environment in which production (of an object or service) can take place, but which do not relate specifically to any particular job (indirect cost).

## Activity 8.3

Sparky Ltd is a business that employs a number of electricians. The business undertakes a range of work for its customers, from replacing fuses to installing complete wiring systems in new houses.

In respect of a particular job done by Sparky Ltd, into which category (direct or indirect) would each of the following cost elements fall

- the wages of the electrician who did the job;
- depreciation of the tools used by the electrician;
- the salary of Sparky Ltd's accountant;
- the cost of cable and other materials used on the job;
- rent of the premises where Sparky Ltd stores its inventories of cable and other materials?

Only the electrician's wages earned while working on the particular job and the cost of the materials used on the job are included in direct cost. This is because it is possible to measure how much time was spent on the particular job (and therefore its direct labour cost) and the amount of materials used (and therefore the direct material cost) in the job.

All the other elements are included in the general cost of running the business and, as such, must form part of the indirect cost of doing the job, but they cannot be directly measured in respect of the particular job.

It is important to note that whether a cost is direct or indirect depends on the item being costed – the cost objective. To refer to indirect cost without identifying the cost objective is incorrect.

## Activity 8.4

Into which category, direct or indirect, would each of the elements of cost listed in Activity 8.3 fall, if we were seeking to find the cost of operating the entire business of Sparky Ltd for a month?

The answer is that all of them will form part of the direct cost, since they can all be related to, and measured in respect of, running the business for a month.

Naturally, broader-reaching cost objectives, such as operating Sparky Ltd for a month, tend to include a higher proportion of direct cost than do more limited ones, such as a particular job done by Sparky Ltd. As we shall see shortly, this makes costing broader cost objectives rather more straightforward than costing narrower ones. It is generally the case that direct cost is easier to deal with than indirect cost.

## Full (absorption) costing and the behaviour of cost

We saw in Chapter 7 that the full cost of doing something (or total cost, as it is usually known in the context of marginal analysis) can be analysed between the fixed and the variable elements. This is illustrated in Figure 8.3.

**Figure 8.3** The relationship between fixed cost, variable cost and total cost

The total cost of a job is the sum of the cost that remains the same irrespective of the level of activity (fixed cost) and that which varies according to the level of activity (variable cost).

The apparent similarity of Figure 8.3 to Figure 8.2 seems to lead some people to believe that variable cost and direct cost are the same and that fixed cost and indirect cost (overheads) are the same. This is incorrect.

The notions of fixed and variable are concerned with cost behaviour in the face of changes in the volume of activity. The notions of direct and indirect, on the other hand, are concerned with the extent to which cost elements can be measured in respect of particular cost units (jobs). The two sets of notions are entirely different. Though it may be true that there is a tendency for fixed cost elements to be indirect (overheads) and for variable cost elements to be direct, there is no link, and there are many exceptions to this tendency. Most activities, for example, have variable indirect cost. Furthermore, labour is a significant element of direct cost in most types of business activity (14 per cent of the total cost of manufacture – see Real World 8.2) but it is usually a fixed cost.

The relationship between the reaction of cost to volume changes (cost behaviour), on the one hand, and how cost elements need to be gathered to deduce the full cost (cost collection), on the other, in respect of a particular job is shown in Figure 8.4.

Total cost is the sum of direct and indirect costs. It is also the sum of fixed and variable costs. These two facts are independent of one another. Thus a particular element of cost may be fixed, but that tells us nothing about whether it is a direct or an indirect cost.

## The problem of indirect cost

It is worth emphasising that the distinction between direct and indirect cost is only important in a job costing environment, that is, where units of output differ. When

**Figure 8.4** The relationship between direct, indirect, variable and fixed costs of a particular job

Fixed cost

Variable cost

Indirect cost (overheads)

Direct cost

Total (or full) cost of a particular job

A particular job's full (or total) cost will be made up of some variable and some fixed cost elements. It will also be made up of some direct and some indirect (overhead) elements.

we were considering costing a litre of Orange Fizz in Activity 8.1, whether particular elements of cost were direct or indirect was of no consequence, because all elements of cost were shared equally between the individual litres of Orange Fizz. Where we have units of output that are not identical, however, we have to look more closely at the make-up of the cost to achieve a fair measure of the full cost of a particular job.

Although the indirect cost of any activity must form part of the cost of each cost unit, it cannot, by definition, be directly related to individual cost units. This raises a major practical issue: how is the indirect cost to be apportioned to individual cost units?

## Overheads as service renderers

It is reasonable to view the indirect cost (overheads) as rendering a service to the cost units. Take, for example, a legal case undertaken by a firm of solicitors for a particular client. This job can be seen as being rendered a service by the office in which the work is done. In this sense, it is reasonable to charge each legal case (cost unit) with a share of the cost of running the office (rent, lighting, heating, cleaning, building maintenance and so on). It also seems reasonable to relate the charge for the 'use' of the office to the level of service that the particular case has received from the office.

The next step is the difficult one. How might the cost of running the office, which is a cost of all work done by the firm, be divided between individual cases that are not similar in size and complexity?

One possibility is sharing this overhead cost equally between each case handled by the firm within the period. This method, however, has little to commend it unless the cases were close to being identical in terms of the extent to which they had 'benefited' from the overheads.

If we are not to propose equal shares, we must identify something observable and measurable about the cases that we feel provides a reasonable basis for distinguishing between one case and the next. In practice, time spent working on each particular cost unit by direct labour is the most popular basis. It must be stressed that this is not the 'correct' way. It is certainly not the only way.

## How job costing works

To see how job costing works, let us consider Example 8.1.

### Example 8.1

Johnson Ltd, a business that provides a personal computer maintenance and repair service to its customers, has overheads of £10,000 each month. Each month 1,000 direct labour hours are worked and charged to cost units (jobs carried out by the business). A particular PC repair undertaken by the business used direct materials costing £15. Direct labour worked on the repair was 3 hours and the wage rate is £16 an hour. Overheads are charged to jobs on a direct labour hour basis. What is the full (absorption) cost of the repair?

First, let us establish the overhead absorption (recovery) rate, that is, the rate at which individual repairs will be charged with overheads. This is £10 (£10,000/ 1,000) per direct labour hour.

Thus, the full cost of the repair is:

|                             | £  |
|-----------------------------|----|
|                             | £  |
| Direct materials            | 15 |
| Direct labour (3 × £16)     | 48 |
|                             | 63 |
| Overheads (3 × £10)         | 30 |
| Full cost of the job        | 93 |

Note, in Example 8.1, that the number of labour hours (3 hours) appears twice in deducing the full cost: once to deduce the direct labour cost and a second time to deduce the overheads to be charged to the repair. These are really two separate issues, though they are both based on the same number of labour hours.

Note also that, if all the jobs undertaken during the month are assigned overheads in a similar manner, all £10,000 of overheads will be charged to the jobs between them. Jobs that involve a lot of direct labour will be assigned a large share of overheads. Jobs that involve little direct labour will be assigned a small share of overheads.

## Activity 8.5

Can you think of reasons why direct labour hours are regarded as the most logical basis for sharing overheads between cost units?

The reasons that occurred to us are as follows:

■ Large jobs should logically attract large amounts of overheads because they are likely to have been rendered more 'service' by the overheads than small ones. The length of time that they are worked on by direct labour may be seen as a rough way of measuring relative size, though other means of doing this may be found – for example, relative physical size, where the cost unit is a physical object, like a manufactured product.
■ Most overheads are related to time. Rent, heating, lighting, non-current asset depreciation, supervisors' and managers' salaries and interest on borrowings, which are all typical overheads, are all more or less time-based. That is to say, the overhead cost for one week tends to be about half of that for a similar two-week period. Thus, a basis of allotting overheads to jobs that takes account of the length of time that the units of output benefited from the 'service' rendered by the overheads seems logical.
■ Direct labour hours are capable of being measured for each job. They will normally be measured to deduce the direct labour element of cost in any case. Thus, a direct labour hour basis of dealing with overheads is practical to apply in the real world.

It cannot be emphasised enough that there is no 'correct' way to allot overheads to jobs. Overheads, by definition, do not naturally relate to individual jobs. If, nevertheless, we wish to take account of the fact that overheads are part of the cost of all jobs, we must find some logical way of including a share of the total overheads in each job. If a particular approach to doing this is regarded as useful by those who use the full cost information deduced, then the approach is acceptable. Accounting is concerned only with providing useful information to decision makers. In practice, the method that seems to be regarded as being the most useful is the direct labour hour method.

Now let us consider Real World 8.3, which gives an example of one well-known organisation that does not use direct labour hours to cost its output.

## Real World 8.3

### Bed days

As we saw in Real World 8.1, the UK National Health Service (NHS) seeks to ascertain the cost of various medical and surgical procedures that it undertakes for its patients. In determining the costs of a procedure that requires time in hospital as an 'inpatient', the NHS identifies the total direct cost of the particular procedure (staff time, medication and so on). To this it adds a share of the hospital overheads. The total overheads are absorbed by individual procedures ('jobs') by taking this overheads total and dividing it by the number of 'bed days' throughout the hospital for the period, to establish a 'bed day rate'. A bed day is one patient spending one day occupying a bed in the hospital. To cost the procedure for a particular patient, the bed day rate is applied to the cost of the procedure according to how many bed days the particular patient had.

Note that the NHS does not use the direct labour hour basis of absorption; however, the bed day rate alternative is also a logical, time-based approach.

*Source*: NHS Costing Manual 2009/2010, Department of Health Gateway, reference 13659, February 2010.

## Activity 8.6

Marine Suppliers Ltd undertakes a range of work, including making sails for small sailing boats on a made-to-measure basis.

The business expects the following to arise during the next month:

| | |
|---|---|
| Direct labour cost | £60,000 |
| Direct labour time | 6,000 hours |
| Indirect labour cost | £9,000 |
| Depreciation of machinery | £3,000 |
| Rent and rates | £5,000 |
| Heating, lighting and power | £2,000 |
| Machine time | 2,000 hours |
| Indirect materials | £500 |
| Other miscellaneous indirect cost elements (overheads) | £200 |
| Direct materials cost | £3,000 |

The business has received an enquiry about a sail. It is estimated that the particular sail will take 12 direct labour hours to make and will require 20 square metres of sailcloth, which costs £2 per square metre.

The business normally uses a direct labour hour basis of charging indirect cost (overheads) to individual jobs.

What is the full (absorption) cost of making the sail?

The direct cost of making the sail can be identified as follows:

| | £ |
|---|---|
| Direct materials (20 × £2) | 40.00 |
| Direct labour (12 × (£60,000/6,000)) | 120.00 |
| | 160.00 |

To deduce the indirect cost (overhead) element that must be added to derive the full cost of the sail, we first need to total these cost elements as follows:

| | £ |
|---|---|
| Indirect labour | 9,000 |
| Depreciation | 3,000 |
| Rent and rates | 5,000 |
| Heating, lighting and power | 2,000 |
| Indirect materials | 500 |
| Other miscellaneous indirect cost (overhead) elements | 200 |
| Total indirect cost (overheads) | 19,700 |

Since the business uses a direct labour hour basis of charging indirect cost to jobs, we need to deduce the indirect cost (or overhead) recovery rate per direct labour hour. This is simply

$$£19,700/6,000 = £3.28 \text{ per direct labour hour}$$

Thus, the full cost of the sail would be expected to be:

| | £ |
|---|---|
| Direct materials (20 × £2) | 40.00 |
| Direct labour (12 × (£60,000/6,000)) | 120.00 |
| Indirect cost (12 × £3.28) | 39.36 |
| Full cost | 199.36 |

Figure 8.5 shows the process for applying indirect (overheads) and direct cost to the sail that was the subject of Activity 8.6.

**Figure 8.5** How the full cost is derived for the sail to be made by Marine Suppliers Ltd in Activity 8.6

The full cost is made up of the sail's (job's) 'fair' share of the total overheads, plus the direct cost element that is measured specifically in relation to the particular sail.

## Activity 8.7

Suppose that Marine Suppliers Ltd (see Activity 8.6) used a machine hour basis of charging overheads to jobs. What would be the cost of the job detailed if it was expected to take 5 machine hours (as well as 12 direct labour hours)?

The total overheads of the business will of course be the same irrespective of the method of charging them to jobs. Thus, the overhead recovery rate, on a machine hour basis, will be

£19,700/2,000 = £9.85 per machine hour

Thus, the full cost of the sail would be expected to be:

|  | £ |
| --- | --- |
| Direct materials (20 × £2) | 40.00 |
| Direct labour (12 × (£60,000/6,000)) | 120.00 |
| Indirect cost (5 × £9.85) | 49.25 |
| Full cost | 209.25 |

## Selecting a basis for charging overheads

We saw earlier that there is no single correct way of charging overheads. The final choice is a matter of judgement. It seems reasonable to say, however, that the nature of the overheads should influence the choice of the basis of charging the overheads to jobs. Where production is capital-intensive and overheads are primarily machine-based (such as depreciation, machine maintenance, power and so on), machine hours might be favoured. Otherwise direct labour hours might be preferred.

It would be irrational to choose one of these bases in preference to the other simply because it apportions either a higher or a lower amount of overheads to a particular job. The total overheads will be the same irrespective of the method of dividing that total between individual jobs. Thus a method that gives a higher share of overheads to one particular job must give a lower share to the remaining jobs. There is one cake of fixed size: if one person receives a relatively large slice, others must on average receive relatively small slices. To illustrate further this issue of apportioning overheads, consider Example 8.2.

### Example 8.2

A business that provides a service expects to incur overheads totalling £20,000 next month. The total direct labour time worked is expected to be 1,600 hours and machines are expected to operate for a total of 1,000 hours.

During the next month, the business expects to do just two large jobs. Information concerning each job is as follows:

|  | Job 1 | Job 2 |
|---|---|---|
| Direct labour hours | 800 | 800 |
| Machine hours | 700 | 300 |

How much of the total overheads will be charged to each job if overheads are to be charged on:

(a) a direct labour hour basis; and
(b) a machine hour basis?

What do you notice about the two sets of figures that you calculate?

**(a) Direct labour hour basis**

Overhead recovery rate = £20,000/1,600 = £12.50 per direct labour hour.

| Job 1 | £12.50 × 800 = £10,000 |
|---|---|
| Job 2 | £12.50 × 800 = £10,000 |

**(b) Machine hour basis**

Overhead recovery rate = £20,000/1,000 = £20.00 per machine hour.

| Job 1 | £20.00 × 700 = £14,000 |
|---|---|
| Job 2 | £20.00 × 300 = £6,000 |

It is clear from these calculations that the total overheads charged to jobs is the same (that is, £20,000) whichever method is used. So, whereas the machine hour basis gives Job 1 a higher share than does the direct labour hour method, the opposite is true for Job 2.

Charging overheads on one basis to one job and on the other basis to the other job would not be practical. It would result in either total overheads not being fully charged to the jobs, or jobs being overcharged with overheads. For example, using the direct labour hour method for Job 1 (£10,000) and the machine hour basis for Job 2 (£6,000) will mean that only £16,000 of a total £20,000 of overheads will be charged to jobs. As a result, the objective of full (absorption) costing, which is to charge all overheads to jobs done, will not be achieved. In this particular case, if selling prices are based on full cost, the business may not charge high enough prices to cover all of its costs.

Figure 8.6 shows the effect of the two different bases of charging overheads to Jobs 1 and 2.

---

**Figure 8.6** The effect of different bases of charging overheads to jobs in Example 8.2

The share of the total overheads for the month charged to jobs can differ significantly depending on the basis used.

---

## Activity 8.8

The point was made above that it would normally be irrational to prefer one basis of charging overheads to jobs simply because it apportions either a higher or a lower amount of overheads to a particular job. This is because the total overheads are the same irrespective of the method of charging the total to individual jobs. Can you think of any circumstances where it would not necessarily be so irrational?

This might apply where, for a particular job, a customer has agreed to pay a price based on full cost plus an agreed fixed percentage for profit. Here it would be beneficial to the producer for the total cost of the job to be as high as possible. This would be relatively unusual, but sometimes public-sector organisations, particularly central and local government departments, have entered into contracts to have work done with the price to be deduced, after the work has been completed, on a 'cost-plus' basis. Such contracts are pretty rare these days, probably because they are open to abuse in the way just described. Usually, contract prices are agreed in advance, typically in conjunction with competitive tendering.

Survey evidence from the early 1990s (Drury, Braund, Osborne and Tayles: *A Survey of Management Accounting Practices in UK Manufacturing Companies*, 1993) showed that the direct labour hour basis of charging overheads to cost units was overwhelmingly the most popular, even where activities were automated. There is no reason to believe that current practice is very different from this and, in the absence of more recent information, it provides some impression of what happens in practice.

## Segmenting the overheads

As we have just seen, charging the same overheads to different jobs on different bases is not logical. It is perfectly reasonable, however, to charge one segment of the total overheads on one basis and another segment (or other segments) on another basis (or bases).

### Activity 8.9

Taking the same business as in Example 8.2, on closer analysis we find that of the overheads totalling £20,000 next month, £8,000 relate to machines (depreciation, maintenance, rent of the space occupied by the machines and so on) and the remaining £12,000 to more general overheads. The other information about the business is exactly as it was before.

How much of the total overheads will be charged to each job if the machine-related overheads are to be charged on a machine hour basis and the remaining overheads are charged on a direct labour hour basis?

*Direct labour hour basis*

Overhead recovery rate = £12,000/1,600 = £7.50 per direct labour hour

*Machine hour basis*

Overhead recovery rate = £8,000/1,000 = £8.00 per machine hour

*Overheads charged to jobs*

|  | Job 1 £ | Job 2 £ |
|---|---|---|
| Direct labour hour basis |  |  |
| £7.50 × 800 | 6,000 |  |
| £7.50 × 800 |  | 6,000 |
| Machine hour basis |  |  |
| £8.00 × 700 | 5,600 |  |
| £8.00 × 300 |  | 2,400 |
| Total | 11,600 | 8,400 |

We can see from this that the expected overheads of £20,000 are charged in total.

Segmenting the overheads in this way may well be seen as providing a better basis of charging overheads to jobs. This is quite often found in practice, usually by dividing a business into separate 'areas' for costing purposes, charging overheads differently from one area to the next, according to the nature of the work done in each.

## Dealing with overheads on a cost centre basis

In practice, all but the smallest businesses are divided into departments. Normally, each department deals with a separate activity. The reasons for dividing a business into departments include the following:

- *Size and complexity*. Many businesses are too large and complex to be managed as a single unit. It is usually more practical to operate each business as a series of relatively independent units with each one having its own manager.
- *Expertise*. Each department normally has its own area of specialism and is managed by a specialist.
- *Accountability*. Each department can have its own accounting records that enable its performance to be assessed. This can lead to greater management control and motivation among the staff.

Most businesses charge overheads to cost units on a department-by-department basis. The aim is to provide a more accurate means of charging overheads to cost units. Each department is treated as a separate cost centre where overheads are accumulated and then charged to those cost units to which it provides a service. A cost centre can be defined as a particular physical area or some activity or function for which the cost is separately identified.

Although it is probably only in a minority of cases that it leads to any great improvement in the quality of information provided, it is not normally an expensive exercise. Since cost elements are collected department by department for other purposes (particularly accountability), to apply overheads on a department-by-department basis is a relatively simple matter.

We shall now take a look at how the departmental approach to deriving full cost works, in a service-industry context, through Example 8.3.

### Example 8.3

Autosparkle Ltd offers a motor vehicle paint-respray service. The jobs that it undertakes range from painting a small part of a saloon car, usually following a road accident, to a complete respray of a double-decker bus.

Each job starts life in the Preparation Department, where it is prepared for the Paintshop. In the Preparation Department the job is worked on by direct workers, in most cases taking some direct materials from the stores with which to treat the old paintwork to render the vehicle ready for respraying. Thus the job will be charged with direct materials, direct labour and a share of the Preparation Department's overheads. The job then passes into the Paintshop Department, already valued at the cost that it picked up in the Preparation Department.

In the Paintshop, the staff draw direct materials (mainly paint) from the stores, and direct workers spend time respraying, using sophisticated spraying apparatus as well as working by hand. So, in the Paintshop, the job is charged with direct materials, direct labour and a share of that department's overheads. The job now passes into the Finishing Department, valued at the cost of the materials, labour and overheads that it accumulated in the first two departments.

In the Finishing Department, vehicles are cleaned and polished ready to go back to the customers. Further direct labour and, in some cases, materials are added. All jobs also pick up a share of that department's overheads. The vehicle, with the job now complete, passes back to the customer.

Figure 8.7 shows graphically how this works for a particular job.

**Figure 8.7** A cost unit (Job A) passing through Autosparkle Ltd's process

As the particular paint job passes through the three departments, where work is carried out on it, the job 'gathers' cost of various types.

The basis of charging overheads to jobs (for example, direct labour hours) might be the same for all three departments, or it might be different from one department to another. It is possible that spraying apparatus cost elements dominate the Paintshop cost, so that department's overheads might well be charged to jobs on a machine hour basis. The other two departments are probably labour intensive, so that direct labour hours may be seen as being appropriate there.

The passage of a job through the departments, picking up cost as it goes, can be compared to a snowball being rolled across snow: as it rolls, it picks up more and more snow.

Charging direct cost to jobs, in a departmental system, is exactly the same as where the whole business is one single cost centre. It is simply a matter of keeping a record of

- the number of hours of direct labour worked on the particular job and the grade of labour, assuming that there are different grades with different rates of pay;
- the cost of the direct materials taken from stores and applied to the job; and
- any other direct cost elements, for example some subcontracted work, associated with the job.

This record keeping will normally be done cost centre by cost centre.

It is obviously necessary to break down the production overheads of the entire business on a cost centre basis. This means that the total overheads of the business must be divided between the cost centres, such that the sum of the overheads of all of the cost centres equals the overheads for the entire business. By charging all of their overheads to jobs, the cost centres will, between them, charge all of the overheads of the business to jobs. Real World 8.4 provides an indication of the number of different cost centres that businesses tend to use in practice.

## Real World 8.4

### Cost centres in practice

It is not unusual for businesses to have several cost centres. Results of a recent survey by Drury and Tayles of 186 larger UK businesses involved in various activities are shown in Figure 8.8.

**Figure 8.8** Analysis of the number of cost centres within a business

The survey of larger businesses shows, as might be expected, that they tend to have several cost centres.

From this we can see that 86 per cent of businesses surveyed had 6 or more cost centres and that 36 per cent of businesses had more than 20 cost centres. Only 3 per cent of businesses surveyed had a single cost centre (that is, there was a business-wide or overall overhead rate used). Clearly, businesses that deal with overheads on a business-wide basis are very rare.

*Source*: based on information taken from Drury, C. and Tayles, M., 'Profitability analysis in UK organisations', *British Accounting Review*, December 2006.

## Batch costing

The production of many types of goods and services (particularly goods) involves producing in a batch of identical, or nearly identical, units of output, but where each batch is distinctly different from other batches. For example, a theatre may put on a production whose nature (and therefore cost) is very different from that of other productions. On the other hand, ignoring differences in the desirability of the various types of seating, all of the individual units of output (tickets to see the production) are identical.

In these circumstances, the cost per ticket would normally be deduced by

■ using a job costing approach (taking account of direct and indirect costs and so on) to find the cost of mounting the production; and then
■ dividing the cost of mounting the production by the expected number of tickets to be sold to find the cost per ticket.

→   This is known as batch costing.

Figure 8.9 shows the process for deriving the cost of one cost unit (product) in a batch.

---

**Figure 8.9 Deriving the cost of one cost unit where production is in batches**

The full cost of the batch, delivered on a 'job costing' basis

*divided by*

The number of cost units (products) in the batch

*equals*

The full cost of one cost unit (product)

The cost for the batch is derived using a job costing basis and this is divided by the number in the batch to determine the cost for each cost unit.

---

## Full (absorption) cost as the break-even price

For decision-making purposes, it can be helpful to allocate non-manufacturing costs, as well as manufacturing costs, to products using some sensible basis of allocation. When this is done and everything proves to be as expected, then selling the output for its full cost should cause the business to break even exactly. Therefore, whatever profit (in total) is loaded onto full cost to set actual selling prices will, if plans are achieved, result in that level of profit being earned for the period.

### The forward-looking nature of full (absorption) costing

Though deducing full cost can be done after the work has been completed, it is often done in advance. In other words, cost is frequently predicted. Where, for example, the full cost is needed as a basis on which to set a selling price, that price will usually need to be set before the customer will place the order. Even where no particular customer has been identified, some idea of the ultimate price will need to be known before the business will be able to make a judgement as to whether potential customers will buy the product, and in what quantities. There is a risk, of course, that the actual outcome will differ from that predicted. This is, however, one of the risks of being in business.

### ? Self-assessment question 8.1

Promptprint Ltd, a printing business, has received an enquiry from a potential customer for the quotation of a price for a job. The pricing policy of the business is based on the plans for the next financial year shown below.

|  | £ |
|---|---|
| Sales revenue (billings to customers) | 196,000 |
| Materials (direct) | (38,000) |
| Labour (direct) | (32,000) |
| Variable overheads | (2,400) |
| Advertising (for business) | (3,000) |
| Depreciation | (27,600) |
| Administration | (36,000) |
| Interest | (8,000) |
| Profit (before taxation) | 49,000 |

A first estimate of the direct costs for the particular job is:

Direct materials: £4,000
Direct labour:    £3,600

**Required:**
(a) Prepare a recommended price for the job based on the plans, commenting on your method.
(b) Comment on the validity of using financial plans in pricing, and recommend any improvements you consider desirable for the pricing policy used in (a).

The answer to this question can be found at the back of the book, in Appendix B.

## Activity-based costing

What we have considered so far is the traditional approach to job/batch costing (deriving the full cost of output where one unit/batch of output differs from another). This approach is to collect, for each job/batch, that part of the cost that can be unequivocally linked to, and measured in respect of, the particular job/batch (direct cost). All other cost elements (overheads) are thrown into a pool of cost and charged to individual jobs/batches according to some formula, often the number of direct labour hours worked on each particular job/batch.

## Costing: the traditional way

This traditional, and still widely-used, approach to product costing was developed when the notion of trying to determine the cost of industrial production first emerged This was around the time of the UK Industrial Revolution, when industry was characterised by:

- *Direct-labour-intensive and direct-labour-paced production.* Labour was at the heart of production. To the extent that machinery was used, it was to support the efforts of direct labour. The speed of production was, however, dictated by direct labour.
- *A low level of overheads relative to direct cost.* Little was spent on power, personnel services, machinery (leading to low depreciation charges) or other areas typical of the overheads of modern businesses.
- *A relatively uncompetitive market.* Transport difficulties, limited industrial production worldwide and customers' lack of knowledge of competitors' prices meant that businesses could prosper without being too scientific in costing and pricing their output. Customers tended to accept the products that the supplier offered, rather than demanding precisely what they wanted.

Since overheads at that time represented a relatively small element of total costs, it was acceptable and practical to deal with them in a fairly arbitrary manner. Little effort was devoted to controlling the cost of overheads because the benefits of better control were relatively small, certainly when compared with the benefits from firmer control of direct labour and material costs. It was also reasonable to charge overheads to individual jobs on a direct labour hour basis. Most of the overheads were incurred directly in support of direct labour: providing direct workers with a place to work, heating and lighting that workplace, employing people to supervise the direct workers and so on. Direct workers, perhaps aided by machinery, carried out all production.

At that time, service industries were a relatively unimportant part of the economy and would have largely consisted of self-employed individuals. These individuals would probably have been uninterested in trying to do more than work out a rough hourly/daily rate for their time and to try to base prices on this.

# Costing: the new environment

In recent years, the world of industrial production has fundamentally altered. Most of it is now characterised by:

- *Capital-intensive and machine-paced production.* Machines are at the heart of much production, including both manufacture of goods and the provision of services. Most labour supports the efforts of machines, for example technically maintaining them. Also, machines often dictate the pace of production. According to evidence in Real World 8.2 (page 281), direct labour accounts for just 14 per cent of manufacturers' total cost.
- *A high level of overheads relative to direct costs.* Modern businesses tend to have very high depreciation, servicing and power costs. There are also high costs of personnel and staff welfare and training which were scarcely envisaged in the early days of industrial production. At the same time, there are very low (sometimes no) direct labour costs. Although direct material cost often remains an important element of total cost, more efficient production methods lead to less waste and, therefore, less total material cost, again tending to make overheads more dominant.
- *A highly competitive, international market.* Production, much of it highly sophisticated, is carried out worldwide. Transport, including fast airfreight, is relatively cheap. Fax, telephone and, particularly, the Internet ensure that potential customers can quickly and cheaply find the prices of a range of suppliers. Markets now tend to be highly price-competitive. Customers increasingly demand products custom-made to their own requirements. This means that businesses need to know their product costs with a greater degree of accuracy than in the past. Businesses also need to take a considered and informed approach to pricing their output.

In the UK, as in many developed countries, service industries now dominate the economy, employing the great majority of the workforce and producing most of the value of productive output. Although there are many self-employed individuals supplying services, many service providers are vast businesses such as train and bus operators, banks, insurance companies and cinema operators. For most of these larger service providers, the activities closely resemble modern manufacturing activity. They too are characterised by high capital intensity, overheads dominating direct costs and a competitive international market.

In the past, overhead recovery rates (that is, rates at which overheads are absorbed by jobs/batches) were typically of a much lower value for each direct labour hour than the rate paid to direct workers as wages or salaries. It is now, however, becoming increasingly common for overhead recovery rates to be between five and ten times the hourly rate of pay, because overheads are now much more significant and the direct labour input much less so. When production is dominated by direct labour paid, say, £8 an hour, it might be reasonable to have an overhead recovery rate of, say, £1 an hour. When, however, direct labour plays a relatively small part in production, to have overhead recovery rates of, say, £50 for each direct labour hour is likely to lead to very arbitrary costing. Even a small change in the amount of direct labour worked on a job/batch could massively affect the total cost deduced. This is not because the direct worker is very highly paid, but because of the effect of the direct labour change on the overhead loading. A further problem is that overheads are still typically charged on a direct labour hour basis even though those overheads may not be particularly closely related to direct labour.

Real World 8.5 provides a rather disturbing view of costing and cost control in large banks.

### Real World 8.5

## Bank accounts

In a study of the cost structures of 52 international banks, the German consultancy firm, Droege, found that indirect costs could represent as much as 85 per cent of total costs. However, whilst direct costs were generally under tight management control, indirect costs were not. The indirect costs, which include such items as IT development, risk control, auditing, marketing and public relations, were often not allocated between operating divisions or were allocated in a rather arbitrary manner.

*Source*: based on information in Skorecki, A., 'Banks have not tackled indirect costs', FT.com, 7 January 2004.

## An alternative approach to full costing

As a result of changes in the business environment, the whole question of overheads, what causes them and how they are charged to jobs/batches, has been receiving much closer attention. Historically, businesses have been content to accept that overheads exist and, therefore, for product costing purposes they must be dealt with in as practical a way as possible. In recent years, however, there has been an increasing acceptance of the fact that overheads do not just happen; they must be caused by something. To illustrate this point, let us consider Example 8.4.

### Example 8.4

Modern Producers Ltd has, like virtually all manufacturers, a storage area that is set aside for its inventories of finished goods. The costs of running the stores include a share of the factory rent and other establishment costs, such as heating and lighting. They also include the salaries of staff employed to look after the inventories, and the cost of financing the inventories held in the stores.

The business has two product lines: A and B. Product A tends to be made in small batches, and low levels of finished inventories are held. The business prides itself on its ability to supply Product B in relatively large quantities instantly. As a consequence, most of the space in the finished goods store is filled with finished Product Bs ready to be dispatched immediately an order is received.

Traditionally, the whole cost of operating the stores would have been treated as a general overhead and included in the total of overheads charged to batches, probably on a direct labour hour basis. This means that when assessing the cost of Products A and B, the cost of operating the stores has fallen on them according to the number of direct labour hours worked on each one, a factor that has nothing to do with storage.

In fact, most of the stores cost should be charged to Product B, since this product causes (and benefits from) the stores cost much more than does Product A. Failure to account more precisely for the cost of running the stores is masking the fact that Product B is not as profitable as it seems to be. It may even be leading to losses as a result of the relatively high stores-operating cost that it causes. So far, much of this cost has been charged to Product A without regard to the fact that Product A causes little of it.

## What drives the costs?

 Realisation that overheads do not just occur, but are caused by activities – such as holding products in stores – that 'drive' the costs, is at the heart of activity-based costing (ABC). The traditional approach is that direct labour hours are the cost driver, which probably used to be true in many cases. ABC recognises that this is now often not the case.

There is a basic philosophical difference between the traditional and the ABC approaches. Traditionally we tend to think of overheads as *rendering a service to cost units*, the cost of which must be charged to those units. ABC sees overheads as being *caused by activities*, and so it is the cost units that cause the activities that must be charged with the costs that they cause.

### Activity 8.10

Can you think of any other purpose that identification of the cost drivers serves, apart from deriving more accurate costs?

Identification of the activities that cause costs puts management in a position where it may well be able to control them more effectively.

It is not always easy to see how and why some overhead costs have arisen. This has traditionally made them more difficult to control than direct labour and material costs. If, however, an analysis of overheads can identify the cost drivers, questions can be asked about whether the activity driving certain costs is necessary at all, and whether the cost justifies the benefit. In Example 8.4, it may well be a good marketing policy that Product B can be supplied immediately from inventories held, but this causes a cost that should be recognised and assessed against the benefit.

Adopting ABC requires that most overheads can be analysed and the cost drivers identified. This means that it might be possible to gain much clearer insights about the overhead costs that are caused, activity by activity, so that fairer and more accurate product costs can be identified, and costs can be controlled more effectively.

## Cost pools

Under ABC, an overhead cost pool is established for each activity that gives rise to cost. All of the costs relating to the particular activity will be placed in its cost pool. The cost driver for the particular activity will then need to be identified. So, the business in Example 8.4 would create a cost pool for the activity of operating the stores. All costs associated with this activity would be allocated to that cost pool. The total costs in that pool would then be allocated to output (Products A and B, in this case), using the cost driver identified, according to the extent to which each unit of output gave rise to the activity that 'drove' those costs.

### Example 8.5

The management accountant at Modern Producers Ltd (see Example 8.4) has estimated that the costs of running the finished goods stores for next year will be £90,000. This will be the amount allocated to the 'finished goods stores cost pool'.

It is estimated that each Product A will spend an average of one week in the stores before being sold. With Product B, the equivalent period is four weeks. Both products are of roughly similar size and have similar storage needs. It is felt, therefore, that the period spent in the stores ('product weeks') is the cost driver.

It is estimated that, next year, 50,000 Product As and 25,000 Product Bs will pass through the stores. So the total number of 'product weeks' in store will be:

|  |  |
|---|---:|
| Product A (50,000 × 1 week) | 50,000 |
| Product B (25,000 × 4 weeks) | 100,000 |
|  | 150,000 |

The cost per unit of cost driver is the total cost of the stores divided by the number of 'product weeks', as calculated above. This is

$$£90,000/150,000 = £0.60$$

To determine the cost to be attached to a particular unit of product, the figure of £0.60 must be multiplied by the number of 'product weeks' that a product stays in the finished goods store. Thus, each unit of Product A will be charged with £0.60 (that is, £0.60 × 1), and each Product B with £2.40 (that is, £0.60 × 4).

Allocating overhead costs to cost pools, as is necessary with ABC, contrasts with the traditional approach, where the overheads are normally allocated to production departments (cost centres). In both cases, however, the overheads are then charged to cost units (goods or services). The two different approaches are illustrated in Figure 8.10.

### Figure 8.10 Traditional versus activity-based costing

**Traditional approach**

**ABC approach**

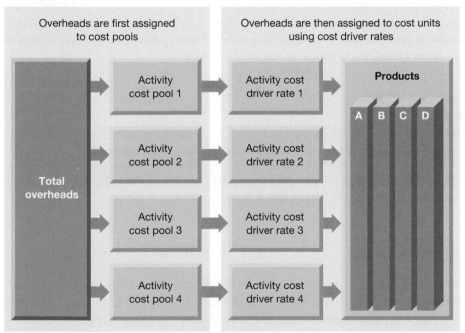

With the traditional approach, overheads are first assigned to product cost centres and then absorbed by cost units based on an overhead recovery rate (using direct labour hours worked on the cost units, or some other approach) for each cost centre. With activity-based costing, overheads are assigned to cost pools and then cost units are charged with overheads to the extent that they drive the costs in the various pools.

*Source*: adapted from Innes, J. and Mitchell, F., *Activity Based Costing: A Review with Case Studies*, CIMA Publishing, 1990.

With the traditional approach, overheads are apportioned to product departments (cost centres). Each department would then derive an overhead recovery rate, typically overheads per direct labour hour. Overheads would then be applied to units of output according to how many direct labour hours were worked on them.

With ABC, the overheads are analysed into cost pools, with one cost pool for each cost-driving activity. The overheads are then charged to units of output, through activity cost driver rates (for example, £0.60 per 'product week' for the stores cost in Example 8.5). These rates are an attempt to represent the extent to which each cost unit is believed to cause the particular part of the overheads.

Cost pools are much the same as cost centres, except that each cost pool is linked to a particular *activity* (operating the stores in Examples 8.4 and 8.5), rather than being more general, as is the case with cost centres in traditional product costing.

## ABC and service industries

Much of our discussion of ABC has concentrated on manufacturing industry, perhaps because early users of ABC were manufacturing businesses. In fact, ABC is possibly even more relevant to service industries because, in the absence of a direct material element, a service business's total costs are likely to be largely made up of overheads. There is certainly evidence that ABC has been adopted more readily by businesses that sell services rather than goods, as we shall see later.

### Activity 8.11

**What is the difference in the way that direct costs are accounted for when using ABC, relative to their treatment taking a traditional approach to full costing?**

The answer is that there is no difference at all. ABC is concerned only with the way in which overheads are charged to jobs to derive the full cost.

## Criticisms of ABC

Critics of ABC argue that analysing overheads in order to identify cost drivers is time-consuming and costly. They further argue that the benefit of doing this, in terms of more accurate product costing and the potential for cost control, does not justify the cost of carrying out the analysis.

ABC is also criticised for the same reason that full costing is generally criticised, which is that it does not provide relevant information for decision making. This point will be addressed in the following section.

Supporters of ABC would tend to respond by saying that even if ABC-derived product costs were not really helpful (and many would argue that they *are* helpful), identifying the activities that cause the costs may still be well worth doing. As was pointed out earlier, knowing what drives the costs may make cost control more effective.

Real World 8.6 shows how ABC came to be used at Royal Mail.

## Delivering ABC

Early in the 2000s the publicly owned Royal Mail adopted ABC and used it to find the cost of making postal deliveries. Royal Mail identified 340 activities that gave rise to costs, and created a cost pool and identified a cost driver for each of these.

Roger Tabour, Royal Mail's Enterprise Systems Programme Director, explained 'A new regulatory and competitive environment, plus a down-turned economy, led management to seek out more reliable sources of information on performance and profitability', and this led to the introduction of ABC.

Royal Mail is a public sector organisation that is subject to supervision by Postcomm, the UK-government-appointed regulatory body. The government requires Royal Mail to operate on a commercial basis and to make profits.

*Source*: www.sas.com.

Real World 8.7 provides some indication of the extent to which ABC is used in practice.

## ABC in practice

The recent survey of 176 UK businesses operating in various industries, all with annual sales revenue of more than £50 million, by Al-Omiri and Drury, referred to in Real World 8.2, indicated that 29 per cent of larger UK businesses use ABC.

The adoption of ABC in the UK varies widely between industries, as is shown in Figure 8.11.

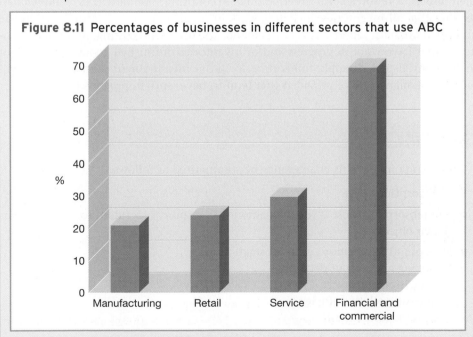

**Figure 8.11 Percentages of businesses in different sectors that use ABC**

Al-Omiri and Drury took their analysis a step further by looking at the factors that apparently tend to lead a particular business to adopt ABC. They found that businesses that used ABC tended to be

■ large;
■ sophisticated, in terms of using advanced management accounting techniques generally;
■ in an intensely competitive market for their products;
■ operating in a service industry, particularly in the financial services.

All of these findings are broadly in line with other recent research evidence involving businesses from around the world.

*Source*: Al-Omiri, M. and Drury, C., 'A survey of factors influencing the choice of product costing systems in UK organisations', *Management Accounting Research*, December 2007.

## Using full (absorption) cost information

Both the traditional and the ABC methods have been criticised because, in practice, they tend to use past (historic) costs. It can be argued that past costs are irrelevant, irrespective of the purpose for which the information is to be used. This is basically because it is not possible to make decisions about the past, only about the future. Advocates of full costing methods would argue, however, that they provide a useful guide to long-run average cost.

Despite the criticisms made of full costing methods, research evidence suggests that their use is widespread. An International Accounting Standard (IAS 2 *Inventories*) requires that all inventories, including work in progress, be valued at full cost in the published financial reports. This fact demands the use of full costing. As a result, businesses that have work in progress and/or inventories of finished goods at the end of their financial periods apply full costing for profit measurement purposes. (This will include the many service providers that tend to have work in progress.)

## Summary

The main points in this chapter may be summarised as follows.

### Full (absorption) cost

■ Full (absorption) cost is the total amount of resources sacrificed to achieve a particular objective.
■ Uses of full (absorption) cost information are
 – pricing and output decisions
 – exercising control
 – assessing relative efficiency
 – profit measurement.

### Single-product businesses

■ Where all the units of output are identical, the full cost can be calculated as follows:

$$\text{Cost per unit} = \frac{\text{Total cost of output}}{\text{Number of units produced}}$$

### Multi-product businesses – job costing

■ Where units of output are not identical, it is necessary to divide the cost into two categories: direct cost and indirect cost (overheads).

■ Direct cost = cost that can be identified with specific cost units (for example, labour of a garage mechanic, in relation to a particular job).

■ Indirect cost (overheads) = cost that cannot be directly measured in respect of a particular job (for example, the rent of a garage).

■ Full (absorption) cost = direct cost + indirect cost.

■ Direct/indirect is not linked to variable/fixed.

■ Indirect cost is difficult to relate to individual cost units – arbitrary bases are used and there is no single correct method.

■ Traditionally, indirect cost is seen as the cost of providing a 'service' to cost units.

■ Direct labour hour basis of applying indirect cost to cost units is the most popular in practice.

### Dealing with indirect cost on a cost centre (departmental) basis

■ Indirect cost (overheads) can be segmented – usually on cost centre basis; each product cost centre has its own overhead recovery rate.

■ Cost centres are areas, activities or functions for which costs are separately determined.

### Batch costing

■ A variation of job costing where each job consists of a number of identical (or near identical) cost units:

$$\text{Cost per unit} = \frac{\text{Cost of the batch (direct + indirect)}}{\text{Number of units in the batch}}$$

### Break-even price and full (absorption) costing

■ If the full (absorption) cost is charged as the sales price and things go according to plan, the business will break even.

### Criticisms of full (absorption) costing

■ Full cost information is seen by some as not very useful because it can be backward-looking: it includes information irrelevant to decision making, but excludes some relevant information.

### Activity-based costing

- Activity-based costing is an approach to dealing with overheads (in full costing) that treats all costs as being caused or 'driven' by activities.

- Advocates argue that it is more relevant to the modern commercial environment than is the traditional approach.

- Identification of the cost drivers can lead to more relevant indirect cost treatment in full costing.

- Identification of the cost drivers can also lead to better control of overheads.

- Critics argue that ABC is time-consuming and expensive to apply – not justified by the possible improvement in the quality of information.

*MyAccountingLab* **Now check your progress in your personal Study Plan**

### → Key terms

full cost p. 278
full costing p. 279
cost unit p. 279
process costing p. 280
direct cost p. 280
indirect cost p. 281
overheads p. 281
common cost p. 281
job costing p. 282

absorption costing p. 282
cost behaviour p. 284
overhead absorption (recovery) rate
    p. 286
cost centre p. 293
batch costing p. 296
activity-based costing (ABC) p. 301
cost driver p. 301
cost pool p. 302

## Further reading

If you would like to explore the topics covered in this chapter in more depth, we recommend the following books:

Atkinson, A., Kaplan, R., Matsumura, E.M. and Young, S.M., *Management Accounting* (5th edn), Prentice Hall, 2007, chapter 3.

Atrill, P. and McLaney, E., *Management Accounting for Decision Makers* (6th edn), FT/Prentice Hall, 2009, chapters 4 and 5.

Drury, C., *Management and Cost Accounting* (7th edn), South Western Cengage Learning, 2007, chapters 3, 4 and 5.

Horngren, C., Foster, G., Datar, S., Rajan, M. and Ittner, C., *Cost Accounting: A Managerial Emphasis* (13th edn), Prentice Hall International, 2008, chapter 4.

#  Review questions

Solutions to these questions can be found at the back of the book, in Appendix C.

**8.1** What problem does the existence of work in progress cause in process costing?

**8.2** What is the point of distinguishing direct cost from indirect cost? Why is this not necessary in process costing environments?

**8.3** Are direct cost and variable cost the same thing? Explain your answer.

**8.4** It is sometimes claimed that the full cost of pursuing some objective represents the long-run break-even selling price. Why is this said and what does it mean?

# ✳ Exercises

Exercises 8.4 and 8.5 are more advanced than 8.1 to 8.3. Those with a coloured number have solutions at the back of the book, in Appendix D.

If you wish to try more exercises, visit the website at www.myaccountinglab.com.

**8.1** Distinguish between job costing, process costing, and batch costing.
What tend to be the problems specifically associated with each of these?

**8.2** Pieman Products Ltd makes road trailers to the precise specifications of individual customers. The following are predicted to occur during the forthcoming year, which is about to start:

| | |
|---|---|
| Direct materials cost | £50,000 |
| Direct labour cost | £160,000 |
| Direct labour time | 16,000 hours |
| Indirect labour cost | £25,000 |
| Depreciation of machine | £8,000 |
| Rent and rates | £10,000 |
| Heating, lighting and power | £5,000 |
| Indirect materials | £2,000 |
| Other indirect cost (overhead) elements | £1,000 |
| Machine time | 3,000 hours |

All direct labour is paid at the same hourly rate.

A customer has asked the business to build a trailer for transporting a racing motor-cycle to race meetings. It is estimated that this will require materials and components that will cost £1,150. It will take 250 direct labour hours to do the job, of which 50 will involve the use of machinery.

**Required:**

Deduce a logical cost for the job and explain the basis of dealing with overheads that you propose.

**8.3** Athena Ltd is an engineering business doing work for its customers to their particular requirements and specifications. It determines the full cost of each job taking a 'job costing' approach, accounting for overheads on a cost centre (departmental) basis. It bases its prices to customers on this full cost figure. The business has two departments (both of which are cost centres): a Machining Department, where each job starts, and a Fitting Department, which completes all of the jobs. Machining Department overheads are charged to jobs on a machine hour basis and those of the Fitting Department on a direct labour hour basis. The budgeted information for next year is as follows:

| | | |
|---|---|---|
| Heating and lighting | £25,000 | (allocated equally between the two departments) |
| Machine power | £10,000 | (all allocated to the Machining Department) |
| Direct labour | £200,000 | (£150,000 allocated to the Fitting Department and £50,000 to the Machining Department; all direct workers are paid £10 an hour) |
| Indirect labour | £50,000 | (apportioned to the departments in proportion to the direct labour cost) |
| Direct materials | £120,000 | (all applied to jobs in the Machining Department) |
| Depreciation | £30,000 | (all relates to the Machining Department) |
| Machine time | 20,000 hours | (all worked in the Machining Department) |

**Required:**

(a) Prepare a statement showing the budgeted overheads for next year, analysed between the two cost centres. This should be in the form of three columns: one for the total figure for each type of overhead and one column each for the two cost centres, where each type of overhead is analysed between the two cost centres. Each column should also show the total of overheads for the year.

(b) Derive the appropriate rate for charging the overheads of each cost centre to jobs (that is, a separate rate for each cost centre).

(c) Athena Ltd has been asked by a customer to specify the price that it will charge for a particular job that will, if the job goes ahead, be undertaken early next year. The job is expected to use direct materials costing Athena Ltd £1,200, to need 50 hours of machining time, 10 hours of Machine Department direct labour and 20 hours of Fitting Department direct labour. Athena Ltd charges a profit loading of 20% to the full cost of jobs to determine the selling price.

Show workings to derive the proposed selling price for this job.

**8.4** Kaplan plc makes a range of suitcases of various sizes and shapes. There are ten different models of suitcase produced by the business. In order to keep inventories of finished suitcases to a minimum, each model is made in a small batch. Each batch is costed as a separate job and the cost for each suitcase deduced by dividing the batch cost by the number of suitcases in the batch.

At present, the business derives the cost of each batch using a traditional job costing approach. Recently, however, a new management accountant was appointed, who is advocating the use of activity-based costing (ABC) to deduce the cost of the batches. The management accountant claims that ABC leads to much more reliable and relevant costs and that it has other benefits.

**Required:**
(a) Explain how the business deduces the cost of each suitcase at present.
(b) Explain how ABC could be applied to costing the suitcases, highlighting the differences between ABC and the traditional approach.
(c) Explain what advantages the new management accountant probably believes ABC to have over the traditional approach.

**8.5** Consider this statement:

> In a job costing system, it is necessary to divide up the business into departments. Fixed cost (or overheads) will be collected for each department. Where a particular fixed cost relates to the business as a whole, it must be divided between the departments. Usually this is done on the basis of area of floor space occupied by each department relative to the entire business. When the total fixed cost for each department has been identified, this will be divided by the number of hours that were worked in each department to deduce an overhead recovery rate. Each job that was worked on in a department will have a share of fixed cost allotted to it according to how long it was worked on. The total cost for each job will therefore be the sum of the variable cost of the job and its share of the fixed cost. It is essential that this approach is taken in order to deduce a selling price for the business's output.

**Required:**
Prepare a table of two columns. In the first column you should show any phrases or sentences in the above statement with which you do not agree. In the second column you should show your reason for disagreeing with each one.

## Chapter 9

# Budgeting

## Introduction

In this chapter we consider the role and nature of budgets. We shall see that budgets set out short-term plans that help managers to run the business. They provide the means to assess whether actual performance has gone as planned and, where it has not, to identify the reasons for this.

It is important to recognise that budgets do not exist in a vacuum; they are an integral part of a planning framework that is adopted by well-run businesses. To understand fully the nature of budgets we must, therefore, understand the strategic planning framework within which they are set.

Preparing budgets relies on an understanding of the financial statements (statement of financial position and income statement), which we considered in Chapters 2 and 3. It also requires an understanding of issues relating to the behaviour of costs and full costing, which we considered in Chapters 7 and 8.

The chapter begins with a discussion of the budgeting framework and then goes on to consider detailed aspects of the budgeting process. It ends by considering the use of budgets in monitoring performance and exercising control.

## Learning outcomes

**When you have completed this chapter, you should be able to:**

■ define a budget and show how budgets, strategic objectives and strategic plans are related;

- explain the budgeting process and the interlinking of the various budgets within the business;

- indicate the uses of budgeting and construct various budgets, including the cash budget, from relevant data;

- show how flexing the budget can be used to exercise control over the business.

 Remember to create your own personalised Study Plan

## Budgets and budgeting

In its 2009 annual report, BSkyB Group plc, the satellite television broadcaster said (about itself):

> There is a comprehensive budgeting and forecasting process, and the annual budget, which is regularly reviewed and updated, is approved by the Board [of directors]. Performance is monitored against budget through weekly and monthly reporting cycles.

As we shall see later, the practice at BSkyB is typical of businesses of all sizes.

What is a budget? What is it for? How is it prepared? Who prepares it? Why does the board regard the budget as important enough to warrant its concern? Why is performance monitored against the budget and how is this achieved? We shall be looking at the answers to each of these questions in the course of this chapter.

## How budgets link with strategic plans and objectives

It is vital that businesses develop plans for the future. What a business is trying to achieve is unlikely to come about unless its managers are clear what the future direction of the business is going to be. The development of plans involves five key steps:

 1 *Establish mission and objectives*. The mission statement sets out the ultimate purpose of the business. It is a broad statement of intent, whereas the strategic objectives are more specific and will usually include quantifiable goals.

2 *Undertake a position analysis*. This involves an assessment of where the business is currently placed in relation to where it wants to be, as set out in its mission and strategic objectives.

3 *Identify and assess strategic options*. The business must explore the various ways in which it might move from where it is now (identified in step 2) to where it wants to be (identified in step 1).

4 *Select strategic options and formulate plans*. This involves selecting what seems to be the best of the courses of action or strategies (identified in step 3) and formulating a long-term strategic plan. This strategic plan is then normally broken down into a series of short-term plans, one for each element of the business. These plans are

the budgets. Thus, a budget is a business plan for the short term – typically one year – and is expressed mainly in financial terms. Its role is to convert the strategic plans into actionable blueprints for the immediate future. Budgets will define precise targets concerning such things as

- cash receipts and payments,
- sales volumes and revenues, broken down into amounts and prices for each of the products or services provided by the business,
- detailed inventories requirements,
- detailed labour requirements, and
- specific production requirements.

5 *Perform, review and control.* Here the business pursues the budgets derived in step 4. By comparing the actual outcome with the budgets, managers can see if things are going according to plan or not. Action would be taken to exercise control where actual performance appears not to be matching the budgets.

From the above description of the planning process, we can see that the relationship between the mission, strategic objectives, strategic plans and budgets can be summarised as follows:

- the mission sets the overall direction and, once set, is likely to last for quite a long time – perhaps throughout the life of the business;
- the strategic objectives, which are also long-term, will set out how the mission can be achieved;
- the strategic plans identify how each objective will be pursued; and
- the budgets set out, in detail, the short-term plans and targets necessary to fulfil the strategic objectives.

An analogy might be found in terms of a student enrolling on a course of study. His or her mission might be to have a happy and fulfilling life. A key strategic objective flowing from this mission might be to embark on a career that will be rewarding in various ways. He or she might have identified the particular study course as the most effective way to work towards this objective. Successfully completing the course would then be the strategic plan. In working towards this strategic plan, passing a particular stage of the course might be identified as the target for the forthcoming year. This short-term target is analogous to the budget. Having achieved the 'budget' for the first year, the budget for the second year becomes passing the second stage.

## Collecting information on performance and exercising control

However well planned the activities of a business might be, they will come to nothing unless steps are taken to try to achieve them in practice. The process of making planned events actually occur is known as control. This is part of step 5 (above).

Control can be defined as compelling events to conform to plan. This definition is valid in any context. For example, when we talk about controlling a motor car, we mean making the car do what we plan that it should do. In a business context, management accounting is very useful in the control process. This is because it is possible to state many plans in accounting terms (as budgets). Since it is also possible to state *actual* outcomes in the same terms, making comparison between actual and planned outcomes is a relatively simple matter. Where actual outcomes are at variance with budgets, this variance should be highlighted by accounting information. Managers can then take steps to get the business back on track towards the achievement of the budgets. We shall be looking more closely at the control aspect of budgeting later in the chapter.

Figure 9.1 shows the planning and control process in diagrammatic form.

**Figure 9.1 The planning and control process**

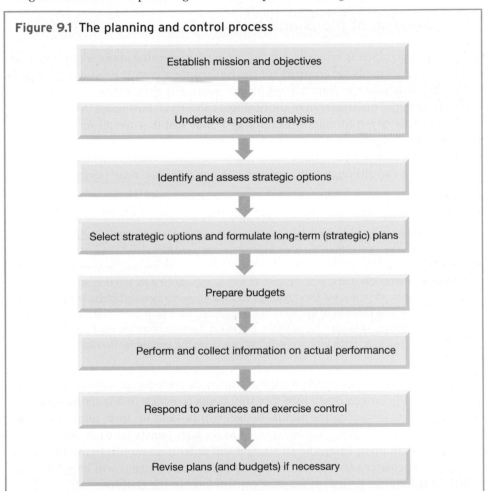

Once the mission and objectives of the business have been determined, the various strategic options available must be considered and evaluated in order to derive a strategic plan. The budget is a short-term financial plan for the business that is prepared within the framework of the strategic plan. Control can be exercised through the comparison of budgeted and actual performance. Where a significant divergence emerges, some form of corrective action should be taken. If the budget figures prove to be based on incorrect assumptions about the future, it might be necessary to revise the budget.

It should be emphasised that planning (including budgeting) is the responsibility of managers rather than accountants. Though accountants should play a role in the planning process, by supplying relevant information to managers and by contributing to decision making as part of the management team, they should not dominate the process. In practice, it seems that the budgeting aspect of planning is often in danger of being dominated by accountants, perhaps because most budgets are expressed in financial terms. However, managers are failing in their responsibilities if they allow this to happen.

## Time horizon of plans and budgets

Setting strategic plans is typically a major exercise performed about every five years and budgets are usually set annually for the forthcoming year. It need not necessarily be the case that strategic plans are set for five years and that budgets are set for one year; it is up to the management of the business concerned. Businesses involved in certain industries – say, information technology – may feel that five years is too long a planning period since new developments can, and do, occur virtually overnight. Here, a planning horizon of two or three years is more feasible. Similarly, a budget need not be set for one year, although this appears to be a widely used time horizon.

### Activity 9.1

Can you think of any reason why most businesses prepare detailed budgets for the forthcoming year, rather than for a shorter or longer period?

The reason is probably that a year represents a long enough time for the budget preparation exercise to be worthwhile, yet short enough into the future for detailed plans to be capable of being made. The process of formulating budgets can be a time-consuming exercise, but there are economies of scale – for example, preparing the budget for the next year would not normally take twice as much time and effort as preparing the budget for the next six months.

An annual budget sets targets for the forthcoming year for all aspects of the business. It is usually broken down into monthly budgets, which define monthly targets. Indeed, in many instances, the annual budget will be built up from monthly figures. For example, the sales staff may be required to set sales targets for each month of the budget period. In many cases, the sales target will differ from month to month – many businesses experience seasonal demand variations. Other budgets will be set, for each month of the budget period, as we shall explain later in the chapter.

## Limiting factors

Some aspect of the business will, inevitably, stop it achieving its objectives to the maximum extent. This is often a limited ability of the business to sell its products.

Sometimes, it is some production shortage (such as labour, materials or plant) that is the limiting factor, or, linked to these, a shortage of funds. Often, production shortages can be overcome by an increase in funds – for example, more plant can be bought or leased. This is not always a practical solution, because no amount of money will buy certain labour skills or increase the world supply of some raw material.

Easing an initial limiting factor may sometimes be possible. For example, sub-contracting can eliminate a plant capacity problem. This means that some other factor, perhaps lack of sales demand, will replace the production problem, though at a higher level of output. Ultimately, however, the business will hit a ceiling; some limiting factor will prove impossible to ease.

The limiting factor must be identified. Ultimately, most, if not all, budgets will be affected by the limiting factor, and so if it can be identified at the outset, all managers can be informed of the restriction early in the process. When preparing the budgets, account can then be taken of the limiting factor.

## Budgets and forecasts

A budget may, as we have already seen, be defined as a business plan for the short term. Budgets are, to a great extent, expressed in financial terms. Note particularly that a budget is a *plan*, not a forecast. To talk of a plan suggests an intention or determination to achieve the targets; forecasts tend to be predictions of the future state of the environment.

Clearly, forecasts are very helpful to the planner/budget-setter. If, for example, a reputable forecaster has predicted the number of new cars to be purchased in the UK during next year, it will be valuable for a manager in a car manufacturing business to take account of this information when setting next year's sales budgets. However, a forecast and a budget are distinctly different.

## Periodic and continual budgets

Budgeting can be undertaken on a periodic or a continual basis. A periodic budget is prepared for a particular period (usually one year). Managers will agree the budget for the year and then allow the budget to run its course. Although it may be necessary to revise the budget on occasions, preparing the budget is in essence a one-off exercise during each financial year. A continual budget, as the name suggests, is continually updated. We have seen that an annual budget will normally be broken down into smaller time intervals (usually monthly periods) to help control the activities of a business. A continual budget will add a new month to replace the month that has just passed, thereby ensuring that, at all times, there will be a budget for a full planning period. Continual budgets are also referred to as rolling budgets.

## Activity 9.2

Which method of budgeting do you think is likely to be more costly and which method is likely to be more beneficial for forward planning?

Periodic budgeting will usually take less time and effort and will, therefore, be less costly. However, as time passes, the budget period shortens, and towards the end of the financial year managers will be working to a very short planning period indeed. Continual budgeting, on the other hand, will ensure that managers always have a full year's budget to help them make decisions. It is claimed that continual budgeting ensures that managers plan throughout the year rather than just once each year. In this way it encourages a forward-looking attitude.

While continual budgeting encourages a forward-looking attitude, there is a danger that budgeting will become a mechanical exercise, as managers may not have time to step back from their other tasks each month and consider the future carefully. Continually taking this future-oriented perspective may be difficult for managers to sustain.

Continual budgets do not appear to be very popular in practice. A recent study of 340 senior financial staff of small, medium and large businesses in North America revealed that only 9 per cent of businesses use them (see reference 1 at the end of the chapter).

## How budgets link to one another

A business will prepare more than one budget for a particular period. Each budget prepared will relate to a specific aspect of the business. The ideal situation is probably that there should be a separate operating budget for each person who is in a managerial position, no matter how junior. The contents of all of the individual operating  budgets will be summarised in master budgets, usually consisting of a budgeted income statement and statement of financial position (balance sheet). The cash budget is considered by some to be a third master budget.

Figure 9.2 illustrates the interrelationship and interlinking of individual operating budgets, in this particular case using a manufacturing business as an example.

The sales budget is usually the first one to be prepared (at the left of Figure 9.2), as the level of sales often determines the overall level of activity for the forthcoming period. This is because it is probably the most common limiting factor (see page 317). The finished inventories requirement tends to be set by the level of sales, though it would also be dictated by the policy of the business on the level of the finished products inventories. The requirement for finished inventories will define the required production levels, which will, in turn, dictate the requirements of the individual production departments or sections. The demands of manufacturing, in conjunction with

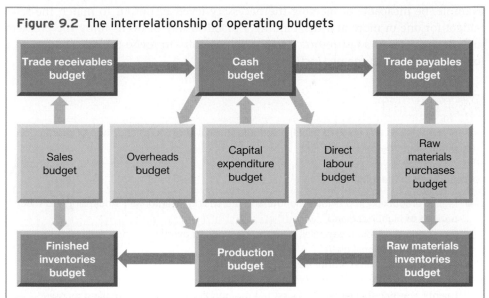

**Figure 9.2** The interrelationship of operating budgets

The starting point is usually the sales budget. The expected level of sales normally defines the overall level of activity for the business, and the other operating budgets will be drawn up in accordance with this. Thus, the sales budget will largely define the finished inventories requirements, and from this we can define the production requirements and so on. This shows the interrelationship of operating budgets for a manufacturing business.

the business's policy on how long it holds raw materials before they enter production, define the raw materials inventories budget. The purchases budget will be dictated by the materials inventories budget, which will, in conjunction with the policy of the business on taking credit from suppliers, dictate the trade payables budget. One of the determinants of the cash budget will be the trade payables budget; another will be the trade receivables budget, which itself derives, through the business's policy on credit periods granted to credit customers, from the sales budget. Cash will also be affected by overheads and direct labour costs (themselves linked to production) and by capital expenditure. Cash will also be affected by new finance and redemption of existing sources. (This is not shown in Figure 9.2 because the diagram focuses only budgets concerned with operational matters.) The factors that affect policies on matters such as inventories holding and trade receivables collection and trade payables payment periods will be discussed in some detail in Chapter 12.

A manufacturing business has been used as the example in Figure 9.2 simply because it has all of the types of operating budgets found in practice. Service businesses have similar arrangements of budgets, but obviously may not have inventories budgets. All of the issues relating to budgets apply equally well to all types of business.

Sales demand is not necessarily the limiting factor. Assuming that the budgeting process takes the order just described, it might be found in practice that there is some constraint other than sales demand. The production capacity of the business may, for example, be incapable of meeting the necessary levels of output to match the sales budget for one or more months. Finding a practical way of overcoming the problem may be possible. As a last resort, it might be necessary to revise the sales budget to a lower level to match the production limitation.

### Activity 9.3

**Can you think of any ways in which a manufacturer's short-term shortage of production facilities might be overcome?**

We thought of the following:

- higher production in previous months and increasing inventories ('stockpiling') to meet periods of higher demand
- increasing production capacity, perhaps by working overtime and/or acquiring (buying or leasing) additional plant
- subcontracting some production
- encouraging potential customers to change the timing of their purchases by offering discounts or other special terms during the months that have been identified as quiet.

You might well have thought of other approaches.

There will be the horizontal relationships between budgets, which we have just looked at, but there will usually be vertical ones as well. Breaking down the sales budget into a number of subsidiary budgets, perhaps one for each regional sales manager, is a common approach. The overall sales budget will be a summary of the subsidiary ones. The same may be true of virtually all of the other budgets, most particularly the production budget.

Figure 9.3 shows the vertical relationship of the sales budgets for a business. The business has four geographical sales regions each one the responsibility of a separate

**Figure 9.3** The vertical relationship between a business's sales budgets

Overall sales budget

| Sales budget North region | Sales budget South region | Sales budget East region | Sales budget West region |

This business manages its sales through four geographical areas. The overall sales budget for the business as a whole is the sum of the four regional sales budgets.

manager, who is probably located in the region concerned. Each regional manager is responsible to the overall sales manager of the business. The overall sales budget is the sum of the budgets for the four sales regions.

Though sales are often managed on a geographical basis, and so their budgets reflect this, sales may be managed on some other basis. For example, a business that sells a range of products may manage sales on a product-type basis, with a specialist manager responsible for each type of product. Thus, an insurance business may have separate sales managers, and so separate sales budgets, for life insurance, household insurance, motor insurance and so on. Very large businesses may even have separate product-type managers for each geographical region. Each of these managers would have a separate budget, which would combine to form the overall sales budget for the business as a whole.

All of the operating budgets that we have just reviewed must mesh with the master budgets, that is, the budgeted income statement and statement of financial position.

## How budgets help managers

Budgets are generally regarded as having five areas of usefulness:

1 *Budgets tend to promote forward thinking and the possible identification of short-term problems.* We saw above that a shortage of production capacity might be identified during the budgeting process. Making this discovery in good time could leave a number of means of overcoming the problem open to exploration. If the potential production problem is picked up early enough, all of the suggestions in the answer to Activity 9.3 and, possibly, other ways of overcoming the problem, can be explored. Early identification of the potential problem gives managers time for calm and rational consideration of the best way of overcoming it. The best solution to the potential problem may possibly only be feasible if action can be taken well in advance. This would be true of all of the suggestions made in the answer to Activity 9.3.

2 *Budgets can be used to help co-ordination between the various sections of the business.* It is crucially important that the activities of the various departments and sections of the business are linked so that the activities of one are complementary to those of another. The activities of the purchasing/procurement department of a manufacturing business, for example, should dovetail with the raw materials needs of the production departments. If they do not, production could run out of raw materials, leading to expensive production stoppages. Possibly, just as undesirable, excessive amounts of raw materials could be bought, leading to large and unnecessary inventories-holding costs. We shall see how this co-ordination tends to work in practice later in this chapter.

3 *Budgets can motivate managers to better performance.* Having a stated task can motivate managers and staff in their performance. Simply to tell a manager to do his or her best is not very motivating, but to define a required level of achievement is more

likely to be so. Managers will be better motivated by being able to relate their particular role in the business to its overall objectives. Since budgets are directly derived from strategic objectives, budgeting makes this possible. It is clearly not possible to allow managers to operate in an unconstrained environment. Having to operate in a way that matches the goals of the business is a price of working in an effective business.

4 *Budgets can provide a basis for a system of control.* As we saw earlier in the chapter, control is concerned with ensuring that events conform to plans. If senior management wishes to control and to monitor the performance of more junior staff, it needs some yardstick against which to measure and assess performance. Current performance could possibly be compared with past performance or perhaps with what happens in another business. However, planned performance is usually the most logical yardstick. If there is information available concerning the actual performance for a period, and this can be compared with the planned performance, then a basis for control will have been established. This will enable the use of management by exception, a technique where senior managers can spend most of their time dealing with those staff or activities that have failed to achieve the budget (the exceptions). Thus senior managers do not have to spend too much time on those that are performing well. It also allows junior managers to exercise self-control. By knowing what they are expected to do and what they have actually achieved, they can assess how well they are performing and take steps to correct matters where they are failing to achieve.

5 *Budgets can provide a system of authorisation for managers to spend up to a particular limit.* Some activities (for example, staff development and research expenditure) are allocated a fixed amount of funds at the discretion of senior management. This provides the authority to spend.

Figure 9.4 shows the benefits of budgets in diagrammatic form.

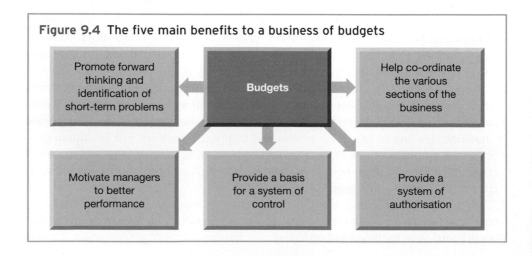

**Figure 9.4** The five main benefits to a business of budgets

Promote forward thinking and identification of short-term problems

**Budgets**

Help co-ordinate the various sections of the business

Motivate managers to better performance

Provide a basis for a system of control

Provide a system of authorisation

The following two activities pick up issues that relate to some of the uses of budgets.

## Activity 9.4

The third on the above list of the uses of budgets (motivation) implies that managers are set stated tasks. Do you think there is a danger that requiring managers to work towards such predetermined targets will stifle their skill, flair and enthusiasm?

If the budgets are set in such a way as to offer challenging yet achievable targets, the manager is still required to show skill, flair and enthusiasm. There is the danger, however, that if targets are badly set (either unreasonably demanding or too easy to achieve), they could be demotivating and have a stifling effect.

## Activity 9.5

The fourth on the above list of the uses of budgets (control) implies that current management performance is compared with some yardstick. What is wrong with comparing actual performance with past performance, or the performance of others, in an effort to exercise control?

What happened in the past, or is happening elsewhere, does not necessarily represent a sensible target for this year in this business. Considering what happened last year, and in other businesses, may help in the formulation of plans, but past events and the performance of others should not automatically be seen as the target.

The five identified uses of budgets can conflict with one another on occasions. Using the budget as a motivational device provides a possible example of this. Some businesses set the budget targets at a more difficult level than the managers are expected to achieve in an attempt to motivate managers to strive to reach their targets. For control purposes, however, the budget becomes less meaningful as a benchmark against which to compare actual performance. Incidentally, there is good reason to doubt the effectiveness of setting excessive targets as a motivational device, as we shall see later in the chapter.

Conflict between the different uses will mean that managers must decide which particular uses for budgets should be given priority. Managers must be prepared, if necessary, to trade off the benefits resulting from one particular use for the benefits of another.

## Using budgets in practice

This section attempts to give a flavour of how budgets are used, the extent to which they are used, and their level of accuracy.

Real World 9.1 shows how the UK-based international engineering and support services business Babcock International Group plc undertakes its budgeting process.

**Real World 9.1**

### Budgeting at Babcock

According to its annual report, Babcock has the following arrangements:

> Comprehensive systems are in place to develop annual budgets and medium-term financial plans. The budgets are reviewed by central management before being submitted to the Board for approval. Updated forecasts for the year are prepared at least quarterly. The Board is provided with details of actual performance each month compared with budgets, forecasts and the prior year, and is given a written commentary on significant variances from approved.

*Source*: Babcock International Group plc Annual Report 2009, p. 45.

There is quite a lot of recent survey evidence that reveals the extent to which budgeting is used by businesses in practice. Real World 9.2 reviews some of this evidence, which shows that most businesses prepare and use budgets.

**Real World 9.2**

### Budgeting in practice

A fairly recent survey of 41 UK manufacturing businesses found that 40 of the 41 prepared budgets.

*Source*: Dugdale, D., Jones, C. and Green, S., *Contemporary Management Accounting Practices in UK Manufacturing*, CIMA Publication, Elsevier, 2006.

Another fairly recent survey of UK businesses, but this time businesses involved in the food and drink sector, found that virtually all of them used budgets.

*Source*: Abdel-Kader, M. and Luther, R., *An Empirical Investigation of the Evolution of Management Accounting Practices*, Working Paper No. 04/06, University of Essex, October 2004.

A survey of the opinions of senior finance staff at 340 businesses of various sizes and operating in a wide range of industries in North America revealed that 97 per cent of those businesses had a formal budgeting process.

*Source*: BPM Forum, *Perfect How You Project*, 2008.

Though these three surveys relate to UK and North American businesses, they provide some idea of what is likely also to be practice elsewhere in the developed world.

A survey of budgeting practice in small and medium-sized enterprises (SMEs) (see Real World 9.3) revealed that not all such businesses fully use budgeting. It seems that some smaller businesses prepare budgets only for what they see as key areas.

The budget that is most frequently prepared by such businesses is the sales budget, followed by the budgeted income statement and the overheads budget. Perhaps surprisingly, the cash budget is prepared by less than two-thirds of the small businesses surveyed.

## Preparation of budgets in SMEs

A study of budgeting practice in small and medium-sized enterprises (SMEs) revealed that the budget that most businesses prepare is the sales budget (78 per cent prepared it), followed by the budgeted income statement and the overheads budget, as shown in Figure 9.5.

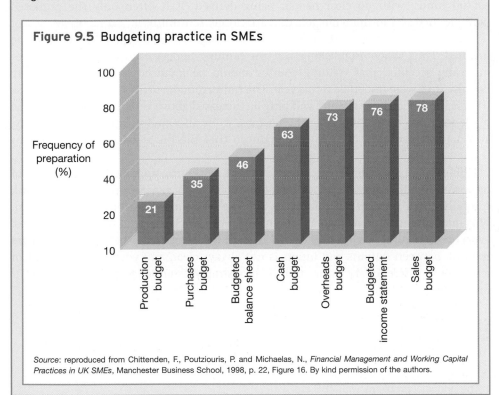

**Figure 9.5** Budgeting practice in SMEs

Source: reproduced from Chittenden, F., Poutziouris, P. and Michaelas, N., *Financial Management and Working Capital Practices in UK SMEs*, Manchester Business School, 1998, p. 22, Figure 16. By kind permission of the authors.

## Incremental and zero-base budgeting

There is a tendency with some types of budget for the budget-setting to be done on the basis of what happened last year, with some adjustment for any changes in factors that are expected to affect the forthcoming budget period (for example, inflation). This approach is known as incremental budgeting and is often used for 'discretionary' budgets, such as research and development and staff training. With this type of budget, the budget holder (the manager responsible for the budget) is allocated a sum of money to be spent in the area of activity concerned. They are referred to as discretionary budgets because the sum allocated is normally at the discretion of senior management. These budgets are very common in local and central government (and in other public bodies), but are also used in commercial businesses to cover the types of activity that we have just referred to.

Discretionary budgets are often found in areas where there is no clear relationship between inputs (resources applied) and outputs (benefits). Compare this with, say, a raw materials usage budget in a manufacturing business, where the amount of material used and, therefore, the amount of funds involved, is clearly related to the level of production and, ultimately, to sales volumes. Discretionary budgets can easily eat up funds, with no clear benefit being derived. It is often only the proposed periodic increases in these budgets that are closely scrutinised.

Zero-base budgeting (ZBB) rests on the philosophy that all spending needs to be justified. Thus, when establishing, say, the training budget each year, it is not automatically accepted that training courses should be financed in the future simply because they were undertaken this year. The training budget will start from a zero base (that is, no resources at all) and will only be increased above zero if a good case can be made for the scarce resources of the business to be allocated to this form of activity. Top management will need to be convinced that the proposed activities represent 'value for money'.

ZBB encourages managers to adopt a more questioning approach to their areas of responsibility. To justify the allocation of resources, managers are often forced to think carefully about the particular activities and the ways in which they are undertaken. This questioning approach should result in a more efficient use of business resources. With an increasing portion of the total costs of most businesses being in areas where the link between outputs and inputs is not always clear, and where commitment of resources is discretionary rather than demonstrably essential to production, ZBB is increasingly relevant.

## Activity 9.6

**Can you think of any disadvantages of using ZBB?**

The principal problems with ZBB are:

- It is time-consuming and therefore expensive to undertake.
- Managers whose sphere of responsibility is subjected to ZBB can feel threatened by it.

The benefits of a ZBB approach can be gained to some extent – perhaps at not too great a cost – by using the approach on a selective basis. For example, a particular budget area could be subjected to ZBB-type scrutiny only every third or fourth year. In any case, if ZBB is used more frequently, there is the danger that managers will use the same arguments each year to justify their activities. The process will simply become a mechanical exercise and the benefits will be lost. For a typical business, some areas are likely to benefit from ZBB more than others. As mentioned earlier, the areas most likely to benefit from ZBB involve discretionary spending, such as training, advertising, and research and development.

If senior managers are aware that their subordinates are likely to feel threatened by the nature of this form of budgeting, care can be taken to apply ZBB with sensitivity. However, in the quest for cost control and value for money, the application of ZBB can result in some tough decisions being made.

Real World 9.4 provides some insight to the extent that ZBB is used in practice.

---

**Real World 9.4**

## ZBB is not food and drink to many businesses

The survey of businesses in the UK food and drink sector referred to in Real World 9.2 found that ZBB is not much used by them. Only 48 per cent ever use it and only 16 per cent use it 'often' or 'very often'.

ZBB seems to be most appropriate, however, with 'spending' budgets, such as training, advertising and so on. Such budgets probably represent a minority for the types of business in this survey.

*Source*: Abdel-Kader, M. and Luther, R., *An Empirical Investigation of the Evolution of Management Accounting Practices*, Working Paper No. 04/06, University of Essex, October 2004.

---

## Preparing the cash budget

We shall now look in some detail at how the various budgets used by the typical business are prepared, starting with the cash budget and then looking at the others. It is helpful for us to start with the cash budget because

- it is a key budget (some people see it as a 'master budget' along with the budgeted income statement and budgeted statement of financial position);
- most economic aspects of a business are reflected in cash sooner or later, so that for a typical business the cash budget reflects the whole business more comprehensively than any other single budget;
- very small, unsophisticated businesses (for example, corner shops) may feel that full-scale budgeting is not appropriate to their needs, but almost certainly they should prepare a cash budget as a minimum (though many do not, as mentioned above).

Since budgets are documents that are to be used only internally by a business, their style is a question of management choice and will vary from one business to the next. However, as managers, irrespective of the business, are likely to be using budgets for similar purposes, some consistency of approach tends to be found. In most businesses, the cash budget will probably possess the following features:

1  The budget period will be broken down into sub-periods, typically months.
2  The budget will be in columnar form, with one column for each month.
3  Receipts of cash will be identified under various headings and a total for each month's receipts shown.
4  Payments of cash will be identified under various headings and a total for each month's payments shown.
5  The surplus of total cash receipts over payments, or of payments over receipts, for each month will be identified.
6  The running cash balance will be identified. This can be achieved by taking the balance at the end of the previous month and adjusting it for the surplus (or deficit) of receipts over payments (or payments over receipts) for the current month.

Typically, all of the pieces of information in points 3 to 6 in this list would be useful to management for one reason or another.

Probably the best way to deal with this topic is through an example.

## Example 9.1

Vierra Popova Ltd is a wholesale business. The budgeted income statements for each of the next six months are as follows:

|  | Jan £000 | Feb £000 | Mar £000 | Apr £000 | May £000 | June £000 |
|---|---|---|---|---|---|---|
| Sales revenue | 52 | 55 | 55 | 60 | 55 | 53 |
| Cost of goods sold | (30) | (31) | (31) | (35) | (31) | (32) |
| Salaries and wages | (10) | (10) | (10) | (10) | (10) | (10) |
| Electricity | (5) | (5) | (4) | (3) | (3) | (3) |
| Depreciation | (3) | (3) | (3) | (3) | (3) | (3) |
| Other overheads | (2) | (2) | (2) | (2) | (2) | (2) |
| Total expenses | (50) | (51) | (50) | (53) | (49) | (50) |
| Profit for the month | 2 | 4 | 5 | 7 | 6 | 3 |

The business allows all of its customers one month's credit (this means, for example, that cash from January sales will be received in February). Sales revenue during December totalled £60,000.

The business plans to maintain inventories at their existing level until some time in March, when they are to be reduced by £5,000. Inventories will remain at this lower level indefinitely. Inventories purchases are made on one month's credit. December purchases totalled £30,000. Salaries, wages and 'other overheads' are paid in the month concerned. Electricity is paid quarterly in arrears in March and June. The business plans to buy and pay for a new delivery van in March. This will cost £15,000, but an existing van will be traded in for £4,000 as part of the deal.

The business expects to have £12,000 in cash at the beginning of January.

The cash budget for the six months ending in June will look as follows:

| | Jan £000 | Feb £000 | Mar £000 | Apr £000 | May £000 | June £000 |
|---|---|---|---|---|---|---|
| Receipts | | | | | | |
| Trade receivables (Note 1) | 60 | 52 | 55 | 55 | 60 | 55 |
| Payments | | | | | | |
| Trade payables (Note 2) | (30) | (30) | (31) | (26) | (35) | (31) |
| Salaries and wages | (10) | (10) | (10) | (10) | (10) | (10) |
| Electricity | – | – | (14) | – | – | (9) |
| Other overheads | (2) | (2) | (2) | (2) | (2) | (2) |
| Van purchase | – | – | (11) | – | – | – |
| Total payments | (42) | (42) | (68) | (38) | (47) | (52) |
| Cash surplus for the month | 18 | 10 | (13) | 17 | 13 | 3 |
| Opening balance (Note 3) | 12 | 30 | 40 | 27 | 44 | 57 |
| Closing balance | 30 | 40 | 27 | 44 | 57 | 60 |

Notes:
1 The cash receipts from trade receivables lag a month behind sales because customers are given a month in which to pay for their purchases. So, December sales will be paid for in January and so on.
2 In most months, the purchases of inventories will equal the cost of goods sold. This is because the business maintains a constant level of inventories. For inventories to remain constant at the end of each month, the business must replace exactly the amount that has been used. During March, however, the business plans to reduce its inventories by £5,000. This means that inventories purchases will be lower than inventories usage in that month. The payments for inventories purchases lag a month behind purchases because the business expects to be allowed a month to pay for what it buys.
3 Each month's cash balance is the previous month's figure plus the cash surplus (or minus the cash deficit) for the current month. The balance at the start of January is £12,000 according to the information provided earlier.
4 Depreciation does not give rise to a cash payment. In the context of profit measurement (in the income statement), depreciation is a very important aspect. Here, however, we are interested only in cash.

## Activity 9.7

Looking at the cash budget of Vierra Popova Ltd, what conclusions do you draw and what possible course of action do you recommend regarding the cash balance over the period concerned?

There appears to be a fairly large cash balance, given the size of the business, and it seems to be increasing. Management might give consideration to putting some of the cash into an income-yielding deposit. Alternatively, it could be used to expand the trading activities of the business by, for example, increasing the investment in non-current (fixed) assets. Another possibility, if the funds will not be used in the business, is to return some cash to the owners.

## Activity 9.8

Vierra Popova Ltd (Example 9.1) now wishes to prepare its cash budget for the second six months of the year. The budgeted income statements for each month of the second half of the year are as follows:

|  | July £000 | Aug £000 | Sept £000 | Oct £000 | Nov £000 | Dec £000 |
|---|---|---|---|---|---|---|
| Sales revenue | 57 | 59 | 62 | 57 | 53 | 51 |
| Cost of goods sold | (32) | (33) | (35) | (32) | (30) | (29) |
| Salaries and wages | (10) | (10) | (10) | (10) | (10) | (10) |
| Electricity | (3) | (3) | (4) | (5) | (6) | (6) |
| Depreciation | (3) | (3) | (3) | (3) | (3) | (3) |
| Other overheads | (2) | (2) | (2) | (2) | (2) | (2) |
| Total expenses | (50) | (51) | (54) | (52) | (51) | (50) |
| Profit for the month | 7 | 8 | 8 | 5 | 2 | 1 |

The business will continue to allow all of its customers one month's credit.

It plans to increase inventories from the 30 June level by £1,000 each month until, and including, September. During the following three months, inventories levels will be decreased by £1,000 each month.

Inventories purchases, which had been made on one month's credit until the June payment, will, starting with the purchases made in June, be made on two months' credit.

Salaries, wages and 'other overheads' will continue to be paid in the month concerned. Electricity is paid quarterly in arrears in September and December.

At the end of December, the business intends to pay off part of some borrowings. This payment is to be such that it will leave the business with a cash balance of £5,000 with which to start next year.

Prepare the cash budget for the six months ending in December. (Remember that any information you need that relates to the first six months of the year, including the cash balance that is expected to be brought forward on 1 July, is given in Example 9.1.)

The cash budget for the six months ended 31 December is:

|  | July £000 | Aug £000 | Sept £000 | Oct £000 | Nov £000 | Dec £000 |
|---|---|---|---|---|---|---|
| *Receipts* | | | | | | |
| Trade receivables | 53 | 57 | 59 | 62 | 57 | 53 |
| *Payments* | | | | | | |
| Trade payables (Note 1) | – | (32) | (33) | (34) | (36) | (31) |
| Salaries and wages | (10) | (10) | (10) | (10) | (10) | (10) |
| Electricity | – | – | (10) | – | – | (17) |
| Other overheads | (2) | (2) | (2) | (2) | (2) | (2) |
| Borrowings repayment (Note 2) | – | – | – | – | – | (131) |
| Total payments | (12) | (44) | (55) | (46) | (48) | (191) |
| Cash surplus for the month | 41 | 13 | 4 | 16 | 9 | (138) |
| Opening balance | 60 | 101 | 114 | 118 | 134 | 143 |
| Closing balance | 101 | 114 | 118 | 134 | 143 | 5 |

Notes:
1 There will be no payment to suppliers (trade payables) in July because the June purchases will be made on two months' credit and will therefore be paid for in August. The July purchases, which will equal the July cost of sales figure plus the increase in inventories made in July, will be paid for in September and so on.
2 The borrowings repayment is simply the amount that will cause the balance at 31 December to be £5,000.

## Preparing other budgets

Though each one will have its own particular features, other budgets will tend to follow the same sort of pattern as the cash budget, that is, they will show inflows and outflows during each month and the opening and closing balances in each month.

### Example 9.2

To illustrate some of the other budgets, we shall continue to use the example of Vierra Popova Ltd that we considered in Example 9.1. To the information given there, we need to add the fact that the inventories balance at 1 January was £30,000.

#### Trade receivables budget

This will normally show the planned amount owed to the business by credit customers at the beginning and at the end of each month, the planned total credit sales revenue for each month and the planned total cash receipts from credit customers (trade receivables). The layout will be something like this:

| | Jan £000 | Feb £000 | Mar £000 | Apr £000 | May £000 | June £000 |
|---|---|---|---|---|---|---|
| Opening balance | 60 | 52 | 55 | 55 | 60 | 55 |
| Sales revenue | 52 | 55 | 55 | 60 | 55 | 53 |
| Cash receipts | (60) | (52) | (55) | (55) | (60) | (55) |
| Closing balance | 52 | 55 | 55 | 60 | 55 | 53 |

The opening and closing balances represent the amount that the business plans to be owed (in total) by credit customers (trade receivables) at the beginning and end of each month, respectively.

#### Trade payables budget

Typically this shows the planned amount owed to suppliers by the business at the beginning and at the end of each month, the planned credit purchases for each month and the planned total cash payments to trade payables. The layout will be something like this:

|                 | Jan £000 | Feb £000 | Mar £000 | Apr £000 | May £000 | June £000 |
|-----------------|----------|----------|----------|----------|----------|-----------|
| Opening balance | 30       | 30       | 31       | 26       | 35       | 31        |
| Purchases       | 30       | 31       | 26       | 35       | 31       | 32        |
| Cash payments   | (30)     | (30)     | (31)     | (26)     | (35)     | (31)      |
| Closing balance | 30       | 31       | 26       | 35       | 31       | 32        |

The opening and closing balances represent the amount planned to be owed (in total) by the business to suppliers (trade payables), at the beginning and end of each month respectively.

## Inventories budget

This will normally show the planned amount of inventories to be held by the business at the beginning and at the end of each month, the planned total inventories purchases for each month and the planned total monthly inventories usage. The layout will be something like this:

|                 | Jan £000 | Feb £000 | Mar £000 | Apr £000 | May £000 | June £000 |
|-----------------|----------|----------|----------|----------|----------|-----------|
| Opening balance | 30       | 30       | 30       | 25       | 25       | 25        |
| Purchases       | 30       | 31       | 26       | 35       | 31       | 32        |
| Inventories used| (30)     | (31)     | (31)     | (35)     | (31)     | (32)      |
| Closing balance | 30       | 30       | 25       | 25       | 25       | 25        |

The opening and closing balances represent the amount of inventories, at cost, planned to be held by the business at the beginning and end of each month respectively.

A *raw materials inventories budget*, for a manufacturing business, would follow a similar pattern, with the 'inventories usage' being the cost of the inventories put into production. A *finished inventories budget* for a manufacturer would also be similar to the above, except that 'inventories manufactured' would replace 'purchases'. A manufacturing business would normally prepare both a raw materials inventories budget and a finished inventories budget. Both of these would typically be based on the full cost of the inventories (that is, including overheads). There is no reason why the inventories should not be valued on the basis of either variable cost or direct costs, should managers feel that this would provide more useful information.

The inventories budget will normally be expressed in financial terms, but may also be expressed in physical terms (for example, kg or metres) for individual inventories items.

Note how the trade receivables, trade payables and inventories budgets in Example 9.2 link to one another, and to the cash budget, for the same business in Example 9.1. Note particularly that:

■ the purchases figures in the trade payables budget and in the inventories budget are identical;
■ the cash payments figures in the trade payables budget and in the cash budget are identical;
■ the cash receipts figures in the trade receivables budget and in the cash budget are identical.

Other values would link different budgets in a similar way. For example, the row of sales revenue figures in the trade receivables budget would be identical to the sales revenue figures that will be found in the sales budget. This is how the linking (co-ordination), which was discussed earlier in this chapter, is achieved.

## Activity 9.9

**Have a go at preparing the trade receivables budget for Vierra Popova Ltd for the six months from July to December (see Activity 9.8 and Example 9.2).**

The trade receivables budget for the six months ended 31 December is:

|  | July £000 | Aug £000 | Sept £000 | Oct £000 | Nov £000 | Dec £000 |
|---|---|---|---|---|---|---|
| Opening balance (Note 1) | 53 | 57 | 59 | 62 | 57 | 53 |
| Sales revenue (Note 2) | 57 | 59 | 62 | 57 | 53 | 51 |
| Cash receipts (Note 3) | (53) | (57) | (59) | (62) | (57) | (53) |
| Closing balance (Note 4) | 57 | 59 | 62 | 57 | 53 | 51 |

Notes:
1 The opening trade receivables figure is the previous month's sales revenue figure (sales are on one month's credit).
2 The sales revenue is the current month's figure.
3 The cash received each month is equal to the previous month's sales revenue figure.
4 The closing balance is equal to the current month's sales revenue figure.

Note that if we knew any three of the four figures each month, we could deduce the fourth.
This budget could be set out in any manner that would have given the sort of information that management would require in respect of planned levels of trade receivables and associated transactions.

## Activity 9.10

**Have a go at preparing the trade payables budget for Vierra Popova Ltd for the six months from July to December (see Activity 9.8 and Example 9.2). (*Hint*: Remember that the trade payables payment period alters from the June purchases onwards.)**

The trade payables budget for the six months ended 31 December is:

| | July £000 | Aug £000 | Sept £000 | Oct £000 | Nov £000 | Dec £000 |
|---|---|---|---|---|---|---|
| Opening balance | 32 | 65 | 67 | 70 | 67 | 60 |
| Purchases | 33 | 34 | 36 | 31 | 29 | 28 |
| Cash payments | – | (32) | (33) | (34) | (36) | (31) |
| Closing balance | 65 | 67 | 70 | 67 | 60 | 57 |

This, again, could be set out in any manner that would have given the sort of information that management would require in respect of planned levels of trade payables and associated transactions.

# Non-financial measures in budgeting

The efficiency of internal operations and customer satisfaction levels have become of critical importance to businesses striving to survive in an increasingly competitive environment. Non-financial performance indicators have an important role to play in assessing performance in such key areas as customer/supplier delivery times, set-up times, defect levels and customer satisfaction levels.

There is no reason why budgeting need be confined to financial targets and measures. Non-financial measures can also be used as the basis for targets and these can be brought into the budgeting process and reported alongside the financial targets for the business.

Self-assessment question 9.1 should pull together what we have just seen about preparing budgets.

## ? Self-assessment question 9.1

Antonio Ltd has planned production and sales for the next nine months as follows:

| | Production units | Sales units |
|---|---|---|
| May | 350 | 350 |
| June | 400 | 400 |
| July | 500 | 400 |
| August | 600 | 500 |
| September | 600 | 600 |
| October | 700 | 650 |
| November | 750 | 700 |
| December | 750 | 800 |
| January | 750 | 750 |

During the period, the business plans to advertise so as to generate these increases in sales. Payments for advertising of £1,000 and £1,500 will be made in July and October respectively.

The selling price per unit will be £20 throughout the period. Forty per cent of sales are normally made on two months' credit. The other 60 per cent are settled within the month of the sale.

Raw materials will be held for one month before they are taken into production. Purchases of raw materials will be on one month's credit (buy one month, pay the next). The cost of raw materials is £8 per unit of production.

Other direct production expenses, including labour, are £6 per unit of production. These will be paid in the month concerned.

Various production overheads, which during the period to 30 June had run at £1,800 a month, are expected to rise to £2,000 each month from 1 July to 31 October. These are expected to rise again from 1 November to £2,400 a month and to remain at that level for the foreseeable future. These overheads include a steady £400 each month for depreciation. Overheads are planned to be paid 80 per cent in the month of production and 20 per cent in the following month.

To help to meet the planned increased production, a new item of plant will be bought and delivered in August. The cost of this item is £6,600; the contract with the supplier will specify that this will be paid in three equal amounts in September, October and November.

The business plans to hold raw materials inventories of 500 units on 1 July. The balance at the bank on the same day is planned to be £7,500.

**Required:**
(a) Draw up the following for the six months ending 31 December:
   (i)   A raw materials inventories budget, showing both physical quantities and financial values.
   (ii)  A trade payables budget.
   (iii) A cash budget.
(b) The cash budget reveals a potential cash deficiency during October and November. Can you suggest any ways in which a modification of plans could overcome this problem?

**The answer to this question can be found at the back of the book, in Appendix B.**

## Budgeting for control

We have seen that budgets provide a useful basis for exercising control over a business as they provide a yardstick against which performance can be assessed. We must, however, measure actual performance in the same terms as those in which the budget is stated. If they are not in the same terms, valid comparison will not be possible.

Exercising control involves finding out where and why things did not go according to plan and then seeking ways to put them right for the future. One reason why things may not have gone according to plan is that the budget targets were unachievable. In this case, it may be necessary to revise the budgets for future periods so that targets become achievable.

This last point should not be taken to mean that budget targets can simply be ignored if the going gets tough; rather that they should be adaptable. Unrealistic budgets cannot form a basis for exercising control and little can be gained by sticking with them. Budgets may become unrealistic for a variety of reasons, including unexpected changes in the commercial environment (for example, an unexpected collapse in demand for services of the type that the business provides).

Real World 9.5 reveals how one important budget had to be revised because it had become so unrealistic.

---

**Real World 9.5**

## No medals for budgeting

Organisers of the London 2012 Olympic Games came under renewed pressure on Thursday after the government revealed that the bill for venues is now forecast to be £196m over budget.

The revised budget for the Olympic stadium, aquatics centre and other venues is now £1.36bn, compared with the £1.17bn that the government assigned to venue costs in November 2007.

That means that venue costs have risen a further £97m since the department for culture, media and sport (DCMS) last published an update on the Olympic budget in July. . . .

The DCMS sought to offset criticism of the venue costs increase by saying it was forecasting savings of £193m between now and the end of construction.

Costs for the Olympic stadium have risen by £22m because of the lack of competition for contract tenders and extra requirements, such as amendments to the roof and the need to erect a perimeter 'wrap'. The velodrome is costing £25m more because of 'more complex foundations and ground conditions'.

*Source:* Blitz, R., 'London Olympics venues over budget by £196m', FT.com, 5 February 2009.

---

We saw earlier that budgets enable a management-by-exception environment to be created where senior management can focus on areas where things are not going according to plan (the exceptions – it is to be hoped). To create this environment, a comparison of the budget and the actual results must be undertaken to see whether any variances between the two exist. We are now going to discuss the way in which this may be done.

## Measuring variances from budget

We saw in Chapter 1 that the key financial objective of a business is to increase the wealth of its owners (shareholders). Since profit is the net increase in wealth from business operations, the most important budget target to meet is the profit target. We shall therefore take this as our starting point when comparing the budget with the actual results. Example 9.3 shows the budgeted and actual income statement for Baxter Ltd for the month of May.

## Example 9.3

The following are the budgeted and actual income statements for Baxter Ltd, a manufacturing business, for the month of May:

|  | Budget | Actual |
|---|---|---|
| Output (production and sales) | 1,000 units | 900 units |
|  | £ | £ |
| Sales revenue | 100,000 | 92,000 |
| Raw materials | (40,000) (40,000 metres) | (36,900) (37,000 metres) |
| Labour | (20,000) (2,500 hours) | (17,500) (2,150 hours) |
| Fixed overheads | (20,000) | (20,700) |
| Operating profit | 20,000 | 16,900 |

From these figures it is clear that the budgeted profit was not achieved. As far as May is concerned, this is a matter of history. However, the business (or at least one aspect of it) is out of control. Senior management must discover where things went wrong during May and try to ensure that these mistakes are not repeated in later months. It is not enough to know that things went wrong overall. We need to know where and why. The approach taken is to compare the budgeted and actual figures for the various items (sales revenue, raw materials and so on) in the above statement.

## Activity 9.11

Can you see any problems in comparing the various items (sales, raw materials and so on) for the budget and the actual performance of Baxter Ltd in order to draw conclusions as to which aspects were out of control?

The problem is that the actual level of output was not as budgeted. The actual level of output was 10 per cent less than budget. This means that we cannot, for example, say that there was a labour cost saving of £2,500 (that is, £20,000 – £17,500) and conclude that all is well in that area.

## Flexing the budget

One practical way to overcome our difficulty is to 'flex' the budget to what it would have been had the planned level of output been 900 units rather than 1,000 units. Flexing a budget simply means revising it, assuming a different volume of output.

To exercise control, the budget is usually flexed to reflect the volume that actually occurred, where this is higher or lower than that originally planned. This means that we need to know which revenues and costs are fixed and which are variable relative to the volume of output. Once we know this, flexing is a simple operation. We shall assume that sales revenue, material cost and labour cost vary strictly with volume. Fixed overheads, by definition, will not. Whether, in real life, labour cost does vary with the volume of output is not so certain, but it will serve well enough as an assumption for our purposes. Were labour costs actually fixed, we should simply take this into account in the flexing process.

On the basis of our assumptions regarding the behaviour of revenues and costs, the flexed budget would be as follows:

|  | Flexed budget |
| --- | --- |
| Output (production and sales) | 900 units |
|  | £ |
| Sales revenue | 90,000 |
| Raw materials | (36,000) (36,000 metres) |
| Labour | (18,000) (2,250 hours) |
| Fixed overheads | (20,000) |
| Operating profit | 16,000 |

This is simply the original budget, with the sales revenue, raw materials and labour cost figures scaled down by 10 per cent (the factor by which the actual output fell short of the budgeted one).

Putting the original budget, the flexed budget and the actual figures for May together, we obtain the following:

|  | Original budget | Flexed budget | Actual |
| --- | --- | --- | --- |
| Output (production and sales) | 1,000 units | 900 units | 900 units |
|  | £ | £ | £ |
| Sales revenue | 100,000 | 90,000 | 92,000 |
| Raw materials | (40,000) | (36,000) (36,000 m) | (36,900) (37,000 m) |
| Labour | (20,000) | (18,000) (2,250 hr) | (17,500) (2,150 hr) |
| Fixed overheads | (20,000) | (20,000) | (20,700) |
| Operating profit | 20,000 | 16,000 | 16,900 |

 Flexible budgets enable us to make a more valid comparison between the budget (using the flexed figures) and the actual results. Key differences, or variances, between budgeted and actual results for each aspect of the business's activities can then be calculated.

It may seem as if we are saying that it does not matter if there are volume shortfalls because we just revise the budget and carry on as if all is well. However, this is not the case, because losing sales means losing profit. The first point that we must pick up therefore is the loss of profit arising from the loss of sales of 100 units.

## Activity 9.12

**What will be the loss of profit arising from the sales volume shortfall, assuming that everything except sales volume was as planned?**

The answer is simply the difference between the original and flexed budget profit figures. The only difference between these two profit figures is the volume of sales; everything else was the same. (That is to say that the flexing was carried out assuming that the per-unit sales revenue, raw material cost and labour cost were all as originally budgeted.) This means that the figure for the loss of profit due to the volume shortfall, taken alone, is £4,000 (that is, £20,000 – £16,000).

Where a variance between the flexed budget and the actual results has the effect of making the actual profit lower than the budgeted profit, it is known as an adverse variance. The variance arising from the sales volume shortfall is, therefore an adverse variance. Where a variance has the opposite effect, it is known as a favourable variance. We can therefore say that a variance is the effect of a factor (taken alone) on the budgeted profit. When looking at some particular aspect, such as sales volume, we assume that all other factors went according to plan. This is shown in Figure 9.6.

**Figure 9.6 Relationship between the budgeted and actual profit**

The variances represent the differences between the budgeted and actual profit, and so can be used to reconcile the two profit figures.

For the month of May, we have already identified one of the reasons that the budgeted profit of £20,000 was not achieved and that the actual profit was only £16,900. This was the £4,000 loss of profit (adverse variance) that arose from the sales volume shortfall. Now that the budget is flexed, we can compare like with like and reach further conclusions about May's trading.

The fact that the sales revenue, raw materials and labour figures differ between the flexed budget and the actual results (see page 338) suggests that the adverse sales volume variance was not the only problem area. To identify the value of the differences that arose from these other three areas (sales revenue, raw materials and labour), we need to compare the flexed budget and actual values for each of them.

## Activity 9.13

Compare the sales revenue, raw materials and labour values between the flexed budget and the actual results and reconcile the original budget and the actual profit for Baxter Ltd. Remember that the sales volume variance is also part of the difference.

This is calculated as follows:

|  | £ |
|---|---|
| Budgeted profit | 20,000 |
| Favourable variances | |
| Sales price (92,000 – 90,000) | 2,000 |
| Labour (18,000 – 17,500) | 500 |
| Total favourable variances | 2,500 |
| Adverse variances | |
| Sales volume (as above) | (4,000) |
| Raw materials (36,000 – 36,900) | (900) |
| Fixed overheads (20,000 – 20,700) | (700) |
| | (5,600) |
| Actual profit | 16,900 |

The variance between flexed budget sales revenue and actual sales revenue (£2,000) can only arise from higher prices being charged than were envisaged in the original budget. This is because any variance arising from volume difference has already been 'stripped out' in the flexing process. Less was spent on labour than was allowed for a volume of 900 units. More was spent on raw materials than should have been for an output of 900 units. There was also an overspend on fixed overheads.

## Activity 9.14

If you were the chief executive of Baxter Ltd, what attitude would you take to the overall variance between the budgeted profit and the actual one?

How would you react to the five individual variances that are the outcome of the analysis shown in the solution to Activity 9.13?

You would probably be concerned about how large the variances are and their direction (favourable or adverse). In particular you may have thought of the following:

- The overall adverse profit variance is £3,100 (that is £20,000 – £16,900). This represents 15.5 per cent of the budgeted profit (that is £3,100/£20,000 × 100%) and you (as chief executive) would pretty certainly see it as significant and worrying.
- The £4,000 adverse sales volume variance represents 20 per cent of budgeted profit and it too would be a major cause of concern.
- The £2,000 favourable sales price variance represents 10 per cent of budgeted profit. Since this is favourable it might be seen as a cause for celebration rather than concern.

On the other hand it means that Baxter's output was, on average, sold at prices 10 per cent above the planned price. This could have been the cause of the worrying adverse sales volume variance. Baxter may have sold fewer units because it charged higher prices.

■ The £900 adverse raw materials variance represents 4.5 per cent of budgeted profit. It would be unrealistic to expect the actuals to hit the precise budget figure each month. The question is whether 4.5 per cent for this variance represents a significant amount and a cause for concern.

■ The £500 favourable labour variance represents 2.5 per cent of budgeted profit. Since this is favourable and relatively small it may not be seen as a major cause for concern.

■ The £700 fixed overhead adverse variance represents 3.5 per cent of budgeted profit. The chief executive may be concerned about this.

The chief executive will now need to ask some questions as to why things went so badly wrong in several areas and what can be done to improve things for the future.

The variance between the actual and flexed figures that has been calculated for both raw materials and labour overheads can be broken down further. The total raw materials variance (£900) can be analysed to see the extent to which it is caused by a difference (between budget and actual) in the amount of raw material used and by a difference in the prices at which the materials were bought. A similar analysis can be carried out for the total labour variance (£500). These further analyses may provide much more helpful information than the broad variances for each of these two areas. A detailed discussion of the ways in which these overhead variances can be broken down is beyond the scope of this book. If you would like to pursue this topic, the further reading at the end of the chapter provides some appropriate references.

Real World 9.6 shows how two UK-based businesses, Next plc, a retailer, and British Airways plc, an airline operator, use variance analysis to exercise control over their operations. Many businesses explain in their annual reports how they operate systems of budgetary control.

## Real World 9.6

### Exercising control

**What Next?**
According to its annual report, Next plc has the following arrangements:

> The Board is responsible for approving semi-annual Group budgets. Performance against budget is reported to the Board monthly and any substantial variances are explained.

**BA at the controls**
BA plc makes it clear that it too uses budgets and variance analysis to help keep control over its activities. The annual report says:

A comprehensive management accounting system is in place providing financial and operational performance measurement indicators. Detailed management accounts are prepared monthly to cover each major area of the business. Variances from plan and previous forecast are analysed, explained and acted on in a timely manner.

The boards of directors of these businesses will not seek explanations of variances arising at each branch/flight/department, but they will be looking at figures for the businesses as a whole or the results for major divisions of them.

Equally certainly, branch/department managers will receive a monthly (or perhaps more frequent) report of variances arising within their area of responsibility alone.

*Sources*: Next plc Annual Report 2009, p. 23; British Airways plc Annual Report 2009, p. 58.

Real World 9.7 gives some indication of the importance of flexible budgeting in practice.

### Real World 9.7

## Being flexible about budgeting

A study of the UK food and drink industry by Abdel-Kader and Luther provides some insight as to the importance attached by management accountants to flexible budgeting. The study asked those in charge of the management accounting function to rate the importance of flexible budgeting by selecting one of three possible categories: 'not important', 'moderately important' or 'important'. Figure 9.7 sets out the results, from the sample of 117 respondents.

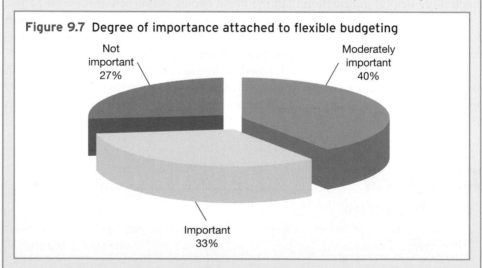

**Figure 9.7  Degree of importance attached to flexible budgeting**

Not important 27%

Moderately important 40%

Important 33%

We can see that although flexible budgeting is regarded as important by a significant proportion of management accountants and is being used in practice, not all businesses use it.

Respondents were also asked to state the frequency with which flexible budgeting was used within the business, using a five-point scale ranging from 1 (never) through to 5 (very often). Figure 9.8 sets out the results.

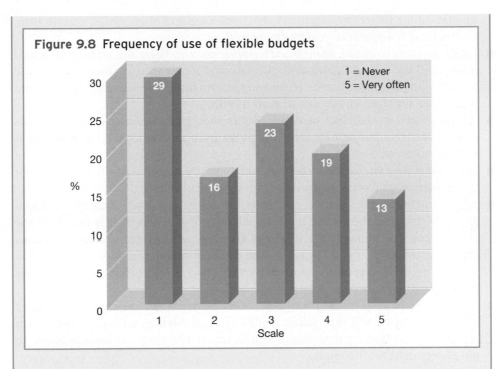

Figure 9.8 Frequency of use of flexible budgets

1 = Never
5 = Very often

Source: based on information in Abdel-Kader, M. and Luther, R., *An Empirical Investigation of the Evolution of Management Accounting Practices*, Working Paper No. 04/06, University of Essex, October 2004.

## Making budgetary control effective

→ It should be clear from what we have seen of budgetary control that a system, or a set of routines, must be put in place to enable the potential benefits to be gained. Most businesses that operate successful budgetary control systems tend to share some common features. These include the following:

- *A serious attitude taken to the system.* This approach should apply to all levels of management, right from the very top. For example, senior managers need to make clear to junior managers that they take notice of the monthly variance reports and base some of their actions and decisions upon them.
- *Clear demarcation between areas of managerial responsibility.* It needs to be clear which manager is responsible for each business area, so that accountability can more easily be ascribed for any area that seems to be going out of control.
- *Budget targets that are challenging yet achievable.* Setting unachievable targets is likely to have a demotivating effect. There may be a case for getting managers to participate

343

in establishing their own targets to help create a sense of 'ownership'. This, in turn, can increase the managers' commitment and motivation.

■ *Established data collection, analysis and reporting routines*. These should take the actual results and the budget figures, and calculate and report the variances. This should be part of the business's regular accounting information system, so that the required reports are automatically produced each month.

■ *Reports aimed at individual managers, rather than general-purpose documents*. This avoids managers having to wade through reams of reports to find the part that is relevant to them.

■ *Fairly short reporting periods*. These would typically be one month long, so that things cannot go too far wrong before they are picked up.

■ *Timely variance reports*. Reports should be produced and made available to managers shortly after the end of the relevant reporting period. If it is not until the end of June that a manager is informed that the performance in May was below the budgeted level, it is quite likely that the performance for June will be below target as well. Reports on the performance in May ideally need to emerge in early June.

■ *Action being taken to get operations back under control if they are shown to be out of control*. The report will not change things by itself. Managers need to take action to try to ensure that the reporting of significant adverse variances leads to action to put things right for the future.

## Behavioural issues

Budgets are prepared with the objective of affecting the attitudes and behaviour of managers. We saw earlier that budgets are intended to motivate managers, and research evidence generally shows that budgets can be effective in achieving this. More specifically, the research shows that

■ the existence of budgets generally tends to improve performance;

■ demanding, yet achievable, budget targets tend to motivate better than less demanding targets – it seems that setting the most demanding targets that will be accepted by managers is a very effective way to motivate them;

■ unrealistically demanding targets tend to have an adverse effect on managers' performance;

■ the participation of managers in setting their targets tends to improve motivation and performance. This is probably because those managers feel a sense of commitment to the targets and a moral obligation to achieve them.

It has been suggested that allowing managers to set their own targets will lead to slack (that is, easily achievable targets) being introduced. This would make achievement of the target that much easier. On the other hand, in an effort to impress, a manager may select a target that is not really achievable. These points imply that care must be taken in the extent to which managers have unfettered choice of their own targets.

## Summary

The main points of this chapter may be summarised as follows.

### Budgets

- A budget is a short-term business plan, mainly expressed in financial terms.
- Budgets are the short-term means of working towards the business's objectives.
- They are usually prepared for a one-year period with sub-periods of a month.
- There is usually a separate budget for each key area.
- The budgets for each area are summarised in master budgets (budgeted income statement and statement of financial position).
- Budgets are plans rather than forecasts.
- Periodic budgets are usually agreed for a year and then allowed to run their course.
- Continual budgets are updated each month to replace the month just passed.

### Uses of budgets

- Budgets promote forward thinking.
- They help co-ordinate the various aspects of the business.
- They motivate performance.
- They provide the basis of a system of control.
- They provide a system of authorisation.

### Zero-base budgeting

- Zero-base budgeting seeks to ensure that all spending is justified.
- It encourages a questioning approach but can be time-consuming.
- It is probably best used selectively.

### Preparing budgets

- There is no standard style – practicality and usefulness are the key issues.
- They are usually prepared in columnar form, with a column for each month (or similarly short period).
- Each budget must link (co-ordinate) with others.
- Non-financial measures (such as units of output) can be used when budgeting.

### Controlling through budgets

- To exercise control, budgets can be flexed to match actual volume of output.
- A variance is an increase (favourable) or decrease (adverse) in profit, relative to the budgeted profit, as a result of some aspect of the business's activities when taken alone.
- Budgeted profit plus all favourable variances less all adverse variances equals actual profit.

### Effective budgetary control

- Good budgetary control requires establishing systems and routines to ensure such things as a clear distinction between individual managers' areas of responsibility; prompt, frequent and relevant variance reporting; and senior management commitment.

- There are behavioural aspects of control relating to management style, participation in budget-setting and the failure to meet budget targets that should be taken into account by senior managers.

**MyAccountingLab** | *Now check your progress in your personal Study Plan*

### → Key terms

mission statement p. 313
budget p. 314
control p. 314
limiting factor p. 317
forecast p. 317
periodic budget p. 317
continual budget p. 317
rolling budget p. 317
master budget p. 318
management by exception p. 322
incremental budgeting p. 325

budget holder p. 326
discretionary budget p. 326
zero-base budgeting (ZBB) p. 326
flexing a budget p. 337
flexible budgets p. 338
adverse variance p. 339
favourable variance p. 339
variance p. 339
variance analysis p. 341
budgetary control p. 343

## Reference

1  BPM Forum, *Perfect How You Project*, 2008.

## Further reading

If you would like to explore the topics covered in this chapter in more depth, we recommend the following books:

Atkinson, A., Kaplan R., Matsumura, E.M. and Young, S.M., *Management Accounting*, (5th edn), Prentice Hall, 2007, chapter 11.

Atrill, P. and McLaney, E., *Management Accounting for Decision Makers* (6th edn), Prentice Hall, 2009, chapters 6 and 7.

Drury, C., *Management and Cost Accounting* (7th edn), South Western Cengage Learning, 2007, chapter 15.

Horngren, C., Foster, G., Datar, S., Rajan, M. and Ittner, C., *Cost Accounting: A Managerial Emphasis* (13th edn), Prentice Hall International, 2008, chapter 6.

## Review questions

Solutions to these questions can be found at the back of the book, in Appendix C.

**9.1** Define a budget. How is a budget different from a forecast?

**9.2** What were the five uses of budgets that were identified in the chapter?

**9.3** What is meant by a *variance*? What is the point in analysing variances?

**9.4** What is the point in flexing the budget in the context of variance analysis? Does flexing imply that differences between budgeted and actual volume of output are ignored in variance analysis?

## ✳ Exercises

Exercises 9.3 to 9.5 are more advanced than 9.1 and 9.2. Those with coloured numbers have solutions at the back of the book, in Appendix D.

> If you wish to try more exercises, visit the website at www.myaccountinglab.com.

**9.1** You have overheard the following statements:

(a) 'A budget is a forecast of what is expected to happen in a business during the next year.'
(b) 'Monthly budgets must be prepared with a column for each month so that you can see the whole year at a glance, month by month.'
(c) 'Budgets are OK but they stifle all initiative. No manager worth employing would work for a business that seeks to control through budgets.'
(d) 'Activity-based budgeting is an approach that takes account of the planned volume of activity in order to deduce the figures to go into the budget.'
(e) 'Any sensible person would start with the sales budget and build up the other budgets from there.'

**Required:**
Critically discuss these statements, explaining any technical terms.

**9.2** Daniel Chu Ltd, a new business, will start production on 1 April, but sales will not start until 1 May. Planned sales for the next nine months are as follows:

|  | Sales units |
|---|---|
| May | 500 |
| June | 600 |
| July | 700 |
| August | 800 |
| September | 900 |
| October | 900 |
| November | 900 |
| December | 800 |
| January | 700 |

The selling price of a unit will be a consistent £100 and all sales will be made on one month's credit. It is planned that sufficient finished goods inventories for each month's sales should be available at the end of the previous month.

Raw materials purchases will be such that there will be sufficient raw materials inventories available at the end of each month precisely to meet the following month's planned production. This planned policy will operate from the end of April. Purchases of raw materials will be on one month's credit. The cost of raw material is £40 a unit of finished product.

The direct labour cost, which is variable with the level of production, is planned to be £20 per unit of finished production. Production overheads are planned to be £20,000 each month, including £3,000 for depreciation. Non-production overheads are planned to be £11,000 a month, of which £1,000 will be depreciation.

Various non-current (fixed) assets costing £250,000 will be bought and paid for during April.

Except where specified, assume that all payments take place in the same month as the cost is incurred.

The business will raise £300,000 in cash from a share issue in April.

**Required:**
Draw up the following for the six months ending 30 September:

(a) A finished inventories budget, showing just physical quantities.
(b) A raw materials inventories budget showing both physical quantities and financial values.
(c) A trade payables budget.
(d) A trade receivables budget.
(e) A cash budget.

9.3 A nursing home, which is linked to a large hospital, has been examining its budgetary control procedures, with particular reference to overhead costs.

The level of activity in the facility is measured by the number of patients treated in the budget period. For the current year, the budget stands at 6,000 patients and this is expected to be met.

For months 1 to 6 of this year (assume 12 months of equal length), 2,700 patients were treated. The actual variable overhead costs incurred during this six-month period were as follows:

| Expense | £ |
|---|---|
| Staffing | 59,400 |
| Power | 27,000 |
| Supplies | 54,000 |
| Other | 8,100 |
| Total | 148,500 |

The hospital accountant believes that the variable overhead costs will be incurred at the same rate during months 7 to 12 of the year.

Fixed overheads are budgeted for the whole year as follows:

| Expense | £ |
|---|---|
| Supervision | 120,000 |
| Depreciation/financing | 187,200 |
| Other | 64,800 |
| Total | 372,000 |

**Required:**
(a) Present an overheads budget for months 7 to 12 of the year. You should show each expense, but should not separate individual months. What is the total overheads cost for each patient that would be incorporated into any statistics?
(b) The home actually treated 3,800 patients during months 7 to 12, the actual variable overheads were £203,300 and the fixed overheads were £190,000. In summary form, examine how well the home exercised control over its overheads.
(c) Interpret your analysis and point out any limitations or assumptions.

**9.4** Linpet Ltd is to be incorporated on 1 June. The opening statement of financial position of the business will then be as follows:

| | £ |
|---|---|
| *Assets* | |
| Cash at bank | 60,000 |
| *Share capital* | |
| £1 ordinary shares | 60,000 |

During June, the business intends to make payments of £40,000 for a leasehold property, £10,000 for equipment and £6,000 for a motor vehicle. The business will also purchase initial trading inventories costing £22,000 on credit.

The business has produced the following estimates:

1  Sales revenue for June will be £8,000 and will increase at the rate of £3,000 a month until September. In October, sales revenue will rise to £22,000 and in subsequent months will be maintained at this figure.
2  The gross profit percentage on goods sold will be 25 per cent.
3  There is a risk that supplies of trading inventories will be interrupted towards the end of the financial year. The business therefore intends to build up its initial level of inventories (£22,000) by purchasing £1,000 of inventories each month in addition to the monthly purchases necessary to satisfy monthly sales requirements. All purchases of inventories (including the initial inventories) will be on one month's credit.
4  Sales revenue will be divided equally between cash and credit sales. Credit customers are expected to pay two months after the sale is agreed.

5 Wages and salaries will be £900 a month. Other overheads will be £500 a month for the first four months and £650 thereafter. Both types of expense will be payable when incurred.

6 Eighty per cent of sales revenue will be generated by salespeople who will receive 5 per cent commission on sales revenue. The commission is payable one month after the sale is agreed.

7 The business intends to purchase further equipment in November for £7,000 cash.

8 Depreciation will be provided at the rate of 5 per cent a year on property and 20 per cent a year on equipment. (Depreciation has not been included in the overheads mentioned in 5 above.)

**Required:**

(a) State why a cash budget is required for a business.

(b) Prepare a cash budget for Linpet Ltd for the six-month period to 30 November.

**9.5** Newtake Records Ltd owns a small chain of shops selling DVDs and CDs. At the beginning of June the business had an overdraft of £35,000 and the bank had asked for this to be eliminated by the end of November. As a result, the directors have recently decided to review their plans for the next six months.

The following plans were prepared for the business some months earlier:

| | May £000 | June £000 | July £000 | Aug £000 | Sept £000 | Oct £000 | Nov £000 |
|---|---|---|---|---|---|---|---|
| Sales revenue | 180 | 230 | 320 | 250 | 140 | 120 | 110 |
| Purchases | 135 | 180 | 142 | 94 | 75 | 66 | 57 |
| Administration expenses | 52 | 55 | 56 | 53 | 48 | 46 | 45 |
| Selling expenses | 22 | 24 | 28 | 26 | 21 | 19 | 18 |
| Taxation payment | – | – | – | 22 | – | – | – |
| Finance payments | 5 | 5 | 5 | 5 | 5 | 5 | 5 |
| Shop refurbishment | – | – | 14 | 18 | 6 | – | – |

**Notes:**

1 The inventories level at 1 June was £112,000. The business believes it is preferable to maintain a minimum inventories level of £40,000 over the period to 30 November.

2 Suppliers allow one month's credit.

3 The gross profit margin is 40 per cent.

4 All sales proceeds are received in the month of sale. However, 50 per cent of customers pay with a credit card. The charge made by the credit card business to Newtake Records Ltd is 3 per cent of the sales revenue value. These charges are in addition to the selling expenses identified above. The credit card business pays Newtake Records Ltd in the month of sale.

5 The business has a bank loan, which it is paying off in monthly instalments of £5,000. The interest element represents 20 per cent of each instalment.

6 Administration expenses are paid when incurred. This item includes a charge of £15,000 each month in respect of depreciation.

7 Selling expenses are payable in the following month.

**Required** (working to the nearest £1,000):

(a) Prepare an inventories budget for the six months to 30 November also based on the table of plans above.

(b) Prepare a cash budget for the six months ending 30 November, showing the cash balance at the end of each month, based on the plans set out in the table above.

(c) Prepare a budgeted income statement for the whole of the six-month period ending 30 November. (A monthly breakdown of profit is *not* required.)

(d) What problems is Newtake Records Ltd likely to face in the next six months? Can you suggest how the business might deal with these problems?

# Part 3

# FINANCIAL MANAGEMENT

10 Making capital investment decisions

11 Financing a business

12 Managing working capital

## Chapter 10

# Making capital investment decisions

## Introduction

This chapter is the first of three dealing with the area generally known as *financial management*.

In this chapter we shall look at how businesses can make decisions involving investments in new plant, machinery, buildings and other long-term assets. In making these decisions, businesses should be trying to pursue their key financial objective, which is to enhance the wealth of the owners (shareholders).

Investment appraisal is a very important area for businesses; expensive and far-reaching consequences can flow from bad investment decisions.

## Learning outcomes

**When you have completed this chapter, you should be able to:**

- explain the nature and importance of investment decision making;
- identify the four main investment appraisal methods found in practice;
- use each method to reach a decision on a particular investment opportunity;
- discuss the attributes of each of the methods.

 **Remember to create your own personalised Study Plan**

## The nature of investment decisions

The essential feature of investment decisions is *time*. Investment involves making an outlay of something of economic value, usually cash, at one point in time, which is expected to yield economic benefits to the investor at some other point in time. Usually, the outlay precedes the benefits. Also, the outlay is typically one large amount and the benefits arrive as a series of smaller amounts over a fairly protracted period.

Investment decisions tend to be of profound importance to the business because:

- *Large amounts of resources are often involved.* Many investments made by businesses involve laying out a significant proportion of their total resources (see Real World 10.2). If mistakes are made with the decision, the effects on the businesses could be significant, if not catastrophic.
- *It is often difficult and/or expensive to bail out of an investment once it has been undertaken.* Investments made by a business are often specific to its needs. For example, a hotel business may invest in a new, custom-designed hotel complex. The specialist nature of this complex will probably lead to its having a rather limited secondhand value to another potential user with different needs. If the business found, after having made the investment, that room occupancy rates were not as buoyant as was planned, the only possible course of action might be to close down and sell the complex. This would probably mean that much less could be recouped from the investment than it had originally cost, particularly if the costs of design are included as part of the cost, as they logically should be.

Real World 10.1 gives an illustration of a major investment by a well-known business operating in the UK.

### Real World 10.1

### Brittany Ferries launches an investment

Brittany Ferries, the cross-channel ferry operator, recently bought an additional ship, named *Cap Finistère*. The ship cost the business €81.5 million and has been used on the Portsmouth to Santander route since Spring 2010. Although Brittany Ferries is a substantial business, this level of expenditure was significant. Clearly, the business believed that acquiring the new ship would be profitable for it, but how would it have reached this conclusion? Presumably the anticipated future cash flows from passengers and freight operators will have been major inputs to the decision.

*Source*: www.brittany-ferries.co.uk.

The kind of issues raised by Brittany Ferries' investment will be the main subject of this chapter.

Real World 10.2 indicates the level of annual net investment for a number of randomly selected, well-known UK businesses. It can be seen that the scale of investment varies from one business to another. (It also tends to vary from one year to the next for a particular business.) In nearly all of these businesses the scale of investment was significant, despite the fact that many businesses were cutting back on investment during the economic recession.

## The scale of investment by UK businesses

| | Expenditure on additional non-current assets as a percentage of: | |
| --- | --- | --- |
| | Annual sales revenue | End-of-year non-current assets |
| British Airways plc (airline) | 6.7 | 7.4 |
| British Sky Broadcasting plc (television) | 7.5 | 15.3 |
| Go-Ahead Group plc (transport) | 2.6 | 11.1 |
| Marks and Spencer plc (stores) | 7.4 | 11.4 |
| Wm Morrison Supermarkets plc (supermarkets) | 4.7 | 9.5 |
| Ryanair Holdings plc (airline) | 23.9 | 19.3 |
| Severn Trent Water Ltd (water and sewerage) | 47.1 | 11.0 |
| Tate and Lyle plc (sugar and allied products) | 9.3 | 16.1 |

Source: Annual reports of the businesses concerned for the financial year ending in 2009.

Real World 10.2 is limited to considering the non-current asset investment, but most non-current asset investment also requires a level of current asset investment to support it (additional inventories, for example), meaning that the real scale of investment is even greater, typically considerably so, than indicated above.

When managers are making decisions involving capital investments, what should the decision seek to achieve?

Investment decisions must be consistent with the objectives of the particular business. For a private sector business, maximising the wealth of the owners (shareholders) is usually assumed to be the key financial objective.

## Investment appraisal methods

Given the importance of investment decisions, it is essential that there is proper screening of investment proposals. An important part of this screening process is to ensure that the business uses appropriate methods of evaluation.

Research shows that there are basically four methods used in practice by businesses throughout the world to evaluate investment opportunities. They are:

- accounting rate of return (ARR)
- payback period (PP)
- net present value (NPV)
- internal rate of return (IRR).

It is possible to find businesses that use variants of these four methods. It is also possible to find businesses, particularly smaller ones, that do not use any formal appraisal method but rely instead on the 'gut feeling' of their managers. Most businesses, however, seem to use one (or more) of these four methods.

We are going to assess the effectiveness of each of these methods and we shall see that only one of them (NPV) is a wholly logical approach. The other three all have flaws. We shall also see how popular these four methods seem to be in practice.

To help us to examine each of the methods, it might be useful to consider how each of them would cope with a particular investment opportunity. Let us consider the following example.

## Example 10.1

Billingsgate Battery Company has carried out some research that shows that the business could provide a standard service that it has recently developed.

Provision of the service would require investment in a machine that would cost £100,000, payable immediately. Sales of the service would take place throughout the next five years. At the end of that time, it is estimated that the machine could be sold for £20,000.

Inflows and outflows from sales of the service would be expected to be as follows:

| Time | | £000 |
|---|---|---|
| Immediately | Cost of machine | (100) |
| 1 year's time | Operating profit before depreciation | 20 |
| 2 years' time | Operating profit before depreciation | 40 |
| 3 years' time | Operating profit before depreciation | 60 |
| 4 years' time | Operating profit before depreciation | 60 |
| 5 years' time | Operating profit before depreciation | 20 |
| 5 years' time | Disposal proceeds from the machine | 20 |

Note that, broadly speaking, the operating profit before deducting depreciation (that is, before non-cash items) equals the net amount of cash flowing into the business. Broadly, apart from depreciation, all of this business's expenses cause cash to flow out of the business. Sales revenues tend to lead to cash flowing in. Expenses tend to lead to it flowing out. For the time being, we shall assume that inventories, trade receivables and trade payables remain constant. This means that operating profit before depreciation will tend to equal the net cash inflow.

To simplify matters, we shall assume that the cash from sales and for the expenses of providing the service are received and paid, respectively, at the end of each year. This is clearly unlikely to be true in real life. Money will have to be paid to employees (for salaries and wages) on a weekly or a monthly basis. Customers will pay within a month or two of buying the service. On the other hand, making the assumption probably does not lead to a serious distortion. It is a simplifying assumption that is often made in real life, and it will make things more straightforward for us now. We should be clear, however, that there is nothing about any of the four methods that *demands* that this assumption is made.

Having set up the example, we shall now go on to consider how each of the appraisal methods works.

## Accounting rate of return (ARR)

The first method that we shall consider is the accounting rate of return (ARR). This method takes the average accounting operating profit that the investment will generate and expresses it as a percentage of the average investment made over the life of the project. Thus:

$$\text{ARR} = \frac{\text{Average annual operating profit}}{\text{Average investment to earn that profit}} \times 100\%$$

We can see from the equation that, to calculate the ARR, we need to deduce two pieces of information about the particular project:

■ the annual average operating profit; and
■ the average investment.

In our example, the average annual operating profit *before depreciation* over the five years is £40,000 (that is, £000(20 + 40 + 60 + 60 + 20)/5). Assuming 'straight-line' depreciation (that is, equal annual amounts), the annual depreciation charge will be £16,000 (that is, £(100,000 − 20,000)/5). Thus, the average annual operating profit *after depreciation* is £24,000 (that is, £40,000 − £16,000).

The average investment over the five years can be calculated as follows:

$$\text{Average investment} = \frac{\text{Cost of machine} + \text{Disposal value}}{2}$$

$$= \frac{£100,000 + £20,000}{2} = £60,000$$

Thus, the ARR of the investment is

$$\text{ARR} = \frac{£24,000}{£60,000} \times 100\% = 40\%$$

Users of ARR should apply the following decision rules:

- For any project to be acceptable it must achieve a target ARR as a minimum.
- Where there are competing projects that all seem capable of exceeding this minimum rate (that is, where the business must choose between more than one project), the one with the higher (or highest) ARR would normally be selected.

To decide whether the 40 per cent return is acceptable, we need to compare this percentage return with the minimum rate required by the business.

### Activity 10.2

Chaotic Industries is considering an investment in a fleet of ten delivery vans to take its products to customers. The vans will cost £15,000 each to buy, payable immediately. The annual running costs are expected to total £50,000 for each van (including the driver's salary). The vans are expected to operate successfully for six years, at the end of which period they will all have to be sold, with disposal proceeds expected to be about £3,000 a van. At present, the business outsources transport, for all of its deliveries, to a commercial carrier. It is expected that this carrier will charge a total of £530,000 each year for the next six years to undertake the deliveries.

What is the ARR of buying the vans? (Note that cost savings are as relevant a benefit from an investment as are net cash inflows.)

The vans will save the business £30,000 a year (that is, £530,000 − (£50,000 × 10)), before depreciation, in total. Thus, the inflows and outflows will be:

| Time | | £000 |
|---|---|---|
| Immediately | Cost of vans (10 × £15,000) | (150) |
| 1 year's time | Saving before depreciation | 30 |
| 2 years' time | Saving before depreciation | 30 |
| 3 years' time | Saving before depreciation | 30 |
| 4 years' time | Saving before depreciation | 30 |
| 5 years' time | Saving before depreciation | 30 |
| 6 years' time | Saving before depreciation | 30 |
| 6 years' time | Disposal proceeds from the vans (10 × £3,000) | 30 |

The total annual depreciation expense (assuming a straight-line method) will be £20,000 (that is, (£150,000 − £30,000)/6). Thus, the average annual saving, *after depreciation*, is £10,000 (that is, £30,000 − £20,000).

The average investment will be

$$\text{Average investment} = \frac{£150,000 + £30,000}{2} = £90,000$$

and the ARR of the investment is

$$\text{ARR} = \frac{£10,000}{£90,000} \times 100\% = 11.1\%$$

## ARR and ROCE

We should note that ARR and the return on capital employed (ROCE) ratio (which we met in Chapter 6) take the same approach to performance measurement. They both relate accounting profit to the cost of the assets invested to generate that profit. ROCE is a popular means of assessing the performance of a business, as a whole, *after* it has performed. ARR is an approach that assesses the potential performance of a particular investment, taking the same approach as ROCE, but *before* it has performed.

As we have just seen, managers using ARR will require that any investment undertaken should achieve a target ARR as a minimum. Perhaps the minimum target ROCE would be based on the rate that previous investments had actually achieved (as measured by ROCE). Perhaps it would be based on the industry-average ROCE.

Since private sector businesses are normally seeking to increase the wealth of their owners, ARR may seem to be a sound method of appraising investment opportunities. Operating profit can be seen as a net increase in wealth over a period. This implies that relating operating profit to the size of investment made to achieve it seems a logical approach.

ARR is said to have a number of advantages as a method of investment appraisal. ROCE seems to be a widely used measure of business performance. Shareholders seem to use this ratio to evaluate management performance. Some businesses even express their financial objective in terms of a target ROCE. It therefore seems sensible to use a method of investment appraisal that is consistent with this overall approach to measuring business performance. It also gives the result expressed as a percentage. It seems that many managers feel comfortable using measures expressed in percentage terms.

## Problems with ARR

### Activity 10.3

ARR suffers from a very major defect as a means of assessing investment opportunities. Can you reason out what this is? Consider the three competing projects whose profits are shown below. All three involve investment in a machine that is expected to have no residual value at the end of the five years. Note that all of the projects have the same total operating profits over the five years.

| Time | | Project A £000 | Project B £000 | Project C £000 |
|---|---|---|---|---|
| Immediately | Cost of machine | (160) | (160) | (160) |
| 1 year's time | Operating profit after depreciation | 20 | 10 | 160 |
| 2 years' time | Operating profit after depreciation | 40 | 10 | 10 |
| 3 years' time | Operating profit after depreciation | 60 | 10 | 10 |
| 4 years' time | Operating profit after depreciation | 60 | 10 | 10 |
| 5 years' time | Operating profit after depreciation | 20 | 160 | 10 |

→

> (*Hint*: The defect is not concerned with the ability of the decision maker to forecast future events, though this too can be a problem. Try to remember the essential feature of investment decisions, which we identified at the beginning of this chapter.)

The problem with ARR is that it almost completely ignores the time factor. In this example, exactly the same ARR would have been computed for each of the three projects.

Since the same total operating profit over the five years (£200,000) arises in all three of these projects, and the average investment in each project is £80,000 (that is, £160,000/2), each project will give rise to the same ARR of 50 per cent (that is, £40,000/£80,000).

Given a financial objective of maximising the wealth of the owners of the business, any rational decision maker faced with a choice between the three projects set out in Activity 10.3 would strongly prefer Project C. This is because most of the benefits from the investment arise within twelve months of investing the £160,000 to establish the project. Project A would rank second and Project B would come a poor third. Any appraisal technique that is not capable of distinguishing between these three situations is seriously flawed. We shall look at why timing is so important later in the chapter.

There are further problems associated with the use of ARR. One of these problems concerns the approach taken to derive the average investment in a project.

Example 10.2 illustrates the daft result that ARR can produce.

## Example 10.2

George put forward an investment proposal to his boss. The business uses ARR to assess investment proposals using a minimum 'hurdle' rate of 27 per cent. Details of the proposal were as follows:

| | |
|---|---|
| Cost of equipment | £200,000 |
| Estimated residual value of equipment | £40,000 |
| Average annual operating profit before depreciation | £48,000 |
| Estimated life of project | 10 years |
| Annual straight-line depreciation charge | £16,000 (that is, (£200,000 − £40,000)/10) |

The ARR of the project will be

$$\text{ARR} = \frac{48,000 - 16,000}{(200,000 + 40,000)/2} \times 100\% = 26.7\%$$

The boss rejected George's proposal because it failed to achieve an ARR of at least 27 per cent. Although George was disappointed, he realised that there was still hope. In fact, all that the business had to do was to give away the piece of equipment at the end of its useful life rather than to sell it. The residual value of the equipment then became zero and the annual depreciation charge became ([£200,000 − £0]/10) = £20,000 a year. The revised ARR calculation was then as follows:

$$\text{ARR} = \frac{48,000 - 20,000}{(200,000 + 0)/2} \times 100\% = 28\%$$

ARR is based on the use of accounting profit. When measuring performance over the whole life of a project, however, it is cash flows rather than accounting profits that are important. Cash is the ultimate measure of the economic wealth generated by an investment. This is because it is cash that is used to acquire resources and for distribution to owners. Accounting profit, on the other hand, is more appropriate for reporting achievement on a periodic basis. It is a useful measure of productive effort for a relatively short period, such as a year or half year. It is really a question of 'horses for courses'. Accounting profit is fine for measuring performance over a short period, but cash is the appropriate measure when considering the performance over the life of a project.

The ARR method can also create problems when considering competing investments of different size.

Sinclair Wholesalers plc is currently considering opening a new sales outlet in Coventry. Two possible sites have been identified for the new outlet. Site A has an area of 30,000 sq m. It will require an average investment of £6m and will produce an average operating profit of £600,000 a year. Site B has an area of 20,000 sq m. It will require an average investment of £4m and will produce an average operating profit of £500,000 a year.

What is the ARR of each investment opportunity? Which site would you select and why?

The ARR of Site A is £600,000/£6m = 10 per cent. The ARR of Site B is £500,000/£4m = 12.5 per cent. Thus, Site B has the higher ARR. However, in terms of the absolute operating profit generated, Site A is the more attractive. If the ultimate objective is to increase the wealth of the shareholders of Sinclair Wholesalers plc, it might be better to choose Site A even though the percentage return is lower. It is the absolute size of the return rather than the relative (percentage) size that is important. This is a general problem of using comparative measures, such as percentages, when the objective is measured in absolute ones, like an amount of money. If businesses were seeking through their investments to generate a percentage rate of return on investment, ARR would be more helpful. The problem is that most businesses seek to achieve increases in their absolute wealth (measured in pounds, euros, dollars and so on), through their investment decisions.

Real World 10.3 illustrates how using percentage measures can lead to confusion.

### Increasing road capacity by sleight of hand

During the 1970s, the Mexican government wanted to increase the capacity of a major four-lane road. It came up with the idea of repainting the lane markings so that there were six narrower lanes occupying the same space as four wider ones had previously done. This increased the capacity of the road by 50 per cent (that is, $2/4 \times 100$). A tragic outcome of the narrower lanes was an increase in deaths from road accidents. A year later the Mexican government had the six narrower lanes changed back to the original four wider ones. This reduced the capacity of the road by 33 per cent (that is, $\frac{2}{6} \times 100$). The Mexican government reported that, overall, it had increased the capacity of the road by 17 per cent (that is, 50% − 33%), despite the fact that its real capacity was identical to that which it had been originally. The confusion arose because each of the two percentages (50 per cent and 33 per cent) is based on different bases (four and six).

*Source: Gigerenzer, G., Reckoning with Risk, Penguin, 2002.*

##  Payback period (PP)

The second approach to appraising possible investments is the payback period (PP). This is the length of time it takes for an initial investment to be repaid out of the net cash inflows from a project. Since it takes time into account, the PP method seems to go some way to overcoming the timing problem of ARR – or at first glance it does.

Let us consider PP in the context of the Billingsgate Battery example (Example 10.1). We should recall that essentially the project's cash flows are:

| Time | | £000 |
|---|---|---|
| Immediately | Cost of machine | (100) |
| 1 year's time | Operating profit before depreciation | 20 |
| 2 years' time | Operating profit before depreciation | 40 |
| 3 years' time | Operating profit before depreciation | 60 |
| 4 years' time | Operating profit before depreciation | 60 |
| 5 years' time | Operating profit before depreciation | 20 |
| 5 years' time | Disposal proceeds | 20 |

Note that all of these figures are amounts of cash to be paid or received (we saw earlier that operating profit before depreciation is a rough measure of the cash flows from the project).

We can see that if this investment is made, it will be three years before the £100,000 outlay is covered by the inflows. (This is still assuming that the cash flows occur at year ends.) We can demonstrate derivation of the payback period by calculating the cumulative cash flows as follows:

| Time | | Net cash flows £000 | Cumulative cash flows £000 | |
|---|---|---|---|---|
| Immediately | Cost of machine | (100) | (100) | |
| 1 year's time | Operating profit before depreciation | 20 | (80) | (−100 + 20) |
| 2 years' time | Operating profit before depreciation | 40 | (40) | (−80 + 40) |
| 3 years' time | Operating profit before depreciation | 60 | 20 | (−40 + 60) |
| 4 years' time | Operating profit before depreciation | 60 | 80 | (20 + 60) |
| 5 years' time | Operating profit before depreciation | 20 | 100 | (80 + 20) |
| 5 years' time | Disposal proceeds | 20 | 120 | (100 + 20) |

We can see that the cumulative cash flows become positive at the end of the third year. Had we assumed that the cash flows arise evenly over the year, the precise payback period would be

$$2 \text{ years} + (^{40}/_{60}) \text{ years} = 2^2/_3 \text{ years}$$

where 40 represents the cash flow still required at the beginning of the third year to repay the initial outlay and 60 is the projected cash flow during the third year.

The decision rule for using PP is:

- For a project to be acceptable it would need to have a payback period shorter than a maximum payback period set by the business.
- If there were two (or more) competing projects whose payback periods were all shorter than the maximum payback period requirement, the project with the shorter (or shortest) payback period should be selected.

If, for example, Billingsgate Battery had a maximum acceptable payback period of four years, the project would be undertaken. A project with a longer payback period than four years would not be acceptable.

## Activity 10.5

What is the payback period of the Chaotic Industries project from Activity 10.2?

The inflows and outflows are expected to be:

| Time | | Net cash flows £000 | Cumulative net cash flows £000 |
|---|---|---|---|
| Immediately | Cost of vans | (150) | (150) |
| 1 year's time | Saving before depreciation | 30 | (120) (−150 + 30) |
| 2 years' time | Saving before depreciation | 30 | (90) (−120 + 30) |
| 3 years' time | Saving before depreciation | 30 | (60) (−90 + 30) |
| 4 years' time | Saving before depreciation | 30 | (30) (−60 + 30) |
| 5 years' time | Saving before depreciation | 30 | 0 (−30 + 30) |
| 6 years' time | Saving before depreciation | 30 | 30 (0 + 30) |
| 6 years' time | Disposal proceeds from the machine | 30 | 60 (30 + 30) |

The payback period here is five years; that is, it is not until the end of the fifth year that the vans will pay for themselves out of the savings that they are expected to generate.

The PP method has certain advantages. It is quick and easy to calculate. Also, it can be easily understood by managers. The logic of using PP is that projects that can recoup their cost quickly are economically more attractive than those with longer payback periods, that is, it emphasises liquidity. PP is probably an improvement on ARR in respect of the timing of the cash flows. PP is not, however, the whole answer to the problem.

## Problems with PP

### Activity 10.6

In what respect is PP not the whole answer as a means of assessing investment opportunities? Consider the cash flows arising from three competing projects:

| Time | | Project 1 £000 | Project 2 £000 | Project 3 £000 |
|---|---|---|---|---|
| Immediately | Cost of machine | (200) | (200) | (200) |
| 1 year's time | Operating profit before depreciation | 70 | 20 | 70 |
| 2 years' time | Operating profit before depreciation | 60 | 20 | 100 |
| 3 years' time | Operating profit before depreciation | 70 | 160 | 30 |
| 4 years' time | Operating profit before depreciation | 80 | 30 | 200 |
| 5 years' time | Operating profit before depreciation | 50 | 20 | 440 |
| 5 years' time | Disposal proceeds | 40 | 10 | 20 |

(*Hint*: Again, the defect is not concerned with the ability of the manager to forecast future events. This is a problem, but it is a problem whatever approach we take.)

The PP for each project is three years and so the PP method would regard the projects as being equally acceptable. It cannot distinguish between those projects that pay back a significant amount early in the three-year payback period and those that do not.

In addition, this method ignores cash flows after the payback period. A decision maker concerned with increasing owners' wealth would prefer Project 3 because the cash flows come in earlier. In fact, most of the initial cost of making the investment has been repaid by the end of the second year. Also, the cash flows are greater in total.

The cumulative cash flows of each project in Activity 10.6 are set out in Figure 10.1. We can see that the PP method is not concerned with the profitability of projects; it is concerned simply with their payback period. Thus cash flows arising beyond the payback period are ignored. While this neatly avoids the practical problems of forecasting cash flows over a long period, it means that relevant information could be ignored.

We may feel that, by favouring projects with a short payback period, the PP method does at least provide a means of dealing with the problems of risk and uncertainty. However, this is a fairly crude approach to the problem. It looks only at the risk that the project will end earlier than expected. However, this is only one of many risk areas. What, for example, about the risk that the demand for the product may be less than expected? There are more systematic approaches to dealing with risk that can be used.

PP takes some note of the timing of the costs and benefits from the project. Its key deficiency, however, is that it is not linked to promoting increases in the wealth of the business and its owners. PP will tend to recommend undertaking projects that pay for themselves quickly.

**Figure 10.1** The cumulative cash flows of each project in Activity 10.6

The payback method of investment appraisal would view Projects 1, 2 and 3 as being equally attractive. In doing so, the method completely ignores the fact that Project 3 provides most of the payback cash earlier in the three-year period and goes on to generate large benefits in later years.

The PP method requires the managers of a business to select a maximum acceptable payback period. This maximum period, in practice, will vary from one business to the next. Real World 10.4 looks at a power-saving device used by Tesco, the supermarket chain, and the payback period involved.

## Real World 10.4

### It's payback time at Tesco

According to the Confederation of British Industry, £8.5bn a year is wasted on energy just in the UK. That adds up to about 22m tonnes of $CO_2$ – or the equivalent of Scotland's total commercial carbon emissions in a year.

There are a number of reasons why so much energy is wasted. But one is a mismatch between the electricity required to run equipment in organisations and the power that is delivered to their premises.

That is where voltage power optimisation comes in – a technology that one company, powerPerfector, has a licence to sell in the UK.

Angus Robertson, its chief executive, points out that all electrical equipment intended for use on commercial three-phase circuits in Europe is designed to run on 380 volts – the equivalent of 220V in domestic, single-phase circuits. Yet the average voltage supplied in the UK is 419V (242 in single phase), a figure which cannot be changed without a whole-sale revamp of the grid, which is out on cost grounds.

Mr Robertson explains the problem. 'Take an electric motor. If you put 419V into a motor rated at 380V it doesn't go faster or more efficiently. But it does have to dissipate the extra energy – mostly in the form of heat, which is wasted. If you go into a Tesco with one of our VPO units, the compressors for the refrigerators are not running so hot, so the air conditioning doesn't have to work so hard – so there's a compounding of benefits.'

There are further bonuses. 'We expect light bulbs to last twice as long,' says Mr Robertson. 'And when we installed a unit at Buxton Press, the decibel level dropped drastically. The electric motors were less hot, so making less noise. Maintenance intervals increased too.'

The maintenance-free unit, which is fitted at the point where a three-phase power supply enters the building, can save up to 20 per cent in energy costs, says powerPerfector, depending on the quality of the supply and the types of electrical equipment in use.

Nationwide, the company says, it can provide an average 13 per cent kWh reduction, which, it says, means the approximate payback period for a supermarket is 18 months, an office two years, and a school three years.

Tesco is putting in about 500 powerPerfector units this year, at a cost of about £25m, as part of a rolling programme that will see the equipment in most of its 2,300 stores and distribution centres across the UK. 'We expect to save 5 to 8 per cent of each store's total energy usage,' says Bukky Adegbeyeni, head of the environmental team at the store chain. 'We expect our return on investment to be about 20 per cent, so we will achieve payback in five years.'

*Source*: adapted from 'Case study: power efficiency', *The Financial Times*, 25/11/2009 (Jaggi, R.), copyright © The Financial Times Ltd.

## Net present value (NPV)

From what we have seen so far, it seems that to make sensible investment decisions, we need a method of appraisal that both

- considers *all* of the costs and benefits of each investment opportunity; and
- makes a logical allowance for the *timing* of those costs and benefits.

 The third of the four methods of investment appraisal, the net present value (NPV) method, provides us with this.

Consider the Billingsgate Battery example's cash flows, which we should recall can be summarised as follows:

| Time | | £000 |
|---|---|---|
| Immediately | Cost of machine | (100) |
| 1 year's time | Operating profit before depreciation | 20 |
| 2 years' time | Operating profit before depreciation | 40 |
| 3 years' time | Operating profit before depreciation | 60 |
| 4 years' time | Operating profit before depreciation | 60 |
| 5 years' time | Operating profit before depreciation | 20 |
| 5 years' time | Disposal proceeds | 20 |

Given that the principal financial objective of the business is to increase owners' wealth, it would be very easy to assess this investment if all of the cash inflows and outflows were to occur now (all at the same time). All that we should need to do would be to add up the cash inflows (total £220,000) and compare them with the cash outflows (£100,000). This would lead us to the conclusion that the project should go ahead because the business, and its owners, would be better off by £120,000. Of course, it is not as easy as this because time is involved. The cash outflow (payment) will occur immediately if the project is undertaken. The inflows (receipts) will arise at a range of later times.

The time factor is an important issue because people do not normally see £100 paid out now as equivalent in value to £100 receivable in a year's time. If we were to be offered £100 in twelve months' time in exchange for paying out £100 now, we should not be prepared to accept the offer unless we wished to do someone a favour.

## Activity 10.7

Why would you see £100 to be received in a year's time as not equal in value to £100 to be paid immediately? (There are basically three reasons.)

The reasons are:

- interest lost
- risk
- effects of inflation.

We shall now take a closer look at these three reasons in turn.

## Interest lost

If we are to be deprived of the opportunity to spend our money for a year, we could equally well be deprived of its use by placing it on deposit in a bank or building society. In this case, at the end of the year we could have our money back and have interest as well. Thus, by investing the funds in some other way, we shall be incurring an *opportunity cost*. An opportunity cost occurs where one course of action, for example making a business investment, deprives us of the opportunity to derive some benefit from an alternative action, for example putting the money in the bank and earning interest.

From this we can see that any investment opportunity must, if it is to make us wealthier, do better than the returns that are available from the next best opportunity. Thus, if Billingsgate Battery Company sees putting the money in the bank on deposit as the alternative to investment in the machine, the return from investing in the machine must be better than that from investing in the bank, if the machine investment is worth making. If the bank offered a better return, the business, and its owners, would become wealthier by putting the money on deposit.

## Risk

→ All investments expose their investors to risk. For example, buying a machine to manufacture a product, or to provide a service, to be sold in the market, on the strength of various estimates made in advance of buying the machine, exposes the business to risk. Things may not turn out as expected.

---

### Activity 10.8

Can you suggest some areas where things could go other than according to plan in the Billingsgate Battery Company example (basically, buying a machine and using it to render a service for five years)?

We have come up with the following:

■ The machine might not work as well as expected; it might break down, leading to loss of the business's ability to provide the service.
■ Sales of the service may not be as buoyant as expected.
■ Labour costs may prove to be higher than expected.
■ The sale proceeds of the machine could prove to be less than were estimated.

---

It is important to remember that the decision whether to invest in the machine must be taken *before* any of these things are known. For example, it is only after the machine has been purchased that we could discover that the level of sales which had been estimated before the event is not going to be achieved. It is not possible to wait until we know for certain whether the market will behave as we expected before we buy the machine. We can study reports and analyses of the market. We can commission sophisticated market surveys and these may give us more confidence in the likely outcome. We can advertise widely and try to promote sales. Ultimately, however, we have to decide whether to jump off into the dark and accept the risk if we want the opportunity to make profitable investments.

Real World 10.5 gives some some impression of the extent to which businesses believe that investment outcomes turn out as expected.

---

### Real World 10.5

## Size matters

Senior finance managers of 99 Cambridgeshire manufacturing businesses were asked how their investments were performing compared to expectations at the time of making the investment decision. The results, broken down according to business size, are set out below.

| Actual performance | Size of business | | | |
| relative | Large | Medium | Small | All |
| to expectations | % | % | % | % |
| Underperformed | 8 | 14 | 32 | 14 |
| Performed as expected | 82 | 72 | 68 | 77 |
| Overperformed | 10 | 14 | 0 | 9 |

It seems that smaller businesses are much more likely to get it wrong than medium-size or larger businesses. This may be because small businesses are often younger and, therefore, less experienced in the techniques of both forecasting and managing investment projects. They are also likely to have less financial expertise. It also seems that small businesses have a distinct bias towards overoptimism and do not take full account of the possibility that things will turn out worse than expected.

*Source*: Baddeley, M., 'Unpacking the black box: an econometric analysis of investment strategies in real world firms', CEPP Working Paper No. 08/05, University of Cambridge, 2006, p. 14.

Normally, people expect to receive greater returns where they perceive risk to be a factor. Examples of this in real life are not difficult to find. One such example is that banks tend to charge higher rates of interest to borrowers whom the bank perceives as more risky. Those who can offer good security for a loan and who can point to a regular source of income tend to be charged lower rates of interest.

Going back to Billingsgate Battery Company's investment opportunity, it is not enough to say that we should advise making the investment provided that the returns from it are as high as those from investing in a bank deposit. Clearly we should want returns greater than the level of bank deposit interest rates, because the logical equivalent of investing in the machine is not putting the money on deposit but making an alternative investment that is of similar risk.

We have just seen that investors tend to expect a higher rate of return from investment projects where the risk is perceived as being higher. How risky a particular project is and, therefore, how large this risk premium should be are, however, matters that are difficult to handle. It is usually necessary to make some judgement on these questions.

## Inflation

If we are to be deprived of £100 for a year, when we come to spend that money it will not buy as much of goods and services as it would have done a year earlier. Generally, we shall not be able to buy as many tins of baked beans or loaves of bread or bus tickets as we could have done a year earlier. This is because of the loss in the purchasing power of money, or inflation, which occurs over time. Clearly, the investor needs compensating for this loss of purchasing power if the investment is to be made. This compensation is on top of a return that takes account of what could have been gained from an alternative investment of similar risk.

In practice, interest rates observable in the market tend to take inflation into account. Rates that are offered to potential building society and bank depositors tend to include an allowance for the rate of inflation that is expected in the future.

## What will logical investors do?

As we have seen, logical investors who are seeking to increase their wealth will only be prepared to make investments that will compensate for the loss of interest and purchasing power of the money invested and for the fact that the returns expected may not materialise (risk). This is usually assessed by seeing whether the proposed investment will yield a return that is greater than the basic rate of interest (which would include an allowance for inflation) plus a risk premium.

These three factors (interest lost, risk and inflation) are set out in Figure 10.2.

**Figure 10.2  The factors influencing the returns required by investors from a project**

There are three factors that influence the required returns to investors (opportunity cost of finance).

Naturally, investors need at least the minimum returns before they are prepared to invest. However, it is in terms of the effect on their wealth that they should logically assess an investment project. Usually it is the investment with the highest percentage return that will make the investor most wealthy, but we shall see later in this chapter that this is not always the case. For the time being, therefore, we shall concentrate on wealth.

Let us now return to the Billingsgate Battery Company example. We should recall that the cash flows expected from this investment are:

| Time | | £000 |
|---|---|---|
| Immediately | Cost of machine | (100) |
| 1 year's time | Operating profit before depreciation | 20 |
| 2 years' time | Operating profit before depreciation | 40 |
| 3 years' time | Operating profit before depreciation | 60 |
| 4 years' time | Operating profit before depreciation | 60 |
| 5 years' time | Operating profit before depreciation | 20 |
| 5 years' time | Disposal proceeds | 20 |

We have already seen that it is not sufficient just to compare the basic cash inflows and outflows for the investment. It would be useful if we could express each of these cash flows in similar terms, so that we could make a direct comparison between the sum of the inflows over time and the immediate £100,000 investment. Fortunately, we can do this.

Let us assume that, instead of making this investment, the business could make an alternative investment with similar risk and obtain a return of 20 per cent a year.

## Activity 10.9

We know that Billingsgate Battery Company could alternatively invest its money at a rate of 20 per cent a year. How much do you judge the present (immediate) value of the expected first year receipt of £20,000 to be? In other words, if instead of having to wait a year for the £20,000, and being deprived of the opportunity to invest it at 20 per cent, you could have some money now, what sum to be received now would you regard as exactly equivalent to getting £20,000 but having to wait a year for it?

We should obviously be happy to accept a lower amount if we could get it immediately than if we had to wait a year. This is because we could invest it at 20 per cent (in the alternative project). Logically, we should be prepared to accept the amount that, with a year's income, will grow to £20,000. If we call this amount PV (for present value) we can say:

$$PV + (PV \times 20\%) = £20,000$$

– that is, the amount plus income from investing the amount for the year equals the £20,000.

If we rearrange this equation we find:

$$PV \times (1 + 0.2) = £20,000$$

(Note that 0.2 is the same as 20 per cent, but expressed as a decimal.) Further rearranging gives:

$$PV = £20,000/(1 + 0.2) = £16,667$$

Thus, rational investors who have the opportunity to invest at 20 per cent a year would not mind whether they have £16,667 now or £20,000 in a year's time. In this sense we can say that, given a 20 per cent alternative investment opportunity, the present value of £20,000 to be received in one year's time is £16,667.

If we derive the present value (PV) of each of the cash flows associated with Billingsgate's machine investment, we could easily make the direct comparison between the cost of making the investment (£100,000) and the various benefits that will derive from it in years 1 to 5.

We can make a more general statement about the PV of a particular cash flow. It is:

**PV of the cash flow of year $n$ = actual cash flow of year $n$ divided by $(1 + r)^n$**

where $n$ is the year of the cash flow (that is, how many years into the future) and $r$ is the opportunity financing cost expressed as a decimal (instead of as a percentage).

We have already seen how this works for the £20,000 inflow for year 1 for the Billingsgate project. For year 2 the calculation would be:

$$\text{PV of year 2 cash flow (that is, £40,000)} = £40,000/(1 + 0.2)^2 = £40,000/(1.2)^2$$
$$= £40,000/1.44 = £27,778$$

Thus the present value of the £40,000 to be received in two years' time is £27,778.

## Activity 10.10

See if you can show that an investor would find £27,778, receivable now, equally acceptable to receiving £40,000 in two years' time, assuming that there is a 20 per cent investment opportunity.

The reasoning goes like this:

|  | £ |
|---|---|
| Amount available for immediate investment | 27,778 |
| Income for year 1 (20% × 27,778) | 5,556 |
|  | 33,334 |
| Income for year 2 (20% × 33,334) | 6,667 |
|  | 40,001 |

(The extra £1 is only a rounding error.)

This is to say that since the investor can turn £27,778 into £40,000 in two years, these amounts are equivalent. We can say that £27,778 is the present value of £40,000 receivable after two years given a 20 per cent cost of finance.

Now let us calculate the present values of all of the cash flows associated with the Billingsgate machine project and from them the *net present value (NPV)* of the project as a whole.

The relevant cash flows and calculations are as follows:

| Time | Cash flow £000 | Calculation of PV | PV £000 |
|---|---|---|---|
| Immediately (time 0) | (100) | $(100)/(1 + 0.2)^0$ | (100.00) |
| 1 year's time | 20 | $20/(1 + 0.2)^1$ | 16.67 |
| 2 years' time | 40 | $40/(1 + 0.2)^2$ | 27.78 |
| 3 years' time | 60 | $60/(1 + 0.2)^3$ | 34.72 |
| 4 years' time | 60 | $60/(1 + 0.2)^4$ | 28.94 |
| 5 years' time | 20 | $20/(1 + 0.2)^5$ | 8.04 |
| 5 years' time | 20 | $20/(1 + 0.2)^5$ | 8.04 |
| Net present value (NPV) |  |  | 24.19 |

Note that $(1 + 0.2)^0 = 1$.

Once again, we must ask how we can decide whether the machine project is acceptable to the business. In fact, the decision rule for NPV is simple:

■ If the NPV is positive the project should be accepted; if it is negative the project should be rejected.
■ If there are two (or more) competing projects that have positive NPVs, the project with the higher (or highest) NPV should be selected.

In this case, the NPV is positive, so we should accept the project and buy the machine. The reasoning behind this decision rule is quite straightforward. Investing in the machine will make the business, and its owners, £24,190 better off than they would be by taking up the next best available opportunity. The gross benefits from investing in this machine are worth a total of £124,190 today. Since the business can 'buy' these benefits for just £100,000 today, the investment should be made. If, however, the present value of the gross benefits were below £100,000, it would be less than the cost of 'buying' those benefits and the opportunity should, therefore, be rejected.

### Activity 10.11

What is the *maximum* the Billingsgate Battery Company would be prepared to pay for the machine, given the potential benefits of owning it?

The business would logically be prepared to pay up to £124,190 since the wealth of the owners of the business would be increased up to this price – although the business would prefer to pay as little as possible.

## Using discount tables

To deduce each PV in the Billingsgate Battery Company project, we took the relevant cash flow and multiplied it by $1/(1 + r)^n$. There is a slightly different way to do this. Tables exist that show values of this discount factor for a range of values of $r$ and $n$. Such a table appears at the end of this book, in Appendix E on pages 563–564. Take a look at it.

Look at the column for 20 per cent and the row for one year. We find that the factor is 0.833. This means that the PV of a cash flow of £1 receivable in one year is £0.833. So the present value of a cash flow of £20,000 receivable in one year's time is £16,660 (that is, 0.833 × £20,000), the same result as we found doing it in longhand.

### Activity 10.12

What is the NPV of the Chaotic Industries project from Activity 10.2, assuming a 15 per cent opportunity cost of finance (discount rate)?

Remember that the inflows and outflow are expected to be:

| Time | | £000 |
| --- | --- | --- |
| Immediately | Cost of vans | (150) |
| 1 year's time | Saving before depreciation | 30 |
| 2 years' time | Saving before depreciation | 30 |
| 3 years' time | Saving before depreciation | 30 |
| 4 years' time | Saving before depreciation | 30 |
| 5 years' time | Saving before depreciation | 30 |
| 6 years' time | Saving before depreciation | 30 |
| 6 years' time | Disposal proceeds from the vans | 30 |

The calculation of the NPV of the project is as follows:

| Time | Cash flows £000 | Discount factor (15%) | Present value £000 |
| --- | --- | --- | --- |
| Immediately | (150) | 1.000 | (150.00) |
| 1 year's time | 30 | 0.870 | 26.10 |
| 2 years' time | 30 | 0.756 | 22.68 |
| 3 years' time | 30 | 0.658 | 19.74 |
| 4 years' time | 30 | 0.572 | 17.16 |
| 5 years' time | 30 | 0.497 | 14.91 |
| 6 years' time | 30 | 0.432 | 12.96 |
| 6 years' time | 30 | 0.432 | 12.96 |
| | | NPV | (23.49) |

## Activity 10.13

How would you interpret this result?

The fact that the project has a negative NPV means that the present values of the benefits from the investment are worth less than the cost of entering into it. Any cost up to £126,510 (the present value of the benefits) would be worth paying, but not £150,000.

The discount table in Appendix E shows how the value of £1 diminishes as its receipt goes further into the future. Assuming an opportunity cost of finance of 20 per cent a year, £1 to be received immediately, obviously, has a present value of £1. However, as the time before it is to be received increases, the present value diminishes significantly, as is shown in Figure 10.3.

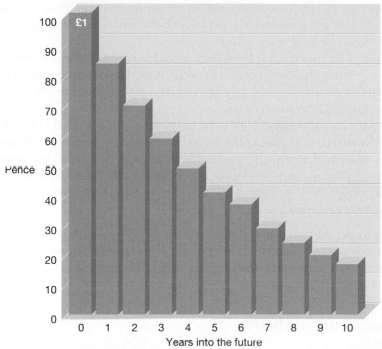

**Figure 10.3** Present value of £1 receivable at various times in the future, assuming an annual cost of capital of 20 per cent

The present value of a future receipt (or payment) of £1 depends on how far in the future it will occur. Those that will occur in the near future will have a larger present value than those whose occurrence is more distant in time.

## The discount rate and the cost of capital

We have seen that the appropriate discount rate to use in NPV assessments is the opportunity cost of finance. This is, in effect, the cost to the business of the finance needed to fund the investment. It will normally be the cost of a mixture of funds (shareholders' funds and borrowings) employed by the business and is often referred to as the cost of capital. We shall refer to it as cost of capital from now on.

## Why NPV is better

From what we have seen, NPV seems to be a better method of appraising investment opportunities than either ARR or PP. This is because it fully takes account of each of the following:

- *The timing of the cash flows.* By discounting the various cash flows associated with each project according to when each one is expected to arise, NPV takes account of the time value of money. Associated with this is the fact that by discounting, using the opportunity cost of capital (that is, the return that the next best alternative opportunity would generate), the net benefit *after* financing costs have been met is identified (as the NPV of the project).

- *The whole of the relevant cash flows.* NPV includes *all* of the relevant cash flows irrespective of when they are expected to occur. It treats them differently according to their date of occurrence, but they are all taken into account in the NPV. They all have an influence on the decision.

- *The objectives of the business.* NPV is the only method of appraisal in which the output of the analysis has a direct bearing on the wealth of the owners of the business (with a limited company, the shareholders). Positive NPVs enhance wealth; negative ones reduce it. Since we assume that private sector businesses seek to increase owners' wealth, NPV is superior to the other two methods (ARR and PP) that we have already discussed.

We saw earlier that a business should take on all projects with positive NPVs, when their cash flows are discounted at the opportunity cost of capital. Where a choice has to be made between projects, the business should normally select the one with the higher or highest NPV.

## NPV's wider application

NPV is considered the most logical approach to making business decisions about investments in productive assets. The same logic makes NPV equally valid as the best approach to take when trying to place a value on any economic asset, that is, an asset that seems capable of yielding financial benefits. This would include a share in a limited company and a loan. In fact, when we talk of *economic value*, we mean a value that has been derived by adding together the discounted (present) values of all future cash flows from the asset concerned.

Real World 10.6 provides an estimate of the NPV expected from one interesting project.

### Real World 10.6

## A real diamond geezer　

Alan Bond, the disgraced Australian businessman and America's Cup winner, is looking at ways to raise money in London for an African diamond mining project. Lesotho Diamond Corporation (LDC) is a private company in which Mr Bond has a large interest. LDC's main asset is a 93 per cent stake in the Kao diamond project in the southern African kingdom of Lesotho.

Mr Bond says, on his personal website, that the Kao project is forecast to yield 5m carats of diamonds over the next 10 years and could become Lesotho's biggest foreign currency earner.

SRK Consulting (mining consultant), has estimated the net present value of the project at £129m.

It is understood that Mr Bond and his family own about 40 per cent of LDC. Mr Bond has described himself as 'spearheading' the Kao project.

*Source*: adapted from 'Bond seeks funds in London to mine African diamonds', *The Financial Times*, 22/04/2007 (Bream, R.), copyright © The Financial Times Ltd.

## Internal rate of return (IRR)

This is the last of the four major methods of investment appraisal that are found in practice. It is quite closely related to the NPV method in that, like NPV, it also involves discounting future cash flows. The internal rate of return (IRR) of a particular investment is the discount rate that, when applied to its future cash flows, will produce an NPV of precisely zero. In essence, it represents the yield from an investment opportunity.

**Activity 10.14**

We should recall that, when we discounted the cash flows of the Billingsgate Battery Company machine investment opportunity at 20 per cent, we found that the NPV was a positive figure of £24,190 (see page 374). What does the NPV of the machine project tell us about the rate of return that the investment will yield for the business (that is, the project's IRR)?

The fact that the NPV is positive when discounting at 20 per cent implies that the rate of return that the project generates is more than 20 per cent. The fact that the NPV is a pretty large figure implies that the actual rate of return is quite a lot above 20 per cent. We should expect increasing the size of the discount rate to reduce NPV, because a higher discount rate gives a lower discounted figure.

It is somewhat laborious to deduce the IRR by hand, since it cannot usually be calculated directly. Iteration (trial and error) is the approach that must usually be adopted. Fortunately, computer spreadsheet packages can deduce the IRR with ease. The package will also use a trial and error approach, but at high speed.

Despite it being laborious, we shall now go on and derive the IRR for the Billingsgate project by hand.

Let us try a higher rate, say 30 per cent, and see what happens.

| Time | Cash flow £000 | Discount factor (30%) | PV £000 |
|------|----------------|----------------------|---------|
| Immediately (time 0) | (100) | 1.000 | (100.00) |
| 1 year's time | 20 | 0.769 | 15.38 |
| 2 years' time | 40 | 0.592 | 23.68 |
| 3 years' time | 60 | 0.455 | 27.30 |
| 4 years' time | 60 | 0.350 | 21.00 |
| 5 years' time | 20 | 0.269 | 5.38 |
| 5 years' time | 20 | 0.269 | 5.38 |
|  |  | NPV | (1.88) |

In increasing the discount rate from 20 per cent to 30 per cent, we have reduced the NPV from £24,190 (positive) to £1,880 (negative). Since the IRR is the discount rate that will give us an NPV of exactly zero, we can conclude that the IRR of Billingsgate Battery Company's machine project is very slightly below 30 per cent. Further trials could lead us to the exact rate, but there is probably not much point, given the likely inaccuracy of the cash flow estimates. It is probably good enough, for practical purposes, to say that the IRR is about 30 per cent.

The relationship between the NPV method discussed earlier and the IRR is shown graphically in Figure 10.4 using the information relating to the Billingsgate Battery Company.

**Figure 10.4** The relationship between the NPV and IRR methods

If the cost of capital were zero, the NPV would be the sum of the net cash flows. In other words, no account would be taken of the time value of money. However, if we assume increasing costs of capital, there is a corresponding decrease in the NPV of the project. When the NPV line crosses the horizontal axis there will be a zero NPV. The point where it crosses is the IRR.

In Figure 10.4, where the cost of capital is equal to zero, the NPV will be the sum of the net cash flows. In other words, no account is taken of the time value of money. However, as the cost of capital increases there is a corresponding decrease in the NPV of the project. When the NPV line crosses the horizontal axis there will be a zero NPV. That point represents the IRR.

## Activity 10.15

What is the internal rate of return of the Chaotic Industries project from Activity 10.2?
(*Hint*: Remember that you already know the NPV of this project at 15 per cent (from Activity 10.12).)

Since we know that, at a 15 per cent discount rate, the NPV is a relatively large negative figure, our next trial is using a lower discount rate, say 10 per cent:

| Time | Cash flows £000 | Discount factor (10% – from the table) | Present value £000 |
|------|------|------|------|
| Immediately | (150) | 1.000 | (150.00) |
| 1 year's time | 30 | 0.909 | 27.27 |
| 2 years' time | 30 | 0.826 | 24.78 |
| 3 years' time | 30 | 0.751 | 22.53 |
| 4 years' time | 30 | 0.683 | 20.49 |
| 5 years' time | 30 | 0.621 | 18.63 |
| 6 years' time | 30 | 0.564 | 16.92 |
| 6 years' time | 30 | 0.564 | 16.92 |
| | | NPV | (2.46) |

This figure is close to zero NPV. However, the NPV is still negative and so the precise IRR will be a little below 10 per cent.

We could undertake further trials in order to derive the precise IRR. If, however, we have to derive the IRR manually, further trials can be time-consuming.

We can get an acceptable approximation to the answer fairly quickly by first calculating the change in NPV arising from a 1 per cent change in the discount rate. This can be done by taking the difference between the two trials (that is, 15 per cent and 10 per cent) that we have already carried out (in Activities 10.12 and 10.15):

| Trial | Discount factor % | Net present value £000 |
|------|------|------|
| 1 | 15 | (23.49) |
| 2 | 10 | (2.46) |
| Difference | 5 | 21.03 |

The change in NPV for every 1 per cent change in the discount rate will be

$$(21.03/5) = 4.21$$

The reduction in the 10% discount rate required to achieve a zero NPV would therefore be:

$$[(2.46)/4.21] \times 1\% = 0.58\%$$

The IRR is therefore

$$(10.00 - 0.58)\% = 9.42\%$$

However, to say that the IRR is about 9 or 10 per cent is near enough for most purposes.

Note that this approach assumes a straight-line relationship between the discount rate and NPV. We can see from Figure 10.4 that this assumption is not strictly correct. Over a relatively short range, however, this simplifying assumption is not usually a problem and so we can still arrive at a reasonable approximation using the approach that we took in deriving the 9.42 per cent IRR.

In practice, most businesses have computer software packages that will derive a project's IRR very quickly. Thus, it is not usually necessary either to make a series of trial discount rates or to make the approximation that we have just considered.

Users of the IRR method should apply the following decision rules:

- For any project to be acceptable, it must meet a minimum IRR requirement. This is often referred to as the *hurdle rate* and, logically, this should be the opportunity cost of capital.
- Where there are competing projects (that is, the business can choose only one of two or more viable projects), the one with the higher (or highest) IRR should be selected.

IRR has certain attributes in common with NPV. All cash flows are taken into account and their timing is logically handled.

Real World 10.7 provides some idea of the IRR for one form of renewable energy.

### Real World 10.7

## The answer is blowin' in the wind

'Wind farms are practically guaranteed to make returns once you have a licence to operate,' says Bernard Lambilliotte, chief investment officer at Ecofin, a financial group that runs Ecofin Water and Power Opportunities, an investment trust.

'The risk is when you have bought the land and are seeking a licence,' says Lambilliotte. 'But once it is built and you are plugged into the grid it is risk-free. It will give an internal rate of return in the low to mid teens.' Ecofin's largest investment is in Sechilienne, a French company that operates wind farms in northern France and generates capacity in the French overseas territories powered by sugar cane waste.

*Source*: Batchelor, C., 'A hot topic, but poor returns', FT.com, 27 August 2005.

Real World 10.8 gives some examples of IRRs sought in practice.

## Real World 10.8

# Rates of return

IRRs for investment projects can vary considerably. Here are a few examples of the expected or target returns from investment projects of large businesses.

- GlaxoSmithKline plc, the leading pharmaceuticals business, is aiming to increase its IRR from investments in new products from 11 per cent to 14 per cent.
- Signet Group plc, the jewellery retailer, requires an IRR of 20 per cent over five years when appraising new stores.
- Apache Capital Partners, a property investment fund, has a target annual IRR of more than 20 per cent.
- Forth Ports plc, a port operator, concentrates on projects that generate an IRR of at least 16 per cent.

*Sources*: Doherty, J., 'GSK sales jump in emerging markets', FT. com, 4 February 2010; Signet Group plc Annual Report 2009, p. 56; Thomas, D., 'Vultures need to pick time to swoop', FT.com, 12 June 2009; FAQs, Forth Ports plc, www.forthports.co.uk, accessed 9 February 2010.

## Problems with IRR

The main disadvantage of IRR, relative to NPV, is the fact that it does not directly address the question of wealth generation. It could therefore lead to the wrong decision being made. This is because the IRR approach will always rank a project with, for example, an IRR of 25 per cent above a project with an IRR of 20 per cent. Although accepting the project with the higher percentage return will often generate more wealth, this may not always be the case. This is because IRR completely ignores the *scale of investment*.

With a 15 per cent cost of capital, £15 million invested at 20 per cent for one year will make us wealthier by £0.75 million (15 × (20 − 15)% = 0.75). With the same cost of capital, £5 million invested at 25 per cent for one year will make us only £0.5 million (5 × (25 − 15)% = 0.50). IRR does not recognise this. It should be acknowledged that it is not usual for projects to be competing where there is such a large difference in scale. Even if the problem is rare and so, typically, IRR will give the same signal as NPV, a method that is always reliable (NPV) must be better to use than IRR. This problem with percentages is another example of the one illustrated in Real World 10.3.

A further problem with the IRR method is that it has difficulty handling projects with unconventional cash flows. In the examples studied so far, each project has a negative cash flow arising at the start of its life and then positive cash flows thereafter. However, in some cases, a project may have both positive and negative cash flows at future points in its life. Such a pattern of cash flows can result in there being more than one IRR, or even no IRR at all. This would make the IRR method difficult to use, although it should be said that this problem is also quite rare in practice. This is never a problem for NPV, however.

## Some practical points

When undertaking an investment appraisal, there are several practical points that we should bear in mind:

→ ■ *Past costs*. As with all decisions, we should take account only of relevant cost in our analysis. This means that only costs that vary with the decision should be considered. Thus, all past costs should be ignored as they cannot vary with the decision. A business may incur costs (such as development costs and market research costs) *before* the evaluation of an opportunity to launch a new product. As those costs have already been incurred, they should be disregarded, even though the amounts may be substantial. Costs that have already been committed but not yet paid should also be disregarded. Where a business has entered into a binding contract to incur a particular cost, it becomes in effect a past cost even though payment may not be due until some point in the future.

■ *Common future costs*. It is not only past costs that do not vary with the decision; some future costs may also be the same. For example, the cost of raw materials may not vary with the decision whether to invest in a new piece of manufacturing plant or to continue to use existing plant.

■ *Opportunity costs*. Opportunity costs arising from benefits forgone must be taken into account. Thus, for example, when considering a decision concerning whether or not to continue to use a machine already owned by the business, the realisable
→ value of the machine might be an important opportunity cost.

These points concerning costs are brought together in Activity 10.16.

### Activity 10.16

A garage has an old car that it bought several months ago for £3,000. The car needs a replacement engine before it can be sold. It is possible to buy a reconditioned engine for £300. This would take seven hours to fit by a mechanic who is paid £12 an hour. At present, the garage is short of work, but the owners are reluctant to lay off any mechanics or even cut down their basic working week because skilled labour is difficult to find and an upturn in repair work is expected soon.

Without the engine, the car could be sold for an estimated £3,500. What is the minimum price at which the garage should sell the car, with a reconditioned engine fitted, to avoid making a loss? (Ignore any timing differences in receipts and payments.)

The minimum price is the amount required to cover the relevant costs of the job. At this price, the business will make neither a profit nor a loss. Any price below this amount will result in a reduction in the wealth of the business. Thus, the minimum price is:

|  | £ |
|---|---|
| Opportunity cost of the car | 3,500 |
| Cost of the reconditioned engine | 300 |
| Total | 3,800 |

The original cost of the car is a past cost and is, therefore, irrelevant. However, we are told that, without the engine, the car could be sold for £3,500. This is the opportunity cost of the car, which represents the real benefits forgone, and should be taken into account.

The cost of the new engine is relevant because, if the work is done, the garage will have to pay £300 for the engine; it will pay nothing if the job is not done. The £300 is a future cost that varies with the decision and should be taken into account.

The labour cost is irrelevant because the same cost will be incurred whether the mechanic undertakes the work or not. This is because the mechanic is being paid to do nothing if this job is not undertaken; thus the additional labour cost arising from this job is zero.

■ *Taxation.* Owners will be interested in the after-tax returns generated from the business. Thus taxation will usually be an important consideration when making an investment decision. The profits from the project will be taxed, the capital investment may attract tax relief and so on. Tax is levied on these at significant rates. This means that, in real life, unless tax is formally taken into account, the wrong decision could easily be made. The timing of the tax outflow should also be taken into account when preparing the cash flows for the project.

■ *Cash flows not profit flows.* We have seen that for the NPV, IRR and PP methods, it is cash flows rather than profit flows that are relevant to the assessment of investment projects. In an investment appraisal requiring the application of any of these methods we may be given details of the profits for the investment period. These need to be adjusted in order to derive the cash flows. We should remember that the operating profit *before* non-cash items (such as depreciation) is an approximation to the cash flows for the period. We should, therefore, work back to this figure.

When the data are expressed in profit rather than cash flow terms, an adjustment in respect of working capital may also be necessary. Some adjustment should be made to take account of changes in working capital. For example, launching a new product may give rise to an increase in the net investment made in trade receivables and inventories less trade payables. This working capital investment would normally require an immediate outlay of cash. This outlay for additional working capital should be shown in the NPV calculations as an initial cash outflow. However, at the end of the life of the project, the additional working capital will be released. This divestment results in an effective inflow of cash at the end of the project. It should also be taken into account at the point at which it is received.

■ *Year-end assumption.* In the examples and activities that we have considered so far in this chapter, we have assumed that cash flows arise at the end of the relevant year. This is a simplifying assumption that is used to make the calculations easier. (However, it is perfectly possible to deal more precisely with the timing of the cash flows.) As we saw earlier, this assumption is clearly unrealistic, as money will have to be paid to employees on a weekly or monthly basis, credit customers will pay within a month or two of buying the product or service and so on. Nevertheless, it is probably not a serious distortion. We should be clear, however, that there is nothing about any of the four appraisal methods that demands that this assumption be made.

- *Interest payments.* When using discounted cash flow techniques (NPV and IRR), interest payments should not be taken into account in deriving the cash flows for the period. The discount factor already takes account of the costs of financing. To take account of interest charges in deriving cash flows for the period would be double counting.

- *Other factors.* Investment decision making must not be viewed as simply a mechanical exercise. The results derived from a particular investment appraisal method will be only one input to the decision-making process. There may be broader issues connected to the decision that have to be taken into account but which may be difficult or impossible to quantify.

    The reliability of the forecasts and the validity of the assumptions used in the evaluation will also have a bearing on the final decision.

## Activity 10.17

The directors of Manuff (Steel) Ltd are considering closing one of the business's factories. There has been a reduction in the demand for the products made at the factory in recent years. The directors are not optimistic about the long-term prospects for these products. The factory is situated in the north of England, in an area where unemployment is high.

The factory is leased with four years of the lease remaining. The directors are uncertain whether the factory should be closed immediately or at the end of the period of the lease. Another business has offered to sublease the premises from Manuff (Steel) Ltd at a rental of £40,000 a year for the remainder of the lease period.

The machinery and equipment at the factory cost £1,500,000. The value at which they appear on the statement of financial position is £400,000. In the event of immediate closure, the machinery and equipment could be sold for £220,000. The working capital at the factory is £420,000. It could be liquidated for that amount immediately, if required. Alternatively, the working capital can be liquidated in full at the end of the lease period. Immediate closure would result in redundancy payments to employees of £180,000.

If the factory continues in operation until the end of the lease period, the following operating profits (losses) are expected:

|  | Year 1 £000 | Year 2 £000 | Year 3 £000 | Year 4 £000 |
|---|---|---|---|---|
| Operating profit (loss) | 160 | (40) | 30 | 20 |

The above figures include a charge of £90,000 a year for depreciation of machinery and equipment. The residual value of the machinery and equipment at the end of the lease period is estimated at £40,000.

Redundancy payments are expected to be £150,000 at the end of the lease period if the factory continues in operation. The business has an annual cost of capital of 12 per cent.

(a) Determine the relevant cash flows arising from a decision to continue operations until the end of the lease period rather than to close immediately.

(b) Calculate the net present value of continuing operations until the end of the lease period, rather than closing immediately.

(c) What other factors might the directors take into account before making a final decision on the timing of the factory closure?

(d) State, with reasons, whether or not the business should continue to operate the factory until the end of the lease period.

Ignore taxation.

Your answer should be as follows:

(a) Relevant cash flows

|  | Years | | | | |
|---|---|---|---|---|---|
|  | 0 | 1 | 2 | 3 | 4 |
|  | £000 | £000 | £000 | £000 | £000 |
| Operating cash flows (Note 1) | – | 250 | 50 | 120 | 110 |
| Sale of machinery (Note 2) | (220) | – | – | – | 40 |
| Redundancy costs (Note 3) | 180 | – | – | – | (150) |
| Sublease rentals (Note 4) | – | (40) | (40) | (40) | (40) |
| Working capital invested (Note 5) | (420) | – | – | – | 420 |
|  | (460) | 210 | 10 | 80 | 380 |

Notes:
1 Each year's operating cash flows are calculated by adding back the depreciation charge for the year to the operating profit for the year. In the case of the operating loss, the depreciation charge is deducted.
2 In the event of closure, machinery could be sold immediately. Thus an opportunity cost of £220,000 is incurred if operations continue.
3 Continuing operations, there will be a saving in immediate redundancy costs of £180,000. However, redundancy costs of £150,000 will be paid in four years' time.
4 Continuing operations will mean that the opportunity to sublease the factory will be forgone.
5 Immediate closure would mean that working capital could be liquidated. If operations continue this opportunity is forgone. However, working capital can be liquidated in four years' time.

(b)

|  | Years | | | | |
|---|---|---|---|---|---|
|  | 0 | 1 | 2 | 3 | 4 |
| Discount rate 12 per cent | 1.000 | 0.893 | 0.797 | 0.712 | 0.636 |
| Present value (£000) | (460) | 187.5 | 8.0 | 57.0 | 241.7 |
| Net present value (£000) | 34.2 | | | | |

(c) Other factors that may influence the decision include:
■ *The overall strategy of the business.* The business may need to set the decision within a broader context. It may be necessary to manufacture the products at the factory because they are an integral part of the business's product range. The business may wish to avoid redundancies in an area of high unemployment for as long as possible.

- *Flexibility*. A decision to close the factory is probably irreversible. If the factory continues, however, there may be a chance that the prospects for the factory will brighten in the future.
- *Creditworthiness of sub-lessee*. The business should investigate the creditworthiness of the sub-lessee. Failure to receive the expected sublease payments would make the closure option far less attractive.
- *Accuracy of forecasts*. The forecasts made by the business should be examined carefully. Inaccuracies in the forecasts or any underlying assumptions may change the expected outcomes.

(d) The NPV of the decision to continue operations rather than close immediately is positive. Hence, shareholders would be better off if the directors took this course of action. The factory should therefore continue in operation rather than close down. This decision is likely to be welcomed by employees and would allow the business to maintain its flexibility.

## Investment appraisal in practice

Many surveys have been conducted in the UK into the methods of investment appraisal used by businesses. They have shown the following features:

- Businesses tend to use more than one method to assess each investment decision.
- The discounting methods (NPV and IRR) have become increasingly popular over time. NPV and IRR are now the most popular of the four methods.
- PP continues to be popular and, to a lesser extent, so does ARR. This is despite the theoretical shortcomings of both of these methods.
- Larger businesses tend to rely more heavily on discounting methods than smaller businesses do.

Real World 10.9 shows the results of a fairly recent survey of a number of UK manufacturing businesses regarding their use of investment appraisal methods.

### Real World 10.9

### A survey of UK business practice

Senior financial managers at 83 of the UK's largest manufacturing businesses were asked about the investment appraisal methods used to evaluate both strategic and non-strategic projects. Strategic projects usually aim to increase or change the competitive capabilities of a business, for example by introducing a new manufacturing process.

| Method | Non-strategic projects Mean score | Strategic projects Mean score |
|---|---|---|
| Net present value | 3.6829 | 3.9759 |
| Payback | 3.4268 | 3.6098 |
| Internal rate of return | 3.3293 | 3.7073 |
| Accounting rate of return | 1.9867 | 2.2667 |

Response scale: 1= never, 2 = rarely, 3 = often, 4 = mostly, 5 = always.

We can see that, for both non-strategic and for strategic investments, the NPV method is the most popular. As the sample consists of large businesses (nearly all with total sales revenue in excess of £100 million), a fairly sophisticated approach to evaluation might be expected. Nevertheless, for non-strategic investments, the payback method comes second in popularity. It drops to third place for strategic projects.

The survey also found that 98 per cent of respondents used more than one method and 88 per cent used more than three methods of investment appraisal.

*Source*: based on information in Alkaraan, F. and Northcott, D., 'Strategic capital investment decision-making: a role for emergent analysis tools? A study of practice in large UK manufacturing companies', *British Accounting Review*, June 2006.

A survey of US businesses also shows considerable support for the NPV and IRR methods. There seems, however, to be less support for the payback method and ARR than there is in the UK. Real World 10.10 sets out some of the main findings.

### Real World 10.10

## A survey of US practice

A survey of the chief financial officers (CFOs) of 392 US businesses examined the popularity of various methods of investment appraisal. Figure 10.5 shows the percentage of businesses surveyed that always, or almost always, used the four methods discussed in this chapter.

**Figure 10.5** The use of investment appraisal methods among US businesses

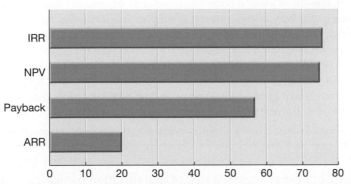

Percentage of CFOs who always or almost always use a given technique

The IRR and NPV methods are both widely used and are much more popular than the payback and accounting rate of return methods. Nevertheless, the payback method is still used always, or almost always, by a majority of US businesses.

*Source*: based on information in Graham, R. and Harvey, C., 'How do CFOs make capital budgeting and capital structure decisions?', *Journal of Applied Corporate Finance*, vol. 15, no. 1, 2002.

## Activity 10.18

Earlier in the chapter we discussed the theoretical limitations of the PP method. Can you explain the fact that it still seems to be a popular method of investment appraisal among businesses?

A number of possible reasons may explain this finding:

- PP is easy to understand and use.
- It can avoid the problems of forecasting far into the future.
- It gives emphasis to the early cash flows when there is greater certainty concerning the accuracy of their predicted value.
- It emphasises the importance of liquidity. Where a business has liquidity problems, a short payback period for a project is likely to appear attractive.

PP can provide a convenient, though rough and ready, assessment of the profitability of a project, in the way that it is used in Real World 10.11.

## Real World 10.11

### An investment lifts off

SES Global is the world's largest commercial satellite operator. This means that it rents satellite capacity to broadcasters, governments, telecommunications groups and Internet service providers. It is a risky venture that few are prepared to undertake. As a result, a handful of businesses dominates the market.

Launching a satellite requires a huge initial outlay of capital, but relatively small cash outflows following the launch. Revenues only start to flow once the satellite is in orbit. A satellite launch costs around €250m. The main elements of this cost are the satellite (€120m), the launch vehicle (€80m), insurance (€40m) and ground equipment (€10m).

According to Romain Bausch, president and chief executive of SES Global, it takes three years to build and launch a satellite. However, the average lifetime of a satellite is fifteen years during which time it is generating revenues. The revenues generated are such that the payback period is around four to five years.

*Source*: 'Satellites need space to earn', *The Financial Times*, 14/07/2003 (Burt, T.), copyright © The Financial Times Ltd.

The popularity of PP may suggest a lack of sophistication by managers concerning investment appraisal. This criticism is most often made against managers of smaller businesses. This point is borne out by the fact that both of the surveys discussed above have found that smaller businesses are much less likely to use discounted cash flow methods (NPV and IRR) than are larger ones. Other surveys have tended to reach a similar conclusion.

IRR may be popular because it expresses outcomes in percentage terms rather than in absolute terms. This form of expression appears to be more acceptable to managers, despite the problems of percentage measures that we discussed earler. This may be because managers are used to using percentage figures as targets (for example, return on capital employed).

Real World 10.12 shows extracts from the 2008 annual report of a well-known business: Rolls-Royce plc, the builder of engines for aircraft and other purposes.

---

**Real World 10.12**

## The use of NPV at Rolls-Royce

In its 2008 annual report and accounts, Rolls-Royce plc stated:

> The Group continues to subject all investments to rigorous examination of risks and future cash flows to ensure that they create shareholder value. All major investments require Board approval.
>
> The Group has a portfolio of projects at different stages of their life cycles. Discounted cash flow analysis of the remaining life of projects is performed on a regular basis.

*Source*: Rolls-Royce plc Annual Report 2008, p. 59.

---

Rolls-Royce makes clear that it uses NPV (the report refers to creating shareholder value and to discounted cash flow, which strongly imply NPV). It is interesting to note that Rolls-Royce not only assesses new projects but also reassesses existing ones. This must be a sensible commercial approach. Businesses should not continue with existing projects unless those projects have a positive NPV based on future cash flows. Just because a project seemed to have a positive NPV before it started does not mean that this will persist in the light of changing circumstances. Activity 10.17 (pages 386–388) considered a decision to close down a project.

---

**? Self-assessment question 10.1**

Beacon Chemicals plc is considering buying some equipment to produce a chemical named X14. The new equipment's capital cost is estimated at £100 million. If its purchase is approved now, the equipment can be bought and production can commence by the end of this year. £50 million has already been spent on research and development work. Estimates of revenues and costs arising from the operation of the new equipment appear below.

| | Year 1 | Year 2 | Year 3 | Year 4 | Year 5 |
|---|---|---|---|---|---|
| Sales price (£/litre) | 100 | 120 | 120 | 100 | 80 |
| Sales volume (million litres) | 0.8 | 1.0 | 1.2 | 1.0 | 0.8 |
| Variable cost (£/litre) | 50 | 50 | 40 | 30 | 40 |
| Fixed cost (£m) | 30 | 30 | 30 | 30 | 30 |

If the equipment is bought, sales of some existing products will be lost resulting in a loss of contribution of £15 million a year, over the life of the equipment.

The accountant has informed you that the fixed cost includes depreciation of £20 million a year on the new equipment. It also includes an allocation of £10 million for fixed overheads. A separate study has indicated that if the new equipment were bought, additional overheads, excluding depreciation, arising from producing the chemical would be £8 million a year. Production would require additional working capital of £30 million.

For the purposes of your initial calculations ignore taxation.

**Required:**
(a) Deduce the relevant annual cash flows associated with buying the equipment.
(b) Deduce the payback period.
(c) Calculate the net present value using a discount rate of 8 per cent.

(*Hint*: You should deal with the investment in working capital by treating it as a cash outflow at the start of the project and an inflow at the end.)

**The answer to this question can be found at the back of the book, in Appendix B.**

As a footnote to our discussion of business investment decision making, Real World 10.13 looks at one of the world's biggest investment projects which has proved to be a commercial disaster, despite being a technological success.

### Real World 10.13

## Wealth lost in the chunnel

The tunnel, which runs for 31 miles between Folkestone in the UK and Sangatte in Northern France, was started in 1986 and opened for public use in 1994. From a technological and social perspective it has been a success, but from a financial point of view it has been a disaster. The tunnel was purely a private sector venture for which a new business, Eurotunnel plc, was created. Relatively little public money was involved. To be a commercial success the tunnel needed to cover all of its costs, including interest charges, and leave sufficient to enhance the shareholders' wealth. In fact the providers of long-term finance (lenders and shareholders) have lost virtually all of their investment. Though the main losers were banks and institutional investors, many individuals, particularly in France, bought shares in Eurotunnel.

Since the accounting year ended 31 December 2007, the business has made a profit and, in 2009, paid its first dividend. This was, however, only achieved as a result of the business forcing lenders, who would expect to be paid interest, to convert their investment to ordinary shares. This meant that the business eliminated the cost of financing some of the cost of building the tunnel.

Key inputs to the pre-1986 assessment of the project were the cost of construction and creating the infrastructure, the length of time required to complete construction and the level of revenue that the tunnel would generate when it became operational.

In the event,

- construction cost was £10 billion – it was originally planned to cost £5.6 billion;
- construction time was seven years – it was planned to be six years;
- revenues from passengers and freight have been well below projections – for example, 21 million annual passenger journeys on Eurostar trains were projected; the numbers have consistently remained at around 7 million.

The failure to generate revenues at the projected levels has probably been the biggest contributor to the problem. When preparing the pre-1986 projection, planners failed to take adequate account of two crucial factors:

1 fierce competition from the ferry operators. At the time many thought that the ferries would roll over and die; and
2 the rise of no-frills, cheap air travel between the UK and the continent.

The commercial failure of the tunnel means that it will be very difficult in future for projects of this nature to be financed from private sector funds.

*Sources*: Annual Reports of Eurotunnel plc; Randall, J., 'How Eurotunnel went wrong', BBC news, www.newsvote.bbc.co.uk, 13 June 2005.

## Summary

The main points of this chapter may be summarised as follows:

### Accounting rate of return

- Accounting rate of return (ARR) is the average accounting profit from the project expressed as a percentage of the average investment.
  - Decision rule – projects with an ARR above a defined minimum are acceptable; the greater the ARR, the more attractive the project becomes.
  - Conclusions on ARR:
    - does not relate directly to shareholders' wealth – can lead to illogical conclusions;
    - takes almost no account of the timing of cash flows;
    - ignores some relevant information and may take account of some irrelevant;
    - relatively simple to use;
    - much inferior to NPV.

### Payback period

- Payback period (PP) is the length of time that it takes for the cash outflow for the initial investment to be repaid out of resulting cash inflows.
  - Decision rule – projects with a PP up to a defined maximum period are acceptable, the shorter the PP, the more attractive the project.

- ❏ Conclusions on PP:
  - – does not relate to shareholders' wealth;
  - – ignores inflows after the payback date;
  - – takes little account of the timing of cash flows;
  - – ignores much relevant information;
  - – does not always provide clear signals and can be impractical to use;
  - – much inferior to NPV, but it is easy to understand and can offer a liquidity insight, which might be the reason for its widespread use.

### Net present value

- ■ Net present value (NPV) is the sum of the discounted values of the net cash flows from the investment.
  - ❏ Money has a time value.
  - ❏ Decision rule – all positive NPV investments enhance shareholders' wealth; the greater the NPV, the greater the enhancement and the greater the attractiveness of the project.
  - ❏ PV of a cash flow = cash flow $\times 1/(1 + r)^n$, assuming a constant cost of capital.
  - ❏ Discounting brings cash flows at different points in time to a common valuation basis (their present value), which enables them to be directly compared.
  - ❏ Conclusions on NPV:
    - – relates directly to shareholders' wealth objective;
    - – takes account of the timing of cash flows;
    - – takes all relevant information into account;
    - – provides clear signals and practical to use.

### Internal rate of return

- ■ Internal rate of return (IRR) is the discount rate that, when applied to the cash flows of a project, causes it to have a zero NPV.
  - ❏ IRR represents the average percentage return on the investment, taking account of the fact that cash may be flowing in and out of the project at various points in its life.
  - ❏ Decision rule – projects that have an IRR greater than the cost of capital are acceptable; the greater the IRR, the more attractive the project.
  - ❏ IRR cannot normally be calculated directly; a trial and error approach is usually necessary.
  - ❏ Conclusions on IRR:
    - – does not relate directly to shareholders' wealth;
    - – usually gives the same signals as NPV but can mislead where there are competing projects of different size;
    - – takes account of the timing of cash flows;
    - – takes all relevant information into account;
    - – problems of multiple IRRs when there are unconventional cash flows;
    - – inferior to NPV.

### Use of appraisal methods in practice

- All four methods identified are widely used.
- The discounting methods (NPV and IRR) show a steady increase in usage over time.
- Many businesses use more than one method.
- Larger businesses seem to be more sophisticated in their choice and use of appraisal methods than smaller ones.

**MyAccountingLab** | *Now check your progress in your personal Study Plan*

### → Key terms

accounting rate of return (ARR) p. 359
payback period (PP) p. 364
net present value (NPV) p. 368
risk p. 370
risk premium p. 371
inflation p. 371

discount factor p. 375
cost of capital p. 377
internal rate of return (IRR) p. 379
relevant cost p. 384
opportunity cost p. 384

## Further reading

If you would like to explore the topics covered in this chapter in more depth, we recommend the following books:

Arnold, G., *Corporate Financial Management* (4th edn), Financial Times Prentice Hall, 2008, chapters 2, 3 and 4.

Drury, C., *Management and Cost Accounting*, 7th edn, South Western Cengage Learning, 2007, chapters 13 and 14.

McLaney, E., *Business Finance: Theory and Practice* (8th edn), Financial Times Prentice Hall, 2009, chapters 4, 5 and 6.

Pike, R. and Neale, B., *Corporate Finance and Investment*, (6th edn), Prentice Hall, 2009, chapters 5, 6 and 7.

# ? Review questions

Solutions to these questions can be found at the back of the book, in Appendix C.

**10.1** Why is the net present value method of investment appraisal considered to be theoretically superior to other methods that are found in practice?

**10.2** The payback method has been criticised for not taking the time value of money into account. Could this limitation be overcome? If so, would this method then be preferable to the NPV method?

**10.3** Research indicates that the IRR method is extremely popular even though it has shortcomings when compared to the NPV method. Why might managers prefer to use IRR rather than NPV when carrying out discounted cash flow evaluations?

**10.4** Why are cash flows rather than profit flows used in the IRR, NPV and PP methods of investment appraisal?

# ✳ Exercises

Exercises 10.3 to 10.5 are more advanced than 10.1 and 10.2. Those with coloured numbers have solutions at the back of the book, in Appendix D.

If you wish to try more exercises, visit the website at www.myaccountinglab.com.

**10.1** The directors of Mylo Ltd are currently considering two mutually exclusive investment projects. Both projects are concerned with the purchase of new plant. The following data are available for each project:

|  | Project 1 £000 | Project 2 £000 |
|---|---|---|
| Cost (immediate outlay) | 100 | 60 |
| Expected annual operating profit (loss): | | |
| Year 1 | 29 | 18 |
| Year 2 | (1) | (2) |
| Year 3 | 2 | 4 |
| Estimated residual value of the plant | 7 | 6 |

The business has an estimated cost of capital of 10 per cent. It uses the straight-line method of depreciation for all non-current assets when calculating operating profit. Neither project would increase the working capital of the business. The business has sufficient funds to meet all capital expenditure requirements.

**Required:**

(a) Calculate for each project:
   (i) The net present value.
   (ii) The approximate internal rate of return.
   (iii) The payback period.

(b) State which, if either, of the two investment projects the directors of Mylo Ltd should accept and why.

**10.2** C. George (Controls) Ltd manufactures a thermostat that can be used in a range of kitchen appliances. The manufacturing process is, at present, semi-automated. The equipment used cost £540,000 and has a carrying amount of £300,000. Demand for the product has been fairly stable and output has been maintained at 50,000 units a year in recent years.

The following data, based on the current level of output, have been prepared in respect of the product:

| Using existing equipment | Per unit | |
|---|---|---|
| | £ | £ |
| Selling price | | 12.40 |
| Labour | (3.30) | |
| Materials | (3.65) | |
| Overheads: Variable | (1.58) | |
| Fixed | (1.60) | |
| | | (10.13) |
| Operating profit | | 2.27 |

Although the existing equipment is expected to last for a further four years before it is sold for an estimated £40,000, the business has recently been considering purchasing new equipment that would completely automate much of the production process. This would give rise to production cost savings. The new equipment would cost £670,000 and would have an expected life of four years, at the end of which it would be sold for an estimated £70,000. If the new equipment is purchased, the old equipment could be sold for £150,000 immediately.

The assistant to the business's accountant has prepared a report to help assess the viability of the proposed change, which includes the following data:

| Using new equipment | Per unit | |
|---|---|---|
| | £ | £ |
| Selling price | | 12.40 |
| Labour | (1.20) | |
| Materials | (3.20) | |
| Overheads: Variable | (1.40) | |
| Fixed | (3.30) | |
| | | (9.10) |
| Operating profit | | 3.30 |

Depreciation charges will increase by £85,000 a year as a result of purchasing the new machinery; however, other fixed costs are not expected to change.

In the report the assistant wrote:

> The figures shown above that relate to the proposed change are based on the current level of output and take account of a depreciation charge of £150,000 a year in respect of the new equipment. The effect of purchasing the new equipment will be to increase the operating profit to sales revenue ratio from 18.3% to 26.6%. In addition, the purchase of the new equipment will enable us to reduce our inventories level immediately by £130,000.
>
> In view of these facts, I recommend purchase of the new equipment.

The business has a cost of capital of 12 per cent.

**Required:**

(a) Prepare a statement of the incremental cash flows arising from the purchase of the new equipment.
(b) Calculate the net present value of the proposed purchase of new equipment.
(c) State, with reasons, whether the business should purchase the new equipment.
(d) Explain why cash flow projections are used rather than profit forecasts to assess the viability of proposed capital expenditure projects.

Ignore taxation.

**10.3** The accountant of your business has recently been taken ill through overwork. In his absence his assistant has prepared some calculations of the profitability of a project, which are to be discussed soon at the board meeting of your business. His workings, which are set out below, include some errors of principle. You can assume that the statement below includes no arithmetical errors.

|  | Year 1 £000 | Year 2 £000 | Year 3 £000 | Year 4 £000 | Year 5 £000 | Year 6 £000 |
|---|---|---|---|---|---|---|
| Sales revenue | – | 450 | 470 | 470 | 470 | 470 |
| *Less* Costs |  |  |  |  |  |  |
| Materials | – | 126 | 132 | 132 | 132 | 132 |
| Labour | – | 90 | 94 | 94 | 94 | 94 |
| Overheads | – | 45 | 47 | 47 | 47 | 47 |
| Depreciation | – | 120 | 120 | 120 | 120 | 120 |
| Working capital | 180 | – | – | – | – | – |
| Interest on working capital | – | 27 | 27 | 27 | 27 | 27 |
| Write-off of development costs | – | 30 | 30 | 30 | – | – |
| Total costs | 180 | 438 | 450 | 450 | 420 | 420 |
| Operating profit/(loss) | (180) | 12 | 20 | 20 | 50 | 50 |

$$\frac{\text{Total profit (loss)}}{\text{Cost of equipment}} = \frac{(£28,000)}{£600,000} = \text{Return on investment (4.7\%)}$$

You ascertain the following additional information:

■ The cost of equipment contains £100,000, being the carrying amount of an old machine. If it were not used for this project it would be scrapped with a zero net realisable value. New equipment costing £500,000 will be purchased on 31 December Year 0. You should assume that all other cash flows occur at the end of the year to which they relate.

■ The development costs of £90,000 have already been spent.

■ Overheads have been costed at 50 per cent of direct labour, which is the business's normal practice. An independent assessment has suggested that incremental overheads are likely to amount to £30,000 a year.

■ The business's cost of capital is 12 per cent.

**Required:**

(a) Prepare a corrected statement of the incremental cash flows arising from the project. Where you have altered the assistant's figures you should attach a brief note explaining your alterations.

(b) Calculate:

    (i) The project's payback period.

    (ii) The project's net present value as at 31 December Year 0.

(c) Write a memo to the board advising on the acceptance or rejection of the project.

Ignore taxation in your answer.

**10.4** Newton Electronics Ltd has incurred expenditure of £5 million over the past three years researching and developing a miniature hearing aid. The hearing aid is now fully developed. The directors are now considering which of three mutually exclusive options should be taken to exploit the potential of the new product. The options are as follows:

1 Newton Electronics Ltd could manufacture the hearing aid itself. This would be a new departure, since the business has so far concentrated on research and development projects. However, the business has manufacturing space available that it currently rents to another business for £100,000 a year. Newton Electronics Ltd would have to purchase plant and equipment costing £9 million and invest £3 million in working capital immediately for production to begin.

A market research report, for which the business paid £50,000, indicates that the new product has an expected life of five years. Sales of the product during this period are predicted as follows:

| | Predicted sales for the year ended 30 November | | | | |
| --- | --- | --- | --- | --- | --- |
| | Year 1 | Year 2 | Year 3 | Year 4 | Year 5 |
| Number of units (000s) | 800 | 1,400 | 1,800 | 1,200 | 500 |

The selling price per unit will be £30 in the first year but will fall to £22 for the following three years. In the final year of the product's life, the selling price will fall to £20. Variable production costs are predicted to be £14 a unit. Fixed production costs (including depreciation) will be £2.4 million a year. Marketing costs will be £2 million a year.

Newton Electronics Ltd intends to depreciate the plant and equipment using the straight-line method and based on an estimated residual value at the end of the five years of £1 million. The business has a cost of capital of 10 per cent a year.

2 Newton Electronics Ltd could agree to another business manufacturing and marketing the product under licence. A multinational business, Faraday Electricals plc, has offered to undertake the manufacture and marketing of the product and, in return, will make a royalty payment to Newton Electronics Ltd of £5 per unit. It has been estimated that the annual number of sales of the hearing aid will be 10 per cent higher if the multinational business, rather than Newton Electronics Ltd, manufactures and markets the product.

3 Newton Electronics Ltd could sell the patent rights to Faraday Electricals plc for £24 million, payable in two equal instalments. The first instalment would be payable immediately and the second at the end of two years. This option would give Faraday Electricals the exclusive right to manufacture and market the new product.

### Required:

(a) Calculate the net present value (as at 1 January Year 1) of each of the options available to Newton Electronics Ltd.

(b) Identify and discuss any other factors that Newton Electronics Ltd should consider before arriving at a decision.

(c) State what you consider to be the most suitable option and why.

Ignore taxation.

10.5 Chesterfield Wanderers is a professional football club that has enjoyed considerable success in recent years. As a result, the club has accumulated £10 million to spend on its further development. The board of directors is currently considering two mutually exclusive options for spending the funds available.

The first option is to acquire another player. The team manager has expressed a keen interest in acquiring Basil ('Bazza') Ramsey, a central defender, who currently plays for a rival club. The rival club has agreed to release the player immediately for £10 million if required. A decision to acquire 'Bazza' Ramsey would mean that the existing central defender, Vinnie Smith, could be sold to another club. Chesterfield Wanderers has recently received an offer of £2.2 million for this player. This offer is still open but will only be accepted if 'Bazza' Ramsey joins Chesterfield Wanderers. If this does not happen, Vinnie Smith will be expected to stay on with the club until the end of his playing career in five years' time. During this period, Vinnie will receive an annual salary of £400,000 and a loyalty bonus of £200,000 at the end of his five-year period with the club.

Assuming 'Bazza' Ramsey is acquired, the team manager estimates that gate receipts will increase by £2.5 million in the first year and £1.3 million in each of the four following years. There will also be an increase in advertising and sponsorship revenues of £1.2 million for each of the next five years if the player is acquired. At the end of five years, the player can be sold to a club in a lower division and Chesterfield Wanderers will expect to receive £1 million as a transfer fee. During his period at the club, 'Bazza' will receive an annual salary of £800,000 and a loyalty bonus of £400,000 after five years.

The second option is for the club to improve its ground facilities. The west stand could be extended and executive boxes could be built for businesses wishing to offer corporate hospitality to clients. These improvements would also cost £10 million and would take one year to complete. During this period, the west stand would be closed, resulting in a reduction of gate receipts of £1.8 million. However, gate receipts for each of the following four years would be £4.4 million higher than current receipts. In five years' time, the club has plans to sell the existing grounds and to move to a new stadium nearby. Improving the ground facilities is not expected to affect the ground's value when it comes to be sold. Payment for the improvements will be made when the work has been completed at the end of the first year. Whichever option is chosen, the board of directors has decided to take on additional ground staff. The additional wages bill is expected to be £350,000 a year over the next five years.

The club has a cost of capital of 10 per cent.

**Required:**
(a) Calculate the incremental cash flows arising from each of the options available to the club.
(b) Calculate the net present value of each of the options.
(c) On the basis of the calculations made in (b) above, which of the two options would you choose and why?
(d) Discuss the validity of using the net present value method in making investment decisions for a professional football club.

Ignore taxation.

## Chapter 11

# Financing a business

## Introduction

In this chapter we shall examine various aspects of financing a business. We begin by considering the main sources of finance available. Some of these sources have already been touched upon when we discussed the financing of limited companies in Chapter 4. In this chapter, we shall look at these in more detail, and also discuss other sources of finance that have not yet been mentioned. The factors to be taken into account when choosing an appropriate source of finance are also considered.

Following our consideration of the main sources of finance, we shall go on to examine various aspects of the capital markets, including the role of the Stock Exchange, the financing of smaller businesses and the ways in which share capital may be issued.

## Learning outcomes

**When you have completed this chapter, you should be able to:**

- identify the main sources of finance available to a business and explain the advantages and disadvantages of each;
- outline the ways in which share capital may be issued;
- explain the role and nature of the Stock Exchange;
- discuss the ways in which smaller businesses may seek to raise finance.

 *Remember to create your own personalised Study Plan*

## Sources of finance

When considering the various sources of finance available to a business, it is useful to distinguish between *internal* and *external* sources. By internal sources we mean sources that do not require the agreement of anyone beyond the directors and managers of the business. Thus, retained profits are considered an internal source because the directors of the business have power to retain profits without the agreement of the shareholders, whose profits they are. Finance from an issue of new shares, on the other hand, is an external source because it requires the compliance of potential shareholders.

Within each of the two categories just described, we can further distinguish between *long-term* and *short-term* sources of finance. There is no agreed definition concerning each of these terms but, for the purpose of this chapter, long-term sources of finance are defined as those that are expected to provide finance for at least one year. Short-term sources typically provide finance for a shorter period. As we shall see, sources that are seen as short-term when first used by the business often end up being used for quite long periods.

We shall begin the chapter by considering the various sources of internal finance available. We shall then go on to look at the various sources of external finance. This is probably an appropriate order since, in practice, businesses tend to look first to internal sources before going outside when they need to raise new funds.

## Sources of internal finance

Internal sources of finance usually have the advantage that they are flexible. They may also be obtained quickly – particularly from working capital sources – and need not require the compliance of other parties. The main sources of internal funds are described below and are summarised in Figure 11.1.

## Long-term sources of internal finance

### Retained profits

Retained profits (or earnings) are an important source of finance for most businesses. If profits are retained within the business rather than being distributed to shareholders in the form of dividends, the funds of the business are increased.

**Figure 11.1 The major sources of internal finance**

The major long-term source of internal finance is the profits that are retained rather than distributed to shareholders. The major short-term sources of internal finance involve reducing the level of trade receivables and inventories and increasing the level of trade payables.

## Activity 11.1

Are retained profits a free source of finance to the business?

It is tempting to think that retained profits are a cost-free source of funds for a business. However, this is not the case. If profits are reinvested rather than distributed to shareholders in cash, those shareholders cannot invest this cash in other forms of investment. They will therefore expect a rate of return from the profits reinvested that is equivalent to what they would have received had the funds been invested in another opportunity with the same level of risk.

The reinvestment of profits can be a useful way of raising capital from ordinary share investors.

An obvious alternative way to increase equity investment is to issue new shares. When issuing new shares, however, the issue costs may be substantial and there may be uncertainty over the success of the issue. We shall look at these two problem areas later in the chapter. There are no issue costs associated with retaining profits. Also, the amount raised is certain, once the profits have been made.

Retaining profits will have no effect on the extent to which existing shareholders control the business, whereas when new shares are issued to outside investors there will be some dilution of control.

The decision to retain profits rather than pay them out as dividends to the shareholders is made by the directors. They may find it easier simply to retain profits rather than ask investors to subscribe to a new share issue. Retained profits are already held by the business; it does not have to wait to receive the funds. Moreover, there is often less scrutiny when profits are being retained for reinvestment purposes than when new shares are being issued. Investors and their advisers will closely examine the reasons for any new share issue. A problem with the use of profits as a source of finance, however, is that the timing and level of future profits cannot always be reliably predicted.

Some shareholders may prefer profits to be retained by the business, rather than be distributed in the form of dividends. If profits are ploughed back, it may be expected that the business will expand, and that share values will increase, as a result. An important reason for preferring profits to be retained is the effect of taxation on the shareholder. In the UK, dividends are treated as income for tax purposes and, therefore, attract income tax. Gains on the sale of shares attract capital gains tax. Generally, capital gains tax bites less hard than income tax. A further advantage of capital gains over dividends is that the shareholder has a choice as to when to sell the shares and realise the gain. In the UK, it is only when the gain is realised that capital gains tax comes into play. Research indicates that investors may be attracted to particular businesses according to the dividend/retention policies that they adopt.

It would be wrong to get the impression that all businesses either retain all of their profits or pay them all out as dividends. Where businesses pay dividends, and most of the larger ones do pay dividends, they typically pay no more than 50 per cent of the profit, retaining the remainder to fund expansion.

Retained profits are much the most important source of new finance for UK businesses, on average, in terms of value of funds raised.

## Short-term sources of internal finance

We saw in Chapter 5, in the context of the statement of cash flows, that increases and decreases in the working capital items will have a direct and immediate effect on cash. Thus, decreasing levels of trade receivables and inventories and increasing trade payables are, in effect, ways of raising finance that can be used elsewhere in the business.

### Tighter credit control

By exerting tighter control over amounts owed by credit customers, it may be possible for a business to reduce the proportion of assets held in this form and so release funds for other purposes. Having funds tied up in trade receivables represents an opportunity cost in that those funds could be used for profit-generating activities. It is important, however, to weigh the benefits of tighter credit control against the likely costs in the form of lost customer goodwill and lost sales. To remain competitive, a business must take account of the needs of its customers and the credit policies adopted by rival businesses within the industry. We shall consider this further in Chapter 12.

## Activity 11.2

Rusli Ltd provides a car valet service for car-hire businesses when their cars are returned from hire. The business has a large overdraft and the bank is pressing Rusli Ltd to reduce this. The business sees reducing the level of its investment in trade receivables as one possible way to reduce the overdraft.

Details of the car valet service costs are as follows:

|  | Per car £ |
|---|---|
| Car valet charge | 20 |
| Variable cost | (14) |
| Fixed cost | (4) |
| Profit | 2 |

Sales revenue is £10 million a year and is all on credit. The average credit period taken by Rusli Ltd's customers is 45 days, although the terms of credit state that payment should be made within 30 days. Bad debts are currently £100,000 a year. The bank overdraft has an interest rate of 10 per cent a year.

Rusli Ltd's credit control department believes it can reduce the average credit period to 30 days if new credit control procedures are implemented. These procedures should also completely eliminate bad debts. These procedures will cost £50,000 a year and are likely to result in a loss of business leading to a reduction in sales revenue of 5 per cent a year.

On the basis of cost, should Rusli Ltd implement the new credit control procedures? (*Hint*: To answer this activity it is useful to compare the current cost of trade credit with the costs under the proposed approach.)

The current annual cost of trade credit is:

|  | £ |
|---|---|
| Bad debts | 100,000 |
| Overdraft interest ((£10m × 45/365) × 10%) | 123,288 |
|  | 223,288 |

The annual cost of trade credit under the new policy would be:

|  | £ |
|---|---|
| Overdraft interest ((95% × £10m × (30/365)) × 10%) | 78,082 |
| Cost of control procedures | 50,000 |
| Net cost of lost sales ((£10m × 5%) × 0.3*) | 150,000 |
|  | 278,082 |

* The loss will be the contribution per £ of sales revenue (that is, (sales revenue per unit − variable cost per unit)/sales revenue per unit = (20 − 14)/20 = 0.3).

These calculations show that the business will be worse off if the new policies are adopted.

## Reducing inventories levels

Reducing the level of inventories is an internal source of funds that may prove attractive to a business. If the business has a proportion of its assets in the form of inventories there is an opportunity cost, as the funds tied up cannot be used for other purposes. By reducing inventories, funds become available for those opportunities. However, a business must try to ensure that there are sufficient inventories available to meet likely future sales demand. Failure to do so will result in lost customer good-will and lost sales revenue.

The nature and condition of the inventories held will determine whether it is possible to exploit this form of finance. A business may have excess inventories as a result of poor buying decisions. This may mean that a significant proportion of the inventories held are slow-moving or obsolete and cannot, therefore, be reduced easily. These issues will be picked up again in Chapter 12.

## Delaying payment to trade payables

By providing a period of credit, suppliers are in effect offering a business an interest-free loan. If the business delays payment, the period of the 'loan' is extended and funds can be retained within the business. This can be a cheap form of finance for a business, though this is not always the case. If a business fails to pay within the agreed credit period, there may be significant costs. For example, the business may find it difficult to buy on credit when it has a reputation as a slow payer. This too will be picked up again in Chapter 12.

## The practicality of raising funds from working capital

These so-called short-term sources are short-term to the extent that they can be reversed at short notice. For example, a reduction in the level of trade receivables can be reversed within a couple of weeks. Typically, however, once a business has established a reduced receivable collection period, a reduced inventories turnover period and/or an expanded payables payment period, it will tend to maintain these new levels.

As we shall see in Chapter 12, for the typical business, the level of funds involved with the working capital items is vast. This means that substantial amounts of funds can be raised through exercising tighter control of trade receivables and inventories and by exploiting opportunities to delay payment to trade payables.

## Sources of external finance

Figure 11.2 summarises the main sources of long-term and short-term external finance.

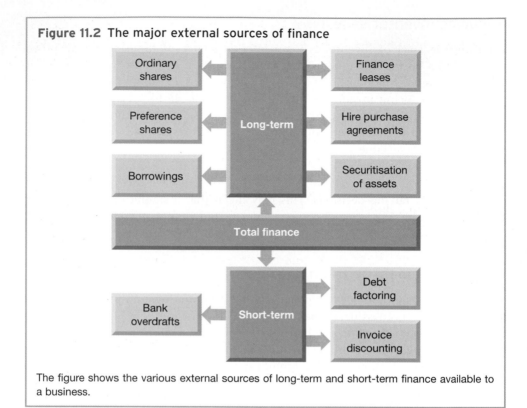

**Figure 11.2 The major external sources of finance**

The figure shows the various external sources of long-term and short-term finance available to a business.

## Long-term sources of external finance

As Figure 11.2 shows, the major forms of long-term external finance are

- ordinary shares
- preference shares
- borrowings
- finance leases, including sale-and-leaseback arrangements
- hire-purchase agreements
- securitisation of assets.

We shall now discuss each of the sources identified.

### Ordinary shares

As we saw in Chapter 4, ordinary shares form the backbone of the financial structure of the business. Ordinary share capital represents the business's risk capital. There is no fixed rate of dividend and ordinary shareholders can receive a dividend only if profits available for distribution still remain after other investors (preference shareholders and lenders, if any) have received their dividend or interest payments. If the business is wound up, the ordinary shareholders will receive any proceeds from asset disposals only after any lenders (including trade payables) and preference shareholders have received their entitlements. Because of the high risks associated with this form of investment, ordinary shareholders will normally require a comparatively high rate of return.

Although ordinary shareholders have a potential loss liability that is limited to the amount that they have invested or agreed to invest, the potential returns from their investment are unlimited. In other words, their downside risk is limited whereas their upside potential is not. Ordinary shareholders have control over the business, through their voting rights. This gives them the power both to elect the directors and to remove them from office.

From the business's (existing shareholders') perspective, ordinary shares can be an attractive form of financing, relative to borrowing. At times, it can be useful to be able to avoid paying a dividend. It is not usually possible to avoid paying interest on borrowings.

## Activity 11.3

Under what circumstances might a business find it useful to avoid paying a dividend?

We feel that there are two main situations where this would apply:

- An expanding business may prefer to retain funds to help fuel future growth.
- A business in difficulties may need the funds to meet its operating costs and so may find making a dividend payment a real burden.

Real World 11.1 looks at the attitude of one well-known businessman to paying dividends.

## Real World 11.1

### No frills, no dividends and no brains

Michael O'Leary, the colourfully-spoken chief executive of the 'no frills' airline Ryanair Holdings plc, was very clear on his attitude to dividends. He said, 'We are never paying a dividend as long as I live and breathe and as long as I'm the largest shareholder. If you are stupid enough to invest in an airline for its dividend flow you should be put back in the loony bin where you came from.'

It is not necessarily the case that Ryanair is expanding at a rate that eats up all available finances. According to its 2009 statement of financial position, the business has a vast amount of cash. The 2009 annual report reasserted Ryanair's intention not to pay a dividend. Nevertheless, a dividend for €500m was eventually paid in October 2010.

*Sources*: Osborne, A., 'Ryanair blunted by Buzz takeover', *Daily Telegraph*, 6 August 2004; Ryanair Holdings plc Annual Report 2009.

Although a business financed by ordinary shares can avoid making cash payments to shareholders when it is not prudent to do so, the market value of the shares may go down. The cost to the business of financing through ordinary shares may become higher if shareholders feel uncertain about future dividends. On the other hand, for a business like Ryanair, which was clearly expanding its operations in a profitable way, share prices are likely to reflect this despite the lack of dividends.

It should be noted that the business does not obtain any tax relief on dividends paid to shareholders, whereas interest on borrowings is tax-deductible. This makes it more expensive to the business to pay £1 of dividend than £1 of interest on borrowings.

## Preference shares

Preference shares offer investors a lower level of risk than ordinary shares. Provided there are sufficient profits available, preference shares will normally be given a fixed rate of dividend each year. Preference shareholders will be paid the first slice of any dividend paid. Should the business be wound up, preference shareholders usually have priority over the claims of ordinary shareholders. (The business's own particular documents of incorporation will state the precise rights of preference shareholders in this respect.)

### Activity 11.4

**Would you expect the returns on preference shares to be higher or lower than those of ordinary shares?**

Preference shareholders will expect to receive a lower level of return than ordinary share-holders. This is because of the lower level of risk associated with this form of investment (preference shareholders have priority over ordinary shareholders regarding dividends).

Preference shares are no longer an important source of new finance. A major reason for this is that dividends paid to preference shareholders, like those paid to ordinary shareholders, are not allowable against taxable profits, whereas interest on borrowings is an allowable expense. From the business's point of view, preference shares and borrowings are quite similar, so the tax-deductibility of interest on borrowings is an important issue. Also, over recent years interest rates on borrowing have been at historically low levels.

### Activity 11.5

**Would you expect the market price of ordinary shares or of preference shares to be the more volatile? Why?**

The share price, which reflects the expected future returns from the share, will normally be less volatile for preference shares than for ordinary shares. The dividends of preference shares tend to be fairly stable over time. Also, there is usually an upper limit on the returns that can be received.

Both preference shares and ordinary shares are, in effect, *redeemable*. The business is allowed to buy back the shares from shareholders at any time.

## Borrowings

Most businesses rely on borrowings as well as equity to finance operations. Lenders enter into a contract with the business in which the rate of interest, dates of interest payments, capital repayments and security for the borrowings are clearly stated. Should interest payments or capital repayments not be made on the due dates, the lender will usually have the right, under the terms of the contract, to seize the assets on which their loan is secured and sell them in order to repay the amount outstanding. Security for a loan may take the form of a fixed charge on particular assets of the borrowing business (land and buildings are often favoured by lenders) or a floating charge on the whole of its assets. A floating charge will 'float' over the assets and will only fix on particular assets in the event that the business defaults on its borrowing obligations. Precisely which assets the charge will fix on is usually at the choice of the unpaid lender.

### Activity 11.6

**What do you think is the advantage for the business of having a floating charge rather than a fixed charge on its assets?**

A floating charge on assets allows the managers greater flexibility in their day-to-day operations than a fixed charge. Individual assets can be sold without reference to the lenders.

### Term loans

A term loan is a type of borrowing offered by banks and other financial institutions, which is usually tailored to the needs of the client business. The amount borrowed, the time period, the repayment terms and the interest payable are all open to negotiation and agreement, which can be very useful. For example, where all of the funds to be borrowed are not required immediately, a business may agree with the lender that funds are drawn only as and when required. This means that interest will be paid only on amounts drawn and so the business will not have to pay interest on amounts borrowed that are temporarily surplus to requirements. Term loans tend to be cheap to set up (from the borrower business's perspective) and can be quite flexible as to conditions. For these reasons they tend to be popular in practice.

### Loan notes (or loan stock)

Another form of long-term borrowing is through loan notes (or loan stock). Loan notes are frequently divided into units (rather like share capital) and investors are invited to purchase the number of units they require. They may be redeemable or irredeemable. Loan notes of public limited companies are often traded on the Stock Exchange, and their listed value will fluctuate according to the fortunes of the business, movements in interest rates and so on.

Loan notes are usually referred to as *bonds* in the US and increasingly also in the UK. Real World 11.2 describes how Manchester United made a bond issue that, though fully taken up by investors, lost them money within the first two weeks. There are fears that this may make it difficult for the club to raise future funds through a bond issue.

---

**Real World 11.2**

## Manchester United loses heavily

Manchester United may be battling to retain the Premier League title but success on the pitch has worked little magic in the City. The club's first bond issue, launched barely two weeks ago, has become one of the market's worst performers this year.

While the club has secured the £500m funding that it needs to refinance its bank debt, the paper losses suffered by investors could affect its ability to return to bond markets.

If an investor had bought a £100,000 bond, he would have made a paper loss of £5,000. Analysts suggested the bonds had been priced too highly at launch and cited the lack of a credit rating.

Other recent issues that have fallen have not declined as heavily. 'In a benign credit market, Manchester United is one of the worst performing bonds since the beginning of 2009,' said Suki Mann, credit strategist at Société Générale.

While the club could issue more debt by increasing the size of the outstanding bond, people close to Manchester United said a return to the market was 'not on the agenda' and that the priority was to placate fans angered by the bond issue and plans by the Glazer family, United's US-based owners, to start paying down 'payment-in-kind' loans with club proceeds. The club declined to comment.

*Source*: adapted from 'Man Utd's first bond suffers from lack of support', *The Financial Times*, 03/02/2010 (Sakou, A. and Blitz, R.), copyright © The Financial Times Ltd.

---

### Eurobonds

 Eurobonds are unsecured loan notes denominated in a currency other than the home currency of the business that issued them. Eurobonds are issued by businesses (and other large organisations) in various countries, and the finance is raised on an international basis. They are often denominated in US dollars, but many are issued in other major currencies. Interest is normally paid annually. Eurobonds are part of an ever-expanding international capital market, and they are not subject to regulations imposed by authorities in particular countries. Numerous financial institutions throughout the world have created a market for eurobonds, where holders of eurobonds are able to sell them to would-be holders. The business issuing the eurobonds usually makes them available to large banks and other financial institutions, which may either retain them as an investment or sell them to their clients.

The extent of borrowing by UK businesses in currencies other than sterling has expanded massively in recent years. Businesses are often attracted to issuing eurobonds because of the size of the international capital market. Access to a large number of international investors is likely to increase the chances of a successful issue.

In addition, the lack of regulation in the eurobond market means that national restrictions regarding loan notes issues may be overcome.

Real World 11.3 provides an example of eurobond financing by a well-known business.

---

**Real World 11.3**

## Eurobonds taking off

British Airways had eurobond financing totalling £248 million at 31 March 2009. This represented 8 per cent of the business's borrowings.

*Source*: British Airways plc Annual Report 2009.

---

**Activity 11.7**

**Would you expect the returns to lenders to be higher or lower than those to preference shareholders?**

Lenders are usually prepared to accept a lower rate of return. This is because they will normally view loans as being less risky than preference shares. Lenders have priority over any claims from preference shareholders. Also, they usually have security for their loans.

---

The risk/return characteristics of borrowing, preference share financing and ordinary share financing (from the investor's point of view) are shown graphically in Figure 11.3. Note that from the viewpoint of the business (the existing shareholders) the level of risk associated with each form of finance is in reverse order. Thus, borrowing is the most risky because it exposes shareholders to the legally enforceable obligation to make regular interest payments and, usually, repayment of the amount borrowed.

### Interest rates

Interest rates on borrowings may be either floating or fixed. A floating rate means that the rate of return required by lenders will rise and fall with market rates of interest. However, the market value of the lender's investment in the business is likely to remain fairly stable over time. The converse will normally be true for fixed-interest borrowings. The interest payments will remain unchanged with rises and falls in market rates of interest, but the value of the lender's investment will fall when interest rates rise and will rise when interest rates fall.

### Convertible loan notes

Convertible loan notes (or convertible bonds) give investors the right, but not the obligation, to exchange the loan notes for ordinary shares in the business at a specified price (the 'exercise' price) on a given future specified date or within a range of specified

**Figure 11.3** The risk/return characteristics of long-term financing

The higher the level of risk associated with a particular form of long-term finance, the higher will be the returns expected by investors. From the investor's point of view, ordinary shares are the most risky and have the highest expected return, and, as a general rule, borrowing is the least risky and has the lowest expected return.

dates. The exercise price is usually higher than the market price of those ordinary shares at the time of issue of the convertible loan notes. In effect, the investor swaps the loan notes for a particular number of shares. The investor remains a lender to the business, and will receive interest on the amount of the loan notes, until such time as the conversion takes place. The investor is not obliged to convert the loan notes to ordinary shares. This will be done only if the market price of the shares at the conversion date exceeds the specified conversion price.

An investor may find this form of investment a useful hedge against risk. This may be particularly useful when investment in a new business is being considered. Initially, the investment is in the form of a loan and regular interest payments will be made. If the business is successful, the investor can then decide to benefit from the success by converting the investment into ordinary shares.

The business may also find this form of financing useful. If the business is successful, the borrowings become self-liquidating (no cash payment is required), as investors will exercise their option to convert. The business may also be able to offer a lower rate of interest to investors because they expect future benefits to arise from conversion. There will be, however, some dilution of both control and earnings for existing shareholders if holders of convertible loan notes exercise their option to convert.

Real World 11.4 outlines a convertible loan notes (bonds) issue made by Tata Group, the Indian conglomerate. The business is one of the world's largest steel producers (it owns Corus, the UK steel maker). Tata also owns Tetley Tea, Jaguar Cars and Land Rover.

**Real World 11.4**

## Property conversion

In November 2009 Tata Group issued convertible bonds. They will have a 4.5 per cent interest rate. They may be converted into fully paid-up ordinary Tata shares. They will be convertible on 21 November 2014 (five years after issue) at a price of 605.53 rupees a share. The conversion share price is 15 per cent above the share price on the date of the issue of the bonds.

*Source*: information taken from 'Tata Steel to switch 56 per cent of securities into convertible bonds', www.tata.com.

Convertibles are an example of a financial derivative. This is any form of financial instrument, based on equity or loans/borrowings, that can be used by investors to increase their returns or reduce risk.

### Mortgages

A mortgage is a form of borrowing that is secured on an asset, typically land. Financial institutions such as banks, insurance businesses and pension funds are often prepared to lend to businesses on this basis. The mortgage may be over a long period (twenty years or more).

### Loan covenants

Lenders often impose certain obligations and restrictions on borrowers in an attempt to protect their loan. Loan covenants (as they are called) often form part of a loan agreement, and may deal with such matters as:

- *Financial statements.* The lender may require access to the financial statements of the borrowing business on a regular basis.
- *Other borrowings.* The lender may require the business to ask the lender's permission before borrowing further from other sources.
- *Dividend payments.* The lender may require dividend payments to be limited during the period of the loan.
- *Liquidity.* The lender may require the business to maintain a certain level of liquidity during the period of the loan. This would typically be a requirement that the borrower business's current ratio is maintained at, or above, a specified level.

Any breach of these restrictive covenants can have serious consequences for the business. The lender may require immediate repayment of the loan in the event of a material breach.

Real World 11.5 relates to EMI Group Ltd, the music business, which is owned by Terra Firma Capital Partners, a private equity fund, run by Guy Hands. It shows how, in early 2010, EMI was fighting to avoid breaching the loan covenants imposed by its lenders. The business was particularly hard hit by the recession and by the fact that much of its borrowings were in US dollars and in euros.

## Real World 11.5

### EMI to face the music about loan covenants

EMI's accountants have raised 'significant doubt' about its ability to continue as a going concern in a report that lays bare the parlous state of Terra Firma's £4.2bn ($6.6bn) investment in the music group behind Katy Perry and the Beatles.

Guy Hands, Terra Firma's founder and chairman, has asked investors in two of its private equity funds to inject another £120m. He must come up with the money by June 14 or risk losing the company to Citigroup, his bankers.

But accounts for the year to March 2009, released yesterday, make clear that even if Terra Firma secures this equity, it will face another 'significant shortfall' against a test on covenants in its loans by March 2011.

Unless it can persuade Citi to restructure its £3.2bn in loans by then, investors face further cash calls. Terra Firma spent £105m to make up shortfalls against the quarterly covenant tests last year but has less than £10m left for future payments.

Directors of Maltby Capital [a subsidiary of Terra Firma], the vehicle that bought EMI just before credit markets collapsed in 2007, said there was no certainty that investors would put new equity into an investment that Terra Firma has already written down by 90 per cent.

Maltby's directors said they had 'a reasonable expectation' that the group could continue as a going concern, in a report that showed interest costs and impairment charges wiping out operational improvements.

Pre-tax losses for the year to March 2009 widened to £1.7bn, against a £414m loss for the previous period, which covered the first eight months and 21 days of Terra Firma's ownership.

Maltby booked a £1.04bn impairment charge, of which two-thirds fell on the more stable music publishing arm which had accounted for two-thirds of the group's original valuation.

The bottom line was also hit by £279m in interest payments and £297m of foreign exchange losses on its borrowings.

*Source*: adapted from '"Significant doubt" over EMI's viability', *The Financial Times*, 05/02/2010 (Edgecliffe-Johnson, A. and Davoudi, S.), copyright © The Financial Times Ltd.

## Activity 11.8

Both preference shares and loan notes are forms of finance whose holders expect the business to provide a particular rate of return. What are the factors that may be taken into account by a business when deciding between these two sources of finance?

The main factors are as follows:

■ Preference shares tend to have a higher rate of return than loan notes. From the investor's point of view, preference shares are more risky. The amount invested cannot be secured, and the return is paid after the returns paid to lenders.

■ A business has a legal obligation to pay interest and, typically, make capital repayments on loan notes at the agreed dates. It will usually make every effort to meet its obligations because failure to do so can have serious consequences. (These consequences have been mentioned earlier.) Failure to pay a preference dividend, on the other hand, is less important. There is no legal obligation to pay if profits are not available for distribution. Failure to pay a preference dividend may prove an embarrassment for the business, however, because it may make it difficult to persuade investors to take up future preference share issues.

■ It was mentioned above that the taxation system in the UK permits interest on borrowing to be allowable against profits for taxation, whereas preference dividends are not. As a result, the cost of servicing borrowings is, pound for pound, usually much lower for a business than the cost of servicing preference shares.

■ The issue of loan notes may result in the management of a business having to accept some restrictions on its freedom of action. We saw earlier that borrowing agreements often contain covenants that can be onerous. Preference shareholders can impose no such restrictions.

A further point is that preference shares issued form part of the permanent capital base of the business. If they are redeemed, the law requires that they be replaced, either by a new issue of shares or by a transfer from revenue reserves, so that the business's capital base stays intact. Borrowings, however, are not viewed in law as part of the business's permanent capital base, and therefore there is no legal requirement to replace any loan notes that have been redeemed.

## Finance leases and sale-and-leaseback arrangements

When a business needs a particular asset (for example, an item of plant), instead of buying it direct from a supplier, the business may decide to arrange for another business (typically a bank) to buy it and then lease it to the first business. The business that owns the asset and leases it out is known as a 'lessor'. The one that uses it is known as the 'lessee'.

 A finance lease, as such an arrangement is known, is, in essence, a form of lending. This is because, had the lessee borrowed the funds and then used them to buy the asset itself, the effect would be much the same. The lessee would have use of the asset, but have a financial obligation to the lender – much the same position as the leasing arrangement would lead to.

With finance leasing, legal ownership of the asset rests with the financial institution (the lessor); however, the lease agreement transfers to the user (the lessee) virtually all the rewards and risks that are associated with the item being leased. The finance lease agreement covers a significant part of the life of the item being leased, and often cannot be cancelled.

Finance leasing is a very important source of finance for UK businesses. The Finance and Leasing Association estimates that 28 per cent of finance for non-current assets (excluding land and buildings) comes from finance leasing.

Real World 11.6 gives an example of the use of finance leasing in a leading airline business.

417

---

**Real World 11.6**

## BA's leased assets are taking off

Many airline businesses use finance leasing as a means of acquiring new aeroplanes. The financial statements for British Airways plc (BA) for the year ended 31 March 2009 show that 33 per cent (totalling £2,004 million) of the net carrying amount of its fleet of aircraft had been acquired through this method.

*Source*: British Airways plc Annual Report 2009, p. 98.

---

A finance lease can be contrasted with an operating lease, where the rewards and risks of ownership stay with the owner and where the lease is short-term. An example of an operating lease is where a builder hires some earthmoving equipment for a week to carry out a particular job.

Finance leasing grew greatly in popularity in the UK during the 1970s and 1980s. At that time, there were some important benefits associated with finance leasing. These included a favourable tax treatment and the fact that such financing arrangements did not have to be disclosed on the statement of financial position. More recently these benefits have disappeared. Changes in UK tax law mean that it is no longer such a tax-efficient form of financing, and changes in accounting disclosure requirements mean that businesses are no longer allowed to conceal this form of 'borrowing' from investors. Nevertheless, the popularity of finance leases has continued. Other reasons must therefore exist for businesses to adopt this form of financing. These reasons are said to include the following:

- *Ease of borrowing*. Leasing may be obtained more easily than other forms of long-term finance. Lenders normally require some form of security and a profitable track record before making advances to a business. However, a lessor may be prepared to lease assets to a new business without a track record. It can use the leased assets as security for the amounts owing.
- *Cost*. Leasing agreements may be offered at reasonable cost. As the asset leased is used as security, standard lease arrangements can be applied and detailed credit checking of lessees may be unnecessary. This can reduce administrative costs for the lessor, and thereby help in providing competitive lease rentals.
- *Flexibility*. Leasing can help provide flexibility where there are rapid changes in technology. If an option to cancel can be incorporated into the lease, the business may be able to exercise this option and invest in new technology as it becomes available. This will help the business to avoid the risk of obsolescence.
- *Cash flows*. Leasing, rather than purchasing an asset outright, means that large cash outflows can be avoided. The leasing option allows cash outflows to be smoothed out over the asset's life. In some cases, it is possible to arrange for low lease payments to be made in the early years of the asset's life, when cash inflows may be low, and for these to increase over time as the asset generates positive cash flows.

Real World 11.7 provides some impression of the importance of finance leasing over recent years.

## Real World 11.7

### A new lease. . . .

The amount of asset finance provided through finance leasing by members of the Finance and Leasing Association has slightly increased over the period from 2004 to 2008 (see Figure 11.4).

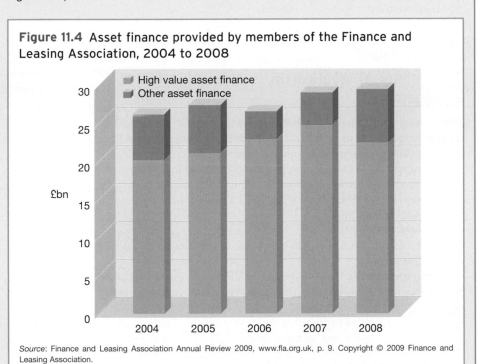

**Figure 11.4** Asset finance provided by members of the Finance and Leasing Association, 2004 to 2008

*Source*: Finance and Leasing Association Annual Review 2009, www.fla.org.uk, p. 9. Copyright © 2009 Finance and Leasing Association.

A sale-and-leaseback arrangement involves a business raising finance by selling an asset to a financial institution. The sale is accompanied by an agreement to lease the asset back to the business to allow it to continue to use the asset. The lease payment is allowable against profits for taxation purposes. There are usually reviews at regular intervals throughout the period of the lease. Thus the amounts payable in future years may be difficult to predict. At the end of the lease agreement, the business must try either to renew the lease or to find an alternative asset. Although the sale of the asset will result in an immediate injection of cash for the business, the business will lose benefits from any future capital appreciation on the asset. Where a capital gain arises on the sale of the asset to the financial institution, a liability for taxation may also arise. Freehold property is often the asset that is the subject of such an arrangement. Many of the well-known UK high street retailers (for example, Boots, Debenhams, Marks and Spencer, Sainsbury and Tesco) have recently sold off some of their store sites under sale-and-leaseback arrangements.

A sale-and-leaseback agreement can be used to help a business focus on its core areas of competence. In recent years, many hotel businesses have entered into sale-and-leaseback agreements to enable them to become purely hotel operators rather than a combination of hotel operators and owners.

Real World 11.8 is a *Financial Times* article that explains how Woolworths' sale-and-leaseback arrangements contributed to the collapse of the business.

---

### Real World 11.8

## The wonder of Woolworths' sale and leaseback arrangements

At Woolworths' annual meeting this summer a perennially cheerful Trevor Bish-Jones cut a rather forlorn figure as he told his audience that making '£3bn of [group] sales for £30m of net profit is hard work this side of the fence'.

The imperturbable chief executive could be forgiven for feeling a little sorry for himself: Mr Bish-Jones had just been ousted from the variety retailer having laboured for six-and-a-half years to keep Woolworths afloat under the weight of rising rents, shabby stores and an outdated business model.

This week the fight to save the much-loved but very under-shopped Woolworths chain finally drew to a close as the 800 stores and the wholesale distribution arm were placed into administration.

Having limped along for seven years, with the profit line gradually shifting from black to red, the directors finally called it a day after the retailer, labouring under £385m ($591m) of debt, succumbed to a cash crisis.

But how did it come to pass that the near 100-year-old chain, which in its heyday was opening a store a week and was still selling £1.7bn of goods a year through its stores at the time of its collapse, should end up in such a dire predicament?

Those close to Woolworths place this week's collapse firmly at the feet of those who de-merged the retailer from Kingfisher in August 2001.

They argue that the decision to carry out a sale-and-leaseback deal for 182 Woolworths stores in return for £614m of cash – paid back to Kingfisher shareholders – crippled the chain.

For in return for the princely price tag, Woolworths was saddled with onerous leases that guaranteed the landlords a rising income stream.

One person who knows Woolworths well says the rent bill rose from £70m a decade ago to £160m today.

'There is no doubt that back in 2001, with the de-merger and the sale of these stores, the company was saddled with a huge amount of quasi debt in terms of these leases,' says one former adviser. 'I think probably that is really where this goes back to. If Woolworths had more financial flexibility they might have been able to do more of the stuff they needed to. . . . To build a sustainable business requires investment but they were not in a position to incur more costs.'

Tony Shiret, analyst at Credit Suisse, says Woolworths' lease-adjusted debt was the highest in the retail sector. 'They didn't really have enough cash flow to cover debt repayments.'

*Source:* 'Seeds of Woolworths' demise sown long ago', *The Financial Times*, 29/11/2008 (Rigby, E.), copyright © The Financial Times Ltd.

## Hire purchase

→ Hire purchase is a form of credit used to buy an asset. Under the terms of a hire purchase (HP) agreement, a customer pays for an asset by instalments over an agreed period. Normally, the customer will pay an initial deposit (down payment) and then make instalment payments at regular intervals (perhaps monthly) until the balance outstanding has been paid. The customer will usually take possession of the asset after payment of the initial deposit, although legal ownership of the asset will not be transferred until the final instalment has been paid.

HP agreements will often involve three parties:

- the supplier,
- the customer, and
- a financial institution.

Although the supplier will deliver the asset to the customer, the financial institution will buy the asset from the supplier and then enter into an HP agreement with the customer. This intermediary role played by the financial institution enables the supplier to receive immediate payment for the asset but allows the customer a period of extended credit. Figure 11.5 sets out the relationship between the three parties in diagrammatic form.

**Figure 11.5 The hire purchase process**

There are usually three parties to a hire purchase agreement. The relationship between these parties is as shown above.

Real World 11.9 describes how one well-known airline operator uses HP to help finance its assets.

**Real World 11.9**

### Flying by instalments

British Airways plc finances some of its aircraft by HP. At 31 March 2009, over 22 per cent (£1,342 million) of the carrying value of its fleet was financed in this way.

*Source*: British Airways plc Annual Report 2009, p. 90.

Generally speaking, HP agreements can be quickly arranged and are readily available (as the financial institution will accept the asset as security). They are similar to finance leases in so far that they allow a customer to obtain possession of the asset, without first paying its full cost. Under the terms of an HP agreement, however, the customer will eventually become the legal owner of the asset, whereas under the terms of a finance lease, ownership will stay with the lessor. HP is probably a more common source of finance among smaller businesses. The British Airways plc example shows, however, that larger businesses also use this source.

## Securitisation

Where a business expects to receive a stream of positive future cash flows, it effectively owns an asset (whose value is the (discounted) present value of those cash flows). An example of such a stream is the monthly repayments, made by those who borrowed money to buy their homes, to a mortgage lender. It is possible for the mortgage lender to raise funds on the basis of these expected future cash receipts by bundling them together to provide asset backing for the issue of bonds to investors (a process known  as securitisation).

Securitising mortgage loan repayments became popular among US mortgage lenders during the early years of the 2000s. The monthly repayments were 'securitised' and sold to many of the major banks, particularly in the US. Unfortunately, many of the mortgage loans were made to people on low incomes who were not good credit risks (sub-prime loans). When the borrowers started to default on their obligations, it became clear that the securities, now owned by the banks, were worth much less than the banks had paid the mortgage lenders for them. This led to the so-called 'sub-prime' crisis that triggered the worldwide economic problems that emerged during 2008.

There is no inherent reason for securitisation to be a problem and it is unfortunate that the practice is linked with the sub-prime crisis. It is a perfectly legitimate and practical way for a business to raise finance.

Real World 11.10 shows that securitisation of household mortgage loans is not restricted to the United States. It is generally believed, however, that the UK securitised mortgage loans are not quite as toxic as some of their US counterparts.

---

**Real World 11.10**

### Banking on bonds

Securitisation of mortgage loans has become an important means of raising finance by UK banks. However, there is a wide variation in the use of this form of finance between the leading banks.

At one end of the scale, HSBC, RBS and Barclays have issued relatively few mortgage-backed bonds. But HBOS, the biggest mortgage lender, funds 17 per cent of all lending with securitisation. Abbey National uses securitisation for 22 per cent of its mortgage lending. Northern Rock used securitisation to fund 57 per cent of its loan book, according to Deutsche Bank data. Following a crisis in the money markets in August 2007, banks found it almost impossible to sell any mortgage-backed bonds. It is clear, however, that some banks will have suffered more than others as a result.

*Source*: adapted from 'King fails to soothe lenders', *The Financial Times*, 23/01/2008 (Strauss, D.), copyright © The Financial Times Ltd.

# Gearing and long-term financing decisions

In Chapter 6 we saw that financial gearing (known as 'leverage' in the US) occurs when a business is financed, at least in part, by contributions from fixed-charge capital (preference shares and borrowings). We also saw that the level of gearing associated with a business is often an important factor in assessing the risk and returns to ordinary shareholders. In Example 11.1, we consider the implications of gearing when raising new long-term finance.

## Example 11.1

The following are the summarised financial statements of Woodhall Engineers plc.

**Woodhall Engineers plc**
**Income statement for the year ended 31 December**

|  | Year 1 | Year 2 |
|---|---|---|
|  | £m | £m |
| Revenue | 47 | 50 |
| Operating costs | (42) | (48) |
| Operating profit | 5 | 2 |
| Interest payable | (1) | (1) |
| Profit before tax | 4 | 1 |
| Taxation | – | – |
| Profit for the year | 4 | 1 |

**Statement of financial position as at 31 December**

|  | Year 1 | Year 2 |
|---|---|---|
| ASSETS | £m | £m |
| Non-current assets (less depreciation) | 21 | 20 |
| Current assets |  |  |
| Inventories | 10 | 18 |
| Trade receivables | 16 | 17 |
| Cash at bank | 3 | 1 |
|  | 29 | 36 |
| Total assets | 50 | 56 |

→

**EQUITY AND LIABILITIES**

| | | |
|---|---|---|
| Equity | | |
| Called-up share capital (25p ordinary shares) | 16 | 16 |
| Retained earnings | 4 | 4 |
| | 20 | 20 |
| Non-current liabilities | | |
| Borrowings – long-term loans (secured) | 15 | 15 |
| Current liabilities | | |
| Trade payables | 10 | 10 |
| Short-term borrowings | 5 | 11 |
| | 15 | 21 |
| Total equity and liabilities | 50 | 56 |

The business is making plans to expand its premises. New plant will cost £8 million, and an expansion in output will increase working capital by £4 million. Over the 15 years' life of the project, incremental operating profit arising from the expansion will be £2 million a year. In addition, Year 3's operating profit from its existing activities is expected to return to the Year 1 level.

Two possible methods of financing the expansion have been discussed by Woodhall's directors. The first is the issue of £12 million of 10 per cent loan notes repayable in Year 18. The second is an issue of 40 million 25p ordinary shares, which will give the business cash of 30p per share after expenses.

The business has substantial tax losses, which can be offset against future profits, so taxation can be ignored in the calculations. The Year 3 total dividend is expected to be £1 million if the expansion is financed by loan notes and £1.6 million if the share issue is made.

Woodhall's projected income statements (excluding revenue and operating costs) for the year ended 31 December Year 3, and statements of its equity and number of shares in issue at that date, assuming that the business issues

(a) loan notes
(b) ordinary shares

are to be prepared.

The projected income statements under each financing option will be as follows:

**Projected income statements for the year ended 31 December Year 3**

| | (a) Loan notes issue | (b) Share issue |
|---|---|---|
| | £m | £m |
| Operating profit (5.0 + 2.0) | 7.0 | 7.0 |
| Interest payable | (2.2) | (1.0) |
| Profit before tax | 4.8 | 6.0 |
| Taxation | – | – |
| Profit for the year | 4.8 | 6.0 |

The equity of the business and number of shares in issue under each option as at the end of Year 3 will be as follows:

| | (a) Loan notes issue £m | (b) Share issue £m |
|---|---|---|
| **Equity** | | |
| Share capital (25p ordinary shares) | 16.0 | 26.0 |
| Share premium account* | – | 2.0 |
| Retained earnings† | 7.8 | 8.4 |
| | 23.8 | 36.4 |
| Number of shares in issue (25p shares) | 64 million | 104 million |

* This represents the amount received from the issue of shares that is above the nominal value of the shares. The amount is calculated as follows:

$$40\text{m shares} \times (30p - 25p) = £2m$$

† This is the retained earnings figure after deducting the dividend paid.

### Activity 11.9

Compute Woodhall's interest cover and earnings per share for the year ended 31 December Year 3 and its gearing on that date, assuming that the business issues

(a) loan notes
(b) ordinary shares.

Your answer should be as follows:

| | (a) Loan notes issue | (b) Share issue |
|---|---|---|
| **Interest cover ratio** | | |
| $\dfrac{\text{Operating profit}}{\text{Interest payable}}$ | $=\dfrac{7.0}{2.2}$ | $=\dfrac{7.0}{1.0}$ |
| | = 3.2 times | = 7.0 times |
| **Earnings per share** | | |
| $\dfrac{\text{Earnings available to ordinary shareholders}}{\text{Number of ordinary shares}}$ | $=\dfrac{£4.8m}{64m}$ | $=\dfrac{£6.0m}{104m}$ |
| | = 7.5p | = 5.8p |
| **Gearing ratio** | | |
| $\dfrac{\text{Non-current liabilities}}{\text{Share capital + Reserves + Non-current liabilities}}$ | $=\dfrac{£27m}{£23.8m + £27m}$ | $=\dfrac{£15m}{£36.4m + £15m}$ |
| | = 53.1% | = 29.2% |

**Activity 11.10**

What would your views of the proposed schemes be in each of the following circumstances?

(a) If you were an investor who had been asked to take up some of the loan notes.
(b) If you were an ordinary shareholder in Woodhall and you were asked to subscribe to a share issue.

(a) Investors may be unenthusiastic about lending money to the business. The gearing ratio of 53.1 per cent is rather high, and would leave the loan notes holders in an exposed position. Their existing loan is already secured on the business's assets, and it is not clear whether the business is in a position to offer an attractive form of security for the new loan. The interest cover ratio of 3.2 times is also rather low. If the business is unable to achieve the expected returns from the new project, or if it is unable to restore profits from the remainder of its operations to Year 1 levels, this ratio would be even lower.

(b) Ordinary share investors may need some convincing that it would be worthwhile to make further investments in the business. The return on ordinary shareholders' funds in Year 1 was 20 per cent (£4 million/£20 million). The incremental profit from the new project is £2 million and the investment required is £12 million, which represents a return of 16.7 per cent. Thus, the returns from the project are expected to be lower than for existing operations. In making their decision, investors should discover whether the new investment is of a similar level of risk to their existing investment and how the returns from the investment compare with those available from other opportunities with similar levels of risk.

# Share issues

A business may issue shares in a number of ways. These may involve direct appeals to investors or the use of financial intermediaries. The most common methods of share issues for cash are

- rights issues;
- offers for sale and public issues;
- private placings.

We shall now discuss these methods.

## Rights issues

As we saw in Chapter 4, rights issues are made when businesses that have been established for some time seek to raise additional funds by issuing new shares to their existing shareholders. The funds may be used for expansion, or even to solve a liquidity problem (cash shortage). Company law gives existing shareholders the first right of refusal to buy any new shares issued by a company, so the new shares would be offered to shareholders in proportion to their existing holding. Only where the existing shareholders agree to waive their right could the shares be offered to the investing public generally, at the same time as to the existing shareholders. Rights issues are a relatively popular form of share issue. Over the period 2005 to 2009, for established businesses already listed on the London Stock Exchange, about 55 per cent of funds raised from new share issues were from rights issues, with the exact proportion varying greatly from one year to the next (see reference 1 at the end of the chapter). The business (in effect, the existing shareholders) would typically prefer that existing shareholders buy the shares through a rights issue, irrespective of the legal position. This is for two reasons:

- The ownership (and, therefore, control) of the business remains in the same hands; there is no 'dilution' of control
- The costs of making the issue (which include advertising and complying with various company law requirements) tend to be less if the shares are to be offered to existing shareholders. It is estimated that the average cost of making a rights issue are 5.8 per cent of the funds raised. Since a lot of the cost is fixed, this percentage will be greater or lesser for smaller and larger rights issues, respectively (see reference 2). This compares with up to 11 per cent for an issue to the public (see reference 3).

To encourage existing shareholders to take up their 'rights' to buy some new shares, those shares are always offered at a price below the current market price of the existing ones. The evidence shows that shares are offered at an average 31 per cent below the current pre-rights price (see reference 2).

## Activity 11.11

In Chapter 4 (Example 4.2, page 127) the point was made that issuing new shares at below their current worth was to the advantage of the new shareholders at the expense of the old ones. In view of this, does it matter that rights issues are always made at below the current value of the shares?

Assume that the new shares are all taken up by existing shareholders in proportion to their existing shareholding.

The answer is that it does not matter *in these particular circumstances*, because, in a rights issue, the existing shareholders and the new shareholders are exactly the same people. Moreover, the shareholders will hold the new shares in the same proportion as they currently hold the existing shares. Thus, shareholders will gain on the new shares exactly as much as they lose on the existing ones: in the end, no one is better or worse off as a result of the rights issue being made at a discount.

Calculating the value of the rights offer received by shareholders is quite straightforward, as shown in Example 11.2.

## Example 11.2

Shaw Holdings plc has 20 million ordinary shares of 50p in issue. These shares are currently valued on the Stock Exchange at £1.60 per share. The directors have decided to make a one-for-four issue (that is, one new share for every four shares held) at £1.30 per share.

The first step in the valuation process is to calculate the price of a share following the rights issue. This is known as the *ex-rights price*, and is simply a weighted average of the price of shares before the issue of rights and the price of the rights shares. In this example, we have a one-for-four rights issue. The theoretical ex-rights price is therefore calculated as follows:

|  | £ |
|---|---|
| Price of four shares before the rights issue (4 × £1.60) | 6.40 |
| Price of taking up one rights share | 1.30 |
|  | 7.70 |
| Theoretical ex-rights price = £7.70/5 | = £1.54 |

As the price of each share, in theory, should be £1.54 following the rights issue and the price of a rights share is £1.30, the value of the rights offer will be the difference between the two:

$$£1.54 - £1.30 = £0.24 \text{ per share}$$

Market forces will usually ensure that the actual and theoretical price of rights shares will be fairly close.

## Activity 11.12

An investor with 2,000 shares in Shaw Holdings plc (see Example 11.2) has contacted you for investment advice. She is undecided whether to take up the rights issue, sell the rights or allow the rights offer to lapse.

Calculate the effect on the net wealth of the investor of each of the options being considered.

Before the rights issue the position of the investor was:

|  | £ |
|---|---|
| Value of shares (2,000 × £1.60) | 3,200 |

If she takes up the rights issue, she will be in the following position:

|  | £ |
|---|---|
| Value of holding after rights issue ((2,000 + 500) × £1.54) | 3,850 |
| Cost of buying the rights shares (500 × £1.30) | 650 |
|  | 3,200 |

If she sells the rights, she will be in the following position:

|  | £ |
|---|---|
| Value of holding after rights issue (2,000 × £1.54) | 3,080 |
| Sale of rights (500 × £0.24) | 120 |
|  | 3,200 |

If she lets the rights offer lapse, she will be in the following position:

|  | £ |
|---|---|
| Value of holding after rights issue (2,000 × £1.54) | 3,080 |

As we can see, the first two options should leave her in the same position concerning net wealth as before the rights issue. Before the rights issue she had 2,000 shares worth £1.60 each, or £3,200 in total. However, she will be worse off if she allows the rights offer to lapse than under the other two options.

In practice, businesses will typically sell the rights on behalf of those investors who seem to be allowing them to lapse. They will then pass on the proceeds. This should mean that shareholders are not worse off as a result of the issue, even if they allow the rights offer to lapse.

When considering a rights issue, the directors must first consider the amount of funds needing to be raised. This will depend on the future plans and needs of the business. The directors must then decide on the issue price of the rights shares. Normally, this decision is not critical. In Example 11.2, the business made a one-for-four issue with the price of the rights shares set at £1.30. However, it could have raised the same amount by making a one-for-two issue and setting the rights price at £0.65, a one-for-one issue and setting the price at £0.325, and so on. The issue price that is finally decided upon will not affect the value of the underlying assets of the business or the proportion of the underlying assets and earnings to which each shareholder is entitled. The directors must ensure that the issue price is not above the current market price of the shares, however, or the issue will be unsuccessful.

Real World 11.11 describes how National Express Group plc, a UK-based bus and train operator, made a rights issue to fund repayment of some of its borrowing and thereby reduce its gearing.

### Real World 11.11

## Express issue

In December 2009, National Express made a seven-for-three rights issue that raised £360 million. Shareholders took up 90.47 per cent of the issue. The remaining 9.53 per cent of the shares were placed with other investors. The rights price was at a discount of 70 per cent to the pre-rights announcement price. This was an unusually large discount.

*Sources*: based on information taken from 'Results of the rights issue' press release, National Express Group plc, 15 December 2009, and Plimmer, G., 'National Express £360m rights issue approved', FT.com, 27 November 2009.

## Offers for sale and public issues

→ An offer for sale usually involves a business that trades as a public limited company selling a new issue of shares to a financial institution known as an *issuing house*. However, shares that are already in issue may also be sold to an issuing house. In this case, existing shareholders agree to sell all or some of their shares to the issuing house. The issuing house will, in turn, sell the shares, purchased from either the business or its shareholders, to the public. The issuing house will publish a prospectus that sets out details of the business and the type of shares to be sold, and investors will be invited to apply for shares. The advantage of this type of issue, from the business's viewpoint, is that the sale proceeds of the shares are certain.

→ A public issue involves the business making a direct invitation to the public to purchase its shares. Typically, this is done through a newspaper advertisement. The shares may, once again, be either a new issue or those already in issue. An offer for sale and a public issue will both result in a widening of share ownership in the business.

In practical terms, the net effect on the business is much the same whether there is an offer for sale or a public issue. As we have seen, the administrative costs of a public issue can be very large. Some share issues by Stock Exchange listed businesses arise from the initial listing of the business. Such issues are usually known as *initial public offerings (IPOs)*. Other share issues are undertaken by businesses that are already listed and that are seeking additional finance from investors, usually such issues are known as *seasoned equity offerings (SEOs)*. Public issues are fairly standard for businesses that have just become listed. Public issues by seasoned businesses (SEOs) are relatively rare. Rights issues are a very much more common way for seasoned businesses to raise new equity finance. IPOs have reduced in number since 2007, reflecting a loss of confidence by investors in the economy generally and, probably, in unseasoned businesses in particular (see reference 1 at the end of the chapter). On the other hand, many seasoned businesses have since 2007 sought to raise additional share capital to shore up their finances and to reduce their levels of borrowing, as with National Express in Real World 11.11.

## Private placings

→ A private placing does not involve an invitation to the public to subscribe for shares. Instead the shares are 'placed' with selected investors, such as large financial institutions. This can be a quick and relatively cheap form of raising funds, because savings can be made in advertising and legal costs. However, it can result in the ownership of the business being concentrated in a few hands. Sometimes, unlisted businesses seeking relatively small amounts of cash will make this form of issue.

Real World 11.12 describes how Blacks Leisure Group plc, the outdoor retail business (Blacks, Millets, Freespirit, Peter Storm, Eurohike and so on), used a combination of a placing and an offer for sale to raise finance. The finance was to be used to refurbish existing stores and to open some entirely new ones.

## Placing confidence in Blacks's future

Blacks Leisure, the outdoor sports retailer, is to raise more than £20m in an open offer and placing, to help accelerate plans to open new stores and refurbish existing ones.

'The business has been massively under-invested,' said Neil Gillis, chief executive of Blacks. 'Twenty-five per cent of our stores have had no investment over the past ten years and some of our stores haven't been invested in for fifteen years. We're at the point where investment is going to make a big difference to our business.'

The group, whose stores trade under the Blacks and Millets brands, will split the proceeds from the fundraising equally between opening 35 new stores and refurbishing 130 existing stores.

'If we had been investing in our business healthily over the past ten years, then I think there might be a case [to be made] that we were over-investing, but I don't think that's the case in this situation,' said Mr Gillis.

'There's also lots and lots of towns where we don't have any representation,' said Mr Gillis, who cited Liverpool, Berwick-upon-Tweed and Newmarket as examples.

*Source*: adapted from 'Blacks set to raise £20m in share sale', *The Financial Times*, 05/02/2010 (Doherty, J.), copyright © The Financial Times Ltd.

Placings are now a very popular way of issuing new shares, both by newly listed and more seasoned listed businesses. They have probably accounted for more than 50 per cent of new shares issued until 2007. Since then, rights issues have tended to take centre stage, certainly for issues by seasoned businesses (see reference 1).

## Bonus issues

We should recall from Chapter 4 that a bonus issue is not a means of raising finance. It is simply converting one part of the equity (reserves) into another (ordinary shares). No cash changes hands; this benefits neither the business nor the shareholders.

## The role of the Stock Exchange

Earlier we considered the various forms of long-term capital that are available to a business. In this section we examine the role that the Stock Exchange plays in providing finance for businesses. The Stock Exchange acts as both an important *primary* and *secondary* capital market for businesses. As a primary market, its function is to enable businesses to raise new finance. As a secondary market, its function is to enable investors to sell their securities (including shares and loan notes) with ease. Thus, it provides a 'second-hand' market where shares and loan notes already in issue may be bought and sold.

To enable it to issue shares or loan notes through the Stock Exchange, a business must be 'listed'. Similarly, it must also be Stock Exchange listed before its existing shares and loan notes can be bought and sold there. Listing means that the business must meet fairly stringent requirements concerning size, profit history, information disclosure and so on.

Real World 11.13 explains how new issues tend to be good investments for those who take up the shares concerned.

### Real World 11.13

## Issues are not problems

It seems that taking up IPOs is profitable, relative to the returns available from investing in stock exchange listed shares generally. This emerged from a research exercise that examined 1,735 separate IPOs that took place through the London Stock Exchange during the period 1995 to 2006.

Among other things, the research looked at the performance (increase in share price and dividends, if any) during the 12 months following the date of the new issue. IPO shares fared about 13 per cent better than did the average stock exchange equity investment. In other words, an investor who took up all of the IPOs between 1995 and 2006 and held them for one year would be 13 per cent better off than one who bought shares in a range of other businesses listed on the stock exchange and held them for a year. This is not to say that all IPOs represented a profitable one-year investment. It simply means that the IPO investor would have lost less in those cases than the other investor.

*Source*: Levis, M., *The London Markets and Private Equity-Backed IPOs*, Cass Business School, April 2008.

## Advantages of a listing

The secondary market role of the Stock Exchange means that shares and other financial claims are easily transferable. Furthermore, their prices are constantly under scrutiny by investors and skilled analysts. This helps to bring the price quoted for a particular business's shares in line with their true worth. These factors can bring real benefits to a business.

### Activity 11.13

**What kinds of benefits might a business gain from its shares being listed?**

If it is generally accepted that shares can easily be sold for prices that tend to reflect their true worth, investors will have more confidence to invest. The business may benefit from this greater investor confidence by finding it easier to raise long-term finance and at a lower cost. This is because investors will view the investment as being less risky.

It is worth pointing out that investors are not obliged to use the Stock Exchange as the means of transferring shares in a listed business. However, it is usually the most convenient way of buying or selling shares.

The Stock Exchange can be a useful vehicle for a successful entrepreneur wishing to realise the value of the business that has been built up. By floating (listing) the shares on the Stock Exchange, and thereby making the shares available to the public, the entrepreneur will usually benefit from a gain in the value of the shares held and will be able to realise that gain easily, if required, by selling some shares. Real World 11.14 describes how two of the owners of moneysupermarket.com, a business that provides online financial information, benefited from its IPO (initial public offering).

---

**Real World 11.14**

## Cashing in

Paul Doughty, the CFO [chief financial officer] of moneysupermarket.com, is nearly £3m richer after his company's IPO despite a below-par fundraising.

The internet broker, which helps consumers to find the cheapest financial products, completed its float last week but ended up with an offer price of £1.70 a share, at the foot of the £1.70 to £2.10 range.

A company spokesperson confirmed that Doughty had cashed in 1.6m shares, but even with the disappointing showing, the CFO of the UK's leading price-comparison website made himself close to £3m.

If the IPO offer price had been set at the top end of the range, Doughty would have earned close to £3.5m. But his windfall was dwarfed by that of chief executive, Simon Nixon, who cashed in 60.3m shares, netting £100m. He still holds more than 57% of the company, which is worth more than £800m.

*Source*: Jetuah, D., 'Internet FD is in the money after floatation', *Accountancy Age*, 2 August 2007, p. 3.

---

## Disadvantages of a listing

A Stock Exchange listing can have certain disadvantages for a business. These include the following:

■ Strict rules are imposed on listed businesses, including requirements for levels of financial disclosure additional to those already imposed by International Financial Reporting Standards (for example, the listing rules require that half-yearly financial reports are published).

■ Financial analysts, financial journalists and others tend to monitor closely the activities of listed businesses, particularly larger ones. Such scrutiny may not be welcome, particularly if the business is dealing with sensitive issues or is experiencing operational problems.

■ It is often suggested that listed businesses are under pressure to perform well over the short term. This pressure may detract from undertaking projects that will yield benefits only in the longer term. If the market becomes disenchanted with the business, and the price of its shares falls, the business may become vulnerable to a takeover bid from another business.

■ The costs of obtaining a listing are huge and this may be a real deterrent for some businesses.

Though there are over a thousand UK businesses listed on the London Stock Exchange, in terms of equity market value, the market is dominated by just a few large ones, as is shown in Real World 11.15.

### Listing to one side

At 31 December 2009 there were 1,026 businesses that had a London Stock Exchange listing. Just 102 of them (9.9 per cent) accounted for 85.6 per cent of their total equity market value.

*Source*: London Stock Exchange Main Market Statistics, December 2009, Table 8.

Real World 11.16 provides an analysis of the ownership of shares in UK listed businesses at the end of 2008.

### Ownership of UK listed shares

At the end of 2008, the proportion of shares of UK listed businesses held by different types of investors was as shown in Figure 11.6.

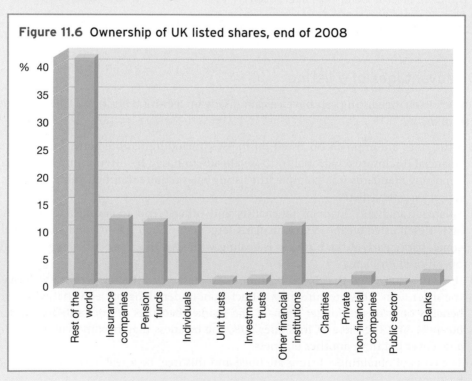

Figure 11.6 Ownership of UK listed shares, end of 2008

A striking feature of the ownership of UK shares is the extent of overseas ownership. At the end of 2008 this accounted for 42 per cent of the total; in 1963 it was 7 per cent and has grown fairly steadily ever since. This is broadly mirrored by the extent to which UK investors own shares of businesses based elsewhere in the world. It reflects increasing levels of globalisation of business.

Another striking feature is the extent that large financial institutions now dominate the ownership of UK listed shares. In 1963, 58 per cent of those UK shares owned by UK investors were owned by individuals. At the end of 2008 it was only 10 per cent.

Of course, ultimately individuals own all of the shares. This may be, for example, through having a life insurance or pension policy, or by investing through unit and investment trusts.

## Going private

Such are the disadvantages of a stock market listing that many businesses have 'delisted'. This has obviously denied them the advantages of a listing, but it has avoided the disadvantages.

## The Alternative Investment Market

The Alternative Investment Market (AIM) was established in June 1995 by the London Stock Exchange for smaller, young and growing businesses. AIM is similar in style to the main London Stock Exchange but it is cheaper for businesses to enter. Obtaining an AIM listing and raising funds costs the typical business about £500,000. Many AIM listed businesses are family-based ones. AIM has proved to be a very successful market where new equity finance can be raised and shares can be traded. Businesses listed on AIM tend to have market values in the range £1 million to £250 million, with only two of them being greater than £1,000 million, as is shown by Real World 11.17.

### Real World 11.17

### Take AIM

At 31 January 2010, there were 1,261 businesses that had an AIM listing. Their distribution according to market value is shown in Figure 11.7.

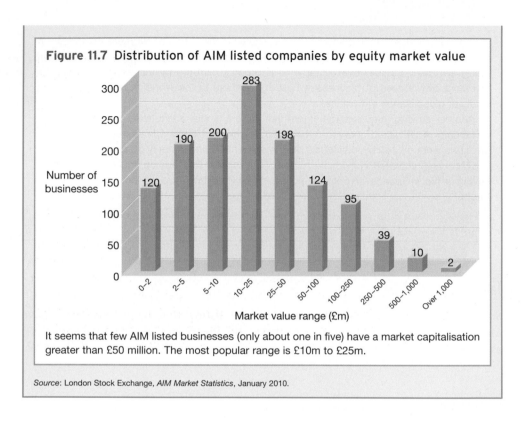

**Figure 11.7** Distribution of AIM listed companies by equity market value

It seems that few AIM listed businesses (only about one in five) have a market capitalisation greater than £50 million. The most popular range is £10m to £25m.

*Source*: London Stock Exchange, *AIM Market Statistics*, January 2010.

The listing requirements of AIM are less stringent than those of a full listing. However, AIM listed businesses tend to be more risky than fully listed ones, which can make AIM listed shares less attractive to investors.

AIM listed companies include the wine retailer Majestic Wine plc and Millwall Football Club. Also AIM listed is LiDCO Group plc, the heart monitoring equipment developer that we met in Real World 5.3 when dealing with the statement of cash flows.

## Short-term sources of external finance

Short-term, in this context, is usually taken to mean up to one year. Figure 11.2 indicated that the major sources of short-term external finance are

- bank overdrafts
- debt factoring
- invoice discounting.

These are discussed below.

## Bank overdrafts

 A bank overdraft enables a business to maintain a negative balance on its bank account. It represents a very flexible form of borrowing as the size of the overdraft can (subject to bank approval) be increased or decreased more or less instantaneously. An overdraft is relatively inexpensive to arrange and interest rates are generally very competitive, though often higher than those for a term loan. As with all borrowing, the rate of interest charged on an overdraft will vary according to how creditworthy the customer is perceived by the bank to be. An overdraft is normally fairly easy to arrange – sometimes by a telephone call to the bank. In view of these advantages, it is not surprising that an overdraft is an extremely popular form of short-term finance.

Banks prefer to grant overdrafts that are self-liquidating, that is, the funds applied will result in cash inflows that will extinguish the overdraft balance. The banks may ask for a cash budget from the business to see when the overdraft will be repaid and how much finance is required. The bank may also require some form of security on amounts advanced. One potential drawback with this form of finance is that the overdraft is repayable on demand. This may pose problems for a business that is short of funds. However, many businesses operate for many years using an overdraft, simply because the bank remains confident of their ability to repay and the arrangement suits the business. Thus the bank overdraft, though in theory regarded as short-term, often becomes a long-term source of finance.

## Debt factoring

Debt factoring is a service offered by a financial institution (known as a *factor*). Many of the large factors are subsidiaries of the commercial banks. Debt factoring involves the factor taking over the business's debt collection. In addition to operating normal credit control procedures, a factor may offer to undertake credit investigations and to provide protection for approved credit sales. The factor is usually prepared to make an advance to the business of a maximum of 80 per cent of approved trade receivables. The charge made for the factoring service is based on total sales revenue and is often 2 to 3 per cent of sales revenue. Any advances made to the business by the factor will attract a rate of interest similar to the rate charged on bank overdrafts.

Debt factoring is, in effect, outsourcing the trade receivables control to a specialist subcontractor. Many businesses find a factoring arrangement very convenient. It can result in savings in credit management and create more certainty with the cash flows. It can also release the time of key personnel for more profitable activities. This may be extremely important for smaller businesses that rely on the talent and skills of a few key individuals. However, there is a possibility that a factoring arrangement will be seen as an indication that the business is experiencing financial difficulties. This may have an adverse effect on the confidence of customers, suppliers and staff. For this reason, some businesses try to conceal the factoring arrangement by collecting debts on behalf of the factor. When considering a factoring agreement, the costs and likely benefits arising must be identified and carefully weighed.

Figure 11.8 shows the factoring process diagrammatically.

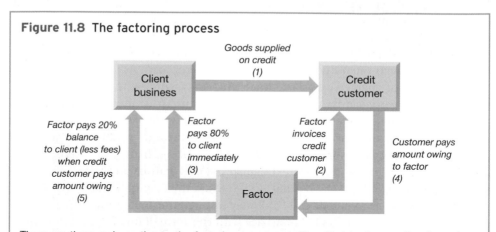

**Figure 11.8 The factoring process**

There are three main parties to the factoring agreement. The client business will sell goods or services on credit and the factor will take responsibility for invoicing the customer and collecting the amount owing. The factor will then pay the client business the invoice amount, less fees and interest, in two stages. The first stage typically represents 80 per cent of the invoice value and will be paid immediately after the goods or services have been delivered to the customer. The second stage will represent the balance outstanding and will usually be paid when the customer has paid the factor the amount owing.

## Invoice discounting

Invoice discounting involves a factor or other financial institution providing a loan based on a proportion of the face value of a business's credit sales outstanding (that is, the trade receivables). The amount advanced is usually 75 to 80 per cent of the value of the approved sales invoices outstanding. The business must agree to repay the advance within a relatively short period, perhaps 60 or 90 days. The responsibility for collecting the trade receivables outstanding remains with the business. Repayment of the advance is not dependent on the trade receivables being collected. Invoice discounting will not result in such a close relationship developing between the business and the financial institution as results with factoring. It may be a short-term arrangement, whereas debt factoring usually involves a longer-term relationship.

Real World 11.18 shows the relative importance of invoice discounting and factoring.

**Real World 11.18**

## The popularity of factoring and invoice discounting

**Figure 11.9** Client sales: domestic invoice discounting and factoring, 2001 to 2008

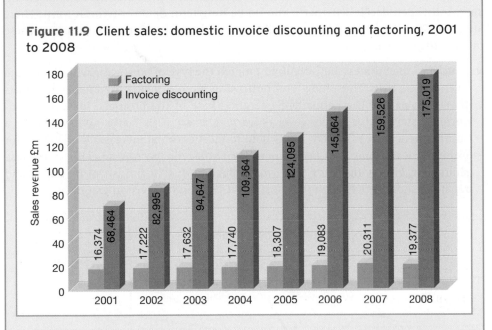

In recent years, invoice discounting has been much more popular and has risen much more sharply than factoring. During 2008, for example, invoice discounting grew by 10 per cent, whereas factoring contracted by 5 per cent. Sales using invoice discounting in 2008 were nine times sales using factoring.

*Source*: compiled from information published by the Asset Based Finance Association, www.abfa.org.uk.

There are three main reasons for the relative popularity of invoice discounting:

- It is a confidential form of financing that the business's customers will know nothing about.
- The service charge for invoice discounting is generally only 0.2 to 0.3 per cent of sales revenue, compared with 2.0 to 3.0 per cent for factoring.
- Many businesses are unwilling to relinquish control of their customers' records. Customers are an important resource of the business, and many wish to retain control over all aspects of their relationship with their customers.

Factoring and invoice discounting are forms of asset-based financing, as the asset of trade receivables is in effect used as security for the cash advances received by the business.

## Long-term versus short-term borrowing

Having decided that some form of borrowing is required to finance the business, managers must then decide whether it should be long-term or short-term in form. There are many issues that should be taken into account when making this decision. These include the following:

■ *Matching.* The business may attempt to match the type of borrowing with the nature of the assets held. Thus, long-term borrowing might provide the finance for assets that form part of the permanent operating base of the business, including non-current assets and a certain level of current assets. This leaves assets held for a short period, such as current assets held to meet seasonal increases in demand (for example, inventories), to be financed by short-term borrowing. This is because short-term borrowing tends to be more flexible in that funds can be raised and repaid at short notice. Figure 11.10 shows this funding division graphically.

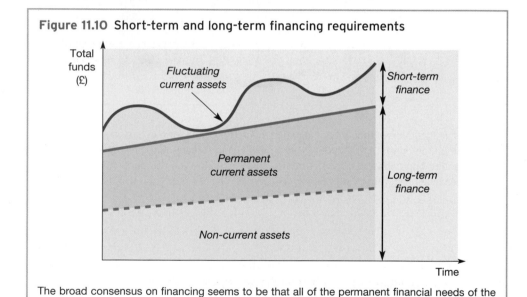

**Figure 11.10** Short-term and long-term financing requirements

The broad consensus on financing seems to be that all of the permanent financial needs of the business should come from long-term sources. Only that part of current assets that fluctuates on a short-term, probably a seasonal, basis should be financed from short-term sources.

A business may wish to match the asset life exactly with the period of the related borrowing. This may not be possible, however, because of the difficulty of predicting the life of many assets.

■ *Flexibility.* Short-term borrowing may be a useful means of postponing a commitment to taking on long-term borrowing. This may be seen as desirable if interest rates are high and it is forecast that they will fall in the future. Short-term borrowing does not usually incur penalties if there is early repayment of the amount outstanding, whereas some form of financial penalty may arise if long-term borrowing is repaid early.

- *Refunding risk*. Short-term borrowing has to be renewed more frequently than long-term borrowing. This may create problems for the business if it is already in financial difficulties or if there is a shortage of funds available for lending.
- *Interest rates*. Interest payable on long-term borrowing tends to be higher than for short-term borrowing, as lenders require a higher return where their funds are locked up for a long period. This fact may make short-term borrowing a more attractive source of finance for a business. However, there may be other costs associated with borrowing (arrangement fees, for example) to be taken into account. The more frequently borrowings must be renewed, the higher these costs will be.

## Activity 11.14

Some businesses may take up a less cautious financing position than that shown in Figure 11.10. Others may take up a more cautious one. How would the balance of financing appear in each of these cases?

A less cautious position would mean relying on short-term finance to help fund part of the permanent capital base. A more cautious position would mean relying on long-term finance to help finance the fluctuating assets of the business.

## Providing long-term finance for the small business

Although the Stock Exchange provides an important source of long-term finance for large businesses, it is not really suitable for small businesses. The aggregate market value of shares that are to be listed on the Stock Exchange must be at least £700,000 and, in practice, the amounts are much higher because of the high costs of listing, even on AIM. Thus, small businesses must look elsewhere for help in raising long-term finance. Some important sources of finance that are available to small businesses are venture capital, finance provided by business angels, and government assistance. We shall now consider these.

### Venture capital

Venture capital is long-term capital provided to small and medium-sized businesses that wish to grow but do not have ready access to stock markets because of the prohibitively large costs of obtaining a listing. The businesses of interest to the venture capitalist will have higher levels of risk than would normally be acceptable to traditional providers of finance, such as the major clearing banks. The attraction for the venture capitalist of investing in higher-risk businesses is the prospect of higher returns.

Many small businesses are designed to provide the owners with a particular lifestyle and with job satisfaction. These kinds of businesses are not of interest to venture capitalists, as they are unlikely to provide the desired financial returns. Instead, venture capitalists look for businesses where the owners are seeking significant sales revenue and profit growth and need some outside help in order to achieve this.

The risks associated with the business can vary in practice. They are often due to the nature of the products or the fact that it is a new business that either lacks a trading record or has new management or both of these.

Venture capitalists provide long-term capital in the form of share and loan finance for different situations, including:

- *Start-up capital.* This is available to businesses that are not fully developed. They may need finance to help refine the business concept or to engage in product development or initial marketing. They have not yet reached the stage where they are trading.
- *Early-stage capital.* This is available for businesses that are ready to start trading.
- *Expansion capital.* This is aimed at providing additional funding for existing, growing businesses.
- *Buy-out or buy-in capital.* This is used to fund the acquisition of a business either by the existing management team ('buy-out') or by a new management team ('buy-in'). Management buy-outs (MBOs) and buy-ins (MBIs) often occur where a large business wishes to divest itself of one of its operating units or where a family business wishes to sell out because of succession problems.
- *Rescue capital.* To help turn around businesses that are in difficulties.

The venture capitalist will often make a substantial investment in the business (usually more than £100,000), and this will often take the form of ordinary shares. However, some of the funding may be in the form of preference shares or loans. To keep an eye on the sum invested, the venture capitalist will usually require a representative on the board of directors as a condition of the investment. The venture capitalist may not be looking for a very quick return and may well be prepared to invest in a business for five years or more. The return may take the form of a capital gain on the realisation of the investment (typically selling the shares).

Though venture capital is extremely important for some small businesses, the vast majority of small businesses obtain their finance from other sources. Real World 11.19 shows the main sources of finance for small businesses in the UK.

### Real World 11.19

## Small business funding

Bank finance, such as overdrafts and loans, is the main source of external finance for small businesses, as the pie chart in Figure 11.11 shows.

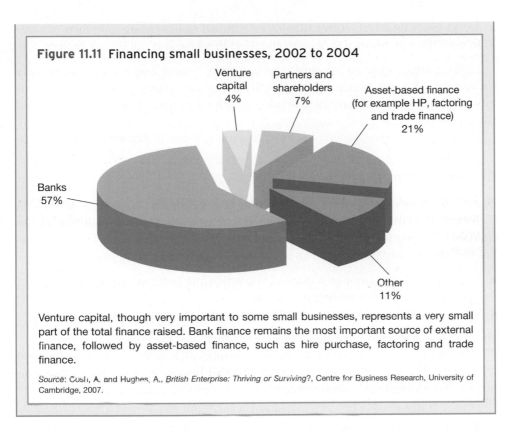

**Figure 11.11** Financing small businesses, 2002 to 2004

Venture capital, though very important to some small businesses, represents a very small part of the total finance raised. Bank finance remains the most important source of external finance, followed by asset-based finance, such as hire purchase, factoring and trade finance.

*Source*: Cosli, A. and Hughes, A., *British Enterprise: Thriving or Surviving?*, Centre for Business Research, University of Cambridge, 2007.

## Business angels

Business angels are often wealthy individuals who have been successful in business. They are usually willing to invest, through a shareholding, between £10,000 and £750,000 in a start-up business or in a business that is wishing to expand. If larger amounts are required, a syndicate of business angels may be formed to raise the money. Business angels typically make one or two investments over a three-year period and will usually be prepared to invest for a period of between three and five years. They normally have a minority stake in the business and, although they do not usually become involved in its day-to-day management, they tend to take an interest, more generally, in the way that the business is managed.

Business angels fill an important gap in the market as the size and nature of investments they find appealing are often not so appealing to venture capitalists. They can be attractive to small businesses because they may

- make investment decisions quickly, particularly if they are familiar with the industry in which the new business operates;
- offer useful skills, experience and business contacts;

■ accept lower financial returns than those required from venture capitalists in order to have the opportunity to become involved in a new and interesting project.

Business angels offer an informal source of share finance and it is not always easy for owners of small businesses to identify a suitable angel. However, numerous business angel networks have now developed to help owners of small businesses find their 'perfect partner'.

The panellists on the popular BBC TV programme *Dragons' Den* are business angels.

## Government assistance

One of the most effective ways in which the UK government assists small businesses is through the Enterprise Finance Guarantee Scheme (formerly the Small Firms Loan Guarantee Scheme). This aims to help small businesses that have viable business plans but lack the security to enable them to borrow. The scheme guarantees:

■ 75 per cent of the amount borrowed, for which the borrower pays a premium of 2 per cent on the outstanding borrowing
■ loans ranging from £1,000 to £1 million for a maximum period of 10 years.

The scheme is available for businesses that have annual sales revenue of up to £25 million.

In addition to other forms of financial assistance, such as government grants and tax incentives for investors to buy shares in small businesses, the government also helps by providing information concerning the sources of finance available.

### ? Self-assessment question 11.1

Helsim Ltd is a wholesaler and distributor of electrical components. The most recent draft financial statements of the business revealed the following:

**Income statement for the year**

|  | £m | £m |
| --- | --- | --- |
| Sales revenue |  | 14.2 |
| Opening inventories | 3.2 |  |
| Purchases | 8.4 |  |
|  | 11.6 |  |
| Closing inventories | (3.8) | (7.8) |
| **Gross profit** |  | 6.4 |
| Administration expenses |  | (3.0) |
| Distribution expenses |  | (2.1) |
| **Operating profit** |  | 1.3 |
| Finance costs |  | (0.8) |
| **Profit before taxation** |  | 0.5 |
| Taxation |  | (0.2) |
| **Profit for the year** |  | 0.3 |

### Statement of financial position as at the end of the year

| ASSETS | £m |
|---|---|
| **Non-current assets** | |
| *Property, plant and equipment* | |
| Land and buildings | 3.8 |
| Equipment | 0.9 |
| Motor vehicles | 0.5 |
| | 5.2 |
| | |
| **Current assets** | |
| Inventories | 3.8 |
| Trade receivables | 3.6 |
| Cash at bank | 0.1 |
| | 7.5 |
| Total assets | 12.7 |
| | |
| **EQUITY AND LIABILITIES** | |
| **Equity** | |
| Share capital | 2.0 |
| Retained earnings | 1.8 |
| | 3.8 |
| | |
| **Non-current liabilities** | |
| Loan notes (secured on land and buildings) | 3.5 |
| **Current liabilities** | |
| Trade payables | 1.8 |
| Short-term borrowings | 3.6 |
| | 5.4 |
| **Total equity and liabilities** | 12.7 |

Notes:
1  Land and buildings are shown at their current market value. Equipment and motor vehicles are shown at their carrying amounts (that is, cost less accumulated depreciation).
2  No dividends have been paid to ordinary shareholders for the past three years.

In recent months, trade payables have been pressing for payment. The managing director has therefore decided to reduce the level of trade payables to an average of 40 days outstanding. To achieve this, he has decided to approach the bank with a view to increasing the overdraft (the short-term borrowings comprise only a bank overdraft). The business is currently paying 10 per cent a year interest on the overdraft.

**Required:**
(a) Comment on the liquidity position of the business.
(b) Calculate the amount of finance required to reduce trade payables, from the level shown on the statement of financial position, to an average of 40 days outstanding.
(c) State, with reasons, how you consider the bank would react to the proposal to grant an additional overdraft facility.
(d) Identify four sources of finance (internal or external, but excluding a bank overdraft) that may be suitable to finance the reduction in trade payables. State, with reasons, which of these you consider the most appropriate.

The solution to this question can be found at the back of the book, in Appendix B.

## Summary

The main points in this chapter may be summarised as follows.

### Sources of finance

- Internal sources of finance do not require the agreement of anyone beyond the directors and managers of the business, whereas external sources of finance do require the compliance of 'outsiders'.

- Long-term sources of finance are not due for repayment within one year whereas short-term sources are due for repayment within one year.

- The higher the level of risk associated with investing in a particular form of finance, the higher the level of return that will be expected by investors.

### Internal sources of finance

- The major internal source of long-term finance is retained profit.

- The main short-term sources of internal finance are tighter credit control of receivables, reducing inventories levels and delaying payments to trade payables.

### External sources of finance

- The main external, *long-term* sources of finance are ordinary shares, preference shares, borrowing, leases, hire-purchase agreements and securitisation.

- Ordinary shares are, from the investor's point of view, normally considered to be the most risky form of investment and, therefore, provide the highest expected returns. Lending is normally the least risky and provides the lowest expected returns to investors.

- Leases and hire purchase agreements allow a business to obtain immediate possession of an asset without having to pay the cost of acquiring the asset.

- The level of gearing associated with a business is often an important factor in assessing the level of risk and returns to ordinary shareholders.

- The main sources of external *short-term* finance are bank overdrafts, debt factoring and invoice discounting.

- When considering the choice between long-term and short-term sources of borrowing, factors such as matching the type of borrowing with the nature of the assets held, the need for flexibility, refunding risk and interest rates should be taken into account.

### Share issues

- Share issues that involve the payment of cash by investors can take the form of a rights issue, a public issue, an offer for sale or a private placing.

- A rights issue is made to existing shareholders. Most share issues are of this type, probably because the issue costs are relatively low. The law requires that shares that are to be issued for cash must first be offered to existing shareholders.

- A public issue involves a direct issue to the public and an offer for sale involves an indirect issue to the public.

- A private placing is an issue of shares to selected investors.

### The Stock Exchange

- The Stock Exchange is an important primary and secondary market in capital for large businesses. However, obtaining a Stock Exchange listing can have certain drawbacks for a business.

### The Alternative Investment Market (AIM)

- AIM is another important primary and secondary market managed by the London Stock Exchange for smaller, growing businesses. It tends to be a cheaper way for a business to become listed.

### Small businesses

- Venture capital is long-term capital for small or medium-sized businesses that are not listed on the Stock Exchange. These businesses often have higher levels of risk but provide the venture capitalist with the prospect of higher levels of return.

- Business angels are wealthy individuals who are willing to invest in businesses at either an early stage or expansion stage of development.

- The government assists small businesses through guaranteeing loans and by providing grants and tax incentives.

**MyAccountingLab** | *Now check your progress in your personal Study Plan*

### → Key terms

term loan p. 411
loan notes p. 411
loan stock p. 411
eurobond p. 412
convertible loan notes p. 413
financial derivative p. 415
mortgage p. 415
loan covenant p. 415
finance lease p. 417
operating lease p. 418
sale-and-leaseback p. 419
hire purchase p. 421
securitisation p. 422

rights issue p. 426
offer for sale p. 430
public issue p. 430
private placing p. 430
Stock Exchange p. 431
Alternative Investment Market
   (AIM) p. 435
bank overdraft p. 437
debt factoring p. 437
invoice discounting p. 438
asset-based financing p. 439
venture capital p. 441
business angel p. 443

## References

1  London Stock Exchange Main Market Statistics, December 2005, 2006, 2007, 2008 and 2009.
2  Armitage, S., 'The direct costs of UK rights issues and open offers', *European Financial Management*, March 2000.
3  London Stock Exchange, *The Cost of Capital: An International Comparison*, 2006.

## Further reading

If you would like to explore the topics covered in this chapter in more depth, we recommend the following books:

Arnold, G., *Corporate Financial Management* (4th edn), Financial Times Prentice Hall, 2008, chapters 9, 10, 11 and 12.
Brealey, R., Myers, S. and Allen, F., *Corporate Finance* (9th edn), McGraw-Hill, 2008, chapters 14, 25 and 26.
McLaney, E., *Business Finance: Theory and Practice* (8th edn), Financial Times Prentice Hall, 2009, chapter 8.
Pike, R. and Neale, B., *Corporate Finance and Investment* (6th edn), Financial Times Prentice Hall, 2009, chapters 15 and 16.

## ? Review questions

Solutions to these questions can be found at the back of the book, in Appendix C.

**11.1**   What are the benefits to a business of issuing convertible loan notes?

**11.2**   Why might a business that has a Stock Exchange listing revert to being unlisted?

**11.3**   Distinguish between an offer for sale and a public issue of shares.

**11.4**   Distinguish between invoice discounting and factoring.

## ✻ Exercises

Exercises 11.3 to 11.5 are more advanced than Exercises 11.1 and 11.2. Those with coloured numbers have solutions at the back of the book, in Appendix D.

If you wish to try more exercises, visit the website at www.myaccountinglab.com.

**11.1**   H. Brown (Portsmouth) Ltd produces a range of central heating systems for sale to builders' merchants. As a result of increasing demand for the business's products, the directors have decided to expand production. The cost of acquiring new plant and machinery and the increase in working capital requirements are planned to be financed by a mixture of long-term and short-term borrowing.

**Required:**
(a) Discuss the major factors that should be taken into account when deciding on the appropriate mix of long-term and short-term borrowing necessary to finance the expansion programme.
(b) Discuss the major factors that a lender should take into account when deciding whether to grant a long-term loan to the business.

**11.2** Carpets Direct plc wishes to increase the number of its retail outlets in the south of England. The board of directors has decided to finance this expansion programme by raising the funds from existing shareholders through a one-for-four rights issue. The most recent income statement of the business is as follows:

### Income statement for the year ended 30 April

|  | £m |
|---|---|
| Sales revenue | 164.5 |
| Operating profit | 12.6 |
| Interest | (6.2) |
| Profit before taxation | 6.4 |
| Taxation | (1.9) |
| Profit for the year | 4.5 |

A £2 million ordinary dividend had been paid in respect of the year.

The share capital consists of 120 million ordinary shares with a nominal value of £0.50 a share. These are currently being traded on the Stock Exchange at a price/earnings ratio of 22 times and the board of directors has decided to issue the new shares at a discount of 20 per cent on the current market value.

**Required:**
(a) Calculate the theoretical ex-rights price of an ordinary share in Carpets Direct plc.
(b) Calculate the price at which the rights in Carpets Direct plc are likely to be traded.
(c) Identify and evaluate, at the time of the rights issue, each of the options arising from the rights issue to an investor who holds 4,000 ordinary shares before the rights announcement.

(*Hint*: To answer part (a), first calculate the earnings per share and then use this and the P/E ratio to calculate the market value per share.)

**11.3** Raphael Ltd is a small engineering business that has annual sales revenue of £2.4 million, all of which is on credit. In recent years, the business has experienced credit control problems. The average collection period for trade receivables has risen to 50 days even though the stated policy of the business is for payment to be made within 30 days. In addition, 1.5 per cent of sales are written off as bad debts each year.

The business has recently been in talks with a factor, which is prepared to make an advance to the business equivalent to 80 per cent of trade receivables, based on the assumption that customers will, in future, adhere to a 30-day payment period. The interest rate for the advance will be 11 per cent a year. The trade receivables are currently financed through a bank overdraft, which has an interest rate of 12 per cent a year. The factor will take over the credit control procedures of the business and this will result in a saving to the business of £18,000 a year. However, the factor will make a charge of 2 per cent of sales revenue for this service. The use of the factoring service is expected to eliminate the bad debts incurred by the business.

**Required:**
Calculate the net cost of the factor agreement to the business and state whether the business should take advantage of the opportunity to factor its trade receivables.
(*Hint*: To answer this question, compare the cost of existing trade credit policies (cost of investment in trade receivables and cost of bad debts) with the cost of using a factor (interest and other charges less the credit control savings.))

**11.4**   Gainsborough Fashions Ltd operates a small chain of fashion shops. In recent months the business has been under pressure from its suppliers to reduce the average credit period taken from three months to one month. As a result, the directors have approached the bank to ask for an increase in the existing overdraft for one year to be able to comply with the suppliers' demands. The most recent financial statements of the business are as follows:

**Statement of financial position as at 31 May**

| ASSETS | £ | £ |
|---|---:|---:|
| **Non-current assets** | | |
| *Property, plant and equipment* | | |
| Fixtures and fittings at cost | 90,000 | |
|    Accumulated depreciation | (23,000) | 67,000 |
| Motor vehicles at cost | 34,000 | |
|    Accumulated depreciation | (27,000) | 7,000 |
| | | 74,000 |
| **Current assets** | | |
| Inventories at cost | | 198,000 |
| Trade receivables | | 3,000 |
| | | 201,000 |
| **Total assets** | | 275,000 |
| | | |
| **EQUITY AND LIABILITIES** | | |
| **Equity** | | |
| £1 ordinary shares | | 20,000 |
| General reserve | | 4,000 |
| Retained earnings | | 17,000 |
| | | 41,000 |
| **Non-current liabilities** | | |
| Borrowings – loan notes repayable in just over one year's time | | 40,000 |
| **Current liabilities** | | |
| Trade payables | | 162,000 |
| Accrued expenses | | 10,000 |
| Borrowings – bank overdraft | | 17,000 |
| Taxation | | 5,000 |
| | | 194,000 |
| **Total equity and liabilities** | | 275,000 |

**Abbreviated income statement for the year ended 31 May**

|  | £ |
|---|---|
| Sales revenue | 740,000 |
| Operating profit | 38,000 |
| Interest charges | (5,000) |
| Profit before taxation | 33,000 |
| Taxation | (10,000) |
| Profit for the year | 23,000 |

A dividend of £23,000 was paid for the year.

Notes:
1 The loan notes are secured by personal guarantees from the directors.
2 The current overdraft bears an interest rate of 12 per cent a year.

Required:
(a) Identify and discuss the major factors that a bank would take into account before deciding whether to grant an increase in the overdraft of a business.
(b) State whether, in your opinion, the bank should grant the required increase in the overdraft for Gainsborough Fashions Ltd. You should provide reasoned arguments and supporting calculations where necessary.

**11.5** Telford Engineers plc, a medium-sized manufacturer of automobile components, has decided to modernise its factory by introducing a number of robots. These will cost £20 million and will reduce operating costs by £6 million a year for their estimated useful life of ten years starting next year (Year 10). To finance this scheme, the business can raise £20 million by issuing either

(i) 20 million ordinary shares at 100p; or
(ii) loan notes at 7 per cent interest a year with capital repayments of £3 million a year commencing at the end of Year 11.

Extracts from Telford Engineers' financial statements appear below.

**Summary of statement of financial position as at 31 December**

|  | Year 6 | Year 7 | Year 8 | Year 9 |
|---|---|---|---|---|
|  | £m | £m | £m | £m |
| ASSETS |  |  |  |  |
| Non-current assets | 48 | 51 | 65 | 64 |
| Current assets | 55 | 67 | 57 | 55 |
| Total assets | 103 | 118 | 122 | 119 |
| EQUITY AND LIABILITIES |  |  |  |  |
| Equity | 48 | 61 | 61 | 63 |
| Non-current liabilities | 30 | 30 | 30 | 30 |
| Current liabilities |  |  |  |  |
| Trade payables | 20 | 27 | 25 | 18 |
| Short-term borrowings | 5 | – | 6 | 8 |
|  | 25 | 27 | 31 | 26 |
| Total equity and liabilities | 103 | 118 | 122 | 119 |
| Number of issued 25p shares | 80m | 80m | 80m | 80m |
| Share price | 150p | 200p | 100p | 145p |

Note that the short-term borrowings consisted entirely of bank overdrafts.

**Summary of income statements for years ended 31 December**

|  | Year 6 | Year 7 | Year 8 | Year 9 |
|---|---|---|---|---|
|  | £m | £m | £m | £m |
| Sales revenue | 152 | 170 | 110 | 145 |
| Operating profit | 28 | 40 | 7 | 15 |
| Interest payable | (4) | (3) | (4) | (5) |
| Profit before taxation | 24 | 37 | 3 | 10 |
| Taxation | (12) | (16) | (0) | (4) |
| Profit for the period | 12 | 21 | 3 | 6 |
| Dividends paid during each year | 6 | 8 | 3 | 4 |

You should assume that the tax rate for Year 10 is 30 per cent, that sales revenue and operating profit will be unchanged from Year 9 except for the £6 million cost saving arising from the introduction of the robots, and that Telford Engineers will pay the same dividend per share in Year 10 as in Year 9.

**Required:**

(a) Prepare, for each financing arrangement, Telford Engineers' projected income statement for the year ending 31 December Year 10 and a statement of its share capital, reserves and borrowings on that date.

(b) Calculate Telford's projected earnings per share for Year 10 for both schemes.

(c) Which scheme would you advise the business to adopt? You should give your reasons and state what additional information you would require.

## Chapter 12

# Managing working capital

## Introduction

This chapter considers the factors that must be taken into account when managing the working capital of a business. The elements of working capital will be identified and the major issues surrounding them will be discussed. Working capital represents a significant investment for many businesses and so its proper management and control can be vital. We saw in Chapter 10 that an investment in working capital is typically an important aspect of many new investment proposals. Some useful tools in the management of working capital are financial ratios, which were considered in Chapter 6, budgets, which we examined in Chapter 9, and NPV, which we considered in Chapter 10.

## Learning outcomes

**When you have completed this chapter, you should be able to:**

- identify the main elements of working capital;
- discuss the purpose of working capital and the nature of the working capital cycle;
- explain the importance of establishing policies for the control of working capital;
- explain the factors that have to be taken into account when managing each element of working capital.

 *Remember to create your own personalised Study Plan*

# What is working capital?

*Working capital* is usually defined as current assets less current liabilities. The major elements of current assets are

- inventories
- trade receivables
- cash (in hand and at bank).

The major elements of current liabilities are

- trade payables
- bank overdrafts.

The size and composition of working capital can vary between industries. For some types of business, the investment in working capital can be substantial. For example, a manufacturing business will typically invest heavily in raw material, work in progress and finished goods. Also, it will normally sell its goods on credit, giving rise to trade receivables. A retailer, on the other hand, will hold only one form of inventories (finished goods) and will usually sell goods for cash. Many service businesses hold no inventories.

Most businesses buy goods and/or services on credit, giving rise to trade payables. Few, if any, businesses operate without a cash balance, though in some cases it is a negative one (a bank overdraft).

Working capital represents a net investment in short-term assets. These assets are continually flowing into and out of the business and are essential for day-to-day operations. The various elements of working capital are interrelated and can be seen as part of a short-term cycle. For a manufacturing business, the working capital cycle can be depicted as shown in Figure 12.1.

For a retailer the situation would be as in Figure 12.1 except that there would be only inventories of finished goods and so no work in progress or raw materials. For a purely service business, the working capital cycle would also be similar to that depicted in Figure 12.1 except that there would be no inventories of finished goods or raw materials. There may well be work in progress, however, since many services, for example a case handled by a firm of solicitors, will take some time to complete and costs will build up before the client is billed for them.

## Managing working capital

The management of working capital is an essential part of the business's short-term planning process. It is necessary for management to decide how much of each element should be held. As we shall see later in this chapter, there are costs associated with holding either too much or too little of each element. Management must be aware of these costs, which include opportunity costs, in order to manage effectively. Hence, potential benefits must be weighed against likely costs in an attempt to achieve the optimum investment.

**Figure 12.1** The working capital cycle

Cash is used to pay trade payables for raw materials, or raw materials are bought for immediate cash settlement. Cash is also spent on labour and other items that turn raw materials into work in progress and, finally, into finished goods. The finished goods are sold to customers either for cash or on credit. In the case of credit customers, there will be a delay before the cash is received from the sales. Receipt of cash completes the cycle.

The working capital needs of a business are likely to vary over time as a result of changes in the business environment. Managers must try to identify these changes to ensure that the level of investment in working capital is appropriate. This means that working capital decisions are frequently being made.

## Activity 12.1

What kinds of changes in the business environment might lead to a decision to change the level of investment in working capital? Try to identify four possible changes that could affect the working capital needs of a business.

These may include the following:

- changes in interest rates
- changes in market demand for the business's output
- changes in the seasons
- changes in the state of the economy.

You may have thought of others.

In addition to changes in the external environment, changes arising within the business could alter the required level of investment in working capital. Such internal changes might include using different production methods (resulting, perhaps, in a need to hold less inventories) and changes in the level of risk that managers are prepared to take.

## The scale of working capital

We might imagine that, compared with the scale of investment in non-current assets by the typical business, the amounts involved with working capital are pretty trivial. However, this is not the case – the scale of the working capital elements for many businesses is vast.

Real World 12.1 gives some impression of the working capital investment for five UK businesses that are very well known by name, or whose products are everyday

### Real World 12.1

## A summary of the statements of financial position (balance sheets) of five UK businesses

| Business | Next plc | British Airways plc | Babcock Int Group plc | Tesco plc | Severn Trent plc |
|---|---|---|---|---|---|
| Statement of financial position date | 24.1.09 | 31.3.09 | 31.3.09 | 28.2.09 | 31.3.09 |
| Non-current assets | 64 | 128 | 116 | 114 | 103 |
| Current assets | | | | | |
| Inventories | 30 | 2 | 13 | 10 | – |
| Trade receivables | 60 | 8 | 45 | 7 | 5 |
| Other receivables | 8 | 5 | – | 16 | – |
| Cash and near cash | 4 | 22 | 17 | 17 | 3 |
| | 102 | 37 | 75 | 50 | 8 |
| Total assets | 166 | 165 | 191 | 164 | 111 |
| Equity and non-current liabilities | 100 | 100 | 100 | 100 | 100 |
| Current liabilities | | | | | |
| Trade payables | 45 | 44 | 70 | 30 | – |
| Taxation | 8 | – | 2 | 1 | – |
| Other short-term liabilities | 2 | 10 | 3 | – | 7 |
| Overdrafts and short-term borrowings | 11 | 11 | 16 | 33 | 4 |
| | 66 | 65 | 91 | 64 | 11 |
| Total equity and liabilities | 166 | 165 | 191 | 164 | 111 |

The non-current assets, current assets and current liabilities are expressed as a percentage of the total net long-term investment (equity plus non-current liabilities) of the business concerned. Next plc is a major retail and home shopping business. British Airways plc (BA) is a major airline. Babcock International Group plc is a major engineering and support business. Tesco plc is one of the major UK supermarkets. Severn Trent plc is a major supplier of water, sewerage services and waste management, mainly in the UK.

*Source*: table constructed from information appearing in the financial statements for the year ended during 2009 for each of the five businesses concerned.

commodities for most of us. These businesses were randomly selected, except that each one is high-profile and from a different industry. For each business the major items appearing on the statement of financial position (balance sheet) are expressed as a percentage of the total investment by the providers of long-term finance (equity and non-current liabilities).

It is quite striking, in Real World 12.1, how different is the make-up of the statement of financial position from one business to the next. Take the current assets and current liabilities for example. Though the totals for current assets are pretty large when compared with the total long-term investment, these percentages vary considerably from one type of business to the next. When we look at the nature of current assets held we can see that Next, Babcock and Tesco, which produce and/or sell goods, are the only ones that hold significant amounts of inventories. The other two businesses are service providers and so inventories are not a significant item. We can see from the table that Tesco does not sell a lot on credit and very few of BA's and Severn Trent's sales are on credit as these businesses have little or nothing invested in trade receivables. It is interesting to note that Tesco's trade payables are much higher than its inventories. Since most of this money will be due to suppliers of inventories, it means that the business is able, on average, to have the cash from a typical trolley load of groceries in the bank quite a long time before it needs to pay the suppliers for the goods concerned.

These types of variation in the amounts and types of working capital elements are typical of other businesses.

In the sections that follow, we shall consider the elements of working capital separately and how they might be properly managed. It seems from the evidence presented in Real World 12.2 that there is much scope for improvement in working capital management among European businesses.

## Real World 12.2

## Working capital not working hard enough!

According to a survey of 1,000 of Europe's largest businesses, working capital is not as well managed as it could be. The survey, conducted in 2009 by REL Consultancy Group and CFO Europe, suggests that larger European businesses had, between them, €813 billion tied up in working capital that could be released through better management of inventories, trade receivables and trade payables. The potential for savings represents a total of 35 per cent of the total working capital invested and is calculated by comparing the results for each business with the results for the upper quartile of the industry within which that business operates.

The overall working capital invested by large European businesses as a percentage of sales for the five-year period ending in 2008 is shown shown in Figure 12.2.

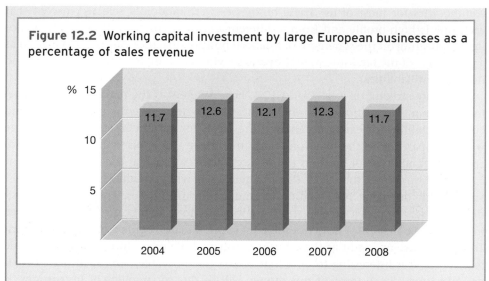

**Figure 12.2** Working capital investment by large European businesses as a percentage of sales revenue

The figure shows that there has been little variation in this percentage over time. In other words, the average performace, in terms of working capital management, has changed little over the five years. Within that average, however, some businesses have improved and some have deteriorated. The report on the survey identifies DSG International plc (the electronics retailer – Currys, Dixons, PC World and so on) as a consistent improver since 2005. It also identifies Rolls-Royce plc (aero and other engines) as a business that has gone backwards in its working capital management over the same period.

*Source*: compiled from information in REL/CFO Europe 2009 European Working Capital Survey, www.relconsult.com.

We should bear in mind that the businesses in the survey discussed in Real World 12.2 are the very largest businesses in Europe. It is probably reasonable to assume that smaller businesses tend to be less well managed than larger ones. Smaller businesses may well have even more excess working capital than the average 35 per cent that is the case with larger businesses.

## Managing inventories

A business may hold inventories for various reasons, the most common of which is to meet the immediate day-to-day requirements of customers and production. However, a business may hold more than is necessary for this purpose if there is a risk that future supplies may be interrupted or scarce. Similarly, if there is a risk that the cost of inventories will rise in the future, a business may decide to stockpile.

For some types of business, the inventories held may represent a substantial proportion of the total assets held. For example, a car dealership that rents its premises may have nearly all of its total assets in the form of inventories. Inventories levels of manufacturers tend to be higher than in many other types of business as they need to hold three kinds of inventories: raw materials, work in progress and finished goods. Each form of inventories represents a particular stage in the production cycle.

For some types of business, the level of inventories held may vary substantially over the year owing to the seasonal nature of the industry. A greetings card manufacturer may provide an example of such a business. For other businesses, inventories levels may remain fairly stable throughout the year.

When businesses hold inventories simply to meet the day-to-day requirements of their customers and for production, they will normally seek to minimise the amount of inventories held. This is because there are significant costs associated with holding inventories. These costs include

- storage and handling costs
- the cost of financing the inventories
- the cost of pilferage and obsolescence
- the cost of opportunities forgone in tying up funds in this form of asset.

To give some impression of the level of cost involved in holding inventories, Real World 12.3 estimates the *financing cost* of inventories for four large businesses.

**Real World 12.3**

## Inventories financing cost

The financing cost of inventories for each of four large businesses, based on their respective opportunity costs of capital, is calculated below.

| Business | Type of operations | Cost of capital | Average inventories held* | Cost of holding inventories | Operating expenses | Cost as percentage of operating expenses |
|---|---|---|---|---|---|---|
| | | (a) | (b) | (a × b) | | |
| | | % | £m | £m | £m | % |
| Associated Britsh Foods | Food producer | 9.5 | 1,152 | 109 | 8,639 | 1.3 |
| British Airways | Airline | 8.9 | 120 | 11 | 9,212 | 0.1 |
| Kingfisher | Home improvement retailer | 8.3 | 1,833 | 152 | 8,606 | 1.8 |
| J Sainsbury | Supermarket | 10.0 | 685 | 69 | 18,448 | 0.4 |

\* Based on opening and closing inventories for the relevant financial period.

We can see that for all of these four businesses, inventories financing costs are significant in relation to their operating expenses. This is particularly true for Associated British Foods and Kingfisher. The nature of the business for these two involves holding fairly large inventories. For the other two, BA and Sainsbury, inventories holding costs are less important. BA is a service provder and has very low levels of inventories. Sainsbury moves its inventories very fast.

Kingfisher spends about £1.80 on financing its inventories for every £100 that it spends on operating expenses. Kingfisher's operating expenses include the cost of the goods sold, salaries, rent, heating and lighting and so on. To spend so much to finance inventories is striking.

These figures do not take account of other costs of inventories holding mentioned above, such as the cost of providing a secure store for the inventories. Clearly, the efficient management of inventories is an important issue for many businesses.

These businesses were not selected because they have particularly high inventories costs but simply because they are among the relatively few businesses that publish their costs of capital.

*Source*: annual reports of the businesses for the financial year ended during 2009.

As we have just seen, the cost of holding inventories can be very large. A business must also recognise, however, that, if the level of inventories held is too low, there will also be associated costs.

## Activity 12.2

**What costs might a business incur as a result of holding too low a level of inventories? Try to jot down at least three types of cost.**

In answering this activity you may have thought of the following costs:

- loss of sales, from being unable to provide the goods required immediately;
- loss of customer goodwill, for being unable to satisfy customer demand;
- high transport costs incurred to ensure that inventories are replenished quickly;
- lost production due to shortage of raw materials;
- inefficient production scheduling due to shortages of raw materials;
- purchasing inventories at a higher price than might otherwise have been possible in order to replenish inventories quickly.

Before dealing with the various approaches that can be taken to managing inventories, let us consider Real World 12.4. It describes how one large international business has sought to reduce its inventories level.

## Real World 12.4

### Back to basics

Wal-Mart has said it will seek further reductions in the levels of backroom inventory it holds at its US stores, in a drive to improve its performance. John Menzer, vice chairman and head of Wal-Mart's US operations, made the retailer's efforts to cut inventory one of the key elements of remarks to reporters this week when he outlined current strategy. Wal-Mart, he said, currently 'has a real focus on reducing our inventory. Inventory that's on trailers behind our stores, in backrooms and on shelves in our stores.' Cutting back on inventory, he said, reduced 'clutter' in the retailer's stores, gave a better return on invested capital, reduced the need to cut prices on old merchandise, and increased the velocity at which goods moved through the stores.

Eduardo Castro-Wright, chief executive of Wal-Mart's US store network, said the inventory reduction marked a return to basics for the retailer, which would be 'getting more disciplined'. Earlier this year, he said Wal-Mart would link inventory reduction to incentive payments to its officers and managers. Wal-Mart is already regarded as one of the most efficient logistical operations in US retailing. It is currently rolling out to all its US stores and distribution centres a new parallel distribution system that speeds the delivery to stores of 5,000 high turnover items. It is also discussing with its suppliers how new RFID radio frequency tagging could be used to further reduce the volume of goods in transit to its stores. But further reductions in its inventory turnover would release working capital that could fund investment in its ongoing initiatives to improve its stores.

Adrienne Shapira, retail analyst at Goldman Sachs, has estimated that the retailer could reduce its annual inventory by 18 per cent, which would lead to a $6bn reduction in working capital needs on a trailing 12-month basis.

*Source*: adapted from 'Wal-Mart aims for further inventory cuts', *The Financial Times*, 19/04/2006 (Birchall, J.), copyright © The Financial Times Ltd.

To try to ensure that the inventories are properly managed, a number of procedures and techniques may be used. These are reviewed below.

## Budgeting future demand

Making and following appropriate plans and budgets is one of the best ways to ensure that there will be inventories available to meet future production and sales requirements. Budgets should deal with each product that the business makes and/or sells. It is important that every attempt is made to ensure that budgets are realistic, as they will determine future ordering and production levels. The budgets may be derived in various ways. They may be developed using statistical techniques such as time series analysis, or they may be based on the judgement of the sales and marketing staff. We considered inventories budgets and their link to production and sales budgets in Chapter 9.

## Financial ratios

One ratio that can be used to help monitor inventories levels is the average inventories turnover period, which we examined in Chapter 6. This ratio is calculated as follows:

$$\text{Average inventories turnover period} = \frac{\text{Average inventories held}}{\text{Cost of sales}} \times 365$$

The ratio provides a picture of the average period for which inventories are held. This can be useful as a basis for comparison. It is possible to calculate the average inventories turnover period for individual product lines as well as for inventories as a whole.

## Recording and reordering systems

A sound system of recording inventories movements is a key element in managing inventories. There must be proper procedures for recording inventories purchases and usages. Periodic checks would normally be made in an attempt to ensure that the amount of physical inventories actually held is consistent with what is indicated by the inventories records.

There should also be clear procedures for the reordering of inventories. Authorisation for both the purchase and the issue of inventories should be confined to a few nominated members of staff. This should avoid problems of duplication and lack of co-ordination. To determine the point at which inventories should be reordered, information will be required concerning the lead time (that is, the time between the placing of an order and the receipt of the goods) and the likely level of demand.

### Activity 12.3

An electrical retailer stocks a particular type of light switch. The annual demand for the light switch is 10,400 units and the lead time for orders is four weeks. Demand for the light switch is steady throughout the year. At what level of inventories of the light switch should the business reorder, assuming that it is confident of the information given above?

The average weekly demand for the switch is 10,400/52 = 200 units. During the time between ordering new switches and receiving them, the quantity sold will be 4 × 200 units = 800 units. So the business should reorder no later than when the level held reaches 800 units. This should avoid running out of inventories.

In most businesses, there will be some uncertainty surrounding the above factors (level of demand, pattern of demand and lead time). Here a buffer or safety inventories level may be maintained in case problems occur. The amount of the buffer to be held is really a matter of judgement. This judgement will depend on

- the degree of uncertainty concerning the above factors;
- the likely costs of running out of the item concerned;
- the cost of holding the buffer inventories.

The effect of holding a buffer will be to raise the inventories level (the reorder point) at which an order for new inventories is placed.

### Activity 12.4

Assume the same facts as in Activity 12.3. However, we are also told that the business maintains buffer inventories of 300 units. At what level should the business reorder?

Reorder point = expected level of demand during the lead time plus the level of buffer inventories

= 800 + 300 = 1,100 units

Carrying buffer inventories will increase the cost of holding inventories; however, this must be weighed against the cost of running out of inventories, in terms of lost sales, production problems and so on.

Real World 12.5 provides an example of how small businesses can use technology in inventories reordering to help compete against their larger rivals.

---

**Real World 12.5**

## Taking on the big boys

The use of technology in inventories recording and reordering may be of vital importance to the survival of small businesses that are being threatened by larger rivals. One such example is that of small independent bookshops. Technology can come to their rescue in two ways. First, electronic point-of-sale (EPOS) systems can record books as they are sold and can constantly update records of inventories held. Thus, books that need to be reordered can be quickly and easily identified. Second, the reordering process can be improved by using web-based technology, which allows books to be ordered in real time. Many large book wholesalers provide free web-based software to their customers for this purpose and try to deliver books ordered during the next working day. This means that a small bookseller, with limited shelf space, may keep one copy only of a particular book but maintain a range of books that competes with that of a large bookseller.

*Source*: information taken from 'Small stores keep up with the big boys', *The Financial Times*, 5 February 2003.

---

## Levels of control

Senior managers must make a commitment to the management of inventories. However, the cost of controlling inventories must be weighed against the potential benefits. It may be possible to have different levels of control according to the nature of the inventories held. The ABC system of inventories control is based on the idea of selective levels of control.

A business may find that it is possible to divide its inventories into three broad categories: A, B and C. Each category will be based on the value of inventories held, as illustrated in Example 12.1.

---

**Example 12.1**

Alascan Products plc makes door handles and door fittings. It makes them in brass, in steel and in plastic. The business finds that brass fittings account for 10 per cent of the physical volume of the finished inventories that it holds, but these represent 65 per cent of its total value. These are treated as Category A inventories. There are sophisticated recording procedures, tight control is exerted over inventories movements and there is a high level of security where the brass inventories are stored. This is economic because the inventories represent a relatively small proportion of the total volume.

The business finds that steel fittings account for 30 per cent of the total volume of finished inventories and represent 25 per cent of its total value. These are treated as Category B inventories, with a lower level of recording and management control being applied.

The remaining 60 per cent of the volume of inventories is plastic fittings, which represent the least valuable items, and account for only 10 per cent of the total value of finished inventories held. These are treated as Category C inventories, so the level of recording and management control would be lower still. Applying to these inventories the level of control that is applied to Category A or even Category B inventories would be uneconomic.

Categorising inventories in this way seeks to direct management effort to the most important areas. It also tries to ensure that the costs of controlling inventories are appropriate to their importance.

Figure 12.3 shows the nature of the ABC approach to inventories control.

**Figure 12.3** ABC method of analysing and controlling inventories

Category A contains inventories that, though relatively few in quantity, account for a large proportion of the total value. Category B inventories consists of those items that are less valuable but more numerous. Category C comprises those inventories items that are very numerous, but relatively low in value. Different inventories' control rules would be applied to each category. For example, only Category A inventories would attract the more expensive and sophisticated controls.

## Inventories management models

### *Economic order quantity*

It is possible to use decision models to help manage inventories. The economic order quantity (EOQ) model is concerned with determining the quantity of a particular inventories item that should be ordered each time. In its simplest form, the EOQ model assumes that demand is constant. This implies that inventories will be depleted evenly over time to be replenished just at the point that they run out. These assumptions would lead to a 'saw-tooth' pattern to represent inventories' movements, as shown in Figure 12.4.

**Figure 12.4 Patterns of inventories movements over time**

Here we assume that there is a constant rate of usage of the inventories item, and that inventories are reduced to zero just as new inventories arrive. At time 0 there is a full level of inventories. This is steadily used as time passes; and just as it falls to zero it is replaced. This pattern is then repeated.

The EOQ model recognises that the key costs associated with inventories management are the cost of holding the inventories and the cost of ordering them. The model can be used to calculate the optimum size of a purchase order by taking account of both of these cost elements. The cost of holding inventories can be substantial. Management may, therefore, try to minimise the average amount of inventories held. This will reduce the level of inventories held and, therefore, the holding cost. It will, however, increase the number of orders placed during the period and so ordering costs will rise.

**Figure 12.5** Inventories holding and order costs

Small inventories levels imply frequent reordering and high annual ordering costs. Small inventories levels also imply relatively low inventories holding costs. High inventories levels imply exactly the opposite. There is, in theory, an optimum order size that will lead to the sum of ordering and holding costs (total costs) being at a minimum.

Figure 12.5 shows how, as the level of inventories and the size of inventories orders increase, the annual costs of placing orders will decrease because fewer orders will be placed. However, the cost of holding inventories will increase, as there will be higher average inventories levels. The total costs curve, which is based on the sum of holding costs and ordering costs, will fall until the point E, which represents the minimum total cost. Thereafter, total costs begin to rise. The EOQ model seeks to identify point E at which total costs are minimised. This will represent half of the optimum amount that should be ordered on each occasion. Assuming, as we are doing, that inventories are used evenly over time and that they fall to zero before being replaced, the average inventories level equals half of the order size.

The EOQ model, which can be used to derive the most economic order quantity, is

$$EOQ = \sqrt{\frac{2DC}{H}}$$

where

$D$ = the annual demand for the inventories item (expressed in units of the inventories item);

$C$ = the cost of placing an order;

$H$ = the cost of holding one unit of the inventories item for one year.

## Activity 12.5

HLA Ltd sells 2,000 bags of cement each year. It has been estimated that the cost of holding one bag of cement for a year is £4. The cost of placing an order for new inventories is estimated at £250.

Calculate the EOQ for bags of cement.

Your answer to this activity should be as follows:

$$EOQ = \sqrt{\frac{2 \times 2,000 \times 250}{4}} = 500 \text{ bags}$$

This will mean that the business will have to order bags of cement four times each year (that is 2,000/500) in batches of 500 bags so that sales demand can be met.

Note that the cost of the inventories concerned, which is the price paid to the supplier, does not directly impact on the EOQ model. The EOQ model is concerned only with the administrative costs of placing each order and the costs of looking after the inventories.

It will tend to be the case that more expensive inventories items will have greater storage costs. Where the business operates an ABC system of inventories control, Category A inventories would tend to have a lower EOQ than Category B ones. Also, higher cost inventories tie up more finance than cheaper ones, again leading to higher holding cost. So the cost of the inventories may have an indirect effect on the economic order size that the model recommends.

The basic EOQ model has a number of limiting assumptions. In particular, it assumes that

- demand for an inventories item can be predicted with accuracy;
- demand is constant over the period and does not fluctuate through seasonality or for other reasons;
- no 'buffer' inventories are required;
- there are no discounts for bulk purchasing.

However, the model can be modified to overcome each of these limiting assumptions. Many businesses use this model (or a development of it) to help in the management of inventories.

### Materials requirement planning systems

A materials requirement planning (MRP) system takes planned sales demand as its starting point. It then uses a computer package to help schedule the timing of deliveries of bought-in parts and materials to coincide with production requirements. It is a co-ordinated approach that links materials and parts deliveries to the scheduled time of their input to the production process. By ordering only those items that are necessary to ensure the flow of production, inventories levels are likely to be reduced. MRP is really a 'top-down' approach to inventories management, which recognises that inventories ordering decisions cannot be viewed as being independent of production decisions. In recent years, this approach has been extended to provide a fully integrated approach to production planning. The approach also takes account of other manufacturing resources such as labour and machine capacity.

### Just-in-time inventories management

In recent years, many businesses have tried to eliminate the need to hold inventories by adopting just-in-time (JIT) inventories management. This approach was originally used in the US defence industry during the Second World War, but was first used on a wide scale by Japanese manufacturing businesses. The essence of JIT is, as the name suggests, to have supplies delivered to the business just in time for them to be used in the production process or in a sale. By adopting this approach, the inventories holding costs rest with suppliers rather than with the business itself. On the other hand, a failure by a particular supplier to deliver on time could cause enormous problems and costs to the business. Thus JIT can save cost, but it tends to increase risk.

For JIT to be successful, it is important that the business informs suppliers of its inventories requirements in advance. Also suppliers, in their turn, must deliver materials of the right quality at the agreed times. Failure to do so could lead to a dislocation of production or supply to customers and could be very costly. Thus a close relationship is required between the business and its suppliers. This close relationship enables suppliers to schedule their own production to that of their customers. This should mean that between supplier and customer there will be a net saving in the amount of inventories that need to be held, relative to what would apply were JIT not in operation.

Adopting JIT may well require re-engineering a business's production process. To ensure that orders are quickly fulfilled, factory production must be flexible and responsive. This may require changes both to the production layout and to working practices. Production flows may have to be redesigned and employees may have to be given greater responsibility to allow them to deal with unanticipated problems and to encourage greater commitment. Information systems must also be installed that facilitate an uninterrupted production flow.

Although a business that applies JIT will not have to hold inventories, there may be other costs associated with this approach. As the suppliers may need to hold inventories for the customer, they may try to recoup this additional cost through increased prices. On the other hand, the close relationship between customer and supplier should enable the supplier to predict its customers' inventories needs. This means that suppliers can tailor their own production to that of the customer. The close relationship necessary between the business and its suppliers may also prevent the business from taking advantage of cheaper sources of supply if they become available.

Many people view JIT as more than simply an inventories control system. The philosophy underpinning this approach is concerned with eliminating waste and striving for excellence. There is an expectation that suppliers will always deliver inventories on time and that there will be no defects in the items supplied. There is also an expectation that, for manufacturers, the production process will operate at maximum efficiency. This means that there will be no production breakdowns and the queuing and storage times of products manufactured will be eliminated, as only that time spent directly on processing the products is seen as adding value. While these expectations may be impossible to achieve, they do help to create a culture that is dedicated to the pursuit of excellence and quality.

Real World 12.6 and Real World 12.7 show how two very well-known businesses operating in the UK (one a retailer, the other a manufacturer) use JIT to advantage.

---

**Real World 12.6**

## JIT at Boots

Boots, the UK's largest healthcare retailer, has improved inventories management at its stores. The business is working towards a JIT system where delivery from its one central warehouse in Nottingham will be made every day to each retail branch, with nearly all of the inventories lines being placed directly on to the sales shelves, not into a store room at the branch. This is expected to bring major savings of stores staff time and lead to significantly lower levels of inventories being held, without any lessening of the service offered to customers. The new system is expected to lead to major economic benefits for the business.

*Source*: information taken from 'Boots £60 million warehouse will improve supply chain', www.thisisnottingham.co.uk, 22 January 2000.

---

**Real World 12.7**

## JIT at Nissan

Nissan Motors UK Limited, the UK manufacturing arm of the world famous Japanese car business, has a plant in Sunderland in the north east of England. Here it operates a fairly well-developed JIT system. For example, Calsonic Kansei supplies car exhausts from a factory close to the Nissan plant. It makes deliveries to Nissan once every 30 minutes on average, so as to arrive exactly as they are needed in production. This is fairly typical of all of the 200 suppliers of components and materials to the Nissan plant.

The business used to have a complete JIT system. More recently, however, Nissan has drawn back from its total adherence to JIT. By using only local suppliers it has cut itself off from the opportunity to exploit low-cost suppliers, particularly some located in China. This has led the business to feel the need to hold buffer inventories of certain items to guard against disruption of supply arising from transport problems when parts are sourced from the Far East.

*Sources*: information taken from 'Planning for quality and productivity', The Times 100 Case Study, www.tt100.biz; Tighe, C., 'Nissan reviews just-in-time parts policy', *The Financial Times*, 23 October 2006; Sunderland Automotive Conference 2010, www.automotiveinternational.co.uk.

## Managing receivables

Selling goods or services on credit will result in costs being incurred by a business. These costs include credit administration costs, bad debts and opportunities forgone to use the funds for other purposes. However, these costs must be weighed against the benefits of increased sales resulting from the opportunity for customers to delay payment.

Selling on credit is very widespread and is the norm outside the retail industry. When a business offers to sell its goods or services on credit, it must have clear policies concerning

- which customers should receive credit;
- how much credit should be offered;
- what length of credit it is prepared to offer;
- whether discounts will be offered for prompt payment;
- what collection policies should be adopted;
- how the risk of non-payment can be reduced.

In this section, we shall consider each of these issues.

### Which customers should receive credit and how much should they be offered?

A business offering credit runs the risk of not receiving payment for goods or services supplied. Thus, care must be taken over the type of customer to whom credit facilities are offered and how much credit is allowed. When considering a proposal from a customer for the supply of goods or services on credit, the business must take a number of factors into account. The following five Cs of credit provide a business with a useful checklist.

- *Capital*. The customer must appear to be financially sound before any credit is extended. Where the customer is a business, its financial statements should be examined. Particular regard should be given to the customer's likely future profitability and liquidity. In addition, any major financial commitments (for example, capital expenditure, contracts with suppliers) must be taken into account.
- *Capacity*. The customer must appear to have the capacity to pay amounts owing. Where possible, the payment record of the customer to date should be examined. If the customer is a business, the type of activity in which it is engaged and the physical resources of the business will be relevant. The value of goods that the customer wishes to buy on credit must be related to the customer's total financial resources.
- *Collateral*. On occasions, it may be necessary to ask for some kind of security for goods supplied on credit. When this occurs, the business must be convinced that the customer is able to offer a satisfactory form of security.
- *Conditions*. The state of the industry in which the customer operates, and the general economic conditions of the particular region or country, may have an

important influence on the ability of a customer to pay the amounts outstanding on the due date.

■ *Character*. It is important for a business to make some assessment of the customer's character. The willingness to pay will depend on the honesty and integrity of the individual with whom the business is dealing. Where the customer is a business, this will mean assessing the characters of its senior managers. The selling business must feel satisfied that the customer will make every effort to pay any amounts owing.

It is clear from the above that the business will need to gather information concerning the ability and willingness of the customer to pay the amounts owing on or before the due dates.

## Activity 12.6

Assume that you are the credit manager of a business and that a limited company approaches you with a view to buying goods on credit. What sources of information might you decide to use to help assess the financial health of the potential customer?

There are various possibilities. You may have thought of some of the following:

■ *Trade references*. Some businesses ask potential customers to supply them with references from other suppliers who have made sales on credit to them. This may be extremely useful provided that the references supplied are truly representative of the opinions of a customer's suppliers. There is a danger that a potential customer will be selective when giving details of other suppliers, in an attempt to create a more favourable impression than is deserved.

■ *Bank references*. It is possible to ask the potential customer for a bank reference. Although banks are usually prepared to supply references, the contents of such references are not always very informative. If customers are in financial difficulties, the bank may be unwilling to add to their problems by supplying poor references. It is worth remembering that the bank's loyalty is likely to be with the customer rather than the enquirer. The bank will usually charge a fee for providing a reference.

■ *Published financial statements*. A limited company is obliged by law to file a copy of its annual financial statements with the Registrar of Companies. These financial statements are available for public inspection and provide a useful source of information. Apart from the information contained in the financial statements, company law requires public limited companies to state (in the directors' report) the average time taken to pay suppliers. The annual reports of many companies are available on their own websites or on computer-based information systems (for example, FAME).

■ *The customer*. Interviews with the directors of the customer business and visits to its premises may be carried out to gain an impression of the way that the customer conducts its business. Where a significant amount of credit is required, the business may ask the customer for access to internal budgets and other unpublished financial information to help assess the level of risk involved.

■ *Credit agencies*. Specialist agencies exist to provide information that can be used to assess the creditworthiness of a potential customer. The information that a credit agency supplies may be gleaned from various sources, including the financial statements of the customer and news items relating to the customer from both published and unpublished sources. The credit agencies may also provide a credit rating for the business. Agencies will charge a fee for their services.

■ *Register of County Court Judgments*. Any money judgments given against the business or an individual in a county court will be maintained on the register for six years. This register is available for inspection by any member of the public for a small fee.

■ *Other suppliers*. Similar businesses will often be prepared to exchange information concerning slow payers or defaulting customers through an industry credit circle. This can be a reliable and relatively cheap way of obtaining information.

## Length of credit period

A business must determine what credit terms it is prepared to offer its customers. The length of credit offered to customers can vary significantly between businesses. It may be influenced by such factors as

■ the typical credit terms operating within the industry;
■ the degree of competition within the industry;
■ the bargaining power of particular customers;
■ the risk of non-payment;
■ the capacity of the business to offer credit;
■ the marketing strategy of the business.

The last point identified may require some explanation. If, for example, a business wishes to increase its market share, it may decide to be more generous in its credit policy in an attempt to stimulate sales. Potential customers may be attracted by the offer of a longer credit period. However, any such change in policy must take account of the likely costs and benefits arising.

To illustrate this point, consider Example 12.2.

### Example 12.2

Torrance Ltd produces a new type of golf putter. The business sells the putter to wholesalers and retailers and has an annual sales revenue of £600,000. The following data relate to each putter produced.

|  | £ |
|---|---|
| Selling price | 40 |
| Variable cost | (20) |
| Fixed cost apportionment | (6) |
| Profit | 14 |

The business's cost of capital is estimated at 10 per cent a year.

Torrance Ltd wishes to expand the sales volume of the new putter. It believes that offering a longer credit period can achieve this. The business's average receivables collection period is currently 30 days. It is considering three options in an attempt to increase sales revenue. These are as follows:

| | Option 1 | Option 2 | Option 3 |
|---|---|---|---|
| Increase in average collection period (days) | 10 | 20 | 30 |
| Increase in sales revenue (£) | 30,000 | 45,000 | 50,000 |

To enable the business to decide on the best option to adopt, it must weigh the benefits of the options against their respective costs. The benefits arising will be represented by the increase in profit from the sale of additional putters. From the cost data supplied we can see that the contribution (that is, selling price (£40) less variable costs (£20)) is £20 a putter, that is, 50 per cent of the selling price. So, whatever increase there may be in sales revenue, the additional contributions will be half of that figure. The fixed costs can be ignored in our calculations, as they will remain the same whichever option is chosen.

The increase in contribution under each option will therefore be:

| | Option 1 | Option 2 | Option 3 |
|---|---|---|---|
| 50% of the increase in sales revenue (£) | 15,000 | 22,500 | 25,000 |

The increase in trade receivables under each option will be as follows:

| | Option 1 £ | Option 2 £ | Option 3 £ |
|---|---|---|---|
| Projected level of trade receivables | | | |
| 40 × £630,000/365 (Note 1) | 69,041 | | |
| 50 × £645,000/365 | | 88,356 | |
| 60 × £650,000/365 | | | 106,849 |
| Current level of trade receivables | | | |
| 30 × £600,000/365 | (49,315) | (49,315) | (49,315) |
| *Increase in trade receivables* | 19,726 | 39,041 | 57,534 |

The increase in receivables that results from each option will mean an additional finance cost to the business.

The net increase in the business's profit arising from the projected change is:

| | Option 1 £ | Option 2 £ | Option 3 £ |
|---|---|---|---|
| Increase in contribution (see above) | 15,000 | 22,500 | 25,000 |
| Increase in finance cost (Note 2) | (1,973) | (3,904) | (5,753) |
| *Net increase in profits* | 13,027 | 18,596 | 19,247 |

The calculations show that Option 3 will be the most profitable one.

Notes:
1 If the annual sales revenue totals £630,000 and 40 days' credit is allowed (both of which will apply under Option 1), the average amount that will be owed to the business by its customers, at any point during the year, will be the daily sales revenue (that is, £630,000/365) multiplied by the number of days that the customers take to pay (that is 40).

   Exactly the same logic applies to Options 2 and 3 and to the current level of trade receivables.
2 The increase in the finance cost for Option 1 will be the increase in trade receivables (£19,726) × 10 per cent. The equivalent figures for the other options are derived in a similar way.

Example 12.2 illustrates the way that a business should assess changes in credit terms. However, if there is a risk that, by extending the length of credit, there will be an increase in bad debts, this should also be taken into account in the calculations, as should any additional trade receivable collection costs that will be incurred.

Real World 12.8 shows how the length of credit taken varies greatly among well-known UK businesses.

## An alternative approach to evaluating the credit decision

It is possible to view the credit decision as a capital investment decision. Granting trade credit involves an opportunity outlay of resources in the form of cash (which has been temporarily forgone) in the expectation that future cash flows will be increased (through higher sales) as a result. A business will usually have choices concerning the level of investment to be made in credit sales and the period over which credit is granted. These choices will result in different returns and different levels of risk. There is no reason in principle why the NPV investment appraisal method, which we considered in Chapter 10, should not be used to evaluate these choices. We have seen that the NPV method takes into account both the time value of money and the level of risk involved.

Approaching the problem as an NPV assessment is not different in principle from the way that we dealt with the decision in Example 12.2. In both approaches the time value of money is considered, but in Example 12.2 we did it by charging a financing cost on the outstanding trade receivables.

## Cash discounts

In an attempt to encourage prompt payment from its credit customers, a business may  decide to offer a cash discount (or discount for prompt payment). The size of any discount will be an important influence on whether a customer decides to pay promptly.

From the business's viewpoint, the cost of offering discounts must be weighed against the likely benefits in the form of a reduction both in the cost of financing receivables and in the amount of bad debts.

In practice, there is always the danger that a customer may be slow to pay and yet may still take the discount offered. Where the customer is important to the business, it may be difficult to insist on full payment. An alternative to allowing the customer to take discounts by reducing payment is to agree in advance to provide discounts for prompt payment through quarterly credit notes. As credit notes will be given only for those debts paid on time, the customer will often make an effort to qualify for the discount.

### ? Self-assessment question 12.1

Williams Wholesalers Ltd at present asks its credit customers to pay by the end of the month after the month of delivery. In practice, customers take rather longer to pay – on average, 70 days. Sales revenue amounts to £4 million a year and bad debts to £20,000 a year.

It is planned to offer customers a cash discount of 2 per cent for payment within 30 days. Williams estimates that 50 per cent of customers will accept this facility but that the remaining customers, who tend to be slow payers, will not pay until 80 days after the sale. At present the business has an overdraft facility at an interest rate of 13 per cent a year. If the plan goes ahead, bad debts will be reduced to £10,000 a year and there will be savings in credit administration expenses of £6,000 a year.

**Required:**
Should Williams Wholesalers Ltd offer the new credit terms to customers? You should support your answer with any calculations and explanations that you consider necessary.

The solution to this question can be found at the back of the book, in Appendix B.

## Debt factoring and invoice discounting

Trade receivables can, in effect, be turned into cash by either factoring them or having sales invoices discounted. Both are forms of asset-based finance, which involves a financial institution providing a business with an advance up to 80 per cent of the value of the trade receivables outstanding. Both of these methods seem to be fairly popular approaches to managing receivables. We discussed both of these, at some length, in Chapter 11.

## Credit insurance

It is possible for a supplier to insure its entire trade receivables, individual accounts (customers) or the outstanding balance relating to a particular transaction.

## Collection policies and reducing the risk of non-payment

A business offering credit must ensure that amounts owing are collected as quickly as possible so that the risk of non-payment is minimised. Various steps can be taken to achieve this, including the following.

### Develop customer relationships

For major customers it is often useful to cultivate a relationship with the key staff responsible for paying sales invoices. If this is done, the chances of prompt payment may be increased. For less important customers, the business should at least identify key staff responsible for paying invoices, who can be contacted in the event of a payment problem.

### Publicise credit terms

The credit terms of the business should be made clear in all relevant correspondence, such as order acknowledgements, invoices and statements. In early negotiations with the prospective customer, credit terms should be openly discussed and an agreement reached.

### Issue invoices promptly

An efficient collection policy requires an efficient accounting system. Invoices (bills) must be sent out promptly to customers, as must monthly statements. Reminders must also be despatched promptly to customers who are late in paying. If a customer fails to respond to a reminder, the accounting system should alert managers so that a stop can be placed on further deliveries.

### Monitor outstanding debts

Management can monitor the effectiveness of collection policies in a number of ways. One method is to calculate the *average settlement period for trade receivables ratio*, which we met in Chapter 6. This ratio is calculated as follows:

$$\text{Average settlement period for trade receivables} = \frac{\text{Average trade receivables}}{\text{Credit sales revenue}} \times 365$$

Although this ratio can be useful, it is important to remember that it produces an *average* figure for the number of days for which debts are outstanding. This average may be badly distorted by a few large customers who are very slow or very fast payers.

### Produce an ageing schedule of trade receivables

A more detailed and informative approach to monitoring receivables may be to produce an ageing schedule of trade receivables. Receivables are divided into categories according to the length of time they have been outstanding. An ageing schedule can be produced, on a regular basis, to help managers see the pattern of outstanding receivables. An example of an ageing schedule is set out in Example 12.3.

---

## Example 12.3

**Ageing schedule of trade receivables at 31 December**

| Customer | 1 to 30 days | 31 to 60 days | 61 to 90 days | More than 90 days | Total |
|---|---|---|---|---|---|
| | £ | £ | £ | £ | £ |
| A Ltd | 20,000 | 10,000 | – | – | 30,000 |
| B Ltd | | 24,000 | – | – | 24,000 |
| C Ltd | 12,000 | 13,000 | 14,000 | 18,000 | 57,000 |
| Total | 32,000 | 47,000 | 14,000 | 18,000 | 111,000 |

*(column heading: Days outstanding spans the four date columns)*

This shows a business's trade receivables figure at 31 December, which totals £111,000. Each customer's balance is analysed according to how long the amount has been outstanding. (This business has just three credit customers.)

Thus we can see from the schedule, for example, that A Ltd has £20,000 outstanding for 30 days or fewer (that is, arising from sales during December) and £10,000 outstanding for between 31 and 60 days (broadly, arising from November sales). This information can be very useful for credit control purposes.

Many accounting software packages now include this ageing schedule as one of the routine reports available to managers. Such packages often have the facility to put customers 'on hold' when they reach their credit limits. Putting a customer on hold means that no further credit sales will be made to that customer until amounts owing from past sales have been settled.

---

### Answer queries quickly

It is important for relevant staff to deal quickly and efficiently with customer queries on goods and services supplied. Payment is unlikely to be made by customers until their queries have been dealt with.

### Deal with slow payers

It is almost inevitably the case that a business making significant sales on credit will be faced with customers who do not pay. When this occurs, there should be agreed procedures for dealing with the situation. However, the cost of any action to be taken against delinquent credit customers must be weighed against the likely returns. For example, there is little point in taking legal action against a customer, incurring large legal expenses, if there is evidence that the customer does not have the necessary resources to pay. Where possible, an estimate of the cost of bad debts should be taken into account when setting prices for products or services.

Real World 12.9 shows that businesses are not always as efficient as they might be with their management of trade receivables.

---

**Real World 12.9**

## Would you credit it?

According to a recent survey of 6,500 UK businesses, 44 per cent of businesses leave it a fortnight, or longer, after the due date for payment before sending reminders to their credit customers, while 13 per cent leave it for a month or more. In other words, many businesses are very slow to react to their customers failing to pay on time.

Intrum Justitia UK, who conducted the survey, said: 'A clear credit policy, consistent checks on overdue payments and robust credit management systems are just some of the critical measures that businesses need to adopt.'

*Source*: information taken from Moules, J., 'Late reminders lead to late payments', *The Financial Times*, 7 January 2006.

---

As a footnote to our consideration of managing receivables, Real World 12.10 outlines some of the excuses that long-suffering credit managers must listen to when chasing payment for outstanding debts.

---

**Real World 12.10**

## It's in the post

The Atradius Group provides trade credit insurance and trade receivables collections services worldwide. It has a presence in 42 countries. Its products and services aim to reduce its customers' exposure to buyers who cannot pay for the products and services customers purchase.

In a press release Atradius said:

Although it happens rarely, some debtors [credit customers] still manage to surprise even us. These excuses have actually been used by credit customers:

- It's not a valid debt as my vindictive ex-wife ran off with the company credit card.
- I just got back from my luxury holiday, it cost more than I thought so I no longer have the funds to pay.
- I wanted to pay but all the invoices were in my briefcase, which was stolen on the street.
- My wife has been kidnapped and I need the money to get her back.

*Source*: www.atradius.us/news/press-releases 13 August 2008.

## Managing cash

### Why hold cash?

Most businesses hold a certain amount of cash. The amount of cash held tends to vary considerably between businesses.

### How much cash should be held?

Although cash can be held for each of the reasons identified, doing so may not always be necessary. If a business is able to borrow quickly, the amount of cash it needs to hold can be reduced. Similarly, if the business holds assets that can easily be converted to cash (for example, marketable securities such as shares in Stock Exchange listed businesses or government bonds), the amount of cash held can be reduced.

The decision as to how much cash a particular business should hold is a difficult one. Different businesses will have different views on the subject.

## Activity 12.8

What do you think are the major factors that influence how much cash a particular business should hold? See if you can think of five possible factors.

You may have thought of the following:

■ *The nature of the business*. Some businesses, such as utilities (for example, water, electricity and gas suppliers), have cash flows that are both predictable and reasonably certain. This will enable them to hold lower cash balances. For some businesses, cash balances may vary greatly according to the time of year. A seasonal business may accumulate cash during the high season to enable it to meet commitments during the low season.

■ *The opportunity cost of holding cash*. Where there are profitable opportunities it may not be wise to hold a large cash balance.

■ *The level of inflation*. Holding cash during a period of rising prices will lead to a loss of purchasing power. The higher the level of inflation, the greater will be this loss.

■ *The availability of near-liquid assets*. If a business has marketable securities or inventories that may easily be liquidated, high cash balances may not be necessary.

■ *The availability of borrowing*. If a business can borrow easily (and quickly) there is less need to hold cash.

■ *The cost of borrowing*. When interest rates are high, the option of borrowing becomes less attractive.

■ *Economic conditions*. When the economy is in recession, businesses may prefer to hold cash so that they can be well placed to invest when the economy improves. In addition, during a recession, businesses may experience difficulties in collecting trade receivables. They may therefore hold higher cash balances than usual in order to meet commitments.

■ *Relationships with suppliers*. Too little cash may hinder the ability of the business to pay suppliers promptly. This can lead to a loss of goodwill. It may also lead to discounts being forgone.

## Controlling the cash balance

Several models have been developed to help businesses control their cash balance. One such model proposes the use of upper and lower control limits for cash balances and the use of a target cash balance. The model assumes that the business will invest in marketable investments that can easily be liquidated. These investments will be purchased or sold, as necessary, in order to keep the cash balance within the control limits.

The model proposes two upper and two lower control limits (see Figure 12.6). If the business exceeds an *outer* limit, the managers must decide whether the cash balance is likely to return over the next few days to a point within the *inner* control limits set. If this seems likely, then no action is required. If, on the other hand, it does not seem likely, management must change the cash position of the business by either buying or selling marketable investments.

**Figure 12.6 Controlling the cash balance**

Management sets the upper and lower limits for the business's cash balance. When the balance goes beyond either of these limits, unless it is clear that the balance will return fairly quickly to within the limit, action will need to be taken. If the upper limit is breached, some cash will be placed on deposit or used to buy some marketable securities. If the lower limit is breached, the business will need to borrow some cash or sell some securities.

In Figure 12.6 we can see that the lower outer control limit has been breached for four days. If a four-day period is unacceptable, managers must sell marketable investments to replenish the cash balance.

The model relies heavily on management judgement to determine where the control limits are set and the period within which breaches of the control limits are acceptable. Past experience may be useful in helping managers decide on these issues. There are other models, however, that do not rely on management judgement. Instead, these use quantitative techniques to determine an optimal cash policy. One model proposed, for example, is the cash equivalent of the inventories economic order quantity model, discussed earlier in the chapter.

## Cash budgets and managing cash

To manage cash effectively, it is useful for a business to prepare a cash budget. This is a very important tool for both planning and control purposes. Cash budgets were considered in Chapter 9 and so we shall not consider them again in detail. However, it is worth repeating that these statements enable managers to see how planned events are expected to affect the cash balance. The cash budget will identify periods when cash surpluses and cash deficits are expected.

When a cash surplus is expected to arise, managers must decide on the best use of the surplus funds. When a cash deficit is expected, managers must make adequate provision by borrowing, liquidating assets or rescheduling cash payments or receipts to deal with this. Cash budgets are useful in helping to control the cash held. The actual cash flows can be compared with the planned cash flows for the period. If there is a significant divergence between the projected cash flows and the actual cash flows, explanations must be sought and corrective action taken where necessary.

To refresh your memory on cash budgets, it would probably be worth looking back at Chapter 9, pages 327–331.

Although cash budgets are prepared primarily for internal management purposes, prospective lenders sometimes require them when a loan to a business is being considered.

## The operating cash cycle

When managing cash, it is important to be aware of the operating cash cycle (OCC) of the business. For a retailer, for example, this may be defined as the period between the outlay of cash necessary for the purchase of inventories and the ultimate receipt of cash from the sale of the goods. In the case of a business that purchases goods on credit for subsequent resale on credit (for example, a wholesaler), the OCC is as shown in Figure 12.7.

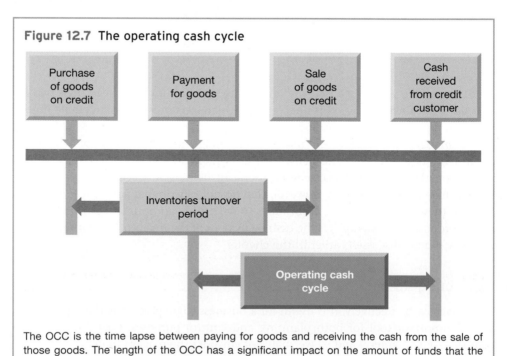

**Figure 12.7 The operating cash cycle**

The OCC is the time lapse between paying for goods and receiving the cash from the sale of those goods. The length of the OCC has a significant impact on the amount of funds that the business needs to apply to working capital.

Figure 12.7 shows that payment for inventories acquired on credit occurs some time after those inventories have been purchased. Therefore, no immediate cash outflow arises from the purchase. Similarly, cash receipts from credit customers will occur some time after the sale is made. There will be no immediate cash inflow as a result of the sale. The OCC is the period between the payment made to the supplier, for the goods concerned, and the cash received from the credit customer. Although Figure 12.7 depicts the position for a wholesaling business, the precise definition of the OCC can easily be adapted for other types of business.

The OCC is important because it has a significant influence on the financing requirements of the business. Broadly, the longer the cycle, the greater the financing requirements of the business and the greater the financial risks. For this reason, the business is likely to want to reduce the OCC to the minimum possible period.

For the type of business mentioned above, which buys and sells on credit, the OCC can be calculated from the financial statements by the use of certain ratios. It is calculated as shown in Figure 12.8.

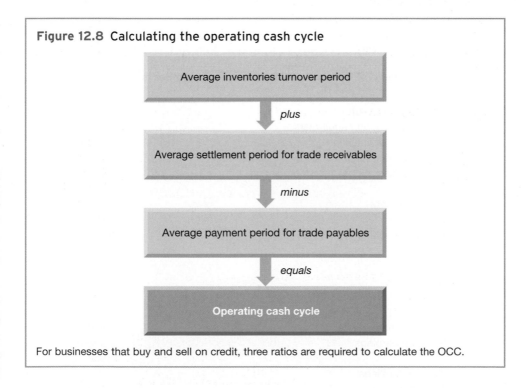

**Figure 12.8** Calculating the operating cash cycle

For businesses that buy and sell on credit, three ratios are required to calculate the OCC.

## Activity 12.9

The financial statements of Freezeqwik Ltd, a distributor of frozen foods, are set out below for the year ended 31 December last year.

### Income statement for the year ended 31 December last year

| | £000 | £000 |
|---|---:|---:|
| Sales revenue | | 820 |
| Cost of sales | | |
| Opening inventories | 142 | |
| Purchases | 568 | |
| | 710 | |
| Closing inventories | (166) | (544) |
| Gross profit | | 276 |
| Administration expenses | | (120) |
| Distribution expenses | | (95) |
| Operating profit | | 61 |
| Financial expenses | | (32) |
| Profit before taxation | | 29 |
| Taxation | | (7) |
| Profit for the year | | 22 |

### Statement of financial position as at 31 December last year

| ASSETS | £000 |
|---|---:|
| Non-current assets | |
| *Property, plant and equipment* | |
| Premises at valuation | 180 |
| Fixtures and fittings at cost less depreciation | 82 |
| Motor vans at cost less depreciation | 102 |
| | 364 |
| Current assets | |
| Inventories | 166 |
| Trade receivables | 264 |
| Cash | 24 |
| | 454 |
| Total assets | 818 |
| EQUITY AND LIABILITIES | |
| Equity | |
| Ordinary share capital | 300 |
| Retained earnings | 352 |
| | 652 |
| Current liabilities | |
| Trade payables | 159 |
| Taxation | 7 |
| | 166 |
| Total equity and liabilities | 818 |

All purchases and sales are on credit. There has been no change in the level of trade receivables or payables over the period.

Calculate the length of the OCC for the business and go on to suggest how the business may seek to reduce this period.

The OCC may be calculated as follows:

|  | *Number of days* |
|---|---|
| Average inventories turnover period: | |
| $\dfrac{\text{(Opening inventories + Closing inventories)/2}}{\text{Cost of sales}} \times 365 = \dfrac{(142 + 166)/2}{544} \times 365$ | 103 |
| Average settlement period for trade receivables: | |
| $\dfrac{\text{Trade receivables}}{\text{Credit sales}} \times 365 = \dfrac{264}{820} \times 365$ | 118 |
| Average settlement period for trade payables: | |
| $\dfrac{\text{Trade payables}}{\text{Credit purchases}} \times 365 = \dfrac{159}{568} \times 365$ | (102) |
| OCC | 119 |

The business can reduce the length of the OCC in a number of ways. The average inventories turnover period seems quite long. At present, average inventories held represent more than three months' sales requirements. Lowering the level of inventories held will reduce this. Similarly, the average settlement period for trade receivables seems long, at nearly four months' sales. Imposing tighter credit control, offering discounts, charging interest on overdue accounts and so on may reduce this. However, any policy decisions concerning inventories and trade receivables must take account of current trading conditions.

Extending the period of credit taken to pay suppliers could also reduce the OCC. However, for reasons that will be explained later, this option must be given careful consideration.

Real World 12.11 shows the average operating cash cycle for large European businesses.

## Cycling along

The annual survey of working capital by REL Consultancy Group and CFO Europe (see Real World 12.2 above) calculates the average operating cash cycle for the top 1,000 European businesses (excluding the financial sector). Comparative figures for the five-year period ending in 2008 are shown in Figure 12.9.

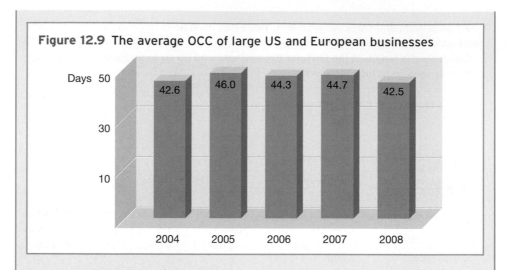

**Figure 12.9** The average OCC of large US and European businesses

The survey calculates the operating cash cycle using year-end figures for trade receivables, inventories and trade payables. We can see that there has been a slight improvement in 2008 compared to the two previous years.

*Source*: compiled from information in REL/CFO Europe 2009 European Working Capital Survey, www.relconsult.com.

## Cash transmission

A business will normally wish to benefit from receipts from customers at the earliest opportunity. The benefit is immediate where payment is made in cash. However, when payment is made by cheque, there may be a delay before it is cleared through the banking system. The business must therefore wait before it can benefit from the amount paid in.

In recent years, however, the CHAPS (Clearing House Automated Payments System) has helped to reduce the time that cheques spend in the system. It is now possible for cheques to be fast tracked so that they reach the recipient's bank account on the same day. A business could require payments to be made in cash. This is not usually very practical, however, mainly because of the risk of theft and/or the expense of conveying cash securely. Another option is to ask for payment to be made by standing order or by direct debit from the customer's bank account. This should ensure that the amount owing is always transferred from the bank account of the customer to the bank account of the business on the day that has been agreed.

It is also possible for funds to be transferred directly to a business's bank account. Customers can pay for items by using debit cards. This results in the appropriate account being instantly debited and the seller's bank account being instantly credited with the required amount. Large retail businesses use this method of payment widely. It can also be extended to other types of business.

## Bank overdrafts

Bank overdrafts are simply bank current accounts that have a negative balance. They are a type of bank loan and can be a useful tool in managing the business's cash flow requirements.

Real World 12.12 shows how Indesit, a large white-goods manufacturer, managed to improve its cash flows through better working capital management.

**Real World 12.12**

### Dash for cash

Despite an impressive working capital track record, a 50% plunge in profit at Indesit in 2005 led to the creation of a new three year plan that meant an even stronger emphasis on cash generation. Operating cash flow was added to the incentive scheme for senior and middle managers, who subsequently released more cash from Indesit's already lean processes by 'attacking the areas that were somehow neglected', says Crenna, the chief financial officer.

Hidden in the dark corners of the accounts-receivable department in the UK's after-sales service operation, for example, were a host of delinquent, albeit small, payments – in some cases overdue by a year or more. 'If you don't put a specific focus on these receivables, it's very easy for them to become neglected,' Crenna says. 'In theory, nobody worries about collecting £20. In reality, we were sitting on a huge amount of receivables, though each individual bill was for a small amount.'

More trapped cash was found in the company's spare-parts inventory. The inventory is worth around €30m today compared with around €40m three years ago. 'This was a good result that came just from paying the same level of attention to spare parts as to finished products,' Crenna says. In general, Indesit has been able to improve working capital performance through 'fine-tuning rather than launching epic projects'. Over the past two years, according to REL, Indesit has released €115m from its working capital processes.

*Source:* Karaian, J., 'Dash for cash', *CFO Europe Magazine*, 8 July 2008, www.CFO.com.

## Managing trade payables

Trade credit arises from the fact that most businesses buy their goods and service requirements on credit. In effect, suppliers are lending the business money, interest-free, on a short-term basis. Trade payables are the other side of the coin from trade receivables. One business's trade payable is another one's trade receivable, in respect of a particular transaction. Trade payables are an important source of finance for most businesses. They have been described as a 'spontaneous' source, as they tend to increase in line with the increase in the level of activity achieved by a business.

Trade credit is widely regarded as a 'free' source of finance and, therefore, a good thing for a business to use. There may be real costs, however, associated with taking trade credit.

First, customers who take credit may not be as well treated as those who pay immediately. For example, when goods are in short supply, credit customers may receive lower priority when allocating the goods available. In addition, credit customers may be less favoured in terms of delivery dates or the provision of technical support services. Sometimes, the goods or services provided may be more costly if credit is required. However, in most industries, trade credit is the norm. As a result, the above costs will not apply except, perhaps, to customers that abuse the credit facilities. A business that purchases supplies on credit will normally have to incur additional administration and accounting costs in dealing with the scrutiny and payment of invoices, maintaining and updating payables accounts, and so on.

These points are not meant to imply that taking credit represents a net cost to a business. There are, of course, real benefits that can accrue. Provided that trade credit is not abused, it can represent a form of interest-free loan. It can be a much more convenient method of paying for goods and services than paying by cash and, during a period of inflation, there will be an economic gain by paying later rather than sooner for goods and services purchased. For most businesses, these benefits will exceed the costs involved.

In some cases, delaying payment to payables can be a sign of financial problems. One such example is given in Real World 12.13.

### Real World 12.13

## Public sector keeps suppliers waiting

The UK government and other public sector bodies fail to pay on time with one in three payments to their small business suppliers. This is according to a survey of its members by the Fedration of Small Businesses, undertaken in late 2009. In 2008, the government pledged that all public sector bodies would pay within ten days of making purchases of goods and services from private sector suppliers.

The worst offenders among the public sector bodies seemed to be the UK government itself, European Union institutions and the National Health Service. Generally, private sector customers were even later payers.

*Source*: information taken from 'One in three payments from the public sector are still being made late', FSB News release, www.fsb.org.uk, 1 February 2010.

## Taking advantage of cash discounts

Where a supplier offers a discount for prompt payment, the business should give careful consideration to the possibility of paying within the discount period. An example may be useful to illustrate the cost of forgoing possible discounts.

## Example 12.4

Hassan Ltd takes 70 days to pay for goods from its supplier. To encourage prompt payment, the supplier has offered the business a 2 per cent discount if payment for goods is made within 30 days.

Hassan Ltd is not sure whether it is worth taking the discount offered.

If the discount is taken, payment could be made on the last day of the discount period (that is, the 30th day). However, if the discount is not taken, payment will be made after 70 days. This means that, by not taking the discount, the business will receive an extra 40 (that is, 70 − 30) days' credit. The cost of this extra credit to the business will be the 2 per cent discount forgone. If we annualise the cost of this discount forgone, we have:

$$(365/40 \times 2)\% = 18.3\%^*$$

We can see that the annual cost of forgoing the discount is very high. It may, therefore, be profitable for the business to pay the supplier within the discount period, even if it means that it will have to borrow to enable it to do so.

\* This is an approximate annual rate. For the more mathematically minded, the precise rate is:

$$\{[(1 + 2/98)^{9.125}] - 1\} \times 100\% = 20.2\%$$

## Controlling trade payables

To help monitor the level of trade credit taken, management can calculate the *average settlement period for trade payables*. As we saw in Chapter 6, this ratio is

$$\text{Average settlement period for trade payables} = \frac{\text{Average trade payables}}{\text{Credit purchases}} \times 365$$

Once again, this provides an average figure, which could be misleading. A more informative approach would be to produce an ageing schedule for payables. This would look much the same as the ageing schedule for receivables described earlier in Example 12.3.

We saw earlier that delaying payment to suppliers may create problems for a business. Real World 12.14, however, describes how cash-strapped businesses may delay payments and still retain the support of their suppliers.

## Real World 12.14

### Credit stretch

According to Gavin Swindell, European managing director of REL, a research and consulting firm, there are 'win-win' ways of extending credit terms. He states: 'A lot of businesses aren't worried about getting paid in 40 or 45 days, but are more interested in the certainty of payment on a specific date.'

Jas Sahota, a partner in Deloitte's UK restructuring practice, says that three-month extensions are common, 'as long as the supplier can see that there is a plan'. In times of stress, he says, it's important to negotiate with only a handful of the most important partners – squeezing suppliers large and small only generates grief and distracts employees with lots of calls.

More fundamentally, the benefits of pulling the payables lever in isolation is 'questionable', notes Andrew Ashby, director of the working capital practice at KPMG in London, 'especially as the impact on the receivables balance is typically a lot more than the payables balance'.

Improving collections, such as achieving longer payment terms, relies on the strength of relationships built over time, notes Robert Hecht, a London-based managing director of turnaround consultancy AlixPartners. 'You can't wait for a crisis and then expect suppliers to step up and be your best friends.'

*Source*: Karaian, J., 'Dash for cash', *CFO Europe Magazine*, 8 July 2008, www.CFO.com.

## Summary

The main points of this chapter may be summarised as follows.

### Working capital

- Working capital is the difference between current assets and current liabilities.
- That is, working capital = inventories + trade receivables + cash – trade payables – bank overdrafts.
- An investment in working capital cannot be avoided in practice – typically large amounts are involved.

### Inventories

- There are costs of holding inventories, which include:
  - lost interest
  - storage cost
  - insurance cost
  - obsolescence.
- There are also costs of not holding sufficient inventories, which include:
  - loss of sales and customer goodwill
  - production dislocation
  - loss of flexibility – cannot take advantage of opportunities
  - reorder costs – low inventories imply more frequent ordering.

- Practical points on inventories management include:
  - identify optimum order size – models can help with this
  - set inventories reorder levels
  - use forecasts
  - keep reliable inventories records
  - use accounting ratios (for example, inventories turnover period ratio)
  - establish systems for security of inventories and authorisation
  - consider just-in-time (JIT) inventories management.

### Trade receivables

- When assessing which customers should receive credit, the five Cs of credit can be used:
  - capital
  - capacity
  - collateral
  - conditions
  - character.
- The costs of allowing credit include:
  - lost interest
  - lost purchasing power
  - costs of assessing customer creditworthiness
  - administration cost
  - bad debts
  - cash discounts (for prompt payment).
- The costs of denying credit include loss of customer goodwill.
- Practical points on receivables management:
  - establish a policy
  - assess and monitor customer creditworthiness
  - establish effective administration of receivables
  - establish a policy on bad debts
  - consider cash discounts
  - use financial ratios (for example, average settlement period for trade receivables ratio)
  - use ageing summaries.

### Cash

- The costs of holding cash include:
  - lost interest
  - lost purchasing power.
- The costs of holding insufficient cash include:
  - loss of supplier goodwill if unable to meet commitments on time
  - loss of opportunities
  - inability to claim cash discounts
  - costs of borrowing (should an obligation need to be met at short notice).

- Practical points on cash management:
  - establish a policy
  - plan cash flows
  - make judicious use of bank overdraft finance – it can be cheap and flexible
  - use short-term cash surpluses profitably
  - bank frequently
  - operating cash cycle (for a wholesaler) = length of time from buying inventories to receiving cash from receivables less payables' payment period (in days)
  - transmit cash promptly.
- An objective of working capital management is to limit the length of the operating cash cycle (OCC), subject to any risks that this may cause.

### Trade payables

- The costs of taking credit include:
  - higher price than purchases for immediate cash settlement
  - administrative costs
  - restrictions imposed by seller.
- The costs of not taking credit include:
  - lost interest-free borrowing
  - lost purchasing power
  - inconvenience – paying at the time of purchase can be inconvenient.
- Practical points on payables management:
  - establish a policy
  - exploit free credit as far as possible
  - use accounting ratios (for example, average settlement period for trade payables ratio).

Now check your progress in your personal Study Plan

 **Key terms**

lead time p. 462
ABC system of inventories control
    p. 463
economic order quantity (EOQ)
    p. 465
materials requirement planning
    (MRP) system p. 467

just-in-time (JIT) inventories
    management p. 468
five Cs of credit p. 470
cash discount p. 475
ageing schedule of trade
    receivables p. 477
operating cash cycle (OCC) p. 482

## Further reading

If you would like to explore the topics covered in this chapter in more depth, we recommend the following books:

Arnold, G., *Corporate Financial Management* (4th edn), Financial Times Prentice Hall, 2008, chapter 13.

Brealey, B., Myers, S. and Allen, F., *Corporate Finance* (9th edn), McGraw-Hill, 2008, chapters 30 and 31.

McLaney, E., *Business Finance: Theory and Practice* (8th edn), Financial Times Prentice Hall, 2009, chapter 13.

Pike, R. and Neale, B., *Corporate Finance and Investment* (6th edn), Financial Times Prentice Hall, 2009, chapters 13 and 14.

## ? Review questions

Solutions to these questions can be found at the back of the book, in Appendix C.

**12.1** Tariq is the credit manager of Heltex plc. He is concerned that the pattern of monthly cash receipts from credit sales shows that credit collection is poor compared with budget. Heltex's sales director believes that Tariq is to blame for this situation, but Tariq insists that he is not. Why might Tariq not be to blame for the deterioration in the credit collection period?

**12.2** How might each of the following affect the level of inventories held by a business?

(a) An increase in the number of production bottlenecks experienced by the business.
(b) A rise in the business's cost of capital.
(c) A decision to offer customers a narrower range of products in the future.
(d) A switch of suppliers from an overseas business to a local business.
(e) A deterioration in the quality and reliability of bought-in components.

**12.3** What are the reasons for holding inventories? Are these reasons different from the reasons for holding cash?

**12.4** Identify the costs of holding:

(a) too little cash;
(b) too much cash.

# ✳ Exercises

Exercises 12.4 and 12.5 are more advanced than 12.1 to 12.3. Those with coloured numbers have solutions at the back of the book, in Appendix D.

If you wish to try more exercises, visit the website at www.myaccountinglab.com.

**12.1** Hercules Wholesalers Ltd has been particularly concerned with its liquidity position in recent months. The most recent income statement and statement of financial position of the business are as follows:

### Income statement for the year ended 31 December last year

|  | £000 | £000 |
|---|---|---|
| Sales revenue |  | 452 |
| Cost of sales |  |  |
| Opening inventories | 125 |  |
| Purchases | 341 |  |
|  | 466 |  |
| Closing inventories | (143) | (323) |
| Gross profit |  | 129 |
| Expenses |  | (132) |
| Loss for the year |  | (3) |

### Statement of financial position as at 31 December last year

|  | £000 |
|---|---|
| **Non-current assets** |  |
| *Property, plant and equipment* |  |
| Premises at valuation | 280 |
| Fixtures and fittings at cost less depreciation | 25 |
| Motor vehicles at cost less depreciation | 52 |
|  | 357 |
| **Current assets** |  |
| Inventories | 143 |
| Trade receivables | 163 |
|  | 306 |
| **Total assets** | 663 |
| **Equity** |  |
| Ordinary share capital | 100 |
| Retained earnings | 158 |
|  | 258 |
| **Non-current liabilities** |  |
| Borrowings – loans | 120 |
| **Current liabilities** |  |
| Trade payables | 145 |
| Borrowings – bank overdraft | 140 |
|  | 285 |
| **Total equity and liabilities** | 663 |

The trade receivables and payables were maintained at a constant level throughout the year.

Required:
(a) Explain why Hercules Wholesalers Ltd is concerned about its liquidity position.
(b) Calculate the operating cash cycle for Hercules Wholesalers Ltd based on the information above.
(c) State what steps may be taken to improve the operating cash cycle of the business.

**12.2** International Electric plc at present offers its customers 30 days' credit. Half the customers, by value, pay on time. The other half take an average of 70 days to pay. The business is considering offering a cash discount of 2 per cent to its customers for payment within 30 days.

The credit controller anticipates that half of the customers who now take an average of 70 days to pay (that is, a quarter of all customers) will pay in 30 days. The other half (the final quarter) will still take an average of 70 days to pay. The scheme will also reduce bad debts by £300,000 a year.

Annual sales revenue of £365 million is made evenly throughout the year. At present the business has a large overdraft (£60 million) with its bank at an interest cost of 12 per cent a year.

Required:
(a) Calculate the approximate equivalent annual percentage cost of a discount of 2 per cent, which reduces the time taken by credit customers to pay from 70 days to 30 days. (*Hint*: This part can be answered without reference to the narrative above.)
(b) Calculate the value of trade receivables outstanding under both the old and new schemes.
(c) How much will the scheme cost the business in discounts?
(d) Should the business go ahead with the scheme? State what other factors, if any, should be taken into account.
(e) Outline the controls and procedures that a business should adopt to manage the level of its trade receivables.

**12.3** The managing director of Sparkrite Ltd, a trading business, has just received summary sets of financial statements for last year and this year:

**Sparkrite Ltd**
**Income statements for years ended 30 September last year and this year**

|  | Last year | | This year | |
| --- | --- | --- | --- | --- |
|  | £000 | £000 | £000 | £000 |
| Sales revenue |  | 1,800 |  | 1,920 |
| Cost of sales |  |  |  |  |
| Opening inventories | 160 |  | 200 |  |
| Purchases | 1,120 |  | 1,175 |  |
|  | 1,280 |  | 1,375 |  |
| Closing inventories | (200) |  | (250) |  |
|  |  | (1,080) |  | (1,125) |
| Gross profit |  | 720 |  | 795 |
| Expenses |  | (680) |  | (750) |
| Profit for the year |  | 40 |  | 45 |

$\rightarrow$

**Statements of financial position as at 30 September last year and this year**

|  | Last year<br>£000 | This year<br>£000 |
|---|---|---|
| Non-current assets | 950 | 930 |
| Current assets |  |  |
| Inventories | 200 | 250 |
| Trade receivables | 375 | 480 |
| Bank | 4 | 2 |
|  | 579 | 732 |
| Total assets | 1,529 | 1,662 |
| Equity |  |  |
| Fully paid £1 ordinary shares | 825 | 883 |
| Retained earnings | 509 | 554 |
|  | 1,334 | 1,437 |
| Current liabilities | 195 | 225 |
| Total equity and liabilities | 1,529 | 1,662 |

The finance director has expressed concern at the increase in inventories and trade receivables levels.

Required:
(a) Show, by using the data given, how you would calculate ratios that could be used to measure inventories and trade receivables levels during last year and this year.
(b) Discuss the ways in which the management of Sparkrite Ltd could exercise control over
    (i)  inventories levels;
    (ii) trade receivables levels.

**12.4** Mayo Computers Ltd has annual sales of £20 million. Bad debts amount to £0.1 million a year. All sales made by the business are on credit and, at present, credit terms are negotiable by the customer. On average, the settlement period for trade receivables is 60 days. Trade receivables are financed by an overdraft bearing a 14 per cent rate of interest per year. The business is currently reviewing its credit policies to see whether more efficient and profitable methods could be employed. Only one proposal has so far been put forward concerning the management of trade credit.

The credit control department has proposed that customers should be given a 2½ per cent discount if they pay within 30 days. For those who do not pay within this period, a maximum of 50 days' credit should be given. The credit department believes that 60 per cent of customers will take advantage of the discount by paying at the end of the discount period. The remainder will pay at the end of 50 days. The credit department believes that bad debts can be effectively eliminated by adopting the above policies and by employing stricter credit investigation procedures, which will cost an additional £20,000 a year. The credit department is confident that these new policies will not result in any reduction in sales revenue.

Required:
Calculate the net annual cost (savings) to the business of abandoning its existing credit policies and adopting the proposals of the credit control department. (*Hint*: To answer this question you must weigh the costs of administration and cash discounts against the savings in bad debts and interest charges.)

**12.5** Boswell Enterprises Ltd is reviewing its trade credit policy. The business, which sells all of its goods on credit, has estimated that sales revenue for the forthcoming year will be £3 million under the existing policy. Credit customers representing 30 per cent of trade receivables are expected to pay one month after being invoiced and 70 per cent are expected to pay two months after being invoiced. These estimates are in line with previous years' figures.

At present, no cash discounts are offered to customers. However, to encourage prompt payment, the business is considering giving a $2\frac{1}{2}$ per cent cash discount to credit customers who pay in one month or less. Given this incentive, the business expects credit customers accounting for 60 per cent of trade receivables to pay one month after being invoiced and those accounting for 40 per cent of trade receivables to pay two months after being invoiced. The business believes that the introduction of a cash discount policy will prove attractive to some customers and will lead to a 5 per cent increase in total sales revenue.

Irrespective of the trade credit policy adopted, the gross profit margin of the business will be 20 per cent for the forthcoming year and three months' inventories will be held. Fixed monthly expenses of £15,000 and variable expenses (excluding discounts), equivalent to 10 per cent of sales revenue, will be incurred and will be paid one month in arrears. Trade payables will be paid in arrears and will be equal to two months' cost of sales. The business will hold a fixed cash balance of £140,000 throughout the year, whichever trade credit policy is adopted.

**Required:**

(a) Calculate the investment in working capital at the end of the forthcoming year under
  (i) the existing policy;
  (ii) the proposed policy.
(b) Calculate the expected profit for the forthcoming year under
  (i) the existing policy;
  (ii) the proposed policy.
(c) Advise the business as to whether it should implement the proposed policy.

Ignore taxation.

(*Hint*: The investment in working capital will be made up of inventories, trade receivables and cash, *less* trade payables and any unpaid expenses at the year end.)

# Appendix A: Glossary of key terms

ABC system of inventories control   A method of applying different levels of inventories control, based on the value of each category of inventories. *p. 463*

Absorption costing   A method of costing in which a 'fair share' of all manufacturing overheads are included when calculating the cost of a particular cost unit. *p. 282*

Accounting   The process of identifying, measuring and communicating information to permit informed judgements and decisions by users of the information. *p. 2*

Accounting conventions   Accounting rules that have evolved over time in order to deal with practical problems rather than to reflect some theoretical ideal. *p. 51*

Accounting information system   The system used within a business to identify, record, analyse and report accounting information. *p. 9*

Accounting rate of return (ARR)   The average profit from an investment, expressed as a percentage of the average investment made. *p. 359*

Accruals accounting   The system of accounting that follows the accruals convention. This is the system followed in drawing up the statement of financial position and income statement. *p. 87*

Accruals convention   The convention of accounting that asserts that profit is the excess of revenue over expenses, not the excess of cash receipts over cash payments. *p. 87*

Accrued expenses   Expenses that are outstanding at the end of an accounting period. *p. 83*

Acid test ratio   A liquidity ratio that relates the current assets (less inventories) to the current liabilities. *p. 208*

Activity-based costing (ABC)   A technique for relating overheads to specific production or provision of a service. It is based on acceptance of the fact that overheads do not just occur but are caused by activities, such as holding products in stores, which 'drive' the costs. *p. 301*

Adverse variance   A difference between planned and actual performance, usually where the difference will cause the actual profit to be lower than the budgeted one. *p. 339*

Ageing schedule of trade receivables   A report dividing trade receivables into categories, depending on the length of time outstanding. *p. 477*

Allotted share capital   *See* Issued share capital.

**Alternative Investment Market (AIM)** A stock market for the shares of smaller, young and growing businesses. AIM is similar in style to the main London Stock Exchange, but is cheaper for a business to enter and has a lighter regulatory regime. *p. 435*

**Amortisation** The term used to describe depreciation of intangible non-current assets. *p. 95*

**Asset** Resource held by a business, that has certain characteristics. *p. 36*

**Asset-based financing** A form of financing where assets are used as security for cash advances to the business. Factoring and invoice discounting, where the security is trade receivables, are examples of asset-based financing. *p. 437*

**Auditors** Professionals whose main duty is to make a report as to whether, in their opinion, the financial statements of a company do what they are supposed to do, namely show a true and fair view and comply with statutory, and financial reporting standard, requirements. *p. 145*

**Average inventories turnover period ratio** An efficiency ratio that measures the average period for which inventories are held by a business. *p. 200*

**Average settlement period for trade payables ratio** The average time taken for a business to pay its trade payables. *p. 202*

**Average settlement period for trade receivables ratio** The average time taken for trade receivables to pay the amounts owing. *p. 201*

**Bad debt** An amount owed to the business that is considered to be irrecoverable. *p. 102*

**Bank overdraft** A flexible form of borrowing that allows an individual or business to have a negative current account balance. *p. 437*

**Batch costing** A technique for identifying full cost, where the production of many types of goods and services – particularly goods – involves producing in a batch of identical or nearly identical cost units, but where each batch is distinctly different from other batches. *p. 296*

**Bonus shares** Reserves that are converted into shares and given 'free' to shareholders. *p. 128*

**Break-even analysis** The activity of deducing the break-even point of some activity through analysing costs and revenue. *p. 245*

**Break-even chart** A graphical representation of the costs and revenue of some activity, at various levels of output, that enables the break-even point to be identified. *p. 246*

**Break-even point (BEP)** The level of activity at which total revenue will equal total cost, so that there is neither profit nor loss. *p. 246*

**Budget** A financial plan for the short term, typically one year or less. *p. 314*

**Budget holder** An individual responsible for a particular budget. *p. 326*

**Budgetary control** Using the budget as a yardstick against which the effectiveness of actual performance may be assessed. *p. 343*

**Business angel**  An individual who supplies finance (usually equity finance) and advice to a small business. Usually the amount of finance supplied falls between £10,000 and £750,000. *p. 443*

**Business entity convention**  The convention that holds that, for accounting purposes, the business and its owner(s) are treated as quite separate and distinct. *p. 51*

**Business review**  A narrative report prepared by the directors that aims to provide a balanced and comprehensive analysis of performance for the period. *p. 146*

**Called-up share capital**  That part of a company's share capital for which the shareholders have been asked to pay the agreed amount. It is part of the claim of the owners against the business. *p. 131*

**Capital reserves**  Reserves that arise from an unrealised 'capital' profits or gains rather than from normal realised trading activities. *p. 126*

**Carrying amount**  The difference between the cost (or fair value) of a non-current asset and the accumulated depreciation relating to the asset. The carrying value is also referred to as the written-down value (WDV) and the net book value (NBV). *p. 91*

**Cash discount**  A reduction in the amount due for goods or services sold on credit in return for prompt payment. *p. 475*

**Claim**  Obligation on the part of a business to provide cash or some other benefit to an outside party. *p. 36*

**Common cost**  *See* Indirect cost.

**Comparability**  The requirement that similar items be treated in the same manner for measurement and reporting purposes. *p. 6*

**Consistency convention**  The accounting convention that holds that, when a particular accounting approach is selected to deal with a transaction, this method should be applied consistently over time. *p. 101*

**Consolidating**  Reducing the number of shares and increasing their nominal value per share to compensate. *p. 125*

**Continual budget**  A budgeting system that continually updates budgets so that there is always a budget for a full planning period. (Also known as a rolling budget.) *p. 317*

**Contribution margin ratio**  The contribution from an activity expressed as a percentage of the sales revenue. *p. 250*

**Contribution per unit**  Sales revenue per unit less variable costs per unit. *p. 250*

**Control**  Compelling events to conform to a plan. *p. 314*

**Convertible loan notes**  Long-term borrowings that can be converted into equity share capital at the option of the holders. *p. 413*

**Corporate governance**  Matters concerned with directing and controlling a company. *p. 119*

**Corporation tax**  Taxation that a limited company is liable to pay on its profits. *p. 118*

Cost   The amount of resources, usually measured in monetary terms, sacrificed to achieve a particular objective. *p. 240*

Cost behaviour   The manner in which costs alter with changes in the level of activity. *p. 284*

Cost centre   Some area, object, person or activity for which costs are separately collected. *p. 293*

Cost driver   An activity that causes costs. *p. 301*

Cost of capital   The cost to the business of the finance needed to fund an investment. *p. 377*

Cost of sales   The cost of the goods sold during a period. Cost of sales can be derived by adding the opening inventories held to the inventories purchases for the period and then deducting the closing inventories held. (Also known as cost of goods sold.) *p. 75*

Cost pool   The sum of the overhead costs that are seen as being caused by the same cost driver. *p. 302*

Cost unit   The objective for which the cost is being deduced, usually a product or service. *p. 279*

Creative accounting   Adopting accounting policies to achieve a particular view of performance and position that preparers would like users to see rather than what is a true and fair view. *p. 146*

Current assets   Assets that are held for the short term. They include cash itself and other assets that are held for sale or consumption in the normal course of a business's operating cycle. *p. 44*

Current liabilities   Claims against the business which are expect to be settled within the normal course of the business's operating cycle or within twelve months of the statement of financial position date, or which are held primarily for trading purposes, or for which the business does not have the right to defer settlement beyond twelve months of the statement of financial position date. *p. 47*

Current ratio   A liquidity ratio that relates the current assets of the business to the current liabilities. *p. 207*

Debt factoring   A service offered by a financial institution (a factor) that involves the factor taking over the management of the trade receivables of the business. The factor is often prepared to make an advance to the business, based on the amount of trade receivables outstanding. *p. 437*

Depreciation   A measure of that portion of the cost (or fair value) of a non-current asset that has been consumed during an accounting period. *p. 87*

Direct cost   A cost that can be identified with a specific cost unit, to the extent that the effect of the cost can be measured in respect of that cost unit. *p. 280*

Direct method   An approach to deducing the cash flows from operating activities, in a statement of cash flows, by analysing the business's cash records. *p. 168*

**Directors**  Individuals who are appointed (normally by being elected) to act as the most senior level of management of a company. *p. 119*

**Directors' report**  A report containing information of a financial and non-financial nature that the directors must produce as part of the annual financial report to shareholders. *p. 145*

**Discount factor**  The rate applied to future cash flows to derive the present value of those cash flows. *p. 375*

**Discretionary budget**  A budget based on a sum allocated at the discretion of senior management. *p. 326*

**Dividend**  The transfer of assets (usually cash) made by a company to its shareholders. *p. 124*

**Dividend cover ratio**  An investment ratio that relates the earnings available for dividends to the dividends announced, to indicate how many times the former covers the latter. *p. 217*

**Dividend payout ratio**  An investment ratio that relates the dividends announced for the period to the earnings available for dividends that were generated in that period. *p. 217*

**Dividend per share**  An investment ratio that relates the dividends announced for a period to the number of shares in issue. *p. 218*

**Dividend yield ratio**  An investment ratio that relates the value the dividend per share announced for a reporting period to the current market value of a share. *p. 218*

**Dual aspect convention**  The accounting convention that holds that each transaction has two aspects and that each aspect must be recorded in the financial statements. *p. 54*

**Earnings per share (EPS)**  An investment ratio that relates the earnings generated by the business during a period, and available to shareholders, to the number of shares in issue. *p. 218*

**Economic order quantity (EOQ)**  The quantity of inventories that should be bought in each order so as to minimise total inventories' costs. *p. 465*

**Equity**  The claim of the owner(s) of the business. In the case of a limited company it comprises the ordinary shares and reserves. *p. 38*

**Eurobond**  A form of long-term borrowing where the finance is raised on an international basis. Eurobonds are issued in a currency that is not that of the country in which the bonds are issued. *p. 412*

**Expense**  A measure of the outflow of assets (or increase in liabilities) incurred as a result of generating revenue. *p. 72*

**Fair values**  The values ascribed to assets as an alternative to historic cost. They are usually the current market value (that is, the exchange values in an arm's-length transaction). *p. 59*

**Favourable variance**   A difference between planned and actual performance, usually where the difference will cause the actual profit to be higher than the budgeted one. *p. 339*

**Final accounts**   The income statement, statement of cash flows and statement of financial position taken together. *p. 35*

**Finance**   A branch of economics concerned with how businesses raise funds and select appropriate investments. *p. 2*

**Finance lease**   A financial arrangement where the asset title remains with the owner (the lessor) but the lease agreement transfers virtually all the rewards and risks to the business (the lessee). *p. 417*

**Financial accounting**   The measuring and reporting of accounting information for external users (those users other than the managers of the business). *p. 10*

**Financial derivative**   Any form of financial instrument, based on share capital or borrowings, which can be used by investors either to increase their returns or to decrease their exposure to risk. *p. 415*

**Financial gearing**   The existence of fixed payment-bearing sources of finance (for example, borrowings) in the capital structure of a business. *p. 209*

**First in, first out (FIFO)**   A method of inventories costing which assumes that the earliest acquired inventories are used (in production or sales) first. *p. 98*

**Five Cs of credit**   A checklist of factors to be taken into account when assessing the creditworthiness of a customer. *p. 470*

**Fixed cost**   A cost that stays the same when changes occur to the volume of activity. *p. 240*

**Flexible budget**   A budget that is adjusted to reflect the actual level of output achieved. *p. 338*

**Flexing a budget**   Revising a budget to what it would have been had the planned level of output been different. *p. 337*

**Forecast**   A prediction of future outcomes, or of the future state of the environment. *p. 317*

**Full cost**   The total amount of resources, usually measured in monetary terms, sacrificed to achieve a particular objective. *p. 278*

**Full costing**   Deducing the total direct and indirect (overhead) costs of pursuing some activity or objective. *p. 279*

**Fully paid shares**   Shares on which the shareholders have paid the full issue price. *p. 131*

**Gearing ratio**   A ratio that relates the contribution of finance that requires a fixed return (such as borrowings) to the total long-term finance of the business. *p. 212*

**Going concern convention**   The accounting convention that holds that it is assumed that the business will continue operations for the foreseeable future, unless there is reason to believe otherwise. In other words, there is no intention, or need, to liquidate the business. *p. 53*

Gross profit   The amount remaining (if positive) after trading expenses (for example, cost of sales) have been deducted from trading revenue. *p. 75*

Gross profit margin ratio   A profitability ratio relating the gross profit to the sales revenue for a period. *p. 197*

Hire purchase   A method of acquiring an asset by paying the purchase price by instalments over a period. Normally, control of the asset will pass as soon as the hire purchase contract is signed and the first instalment is paid, whereas ownership will pass on payment of the final instalment. *p. 421*

Historic cost convention   The accounting convention that holds that assets should be recorded at their historic (acquisition) cost. *p. 51*

Income statement   A financial statement (also known as profit and loss account) that measures and reports the profit (or loss) the business has generated during a period. It is derived by deducting from total revenue for a period, the total expenses associated with that revenue. *p. 31*

Incremental budgeting   Constructing budgets on the basis of what happened in the previous period, with some adjustment for expected changes in the forthcoming budget period. *p. 325*

Indirect cost (or common cost or overheads)   The element of cost that cannot be directly measured in respect of a particular cost unit – that is, all cost except direct cost. *p. 281*

Indirect method   An approach to deducing the cash flows from operating activities, in a statement of cash flows, by analysing the business's financial statements. *p. 168*

Inflation   An increase in the general prices of goods and services resulting in a corresponding decline in the purchasing power of money. *p. 371*

Intangible assets   Assets that do not have a physical substance (for example, patents, goodwill and trade receivables). *p. 38*

Interest cover ratio   A gearing ratio that divides the operating profit (that is, profit before interest and taxation) by the interest payable for a period. *p. 213*

Internal rate of return (IRR)   The discount rate for an investment that will have the effect of producing a zero NPV. *p. 379*

International Accounting Standards   *See* International Financial Reporting Standards.

International Financial Reporting Standards   Transnational accounting rules that have been adopted, or developed, by the International Accounting Standards Board and which should be followed in preparing the published financial statements of listed limited companies. (Also known as International Accounting Standands.) *p. 143*

Inventories   Merchandise held for resale or for use within a business. (Also known as stock.) *p. 33*

**Invoice discounting**   A loan provided by a financial institution based on a proportion of the face value of credit sales outstanding. *p. 438*

**Issued share capital**   That part of the share capital that has been issued to shareholders. Also known as allotted share capital. *p. 131*

**Job costing**   A technique for identifying the full cost per cost unit, where each cost unit is not identical to other cost units produced. *p. 282*

**Just-in-time (JIT) inventories management**   A system of inventories management that aims to have supplies delivered, to production or sales, just in time for their required use. *p. 468*

**Last in, first out (LIFO)**   A method of inventories costing which assumes that the most recently acquired inventories are used (in production or sales) first. *p. 98*

**Lead time**   The time lag between placing an order for goods or services and their delivery to the required location. *p. 162*

**Liabilities**   Claims of individuals and organisations, apart from the owner, that have arisen from past transactions or events such as supplying goods or lending money to the business. *p. 38*

**Limited company**   An artificial legal person that has an identity separate from that of those who own and manage it. *p. 113*

**Limited liability**   The restriction of the legal obligation of shareholders to meet all of the company's debts. *p. 116*

**Limiting factor**   Some aspect of the business (for example, lack of sales demand) that will prevent it achieving its objectives to the maximum extent. *p. 317*

**Loan covenant**   A condition contained within a loan agreement that is designed to help protect the lenders. *p. 415*

**Loan notes**   Long-term borrowings usually made by limited companies, sometimes known as loan stock. *p. 411*

**Loan stock**   *See* Loan notes.

**Management accounting**   The measuring and reporting of accounting information for the managers of a business. *p. 10*

**Management by exception**   A system of control, based on a comparison of planned and actual performance, that allows managers to focus on areas of poor performance rather than dealing with areas where performance is satisfactory. *p. 322*

**Margin of safety**   The extent to which the planned volume of output or sales lies above the break-even point. *p. 251*

**Marginal analysis**   The activity of decision making through analysing variable costs and revenues, ignoring fixed costs. *p. 262*

**Marginal cost**   The additional cost of producing one more unit. This is often the same as the variable cost. *p. 262*

**Master budget**   A summary of individual budgets, usually consisting of a budgeted income statement, a budgeted statement of financial position and a cash budget. *p. 318*

**Matching convention** The accounting convention that holds that, in measuring income, expenses should be matched to revenue which they helped generate in the same reporting period as that revenue was realised. *p. 83*

**Materiality** The requirement that information should only be reported in the financial statements if it is significant and its omission could affect users' decisions. *p. 7*

**Materiality convention** The accounting convention that states that, where the amounts involved are immaterial, only what is expedient should be considered. *p. 86*

**Materials requirement planning (MRP) system** A computer-based system of inventories control that schedules the timing of deliveries of bought-in parts and materials to coincide with production requirements to meet demand. *p. 467*

**Mission statement** A brief statement setting out the aims of the business. *p. 313*

**Mortgage** A loan secured on property (real estate). *p. 415*

**Net book value** *See* Carrying amount.

**Net present value (NPV)** A method of investment appraisal based on the present value of all relevant cash flows associated with an investment. *p. 368*

**Net profit** See Profit for the year.

**Nominal value** The face value of a share in a company. (Also called par value.) *p. 123*

**Non-current assets** Assets held that do not meet the criteria of current assets. They are held for the long-term operations of the business rather than continuously circulating within the business. Non-current assets can be seen as the tools of the business. (They are also known as fixed assets.) *p. 45*

**Non-current liabilities** Those amounts due to other parties that are not current liabilities. *p. 47*

**Offer for sale** An issue of shares that involves a public limited company (or its shareholders) selling the shares to a financial institution that will, in turn, sell the shares to the public. *p. 430*

**Operating cash cycle (OCC)** The period between the outlay of cash to buy supplies and the ultimate receipt of cash from the sale of goods. *p. 482*

**Operating gearing** The relationship between the total fixed and the total variable costs for some activity. *p. 255*

**Operating lease** An arrangement where a business hires an asset, usually for a short time. Hiring an asset under an operating lease tends to be seen as an operating, rather than a financing, decision. *p. 418*

**Operating profit** The profit achieved during a period after all operating expenses have been deducted from revenues from operations. Financing expenses are deducted after the calculation of operating profit. *p. 75*

**Operating profit margin ratio** A profitability ratio relating the operating profit to the sales revenue for the period. *p. 196*

**Opportunity cost** The cost incurred when one course of action prevents an opportunity to derive some benefit from another course of action. *p. 384*

Ordinary shares   Shares of a company owned by those who are due the benefits of the company's activities after all other stakeholders have been satisfied. *p. 124*

Outsourcing   Subcontracting activities to (sourcing goods or services from) organisations outside of the business. *p. 266*

Overhead absorption (recovery) rate   The rate at which overheads are charged to cost units (jobs), usually in a job costing system. *p. 286*

Overheads   *See* Indirect cost.

Paid-up share capital   That part of the share capital of a company that has been called and paid. *p. 131*

Par value   *See* Nominal value.

Payback period (PP)   The time taken for the initial outlay for an investment to be repaid from its future net cash inflows. *p. 364*

Periodic budget   A budget developed on a one-off basis to cover a particular planning period. *p. 317*

Preference shares   Shares of a company owned by those who are entitled to the first part of any dividend that the company may pay. *p. 125*

Prepaid expenses   Expenses that have been paid in advance at the end of the accounting period. *p. 86*

Price/earnings ratio   An investment ratio that relates the market value of a share to the earnings per share. *p. 219*

Private limited company   A limited company for which the directors can restrict the ownership of its shares. *p. 116*

Private placing   An issue of shares that involves a limited company arranging for the shares to be sold to the clients of particular issuing houses or stockbrokers, rather than to the general investing public. *p. 430*

Process costing   A technique for deriving the full cost per unit of output, where the units of output are identical or it is reasonable to treat them as being so. *p. 280*

Profit   The increase in wealth attributable to the owners of a business that arises through business operations. *p. 71*

Profit before taxation   The result when all of the appropriately matched expenses of running a business have been deducted from the revenue for the year, but before the taxation charge is deducted. *p. 137*

Profit for the year   The result when all of the appropriately matched expenses of running a business have been deducted from the revenue for the year and then, in the case of a limited company the taxation charge deducted. *pp. 75, 137*

Profit-volume (PV) chart   A graphical representation of the contribution (revenue less variable cost) of some activity, at various levels, which enables the break-even point and the profit at various activity levels to be identified. *p. 250*

Property, plant and equipment   Those non-current assets that have a physical substance (for example, plant and machinery, motor vehicles). *p. 58*

**Prudence convention** The accounting convention that holds that financial statements should err on the side of caution. *p. 53*

**Public issue** An issue of shares that involves a public limited company (plc) making a direct invitation to the public to buy shares in the company. *p. 430*

**Public limited company** A limited company for which the directors cannot restrict the ownership of its shares. *p. 116*

**Reducing-balance method** A method of calculating depreciation that applies a fixed percentage rate of depreciation to the carrying amount of an asset in each period. *p. 91*

**Relevance** The ability of accounting information to influence decisions; regarded as a key characteristic of useful accounting information. *p. 5*

**Relevant cost** A cost that is relevant to a particular decision. *p. 384*

**Reliability** The requirement that accounting information should be free from significant errors or bias and should represent what it purports to represent. Reliability is regarded as a key characteristic of useful accounting information. *p. 6*

**Reporting period** The time span for which a business prepares its financial statements. (Also known as accounting period.) *p. 73*

**Reserves** Part of the owners' claim (equity) of a limited company that has arisen from profits and gains, to the extent that these have not been distributed to the shareholders or reduced by losses. *p. 123*

**Residual value** The amount for which a non-current asset is sold when the business has no further use for it. *p. 89*

**Return on capital employed ratio (ROCE)** A profitability ratio expressing the relationship between the operating profit (that is, profit before interest and taxation) and the long-term funds (equity and borrowings) invested in the business. *p. 194*

**Return on ordinary shareholders' funds ratio (ROSF)** A profitability ratio that compares the amount of profit for the period available to the ordinary shareholders with their stake in the business. *p. 193*

**Revenue** A measure of the inflow of assets (for example, cash or amounts owed to a business by credit customers), or a reduction in liabilities, arising as a result of trading operations. *p. 71*

**Revenue reserve** Part of the owners' claim (equity) of a company that arises from realised profits and gains, including after-tax trading profits and gains from disposals of non-current assets. *p. 124*

**Rights issue** An issue of shares for cash to existing shareholders on the basis of the number of shares already held. *p. 426*

**Risk** The extent and likelihood that what is projected to occur will not actually occur. *p. 370*

**Risk premium** The additional return required from an investment, owing to a perceived level of risk: the greater the perceived risk, the larger the required risk premium. *p. 371*

Rolling budget   *See* Continual budget.

Sale and leaseback   An agreement to sell an asset (usually property) to another party and simultaneously to lease the asset back in order to continue using it. *p. 419*

Sales revenue per employee ratio   An efficiency ratio that relates the sales revenue generated during a period to the average number of employees of the business. *p. 204*

Sales revenue to capital employed ratio   An efficiency ratio that relates the sales revenue generated during a period to the capital employed. *p. 203*

Securitisation   Raising funds on the basis of expected future cash receipts (for example, interest receipts) by bundling them together to provide asset backing for the issue of bonds to investors. *p. 422*

Semi-fixed (semi-variable) cost   A cost that has an element of both fixed and variable cost. *p. 243*

Shares   Portions of the ownership, or equity, of a company. *p. 113*

Share premium account   A capital reserve reflecting any amount, above the nominal value of shares, that is paid for those shares when issued by a company. *p. 128*

Splitting   Dividing the nominal value of the company's shares into smaller values, so that each shareholder has more shares but with the same total nominal value. *p. 125*

Statement of cash flows   A statement that shows the sources and uses of cash for a period. *p. 31*

Statement of changes in equity   A financial statement, required by IAS 1, which shows the effect of gains/losses and capital injections/withdrawals on the equity base of a company. *p. 140*

Statement of comprehensive income   An extended version of the traditional income statement that includes all gains and losses affecting shareholders' equity. *p. 139*

Statement of financial position   A financial statement that shows the assets of the business and the claims on those assets. (It is also known as a balance sheet). *p. 31*

Stepped fixed cost   A fixed cost that does not remain fixed over all levels of output but which changes in steps as a threshold level of output is reached. *p. 242*

Stock Exchange   A market where 'second-hand' shares may be bought and sold and new capital raised. *p. 431*

Straight-line method   A method of accounting for depreciation that allocates the amount to be depreciated evenly over the useful life of the asset. *p. 90*

Strategic management   The process of setting a course to achieve the business's objectives, taking account of the commercial and economic environment in which the business operates. *p. 15*

Tangible assets   Those assets that have physical substance (for example, plant and machinery, motor vehicles). *p. 38*

**Term loan** Finance provided by financial institutions, such as banks and insurance companies, under a contract with the borrowing business that indicates the interest rate and dates of payments of interest and repayment of the loan. The loan is not normally transferable from one lender to another. *p. 411*

**Trade payables** Amounts owed by a business to suppliers for goods or services purchased on credit. (Also known as trade creditors.) *p. 40*

**Trade receivables** Amounts owed to a business from customers that purchase goods or services on credit. (Also known as trade debtors.) *p. 45*

**UK Corporate Governance Code** A code of practice for companies listed on the London Stock Exchange that deals with corporate governance matters. *p. 121*

**Understandability** The requirement that accounting information should be understood by those for whom the information is primarily compiled. Lack of understandability will limit the usefulness of accounting information. *p. 6*

**Variable cost** A cost that varies according to the volume of activity. *p. 240*

**Variance** The financial effect, usually on the budgeted profit, of a particular factor under consideration being more, or less, than budgeted. *p. 339*

**Variance analysis** Carrying out calculations to find the area of the business's operations that has caused the budgets not to have been met. *p. 341*

**Venture capital** Long-term finance provided by certain institutions to small and medium-sized businesses to exploit relatively high-risk opportunities. *p. 441*

**Weighted average cost (AVCO)** A method of inventories costing which assumes that inventories entering the business lose their separate identity and any issues of inventories reflect the weighted average cost of the inventories held. *p. 98*

**Working capital** Current assets less current liabilities. *p. 170*

**Written-down value (WDV)** *See* Carrying amount.

**Zero-base budgeting (ZBB)** An approach to budgeting based on the philosophy that all spending needs to be justified annually and that each budget should start as a clean sheet. *p. 326*

# Appendix B: Solutions to self-assessment questions

## Chapter 2

### 2.1 Simonson Engineering

The statement of financial position you prepare should be set out as follows:

**Simonson Engineering**
**Statement of financial position as at 30 September 2010**

|  | £ |
|---|---|
| **ASSETS** | |
| **Non-current assets** | |
| *Property, plant and equipment* | |
| Property | 72,000 |
| Plant and machinery | 25,000 |
| Motor vehicles | 15,000 |
| Fixtures and fittings | 9,000 |
|  | 121,000 |
| **Current assets** | |
| Inventories | 45,000 |
| Trade receivables | 48,000 |
| Cash in hand | 1,500 |
|  | 94,500 |
| **Total assets** | 215,500 |
| **EQUITY AND LIABILITIES** | |
| **Equity** | |
| Closing balance* | 120,500 |
| **Non-current liabilities** | |
| Long-term borrowings | 51,000 |
| **Current liabilities** | |
| Trade payables | 18,000 |
| Short-term borrowings | 26,000 |
|  | 44,000 |
| **Total equity and liabilities** | 215,500 |

| * The equity is calculated as follows: | |
|---|---|
| Opening balance | 117,500 |
| Profit | 18,000 |
|  | 135,500 |
| Drawings | (15,000) |
| Closing balance | 120,500 |

## Chapter 3

**3.1**

**TT and Co.**
**Statement of financial position as at 31 December 2009**

| | £ |
|---|---:|
| **ASSETS** | |
| Delivery van (12,000 − 2,500) | 9,500 |
| Inventories (143,000 + 12,000 − 74,000 − 16,000) | 65,000 |
| Trade receivables (152,000 − 132,000 − 400) | 19,600 |
| Cash at bank (50,000 − 25,000 − 500 − 1,200 | |
|   − 12,000 − 33,500 − 1,650 − 12,000 + 35,000 | |
|   + 132,000 − 121,000 − 9,400) | 750 |
| Prepaid expenses (5,000 + 300) | 5,300 |
| **Total assets** | 100,150 |
| **EQUITY AND LIABILITIES** | |
| Equity (50,000 + 26,900) | 76,900 |
| Trade payables (143,000 − 121,000) | 22,000 |
| Accrued expenses (630 + 620) | 1,250 |
| **Total equity and liabilities** | 100,150 |

**Income statement for the year ended 31 December 2009**

| | £ |
|---|---:|
| Sales revenue (152,000 + 35,000) | 187,000 |
| Cost of goods sold (74,000 + 16,000) | (90,000) |
| **Gross profit** | 97,000 |
| Rent | (20,000) |
| Rates (500 + 900) | (1,400) |
| Wages (33,500 + 630) | (34,130) |
| Electricity (1,650 + 620) | (2,270) |
| Bad debts | (400) |
| Van depreciation ((12,000 − 2,000)/4) | (2,500) |
| Van expenses | (9,400) |
| **Profit for the year** | 26,900 |

The statement of financial position could now be rewritten in a more stylish form as follows:

**Statement of financial position as at 31 December 2009**

| | £ |
|---|---:|
| **ASSETS** | |
| **Non-current assets** | |
| *Property, plant and equipment* | |
| Delivery van at cost | 12,000 |
| Accumulated depreciation | (2,500) |
| | 9,500 |
| **Current assets** | |
| Inventories | 65,000 |
| Trade receivables | 19,600 |
| Prepaid expenses | 5,300 |
| Cash | 750 |
| | 90,650 |
| **Total assets** | 100,150 |

EQUITY AND LIABILITIES

| | |
|---|---:|
| Equity | 76,900 |
| **Current liabilities** | |
| Trade payables | 22,000 |
| Accrued expenses | 1,250 |
| | 23,250 |
| Total equity and liabilities | 100,150 |

# Chapter 4

4.1

**Pear Limited**

**Income statement for the year ended 30 September 2010**

| | £000 |
|---|---:|
| Revenue (1,456 + 18) | 1,474 |
| Cost of sales | (768) |
| **Gross profit** | 706 |
| Salaries | (220) |
| Depreciation (249 + 12) | (261) |
| Other operating costs (131 + (2% × 200) + 2) | (137) |
| **Operating profit** | 88 |
| Interest payable (15 + 15) | (30) |
| **Profit before taxation** | 58 |
| Tax (58 × 30%) | (17) |
| **Profit for the year** | 41 |

**Statement of financial position as at 30 September 2010**

| | £000 |
|---|---:|
| **Non-current assets** | |
| *Property, plant and equipment* | |
| Cost (1,570 + 30) | 1,600 |
| Depreciation (690 + 12) | (702) |
| | 898 |
| **Current assets** | |
| Inventories | 207 |
| Receivables (182 + 18 – 4) | 196 |
| Cash at bank | 21 |
| | 424 |
| **Total assets** | 1,322 |
| **Equity** | |
| Share capital | 300 |
| Share premium account | 300 |
| Retained earnings (104 + 41 – 25) | 120 |
| | 720 |
| **Non-current liabilities** | |
| Borrowings – 10% loan ( repayable 2014) | 300 |
| **Current liabilities** | |
| Trade payables | 88 |
| Other payables (20 + 30 + 15 + 2) | 67 |
| Taxation | 17 |
| Dividends approved | 25 |
| Borrowings – bank overdraft | 105 |
| | 302 |
| **Total equity and liabilities** | 1,322 |

## Chapter 5

### 5.1

**Touchstone plc**
**Statement of cash flows for the year ended 31 December 2010**

|  | £m |
|---|---|
| **Cash flows from operating activities** | |
| Profit before taxation (after interest) | |
| (see Note 1 below) | 60 |
| Adjustments for: | |
| Depreciation | 16 |
| Interest expense (Note 2) | 4 |
|  | 80 |
| Increase in trade receivables (26 – 16) | (10) |
| Decrease in trade payables (38 – 37) | (1) |
| Decrease in inventories (25 – 24) | 1 |
| *Cash generated from operations* | 70 |
| Interest paid | (4) |
| Taxation paid (Note 3) | (12) |
| Dividend paid | (18) |
| *Net cash from operating activities* | 36 |
| **Cash flows from investing activities** | |
| Payments to acquire tangible non-current assets (Note 4) | (41) |
| *Net cash used in investing activities* | (41) |
| **Cash flows from financing activities** | |
| Issue of loan notes (40 – 20) | 20 |
| *Net cash used in financing activities* | 20 |
| **Net increase in cash and cash equivalents** | 15 |
| Cash and cash equivalents at 1 January 2010 | |
| Cash | 4 |
| Cash and cash equivalents at 31 December 2010 | |
| Cash | 4 |
| Treasury bills | 15 |
|  | 19 |

To see how this relates to the cash of the business at the beginning and end of the year it can be useful to provide a reconciliation as follows:

**Analysis of cash and cash equivalents during the year ended 31 December 2010**

|  | £m |
|---|---|
| Cash and cash equivalents at 1 January 2010 | 4 |
| Net cash inflow | 15 |
| Cash and cash equivalents at 31 December 2010 | 19 |

**Notes:**
1. This is simply taken from the income statement for the year.
2. Interest payable expense must be taken out, by adding it back to the profit before taxation figure. We subsequently deduct the cash paid for interest payable during the year. In this case the two figures are identical.
3. Companies pay 50% of their tax during their accounting year and the other 50% in the following year. Thus the 2010 payment would have been half the tax on the 2009 profit (that is, the figure that would have appeared in the current liabilities at the end of 2009), plus half of the 2010 tax charge (that is, $4 + (1/2 \times 16) = 12$).
4. Since there were no disposals, the depreciation charges must be the difference between the start and end of the year's non-current asset values, adjusted by the cost of any additions:

|  | £m |
|---|---|
| Carrying amount at 1 January 2010 | 147 |
| Additions (balancing figure) | 41 |
|  | 188 |
| Depreciation (6 + 10) | (16) |
| Carrying amount at 31 December 2010 | 172 |

# Chapter 6

## 6.1 Ali plc and Bhaskar plc

In order to answer this question, you may have used the following ratios:

|  | Ali plc | Bhaskar plc |
|---|---|---|
| Return on ordinary shareholders' funds ratio | $\dfrac{99.9}{687.6} \times 100 = 14.5\%$ | $\dfrac{104.6}{874.6} \times 100 = 12.0\%$ |
| Operating profit margin ratio | $\dfrac{151.3}{1,478.1} \times 100 = 10.2\%$ | $\dfrac{166.9}{1,790.4} \times 100 = 9.3\%$ |
| Average inventories turnover period ratio | $\dfrac{592.0}{1,018.3} \times 12 = 7.0$ months | $\dfrac{403.0}{1,214.9} \times 12 = 4.0$ months |
| Average settlement period for trade receivables ratio | $\dfrac{176.4}{1,478.1} \times 12 = 1.4$ months | $\dfrac{321.9}{1,790.4} \times 12 = 2.2$ months |
| Current ratio | $\dfrac{853.0}{422.4} = 2.0$ | $\dfrac{816.5}{293.1} = 2.8$ |
| Acid test ratio | $\dfrac{(853.0 - 592.0)}{422.4} = 0.6$ | $\dfrac{(816.5 - 403.0)}{293.1} = 1.4$ |
| Gearing ratio | $\dfrac{190}{(687.6 + 190)} \times 100 = 21.6\%$ | $\dfrac{250}{(874.6 + 250)} \times 100 = 22.2\%$ |
| Interest cover ratio | $\dfrac{151.3}{19.4} = 7.8$ times | $\dfrac{166.9}{27.5} = 6.1$ times |

(Note: It is not possible to use any averages in ratios because only the end-of-year figures are provided for each business)

Ali plc seems more effective than Bhaskar plc at generating returns for shareholders indicated by the higher ROSF ratio. This is perhaps partly caused by Ali plc's higher operating profit margin.

Both businesses have a very high inventories turnover period; this probably needs to be investigated, particularly by Ali plc. Ali plc has a lower average settlement period for trade receivables than Bhaskar plc.

Ali plc has a much lower current ratio and acid test ratio than Bhaskar plc. The acid test ratio of Ali plc is substantially below 1.0: this may suggest a liquidity problem.

The gearing ratio of each business is quite similar. Neither business seems to have excessive borrowing. The interest cover ratio for each business is also similar. The ratios indicate that both businesses have good profit coverage for their interest charges.

To draw better comparisons between the two businesses, it would be useful to calculate other ratios from the financial statements. It would also be helpful to calculate ratios for both businesses over (say) five years as well as key ratios of other businesses operating in the same industry.

## Chapter 7

### 7.1 Khan Ltd

(a) The break-even point, if only the Alpha service were rendered, would be:

$$\frac{\text{Fixed costs}}{\text{Sales revenue per unit} - \text{Variable cost per unit}} = \frac{£40,000}{£30 - £(15 + 6)}$$

$$= 4,445 \text{ units (a year)}$$

(Strictly it is 4,444.44, but 4,445 is the smallest number of units of the service that must be rendered to avoid a loss.)

(b)

|  | Alpha | Beta | Gamma |
|---|---|---|---|
| Selling price (£/unit) | 30 | 39 | 20 |
| Variable material cost (£/unit) | (15) | (18) | (10) |
| Variable production cost (£/unit) | (6) | (10) | (5) |
| Contribution (£/unit) | 9 | 11 | 5 |
| Staff time (hr/unit) | 2 | 3 | 1 |
| Contribution/staff hour | £4.50 | £3.67 | £5.00 |
| Order of priority | 2nd | 3rd | 1st |

(c)

| | Hours | | Contribution £ |
|---|---|---|---|
| Render: | | | |
| 5,000 Gamma using | 5,000 | generating (that is, 5,000 × £5 =) | 25,000 |
| 2,500 Alpha using | 5,000 | generating (that is, 2,500 × £9 =) | 22,500 |
| | 10,000 | | 47,500 |
| | | Fixed cost | (40,000) |
| | | Profit | 7,500 |

This leaves a demand for 500 units of Alpha and 2,000 units of Beta unsatisfied.

## Chapter 8

### 8.1 Promptprint

(a) The budget may be summarised as:

| | £ | |
|---|---|---|
| Sales revenue | 196,000 | |
| Direct materials | (38,000) | |
| Direct labour | (32,000) | |
| Total overheads | (77,000) | (2,400 + 3,000 + 27,600 + 36,000 + 8,000) |
| Operating profit | 49,000 | |

The job may be priced on the basis that both overheads and operating profit should be apportioned to it on the basis of direct labour cost, as follows:

|  | £ |  |
|---|---|---|
| Direct materials | 4,000 |  |
| Direct labour | 3,600 |  |
| Overheads | 8,663 | (£77,000 × 3,600/32,000) |
| Operating profit | 5,513 | (£49,000 × 3,600/32,000) |
|  | 21,776 |  |

This answer assumes that variable overheads vary in proportion to direct labour cost. Various other bases of charging overheads and profit loading the job could have been adopted. For example, materials cost could have been included (with direct labour) as the basis for profit loading, or even apportioning overheads.

(b) This part of the question is, in effect, asking for comments on the validity of 'full-cost-plus' pricing. This approach can be useful as an indicator of the effective long-run cost of doing the job. On the other hand, it fails to take account of relevant opportunity costs as well as the state of the market and other external factors. For example, it ignores the price that a competitor printing business may quote.

# Chapter 9

## 9.1 Antonio Ltd

(a) (i) Raw materials inventories budget for the six months ending 31 December (physical quantities):

|  | July units | Aug units | Sept units | Oct units | Nov units | Dec units |
|---|---|---|---|---|---|---|
| Opening inventories (current month's production) | 500 | 600 | 600 | 700 | 750 | 750 |
| Purchases (balancing figure) | 600 | 600 | 700 | 750 | 750 | 750 |
| Issues to production (from question) | (500) | (600) | (600) | (700) | (750) | (750) |
| Closing inventories (next month's production) | 600 | 600 | 700 | 750 | 750 | 750 |

Raw material inventories budget for the six months ending 31 December (in financial terms, that is, the physical quantities × £8):

|  | July £ | Aug £ | Sept £ | Oct £ | Nov £ | Dec £ |
|---|---|---|---|---|---|---|
| Opening inventories | 4,000 | 4,800 | 4,800 | 5,600 | 6,000 | 6,000 |
| Purchases | 4,800 | 4,800 | 5,600 | 6,000 | 6,000 | 6,000 |
| Issues to production | (4,000) | (4,800) | (4,800) | (5,600) | (6,000) | (6,000) |
| Closing inventories | 4,800 | 4,800 | 5,600 | 6,000 | 6,000 | 6,000 |

(ii) Trade payables budget for the six months ending 31 December:

| | July £ | Aug £ | Sept £ | Oct £ | Nov £ | Dec £ |
|---|---|---|---|---|---|---|
| Opening balance | | | | | | |
| (current month's payment) | 4,000 | 4,800 | 4,800 | 5,600 | 6,000 | 6,000 |
| Purchases (from raw | | | | | | |
| materials inventories budget) | 4,800 | 4,800 | 5,600 | 6,000 | 6,000 | 6,000 |
| Payments | (4,000) | (4,800) | (4,800) | (5,600) | (6,000) | (6,000) |
| Closing balance | | | | | | |
| (next month's payment) | 4,800 | 4,800 | 5,600 | 6,000 | 6,000 | 6,000 |

(iii) Cash budget for the six months ending 31 December:

| | July £ | Aug £ | Sept £ | Oct £ | Nov £ | Dec £ |
|---|---|---|---|---|---|---|
| **Inflows** | | | | | | |
| Receipts: | | | | | | |
| Trade receivables (40% | | | | | | |
| of sales revenue of | | | | | | |
| two months previous) | 2,800 | 3,200 | 3,200 | 4,000 | 4,800 | 5,200 |
| Cash sales revenue (60% | | | | | | |
| of current month's | | | | | | |
| sales revenue) | 4,800 | 6,000 | 7,200 | 7,800 | 8,400 | 9,600 |
| Total inflows | 7,600 | 9,200 | 10,400 | 11,800 | 13,200 | 14,800 |
| **Outflows** | | | | | | |
| Payables (from | | | | | | |
| trade payables | | | | | | |
| budget) | (4,000) | (4,800) | (4,800) | (5,600) | (6,000) | (6,000) |
| Direct cost | (3,000) | (3,600) | (3,600) | (4,200) | (4,500) | (4,500) |
| Advertising | (1,000) | – | – | (1,500) | – | – |
| Overheads: 80% | (1,280) | (1,280) | (1,280) | (1,280) | (1,600) | (1,600) |
| 20% | (280) | (320) | (320) | (320) | (320) | (400) |
| New plant | – | – | (2,200) | (2,200) | (2,200) | – |
| Total outflows | (9,560) | (10,000) | (12,200) | (15,100) | (14,620) | (12,500) |
| Net inflows (outflows) | (1,960) | (800) | (1,800) | (3,300) | (1,420) | 2,300 |
| Balance c/f | 5,540 | 4,740 | 2,940 | (360) | (1,780) | 520 |

The balances carried forward are deduced by deducting the deficit (net outflows) for the month from (or adding the surplus for the month to) the previous month's balance.

Note how budgets are linked; in this case the inventories budget to the trade payables budget and the payables budget to the cash budget.

(b) The following are possible means of relieving the cash shortages revealed by the budget:

■ Make a higher proportion of sales on a cash basis.

- Collect the money from credit customers more promptly, for example during the month following the sale.
- Hold lower inventories, both of raw materials and of finished goods.
- Increase the trade payables payment period.
- Delay the payments for advertising.
- Obtain more credit for the overhead cost elements; at present only 20 per cent are on credit.
- Delay the payments for the new plant.

# Chapter 10

## 10.1 Beacon Chemicals plc

(a) Relevant cash flows are as follows:

| | Year 0 £ million | Year 1 £ million | Year 2 £ million | Year 3 £ million | Year 4 £ million | Year 5 £ million |
|---|---|---|---|---|---|---|
| Sales revenue | – | 80 | 120 | 144 | 100 | 64 |
| Loss of contribution | – | (15) | (15) | (15) | (15) | (15) |
| Variable cost | – | (40) | (50) | (48) | (30) | (32) |
| Fixed cost (Note 1) | – | (8) | (8) | (8) | (8) | (8) |
| Operating cash flows | – | 17 | 47 | 73 | 47 | 9 |
| Working capital | (30) | – | – | – | – | 30 |
| Capital cost | (100) | – | – | – | – | – |
| Net relevant cash flows | (130) | 17 | 47 | 73 | 47 | 39 |

Notes:

1 Only the elements of fixed cost that are incremental to the project (only existing because of the project) are relevant. Depreciation is irrelevant because it is not a cash flow.

2 The research and development cost is irrelevant since it has been spent irrespective of the decision on X14 production.

(b) The payback period is deduced as follows:

| | Year 0 £ million | Year 1 £ million | Year 2 £ million | Year 3 £ million |
|---|---|---|---|---|
| Cumulative cash flows | (130) | (113) | (66) | 7 |

Thus the equipment will have repaid the initial investment by the end of the third year of operations. The payback period is, therefore, three years.

(c) The net present value is as follows:

| | Year 0 £ million | Year 1 £ million | Year 2 £ million | Year 3 £ million | Year 4 £ million | Year 5 £ million |
|---|---|---|---|---|---|---|
| Discount factor | 1.00 | 0.926 | 0.857 | 0.794 | 0.735 | 0.681 |
| Present value | (130) | 15.74 | 40.28 | 57.96 | 34.55 | 26.56 |
| Net present value | 45.09 (That is, the sum of the present values for years 0 to 5.) | | | | | |

# Chapter 11

### 11.1 Helsim Ltd

(a) The liquidity position may be assessed by using the liquidity ratios discussed in Chapter 6:

$$\text{Current ratio} = \frac{\text{Current assets}}{\text{Current liabilities}}$$

$$= \frac{£7.5m}{£5.4m}$$

$$= 1.4$$

$$\text{Acid test ratio} = \frac{\text{Current assets (excluding inventories)}}{\text{Current liabilities}}$$

$$= \frac{£3.7m}{£5.4m}$$

$$= 0.7$$

These ratios reveal a fairly weak liquidity position. The current ratio seems quite low and the acid test ratio very low. This latter ratio suggests that the business does not have sufficient liquid assets to meet its maturing obligations. It would, however, be useful to have details of the liquidity ratios of similar businesses in the same industry in order to make a more informed judgement. The bank overdraft represents 67% of the current liabilities and 40% of the total liabilities of the business. The continuing support of the bank is therefore important to the ability of the business to meet its commitments.

(b) The finance required to reduce trade payables to an average of 40 days outstanding is calculated as follows:

|  | £m |
| --- | --- |
| Trade payables at the date of the statement of financial position | 1.80 |
| Trade payables outstanding based on 40 days' credit 40/365 × £8.4m (that is, credit purchases) | (0.92) |
| Finance required | 0.88 (say £0.9m) |

(c) The bank may not wish to provide further finance to the business. The increase in overdraft will reduce the level of trade payables but will increase the risk exposure of the bank. The additional finance invested by the bank will not generate further funds (it will not increase profit) and will not therefore be self-liquidating. The question does not make it clear whether the business has sufficient security to offer the bank for the increase in overdraft facility. The profits of the business will be reduced and the interest cover ratio, based on the profits generated last year, would reduce to about 1.6* times if the additional overdraft were granted (based on interest charged at 10% each year). This is very low and means that only a small decline in profits would leave interest charges uncovered.

* Existing bank overdraft (3.6) + extension of overdraft to cover reduction in trade payables (0.9) + loan notes (3.5) = £8.0m. Assuming a 10% interest rate means a yearly interest payment of £0.8m. The operating profit was £1.3m. Interest cover would be 1.63 (that is, 1.3/0.8).

(d) A number of possible sources of finance might be considered. Four possible sources are as follows:

- *Issue equity shares.* This option may be unattractive to investors. The return on equity is fairly low at 7.9% (that is, profit for the year (0.3)/equity (3.8)) and there is no evidence that the profitability of the business will improve. If profits remain at their current level the effect of issuing more equity will be to reduce further the returns to equity.

- *Make other borrowings.* This option may also prove unattractive to investors. The effect of making further borrowings will have a similar effect to that of increasing the overdraft. The profits of the business will be reduced and the interest cover ratio will decrease to a low level. The gearing ratio of the business is already quite high at 48% (that is, loan notes (3.5)/(loan notes + equity (3.5 + 3.8)) and it is not clear what security would be available for the loan. The gearing ratio would be much higher if the overdraft were to be included.

- *Chase trade receivables.* It may be possible to improve cash flows by reducing the level of credit outstanding from customers. At present, the average settlement period is 93 days (that is, (trade receivables (3.6)/sales revenue (14.2)) × 365), which seems quite high. A reduction in the average settlement period by approximately one-quarter would generate the funds required. However, it is not clear what effect this would have on sales.

- *Reduce inventories.* This appears to be the most attractive of the four options. At present, the average inventories holding period is 178 days (that is, (closing inventories (3.8)/cost of sales (7.8)) × 365), which seems very high. A reduction in this period by less than one-quarter would generate the funds required. However, if the business holds a large amount of slow-moving and obsolete items, it may be difficult to reduce inventories levels.

# Chapter 12

## 12.1 Williams Wholesalers Ltd

|  | £ | £ |
|---|---|---|
| Existing level of trade receivables (£4m × 70/365) |  | 767,123 |
| New level of trade receivables: £2m × 80/365 | 438,356 |  |
| £2m × 30/365 | 164,384 | 602,740 |
| Reduction in trade receivables |  | 164,383 |
| *Cost and benefits of policy* |  |  |
| Cost of discount (£2m × 2%) |  | 40,000 |
| *Less* |  |  |
| Interest saved on the reduction in trade receivables (£164,383* × 13%) | 21,370 |  |
| Administration cost saving | 6,000 |  |
| Cost of bad debts saved (20,000 − 10,000) | 10,000 | 37,370 |
| Net cost of policy |  | 2,630 |

* It could be argued that the interest should be based on the amount expected to be received – that is, the value of the trade receivables *after* taking account of the discount. Basing it on the expected receipt figure would not, however, alter the conclusion that the business should not offer the new credit terms.

These calculations show that the business will be worse off by offering the new credit terms.

# Appendix C: Solutions to review questions

## Chapter 1

**1.1** The purpose of providing accounting information is to enable users to make more informed decisions and judgements about the organisation concerned. Unless the information fulfils this objective, there is no point in providing it.

**1.2** The main users of financial information for a university, and the way in which they are likely to use this information, may be summed up as follows:

| | |
|---|---|
| Students | Whether to enrol on a course of study. This would probably involve an assessment of the university's ability to continue to operate and to fulfil students' needs. |
| Other universities and colleges | How best to compete against the university. This might involve using the university's performance in various aspects as a 'benchmark' when evaluating their own performance. |
| Employees | Whether to take up or to continue in employment with the university. Employees might assess this by considering the ability of the university to continue to provide employment and to reward employees adequately for their labour. |
| Government/ funding authority | How efficient and effective the university is in undertaking its various activities. Possible funding needs that the university may have. |
| Local community representatives | Whether to allow/encourage the university to expand its premises. To assess this, the university's ability to continue to provide employment for the community, to use community resources and to help fund environmental improvements might be considered. |
| Suppliers | Whether to continue to supply the university at all; also whether to supply on credit. This would involve an assessment of the university's ability to pay for any goods and services supplied. |
| Lenders | Whether to lend money to the university and/or whether to require repayment of any existing loans. To assess this, the university's ability to meet its obligations to pay interest and to repay the principal would be considered. |
| Board of governors and managers (faculty deans and so on) | Whether the performance of the university requires improvement. Performance to date would be compared with earlier plans or some other 'benchmark' to decide whether action needs to be taken. Whether there should be a change in the university's future direction. In making such decisions, management will need to look at the university's ability to perform and at the opportunities available to it. |

We can see that the users of accounting information and their needs are similar to those of a private sector business.

**1.3**  Most businesses are far too large and complex for managers to be able to see and assess everything that is going on in their own areas of responsibility merely by personal observation. Managers need information on all aspects within their control. Management accounting reports can provide them with this information, to a greater or lesser extent. These reports, therefore, can be seen as acting as the eyes and ears of the managers, providing insights not necessarily obvious without them.

**1.4**  Since we can never be sure what is going to happen in the future, the best that we can do is to make judgements on the basis of past experience. Thus information concerning flows of cash and of wealth in the recent past is likely to be a useful source on which to base judgements about possible future outcomes.

## Chapter 2

**2.1**  The confusion arises because the owner seems unaware of the business entity convention in accounting. This convention requires a separation of the business from the owner(s) of the business for accounting purposes. The business is regarded as a separate entity and the statement of financial position is prepared from the perspective of the business rather than that of the owner. As a result, funds invested in the business by the owner will be regarded as a claim that the owner has on the business. In the standard layout of the statement of financial position, this claim will be shown alongside other claims on the business from outsiders.

**2.2**  A statement of financial position does not show what a business is worth, for two major reasons:

- Only those items that can be measured reliably in monetary terms are shown on the statement of financial position. Thus, things of value such as the reputation for product quality, skills of employees and so on will not normally appear in the statement of financial position.
- The historic cost convention results in assets normally being recorded at their outlay cost rather than their current value. In the case of certain assets, the difference between historic cost and current value may be significant.

**2.3**  The accounting equation is simply the relationship between a business's assets, liabilities and equity. For the standard layout, it is:

Assets (current and non-current) = Equity + Liabilities (current and non-current)

For the alternative layout mentioned in the chapter, the equation is:

Assets (current and non-current) − Liabilities (current and non-current) = Equity

**2.4**  Some object to the idea of humans being treated as assets for inclusion on the statement of financial position. It can be seen as demeaning for humans to be listed alongside inventories, plant and machinery and other assets. However, others argue that humans are often the most valuable resource of a business and that placing a value on this resource will help bring to the attention of managers the importance of nurturing and developing this 'asset'. There is a saying in management that 'the things that count are the things that get counted'. As the value of the 'human assets' is not stated in the financial statements, there is a danger that managers will treat these 'assets' less favourably than other assets that are on the statement of financial position.

Humans are likely to meet the first criterion of an asset listed in the chapter, that is, a probable future benefit exists. There would be little point in employing people if this were not the case. The second criterion concerning exclusive right of control is more problematic. Clearly a business cannot control humans in the same way as most other assets. However, a business can have the exclusive right to the employment services that a person provides. This distinction between control over the services provided and control over the person makes it possible to argue that the second criterion can be met.

Humans normally sign a contract of employment with the business, and so the third criterion is normally met. The difficulty, however, is with the fourth criterion, that is, whether the value of humans (or their services) can be measured with any degree of reliability. To date, none of the measurement methods proposed enjoy widespread acceptance.

## Chapter 3

**3.1** At the time of preparing the income statement, it is not always possible to determine accurately the expenses that need to be matched to the sales revenue figure for the period. It will only be at some later point in time that the true position becomes clear. However, it is still necessary to try to include all relevant expenses in the income statement and so estimates of the future will have to be made. The income statement would lose its timeliness if the business were to wait for all of the unknowns to become clear.

Examples of estimates that may have to be made include:

- expenses accrued at the end of the period such as the amount of telephone expenses incurred since the last quarter's bill
- the amount of depreciation based on estimates of the life of a non-current asset and its future residual value
- the amount of bad debts incurred.

**3.2** Depreciation attempts to allocate the cost or fair value, less any residual value, of an asset over its useful life. Depreciation does not attempt to measure the fall in value of the asset during a particular accounting period. Thus, the carrying amount of the asset appearing on the statement of financial position normally represents the unexpired cost of the asset rather than its current market value.

**3.3** The convention of consistency is designed to provide a degree of uniformity concerning the application of accounting policies. We have seen that in certain areas there may be more than one method of accounting for an item, for example inventories. The convention of consistency states that, having decided on a particular accounting policy, a business should continue to apply the policy in successive periods. While this policy helps to ensure that users can make valid comparisons concerning business performance *over time*, it does not ensure that valid comparisons can be made *between businesses*. This is because different businesses may consistently apply different accounting policies.

**3.4** An expense is that element of the cost incurred that is used up during the accounting period. An asset is that element of cost which is carried forward on the statement of financial position and which will normally be used up in future periods. Thus, both assets and expenses arise from costs being incurred. The major difference between the two is the period over which the benefits (resulting from the costs incurred) accrue.

## Chapter 4

**4.1** It does not differ. In both cases they are required to meet their debts to the full extent that there are assets available. This means that they both have a liability that is limited to the extent of their assets. This is a particularly important fact for the shareholders of a limited company because they know that those owed money by the company cannot demand that the shareholders contribute additional funds to help meet debts. Thus the liability of the shareholders is limited to the amount that they have paid for their shares, or have agreed to pay in the case of partially unpaid shares. This contrasts with the position of the owner or part owner of an unincorporated (non-company) business. Here all of the individual's assets could be required to meet the unsatisfied liabilities of the business.

Thus, while there is a difference between the position of a shareholder (in a limited company) and that of a sole proprietor or partner, there is no difference between the position of the company itself and a sole proprietor or partner.

**4.2** A private limited company may place restrictions on the transfer of its shares, that is, the directors can veto an attempt by a shareholder to sell his or her shares to another person to whom the directors object. Thus, in effect, the majority can avoid having as a shareholder someone that they would prefer not to have. A public company cannot do this.

A public limited company must have authorised share capital of at least £50,000. There is no minimum for a private limited company.

The main advantage of being a public limited company is that the company may offer its shares and loan notes to the general public; a private company cannot make such an offer.

**4.3** A reserve is that part of the equity (owners' claim) of a company that is not share capital. Reserves represent gains or surpluses that enhance the claim of the shareholders above the nominal value of their shares. For example, the share premium account is a reserve that represents the excess over the nominal value of shares that is paid for them on a share issue. The retained earnings balance is a reserve that arises from ploughed-back profits earned by the company. Revenue reserves arise from realised profits and gains. Capital reserves arise from unrealised profits and gains (for example, the upward revaluation of a non-current asset) or from issuing shares at a premium (share premium).

**4.4** A preference share represents part of the ownership of a company. Preference shares entitle their owners to the first part of any dividend paid by the company, up to a maximum amount. The maximum is usually expressed as a percentage of the nominal or par value of the preference shares.

(a) They differ from ordinary shares to the extent that they only entitle their holders to dividends to a predetermined maximum value. Dividends to ordinary shareholders have no predetermined maximum. Were the company to be liquidated, the preference shareholders would normally receive a maximum of the nominal value of their shares, whereas the ordinary shareholders receive the residue after all other claimants, including the preference shareholders.

(b) They differ from loan notes in that the latter represent borrowings for the company, where normally holders have a contract with the company that specifies the rate of interest, interest payment dates and redemption date. They are often secured on the company's assets. Preference shareholders have no such contract.

# Chapter 5

**5.1** Cash is normally required in the settlement of claims. Thus, employees and contractors want to be paid for their work in cash. A supplier of non-current assets or inventories will normally expect to be paid in cash, perhaps after a short period of credit. When businesses fail, it is their inability to find the cash to pay claimants that actually drives them under. These factors lead to cash being the pre-eminent business asset and, therefore, the one that analysts and others watch carefully in trying to assess the ability of the business to survive and/or to take advantage of commercial opportunities.

**5.2** With the direct method, the business's cash records are analysed for the period concerned. The analysis reveals the amounts of cash, in total, that have been paid and received in respect of each category of the statement of cash flows. This is not difficult in principle, or in practice if it is done by computer as a matter of routine.

The indirect method takes the approach that, while the profit (loss) for the year is not equal to the net inflow (outflow) of cash from operations, they are fairly closely linked to the extent that appropriate adjustment of the profit (loss) for the year figure will produce the correct cash flow one. The adjustment is concerned with depreciation charge for, and movements in relevant working capital items over, the period.

**5.3** (a) *Cash flows from operating activities*. This would normally be positive, even for a business with small profits or even losses. The fact that depreciation is not a cash flow tends to lead to positive cash flows in this area in most cases.

(b) *Cash flows from investing activities*. Normally this would be negative in cash flow terms since assets become worn out and need to be replaced in the normal course of business. This means that, typically, old items of property, plant and equipment are generating less cash on their disposal than is having to be paid out to replace them.

(c) *Cash flows from financing activities*. There is a tendency for businesses either to expand or to fail. In either case, this is likely to mean that, over the years, more finance will be raised than will be redeemed or retired.

**5.4** There are several reasons for this, including the following:

- Changes in inventories, trade receivables and trade payables. For example, an increase in trade receivables during a reporting period would mean that the cash received from credit sales would be less than the credit sales revenue for the same period.
- Cash may have been spent on new non-current assets or received from disposals of old ones; these would not directly affect profit.

- Cash may have been spent to redeem or repay a financial claim, or received as a result of the creation or the increase of a claim. These would not directly affect profit.
- The taxation charged in the income statement would not normally be the same tax that is paid during the same reporting period.

## Chapter 6

**6.1** The fact that a business operates on a low operating profit margin indicates that only a small operating profit is being produced for each £1 of sales revenue generated. However, this does not necessarily mean that the ROCE will be low. If the business is able to generate sufficient sales revenue during a period, the operating profit may be very high even though the operating profit per £1 of sales revenue is low. If the overall operating profit is high, this can lead, in turn, to a high ROCE, since it is the total operating profit that is used as the numerator (top part of the fraction) in this ratio. Many businesses (including supermarkets) pursue a strategy of 'low margin, high turnover'.

**6.2** The statement of financial position is drawn up at a single point in time – the end of the reporting period. As a result, the figures shown on the statement represent the position at that single point in time and may not be representative of the position during the period. Wherever possible, average figures (perhaps based on monthly figures) should be used. However, an external user may only have access to the opening and closing statements of financial position for the year and so a simple average based on these figures may be all that it is possible to calculate. Where a business is seasonal in nature or is subject to cyclical changes, this simple averaging may not be sufficient.

**6.3** Three possible reasons for a long inventories turnover period are:

- poor inventories controls, leading to excessive investment in inventories;
- inventories hoarding in anticipation of price rises or shortages;
- inventories building in anticipation of increased future sales.

A short inventories turnover period may be due to:

- tight inventories controls, reducing excessive investment in inventories and/or the amount of obsolete and slow-moving inventories;
- an inability to finance the required amount of inventories to meet sales demand;
- a difference in the mix of inventories carried by similar businesses (for example, greater investment in perishable goods which are held for a short period only).

These are not exhaustive lists; you may have thought of other reasons.

**6.4** Size may well be an important factor when comparing businesses:

- Larger businesses may be able to generate economies of scale in production and distribution to an extent not available to smaller businesses.
- Larger businesses may be able to raise finance more cheaply, partly through economies of scale (for example, borrowing larger amounts) and partly through being seen as less of a risk to the lender.

- Smaller businesses may be able to be more flexible and 'lighter on their feet' than can the typical larger business.

These and other possible factors may lead to differences in performance and position between larger and smaller businesses.

# Chapter 7

**7.1** A fixed cost is one that is the same irrespective of the level of activity or output. Typical examples of elements of cost that are fixed, irrespective of the level of production or provision of a service, include rent of business premises, salaries of supervisory staff and insurance.

A variable cost is one that varies with the level of activity or output. Examples include raw materials and, where it is rewarded in proportion to the level of output, labour.

Note particularly that it is relative to the level of activity that costs are fixed or variable. Fixed cost will be affected by inflation and it will be greater for a longer period than for a shorter one.

For a particular product or service, knowing which costs are fixed and which are variable enables managers to predict the total cost for any particular level of activity. It also enables them to concentrate only on the variable cost in circumstances where a decision will not alter the fixed cost.

**7.2** The break-even point is the level of activity, measured either in physical units or in value of sales revenue, at which the sales revenue exactly covers all of the costs, both fixed and variable.

Break-even point is calculated as

Fixed cost/(Sales revenue per unit − Variable cost per unit)

which may alternatively be expressed as

Fixed cost/Contribution per unit

Thus break-even will occur when the contributions for the period are sufficient to cover the fixed cost for the period.

Break-even point tends to be useful as a comparison with planned level of activity in an attempt to assess the riskiness of the activity.

**7.3** Operating gearing refers to the extent of fixed cost relative to variable cost in the total cost of some activity. Where the fixed cost forms a relatively high proportion of the total, we say that the activity has high operating gearing.

Typically, high operating gearing is present in environments where there is a relatively high level of automation (that is, capital-intensive environments). This is because such environments tend simultaneously to involve a relatively high fixed cost of depreciation, maintenance and so on and relatively low variable cost.

High operating gearing tends to mean that the effects of increases or decreases in the level of activity have an accentuated effect on operating profit. For example, a 20% decrease in output of a particular service will lead to a greater than 20% decrease in operating profit, assuming no cost or price changes.

**7.4** In the face of a restricting scarce resource, profit will be maximised by using the scarce resource on output where the contribution per unit of the scarce resource is maximised.

This means that the contribution per unit of the scarce resource (for example, hour of scarce labour, unit of scarce raw material and so on) for each competing product or service needs to be identified. It is then a question of allocating the scarce resource to the product or service that provides the highest contribution per unit of the particular scarce resource.

The logic of this approach is that the scarce resource is allocated to the activity that uses it most effectively, in terms of contribution and, therefore, profit.

# Chapter 8

**8.1** In process costing, the total production cost for a period is divided by the number of completed units of output for the period to deduce the full cost per unit. Where there is work in progress at the beginning and/or the end of the period complications arise.

The problem is that some of the completed output incurred cost in the preceding period. Similarly some of the cost incurred in the current period leads to completed production in the subsequent period. Account needs to be taken of these facts, if reliable full cost information is to be obtained.

**8.2** The only reason for distinguishing between direct and indirect costs is to help to deduce the full cost of a unit of output in a job costing environment. In an environment where all units of output are identical, or can reasonably be regarded as being so, a process costing approach will be taken. This avoids the need for identifying direct and indirect costs separately.

Direct cost forms that part of the total cost of pursuing some activity that can unequivocally be associated with that particular activity. Examples of direct cost items in the typical job costing environment include direct labour and direct materials.

Indirect cost is the remainder of the cost of pursuing some activity.

In practice, knowledge of the direct cost tends to provide the basis used to charge overheads to jobs.

The distinction between direct and indirect cost is irrelevant for any other purpose.

Directness and indirectness is dictated as much by the nature of what is being costed as by the nature of the cost.

**8.3** The notion of direct and indirect cost is concerned only with the extent to which particular elements of cost can unequivocally be related to, and measured in respect of, a particular cost unit, usually a product or service. The distinction between direct and indirect costs is made exclusively for the purpose of deducing the full cost of some cost unit, in an environment where each cost unit is not identical, or not close enough to being identical for it to be treated as such. Thus, it is typically in the context of job costing, or some variant of it, that the distinction between direct and indirect cost is usefully made.

The notion of variable and fixed costs is concerned entirely with how costs behave in the face of changes in the volume of output. The benefit of being able to distinguish between fixed and variable cost is that predictions can be made of what total cost will be at particular levels of volume and/or what reduction or addition to cost will occur if the volume of output is reduced or increased.

Thus the notion of direct and indirect cost, on the one hand, and that of variable and fixed cost, on the other, are not linked to one another. Although it is true that, in most contexts, some elements of direct cost are variable, some are fixed. Similarly, indirect cost might be fixed or variable.

**8.4** The full cost includes all of the cost of pursuing the cost objective, including a 'fair' share of the overheads. Generally the full cost represents an average cost of the various elements, rather than a cost that arises because the business finds itself in a particular situation.

The fact that the full cost reflects all aspects of cost should mean that, were the business to sell its output at a price exactly equal to the full cost (manufacturing and non-manufacturing), the sales revenues for the period would exactly cover all of the cost and the business would break even, that is make neither profit nor loss.

## Chapter 9

**9.1** A budget can be defined as a financial plan for a future period of time. Thus it sets out the intentions which management has for the period concerned. Achieving the budget plans should help to achieve the long-term plans of the business. Achievement of the long-term plans should mean that the business is successfully working towards its objectives.

A budget differs from a forecast in that a forecast is a statement of what is expected to happen without the intervention of management, perhaps because they cannot intervene, as with a weather forecast. A plan is an intention to achieve.

Normally management would take account of reliable forecasts when making its plans.

**9.2** The five uses of budgets are:

- They tend to promote forward thinking and the possible identification of short-term problems. Managers must plan and the budgeting process tends to force them to do so. In doing so they are likely to encounter potential problems. If the potential problems can be identified early enough, solutions might be easily found.
- They can be used to help co-ordination between various sections of the business. It is important that the plans of one area of the business fit in with those of other areas; a lack of co-ordination could have disastrous consequences. Having formal statements of plans for each aspect of the business enables a check to be made that plans are complementary.
- They can motivate managers to better performance. It is believed that people are motivated by having a target to aim for. Provided that the inherent goals are achievable, budgets can provide an effective motivational device.
- They can provide a basis for a system of control. Having a plan against which actual performance can be measured provides a potentially useful tool of control.
- They can provide a system of authorisation. Many managers have 'spending' budgets, like research and development, staff training and so on. For these people, the size of their budget defines their authority to spend.

**9.3** A variance is the effect on budgeted operating profit of the particular aspect of the business that is being considered. Thus it is the difference between the budgeted operating profit and what the actual operating profit would have been had all other matters, except the one under consideration, gone according to budget. From this it must be the case that budgeted operating profit plus favourable variances less unfavourable variances equals actual operating profit.

The objective of analysing and assessing variances is to identify whether, and if so where, things are not going according to plan. If this can be done, it may be possible to find out the actual cause of things going out of control. If this can be discovered, it may be possible to put things right for the future.

**9.4** Where the budgeted and actual volumes of output do not coincide, it is impossible to make a valid comparison of budgeted and actual expenses and revenues. Flexing the original budget to reflect the actual output level enables a more informative comparison to be made.

Flexing certainly does not mean that output volume differences do not matter. Flexing will show (as the difference between flexed and original budget operating profits) the effect on operating profit of output volume differences.

## Chapter 10

**10.1** NPV is usually considered the best method of assessing investment opportunities because it takes account of:

- *The timing of the cash flows.* By discounting the various cash flows associated with each project according to when they are expected to arise, it recognises the fact that cash flows do not all occur simultaneously. Associated with this is the fact that, by discounting, using the opportunity cost of capital (that is, the return which the next best alternative opportunity would generate), the net benefit after the financing cost has been met is identified (as the NPV).
- *The whole of the relevant cash flows.* NPV includes all of the relevant cash flows irrespective of when they are expected to occur. It treats them differently according to their date of occurrence, but they are all taken account of in the NPV and they all have, or can have, an influence on the decision.
- *The objectives of the business.* NPV is the only method of appraisal where the output of the analysis has a direct bearing on the wealth of the business. (Positive NPVs enhance wealth; negative ones reduce it.) Since most private sector businesses seek to increase their value and wealth, NPV clearly is the best approach to use.

NPV provides clear decision rules concerning acceptance/rejection of projects and the ranking of projects. It is fairly simple to use, particularly with the availability of modern computer software that takes away the need for routine calculations to be done manually.

**10.2** The payback method, in its original form, does not take account of the time value of money. However, it would be possible to modify the payback method to accommodate this requirement. Cash flows arising from a project could be discounted, using the cost of capital as the appropriate discount rate, in the same way as in the NPV and

IRR methods. The discounted payback approach is used by some businesses and represents an improvement on the original approach described in the chapter. However, it still retains the other flaws of the original payback approach that were discussed. For example it ignores relevant data after the payback period. Thus, even in its modified form, the PP method cannot be regarded as superior to NPV.

**10.3** The IRR method does appear to be preferred to the NPV method among many practising managers. The main reasons for this appear to be as follows:

■ A preference for a percentage return ratio rather than an absolute figure as a means of expressing the outcome of a project. This preference for a ratio may reflect the fact that other financial goals of the business are often set in terms of ratios, for example, return on capital employed.
■ A preference for ranking projects in terms of their percentage return. Managers feel it is easier to rank projects on the basis of percentage returns (though NPV outcomes should be just as easy for them). We saw in the chapter that the IRR method could provide misleading advice on the ranking of projects and that the NPV method was preferable for this purpose.

**10.4** Cash flows are preferred to profit flows because cash is the ultimate measure of economic wealth. Cash is used to acquire resources and for distribution to shareholders. When cash is invested in an investment project an opportunity cost is incurred, as the cash cannot be used in other investment projects. Similarly, when positive cash flows are generated by the project it can be used to re-invest in other investment projects.

Profit, on the other hand, is relevant to reporting the productive effort for a period. This measure of effort may have only a tenuous relationship to cash flows for a period. The conventions of accounting may lead to the recognition of gains and losses in one period and the relevant cash inflows and outflows occurring in another period.

## Chapter 11

**11.1** Convertible loan notes may be particularly useful for young expanding businesses that wish to attract new investors, who may not want to take the risk involved with a pure equity investment. If the business is successful, the loan note holders will convert to equity, meaning that the loan notes will become self-liquidating. The business may be able to pay a lower rate of interest on the loan notes because investors have the possibility of valuable equity conversion, not available with a straightforward loan.

**11.2** A listed business may wish to revert to unlisted status for a number of possible reasons. These include:

■ *Cost.* A Stock Exchange listing can be costly, as the business must adhere to certain administrative regulations and financial disclosures.
■ *Scrutiny.* Listed companies are subject to close scrutiny by analysts and this may not be welcome if the business is engaged in sensitive negotiations or controversial business activities.

- *Takeover risk*. The shares of the business may be purchased by an unwelcome bidder and this may result in a takeover.
- *Investor profile*. If the business is dominated by a few investors who wish to retain their interest in the business and do not wish to raise further equity by public issues, the benefits of a listing are few.

**11.3**  An offer for sale involves an issuing house buying the shares in the business and then, in turn, selling the shares to the public. The issue will be advertised by the publication of a prospectus, which will set out details of the business and the issue price of the shares (or reserve price if a tender issue is being made). The shares issued by the issuing house may be either new shares or shares which have been purchased from existing shareholders. A public issue is where the business undertakes direct responsibility for issuing shares to the public. If an issuing house is employed it will usually be in the role of adviser and administrator of the issue. However, the issuing house may also underwrite the issue. A public issue runs the risk that the shares will not be taken up and is a less popular form of issue for businesses.

**11.4**  Invoice discounting is a service offered to businesses by a financial institution whereby the institution is prepared to advance a sum equivalent to 75% to 80% of outstanding trade receivables. The amount advanced is usually payable within 60 to 90 days. The business will retain responsibility for collecting the amounts owing from credit customers and the advance must be repaid irrespective of whether the trade receivables have been collected. Factoring is a service that is also offered to businesses by financial institutions. In this case, the factor will take over the business's sales and trade receivables records and will undertake to collect trade receivables on behalf of the client business. The factor will also be prepared to make an advance of 80% to 85% of approved trade receivables that is repayable from the amounts received from customers. The service charge for invoice discounting is up to 0.5% of turnover, whereas the service charge for factoring is up to 3% of turnover. This difference explains, in part, why businesses have shown a preference for invoice discounting rather than factoring in recent years. However, the factor provides additional services, as explained.

## Chapter 12

**12.1**  Although the credit manager is responsible for ensuring that receivables pay on time, Tariq may be right in denying blame. Various factors may be responsible for the situation described which are beyond the control of the credit manager. These include:

- a downturn in the economy leading to financial difficulties among credit customers;
- decisions by other managers within the business to liberalise credit policy in order to stimulate sales;
- an increase in competition among suppliers offering credit, which is being exploited by customers;
- disputes with customers over the quality of goods or services supplied;
- problems in the delivery of goods leading to delays.

You may have thought of others.

**12.2** The level of inventories held will be affected in the following ways.

(a) An increase in production bottlenecks is likely to result in an increase in raw materials and work in progress being processed within the plant. Therefore, inventories levels should rise.

(b) A rise in the cost of capital will make holding inventories more expensive. This may, in turn, lead to a decision to reduce inventory levels.

(c) The decision to reduce the range of products should result in a lower level of inventories being held. It would no longer be necessary to hold certain items in order to meet customer demand.

(d) Switching to a local supplier may reduce the lead time between ordering an item and receiving it. This should, in turn, reduce the need to carry such high levels of the particular item.

(e) A deterioration in the quality of bought-in items may result in the purchase of higher quantities of inventories in order to take account of the defective element in inventories acquired. It may also lead to an increase in the inspection time for items received. This too would lead to a rise in inventory levels.

**12.3** Inventories are held:

- to meet customer demand,
- to avoid the problems of running out of inventories, and
- to take advantage of profitable opportunities (for example, buying a product that is expected to rise steeply in price in the future).

The first reason may be described as transactionary, the second precautionary and the third speculative. They are, in essence, the same reasons why a business holds cash.

**12.4** (a) The costs of holding too little cash are:

- failure to meet obligations when they fall due which can damage the reputation of the business and may, in the extreme, lead to the business being wound up;
- having to borrow and thereby incur interest charges;
- an inability to take advantage of profitable opportunities.

(b) The costs of holding too much cash are:

- failure to use the funds available for more profitable purposes;
- loss of value during a period of inflation.

## Chapter 2

**2.1**

**Paul**

**Statement of cash flows for Thursday**

| | £ |
|---|---|
| Opening balance (from Wednesday) | 59 |
| Cash from sale of wrapping paper | 47 |
| Cash paid to purchase wrapping paper | (53) |
| Closing balance | 53 |

**Income statement for Thursday**

| | £ |
|---|---|
| Sales revenue | 47 |
| Cost of goods sold | (33) |
| Profit | 14 |

**Statement of financial position as at Thursday evening**

| | £ |
|---|---|
| Cash | 53 |
| Inventories of goods for resale (23 + 53 − 33) | 43 |
| Total assets | 96 |
| Equity | 96 |

**2.2**

**Helen**

**Income statement for day 1**

| | £ |
|---|---|
| Sales revenue (70 × £0.80) | 56 |
| Cost of sales (70 × £0.50) | (35) |
| Profit | 21 |

**Statement of cash flows for day 1**

| | £ |
|---|---|
| Opening balance | 40 |
| Cash from sales | 56 |
| Cash for purchases (80 × £0.50) | (40) |
| Closing balance | 56 |

**Statement of financial position as at end of day 1**

| | £ |
|---|---|
| Cash balance | 56 |
| Inventories of unsold goods (10 × £0.50) | 5 |
| Total assets | 61 |
| Equity | 61 |

### Income statement for day 2

|  | £ |
|---|---|
| Sales revenue (65 × £0.80) | 52.0 |
| Cost of sales (65 × £0.50) | (32.5) |
| Profit | 19.5 |

### Statement of cash flows for day 2

|  | £ |
|---|---|
| Opening balance | 56.0 |
| Cash from sales | 52.0 |
| Cash for purchases (60 × £0.50) | (30.0) |
| Closing balance | 78.0 |

### Statement of financial position as at end of day 2

|  | £ |
|---|---|
| Cash balance | 78.0 |
| Inventories of unsold goods (5 × £0.50) | 2.5 |
| Total assets | 80.5 |
| Equity | 80.5 |

### Income statement for day 3

|  | £ |
|---|---|
| Sales revenue (20 × £0.80) + (45 × £0.40) | 34.0 |
| Cost of sales (65 × £0.50) | (32.5) |
| Profit | 1.5 |

### Statement of cash flows for day 3

|  | £ |
|---|---|
| Opening balance | 78.0 |
| Cash from sales | 34.0 |
| Cash for purchases (60 × £0.50) | (30.0) |
| Closing balance | 82.0 |

### Statement of financial position as at end of day 3

|  | £ |
|---|---|
| Cash balance | 82.0 |
| Inventories of unsold goods | – |
| Total assets | 82.0 |
| Equity | 82.0 |

**2.4 Crafty Engineering Ltd**

(a) **Statement of financial position as at 30 June last year**

|  | £000 |
|---|---|
| **ASSETS** | |
| **Non-current assets** | |
| *Property, plant and equipment* | |
| Property | 320 |
| Equipment and tools | 207 |
| Motor vehicles | 38 |
| | 565 |

| | |
|---|---:|
| **Current assets** | |
| Inventories | 153 |
| Trade receivables | 185 |
| | 338 |
| **Total assets** | 903 |
| | |
| **EQUITY AND LIABILITIES** | |
| **Equity** (which is the missing figure) | 441 |
| **Non-current liabilities** | |
| Long-term borrowings (loan: Industrial Finance Co.) | 260 |
| **Current liabilities** | |
| Trade payables | 86 |
| Short-term borrowings | 116 |
| | 202 |
| **Total equity and liabilities** | 903 |

(b) The statement of financial position reveals a high level of investment in non-current assets. In percentage terms, we can say that more than 60% of the total investment in assets (565/903) has been in non-current assets. The nature of the business may require a heavy investment in non-current assets. The investment in current assets exceeds the current liabilities by a large amount (approximately 1.7 times). As a result, there is no obvious sign of a liquidity problem. However, the statement of financial position reveals that the business has no cash balance and is, therefore, dependent on the continuing support of short-term borrowing in order to meet obligations when they fall due. When considering the long-term financing of the business, we can see that about 37% (that is, 260/(260 + 441)) of the total long-term finance for the business has been supplied by borrowings and about 63% (that is, 441/(260 + 441)) by the owners. This level of long-term borrowing seems quite high but not excessive. However, we would need to know more about the ability of the business to service the borrowing (that is, make interest payments and repayments of the amount borrowed) before a full assessment could be made.

# Chapter 3

**3.1**  (a) Equity does increase as a result of the owners introducing more cash into the business, but it can also increase as a result of introducing other assets (for example, a motor car) and by the business generating revenue by trading. Similarly, equity decreases not only as a result of withdrawals of cash by owners but also by withdrawals of other assets (for example, inventories for the owners' personal use) and through trading expenses being incurred. For the typical business, in a typical accounting period, equity will alter much more as a result of trading activities than for any other reason.

(b) An accrued expense is not one that relates to next year. It is one that needs to be matched with the revenue of the accounting period under review, but that has yet to be met in terms of cash payment. As such, it will appear on the statement of financial position as a current liability.

(c) The purpose of depreciation is not to provide for asset replacement. Rather, it is an attempt to allocate the cost, or fair value, of the asset (less any residual value) over its useful life. Depreciation is an attempt to provide a measure of the amount of the non-current asset that has been consumed during the period. This amount will then be charged as an expense for the period in deriving the profit figure. Depreciation is a book entry (the outlay of cash occurs when the asset is purchased) and does not normally entail setting aside a separate amount of cash for asset replacement. Even if this were done, there would be no guarantee that sufficient funds would be available at the end of the asset's life for its replacement. Factors such as inflation and technological change may mean that the replacement cost is higher than the original cost of the asset. It is not necessarily the case that a particular asset will be replaced, in any case.

(d) In the short term, it is possible for the current value of a non-current asset to exceed its original cost. However, nearly all non-current assets will wear out over time as a result of being used to generate wealth for the business (land being one of the rare exceptions). This will be the case for freehold buildings. As a result, some measure of depreciation should be calculated to take account of the fact that the asset is being consumed. Some businesses revalue their freehold buildings where the current value is significantly different from the original cost. Where this occurs, the depreciation charged should be based on the revalued amount (fair value). This will normally result in higher depreciation charges than if the asset remained at its historic cost.

**3.3** The existence of profit and downward movement in cash may be for various reasons, which include the following:

■ the purchase of assets for cash during the period (for example, motor cars and inventories), which were not all consumed during the period and are therefore not having as great an effect on expenses as they are on cash

■ the payment of an outstanding liability (for example, borrowings), which will have an effect on cash but not on expenses in the income statement

■ the withdrawal of cash by the owners from the equity invested, which will not have an effect on the expenses in the income statement

■ the generation of revenue on credit where the cash has yet to be received. This will increase the sales revenue for the period but will not have a beneficial effect on the cash balance until a later time.

**3.5   WW Associates**

**WW Associates**
**Income statement for the year ended 31 December 2009**

|  | £ |
|---|---|
| Sales revenue (211,000 + 42,000) | 253,000 |
| Cost of goods sold (127,000 + 25,000) | (152,000) |
| Gross profit | 101,000 |
| Rent (20,000) | (20,000) |
| Rates (400 + 1,500) | (1,900) |
| Wages (−1,700 + 23,800 + 860) | (22,960) |
| Electricity (2,700) | (2,700) |
| Machinery depreciation (9,360) | (9,360) |
| Loss on disposal of the old machinery (13,000 − 3,900 − 9,000) | (100) |
| Van expenses (17,500) | (17,500) |
| Profit for the year | 26,480 |

The loss on disposal of the old machinery is the carrying amount (cost less depreciation) less the disposal proceeds. Since the machinery had only been owned for one year, with a depreciation rate of 30%, the depreciation on it so far is £3,900 (that is, £13,000 × 30%). The effective disposal proceeds were £9,000 because, as a result of trading it in, the business saved £9,000 on the new asset.

The depreciation expense for 2009 is based on the cost less accumulated depreciation of the assets owned at the end of 2009. Accumulated depreciation must be taken into account because the business uses the reducing-balance method.

### Statement of financial position as at 31 December 2009

|  | £ |
|---|---|
| **ASSETS** | |
| Machinery (25,300 + 6,000 + 9,000 − 13,000 + 3,900 − 9,360) | 21,840* |
| Inventories (12,200 + 143,000 + 12,000 − 127,000 − 25,000) | 15,200 |
| Trade receivables (21,300 + 211,000 − 198,000) | 34,300 |
| Cash at bank (overdraft) (8,300 − 23,000 − 25,000 − 2,000 − 6,000 | |
| − 23,800 − 2,700 − 12,000 + 42,000 + 198,000 − 156,000 − 17,500) | (19,700) |
| Prepaid expenses (400 − 400 + 5,000 + 500) | 5,500 |
| **Total assets** | 57,140 |
| **EQUITY AND LIABILITIES** | |
| Equity (owner's capital) (48,900 − 23,000 + 26,480) | 52,380 |
| Trade payables (16,900 + 143,000 − 156,000) | 3,900 |
| Accrued expenses (1,700 − 1,700 + 860) | 860 |
| **Total equity and liabilities** | 57,140 |
| * Cost less accumulated depreciation at 31 December 2008 | 25,300 |
| Carrying amount of machine disposed of (£13,000 − £3,900) | (9,100) |
| Cost of new machine | 15,000 |
| Depreciation for 2009 (£31,200 × 30%) | (9,360) |
| Carrying amount (written-down value) of machine at 31 December 2009 | 21,840 |

The statement of financial position could now be rewritten in a more stylish form as follows:

### WW Associates
### Statement of financial position as at 31 December 2009

|  | £ |
|---|---|
| **ASSETS** | |
| **Non-current assets** | |
| *Property, plant and equipment* | |
| Machinery at cost less depreciation | 21,840 |
| **Current assets** | |
| Inventories | 15,200 |
| Trade receivables | 34,300 |
| Prepaid expenses | 5,500 |
|  | 55,000 |
| **Total assets** | 76,840 |

EQUITY AND LIABILITIES

| | |
|---|---:|
| Equity | 52,380 |
| Current liabilities | |
| Trade payables | 3,900 |
| Accrued expenses | 860 |
| Borrowings – bank overdraft | 19,700 |
| | 24,460 |
| Total equity and liabilities | 76,840 |

# Chapter 4

**4.1**  Limited companies can no more set a limit on the amount of debts they will meet than can human beings. They must meet their debts up to the limit of their assets, just as we as individuals must. In the context of limited companies, 'reserves' mean part of the owners' claim against the assets of the company. These assets may or may not include cash. The legal ability of the company to pay dividends is not related to the amount of cash that it has.

Preference shares do not carry a guaranteed dividend. They simply guarantee that the preference shareholders have a right to the first slice of any dividend that is paid. Shares in those companies that have gained a Stock Exchange listing can, in effect, be bought by one investor from another through the Stock Exchange. Listed companies represent a very small proportion of all companies. One shareholder selling shares to another has no direct effect on the company, however. These are not new shares being offered by the company, but existing shares that are being sold 'second-hand'.

**4.2**

### I. Ching (Booksellers) plc
### Statement of comprehensive income for the year ended 31 December 2009

| | £m |
|---|---:|
| Revenue | 943 |
| Cost of sales | (460) |
| **Gross profit** | 483 |
| Distribution expenses | (110) |
| Administrative expenses | (212) |
| Other expenses | (25) |
| **Operating profit** | 136 |
| Finance charges | (40) |
| **Profit before tax** | 96 |
| Taxation | (24) |
| **Profit for the year** | 72 |
| *Other comprehensive income* | |
| Revaluation of property, plant and equipment | 20 |
| Foreign currency translation differences for foreign operations | (15) |
| Tax on other comprehensive income | (1) |
| Other comprehensive income for the year, net of tax | 4 |
| **Total comprehensive income for the year** | 76 |

**4.4**

**Chips Limited**
**Income statement for the year ended 30 June 2010**

| | £000 |
|---|---:|
| Revenue (1,850 − 16) | 1,834 |
| Cost of sales (1,040 + 23) | (1,063) |
| Gross profit | 771 |
| Depreciation (220 − 2 − 5 + 8 + (94 × 20%)) | (240) |
| Other operating costs | (375) |
| Operating profit | 156 |
| Interest payable (35 + 35) | (70) |
| Profit before taxation | 86 |
| Taxation (86 × 30%) | (26) |
| Profit for the year | 60 |

**Statement of financial position as at 30 June 2010**

| | Cost £000 | Depreciation £000 | £000 |
|---|---:|---:|---:|
| **ASSETS** | | | |
| **Non-current assets** | | | |
| *Property, plant and equipment* | | | |
| Buildings | 800 | (112) | 688 |
| Plant and equipment | 650 | (367) | 283 |
| Motor vehicles (102 − 8); (53 − 5 + 19) | 94 | (67) | 27 |
| | 1,544 | (546) | 998 |
| **Current assets** | | | |
| Inventories | | | 950 |
| Trade receivables (420 − 16) | | | 404 |
| Cash at bank (16 + 2) | | | 18 |
| | | | 1,372 |
| **Total assets** | | | 2,370 |
| **EQUITY AND LIABILITIES** | | | |
| **Equity** | | | |
| Ordinary shares of £1, fully paid | | | 800 |
| Reserves at beginning of the year | | | 248 |
| Retained profit for year | | | 60 |
| | | | 1,108 |
| **Non-current liabilities** | | | |
| Borrowings − secured 10% loan notes | | | 700 |
| **Current liabilities** | | | |
| Trade payables (361 + 23) | | | 384 |
| Other payables (117 + 35) | | | 152 |
| Taxation | | | 26 |
| | | | 562 |
| **Total equity and liabilities** | | | 2,370 |

## Chapter 5

**5.1** (a) An increase in the level of inventories would, ultimately, have an adverse effect on cash.

(b) A rights issue of ordinary shares will give rise to a positive cash flow, which will be included in the 'financing' section of the statement of cash flows.

(c) A bonus issue of ordinary shares has no cash flow effect.

(d) Writing off some of the value of the inventories has no cash flow effect.

(e) A disposal for cash of a large number of shares by a major shareholder has no cash flow effect as far as the business is concerned.

(f) Depreciation does not involve cash at all. Using the indirect method of deducing cash flows from operating activities involves the depreciation expense in the calculation, but this is simply because we are trying to find out from the profit before taxation (after depreciation) figure what the profit before taxation *and* before depreciation must have been.

**5.3**

### Torrent plc
### Statement of cash flows for the year ended 31 December 2010

|  | £m |
|---|---:|
| **Cash flows from operating activities** | |
| Profit before taxation (after interest) (see Note 1 below) | 170 |
| Adjustments for: | |
| Depreciation (Note 2) | 78 |
| Interest expense (Note 3) | 26 |
|  | 274 |
| Decrease in inventories (41 – 35) | 6 |
| Increase in trade receivables (145 – 139) | (6) |
| Decrease in trade payables (54 – 41) | (13) |
| *Cash generated from operations* | 261 |
| Interest paid (Note 3) | (26) |
| Taxation paid (Note 4) | (41) |
| Dividend paid | (60) |
| *Net cash from operating activities* | 134 |
| **Cash flows from investing activities** | |
| Payments to acquire plant and machinery | (67) |
| *Net cash used in investing activities* | (67) |
| **Cash flows from financing activities** | |
| Redemption of loan notes (250 – 150) (Note 5) | (100) |
| *Net cash used in financing activities* | (100) |
| **Net decrease in cash and cash equivalents** | (33) |
| Cash and cash equivalents at 1 January 2010 | |
| Bank overdraft | (56) |
| Cash and cash equivalents at 31 December 2010 | |
| Bank overdraft | (89) |

To see how this relates to the cash of the business at the beginning and end of the year it can be useful to provide a reconciliation as follows:

**Analysis of cash and cash equivalents during the year ended 31 December 2010**

|  | £m |
|---|---|
| Cash and cash equivalents at 1 January 2010 | (56) |
| Net cash outflow | (33) |
| Cash and cash equivalents at 31 December 2010 | (89) |

**Notes:**

1 This is simply taken from the income statement for the year.

2 Since there were no disposals, the depreciation charges must be the difference between the start and end of the year's plant and machinery values, adjusted by the cost of any additions.

|  | £m |
|---|---|
| Carrying amount at 1 January 2010 | 325 |
| Additions | 67 |
| Depreciation (balancing figure) | (78) |
| Carrying amount at 31 December 2010 | 314 |

3 Interest payable expense must be taken out, by adding it back to the profit before taxation figure. We subsequently deduct the cash paid for interest payable during the year. In this case the two figures are identical.

4 Companies pay 50% of their tax during their accounting year and 50% in the following year. Thus the 2010 payment would have been half the tax on the 2009 profit (that is, the figure that would have appeared in the current liabilities at the end of 2009), plus half of the 2010 tax charge (that is, $23 + (\frac{1}{2} \times 36) = 41$).

5 It is assumed that the cash payment to redeem the loan notes was simply the difference between the two statement of financial position figures.

It seems that there was a bonus issue of ordinary shares during the year. These increased by £100m. At the same time, the share premium account balance reduced by £40m (to zero) and the revaluation reserve balance fell by £60m. This had no impact on cash.

**5.5**

**Brownstone plc**

**Statement of cash flows for the year ended 31 March 2010**

|  | £m |
|---|---|
| **Cash flows from operating activities** |  |
| Profit before taxation (after interest) |  |
| (see Note 1 below) | 1,853 |
| Adjustments for: |  |
| Depreciation (Note 2) | 1,289 |
| Interest expense (Note 3) | 456 |
|  | 3,598 |
| Increase in inventories (2,410 – 1,209) | (1,201) |
| Increase in trade receivables (1,173 – 641) | (532) |
| Increase in trade payables (1,507 – 931) | 576 |
| *Cash generated from operations* | 2,441 |
| Interest paid (Note 3) | (456) |
| Taxation paid (Note 4) | (300) |
| Dividend paid | (400) |
| *Net cash from operating activities* | 1,285 |
| **Cash flows from investing activities** |  |
| Proceeds of disposals | 54 |
| Payment to acquire intangible non-current asset | (700) |
| Payments to acquire property, plant and equipment | (4,578) |
| *Net cash used in investing activities* | (5,224) |

| Cash flows from financing activities | |
|---|---|
| Bank borrowings | 2,000 |
| *Net cash from financing activities* | 2,000 |
| **Net decrease in cash and cash equivalents** | (1,939) |
| Cash and cash equivalents at 1 April 2009 | |
| Cash at bank | 123 |
| Cash and cash equivalents at 31 March 2010 | |
| Bank overdraft | (1,816) |

To see how this relates to the cash of the business at the beginning and end of the year it can be useful to provide a reconciliation as follows:

**Analysis of cash and cash equivalents during the year ended 31 March 2010**

| | £m |
|---|---|
| Cash and cash equivalents at 1 April 2009 | 123 |
| Net cash outflow | (1,939) |
| Cash and cash equivalents at 31 March 2010 | (1,816) |

**Notes:**

1 This is simply taken from the income statement for the year.

2 The full depreciation charge was that stated in Note 2 to the question (£1,251m), plus the deficit on disposal of the non-current assets. According to Note 2, these non-current assets had originally cost £581m and had been depreciated by £489m, thus they had a net carrying amount of £92m. They were sold for £54m, leading to a deficit on disposal of £38m. Thus the full depreciation expense for the year was £1,289m (that is, £1,251m + £38m).

3 Interest payable expense must be taken out, by adding it back to the profit before taxation figure. We subsequently deduct the cash paid for interest payable during the year. In this case the two figures are identical.

4 Companies pay tax at 50% during their accounting year and the other 50% in the following year. Thus the 2010 payment would have been half the tax on the 2009 profit (that is, the figure that would have appeared in the current liabilities at 31 March 2009), plus half of the 2010 tax charge (that is, $105 + (^1/_2 \times 390) = 300$).

# Chapter 6

**6.1    I. Jiang (Western) Ltd**

The effect of each of the changes on ROCE is not always easy to predict.

1 On the face of it, an increase in the gross profit margin would tend to lead to an increase in ROCE. An increase in the gross profit margin may, however, lead to a decrease in ROCE in particular circumstances. If the increase in the margin resulted from an increase in sales prices, which in turn led to a decrease in sales revenue, a fall in ROCE can occur. A fall in sales revenue can reduce the operating profit (the numerator (top part of the fraction) in ROCE) if the overheads of the business did not decrease correspondingly.

2 A reduction in sales revenue can reduce ROCE for the reasons mentioned above.

3 An increase in overhead expenses will reduce the operating profit and this in turn will result in a reduction in ROCE.

4 An increase in inventories held would increase the amount of capital employed by the business (the denominator (bottom part of the fraction) in ROCE) where long-term funds are employed to finance the inventories. This will, in turn, reduce ROCE.

5 Repayment of the borrowings at the year end will reduce the capital employed and this will increase the ROCE, assuming that the year-end capital employed figure has been used in the calculation. Since the operating profit was earned during a period in which the borrowings existed, there is a strong argument for basing the capital employed figure on what was the position during the year, rather than at the end of it.

6 An increase in the time taken for credit customers to pay will result in an increase in capital employed if long-term funds are employed to finance the trade receivables. This increase in long-term funds will, in turn, reduce ROCE.

### 6.2 Amsterdam Ltd and Berlin Ltd

The ratios for Amsterdam Ltd and Berlin Ltd reveal that the settlement period for trade receivables for Amsterdam Ltd is three times that for Berlin Ltd. Berlin Ltd is therefore much quicker in collecting amounts outstanding from customers. On the other hand, there is not much difference between the two businesses in the time taken to pay trade payables.

It is interesting to compare the difference in the trade receivables and payables collection periods for each business. As Amsterdam Ltd allows an average of 63 days' credit to its customers, yet pays suppliers within 50 days, it will require greater investment in working capital than Berlin Ltd, which allows an average of only 21 days to its customers but takes 45 days to pay its suppliers.

Amsterdam Ltd has a much higher gross profit margin than Berlin Ltd. However, the operating profit margin for the two businesses is identical. This suggests that Amsterdam Ltd has much higher overheads (as a percentage of sales revenue) than Berlin Ltd. The inventories turnover period for Amsterdam Ltd is more than twice that of Berlin Ltd. This may be due to the fact that Amsterdam Ltd maintains a wider range of inventories in an attempt to meet customer requirements. The evidence therefore suggests that Amsterdam Ltd is the one that prides itself on personal service. The higher average settlement period for trade receivables is consistent with a more relaxed attitude to credit collection (thereby maintaining customer goodwill) and the high overheads are consistent with incurring the additional costs of satisfying customers' requirements. Amsterdam Ltd's high inventories levels are consistent with maintaining a wide range of inventories, with the aim of satisfying a range of customer needs.

Berlin Ltd has the characteristics of a more price-competitive business. Its gross profit margin is much lower than that of Amsterdam Ltd, that is, a much lower gross profit for each £1 of sales revenue. However, overheads have been kept low, the effect being that the operating profit margin is the same as Amsterdam Ltd's. The low inventories turnover period and average collection period for trade receivables are consistent with a business that wishes to minimise investment in current assets, thereby reducing costs.

### 6.5 Bradbury Ltd

(a)

| | | 2009 | 2010 |
|---|---|---|---|
| 1 | Operating profit margin | $\frac{914}{9,482} \times 100\% = 9.6\%$ | $\frac{1,042}{11,365} \times 100\% = 9.2\%$ |
| 2 | ROCE | $\frac{914}{11,033} \times 100\% = 8.3\%$ | $\frac{1,042}{13,943} \times 100\% = 7.5\%$ |
| 3 | Current ratio | $\frac{4,926}{1,508} = 3.3{:}1$ | $\frac{7,700}{5,174} = 1.5{:}1$ |
| 4 | Gearing ratio | $\frac{1,220}{11,033} \times 100\% = 11.1\%$ | $\frac{3,675}{13,943} \times 100\% = 26.4\%$ |
| 5 | Days trade receivables | $\frac{2,540}{9,482} \times 365 = 98$ days | $\frac{4,280}{11,365} \times 365 = 137$ days |
| 6 | Sales revenue to capital employed | $\frac{9,482}{(9,813 + 1,220)} = 0.9$ times | $\frac{11,365}{(10,268 + 3,675)} = 0.8$ times |

(b) The operating profit margin was slightly lower in 2010 than in 2009. Although there was an increase in sales revenue in 2009, this could not prevent a slight fall in ROCE in that year. The lower operating margin and increases in sales revenue may well be due to the new contract. The capital employed by the company increased in 2010 by a larger percentage than the increase in revenue. Hence, the sales revenue to capital employed ratio decreased over the period. The increase in capital employed during 2010 is largely due to an increase in borrowing. However, the gearing ratio is probably still low in comparison with other businesses. Comparison of the premises and borrowings figures indicates possible unused borrowing (debt) capacity.

The major cause for concern has been the dramatic decline in liquidity during 2010. The current ratio has more than halved during the period. There has also been a similar decrease in the acid test ratio, from 1.7:1 in 2009 to 0.8:1 in 2010. The statement of financial position shows that the business now has a large overdraft and the trade payables outstanding have nearly doubled in 2010.

The trade receivables outstanding and inventories have increased much more than appears to be warranted by the increase in sales revenue. This may be due to the terms of the contract that has been negotiated and may be difficult to influence. If this is the case, the business should consider whether it needs more longer-term finance. If the conclusion is that it does, increasing its long-term funding may be a sensible policy.

# Chapter 7

### 7.3 Products A, B and C

(a) Total time required on cutting machines is

$$(2,500 \times 1.0) + (3,400 \times 1.0) + (5,100 \times 0.5) = 8,450 \text{ hours}$$

Total time available on cutting machines is 5,000 hours. Therefore, this is a limiting factor.

Total time required on assembling machines is

$$(2,500 \times 0.5) + (3,400 \times 1.0) + (5,100 \times 0.5) = 7,200 \text{ hours}$$

Total time available on assembling machines is 8,000 hours. Therefore, this is not a limiting factor.

|  | A | B | C |
|---|---|---|---|
| Selling price (£/unit) | 25 | 30 | 18 |
| Variable materials (£/unit) | (12) | (13) | (10) |
| Variable production cost (£/unit) | (7) | (4) | (3) |
| Contribution (£/unit) | 6 | 13 | 5 |
| Time on cutting machines (hours/unit) | 1.0 hour | 1.0 hour | 0.5 hour |
| Contribution per hour on cutting machines | £6 | £13 | £10 |
| Order of priority | 3rd | 1st | 2nd |

Therefore, produce:

| 3,400 product B using | 3,400 hours |
|---|---|
| 3,200 product C using | 1,600 hours |
|  | 5,000 hours |

(b) Assuming that the business would make no saving in variable production cost by subcontracting, it would be worth paying up to the contribution per unit (£5) for product C, which would therefore be £5 × (5,100 − 3,200) = £9,500 in total.

Similarly it would be worth paying up to £6 per unit for product A – that is, £6 × 2,500 = £15,000 in total.

### 7.4 Darmor Ltd

(a) Contribution per hour of skilled labour of product X is

$$\frac{£(30 - 6 - 2 - 12 - 3)}{(6/12)} = £14$$

Given the scarcity of skilled labour, if the management is to be indifferent between the products, the contribution per skilled-labour-hour must be the same. Thus for product Y the selling price must be

$$£((14 \times (9/12)) + 9 + 4 + 25 + 7) = £55.50$$

(that is, the contribution plus the variable cost), and for product Z the selling price must be

$$£((14 \times (3/12)) + 3 + 10 + 14 + 7) = £37.50$$

(b) The business could pay up to £26 an hour (£12 + £14) for additional hours of skilled labour. This is the potential contribution per hour, before taking account of the labour rate of £12 an hour.

### 7.5 Gandhi Ltd

(a) Given that the spare capacity could not be used by other services, the standard service should continue to be offered. This is because it renders a positive contribution.

(b) The standard service renders a contribution per unit of £15 (that is, £80 – £65), or £30 during the time it would take to render one unit of the Nova service. The Nova service would provide a contribution of only £25 (that is, £75 – £50).

The Nova service should, therefore, not replace the standard service.

(c) Under the original plans, the following contributions would be rendered by the basic and standard services:

|  |  | £ |
|---|---|---|
| Basic | 11,000 × (£50 – £25) = | 275,000 |
| Standard | 6,000 × (£80 – £65) = | 90,000 |
|  |  | 365,000 |

If the basic were to take the standard's place, 17,000 units (that is, 11,000 + 6,000) of them could be produced in total. To generate the same total contribution, each unit of the standard service would need to provide £21.47 (that is, £365,000/ 17,000) of contribution. Given the basic's variable cost of £25, this would mean a selling price of £46.47 each (that is, £21.47 + £25.00).

## Chapter 8

**8.1** All three of these costing techniques are means of deducing the full cost of some activity. The distinction between them lies essentially with the difference in the manner of the production of the goods or services involved.

■ *Job costing* is used where each unit of output or 'job' differs from others produced by the same business. Because the jobs are not identical, it is not normally helpful to those who are likely to use the cost information to treat the jobs as if they are identical. This means that costs need to be identified, job by job. For this purpose, cost fall into two categories: direct cost and indirect cost (or overheads).

Direct cost elements are those that can be measured directly in respect of the specific job, such as the cost of the labour that was directly applied to the job, or the cost of material that has been incorporated in it. To this must be added a share of the indirect cost. This is usually done by taking the total overheads for the period concerned and charging part of them to the job. This, in turn, is usually done according to some measure of the job's size and importance, relative to the other jobs done during the period. The number of direct labour hours worked on the job is the most commonly used measure of size and/or importance.

The main problem with job costing tends to be the method of charging indirect cost to jobs. Indirect cost, by definition, cannot be related directly to jobs, yet must, if full cost is to be deduced, be charged on a basis that is more or less arbitrary. If overheads accounted for a small proportion of the total, the arbitrariness of charging them would probably not matter. Overheads, in many cases, however, form the majority of total cost, so arbitrariness is a problem.

■ *Process costing* is the approach taken where all output is of identical units. These can be treated, therefore, as having identical cost. Sometimes a process costing approach is taken even where the units of output are not strictly identical. This is because process costing is much simpler and cheaper to apply than the only other option, job costing. Provided that users of the cost information are satisfied that treating units as identical when they are not strictly so is acceptable, the additional cost and effort of job costing is not justified.

In process costing, the cost per unit of output is found by dividing total costs for the period by the total number of units produced in the period.

The main problem with process costing tends to be that at the end of any period (or the beginning of the next period), there will probably be partly completed units of output. An adjustment needs to be made for this work in progress if the resulting figures for cost per unit are not to be distorted.

- *Batch costing* is really an extension of job costing. Batch costing tends to be used where production is in batches. A batch consists of more than one, perhaps many, identical units of output. The units of output differ from one batch to the next. For example, a clothing manufacturing business may produce 500 identical jackets in one batch, followed by a batch of 300 identical skirts.

Each batch is costed, as one job, using a job-costing approach. The full cost of each unit is then found by dividing the cost of the batch by the number of units in the batch.

The main problem of batch costing is exactly that of job costing, of which it is an extension. This is the problem of dealing with overheads.

### 8.4 Kaplan plc

(a) The business makes each model of suitcase in a batch. The direct cost (materials and labour) will be recorded in respect of each batch. To this cost will be added a share of the overheads of the business for the period in which production of the batch takes place. The basis of the batch absorbing overheads is a matter of managerial judgement. A popular method is direct labour hours spent working on the batch, relative to total direct labour hours worked during the period. This is not the 'correct' way, however. There is no correct way. If the activity is capital intensive, some machine hour basis of dealing with overheads might be more appropriate, though still not 'correct'. Overheads might be collected, cost centre by cost centre (department by department), and charged to the batch as it passes through each product cost centre. Alternatively, all of the overheads for the entire production facility might be totalled and the overheads dealt with more globally. It is only in restricted circumstances that overheads charged to batches will be affected by a decision to deal with them by cost centres, rather than globally.

Once the 'full cost' (direct cost plus a share of indirect cost) has been ascertained for the batch, the cost per suitcase can be established by dividing the batch cost by the number in the batch.

(b) Whereas the traditional approach to dealing with overheads is just to accept that they exist and deal with them in a fairly broad manner, ABC takes a much more enquiring approach. ABC takes the view that overheads do not just 'occur', but that they are caused or 'driven' by 'activities'. It is a matter of finding out which activities are driving the cost and how much cost they are driving.

For example, a significant part of the cost of making suitcases of different sizes might be resetting machinery to cope with a batch of a different size from its predecessor batch. Where a particular model is made in very small batches, because it has only a small market, ABC would advocate that this model is charged directly with its machine-setting cost. The traditional approach would be to treat machine setting as a general overhead that the individual suitcases (irrespective of the model) might bear equally. ABC, it is claimed, leads to more accurate costing and thus to more accurate assessment of profitability.

(c) The other advantage of pursuing an ABC philosophy and identifying cost drivers is that, once the drivers have been identified, they are likely to become much more susceptible to being controlled. Thus the ability of management to assess the benefit of certain activities against their cost becomes more feasible.

### 8.5 Offending phrases and explanations

| Offending phrase | Explanation |
| --- | --- |
| 'Necessary to divide up the business into departments' | This can be done but it will not always be of much benefit. Only in quite restricted circumstances will it give a significantly different job cost. |
| 'Fixed cost (or overheads)' | This implies that fixed cost and overheads are the same thing. They are not really connected with one another. 'Fixed' is to do with how cost behaves as the level of output is raised or lowered; 'overheads' are to do with the extent to which cost can be directly measured in respect of a particular unit of output. Though it is true that many overheads are fixed, not all are. Also, direct labour is usually a fixed cost. <br><br> All of the other references to fixed and variable cost are wrong. The person should have referred to indirect and direct costs. |
| 'Usually this is done on the basis of area' | Where overheads are apportioned to departments, they will be apportioned on some logical basis. For certain elements of cost – for example, rent – the floor area may be the most logical; for others, such as machine maintenance cost, the floor area would be totally inappropriate. |
| 'When the total fixed cost for each department has been identified, this will be divided by the number of hours that were worked' | Where overheads are dealt with on a departmental basis, they may be divided by the number of direct labour hours to deduce a recovery rate. However, this is only one basis of applying overheads to jobs. For example, machine hours or some other basis may be more appropriate to the particular circumstances involved. |
| 'It is essential that this approach is taken in order to deduce a selling price' | It is relatively unusual for the 'job cost' to be able to dictate the price at which the manufacturer can price its output. For many businesses, the market dictates the price. |

# Chapter 9

## 9.3 Nursing Home

(a) The rates per patient for the variable overheads, on the basis of experience during months 1 to 6, are as follows:

| Expense | Amount for 2,700 patients | Amount per patient |
|---|---|---|
| | £ | £ |
| Staffing | 59,400 | 22 |
| Power | 27,000 | 10 |
| Supplies | 54,000 | 20 |
| Other | 8,100 | 3 |
| | 148,500 | 55 |

Since the expected level of activity for the full year is 6,000, the expected level of activity for the second six months is 3,300 (that is, 6,000 – 2,700).

Thus the budget for the second six months will be:

| Variable element: | £ | |
|---|---|---|
| Staffing | 72,600 | (3,300 × £22) |
| Power | 33,000 | (3,300 × £10) |
| Supplies | 66,000 | (3,300 × £20) |
| Other | 9,900 | (3,300 × £3) |
| | 181,500 | (3,300 × £55) |

| Fixed element: | | |
|---|---|---|
| Supervision | 60,000 | (6/12 of the annual figure) |
| Depreciation/finance | 93,600 | (6/12 of the annual figure) |
| Other | 32,400 | (6/12 of the annual figure) |
| | 186,000 | (per patient = £56.36 (that is, £186,000/3,300)) |
| Total (second six months) | 367,500 | (per patient = £111.36 (that is, £56.36 + £55.00)) |

(b) For the second six months the actual activity was 3,800 patients. For a valid comparison with the actual outcome, the budget will need to be revised to reflect this activity.

| | Actual costs | Budget (3,800 patients) | Difference |
|---|---|---|---|
| | £ | £ | £ |
| Variable element | 203,300 | 209,000 (3,800 × £55) | 5,700 (saving) |
| Fixed element | 190,000 | 186,000 | 4,000 (overspend) |
| Total | 393,300 | 395,000 | 1,700 (saving) |

(c) Relative to the budget, there was a saving of nearly 3 per cent on the variable element and an overspend of about 2 per cent on fixed cost. Without further information, it is impossible to deduce much more than this.

The differences between the budget and the actual may be caused by some assumptions made in framing the budget for 3,300 patients in the second part of the year. There may be some element of economies of scale in the variable cost; that is, the cost may not be strictly linear. If this were the case, basing a relatively large activity budget on the experience of a relatively small activity period would tend to overstate the large activity budget. The fixed-cost budget was deduced by dividing the budget for 12 months by two. In fact, there could be seasonal factors or inflationary pressures at work that might make such a crude division of the fixed cost element unfair.

### 9.4 Linpet Ltd

(a) Cash budgets are extremely useful for decision-making purposes. They allow managers to see the likely effect on the cash balance of the plans that they have set in place. Cash is an important asset and it is necessary to ensure that it is properly managed. Failure to do so can have disastrous consequences for the business. Where the cash budget indicates a surplus balance, managers must decide whether this balance should be reinvested in the business or distributed to the owners. Where the cash budget indicates a deficit balance, managers must decide how this deficit should be financed or how it might be avoided.

(b) Cash budget for the six months to 30 November

|  | June £ | July £ | Aug £ | Sept £ | Oct £ | Nov £ |
|---|---|---|---|---|---|---|
| **Receipts** | | | | | | |
| Cash sales revenue (Note 1) | 4,000 | 5,500 | 7,000 | 8,500 | 11,000 | 11,000 |
| Credit sales revenue (Note 2) | – | – | 4,000 | 5,500 | 7,000 | 8,500 |
| | 4,000 | 5,500 | 11,000 | 14,000 | 18,000 | 19,500 |
| **Payments** | | | | | | |
| Purchases (Note 3) | – | 29,000 | 9,250 | 11,500 | 13,750 | 17,500 |
| Overheads | 500 | 500 | 500 | 500 | 650 | 650 |
| Wages | 900 | 900 | 900 | 900 | 900 | 900 |
| Commission (Note 4) | – | 320 | 440 | 560 | 680 | 880 |
| Equipment | 10,000 | – | – | – | – | 7,000 |
| Motor vehicle | 6,000 | – | – | – | – | – |
| Leasehold | 40,000 | – | – | – | – | – |
| | 57,400 | 30,720 | 11,090 | 13,460 | 15,980 | 26,930 |
| Cash flow | (53,400) | (25,220) | (90) | 540 | 2,020 | (7,430) |
| Opening balance | 60,000 | 6,600 | (18,620) | (18,710) | (18,170) | (16,150) |
| Closing balance | 6,600 | (18,620) | (18,710) | (18,170) | (16,150) | (23,580) |

Notes:

1 Fifty per cent of the current month's sales revenue.

2 Fifty per cent of sales revenue of two months previous.

3 To have sufficient inventories to meet each month's sales will require purchases of 75 per cent of the month's sales inventories figures (25 per cent is profit). In addition, each month the business will buy £1,000 more inventories than it will sell. In June, the business will also buy its initial inventories of £22,000. This will be paid for in the following month. For example, June's purchases will be (75% × £8,000) + £1,000 + £22,000 = £29,000, paid for in July.

4 This is 5 per cent of 80 per cent of the month's sales revenue, paid in the following month. For example, June's commission will be 5% × 80% × £8,000 = £320, payable in July.

### 9.5 Newtake Records

(a) The inventories budget for the six months to 30 November is:

| | June £000 | July £000 | Aug £000 | Sept £000 | Oct £000 | Nov £000 |
|---|---|---|---|---|---|---|
| Opening balance | 112 | 154 | 104 | 48 | 39 | 33 |
| Inventories purchased | 180 | 142 | 94 | 75 | 66 | 57 |
| Cost of inventories sold | | | | | | |
| (60% of sales revenue) | (138) | (192) | (150) | (84) | (72) | (66) |
| Closing balance | 154 | 104 | 48 | 39 | 33 | 24 |

(b) The cash budget for the period to 30 November is:

| | June £000 | July £000 | Aug £000 | Sept £000 | Oct £000 | Nov £000 |
|---|---|---|---|---|---|---|
| **Cash receipts** | | | | | | |
| Sales revenue (Note 1) | 227 | 315 | 246 | 138 | 118 | 108 |
| **Cash payments** | | | | | | |
| Administration (Note 2) | (40) | (41) | (38) | (33) | (31) | (30) |
| Goods purchased | (135) | (180) | (142) | (94) | (75) | (66) |
| Repayments of borrowings | (5) | (5) | (5) | (5) | (5) | (5) |
| Selling expenses | (22) | (24) | (28) | (26) | (21) | (19) |
| Tax paid | – | – | (22) | – | – | – |
| Shop refurbishment | – | (14) | (18) | (6) | – | – |
| | (202) | (264) | (253) | (164) | (132) | (120) |
| Cash surplus (deficit) | 25 | 51 | (7) | (26) | (14) | (12) |
| Opening balance | (35) | (10) | 41 | 34 | 8 | (6) |
| Closing balance | (10) | 41 | 34 | 8 | (6) | (18) |

Notes:

1 (50% of the current month's sales revenue) + (97% × 50% of that sales revenue). For example, the June cash receipts = (50% × £230,000) + (97% × 50% × £230,000) = £226,550.

2 The administration expenses figure for the month, *less* £15,000 for depreciation (a non-cash expense).

(c) The budgeted income statement for the six months ending 30 November is:

| | £000 |
|---|---|
| Sales revenue | 1,170 |
| Cost of goods sold | (702) |
| Gross profit | 468 |
| Selling expenses | (136) |
| Admin. expenses | (303) |
| Credit card charges | (18) |
| Interest charges | (6) |
| Profit for the period | 5 |

(d) We are told that the business is required to eliminate the bank overdraft by the end of November. However, the cash budget reveals that this will not be achieved. There is a decline in the overdraft of nearly 50 per cent over the period, but this is not enough and ways must be found to comply with the bank's requirements. It may be possible to delay the refurbishment programme that is included in the forecasts or to obtain an injection of funds from the owners or other investors. It may also be possible to stimulate sales in some way. However, there has been a decline in the sales revenue since the end of July and the November sales revenue is approximately one-third of the July sales revenue. The reasons for this decline should be sought.

The inventories levels will fall below the preferred minimum level for each of the last three months. However, to rectify this situation it will be necessary to purchase more inventories, which will, in turn, exacerbate the cash flow problems of the business.

The budgeted income statement reveals a very low net profit for the period. For every £1 of sales revenue, the business is only managing to generate 0.4p in profit. The business should look carefully at its pricing policies and its overhead expenses. The administration expenses, for example, absorb more than one-quarter of the total sales revenue. Any reduction in overhead expenses will have a beneficial effect on cash flows.

## Chapter 10

### 10.1 Mylo Ltd

(a) The annual depreciation of the two projects is:

$$\text{Project 1:} \frac{£100,000 - £7,000}{3} = £31,000$$

$$\text{Project 2:} \frac{£60,000 - £6,000}{3} = £18,000$$

**Project 1**

(i) Net present value

|  | Year 0 £000 | Year 1 £000 | Year 2 £000 | Year 3 £000 |
|---|---|---|---|---|
| Operating profit/(loss) | – | 29 | (1) | 2 |
| Depreciation | – | 31 | 31 | 31 |
| Capital cost | (100) | – | – | – |
| Residual value | – | – | – | 7 |
| Net cash flows | (100) | 60 | 30 | 40 |
| 10% discount factor | 1.000 | 0.909 | 0.826 | 0.751 |
| Present value | (100.00) | 54.54 | 24.78 | 30.04 |
| **Net present value** | 9.36 | | | |

(ii) Internal rate of return

Clearly the IRR lies above 10%; try 15%:

|  | Year 0 £000 | Year 1 £000 | Year 2 £000 | Year 3 £000 |
|---|---|---|---|---|
| 15% discount factor | 1.000 | 0.870 | 0.756 | 0.658 |
| Present value | (100.00) | 52.20 | 22.68 | 26.32 |
| Net present value | 1.20 | | | |

Thus the IRR lies a little above 15%, perhaps around 16%.

(iii) Payback period

To find the payback period, the cumulative cash flows are calculated:

|  | Year 0 £000 | Year 1 £000 | Year 2 £000 | Year 3 £000 |
|---|---|---|---|---|
| Cumulative cash flows | (100) | (40) | (10) | 30 |

Thus the payback will occur after three years if we assume year-end cash flows.

## Project 2

(i) Net present value

|  | Year 0 £000 | Year 1 £000 | Year 2 £000 | Year 3 £000 |
|---|---|---|---|---|
| Operating profit/(loss) | – | 18 | (2) | 4 |
| Depreciation | – | 18 | 18 | 18 |
| Capital cost | (60) | – | – | – |
| Residual value | – | – | – | 6 |
| Net cash flows | (60) | 36 | 16 | 28 |
| 10% discount factor | 1.000 | 0.909 | 0.826 | 0.751 |
| Present value | (60.00) | 32.72 | 13.22 | 21.03 |
| Net present value | 6.97 | | | |

(ii) Internal rate of return

Clearly the IRR lies above 10%; try 15%:

|  | Year 0 £000 | Year 1 £000 | Year 2 £000 | Year 3 £000 |
|---|---|---|---|---|
| 15% discount factor | 1.000 | 0.870 | 0.756 | 0.658 |
| Present value | (60.00) | 31.32 | 12.10 | 18.42 |
| Net present value | 1.84 | | | |

Thus the IRR lies a little above 15%; perhaps around 17%.

(iii) Payback period

The cumulative cash flows are:

|  | Year 0 £000 | Year 1 £000 | Year 2 £000 | Year 3 £000 |
|---|---|---|---|---|
| Cumulative cash flows | (60) | (24) | (8) | 20 |

Thus, the payback will occur after three years (assuming year-end cash flows).

(b) Assuming that Mylo Ltd is pursuing a wealth-enhancement objective, Project 1 is preferable since it has the higher NPV. The difference between the two NPVs is not significant, however.

### 10.4 Newton Electronics Ltd

(a) **Option 1**

|  | Year 0 £m | Year 1 £m | Year 2 £m | Year 3 £m | Year 4 £m | Year 5 £m |
|---|---|---|---|---|---|---|
| Plant and equipment | (9.0) | – | – | – | – | 1.0 |
| Sales revenue | – | 24.0 | 30.8 | 39.6 | 26.4 | 10.0 |
| Variable cost | – | (11.2) | (19.6) | (25.2) | (16.8) | (7.0) |
| Fixed cost (ex. dep'n) | – | (0.8) | (0.8) | (0.8) | (0.8) | (0.8) |
| Working capital | (3.0) | – | – | – | – | 3.0 |
| Marketing cost | – | (2.0) | (2.0) | (2.0) | (2.0) | (2.0) |
| Opportunity cost | – | (0.1) | (0.1) | (0.1) | (0.1) | (0.1) |
|  | (12.0) | 9.9 | 8.3 | 11.5 | 6.7 | 4.1 |
| Discount factor 10% | 1.000 | 0.909 | 0.826 | 0.751 | 0.683 | 0.621 |
| Present value | (12.0) | 9.0 | 6.9 | 8.6 | 4.6 | 2.5 |
| NPV | 19.6 | | | | | |

**Option 2**

|  | Year 0 £m | Year 1 £m | Year 2 £m | Year 3 £m | Year 4 £m | Year 5 £m |
|---|---|---|---|---|---|---|
| Royalties | – | 4.4 | 7.7 | 9.9 | 6.6 | 2.8 |
| Discount factor 10% | 1.000 | 0.909 | 0.826 | 0.751 | 0.683 | 0.621 |
| Present value | – | 4.0 | 6.4 | 7.4 | 4.5 | 1.7 |
| NPV | 24.0 | | | | | |

**Option 3**

|  | Year 0 £m | Year 2 £m |
|---|---|---|
| Instalments | 12.0 | 12.0 |
| Discount factor 10% | 1.000 | 0.826 |
| Present value | 12.0 | 9.9 |
| NPV | 21.9 | |

(b) Before making a final decision, the board should consider the following factors:
  (i) The long-term competitiveness of the business may be affected by the sale of the patents.
  (ii) At present, the business is not involved in manufacturing and marketing products. Would a change in direction be desirable?
  (iii) The business will probably have to buy in the skills necessary to produce the product itself. This will involve cost, and problems could arise. Has this been taken into account?
  (iv) How accurate are the forecasts made and how valid are the assumptions on which they are based?
(c) Option 2 has the highest NPV and is therefore the most attractive to shareholders. However, the accuracy of the forecasts should be checked before a final decision is made.

## 10.5 Chesterfield Wanderers

(a) and (b)

**Player option**

| Years | 0 £000 | 1 £000 | 2 £000 | 3 £000 | 4 £000 | 5 £000 |
|---|---|---|---|---|---|---|
| Sale of player | 2,200 | – | – | – | – | 1,000 |
| Purchase of player | (10,000) | – | – | – | – | – |
| Sponsorship etc. | – | 1,200 | 1,200 | 1,200 | 1,200 | 1,200 |
| Gate receipts | – | 2,500 | 1,300 | 1,300 | 1,300 | 1,300 |
| Salaries paid | – | (800) | (800) | (800) | (800) | (1,200) |
| Salaries saved | – | 400 | 400 | 400 | 400 | 600 |
| | (7,800) | 3,300 | 2,100 | 2,100 | 2,100 | 2,900 |
| Discount factor 10% | 1.000 | 0.909 | 0.826 | 0.751 | 0.683 | 0.621 |
| Present values | (7,800) | 3,000 | 1,735 | 1,577 | 1,434 | 1,801 |
| NPV | 1,747 | | | | | |

**Ground improvement option**

| Years | 1 £000 | 2 £000 | 3 £000 | 4 £000 | 5 £000 |
|---|---|---|---|---|---|
| Ground improvements | (10,000) | – | – | – | – |
| Increased gate receipts | (1,800) | 4,400 | 4,400 | 4,400 | 4,400 |
| | (11,800) | 4,400 | 4,400 | 4,400 | 4,400 |
| Discount factor 10% | 0.909 | 0.826 | 0.751 | 0.683 | 0.621 |
| Present values | (10,726) | 3,634 | 3,304 | 3,005 | 2,732 |
| NPV | 1,949 | | | | |

(c) The ground improvement option provides the higher NPV and is therefore the preferable option, based on the objective of shareholder wealth enhancement.
(d) A professional football club may not wish to pursue an objective of shareholder wealth enhancement. It may prefer to invest in quality players in an attempt to enjoy future sporting success. If this is the case, the NPV approach will be less appropriate because the club is not pursuing a strict wealth-related objective.

# Chapter 11

## 11.1   H. Brown (Portsmouth) Ltd

(a) The main factors to take into account are:

- *Risk*. If a business borrows, there is a risk that at the maturity date for repayment of the funds the business will not have sufficient to repay the amount owing and will be unable to find a suitable form of replacement borrowing. With short-term borrowing, the maturity dates will arrive more quickly and the type of risk outlined will occur at more frequent intervals.
- *Matching*. A business may wish to match the life of an asset with the maturity date of the borrowing. In other words, long-term assets will be purchased with long-term borrowed funds. A certain level of current assets, which form part of the long-term asset base of the business, may also be funded by long-term borrowing. Those current assets that fluctuate owing to seasonality and so on will be funded by short-term borrowing. This approach to funding assets will help reduce risks for the business.
- *Cost*. Interest rates for long-term borrowings tend to be higher than for short-term ones as investors may seek extra compensation for having their funds locked up for a long period. However, issue costs may be higher for short-term borrowings as there will be a need to refund at more frequent intervals.
- *Flexibility*. Short-term borrowings may be more flexible. It may be difficult to repay long-term ones before the maturity period.

(b) When deciding to grant a loan, a lender should consider the following factors:

- security
- purpose of the loan
- ability of the borrower to repay
- loan period
- availability of funds
- character and integrity of the senior managers.

## 11.2   Carpets Direct plc

(a) The earnings per share (EPS) is:

$$\frac{\text{Profit for the year}}{\text{Number of ordinary shares}} = \frac{£4.5\text{m}}{120\text{m}} = £0.0375$$

The current market value per share is:

$$\text{Earnings per share} \times \text{P/E} = £0.0375 \times 22 = £0.825$$

The rights issue price will be £0.825, less 20% discount = £0.66. The theoretical ex-rights price is calculated as follows:

|  | £ |
|---|---|
| Original shares (4 @ £0.825) | 3.30 |
| Rights share (1 @ £0.66) | 0.66 |
| Value of five shares following rights issue | 3.96 |

Therefore, the value of one share following the rights issue is:

$$\frac{£3.96}{5} = 79.2\text{p}$$

(b) Value of one share after rights issue                        79.2p
      Cost of a rights share                                     (66.0p)
      Value of rights to shareholder                       13.2p

(c) (i) *Taking up rights issue*

|  | £ |
|---|---|
| Shareholding following rights issue ((4,000 + 1,000) × 79.2p) | 3,960 |
| *Less* Cost of rights shares (1,000 × 66p) | (660) |
| Shareholder wealth | 3,300 |

  (ii) *Selling the rights*

|  | £ |
|---|---|
| Shareholding following rights issue (4,000 × 79.2p) | 3,168 |
| *Add* Proceeds from sale of rights (1,000 × 13.2p) | 132 |
| Shareholder wealth | 3,300 |

(iii) *Doing nothing*

As the rights are neither purchased nor sold, the shareholder wealth following the rights issue will be:

|  | £ |
|---|---|
| Shareholding (4,000 × 79.2p) | 3,168 |

We can see that the investor will have the same wealth under the first two options. However, by the investor doing nothing, the rights offer will lapse and so the investor will lose the value of the rights and will be worse off.

## 11.3 Raphael Ltd

The existing credit policies have the following costs:

|  | £ |
|---|---|
| Cost of investment in trade receivables ((50/365) × £2.4m × 12%) | 39,452 |
| Cost of bad debts (1.5% × £2.4m) | 36,000 |
| Total cost | 75,452 |

Employing a factor will result in the following costs and savings:

|  | £ |
|---|---|
| Charges of the factor (2% × £2.4m) | 48,000 |
| Interest charges on advance ((30/365) × (80% × £2.4m) × 11%) | 17,359 |
| Interest charges on overdraft ((30/365) × (20% × £2.4m) × 12%) | 4,734 |
| Total cost | 70,093 |
| Credit control savings | (18,000) |
| Net cost | 52,093 |

We can see the net cost of factoring is lower than the existing costs, and so there would be a benefit gained from entering into an agreement with the factor.

# Chapter 12

## 12.1 Hercules Wholesalers Ltd

(a) The business is probably concerned about its liquidity position because:

- it has a substantial overdraft, which together with its non-current borrowings means that it has borrowed an amount roughly equal to its equity (according to statement of financial position values);
- it has increased its investment in inventories during the past year (as shown by the income statement); and
- it has a low current ratio (ratio of current assets to current liabilities).

(b) The operating cash cycle can be calculated as follows:

|  | Number of days |
|---|---|
| Average inventories holding period: | |
| $\dfrac{((\text{Opening inventories} + \text{Closing inventories})/2) \times 365}{\text{Cost of sales}} = \dfrac{((125 + 143)/2) \times 365}{323}$ | = 151 |
| *Add* Average settlement period for receivables: | |
| $\dfrac{\text{Trade receivables} \times 365}{\text{Credit sales revenue}} = \dfrac{163}{452} \times 365$ | = 132 |
|  | 283 |
| *Less* Average settlement period for payables: | |
| $\dfrac{\text{Trade payables} \times 365}{\text{Credit purchases}} = \dfrac{145}{341} \times 365$ | = 155 |
| Operating cash cycle | 128 |

(c) The business can reduce the operating cash cycle in a number of ways. The average inventories holding period seems quite long. At present, average inventories held represent about five months' inventories usage. Reducing the level of inventories held can reduce this period. Similarly, the average settlement period for receivables seems long at more than four months' sales revenue. Imposing tighter credit control, offering discounts, charging interest on overdue accounts and so on may reduce this. However, any policy decisions concerning inventories and receivables must take account of current trading conditions.

Extending the period of credit taken to pay suppliers would also reduce the operating cash cycle. However, for the reasons mentioned in the chapter, this option must be given careful consideration.

## 12.4 Mayo Computers Ltd

### New proposals from credit control department

|  | £000 | £000 |
|---|---|---|
| Current level of investment in receivables | | |
| (£20m × (60/365)) | | 3,288 |
| Proposed level of investment in receivables | | |
| ((£20m × 60%) × (30/365)) | (986) | |
| ((£20m × 40%) × (50/365)) | (1,096) | (2,082) |
| Reduction in level of investment | | 1,206 |

The reduction in overdraft interest as a result of the reduction in the level of investment will be £1,206,000 × 14% = £169,000.

|  | £000 | £000 |
|---|---|---|
| Cost of cash discounts offered (£20m × 60% × 2.5%) |  | 300 |
| Additional cost of credit administration |  | 20 |
|  |  | 320 |
| Bad debt savings | (100) |  |
| Interest charge savings (see above) | (169) | (269) |
| Net cost of policy each year |  | 51 |

These calculations show that the business would incur additional annual cost if it implemented this proposal. It would therefore be cheaper to stay with the existing credit policy.

### 12.5 Boswell Enterprises Ltd

(a)

|  | Current policy | | New policy | |
|---|---|---|---|---|
|  | £000 | £000 | £000 | £000 |
| Trade receivables |  |  |  |  |
| ((£3m × $^1/_{12}$ × 30%) + (£3m × $^2/_{12}$ × 70%)) |  | 425.0 |  |  |
| ((£3.15m × $^1/_{12}$ × 60%) + (£3.15m × $^2/_{12}$ × 40%)) |  |  |  | 367.5 |
| Inventories |  |  |  |  |
| ((£3m − (£3m × 20%)) × $^3/_{12}$) |  | 600.0 |  |  |
| ((£3.15m − (£3.15m × 20%)) × $^3/_{12}$) |  |  |  | 630.0 |
| Cash (fixed) |  | 140.0 |  | 140.0 |
|  |  | 1,165.0 |  | 1,137.5 |
| Trade payables |  |  |  |  |
| ((£3m − (£3m × 20%)) × $^2/_{12}$) | (400.0) |  |  |  |
| ((£3.15m − (£3.15m × 20%)) × $^2/_{12}$) |  |  | (420.0) |  |
| Accrued variable expenses |  |  |  |  |
| (£3m × $^1/_{12}$ × 10%) | (25.0) |  |  |  |
| (£3.15m × $^1/_{12}$ × 10%) |  |  | (26.3) |  |
| Accrued fixed expenses | (15.0) | (440.0) | (15.0) | (461.3) |
| Investment in working capital |  | 725.0 |  | 676.2 |

(b) The expected profit for the year

|  | Current policy | | New policy | |
|---|---|---|---|---|
|  | £000 | £000 | £000 | £000 |
| Sales revenue |  | 3,000.0 |  | 3,150.0 |
| Cost of goods sold |  | (2,400.0) |  | (2,520.0) |
| Gross profit (20%) |  | 600.0 |  | 630.0 |
| Variable expenses (10%) | (300.0) |  | (315.0) |  |
| Fixed expenses | (180.0) |  | (180.0) |  |
| Discounts (£3.15m × 60% × 2.5%) | − | (480.0) | (47.3) | (542.3) |
| Profit for the year |  | 120.0 |  | 87.7 |

(c) Under the proposed policy we can see that the investment in working capital will be slightly lower than under the current policy. However, profits will be substantially lower as a result of offering discounts. The increase in sales revenue resulting from the discounts will not be sufficient to offset the additional cost of making the discounts to customers. It seems that the business should, therefore, stick with its current policy.

# Appendix E: Present value table

Present value of £1, that is, $1/(1 + r)^n$

where   $r$ = discount rate
          $n$ = number of periods until payment

| | | | | | Discount rates (r) | | | | | | |
| Periods (n) | 1% | 2% | 3% | 4% | 5% | 6% | 7% | 8% | 9% | 10% | |
|---|---|---|---|---|---|---|---|---|---|---|---|
| 1 | 0.990 | 0.980 | 0.971 | 0.962 | 0.952 | 0.943 | 0.935 | 0.926 | 0.917 | 0.909 | 1 |
| 2 | 0.980 | 0.961 | 0.943 | 0.925 | 0.907 | 0.890 | 0.873 | 0.857 | 0.842 | 0.826 | 2 |
| 3 | 0.971 | 0.942 | 0.915 | 0.889 | 0.864 | 0.840 | 0.816 | 0.794 | 0.772 | 0.751 | 3 |
| 4 | 0.961 | 0.924 | 0.888 | 0.855 | 0.823 | 0.792 | 0.763 | 0.735 | 0.708 | 0.683 | 4 |
| 5 | 0.951 | 0.906 | 0.863 | 0.822 | 0.784 | 0.747 | 0.713 | 0.681 | 0.650 | 0.621 | 5 |
| 6 | 0.942 | 0.888 | 0.837 | 0.790 | 0.746 | 0.705 | 0.666 | 0.630 | 0.596 | 0.564 | 6 |
| 7 | 0.933 | 0.871 | 0.813 | 0.760 | 0.711 | 0.665 | 0.623 | 0.583 | 0.547 | 0.513 | 7 |
| 8 | 0.923 | 0.853 | 0.789 | 0.731 | 0.677 | 0.627 | 0.582 | 0.540 | 0.502 | 0.467 | 8 |
| 9 | 0.914 | 0.837 | 0.766 | 0.703 | 0.645 | 0.592 | 0.544 | 0.500 | 0.460 | 0.424 | 9 |
| 10 | 0.905 | 0.820 | 0.744 | 0.676 | 0.614 | 0.558 | 0.508 | 0.463 | 0.422 | 0.386 | 10 |
| 11 | 0.896 | 0.804 | 0.722 | 0.650 | 0.585 | 0.527 | 0.475 | 0.429 | 0.388 | 0.350 | 11 |
| 12 | 0.887 | 0.788 | 0.701 | 0.625 | 0.557 | 0.497 | 0.444 | 0.397 | 0.356 | 0.319 | 12 |
| 13 | 0.879 | 0.773 | 0.681 | 0.601 | 0.530 | 0.469 | 0.415 | 0.368 | 0.326 | 0.290 | 13 |
| 14 | 0.870 | 0.758 | 0.661 | 0.577 | 0.505 | 0.442 | 0.388 | 0.340 | 0.299 | 0.263 | 14 |
| 15 | 0.861 | 0.743 | 0.642 | 0.555 | 0.481 | 0.417 | 0.362 | 0.315 | 0.275 | 0.239 | 15 |

| | | | | | Discount rates (r) | | | | | | |
| Periods (n) | 11% | 12% | 13% | 14% | 15% | 16% | 17% | 18% | 19% | 20% | |
|---|---|---|---|---|---|---|---|---|---|---|---|
| 1 | 0.901 | 0.893 | 0.885 | 0.877 | 0.870 | 0.862 | 0.855 | 0.847 | 0.840 | 0.833 | 1 |
| 2 | 0.812 | 0.797 | 0.783 | 0.769 | 0.756 | 0.743 | 0.731 | 0.718 | 0.706 | 0.694 | 2 |
| 3 | 0.731 | 0.712 | 0.693 | 0.675 | 0.658 | 0.641 | 0.624 | 0.609 | 0.593 | 0.579 | 3 |
| 4 | 0.659 | 0.636 | 0.613 | 0.592 | 0.572 | 0.552 | 0.534 | 0.516 | 0.499 | 0.482 | 4 |
| 5 | 0.593 | 0.567 | 0.543 | 0.519 | 0.497 | 0.476 | 0.456 | 0.437 | 0.419 | 0.402 | 5 |
| 6 | 0.535 | 0.507 | 0.480 | 0.456 | 0.432 | 0.410 | 0.390 | 0.370 | 0.352 | 0.335 | 6 |
| 7 | 0.482 | 0.452 | 0.425 | 0.400 | 0.376 | 0.354 | 0.333 | 0.314 | 0.296 | 0.279 | 7 |
| 8 | 0.434 | 0.404 | 0.376 | 0.351 | 0.327 | 0.305 | 0.285 | 0.266 | 0.249 | 0.233 | 8 |
| 9 | 0.391 | 0.361 | 0.333 | 0.308 | 0.284 | 0.263 | 0.243 | 0.225 | 0.209 | 0.194 | 9 |
| 10 | 0.352 | 0.322 | 0.295 | 0.270 | 0.247 | 0.227 | 0.208 | 0.191 | 0.176 | 0.162 | 10 |
| 11 | 0.317 | 0.287 | 0.261 | 0.237 | 0.215 | 0.195 | 0.178 | 0.162 | 0.148 | 0.135 | 11 |
| 12 | 0.286 | 0.257 | 0.231 | 0.208 | 0.187 | 0.168 | 0.152 | 0.137 | 0.124 | 0.112 | 12 |
| 13 | 0.258 | 0.229 | 0.204 | 0.182 | 0.163 | 0.145 | 0.130 | 0.116 | 0.104 | 0.093 | 13 |
| 14 | 0.232 | 0.205 | 0.181 | 0.160 | 0.141 | 0.125 | 0.111 | 0.099 | 0.088 | 0.078 | 14 |
| 15 | 0.209 | 0.183 | 0.160 | 0.140 | 0.123 | 0.108 | 0.095 | 0.084 | 0.074 | 0.065 | 15 |

Discount rates (r)

| Periods (n) | 21% | 22% | 23% | 24% | 25% | 26% | 27% | 28% | 29% | 30% | |
|---|---|---|---|---|---|---|---|---|---|---|---|
| 1 | 0.826 | 0.820 | 0.813 | 0.806 | 0.800 | 0.794 | 0.787 | 0.781 | 0.775 | 0.769 | 1 |
| 2 | 0.683 | 0.672 | 0.661 | 0.650 | 0.640 | 0.630 | 0.620 | 0.610 | 0.601 | 0.592 | 2 |
| 3 | 0.564 | 0.551 | 0.537 | 0.524 | 0.512 | 0.500 | 0.488 | 0.477 | 0.466 | 0.455 | 3 |
| 4 | 0.467 | 0.451 | 0.437 | 0.423 | 0.410 | 0.397 | 0.384 | 0.373 | 0.361 | 0.350 | 4 |
| 5 | 0.386 | 0.370 | 0.355 | 0.341 | 0.328 | 0.315 | 0.303 | 0.291 | 0.280 | 0.269 | 5 |
| 6 | 0.319 | 0.303 | 0.289 | 0.275 | 0.262 | 0.250 | 0.238 | 0.277 | 0.217 | 0.207 | 6 |
| 7 | 0.263 | 0.249 | 0.235 | 0.222 | 0.210 | 0.198 | 0.188 | 0.178 | 0.168 | 0.159 | 7 |
| 8 | 0.218 | 0.204 | 0.191 | 0.179 | 0.168 | 0.157 | 0.148 | 0.139 | 0.130 | 0.123 | 8 |
| 9 | 0.180 | 0.167 | 0.155 | 0.144 | 0.134 | 0.125 | 0.116 | 0.108 | 0.101 | 0.094 | 9 |
| 10 | 0.149 | 0.137 | 0.126 | 0.116 | 0.107 | 0.099 | 0.092 | 0.085 | 0.078 | 0.073 | 10 |
| 11 | 0.123 | 0.112 | 0.103 | 0.094 | 0.086 | 0.079 | 0.072 | 0.066 | 0.061 | 0.056 | 11 |
| 12 | 0.102 | 0.092 | 0.083 | 0.076 | 0.069 | 0.062 | 0.057 | 0.052 | 0.047 | 0.043 | 12 |
| 13 | 0.084 | 0.075 | 0.068 | 0.061 | 0.055 | 0.050 | 0.045 | 0.040 | 0.037 | 0.033 | 13 |
| 14 | 0.069 | 0.062 | 0.055 | 0.049 | 0.044 | 0.039 | 0.035 | 0.032 | 0.028 | 0.025 | 14 |
| 15 | 0.057 | 0.051 | 0.045 | 0.040 | 0.035 | 0.031 | 0.028 | 0.025 | 0.022 | 0.020 | 15 |

# Index

Note: Page numbers in **bold** indicate highlighted **key terms** and their glossary definitions.

5 Cs of credit **470**, 470–1, **503**

ABC *see* activity-based costing
ABC system of inventories control **463**, 463–4, **498**
absorption costing **282**, **498**
  *see also* full costing
accountability 120
accounting **2**, **498**
  decision-making perspective 3
  financial versus management 10–12
  as information system 9–10
  purpose 2
  as service 5–6
accounting and finance 1
  balancing risk and return 19–20
  and business management 15
  changing face of 14–15
  definitions 2–3
  financial objectives of businesses 15–19
  not-for-profit organisations 20–1
  reasons for studying 21–2
  scandals 13–14
  user needs 3–5
accounting conventions **51**, **498**
  accruals **87**, **498**
  business entity **51**, 54, **500**
  consistency **101**, **500**
  dual aspect **54**, **502**
  going concern **53**, 54, **504**
  historic cost **51**, 51–2, 58, **504**
  influence on statement of financial position 54
  matching **83**, 85, 86, 102, **506**
  materiality **86**, **506**
  prudence **53**, 54, 100, **508**
accounting equation 39, 42, 44, 49–50, 73–4, 85
accounting information 2
  and not-for-profit organisations 20–1
  usefulness of 7–9
  users of 3–5
accounting information systems **9**, 9–10, **498**
accounting periods *see* reporting periods
accounting rate of return (ARR) 358, **359**, 359–64, 365, 377, 378, 388–9, **498**
accounting rules 142–4, 146

accounting standards
  and depreciation 94
  for inventory valuation 100–1
  statements of cash flow (FRS 1) 160
  *see also* International Accounting Standards
accruals accounting **87**, **498**
accruals convention **87**, **498**
accrued expenses **83**, 83–5, **498**
acid test ratio **208**, 208–9, **498**
acquisition costs 51
activity-based costing (ABC) 298–306, **301**, **498**
adverse variances **339**, 339–41, **498**
ageing schedule of trade receivables **477**, **498**
AIM *see* Alternative Investment Market
Air France-KLM 195
Akzo Nobel 61–2
allotted share capital **131**, **499**
Alternative Investment Market (AIM) **435**, 435–6, **499**
Amec plc 81, 214
amortisation 57, **95**, 95–6, **499**
Amstrad 62
annual depreciation charges 91
AOL 260
Apache Capital Partners 383
ARR *see* accounting rate of return
Arsenal Football Club 72
articles and memorandum of association 126
Asda 117
asset-based financing **439**, **499**
  *see also* debt factoring; invoice discounting
assets **36**, **499**
  characteristics 36
  classification of 44–6
  economic life of 89
  examples 39–42, 46
  fair values of 88–9
  intangible **38**, **504**
  net 49
  physical life of 89
  relationship with claims 38–42, 63–4
  residual/disposal values **89**, 89–90, **508**
  and right to control 36
  'ring-fenced' 115
  tangible **38**, **510**
  valuation of 58–63

assets (*continued*)
    *see also* current assets; depreciation;
        intangible assets; non-current assets;
        working capital
Associated British Foods 459
attitudes to budgets 343, 344
audit fees 137
auditors **145**, **499**
authorisation systems, budgets as 322
AVCO *see* weighted average cost
average inventories turnover period **200**,
    200–1, 461, **499**
average settlement periods
    trade payables 202–3, 483, 485
    trade receivables 201–2, 476–7, 483, 485

Babcock International Group 324, 456–7
bad debts **102**, 102–3, **499**
balance sheets *see* statements of financial
    position
bank overdrafts **437**, 487, **499**
banks and bad debts 103
batch costing **296**, **499**
behaviour
    and budgets 344
    of costs 240
benefits
    of accounting information 7–9
    and assets 36, 38
BEP *see* break-even point
best fit, lines of 244–5
BHP 215
Blacks Leisure plc 430–1
BMW 195
bonds 412–15
bonus shares **128**, 128–30, 431, **499**
Boots 469
borrowings 131–2, 411–17
    *see also* bank overdrafts; loan covenants;
        loan notes; loans
bottom line 104
BP 214, 221
brands 55–6
break even, failing to 257–8
break-even analyses **245**, **499**
    contribution 250–1
    weaknesses of 258–61
break-even charts 245–6, **246**, 252, **499**
    and profit–volume (PV) charts 257
break-even point (BEP) 245–50, **246**, 252,
    257–8, 259, **499**
    and margins of safety 251–3
break-even prices 297
British Airways plc 197, 248, 251, 253, 357,
    413, 418, 421, 456–7, 459, 474
British Telecommunications Group plc
    474
Brittany Ferries 356
BSkyB Group plc 82, 195, 313, 357
budget holders **326**, **500**
budgetary control **343**, 343–4, **500**

budgeting 312–46
    and control 335–6, 337
    incremental **325**, 325–6, **504**
    non-financial measures in 334–5
    zero-base (ZBB) 325–7, **326**, **510**
budgets 312, **314**, **499**
    attitudes to 343, 344
    and behaviour 344
    and budgeting 313
    capital expenditure 319
    cash 319, 327–31, 333, 481–2
    continual **317**, 317–8, **500**
    data collection and analysis 344
    direct labour 319
    discretionary 325–6, **326**, **502**
    examples 328–9, 331–2, 337
    flexible **338**, **503**
    flexing **337**, 337–43, **503**
    and forecasts **317**
    interrelationship of types of 318–21
    inventories 318–9, 332–3, 461
    master **318**, **506**
    overheads 319
    periodic **317**, 317–8, **507**
    preparing 327–34
    production 319
    raw materials 319, 332
    reporting 344
    rolling **317**, **509**
    sales 318–20
    SME practice 324–5
    and strategic plans/objectives 313–16
    targets 343–4
    and time horizons 316
    trade payables 319, 331–2, 333
    trade receivables 319, 331, 333
    uses and usage of 321–5
    variances from 336–43
buffer inventories 462–3
Buffett, Warren 13
buildings *see* property
business angels **443**, 443–4, **500**
business entity convention **52**, 54, **500**
business objectives 15–19, 313–14, 378
business reviews **146**, **500**
businesses
    management of 15
    multi-product 259, 280
    single-product 279–80
buy-in/buy-out capital 442
buy-or-make decisions 266–7

called-up share capital **131**, **500**
capacity for payments, customers' 470
capital
    cost of **377**, **501**
    customers' 470
    employed 194–6, 203–7, 361
    venture **441**, 441–3, **510**
    *see also* equity; limited companies; shares;
        working capital

capital expenditure budgets 319
capital investment decisions 355
  appraisals 357–93
  nature of 356–7
capital reserves **126**, 126–7, 128, 133, **500**
capital-intensive production 299
Carphone Warehouse 474
carrying amounts 58, **91**, 91–2, **500**
cash
  definition 161–2
  expenses less than cash paid 86–7
  expenses more than cash paid 83–5
  holding 479–80
  importance of 32, 160–1
  increase or decrease in 164, 174–6
  managing 479–87
  transmission 486
  withdrawals of 44
cash balances 192–3
  controlling 480–1
cash budgets 319, 327–31, 333, 481–2
cash discounts **475**, 488–9, **500**
cash equivalents
  definition 161–2
  increase or decrease in 164, 174–6
cash flow statements *see* statements of cash
  flow
cash flows
  depreciation 171
  direct method of deducing **168**, **502**
  discounted 373–7, 386
  dividends paid 171
  indirect method of deducing **168**, 168–71,
    **504**
  interest 171
  investment appraisal and 363, 364–7,
    368–9, 372–4, 378, 383
  and leasing 418
  measuring and reporting 158–180
  negative 166–7
  normal direction of 166–7
  positive 166
  variances 482
  *see also* statements of cash flow
cash operating cycle *see* operating cash cycle
channel stuffing 147
character of customers 471
charges 411
  *see also* mortgages
claims 36, 38–9, **500**
  classification of 47–8
  examples 39–42
  relationship with assets 38–42, 63–4
  *see also* equity; liabilities
Chelsea Football Club 259–60
closing or continuation decisions 268–9
Cohort 10
collateral, customers' 470
collection policies, trade receivables 476–8
Combined Code *see* UK Corporate
  Governance Code

commission on sales 83–4
common costs **281**, **500**
  *see also* overheads (indirect costs)
common future costs 384
community representatives 4, 5
companies *see* limited companies
Companies House *see* Registrar of
  Companies
comparability 6, 8, **500**
comparison
  of budget and actual 336–43
  using ratios 189–90, 227
competition 298, 299
  competitive forces 16
  competitors as users of information 4, 5
conditions, and customers' ability to pay
  470–1
consistency convention **101**, **500**
consolidating shares **125**, **500**
construction contracts 81
continual budgets **317**, 317–8, **500**
continuation decisions 268–9
contracts
  long-term 80–1
  pricing/assessing 262–3
contribution margin ratio **250**, 250–1, **500**
contribution per unit **250**, 257, 264, **500**
contributions
  and break-even analysis 250–1
  and marginal analysis 261–9
  and operating gearing 255–6
  and profit–volume charts 257
control **314**, **500**
  of assets, right to 36
  budgetary **343**, 343–4, **500**
  of cash balances 480–1
  of credit 404, 405–6
  exercising 277
  of inventories 463–4
  of trade payables 489–90
  *see also* management
conventions *see* accounting conventions
convertible loan notes **413**, 413–5, **500**
co-ordination and budgets 321
copyrights 55
corporate governance **119**, 119–23, **501**
corporate objectives *see* business objectives
corporation tax **118**, **501**
cost behaviour 240, **284**, **501**
cost centres 293, 302, 303, **501**
  and overheads 293–6
cost drivers 301, 301–2, 304, **501**
cost pools 302, 302–4, **501**
cost units 279, 280–2, 284–7, 301, 303,
  **501**
cost–volume–profit analysis 239–71
costing
  batch **296**, **499**
  process 280, **507**
  *see also* activity-based costing; full costing;
    job costing

costs 239–40, **240**, **501**
  of accounting information 7–9
  of assets, depreciation and 88–9, 95–6
  borrowing 480
  of capital **377**, **501**
  common future 384
  direct **280**, 280–1, 284–5, **502**
  future 36
  historic (acquisition) **51**, 51–2, 58–63, **504**
  of inventories 465–7
  of leasing 417
  opportunity 369, 378, 384–5, 480, **507**
  past 384–5
  relevant **384**, **508**
  of sales 72, **75**, 75–7, **501**
  semi-fixed (semi-variable) **243**, 243–5, **509**
  total 284
  weighted average **98**, 99–101, **510**
  *see also* break-even analyses; fixed costs;
    overheads; variable costs
covenants, loan **415**, 415–7, **505**
cover ratio, dividends **217**, **502**
creative accounting **146**, 146–9, **501**
credit 470–7
  customers receiving 470–1
  five Cs of **470**, 470–1, **503**
  and operating cash cycle 482–6
  publicising terms 476
  tightened control 404, 405–6
  *see also* bad debts; trade payables; trade
    receivables
credit agencies 471–2
credit insurance **476**
credit periods 472–7
credit sales 101
creditors *see* trade payables
current assets **44–5**, 455, 456, **501**
  and borrowing 440
  examples 49, 50, 60
  *see also* cash; inventories; trade receivables;
    working capital
current liabilities **47**, **501**
  examples 48, 49, 60
  *see also* trade payables; working capital
current ratio **207**, 207–8, 224, **501**
current value 51–2
customers 3, 5, 16–17, 470–1, 476

data collection and analysis 344
dates 50–1
debentures *see* loan notes
debt capacity 193
debt factoring **437**, 437–8, 439, 476, **501**
debtors *see* trade receivables
debts, bad **102**, 102–3, **499**
decision-making perspective of accounting 2
demarcation between managerial
    responsibility areas 343
departments *see* cost centres
depreciation 58–9, 61, **86**, 359, **501**
  as cash flow 171

  and cost of assets 88–9, 96
  examples 89–93
  of intangible assets 95–6
  judgement and 96–7
  methods 90–5
  and replacement of non-current assets 96
  and residual value of assets 89–90
  and statements of cash flows 174–5
  useful life of 89
  *see also* amortisation
derivatives **415**, **503**
detail, level of 11
direct costs **280**, 280–1, 284–5, **502**
direct labour 280, 286–7, 290–2, 298, 303, 319
direct method of deducing cash flows **168**,
  **502**
directors **119**, 122–3, 145–6, **502**
directors' reports **145**, 145–6, **502**
disasters, accounting for 21
disclosures 120
discount factors 374–6, **375**, **502**
discount (PV) tables 375–7, 563–4
discounted cash flows 373–7, 386
discounts, cash **475**, 488–9, **500**
discretionary budgets 325–6, **326**, **502**
disposal values *see* residual values
dividend cover ratio **217**, **502**
dividend payout ratio **217**, **502**
dividend per share **218**, **502**
dividend yield ratio **218**, 221–2, **502**
dividends **124**, 138, **502**
  as cash flow 171
  and loan covenants 415
  and preference shares 125–6
  and retained profits 404–5
  and statements of cash flow 174
  and statements of changes in equity 140
  and statements of financial position 138, 142
  and taxation 405
dual aspect convention **54**, **502**

early-stage capital 442
earnings per share (EPS) **218**, 218–19, **502**
earnings ratio *see* price/earnings ratio
easyJet plc 747
Ecofin 382
economic benefits of accounting information
  8–9
economic life of assets 89
economic order quantity (EOQ) **465**, 465–7,
  **502**
efficiency
  assessing 277
  ratios 188, 200–7
efficient use of scarce resources 263–6
electronic point-of-sale (EPOS) 463
EMI Group Ltd 415–16
employees
  sales revenue per employee ratio **204**,
    204–5, **509**
  as users of information 4, 5

Enron 13, 147
Enterprise Finance Guarantee Scheme 444
EOQ *see* economic order quantity
EPOS *see* electronic point-of-sale
EPS (earnings per share) **218**, 218–19, **502**
equation of accounting 39, 42, 44, 49–50,
    73–4, 85
equipment *see* property, plant and equipment
equities *see* ordinary shares
equity **38**, 123, **502**
    examples 48, 49, 60
    withdrawing 132–6
equity finance 132
eurobonds **412**, 412–13, **502**
Eurotunnel 259, 392–3
ex-rights prices 428
exception, management by **322**, **505**
expansion capital 442
expenses **72**, 72–3, **502**
    accrued **83**, 83–5, **498**
    classification of 77–8
    examples 72–3
    less than cash paid 86–7
    more than cash paid 83–5
    prepaid **86**, 89, **507**
    recognition of 83–7
    *see also* income statements
external finance sources 403, 407–39

factoring *see* debt factoring
fair values **59**, 88–9, **503**
fairness 120
favourable variances **339**, 339–41, **503**
FIFO *see* first in, first out
final accounts **35**, **503**
    *see also* financial statements
final dividends 138
finance **2–3**, **503**
    *see also* accounting and finance; capital
    investment decisions; financing
    businesses; working capital
finance leases **417**, 417–19, **503**
financial accounting **10–12**, **503**
    *see also* cash flows; limited companies;
    statements of cash flow
financial derivatives **415**, **503**
financial gearing 188, **209**, 209–15, **503**
financial management *see* finance
financial performance, measuring and
    reporting 70–107
    *see also* income statements; profit
    measurement
financial periods *see* reporting periods
financial position, measuring and reporting
    29–66
    *see also* income statements; statements of
    cash flow; statements of changes in
    equity; statements of comprehensive
    income; statements of financial position
financial position statements *see* statements of
    financial position

financial ratios 186–8
    calculation of 190–2
    classification of 188–9
    efficiency 188, 200–7
    examples 191–3, 206, 210–11
    financial gearing 188, 209–15
    gross profit margin **197**, 197–200, **504**
    investment 188, 217–23
    limitations of 226–8
    liquidity 188, 207–9
    need for 189–90
    operating profit margin **196**, 196–7, **507**
    overreliance on 227
    to predict future outcomes 226
    profitability 188, 193–200, 205–7
    trend analysis 224–5
financial reporting standards *see* accounting
    standards; International Financial
    Reporting Standards
Financial Services Authority (FSA) 144
financial statements
    analysis and interpretation 186–230
    limited companies 136–8
    and loan covenants 415
    quality of 146, 226
    *see also* income statements; statements of
    cash flow; statements of changes in
    equity; statements of comprehensive
    income; statements of financial position
financing activities, cash flows from 164, 165,
    174
financing businesses 402
    business angels **443**, 443–4, **500**
    examples 423–5, 428
    government assistance 444
    limited companies 123–31
    share issues 426–31
    small businesses 441–4
    sources of finance 403–45
    Stock Exchange role 431–5
    venture capital **441**, 441–3, **510**
finished inventories budgets 318–9, 332
first in, first out (FIFO) 98, 99–101, **503**
five Cs of credit **470**, 470–1, **503**
fixed assets *see* capital investment decisions;
    depreciation; non-current assets
fixed charges 411
fixed costs **240**, 240–2, **503**
    and break-even analysis 245–50
    and operating gearing 255–6
    full costing and 284
    marginal analysis and 261–2
    semi-fixed **243**, 243–5, **509**
    stepped **242**, 258–9, **509**
flexibility
    of borrowing 440–1
    of leasing 418
flexible budgets **336**, **503**
flexing budgets **337**, 337–43, **503**
floating charges 411
football clubs 57, 72, 259–60, 412

forecasts **317**, **503**
Forth Ports plc 383
forward planning 22
forward thinking and budgets 321, 322
FRS 1 *Cash flow statements* 160
FSA (Financial Services Authority) 144
full costing 276–308, **279**, **503**
    alternative approach to 300–1
    examples 286, 293–4, 300–1, 303
    new environment 299–300
    single-product businesses 279–80
    traditional way 298
full costs 277–9, **278**, **503**
    forward-looking nature of 297
    reasons for knowing 277–8
    using information 306
fully paid shares **131**, **503**

gains 139
Gap 17
gearing
    financial 188, **209**, 209–15, **503**
    long-term finance decisions and 423–6
    operating **255**, 255–6, **506**
gearing ratios 188, **212**, 212–13, **504**
GEC plc 228
General Motors 258
general reserves 138
GlaxoSmithKline plc 383
Global Crossing 147
Go-Ahead Group plc 357, 474
going concern convention **53**, 54, **504**
goodwill 55–6, 60, 62
government
    financing assistance 444
    as users of financial information 4, 5
gross profit margin ratio **197**, 197–200, **504**
gross profits **75**, **504**

hire purchase **421**, 421–2, **504**
historic cost convention **51**, 51–2, 54, 58, **504**
hollow swaps 147
human resources 56–7
hurdle rates 382

IAS 7 *Cash flow statements* 160, 161, 164, 165
IASB *see* International Accounting Standards Board
IFRS *see* International Financial Reporting Standards
impairment of non-current assets 61–2
in-and-out trading 147
income statements **31**, 71–2, **504**
    audit fees 137
    cost of sales 75–7
    examples 32, 33, 74, 190–3
    expenses, classification of 77–8
    layouts 74–5
    and limited companies 116, 136, 137
    reporting periods 78
    and statements of cash flow 35, 159–60, 163, 173
    and statements of comprehensive income 139
    and statements of financial position 35, 73–4, 163
    and taxation 138
    uses and usefulness of 104
    working capital 484
incorporation of limited companies 113
incremental budgeting **325**, 325–6, **504**
indirect costs *see* overheads
indirect method of deducing cash flows **168**, 168–71, **504**
initial public offering (IPO) 430, 432
inflation 57–8, 226–7, 241, 371–2, **371**, 372, 480, **504**
information
    range and quality 11
    from statements of cash flow 175–7
    *see also* accounting information
institutional investors 121
insurance, credit **476**
intangible assets **38**, **504**
    amortisation of 95–6
    depreciation of 95–6
    non-current 55–6, 61–2
interest
    as cash flow 170, 171
    lost 369, 372
    rates 413, 441
    and statements of cash flow 174–5
interest cover ratio **213**, 213–15, **504**
interest payments 386
interim dividends 138
internal finance sources 403–7
internal rate of return (IRR) 358, **379**, 379–83, 385, 386, 388–92, **504**
International Accounting Standards 94, **143**, **504**
    IAS 7 *Cash flow statements* 160, 161, 164, 165
International Accounting Standards Board (IASB) 143–4
International Financial Reporting Standards (IFRS) 58, 97, 100–1, **143**, 143–4, **504–5**
inventories **505**
    buffer/safety 462–3
    control of 463–4
    costing methods 97–101
    economic order quantity (EOQ) **465**, 465–7
    holding periods 482
    managing 458–69
    recording systems 462–3
    reduction in levels 404, 407
    reordering systems 462–3
    and trading transactions 42–4
    valuation of 62–3, 97–101
    volume 464
    turnover period, average **200**, 200–1, 461, 485, **499**
    working capital 454–5

inventories budgets 318–9, 322–3, 461
inventories management
    JIT (just-in-time) **468**, 468–9, **505**
    materials requirement planning (MRP)
        system **467–8**, **506**
investing activities, cash flows from 164, 165,
    166–7
investment 3
    scale of 383
    *see also* shares
investment analysts 4, 5
investment appraisals 357–93
investment ratios 188, 217–23
invoice discounting **438**, 438–9, 476, **505**
invoicing promptly 476
IPO *see* initial public offering
IRR *see* internal rate of return
issued share capital **131**, **505**
ITV 221

J D Wetherspoon 221, 474
Jarvis plc 474
JJB Sports plc 97
job costing **282**, 282–5, 286–95, 296, 298,
    **505**
just-in-time (JIT) inventories management
    **468**, 468–9, **505**

Kesa Electricals 260
key factors (scarce resources) 264
Kingfisher plc 459, 474

labour, direct 280, 286–7, 290–2, 298, 303,
    319
land
    valuation of 59–60
    *see also* property
last in, first out (LIFO) **98**, 98–101, **505**
law and companies 124, 127, 128, 135, 138,
    142, 144
lead time **462**, **505**
leases
    finance **417**, 417–19, **503**
    operating **418**, **506**
    sale and leaseback **419**, 419–20, **509**
least squares regression 245
lenders as users of information 4, 5
Lesotho Diamond Corporation 378–9
leverage *see* gearing
liabilities **38**, **505**
    *see also* claims; current liabilities; expenses;
        non-current liabilities; revenue
liability, limited 114–16, **116**, **505**
licences 55
LiDCO Group plc 176–7
LIFO *see* last in, first out
limited companies 112, **113**, **505**
    auditors **145**
    borrowings 131–2
    dividends 138
    equity (owners' claim) 123, 132–6

examples 123–4, 127, 134–5, 136–7
features 113–19
financial statements 136–8
financing 123–31
income statements 116, 136, 137
incorporation of 113
law 124, 127, 128, 135, 138, 142, 144
legal safeguards 116
limited liability 114–16, **116**, **505**
managing 119–23
perpetual life 113–14
private **116**, 116–17, **507**
public **116**, 116–17, **508**
reserves 126–8
share capital 124–6, 128–31
statements of financial position 116, 122,
    129, 134–5, 136, 138
and Stock Exchange 131–2, 144, 146
and taxation 117–18, 138
    *see also* accounting standards; directors
limited liability 114–16, **116**, **505**
limiting factors (scarce resources) 264,
    316–17, **317**, **505**
liquidation, voluntary 114
liquidity
    and cash control 480
    and loan covenants 415
    ratios 188, 207–9
listed companies 118
    *see also* public limited companies
listing 431–5
listing authority **144**
loan covenants **415**, 415–7, **505**
loan notes 131–2, **411**, 411–12, 416–17, **505**
    convertible **413**, 413–5, **500**
loan stocks *see* loan notes
loans 411–12
    Enterprise Finance Guarantee Scheme
        444
    long-term 132
    mortgages **415**, **506**
    term **411**, **510**
logical investors 372–5
London 2012 Olympic Games 336
long-term contracts 80–1
long-term finance
    external 408–36
    and gearing 423–6
    internal 403–5
    leases 417–19
    sale and leaseback **419**, 419–20, **509**
    sources 403–5, 409–36
    venture capital **441**, 441–3, **510**
    versus short-term 440–1
    *see also* loans; shares
long-term liabilities *see* non-current
    liabilities
long-term loans 132
losses
    calculation of 74
    realised/unrealised 139

make-or-buy decisions 266–7
management
    of cash 479–87
    by exception **322**, **505**
    of inventories 458–69
    motivation and budgets 321–2
    strategic **15**, **510**
    as users of information 4, 5
    *see also* budgets; control
management accounting **10–12**, **505**
    cost–volume–profit analysis 239–71
    *see also* budgets; full costing
managerial responsibility areas, demarcation
        between 343
managing limited companies 119–23
Manchester United Football Club 412
Mango (Management Accounting for Non-
        Governmental Organisations) 21
manufacturing industries, ABC in 304
marginal analysis 261–69, **262**, **505**
marginal costs **262**, **506**
margins
    gross profit **197**, 197–200, **504**
    operating profit **196**, 196–7, **507**
    of safety **135**, **251**, 251–3, **505**
market valuations 56, 59, 61
Marks and Spencer 59, 221, 225, 357, 474
master budgets **318**, **506**
matching borrowing with assets 440
matching convention **83**, 85, 86, 102, **506**
materiality 7, **506**
materiality convention **86**, **506**
materials
    raw materials budgets 319, 332
    variances 341
materials requirements planning (MRP)
        system **467–8**, **506**
Medusa Mining 130
members *see* shareholders
memoranda of association 126
Millward Brown Optimor 56
mission statements **313**, **506**
monetary measurement of assets 36
monetary stability 57–8
money measurement 55–8
moneysupermarket.com 433
Morrison's 117, 224, 357, 474
mortgages **415**, **506**
    securitisation of 422–3
motivation and budgets 321–2
MRP *see* materials requirements planning system
multi-product businesses 280
    break-even analyses 259
    *see also* job costing; overheads

National Express 429
National Health Service (NHS) 278, 287
NBV (net book value) *see* carrying amounts
negative cash flows 166–7
net assets 49
    *see also* working capital

net book value (NBV) *see* carrying amounts
net current assets *see* working capital
net present value (NPV) 358, **368**, 368–79,
        379–82, 385, 386, 388–92, 475, **506**
net profits 75, **506**
net realisable values 100
Next plc 341, 456–7
NHS *see* National Health Service
Nike 17, 18
Nissan 469
nominal value (shares) **123**, 124–5, 127, **506**
    *see also* shares
non-current assets **45–6**, 192, **506**
    and borrowing 440
    examples 48, 49, 60
    impairment 61–2
    intangible 55, 61–2
    replacement of 96
non-current liabilities **47**, 47–8, 60, **506**
non-financial measures in budgeting 334–5
non-linear relationships and break-even
        analyses 258
not-for-profit organisations 20–1
NPV *see* net present value

objectives
    of business 15–19, 313–14, 378
    strategic 313–16
OCC *see* operating cash cycle
offer for sale **430**, **506**
operating activities
    cash flows from 164, 165
    deducing cash flows from 168–71
    and normal direction of cash flows 166
operating cash cycle (OCC) **482**, 482–6,
        **506**
operating gearing **255**, 255–6, **506**
operating leases **418**, **506**
operating profits 75, 136, 137, 192, **506**
    margin ratio **196**, 196–7, **507**
operational gearing *see* operating gearing
opportunity costs 369, 378, 384–5, 480, **507**
options, strategic 313–16
ordinary shares **125**, 125–6, 193–4, 408–10,
        **507**
output decisions 277
outsourcing **266**, 266–7, **507**
overdrafts **437**, 487, **499**
overhead absorption (recovery) rate **286**, 299,
        303, **507**
overheads (indirect costs) **281**, 281–2, **507**
    budgets 319
    charging basis 290–2
    and cost behaviour 284
    on cost centre basis 293–6
    cost drivers of 301–2, 304
    levels of 298, 299
    problem of 284–5
    segmenting 292
    as service renderers 285–6
    variances 341

owners
claim on limited companies 123
partners 115
sole proprietors 115
as users of information 4, 5
see also directors; equity; management;
shareholders

paid-up share capital **131**, **507**
par value see nominal value
partners 115
past costs 384–5
past transactions or events 36
patents 55
payback period (PP) 358, **364**, 364–8, 377,
378, 385, 388–92, **507**
payout ratio, dividend **217**, **502**
P/E see price/earnings ratio
performance
assessing 277
and budgets 321–2, 336–43
financial, measuring and reporting 70–107
planned 190
and statements of financial position 64
periodic budgets **317**, 317–8, **507**
perpetual life of companies 113–14
physical life of assets 89
planning
forward 22
materials requirements (MRP) **467–8**, **506**
planned performance 190
strategic 313–16
time horizons of 316
see also budgets
plant see property, plant and equipment
position analyses 313
position statements see statements of financial
position
positive cash flows 166
PP see payback period
predictions and financial ratios 226
pre-dispatching 147
preference **125**, 125–6, 408, 410–11, 416–17,
**507**
premises see property; property, plant and
equipment
premiums
risk **371**, 372, **509**
shares 128
prepaid expenses **86**, 89, **507**
present values (PV) 373–6
table 563–4
see also net present value
price/earnings ratio (P/E) **219**, 219–23, **507**
prices
break-even 297
decisions 277
effect of change on inventory cost 98
primary market, Stock Exchange as 431
private limited companies **116**, 116–17, 118,
435, **507**

private placing 131, **430**, 430–1, **507**
process costing **280**, **507**
production
budgets 319
capital-intensive 299
direct-labour intensive/paced 298
profit and loss accounts see income
statements
profit before taxation **137**, **507**
profit for the year 75, **137**, **507**
profit measurement
bad debts and 102–3
and cash and accruals accounting 87
inventory costing methods and 97–101
revenue recognition 78–82
see also depreciation
profitability ratios 188, 193–200, 205–7
profits **71**, **507**
achieving target 254
before taxation **137**, **507**
bottom line 104
budget versus actual 339–40
calculation of 74
from change of focus 16
cost–volume–profit analysis 237–71
current year/short-term 17–18
gross 75, 197–200, **504**
net 75
operating 75, 136, 137, 192, **506**
margin ratio **196**, 196–7, **507**
operating gearing effects on 255–6
retained 132, 138, 403–5
see also accounting rate of return; reserves
profit–volume (PV) charts **257**, **508**
promoters of companies 113, 123
property
rent 241–2
sale and leaseback **419**, 419–20, **509**
property, plant and equipment 58, **508**
valuation of 58–60
see also depreciation
prudence convention 53, 54, 100, **508**
public issues 131, **430**, **508**
public limited companies **116**, 116–17, 118,
434, **508**
PV see present values
PV (profit–volume) charts **257**, **508**

ratios see financial ratios
raw materials budgets 319, 332
realisable values, net 100
recognition
of expenses 83–7
of revenue 78–82
recovery (overhead absorption) rate **286**, 299,
303, **507**
redemption of shares 411
reducing balance depreciation method **91**,
91–5, **508**
reducing inventory levels 404, 407
references for credit 471

refunding risk 441
Registrar of Companies 113, 116, 126, 142
regulations 11
relative efficiency, assessing 277
relevance **5**, 8, **508**
relevant costs **384**, **508**
reliability **6**, 8, **508**
remuneration report 146
rent 241–2
reordering and inventories 461–2
replacement of non-current assets 96
reporting intervals 11
reporting periods **73**, **508**
reports 10–11
  auditors 145
  budgets 344
  directors' **145**, 145–6, **502**
  remuneration 146
rescue capital 442
reserves **123**, 126–8, **508**
  capital **126**, 126–7, 128, 133, **500**
  general 138
  revenue **124**, 126, 128, 133–5, **509**
  and statements of financial position 138
residual values of assets **89**, 89–90, **508**
resources
  investment decisions and 356
  most efficient use of scarce 263–6
retained profits 132, 138, 403–5
return, accounting rate of (ARR) 358, **359**,
    359–64, 365, 377, 378, 388–9, **498**
return, balancing risk and 19–20
return, internal rate of (IRR) 358, **379**,
    379–83, 385, 386, 388–92, **504**
return on capital employed (ROCE) **194**,
    194–6, 205–7, 361, **508**
return on ordinary shareholders' funds (ROSF)
    **193**, 193–4, **508**
revenue **71**, **508**
  and break-even analysis 246–50, 257
  examples 71–2
  recognition of 78–82
  from sales ratios 203–5
  see also break-even analyses; income
    statements; reserves
revenue reserve **124**, 126, 128, 133–5, **509**
right to control of assets 36
rights issues 131, **426**, 426–9, **509**
Rio Tinto 215
risk premiums **371**, 372, **509**
risks **509**
  balancing with returns 19–20
  NPV and 370–1, 372
  of refunding borrowing 441
ROCE *see* return on capital employed
rolling budgets **317**, **509**
Rolls-Royce 221, 391
ROSF *see* return on ordinary shareholders' funds
round tripping 147
Royal Mail 305
Ryanair 248, 251, 357, 410

safety
  inventory levels 462–3
  margin of 135, **251**, 251–3, **505**
Sainsbury's 17, 117, 224, 256, 459
sale and leaseback **419**, 419–20, **509**
sales
  commission 83–4
  cost of 72, **75**, 75–7, **501**
  on credit 101
  and profit–volume charts 257
sales budgets 318–20
sales revenue per employee ratio **204**, 204–5,
    **509**
sales revenue to capital employed ratio **203**,
    203–4, **509**
scale of investments 383
scarce resources, most efficient use of 263–6
scrip issues *see* bonus issues
secondary market, Stock Exchange as 431
securitisation **422**, 422–3, **509**
semi-fixed (semi-variable) costs **243**, 243–5,
    **509**
service, accounting as form of 5–6
service industries, ABC in 304
services, revenue recognition of 81–2
SES Global 390
settlement periods *see* average settlement
    periods
Severn Trent Water 215, 357, 456–7, 474
share issues 426–31
  bonus 431
  offer for sale **430**, 430–1, **506**
  private placing 131, **430**, 430–1, **507**
  public issue 131, **430**, **508**
  rights 131, **426**, 426–9, **509**
share premium account **128**, **509**
shareholders 113, 145
  and company management 119–20
  and limited liability 114–16
  and perpetual life, 113–14
  restrictions on 116
  safeguards for 120–1
shares **113**, 113–14, **509**
  bonus **128**, 128–30, 431, **499**
  capital 124–6, 131, 133
  consolidating **125**, **500**
  earnings per share (EPS) **218**, 218–19, **502**
  initial public offering (IPO) 430, 432
  listing 431–5
  nominal value **123**, 124–5, 127, **506**
  ordinary **125**, 125–6, 193–4, 408–10, **507**
  par value **123**
  preference **125**, 125–6, 408, 410–11,
    416–17, **507**
  redemption of 411
  splitting **125**, **509**
  transfer of ownership 118–19
  see also dividends; Stock Exchange
short-term finance 403, 404, 405–7, 436–41
short-term planning *see* budgets
Signet Group plc 383

single-product businesses 279–80
slow payers 478
small and medium-sized enterprises (SMEs), budgeting practice 324–5
Small Firms Loan Guarantee Scheme *see* Enterprise Finance Guarantee Scheme
SMEs *see* small and medium-sized enterprises
Smith Group plc 474
sole proprietors 115, 123
splitting shares **125**, **509**
SSL 147
standards *see* accounting standards; International Accounting Standards; International Financial Reporting Standards
start-up capital 442
statements of cash flow **31**, **509**
  cash and cash equivalents 161–2, 163, 165, 171 6
  depreciation 174–6
  dividends paid 174
  examples 31, 33, 34, 167, 169–70, 173–5
  financing activities 164, 165, 174
  and income statements 35, 159–60, 163, 173
  information from 175–7
  interest 174–5
  investing activities 164, 165, 166–7
  layout 163–4
  normal direction of flows 166–7
  operating activities 164, 165
  and statements of financial position 35, 163, 173
  taxation 138
  *see also* cash flows
statements of changes in equity **140**, 140–1, **509**
statements of comprehensive income **139**, 139–40, **509**
  and income statements 139
statements of financial position **31**, **509**
  dates of 50–1
  and dividends 138
  examples 32, 33, 39–44, 191–3
  financial ratios relating to 227–8
  and general reserve 138
  and income statements 35, 73–4, 163
  influence of accounting conventions 54
  layouts 48–50
  and money measurement 55–8
  as position in point of time 50–1
  and reserves 138
  and statements of cash flow 35, 163, 173
  and taxation 138
  trading transactions effects on 42–4
  and user needs 63–4
  and valuation of assets 59–63
  working capital 456–7, 484
  *see also* assets; claims; limited companies
stepped fixed costs **242**, 258–9, **509**
stock *see* inventories; shares

Stock Exchange **431**, **510**
  financing role 431–5
  and limited companies 131–2, 144, 146
  share ownership transfer role 118–19
  and UK Corporate Governance Code 121
straight-line depreciation method **90**, 90–5, **510**
strategic management **15**, **510**
strategic options 313
strategic plans and objectives 313–16
subcontracting 266–7
suppliers 4, 5, 480

tangible assets **38**, **510**
  *see also* depreciation; property; property, plant and equipment
targets
  budgets 343–4
  profits 254
Tata Group 260, 414–15
Tate and Lyle plc 357, 474
taxation
  as cash flow 171
  and dividends 405
  and income statements 138
  investment appraisals and 385
  and limited companies 117–18, 138
  profit before **137**, **507**
  and shares 405, 410, 417
  and statements of cash flow 174–5
  and statements of financial position 138
Ted Baker plc 63, 474
term loans **411**, **510**
Tesco plc 117, 167, 195, 224, 367–8, 456–7
Thorntons plc 94–5, 128, 474
time horizons of plans and budgets 316
time orientation of reports 11
total costs 284
Tottenham Hotspur plc 57, 474
trade creditors *see* trade payables
trade debtors *see* trade receivables
trade loading 147
trade payables **40**, **510**
  average settlement period for **202**, 202–3, 483, 485, **499**
  delaying payment to 404, 408
  managing 487–90
  working capital 454–5
trade payables budgets 319, 321–2, 333
trade receivables **45**, **510**
  ageing schedule of **477**, **498**
  average settlement period for **201**, 201–2, 476–7, 483, 485, **499**
  cash discounts 475, 488–9
  collection policies 476–8
  managing 470–8
  working capital 454–5
  *see also* bad debts
trade receivables budgets 319, 321, 333
trademarks 55
trading transactions 42–4

transmission of cash 486
trend analysis 224–5
turnover period, average inventories **200**,
    200–1, 461, **499**

UK Corporate Governance Code **121**, 121–3,
    **510**
understandability **6**, 8, **510**
useful life of assets 89
users of accounting information 3–5

valuation
    of assets 58–63
    of inventories 62–3, 97–101
    of land 59–60
    of property, plant and equipment 58–60
    and statements of financial position 58–63
values
    of businesses 63
    fair **59**, 88–9, **503**
    market 56, 59, 61
    net book *see* carrying amounts
    net present (NPV) 358, **368**, 368–79,
        379–82, 385, 386, 388–92, 475, **506**
    net realisable 100
    residual **89**, 89–90, **508**
    nominal (shares) **123**, 124–5, 127, **506**
    written-down (WDV) *see* carrying amounts
    *see also* depreciation
variable costs **240**, 242–3, **510**
    and break-even analysis 245–50, 251, 257
    full costing and 284
    marginal analysis and 262
    semi-variable **243**, 243–5, **509**
variance analyses **341**, 341–2, **510**
variances **510**
    adverse **339**, 339–41, **498**
    favourable **339**, 339–41, **503**
    materials 341
    overheads 341
    reports 344

venture capital **441**, 441–3, **510**
Vodafone 221
Volkswagen 199–200
volume
    cost–volume–profit analysis 239–71
    inventories 464
voluntary liquidation 114

W H Smith plc 16, 474
Wal-Mart 117, 460–1
WDV (written-down values) *see* carrying
    amounts
wealth
    of business 33, 104
    owners' 16–17
    *see also* profits
weighted average cost (AVCO) **98**, 99–101,
    **510**
Weinstock, Lord 228
Woolworths 16, 420
work-in-progress 442
working capital **170**, 192, 454–5, **510**
    cash 479–87
    examples 456–7, 463–4, 472–3, 489
    inventories 454–5
    nature and purpose 454–6
    scale of 456–8
    trade payables 454–5, 487–90
    trade receivables 454–5, 470–8
WorldCom 13
written-down values (WDV) *see* carrying
    amounts

Xstrata 215

year-end assumptions, investment appraisals
    385
year-end dates 50–1
yield ratio, dividends **218**, 221–2, **502**

zero-base budgeting (ZBB) 325–7, **326**, **510**